Not All Is Changed

Not All Is Changed
A Life History of Hingham

LORENA LAING HART
FRANCIS RUSSELL HART

Historical Resources Consultant
John P. Richardson

THE HINGHAM HISTORICAL COMMISSION
Hingham, Massachusetts

FIRST EDITION

LIBRARY OF CONGRESS CATALOG NUMBER 93-079100

ISBN 0-9638083-0-3

The Hingham Historical Commission is grateful for permission to reprint the following copyrighted material:

Excerpt from "An Old Ham Under the Sun," by Francis S. Wright. Copyright © by The New York Times Company. Reprinted by permission.

Excerpts from SOUTH SHORE TOWN by Elizabeth Coatsworth. Copyright 1948 and renewed © 1976 Elizabeth Coatsworth Beston. Reprinted with permission of Macmillan Publishing Company.

PRINTED IN THE UNITED STATES OF AMERICA

*Dedicated to
our families and
especially our children*

Foreword

✠

THE first history of Hingham, a small volume of one hundred and eighty-three pages, was compiled by Solomon Lincoln, Jr., and published privately in 1827. As the two hundred and fiftieth anniversary of our settlement approached, the 1883 annual town meeting voted "that the town cause a History of Hingham to be prepared and published, and that a committee be appointed to have charge of the publication." Using appropriated funds, that committee produced a substantial, four volume History of Hingham, written by George Lincoln and others, which was published by the town in 1893. There has been no comprehensive history written since that year.

In conjunction with our three hundred and fiftieth anniversary in 1985, the annual town meeting similarly voted, at the request of the Historical Commission, "that the Moderator appoint a committee to consider the feasibility of updating the 1893 History of Hingham." That committee was chaired by the late Professor John B. Armstrong and also included the late Louise Wilder Cobleigh, Winona Fredie, Winston I. Hall, the late Judith Kimball, Hilary McCarthy, John F. McKee, Jr., Michael J. Shilhan, Doone H. Williams, John P. Richardson, Eileen A. Whelan. A year later, acting on the recommendation of the study committee, the electorate decreed "that the sum of Twenty Thousand Dollars be appropriated as the first year's production costs of updating the town's history, and that an advisory/editorial committee be appointed" to oversee the project.

The editorial advisory committee consisted initially of members of the Historical Commission: Morton Cole, Mary Frances Gray, Winston I. Hall, the late Judith Kimball, Alexander Macmillan, Virginia D. Pearce and Virginia D. Winslow. Additional members, subsequently recruited, included Dr. W. Robert Carr, who served ably as chairman until he moved to Marshfield in 1992, Carl W. Harris, Jr., Hilary McCarthy, Mary E. Tondorf-Dick and Professor George Smith.

After interviewing numerous candidates, this committee unanimously selected Professor Francis Russell Hart and his wife, Lorena Laing Hart, to write the book, *Not All Is Changed: A Life History of Hingham,* and retained John P. Richardson as a consultant. Varying from the original plan, the committee decided to rely primarily on private contributions in order to publish the new history and to seek no new appropriation.

In addition to our debt to the authors, the consultant and other members of the committee, the Commission, which now includes Frederick A. Copeman, III, Deborah E. Edmundson, Mary Frances Gray, Frederic A. Hills, Winston I. Hall, Alexander Macmillan and Dorothy D. Monroe, gratefully acknowledges the important work of more recent committee members Peter Carr, William C. Hammond, James L. Macedo and Elizabeth Schultz; the technical assistance provided by others, including Kathleen E. Carr, Russell Hart, George Loring, Frances Cooke Macgregor, Barbara Menzies, Warren Noble, Carol Maryanski O'Neill, Tina Samaha, Robert Stella, John D. Stobierski and Philip O. Swanson; the crucial role played by our administrator, Elaine Cusker, who coordinated all aspects of the project; and, of course, the many citizens and institutions whose generous contributions helped make the publication possible.

Alexander Macmillan, Chairman
HINGHAM HISTORICAL COMMISSION

History Makers

⬧

GEORGE LINCOLN SOCIETY

Dr. W. Robert Carr & Kathleen E. Carr
Thomas & Marjorie Curtis
Carol Gardner & Willis Marion Ertman
Winston I. Hall
In Recognition of James Macedo
Mr. & Mrs. Alexander Macmillan
Wilder Charitable & Educational Fund

BENEFACTORS

Hingham Institution for Savings   Monique & Philip Lehner

PATRONS

Edna S. English & William S. English   Mr. & Mrs. Peter W. Hersey

SPONSORS

Mr. & Mrs. John D. Brewer, Jr.
Thomas & Kathleen Bright
Ada Laurie Bryant
Thomas J. Carey, Jr.
Peter Carr
Eugene R. Chamberlain
Terence M. Clarke
Continental Cablevision
Ruth Curry
Deborah & Philip Edmundson
Dr. & Mrs. LeRoy Lincoln
  Eldredge, Jr.
First Parish in Hingham
  (Old Ship Church)
Giarrusso Family
Mary Frances Gray
Victoria & Bill Hammond
Hingham Republican Town
  Committee
Hingham Rotary Club, Inc.
Philip & Elizabeth Howlett

Theodore Iorio
Captain & Mrs. Paul A. Lutz
Mr. & Mrs. Colin S. Marshall
Dorothy & Parker Monroe
Patrick & Mary Ann Nagle
Thomas L. P. O'Donnell
Virginia Fay Pittman
Joseph L. Potz
John & Therese Riley
Kenneth G. Ryder
Mr. & Mrs. William C. Schrader
Dr. Eugene D. & Elizabeth A.
  (O'Brien) Shaw
George W. Smith & Louise Z. Smith
Elbert & Betty Stallard
Mr. & Mrs. Michael F. Stone
Barbara & Carol Sullivan
Mrs. Philip H. Tobey
Thomas J. & Mary G. Wallace
Mrs. Isabelle Wilson

SUBSCRIBERS

Mr. & Mrs. Foster C. Aborn
Mr. & Mrs. Frank G. Achille
Elizabeth Melcher Anderson
Dr. & Mrs. Jeffrey M. Anderson
Anonymous
Kathleen Ryder Arnold
Mrs. Stuart V. Arnold
Ronald Lincoln Bacon
Joan Andre Balerna
Audrey & Emily Banks
Gloria J. Barbuto
Mr. & Mrs. Arthur Barrett
I. H. Bartlett
Mr. Dana S. Baxter &
   Mrs. Ginger F. Baxter
John D. Beal, Jr.
Peter & Diana Bennett
Paul & Nancy Benson
Susan Bickford Berry
Midge & Gene Bickford
Geneva Tower Blaine
Ruth Lincoln Blair
W. Robert & Gisela Boris
Mr. & Mrs. John M. Bradlee
Charles, Jeanette & Janine Bradley
Mrs. Robert D. Brewer, Jr.
Raymond & Dorothy Brown
Bruce & Gail Bunten
Anna M. Calvi
Margaret Osborn Carnes
Dr. & Mrs. A. Alden Carpenter
Joanne C. Carpenter
Bruce Carr
Harriet & Earle Caton
Stephen Certa
Mr. & Mrs. Francis S. Chapman
Loretta T. Cogliano
Ann P. Collins
Ruth Coolen
Fred H. Copeman
Leith Cosman
Martin & Kathleen Crane
Basil F. Cronin
Bill & Kim Cross

J. Robert Crowley
Brian & Margaret Curtis
Winnie & Charlie Cushing
Elaine, Joseph, Jeremy & Erin Cusker
Iris F. & J. Cray Daigle
Stephen C. Daly
Marguerite Boss Davis
Dorothy Hooper Dean
Mr. & Mrs. Charles Debreczeni
Deja Vu
Rich Delmar & Family
Kate Hersey Dickerson & Jack Dickerson
Mr. & Mrs. Frank D. Doble
Mr. & Mrs. Robert W. Dresser, Sr.
John Rogers Duxbury
Wendy Carr Ellison
Dr. & Mrs. Roger H. Emerson, Sr.
Paul A. Epstein & Betsey Wigmore Epstein
Doris E. Evans
Albert Fearing
Curt & Jane Fithian
Mr. & Mrs. James A. Flett
Edward R. & Anne M. Foley
Mr. & Mrs. Samuel Galpin
Michael J. Gardner
Clare C. Garrity
Mr. & Mrs. Andrew Gatturna
Mr. & Mrs. Ebenezer Gay
George Glazebrook, Jr.
Mr. & Mrs. Harold S. Glenzel
Mr. & Mrs. Carleton N. Goff
Leon & Pat Granahan
Joseph & Kimberly Granatino
Ken & Nora Grant
Fran & Greg Hall
Mr. & Mrs. Daniel E. Hanlon III
Carl W. Harris
Elizabeth Hanna Harris
Charles & Virginia Harvey
Fred & Jean Harvie
Mr. & Mrs. Herbert P. Hess
Edwin A. Hills II
Mr. & Mrs. Frederic A. Hills
Hingham Democratic Town Committee

Winthrop & Marjorie Hodges
Mrs. Lucille J. Holliday
William & Elizabeth Holm
Dr. & Mrs. Herbert C. Hoover, Jr.
Alfred E. Housman
Mr. & Mrs. Elwood A. Hoxie
William T. Hurley III
Nancy Robinson Hutchison
Jane Illinger
R. Iredale
Mr. & Mrs. Dale D. Jacobs
Stephen L. Jacobs
Glen F. Johnson & Genevieve M. Johnson
Dr. & Mrs. Jeffrey A. Johnson
Clint & Ellen Jones
Carole & James Kababik
Thomas & Leslie Kehoe
James H. Kelley
William & Jane Kelly
Priscilla Leathers Keniston
Mr. & Mrs. Thomas Lamb
Mr. & Mrs. Frederick S. Lane
Mr. & Mrs. Charles F. Langenhagen, Jr.
Talbert & Irma Lauter
Peter Lehner
Edward & Virginia Lewiecki
Mrs. George Lewis
Mr. & Mrs. John G. Liddell
C. Warren Lincoln
Joseph T. Lincoln
Ronald E. Lincoln
Grace T. Loring
Wanda Ellis Loring
Louise S. Luther
Lynda Boynton Lynch & William
    Benton Lynch
Mr. & Mrs. Donald J. MacKinnon
Mrs. Kenneth Gordon MacLeod
Warren & Dorothy MacPhadden
Mr. & Mrs. William Maddrix
Frank & Kate Mahony
Mr. & Mrs. Charles I. Malme
Donald & Geraldine M. Mann
E. L. Margetts & Sons
Robert & Janet Marlatt
Massachusetts American Water Co.
Mr. & Mrs. William Pratt Mayer
Chris & Mary Maynard

William L. & Janet D. McCarthy
Louise A. McCue
Richard & Carol McCusker
Joseph P. McElaney
Mr. & Mrs. H. T. McMeekin, Jr.
Barbara Menzies
Mr. & Mrs. T. Michael Middleton
Jack & Valerie Mine
James F. Moran
Virginia Tower Moore
Mr. & Mrs. Daniel S. Morrison
August W. & Jean M. Muller
Ellen M. Murphy
The Harry J. Murphy Family
Margaret N. Murphy
Mrs. Peter H. Murphy
Peg & Jack Murray
In Memory of Mary M. O'Brien
Richard & Dorothy O'Brien
David & Kathleen Olsson
Robert & Dorothy Palmer
C. Scott Parker
Barbara Partridge
Mary Burr Paxton
Virginia D. Pearce
Pennell Crosby Peck
Eric Pence & Patti Rosenfield
Robert & Nancy Perry
John & Diane Pica
Mr. & Mrs. Demetrius C. Pilalas
G. Whiton Price
Peter L. & Annie Puciloski
Dr. & Mrs. Joseph J. Pucko
Mr. & Mrs. Michael J. Puzo
Mr. & Mrs. William S. Reardon
Kenneth & Susan Read-Brown
Mr. & Mrs. Harry Renner
Robert & Maryann Rioux
Edward Frankin Ripley
Mr. & Mrs. Charles W. Rizzotto
Brooks & Meg Robbins
The Rockoff Family
Ryland F. & Gunver J. Rogers
Janet Hough Ross in Memory
    of Karl C. Hough
Dorothy Gemma Rowe
St. Paul's Parish
Christine & Richard Samaha

Ronald B. & Carol A. Schram
The Schultz-Bone Family
Russell & Janice Sears
Mr. & Mrs. Jerry K. Seelen
Mr. & Mrs. Stanley C. Shaw
The Shilhan Company
Mr. & Mrs. Francis E. Silva, Jr.
F. Robert Skilling
Matthew B. Sloan
Mrs. Franklin H. Smith
Donald & Beverly Smith
Roberta E. Smith
Dr. & Mrs. Robert F. Sommer
Charles & Paula Souther
Richard Dennis Souther
Stephen C. Spear
Wm. Bradford Sprout, Jr.
Richard H. Starr

Thomas Burr Studley
Carl R. Swett
Dr. & Mrs. Charles E. Taylor
Mr. & Mrs. James B. Tiffin
Gary & Mary Tondorf-Dick
Mr. & Mrs. Stephen Trebino
Terence M. Troyer
William & May Vuilleumier
Joseph & Dorothy Wagstaff
Mrs. Joseph Watkins
Cynthia Wessling
Christopher W. Whitman
Daniel F. & Alice Wigmore
Patricia Wright Wilder
Mrs. Roger H. Williams
Helen S. Wollan
Stephen & Gay Zsigalov

Preface

✠

Our present problems are the result of historical conditions, not of some inevitable historical law. They are the result of actual choices that people have made in history. . . . A better understanding. . . could allow us to make different choices, with different consequences for us all.

Robert N. Bellah, 1991

For the sake of history itself, let us deal honestly and fearlessly with the record our predecessors have left behind them. . . . Let us explore the lives and actions of men and their generations, with pious carefulness, but with impartial fidelity and independence.

John A. Andrew, 1867

HISTORY is often a process of accidentals and timing, and the creation of this book is no exception. The accidentals began over twenty years ago when we made the choice to return to Massachusetts and live in Hingham rather than in more familiar and familial territory west of Boston. The process continued when, some years later, we found ourselves, at the suggestion of our old friend George Smith, in the pool of candidates to write the story. At no other time in our lives could we have committed ourselves to a work of such magnitude.

We have explored with "pious carefulness" out of a sense of obligation to explorers who preceded us, especially George Lincoln, and out of a sense of responsibility to future readers, recognizing that another history of Hingham will not be written for some time. We believe we have told the story truthfully. Truth is relative, but as a friend of ours, a writer, once said, "I never had to make up anything." While dealing frankly with conflict and controversy, history need not be divisive, but should affirm the human community we all share. "Whatever the future may have in order," wrote philosopher John Dewey, "one thing is certain. Unless local communal life can be restored, the public cannot adequately resolve its most urgent problem, to find and identify itself."

We cannot tell Hingham's whole story because we do not know it. Who will discover the documents we could not find? Would they have significantly changed our story? It is surprising how much evidence has been preserved, perhaps because the town and some of its citizens have been and remain intensely aware of its past. But the surviving evidence is only an accidental miscellany. Of many Hingham lives, past and present, we have no knowledge. The "profundity of our unknowing" has served us as a constant monitor and corrective and sometimes even as a comfort. "I'm so glad," said a woman when we admitted we could not answer her question straightaway, "to meet someone who feels they don't know everything."

Historians must not invent what they do not know. And yet, without an act of imagination they cannot connect with the past, cannot share with readers a sense of connection with past lives. This sense begins with a simple realization: no one who lived in the past ever thought of oneself as living in the past. Rather, all lived in constantly forming and re-forming presents, in their own "nows." We invite readers to join us in an act of imagination that sees past times as the nows they were. We all may begin with a fascination with genealogies, old houses, maps. But we must then try to imagine the thoughts and feelings of those who once peopled those families and places. This has been our experience: like the old sexton in Elizabeth Coatsworth's *South Shore Town*, we have seen and talked with many people we never meet on the streets.

How comfortably in the 1640s did Anthony Eames live on the same side of the Centre Common as his arch-rival Bozoan Allen? What were the thoughts of Solomon Lincoln, the leading Whig in the 1840s, about his next-door neighbor on Main Street, the outspoken antislavery advocate Jairus Lincoln? How could Thomas Buttimer have felt in 1902 when, after a recount, he realized he was the town's first state representative of Irish Catholic ancestry? What must have been the frustration of Amy Howard in 1937, when the Hingham Hospital for which she had labored so long was forced to close by covert political pressure?

Harder to imagine are the lives and feelings of those who had no political or social agenda, no power or influence, and who left little trace of their diverse selves: Hingham's common soldiers and sailors, its blacks and Indians, its immigrant minorities, its women and children, and its poor. But their everyday lives sometimes resonate from the matter-of-fact records of town clerks, parishes, and the almshouse. And after 1827, something of their lives can be gleaned from the town newspaper. We have read all of the more than 8400 weekly issues through 1990 in search of the means of connecting with them: the commonplace detail, the delicious anecdote, the haunting verbal image, the vestige of an individual life. As Sam Bass Warner has said, the individual experience—how a person lived and worked in a particular place—takes on fresh value as an antidote to the "floods of public messages," the deluge of information from the media, statisticians, and computer net-works, in our "information age."

How will later writers of Hingham's history cope with the barrage of information from screens? We do not envy them their task of sorting it into meaning. By contrast, a slip of paper with the pencil or penned ink of one hundred or three hundred years ago gives a palpable sense of connection to the hand and mind of the writer.

Ours may be one of the last books to be written "the old-fashioned way" with slips of paper, pencils, pens, and typewriters. We began by looking at the surfaces of past life and town histories for their texture, much as one would look at treasured old fabric. Why and how was it woven the way it was? Why, in past histories of Hingham, are some warp threads missing? An empty space is often as revealing as a full one. The 1893 *History*, however monumental, slighted or left out some groups of the town's people, parts of its communal life, and several important controversies and events. We would have to weave anew. Like Penelope, we often unraveled our cloth and reworked it, for writing history, like history itself, is an erratic and complex process rich in accidentals.

One fruitful accidental was the choice of the working title, *Not All Is Changed,* a simple phrase written nearly a century ago by John D. Long. As the story unfolds, every reader must be struck by the many ways, some delightful, some depressing, in which the present echoes the past. What Governor Long's phrase chiefly suggests is a belief held by many that Hingham has kept its identity, its essential character, through generations of drastic change. Is this true? The identity of a community, like that of a person, cannot be found in anything visible at any one moment. It can be found only in human consciousness, and human consciousness is a blend of fact, myth, and aspiration. The abiding aspiration that identifies Hingham was beautifully expressed in 1963 by Francis Leonard:

> Who wants to live in a town where there is no wild land? No sense of breathing space? No feeling of communal belonging that discourages lawlessness? No awareness of an unbroken thread with the past that is now a kind of folk-wisdom inherited by the people who live here?

This is, in a profound sense, a conservative aspiration, a desire to protect and preserve continuities. It has, over many generations, motivated legions of Hingham citizens to work for the good of the town as they saw it, and often to contend vehemently with others, also sincere and dedicated, who saw the good of the town differently. The interplay of dedication and contentiousness is one persistent theme, one warp thread, of our story. There are others. But beyond themes, we have written a narrative of real life with its cross threads too.

Our story opens with the Civil War, and readers may wonder why. This, too, originated with an accidental. We were expected to "update" the town's 1893 *History* from the time of that war. But who could understand that central, traumatic time without some explanation of the events, "broken bones that wouldn't heal," that led up to it? Twentieth-century scholarship substantially alters our understanding of Hingham's history in the generations prior to the Civil War. Indeed, it revises our knowledge of earlier history beginning in the 1630s. So, after our Prologue we offer in Part One a fresh, abbreviated retrospective of the first 228 years. Part Two, our personal favorite, recreates the town as a lively "island community" in the second half of the nineteenth century. In Part Three, we trace the crucial trends of change before and after World War I. Part Four tells of the momentous decades from the Great Depression to the climax of the Vietnam War. In the Epilogue, we describe and try to make sense of the present from 1971 to the spring of 1990.

Our story grew like Topsy into one far more comprehensive and inclusive than we had envisioned. We sensed we were into it when it took on a life of its own. The principle of inclusiveness significantly affected our work and has been the greatest challenge in composition. The result is a hybrid which must serve several purposes. It must be the inclusive history of a diverse people. It must also be a reference book, and as such, it must be inclusive to have value. And it must set Hingham's local history in the wider contexts of region, nation, and world. Our hope is that every reader, present and future, will find a reflection of him or herself in what we include.

Perhaps the need for human inclusiveness is why Hingham continues to insist on open town meeting. Whatever its imperfections and inefficiencies, town meeting brings people face to face as parts of a now fragile community. While its sometimes fractious nature may be unsettling, it affirms diversity and community. The challenge is to insure that community is inclusive. The grand directive, "Tell me if your civilization is interesting," can apply to a social unit of any size. Hingham will remain interesting if it sustains diversity through what were once central to its being: acts of accommodation and inclusiveness.

Lorena Laing Hart
Francis Russell Hart
Crow Point, May, 1993
P.O. Box 471, Hingham

A Note of Thanks

✠

MANY people have helped during the long labor of producing this history, beginning with members of the Advisory Editorial Committee, whose names are listed earlier. Two who were early participants in the process deserve special mention, Morton Cole and the late Judith Kimball. The members spent countless hours at meetings and in reading and commenting on the text, and their chairman, W. Robert Carr, was a most fastidious and critical editor. John P. Richardson graciously shared with us his unique knowledge of the town's past and spared us errors. Many others who shared memories or tried to help us find wanted illustrations are listed in the Bibliography under "Interviews and Conversations." Individual artists, owners, and institutions who permitted reproduction of graphic work are acknowledged along with the photographers in the List of Illustrations.

The help of local institutions has been crucial. The Historical Society through the agency of its most recent president James Macedo gave us access to its holdings. Nancy Tiffin offered useful suggestions as we sought graphics. Ann Tolman and the Society's new president Eugene Chamberlain agreed with stoic kindness to winter appointments in the chilly confines of the Old Ordinary and Derby Hall, and Thomas Hall in the sacred confines of the town vault. The town's newspapers, the *Journal* and the *Mariner*, helped by printing articles adapted from the text. We appreciate the efforts of their editors, Jane Arena and Mary Ford, in offering readers a prepublication view.

Libraries, of course, have been at the heart of our work. Without the staff of our own public library, our research would have been impossible. We salute Walter Dziura, Ruth Osborn, Jean Beatty, and

Marguerite Sheffield, and offer very special thanks to those wonderful reference specialists Winifred Roberts Grotevant and Kathleen Leahy. Mary Wilhelmi and William Quinn of the Healey Library, University of Massachusetts at Boston, arranged the long-term loan of an unused microfilm reader, which let us work at home at all hours and finish on schedule.

Our kind neighbors May and William Vuilleumier provided four years of safety storage for our work-in-progress and shoveled our snow when sore backs and repaired eyes disabled us, and Herbert Hirsch kept our house from falling down around us as the years passed. Friends and family, particularly our children, tolerated and understood our long monastic withdrawal. When we felt very alone and our morale sagged, they sustained and cheered us by their love and invaluable advice.

When it seemed probable that this book would be published, the copywriting talent of Elizabeth Schultz, the promotional skills of Hilary McCarthy, and the steady coordination of Elaine Cusker pulled everything together. Elaine once said, "I like to make a difference." She has. We thank Alexander Macmillan for his energetic efforts to raise funds and the many donors and subscribers for their confidence and generosity.

Finally, we are *all* indebted to Peter Carr, a master of fine book design and production, and to computer wizard George Smith for their many weeks of volunteered, meticulous, and artful work. Through them, the myriad efforts of many have become *Not All Is Changed: A Life History of Hingham.*

Contents

✠

Contents

List of Illustrations and Maps

✠

WE are indebted to many persons who provided photographs or allowed us to reproduce their own work or privately held materials. Because of the extensive holdings of the Hingham Historical Society and the Public Library, the selection process was both delightful and difficult. We are especially grateful to photographers Frances Cooke Macgregor and Michael Shilhan. This year, photographers Lee Bain, Russell Hart, George Loring, Robert Stella, John Stobierski, and Philip Swanson have made many prints for production purposes, sometimes from very challenging originals. The illustrations are richer and more varied because of their interest and skill.

When we do not give information about images, it is because information is not available. Readers interested in knowing more about the personalities in the illustrations will discover almost all of them by consulting the index.

List of Illustrations and Maps

List of Illustrations and Maps

LIST OF MAPS

Not All Is Changed

Solomon Lincoln (1804-1881).

George Lincoln (1822-1909).

Fearing Burr (1815-1897).

Reverend Donald F. Robinson (1905-1991).

Julian C. Loring (1899-1978).

Mason A. Foley (1903-1968).

SEE THE BIBLIOGRAPHY FOR THEIR CONTRIBUTIONS

The old, old Centre primary and grammar school (later moved to Short Street to become the central fire station, now the tree division building) with a "democrat" carriage and Dot the horse in front; the Lincoln Light Infantry Armory (renovated from the Hingham Centre male schoolhouse in 1857); 36 Spring Street.

Loring Hall; the Fire Insurance Company and Institution for Savings building; the Harding-Whidden house (photograph 1885). Note the gas lanterns, hitching posts, and collared elms.

Recreation by glazier, painter, and postmaster (1863–1888) Edwin Wilder (1829–1906) of the east side of Broad Bridge before the railroad, looking south along Main Street past the commercial buildings (burned 1862) to the Acadian-Hollis House (razed in 1912) and Derby Academy (1818), now home of the Hingham Historical Society.

Broad Bridge looking northwest from South Street after the disastrous fire of May 3, 1862, destroyed the Tilden, Royal Whiton, and Lane buildings. LEFT TO RIGHT: Lincoln Building (1859), Railroad Depot, Thomas Andrews house (today, St. Paul's Rectory), Thayer (formerly Thaxter) Building. FOREGROUND: cellar holes of burned buildings. Southworth's Pharmacy (today, Conte's shop) was built here in 1878. Reverse side of high wooden sign spanning Broad Bridge reads: "Railroad Crossing. Look out for the engine, while the bells rings."

Andrew J. Clark (1837–1927), Civil War soldier (1861–1865) and war correspondent for THE HINGHAM JOURNAL.

Edwin Humphrey (1831–1863), captain of Company A, 11th Regiment, M.V.I., killed at Gettysburg. The GAR Post 104 was named in his honor.

POST 104, G. A. R

Carrara marble statue of Governor John A. Andrew by Thomas Gould, dedicated 1875. In the background is the Soldiers' and Sailors' Monument, dedicated 1870. The iron fence once around the monument was designed by Isaac Sprague.

PROLOGUE

✠

"The Home of My Heart"

AS any local sailor can tell you, the best way to approach Hingham is by water. The weary but elated men who sailed home into the harbor on July 23, 1861, were not sailors but citizen soldiers, the Lincoln Light Infantry, back from their brief war in Virginia. As the steamboat *Nantasket* carefully threaded its way up the channel, they were welcomed home by the same point, the same islands, the same brook and hills seen by the first settlers in the 1630s. Not a house was visible on Crow Point. Sheep grazed on Otis Hill, bare of trees. Old tenements crowded the Cove. And what a bustling throng along the wharf east of the coal and lumber docks. Folks from all of Hingham's villages cheered the returning heroes. Led by the Home Guard and fire engines, a procession moved up Water Street to the home (14) of their leader, Colonel Luther Stephenson, Jr. Bells rang. The band played "Home Again." With a battery of guns and a hundred horses, the parade marched down Main Street to Broad Bridge for speeches of welcome.

The soldiers had been away only three months. They had set out from the little armory near the Centre Common at a few hours' notice. A working box-maker "dropped all, left his shop, rushed home, told his wife he was bound to the war. She assured him if he considered it his duty, she was willing . . . . He opened the door, closed it, and was gone." On April 16, remembered Stephenson long afterwards,

> I received a telegram from Governor Andrew, directing me to report with my company . . . by the first train for Boston. While the men were being notified and were preparing to respond to the order, a man came into the armory and asked permission to join the com-

[3]

pany . . . he was furnished with a uniform, musket, and equipments and Alvin Tower was enlisted as a soldier of the Union . . . he had virtually left the plough in the furrow.

Fourteen months later, after the battle of Fair Oaks, Alvin Tower would become the third Hingham man to die in the Civil War.

On that April day in 1861, he joined men with other old names: Cushing, Humphrey, Jones, Lincoln, Souther, Sprague, Stodder, and Whiton. Twenty-three-year-old Andrew Clark voiced their feelings in Virginia:

> God bless those noble men whose foresight and promptness placed us here . . . . Be assured that when we strike, we shall strike home, and falter not until we have carried our country's flag through the length and breadth of this fair land, and treason is no more . . . ridding our country of a nest of evildoers, rebels, traitors, call them what you will, and, incidentally, of working out the freedom of our poor, enslaved fellow men, in making this what it was intended it should be—a land of *freedom* in every sense of the word.

Their first task was to guard the mouth of the James River against the "rebs." The chief threats they faced were heat, exhaustion, and disease. But in July, they were safely home. A short war! Then in that same July, the bloody survivors of the first battle of Bull Run staggered back to Washington, and hopes for peace faded. Hingham native Elijah Gill lay dead on the battlefield. Charles Marsh, soon to become the second Hingham native casualty, wrote home of the "disastrous retreat," the "most fatal error" of attacking much larger forces. The Union paused to organize and train its troops. Governor John Andrew, who had found in Hingham "the home of my heart," declared: "We went down to Bull Run an aggregation of town meetings. Whenever we march again, we march AN ARMY."

First, an army had to be manned. The war's most lasting and demoralizing impact on a small New England town was the burden of raising recruits to fill state-set quotas. In the early months, a brief ardor of patriotism and a naive romanticizing of war made it easy, especially when jobs were scarce. "Now that shoemaking flags and fishing is ending for the season," recruiting picked up. Looking back from the summer of 1863, the *Journal* recalled: "When the war broke out, business was dull, and volunteers, filled with indignation at the audacity of the rebels, rushed spontaneously to arms. Those left behind found good situations when business revived." Volunteering would not be enough. Even efforts to fill the Lincoln Light Infantry failed, and in September,

1862, it was disbanded. What followed—the "indefensible bounty system" and then the draft—historian Bruce Catton calls "almost uniformly vicious," "an atrocity."

In July, 1862, as Confederate armies threatened Washington itself and President Lincoln sent a frantic call for troops, Hingham held the first of many "large and enthusiastic" rallies at the town house opposite the Orthodox (Congregational) Church. "Animating" speeches urged enlistments and offered bounties, but to little avail. A ladies' committee orchestrated another rally with music and orators. More meetings followed. From General Burnside's expedition in North Carolina, Andrew Clark wrote home:

> I think they could easily raise double the number required if the young men remaining there would take hold of the matter in earnest and say they *will not* be behind others of their own, now that their patriotic services are required to crush this wicked rebellion.

Sumner Trask of the 32nd Mass. Regiment was "afraid the fault lays [sic] with the 'poppas,' 'mommas,' and 'sweethearts.'" Some fellows thought "a town so wealthy as this should be a little more patriotic in the line of dollars and cents," and when the bounty for enlisting was raised to $200 the quota filled in forty-eight hours. In fact, the North would fight the war partly with mercenaries, poor men with dependent families. In September, 1862, the selectmen's "arrangements to fill the . . . quota" required buying recruits from other towns, and Abington declared Hingham "the banner town" in doing so. Other towns followed suit.

On top of the bounties—they rose to over $800 from federal, state, and town governments by 1864—came the threat of the draft. A new conscription bill passed Congress in March, 1863, and subsequent drafts followed every few months. The drafts were "heavily inegalitarian"; men between twenty and forty-five were called up unless they could afford a $300 "commutation" fee, the equivalent of half a year's wages, or hire a substitute for about $700. All over the North, grumbles were heard: "a rich man's war . . . a poor man's fight." Mobs rioted in New York; in Boston, gangs attacked deliverers of draft notices and people of color. Hingham successfully used the threat to promote enlistments and substitutes, but in July, 1863, three men were drafted. Only William Gould survived. Sewall Pugsley, in poor health when called up and lacking $300, died of disease in hospital in November. Dentist Don Pedro Wilson was missing in action in October, probably captured, never found.

In 1864, rallies added the warning, "unless more encouragement be given"—that is, unless men of means show their patriotism with their pocketbooks—the draft will strike again. The January quota was filled because a Boston bounty agent secured recruits at a premium and because Hingham men of the 32nd Regiment reenlisted at the front. The town appropriated more recruiting money, reimbursed men buying substitutes, and borrowed funds to aid soldiers' families and to pay the costs of bringing home and burying the dead. The September quota was filled because Hingham finally received credit for its men in the Navy and for its share of a state surplus.

The whole story, of course, is not so depressing. Many men like Andrew Clark signed up and reenlisted out of sustained patriotism, men of a Hingham both old and new. Clark's father, baker Melzar, served as a nurse. Three of Nathaniel French's sons gave their lives. When William Jones, Sr., died of wounds in Florida, two sons of this forty-eight-year-old bootmaker had gone before him, sixteen-year-old Samuel had just joined up as a drummer boy, and Mrs. Jones was left an indigent widow with six children. Young Horace Burr, disabled at Williamsburg, rejoined his regiment only to die at Gettysburg. Wallace Sprague, taken prisoner at the same terrible battle, was offered parole but refused on conviction to take it. Peter N. Sprague, long rejected for service from "loss of teeth," finally won a commission in the black 55th Regiment. Benjamin Thomas, a "cripple," insisted he could serve on horseback and was commissioned in the cavalry.

From a new Hingham, patriotic Irish immigrants such as Jerry Corcoran and Michael Fee gave their lives. Nineteen-year-old Tom Conway had come from Ireland two years before the war and worked at the Union Hotel stable. "I must have a shot at these infernal rebels who want to break up this fine Union," he announced in 1861, and he kept his word. The schoolboy hero of the 11th Regiment was James Healey, who boarded at the Cove and went to North Grammar School. Not yet fifteen when he signed up as a drummer boy, he spent his last day at school in uniform and was followed to the train by fellow scholars. He served in eighteen battles, was five times wounded, and had two horses shot under him at Gettysburg.

The impact on families and on the town's small labor force was severe. Imagine wartime life in the remote "little village" of Liberty Plain, where, by the war's climax in the fall of 1864, nineteen had enlisted: five fought at the siege of Petersburg, three had died, two were in hospital, four were prisoners taken at the Weldon Railroad, and five were home in various states of health and disability.

What sort of a home was Civil War Hingham? It was already very old, and it felt its age pridefully, liking to call itself "a quaint old place," an "ancient borough," with its own prudent, conservative ways of doing things. Its recent decades of growth and bustle, in fishing, shipbuilding, and new industries, had ended. When young John D. Long, later governor of the Commonwealth, paid his first visit in 1860, he thought he saw "a town decayed and diminished in importance. Its stores are falling down and its wharves are old." Had Long returned after May 3, 1862, he would have been dismayed by the charred ruins of "one of the most extensive conflagrations ever known in this vicinity," of the old commercial buildings by the railroad track east of Broad Bridge.

From David Souther's shoe store in Tilden's building on the northeast corner of Main and South Streets, the fire spread east to Royal Whiton's grocery store and jumped the track northward to the long low store known as Thaxter's building, later replaced by Barba's. "Had a brisk wind sprung up from the northwest, the dye house [in 1990, the site of Hennessy's], the painter's shop of Mr. Edwin Wilder 2d, and all the buildings embraced between the two streets might and would have been consumed." Reading the news, Andrew Clark wrote home, "I know it would not have been so severe if the firemen had all been at home. As it was, I feel personally indebted to those ladies who so gallantly took our places at the brakes," the hand levers of the old fire "tubs."

But Long would also have seen signs of renewal. The new Lincoln's Building arose where a fire of 1858 had devastated the west side of "the Bridge." New public buildings—Loring Hall, the Hingham Fire Insurance Company—graced "the village." Merchants were lighting the streets with gas lanterns; the lower Main Street buildings of the cord and tassel company presented "a splendid appearance" when lit at night. The selectmen had added kerosene lamps to the town house, and on East Street a Boston summer townsman installed the "soft, clear, and beautiful brilliancy" of gas light in his home.

The town's growth had slowed in the 1850s, but with a growth rate of 9 percent—it had increased in population during the decade from 3980 to 4351—it still surpassed other Plymouth County towns, except for the Abingtons and the Bridgewaters, mainline centers of shoemaking and heavy industry. Sons of old families were heading west or to the cities for jobs. The major growth was in the new Irish community, nearly 10 percent of the total population by the time of the war; 45 percent of babies were born to foreign-born parents. For its size, Hingham was wealthy. Its 1861 county tax per capita was $.656, compared with

Plymouth's $.573, Scituate's $.493, and Abington's $.469. Its property values by the war's end averaged $2403, compared with Plymouth's $2155, Scituate's $1227, and Abington's $1530. Its wealthy men were Boston merchants and local industrialists.

To be sure, Hingham's industry and trade had been hurt by the national panic of 1857 and the depression that followed. The glorious days of mackerel fishing were past, and many, "disgusted with the meagre returns," had turned to other jobs. But the business revived in war years, peaking at 14,344 barrels in 1863. The little fleet riding at anchor was a welcome vision in spring and fall, and in winter, the harbor appeared "a small field of standing wood." A single steamer carried passengers to and from Boston; and in 1863, the new *Rose Standish*, "elegant and graceful as a Broadway belle," "squirmed and twisted and curlicued" around the channel, "a corkscrew squat down flat," until she "steamed up proudly and majestically to her berth beside the wharf."

Hingham was still a town of separate villages, each with its farms, workshops, and industries: Broad Bridge's Burr Brown factory; West village's cabinet and shoe factories; Little Plain's scale-making and long, low ropewalk; Hersey village's box coopers. And by Cushing Pond in South Hingham were the edge-tool factory and the Wilder enterprise, which maintained Hingham's fame nationwide as "Bucket Town." The revival of agriculture was transforming town life. New gentleman farmers planted waving acres of experimental corn, wheat, and barley. One progressive farmer raised eight hundred bushels of onions on 1¼ acres; another, 7500 head of cabbage. The newly founded Agricultural and Horticultural Society held its first fair by the town house in 1859, with a huge tent, flags flying, and pens of livestock. In 1862 came the first Flower and Strawberry Festival, and in 1864, the first Harvest Festival.

Picture the streets filled with animals: yokes of "noble oxen," a favorite sight; the glimpse out an office window of "a fine flock of sheep" passing by; the sudden freedom of a "reckless boar" roving "ad libitum about the streets, entering the barnyard of Rev. Mr. Dyer" near Cold Corner. Horses were everywhere, pulling coaches, delivery wagons, carts and chaises, and occasionally showing minds of their own, as when the horses of Foster's new Scituate coach, arriving at the Hingham railroad depot impatient for lunch, started "at top speed for Mr. Wilder's stable" (today's Old Ordinary) and collided with the wagon of wealthiest townsman Thomas F. Whiton; or when the Alfred C. Hersey family, homeward bound across the mill pond bridge, encountered four teams racing furiously. Streets were often scenes of such danger, especially in icy winters, when men skated about, boys sledded down hills into passing wagons, and farmers' sleds sometimes outpaced the oxen dragging them. The noisy, fiery railroad in its second decade worsened the danger, especially when naughty boys put hollowed-out pumpkins filled with stones on the track. In the fall of 1864, a car of the Boston train capsized down an embankment in West Hingham, killing Norton Quincy Thaxter's only son.

Other street scenes were more agreeable. After more than two centuries, Hingham's prize commodity of timber had been depleted, and hills and fields wore a bare look, but private efforts began to restore shade trees to the dusty roadsides. A visitor in 1864 observed "one street nearly four miles long and in some places ten rods wide, all of which is studded with trees," and "many ancient houses are enveloped in shadow." Gardens became popular, and passionate gardeners such as John Todd and George Lincoln led in the new fashion of hothouses, filled with flowers, grape vines, strawberries, peach trees, and tomatoes. A taste for beautification touched the ancient cemeteries, which were assuming grim prominence as the awful war dragged on and the bodies came home for burial.

The lively streets were seldom free of living or partly living human reminders of the faraway carnage. Veterans—ill, maimed, lacking a leg or an arm—made their way about the villages telling their terrible stories. They contrasted in stark irony with signs of the wealth and prosperity war had brought to others. "The past year," noted the *Journal* on January 1, 1864, "has been one of war and tumult, of unparalleled prosperity with many, and of suffering, privation, and hardship with others." For merchants, financiers, and manufacturers, pre-war hard times had given way to huge profits. In July, 1863, when many Hingham men were killed or wounded at Gettysburg, popular summer resort hotels on the South Shore filled up with Boston's wealthy. And in the spring of 1864, while other local men were suffering through the campaign of northern Virginia, weekly reports pictured the city's prosperity and attacked the "outrageous extortion" of speculators and monopolists who sustained high prices of food, fuel, and clothing. For the poor, especially the hard-hit families of men at war, mounting inflation, doubling the cost of living, made sheer survival precarious. The repeated orations of patriotism sounded as hollow as the optimistic predictions of an early end to the bloodbath.

What was it all for, this mounting misery? From many fronts, Union soldiers wrote home of "dashed hopes," wasted money, "knaves and fools" running the show, desires for a compromise peace, and of course, the routine of rain, mud, disease, and suffering. "They may keep us on salt junk", wrote Andrew Clark, "hard bread . . . and poor coffee, until all the army contractors are fat with their gains—they may keep our hard-earned, much needed pay from us, until some of Uncle Sam's agents have made six months' interest." This young idealist's vision of war had faded in the face of "horrid" reality:

> one sight of a wounded man, with blood pouring from his throat or mouth—of mangled limbs—of cold, stiff corpses lying in the road, with their eyes set in their head, staring right at you, all this and more I might describe, is more to me in one short minute, than hours, or even days spent in reading accounts of the Revolution or of Napoleon's campaigns.

For every man who died of battle wounds, four died of disease, some of them months and years afterwards. We cannot say precisely how many "Hingham men" fought and died. Numbers of them had been living and working elsewhere. Some on town quotas came from other places, while some Hingham natives enlisted from other towns. It is most honest simply to approximate. About five hundred served *for* the town. Well over half of them were residents, at a time when the male population between twenty and forty-five years of age numbered only 679, almost 10 percent of them exempt as aliens. They fought in many regiments, most notably the 32nd. Thirty-five "natives" and "residents" served in the Navy, but it took a special effort of Governor Andrew to include seamen in the quotas and thus answer unfair charges that Massachusetts patriotism was lukewarm.

The research of militia historian Richard Shaner has found substantial discrepancies between the list of seventy-six war dead on Hingham's Civil War Monument and the actual numbers who died during or after the war. But a general grim fact is undeniable. By 1876, Fearing Burr and George Lincoln, the town's war historians, knew of ninety-seven who had died of war-related causes, about one in five who had served. Of these, we know the occupations of half. A dozen were shoemakers; others were makers of hatchets, harnesses, and sashes; tinsmiths, painters, and glaziers; a weaver, a cooper, a pump-maker, a wheelwright, and "laborers." We know the jobs of those recruited for the first quota: shoemakers and farmers, bakers, a butcher, a teamster, a blacksmith, a carpenter, a weaver. For them, it was a "poor man's fight."

After waiting months in late 1861 and early 1862 for news, Hingham heard glorious reports from the Mississippi and from Andrew Clark at the conquest of Roanoke Island, North Carolina. Nelson Corthell wrote from Virginia, "The war will end by June, and most of us will be at home before the close of summer." He died at Second Bull Run. By summer, Confederate General Robert E. Lee had destroyed this optimism. Union forces were retreating; Union General George McClellan abandoned the peninsula. By the fall of 1862, Union troops were "reeling" from massacres at Antietam and Fredericksburg, where Hingham men of the 32nd were "for the first time under serious fire." Union armies were bogged down in Tennessee and on the Mississippi. Bloody stalemate settled in. Grumblings grew over the war's mismanagement, and "Copperheads," northern anti-war Democrats, pushed for a compromise peace. "Oh shame," wrote Hingham's Cyrus Bates, "upon the men who, while their brothers are in arms, to put down this rebellion, are behind their backs openly aiding and abetting the enemy." In May, 1863, Lee's "most brilliant victory," at Chancellorsville, opened his way to invade Pennsylvania. Captain Edwin Humphrey of the Mass. 11th was comforting: "Hingham boys . . . in the regiment were unhurt—Horace Burr, Corp. Jackson Healey, and myself."

In these grim months, an unlikely Union hero had emerged on the Mississippi: cigar-smoking, hard-drinking Ulysses S. Grant. While Grant was breaking the South's hold at Vicksburg, Lee made his thrust north. The climax came in the first three days of July, 1863, at Gettysburg, where, in a "cauldron of noise and heat and smoke, of fear and pain and sudden darkness," Lee was beaten. The next day, Vicksburg surrendered to Grant. The Confederacy was henceforth on the defensive. All too many Hingham men knew the horror of Gettysburg. Six died there or later of wounds: a Beal, a Burr, a Haskell, a Stodder, a Thomas. Edwin Humphrey, for whom the Grand Army of the Republic (G.A.R.) Post would be named, fell the first day. Forty-two-year-old Michael Fee helped bury the dead, "a performance no human being can describe," and died later in hospital. Luther Stephenson was severely wounded an inch below his eye and came home for months of recovery. His men joined him on furlough in January: Hingham men of the 32nd rode home from Boston on Turner's and Wilder's omnibuses for a big celebration. But the end was not yet.

They were back on the battlefield for the spring offensive. Grant now led the Army of the Potomac against Lee in a campaign of attrition through the lovely green Virginia countryside. Stephenson called it "the terrible campaign, which might have been traced by a line of blood, extending from the Rapidan to the James"—Wilderness, Spotsylvania, Cold Harbor, and the battle Stephenson called "Laurel Hill" in May, 1864. Lee's army held the hill, and his sharpshooters' aim was as deadly as the weather was wild. Advance was almost hopeless. Stephenson looked back to see his men "exposed to a terrible fire." He reached them under whining bullets and shells. Retreat was even more disastrous, "under an incessant fire . . . reaping down our noble soldiers like grass before the scythe."

About 190 men of the 32nd had gone into the battle. In less than half an hour, 103 were dead or wounded. The severely wounded were jolted over log roads fourteen miles to Fredericksburg, and here Stephenson entered the hospital tents to find his men lying on every side. Washington Irving Stodder had just breathed his last. Dying Jacob Cushing, the color guard, managed to call his commander's name. Albert Wilder, Gardner Jones, and Henry Miller, shoemakers all, were casualties of that day.

Stephenson was called away, and the survivors marched on to the final long sieges of Richmond and Petersburg. Lee retreated, but Grant and Sheridan pursued, while Sherman's army swept "like an avalanche" up through Georgia and the Carolinas. On April 3, 1865, black Union troops were the first to enter captured Richmond, and on April 9, at Appomattox, Lee surrendered. Home in Hingham the town was "radiant with 'red, white, and blue.'" Bells rang, schoolchildren marched, bonfires blazed, fireworks burst. A week later, the town mourned the death of President Lincoln. Townsman John Andrew, the great war governor, had seen the beginning and lived to see the end. On December 22, 1865, veterans paraded to the State House in Boston. Each color bearer stepped forward and presented his regiment's flag to Governor Andrew. At the start of war, he had "ordered the overcoats" for the troops; now "he received the flags."

For two years after he died in 1867 at age forty-nine, Governor Andrew's remains would not come back to Hingham, "the home of my heart." Less famous townsmen had been straggling home for years, some to survive only briefly. Andrew Clark had warned, "As the people of Hingham see their friends who left them full of life and vigor, come back sick, wounded, emaciated, and dead, they begin to realize, as it is brought nearer home to them, some of the realities of war." William Beal, eighth generation descendant of John Beal, was one of those who came home to die of consumption. Daniel Hersey, discharged ill in Virginia, started "on hands and knees" for the depot and had to be carried to the train by a nameless black man. He made it to Hingham but died a few days later.

What did "home" mean to them? It meant one thing to the two Beals, three Cushings, three Frenches, three Joneses, three Gills, three Herseys, two Humphreys, six Lincolns, two Stodders, and two Wilders who died. But when Michael Fee died in a Washington hospital, what home did this Irish native think of? As Daniel Murphy lay dying there, too, what was "home" to this shoemaker? His mother gave a moving answer to historians Burr and Lincoln: Dan must be called a citizen of Hingham, for "if Hingham was not his home, the young man had no home."

At least two other heroes bore unfamiliar names. A color bearer at Laurel Hill, James McCarthy, rescued the state flag from the mortally wounded Cushing and carried it to safety. When Thomas Hickey, a color sergeant, was captured near Petersburg, he managed first, "amidst a shower of bullets," to get to a cabin and destroy the flag before it could be captured. Nor must we forget, among the heroes, one brave woman. Helen Aurelia Dyer, daughter of Hingham's Congregational minister, taught black children in liberated areas of South Carolina. In 1864, she came home to marry, and when she and her bridegroom sailed again for the South, their steamer sank in a snowstorm.

But for now we think of the men, think of three pairs of homecoming brothers. Thomas and James Hickey had their genealogy, but it was left behind when their father John migrated from Ireland to Nova Scotia and came to Hingham in 1831. Edwin and Henry, Constable Gridley Hersey's sons, came home, and so did cooper Nathaniel Hersey's sons Hollis and Albert. Their genealogy stretched back over eight prolific generations to William Hersey, who came to Hingham in 1635. For them, "home" was the whole history of the town, already over 230 years long. Their forebears had lived through many chapters, many conflicts in war and peace, many challenges to community in the face of which Hingham had survived, changed, and grown.

The men of the 1860s were born in the 1830s and 1840s, a time of growth and vitality followed by decline. "When I was a boy," said their grandfathers, recalling their boyhood a half-century earlier in the first years of a new nation born in war and menaced by divisions. *Their* grandfathers had been boys, too, and "When I was a boy" reached back to the 1730s, when old parson Ebenezer Gay was a young man. And *their* grandfathers in turn could remember the "Indian" wars, King Philip's death, and the building of a new meetinghouse. And *their* grandfathers were here at the beginning and could remember a new town of a few hundred souls, facing its first challenges and conflicts, forging its new community.

PART ONE

The Worlds of the Grandfathers

1633 to the Civil War

CHAPTER ONE

✠

First Memories and Modern Guesses

THIS is a story of change, for change is what history is made of. It is also a story of facts, challenges, and aspirations that persist, for not all is changed. Chiefly, the story tells of how an ancient New England town has been transformed in the five generations since Americans fought the war that made them one nation. But when its men fought in that war, Hingham's life history already stretched back over 230 years. For some of those men, immigrants from famine and oppression abroad, Hingham was a new home. For others, whose ancestors had also been, once upon a time, immigrants from famine and oppression, Hingham was already the home of long ancestral memories.

Historian Solomon Lincoln warned in 1827 that "the exact date at which any individual came here to reside cannot be ascertained." Modern historian John P. Richardson reminds us that a settlement here called Bare Cove was taxed by the colonial government in 1634. "Settlement was gradual from 1633 to 1640." Quite possibly, settlers were here before 1633. Numerous coastal settlements from Cape Ann to Wessagusset (Weymouth), some established by fishermen from England's southwest, had failed in the 1620s, and stragglers had moved down the coast as far as Conohasset and Nantasket. Places along Hingham's shoreline from Martin's Cove to Otis Hill, Walton's Cove, and Tucker's Swamp, preserve southwest English names.

In 1633, we know, a handful of families arrived from Hingham and Windham, England—among them Hobarts, Jacobs, Smiths, and Lincolns—after spending a few months in Charlestown. A chain migration started, but its slowness is significant. Eleven towns of the Massachusetts Bay Colony were established earlier than Hingham; Concord, far inland, was formed at the same time. The Hingham plantation had to be surveyed and staked out—we do not know when this was done. A prudent people had to be recruited, screened, and persuaded that the plantation would not fail. Family was a key factor, as the trickle-in of Lincolns suggests. Nicholas Jacob brought with him to Charlestown in 1633 his cousin Thomas Lincoln, a weaver, and after two years in Watertown, Thomas chose to move to Hingham. His brother Samuel decided to join him in 1637 after four years in Salem. Thomas, a miller, came in 1635, and so did Thomas, a cooper. Thomas, a husbandman (farmer), and his brother Stephen did not arrive until 1638.

The small, mixed settlement had lacked a minister and hence a leader for at least two years when a Hobart kinsman, the Rev. Peter Hobart, was persuaded to come. He was thirty years old when he reached Charlestown from England in June, 1635. His boat trip to join his family in Hingham took place after three months' delay in Charlestown, where he reportedly weighed offers from other towns. Probably it took time to recruit and carefully screen the small company of settlers he brought with him. The towns took this process very seriously; no one was admitted without invitation. No "squatters" were allowed.

Who came with Peter Hobart from Charlestown? The evidence is not clear, but it suggests a band of mixed origins, some from East Anglia (Hingham, England, and its vicinity) and others from southwest counties, such as Devon and Dorset. The familiar legend of a cohesive band arriving with Hobart from Hingham, England, must be set aside. So, too, must the modern scholarly speculation that west countrymen had already formed a town and that coordinated waves of East Anglians then "invaded" and drove out most of those first settlers. This modern "myth" includes the unsupported conjecture that the two groups engaged in heated conflict, that the puritanical later arrivals would not tolerate the west country customs—maypoles, pagan rites, sexual license, and heavy drinking—of the earlier settlers. No doubt the customs were very different. Indeed, even daily communication might have been a challenge, for the groups spoke very different dialects of English. But if there was open hostility, why would members of both groups have arrived and been granted land in 1635? And why would later arrivals constitute a similar mixture?

The only concerted "invasion" of East Anglians came by the ship *Diligent* in 1638, when Hingham, England, minister Robert Peck, now a fugitive from episcopal persecution, sought refuge and brought twenty-plus families with him. Among them were Beals, Chamberlains,

[18]

Cushings, Gateses, Gilmans, two Lincolns, Jameses, Ripleys, and Stodders, and Hawkes and Fearings from nearby Cambridge, England.

Hingham's first population was now almost complete; by 1640, migration was slowing to a trickle all over New England. In the next two decades, as few as eight families were admitted—among them, Burr, Dunbar, Garnett (later Gardner), Lasell, and Wyton (later spelled Whiting and Whiton). In the Hingham of 1640, there were about 130 families, about seven hundred persons. Of these, early recorders estimate, about two hundred, 30 percent, came from Old Hingham and nearby. A modern scholar stretches this to 40 percent, with 15 percent from west counties. Where the other 45 percent came from is not known. Hingham began as a mixed town, only slightly more East Anglian than Massachusetts in general. The scholarly impulse to declare Hingham peculiarly "East Anglian" has been tied to another speculation: that Hingham was from the start also unusually "conservative," protective of its East Anglian ways. However, recent historians of Massachusetts find the same conservatism throughout the colony.

West countrymen were among the town's leaders at the start: Joseph Andrews the first constable and first clerk; Thomas Loring the first church deacon and first holder of a liquor license, a dual role that reflects oddly on the stereotype of "puritan." John Otis held important offices through the 1640s, and Anthony Eames, too, until 1645. After 1639, it is true, a few men, chiefly East Anglian, held most power; but this reflected the "population ratio," and besides, such "oligarchies" were the rule throughout the colony. The modern speculation of ethnic conflict is based wholly on a dispute in 1645 over the selection of militia officers. A recent writer fancies that "apparently determined to purge the town of all West Country influence, the East Anglian leaders arranged" to block Eames's nomination to be captain. The only contemporary explanation of why this happened is that he had "offended the greater part of the town." Presumably the offense had nothing to do with his place of birth. But if he was ethnically unacceptable, why would Eames have held prominent positions and been nominated captain in the first place?

Whatever his offense, the aftermath divided Hingham for years in "sad, unbrotherly contention." The town's first historian, Solomon Lincoln, accepts the tradition that "many of the first settlers" moved away as a result. This tradition, too, must be questioned. Of the families who did leave in the next few years, we estimate, seven or eight were west country folks, but twice as many were East Anglian. The population shrank from about seven hundred to four hundred. People moved to various places, notably towns in Plymouth Colony, whose northern border abutted Hingham. This suggests that they had religious-political differences with the Massachusetts Bay Colony. Such mobility was not unusual. Noting that "nearly sixty percent of the original landholders left the town before they died," Daniel Smith comments, "this early sifting out process was a common feature in New England towns." But it was even more common elsewhere than in Hingham. Kenneth Lockridge has studied the unusual stability of Dedham, and he found Hingham even more stable. So, the key question for grasping the uniqueness of Hingham is not why some moved away, but why so many did not.

What were the settlers like? They were neither very rich nor very poor; none was of the aristocracy. Most were of the middle class, some prosperous enough to bring servants. Of the 133 people who arrived in 1638, about thirty were servants. The settlers came with a mix of occupations. They were townsmen who had some familiarity with farming, but they had much to learn in order to manage a self-sufficient agricultural life by their own labor. "The picture of the early time, if it could be reproduced," thought John D. Long, "would present a body of men and women engaged in the most ordinary activities." They were hardly "ordinary" by our standards. A more recent and realistic guess is that "truly the burdens of existence must have appeared endless."

They had small houses to raise, varying in size from less than fifteen feet square to twenty-eight by twenty feet. One room with a loft went up first; later, a second room and a "shed" kitchen would be added. They had grain to grow: Indian corn was easiest, planted in small "hills" with fish to fertilize, if dogs could be kept away until the fish rotted. As Englishmen, they preferred wheat and barley, but wheat did not flourish, and they adjusted to bread made of "rye and Injun." Poor barley made poor beer, so strong cider became popular. This meant planting apple trees for cider, as well as for the preservative vinegar. Next to orchards in their small "home lots" they had kitchen gardens to plant: Indian vegetables—corn, beans, pumpkins, squash—and their own root crops—carrots, turnips, parsnips. Women tended kitchen gardens, small dairies, perhaps a few hens, when not cooking, making cloth, or endlessly bearing children, while men were off at the "common" or the "great lot."

The labors included hauling water, preparing wood for fuel, and herding livestock between home night pasture and daytime on the common or great lot. Salt and fresh meadow hay had to be cut, carried, and cured for winter feed. Livestock was the basis of the first Massachusetts economy; the settlers were livestock raisers and traders. With livestock, they had fences to build and maintain; there were stiff penalties for failure. Predators, primarily wolves, threatened livestock, and livestock on the loose threatened crops. Hogs, allowed to feed where they could, had to be kept out of gardens, horses out of cornfields and meadows, and later, rams had to be exiled to Bumpkin's Island until needed again among the flocks of sheep.

The tools for all this work were few and simple: "a strong man might carry on his shoulder all his ordinary farm implements," wooden shovel and hay fork, iron manure fork, iron reaping hook, scythe, mattock, hatchet. Ploughs were costly, heavy, and few; for a century or more, poorer farmers did not have them.

There were also obligatory civic duties. Frequent town meetings required male attendance; committees came into being early; Sabbath services were long and multiple; the militia, the "trainband," had its drills. A "deal of human nature" animated occasional disputes, as when John Tower and John Magoon were fined twenty shillings each for "quarreling and striking one another in a public town meeting."

Although life was hard, the town was a healthy place. The first settlers were blessed with longevity as well as fertility. The Hobart brothers, Pastor Peter and Captain Joshua, whose presences dominated these years, assured continuity by living into the last quarter of the century. Peter, his three brothers, and a sister, John Beal's wife, had a total of sixty children, of whom at least forty-eight survived childhood. And John Beal himself lived to be one hundred. Insularity in the early towns, into which even visitors were admitted only by consensus, protected them against epidemics. So did the climate, from the malaria, yellow fever, and parasitic diseases common in the South. Settlers along the Massachusetts coast had found

> an inviting shore, formerly well-inhabited by native Indians, but in 1630 almost empty . . . excellent harbors . . . small rivers for access to the interior, and a wealth of forest within reach . . . thousands of acres of natural grass . . . and substantial areas of open, tillable land . . . in comparatively recent Indian cultivation.

The most wondrous gift of "Divine Providence" was the gift of incredible natural resources: pure water in the Town Brook and the Weir River, a protected harbor, abundant wildlife—fish, crustaceans, game birds and beasts, wild fruit, a sufficient annual rainfall, great stands of woodland, land of varying types and soils. It was "the Promised Land."

Land was a major reason why settlers came, but there were other motives not so easily understood. "The mind of any period or people of the past is an indescribable thing, for it is a conglomerate of the ever-changing desires, prejudices, and standards of the incoherent many as well as of the vociferous few." Motives for risking the long, dangerous journey must have been complex: fear, hope, desperation, acquisitiveness, faith. But clearly, one major motive was economic.

Economic conditions across the southern half of England were dismal. Common lands were being enclosed into rental farms, and dispossessed peasants roamed the countryside. Wages dropped, unemployment rose, and textile towns of East Anglia were hard hit. Epidemic diseases struck every few years, but still the population rose, by the standards of the seventeenth century, to overcrowding. In the 1620s, depression made matters worse, and so did the absolutism of a new king, Charles I, who raised taxes for foreign wars, billeted troops in homes, and forced men into the military. John Winthrop remembered "spectacles of misery in all our streets." Meanwhile, English navigators wrote glowing reports of America's east coast. People decided to risk the journey of six to eight weeks, the storms, the shipboard epidemics. They came partly for land, which was life and wealth.

Every story of Hingham has started with the drawing of land lots. Home lots, by a 1635 order of the colonial government in Boston, had to be clustered not far from the meetinghouse, partly to insure physical safety, partly to provide the spiritual safety of covenanted mutual control. This order was meant to correct the sort of land division that had happened in Watertown, where settlers had allotted themselves all of the land in large house-farm lots. The puritan ideal of community had broken down; neighbor did not meet neighbor in the coming and going of everyday life. In Hingham, by contrast, planting grounds, meadows, salt marsh, uplands, "great lots," were assigned separately, outside of two stringlike village nuclei with their nearby "commons."

On September 18, 1635, house lots were "drawn." About this event the evidence is unclear. Some who "drew" lots were here already; some here already did not "draw" lots; some who "drew" lots would come later, if at all. That day, between thirty and thirty-seven lots were assigned, twenty-eight on "Town Street" (later North), two on what became West Street, and (perhaps also on that day) seven on Broad Cove, along the west side of today's Lincoln Street. The Town Street lots lay side by side from the harbor to "Hockley Lane," all but one of them facing south over the Town Brook, protected from the north by hills.

[22]

Francis Smithes 5 Acres,	Thomas Collier 5 Acres,	
30	29	Highway leading to the Great Lots.

28 — George Bacon, 5 Acres. (Lot Mask's)
27 — Andrew Lane, 5 Acres.
26 — Nath. Baker. 5 Acres.
25 — Nicholas Baker. 5 Acres.
24 — George Ludkin. 5 Acres.
23 — George Lane. 5 Acres.

Burton's Lane

22 — George Marsh, 5 Acres.
21 — Richard Osborn. 5 Acres.
20 — Nath. Peck. 5 Acres.
19 — Rev. Peter Hobart, 10 Acres. { Gould and Andrews now.
18 — Joshua Hobart; 5 Acres. (Caleb Theytons now.
17 — Edmund Hobart. Sen. 10 As. { Setts Lincolns now.
16 — John Smart. 5 Acres. (Lanes now.
15 — Edmund Hobart. Jr. 5 Acres.
14 — Nicholas Jacob. 3 Acres. { now Wm Lincolns.
A subsequent grant to Thomas Lincoln. Cooper.

Highway leading to Broad Cove.

12 — Thomas Wakely. 5 Acres.
11 — Richard Betscombe. 5 Acres.
10 — William Walton. 5 Acres.
9 — Joseph Andrews, 5 Acres. { Son of No 8.
8 — Thomas Andrews. 5 Acres.
7 — David Phippen. 5 Acres.
6 — John Strong. 5 Acres.
5 — Thomas Loring. 5 Acres.
4 — John Otis. 5 Acres.
3 — William Nolton. 5 Acres.
2 — Abraham Martin. 2 Acres.
1 — James Cady. 2 Acres.

The Sea.

Town Street.
now North Street,

13
Wm. Arnall.
5 Acres.
(Now Soules.)

Errata. There is a lot between Nos 19 and 20 not numbered on the copy, which we left out here for want of room. It is subsequent-rant to Anthony Cooper Jr.

In the number of acres given, a certain proportion is in Back Lands. Hon. Solomon Lincoln's plan explains this matter.

George Lincoln Jr.'s chart of 1635 house lot assignments along North and West Streets

The lots were long and narrow: a house was raised in front; behind was land for a kitchen garden, orchard, and night pasture. With a few exceptions—Peter Hobart and his father received ten acres apiece—each lot was about five acres.

The locations appear to have been planned, perhaps to legitimize where some already lived, perhaps to create the neighborhoods that resulted. Of the twelve families settled between the harbor and today's Lincoln Street, most, possibly all, came from England's southwest seafaring counties, Devon and Dorset. West of them, beginning with Nicholas Jacob (185 North Street), gathered the neighborhood of Old Hinghamites with their leaders, Edmund Hobart and his three sons, in their midst and Hobart's Bridge in front of them. Reverend Peter's house probably stood astride present-day Thaxter Street on the slope above today's Methodist Church, an historical irony that would not have pleased that staunch presbyterian.

With more arrivals in 1636, the south branch of Town Street across the Town Brook, today's South Street, was assigned. Near the middle, Jarvis Goold left his name in Goold's Bridge, today's West Hingham crossing. In 1638, the Hobart domain was enlarged when old Edmund's son-in-law John Beal arrived with his family, received land across the brook, and raised his house where Beals would center for generations at the southwest corner of Hersey Street. In 1637, the village nucleus expanded west and south—west to "Nichols' Hill," the origin of Fort Hill village, and south along "Bachelors' Row" below the hill which lower Main Street now cuts through. In 1638, the arrival of the large *Diligent* party necessitated a second village nucleus, winding up Pear Tree Hill, steeper then, to "the Playne," now the Centre.

Here was a village with a difference. Most of these newcomers had voyaged together from Old Hingham and its vicinity with the same customs and occupations, weaver, cooper, tanner, and farmer. Their leaders, Robert and Joseph Peck and Matthew Cushing, received prize lots below Pear Tree Hill. On "the Playne," south from what later became East Street to "Cold" or "Cole" Corner, clustered Chamberlain, Foulsham, Fearing, Hawke, James, Pitts, Ripley, Smith, Wilder. If Hingham Centre has kept its distinctive and cohesive character over the centuries, perhaps it took root in this, the only transplanted Old Hingham village.

A few "Playne" settlers already lived at some distance from this enclave, beyond the training field of the militia, bounded by Main, Leavitt, School, and Pleasant Streets, and beyond the fort near today's Common. Joneses were "over the river" at Leavitt's Bridge, Leavitts further on, Spragues on the southern edge of the training field. "Over the river" was good planting ground, "flat, deep, alluvial soil," and they were farmers.

So lay the town's villages of seven hundred souls as of 1639. But within a generation, Hingham spread out from its two stringlike nuclei. This important change evolved from the original practice of assigning "planting lots" and "great lots" at a considerable distance from house lots, in order to keep the residential town close together. Great lots, twelve to twenty acres each, were for timber, hay, and pasture. Often they were far from home, on "Great Playne" from Crooked Meadow River to Accord Pond, at "Nutty Hill" (the west end of High Street), at Hockley (the region of Bare Cove Park), Old Planter's Hill (World's End), and elsewhere. Imagine the slow traffic of two-wheeled carts and livestock over the rough, unleveled tracks, sometimes forty feet wide. Imagine, too, the townsmen's daily encounters in their slow treks.

What soon happened was this. Some owners moved away, and a few townsmen bought their holdings, accumulating in a generation huge tracts of land from which to draw wealth and on which to settle their heirs. Daniel Cushing bought the most, and some of his sons settled on East Street and in South Hingham. The large great lot of Robert Peck passed, when he returned to England in 1641, to the first Thaxter, whose three granddaughters married Cushings. When William Hersey died in 1658, he left land all over town, "formerly Palmer's, formerly Chaffee's, formerly Jacob's, formerly Ripley's, formerly Austin's," etc. His Fort Hill neighbor, Thomas Lincoln the husbandman, included in his estate (1692) land on Great Plain, in Conyhassett, fresh and salt meadow all over town, acres at Weariall (Otis) Hill and Hockley, and so on. A few late-comers had begun building further south: Lasells, Garnetts, and Dunbars. Further on settled James Wyton, who arrived no earlier than 1647 and by 1681 had become one of the town's largest landowners.

Thus did the first Cushings, Herseys, Lincolns, and Whitons plant their progeny all over Hingham, while others formed clan compounds. Thus, too, began the transformation of a Puritan village into a network of landed families.

Early town records are filled with grants, swaps, and sales of land, all recorded by Town Clerk Joseph Andrews, who received fourpence for each transaction. Land was assigned by collective decision. No land held "in common" could be distributed except by special town meeting. Periodically, the "select men"—the term appears in 1649—chosen to "order the affairs of the town" were reminded that they could not give, sell, exchange, lease, or divide town land, or make decisions regarding its timber, even though they were expected to enforce orders to protect it. Already, selectmen were given large responsibilities and little power.

The powers of individuals were limited, too. Land could be sold privately to an "honest man", but only after it had been offered to the town. The town could recall a parcel if, for example, it turned out to interfere with access to common land, or if it was needed for a "highway." Another lot or lots were then given. This was an early expression of the power of eminent domain. Defining land as "more or less" so many acres, whose boundary markers were often trees, stumps, and boulders, invariably called for arbitration about straightening and measuring lots and maintaining fences. Almost from the town's inception, there were fence-viewers, and by the 1660s, surveyors were appointed.

When and how towns distributed land, and the reasons for such assignments, varied widely. Pilgrim Plymouth had no English title to its land. Unable to pay the stockholders of its sponsoring merchant company, Plymouth decided to buy out the company. To do so, it aggressively developed trade based on hatchets and knives, livestock and grain, to pay off the debt. Before 1640, fifty-three men owned all the land. For a different reason (the desire to divide inheritance equally among heirs) the inhabitants of the huge Dedham plantation decided in 1657 to admit no more settlers. Seventy-nine men made themselves proprietors in common of all public land. Sudbury's division of land favored the most influential and powerful. As a result of protracted debate and political skirmishing, the colonial government granted adjacent land and allowed the dissatisfied to form a new town, Marlborough. In Hingham, the tradition of common lands remained strong at least until the 1660s.

With land came wealth and power. In 1637, when Hingham still had about one hundred families and thirty-two square miles, land hunger became an early source of conflict. A town committee argued at the General Court for a portion of Nantasket. The petition was summarily denied. Land hunger caused conflict for years with Scituate. The border, now Norwell, was rich in marsh hay, "most desirable of all fodder for an Englishman's cattle," and Hingham's first commerce was raising and selling livestock to later arrivals. When immigration almost ended after 1640, new markets had to be found in far-off Virginia and the West Indies.

Hingham's other early industry came from its considerable stand of primeval forest and port location. By the 1650s, it had become famous for lumber: "The people have much profited themselves by transporting Timber, Planke, and Mast for shipping to the town of Boston; as also cedar and Pine-board, to supply the wants of other townes, and also to remote parts, even as far as Barbadoes." Lumber was paid for in scarce currency, not the "country pay" of bartered goods and crops. This may explain how some families had the money to buy so much land so soon.

Such economic motives came into conflict early with the political ideal of the town as a commonwealth. The immigrants had fled distressing new political trends in England. Their traditional "localism" had been threatened by meddling bishops, grasping courtiers, demanding military officers, and tax collectors. They "departed England determined to maintain their local attachments against outside interference," and they shaped their politics accordingly. John Winthrop's colonial government in Boston had the impossible task of balancing the central authority of the colony with the local autonomy of the towns.

Recent historians agree that the majority of settlers in the Bay Colony brought an agrarian, village-county mind-set. They consented to a covenanted society, a concept eloquently articulated by Winthrop. It was to be an ordered, peaceable society of the like-minded, in which the individual was subordinate to a "corporate Christian community." Ideally, all disputes were settled by peaceful arbitration leading to consensus. The town ideal was expressed in the General Court's allotting "plantations" only to *groups*. The group was expected to form a municipal government, elect town officers, make bylaws, and enjoy *almost* total self-determination in local matters. It had the right to send representatives ("deputies") to the lower house of the legislature ("General Court") and the obligation to levy taxes for both local and colonial governments. Initially, only covenanted church members—they were called "visible saints"—and their families were admitted to a plantation. These heads of households, "freemen," were obliged to participate in and make decisions regarding local covenanted institutions: church, militia, town meeting. They lived by a voluntary, enveloping social contract.

But to this ideal—it became known as "The New England Way"— Peter Hobart and the ministers of a few other towns were not entirely sympathetic. They preferred what we will later describe as the presbyterian model, which, paradoxically, was more authoritarian, but also less exclusive and rigid. As a result of his "strong opinions," Hobart and Hingham were involved in five clashes with Boston during the 1640s, the "crucial decade" of the young colony. These were not just disputes of personalities; they were parts and symptoms of a crisis in these formative years of Massachusetts. The struggle centered on the desire of the deputies of the General Court for sharing of power with the upper legislative house, the elected magistrates. Of greatest impact was the Hingham militia affair.

The "jealous localism" of colonial militias or "trainbands" in seeking to choose their own officers, and the political importance of militias as voluntary town institutions, had evolved in reaction to the settlers' experiences in England. King Charles I had tried to centralize authority through a standing army; the "trainbands," pillars of local autonomy, were a bulwark against such centralization. But they were also radical early experiments in "democracy," not yet a popular idea, and as such, they were bound to cause conflicts. They did so throughout the colony; Hingham was not peculiar when its conflict broke out in 1645. However, the challenge it posed to John Winthrop was the most serious he would ever face.

Lieutenant Anthony Eames was nominated by the Hingham militia to be captain. His name was presented to the Standing Council in Boston, composed of magistrates, who alone had the power to *appoint* officers. For reasons no document reveals, the men of the militia then changed their minds and nominated Bozoan Allen. The magistrates denied this changed nomination and reaffirmed the appointment of Eames. Without notifying Eames, Ensign Joshua Hobart called a drill session. Arriving tardily on the field, Eames received no response to his commands but instead, much contentious verbal opposition. This angry quarrel moved next Sunday into the meetinghouse. According to Winthrop, Peter Hobart threatened to excommunicate Eames, a serious threat, since only freemen (church members) could serve as officers. Although more judicious opinion prevailed that day, Eames and twelve others later left the congregation.

The four Hobart brothers, Bozoan Allen, Daniel Cushing, and William Hersey were chief among the eighty-one petitioners who now challenged the authority and procedures of the magistrates, particularly John Winthrop, in denying the choice of a local majority. Before a joint session of the General Court in June, 1645, a proceeding to impeach Winthrop began. Hingham's deputies, Joshua Hobart and Bozoan Allen, described what the petitioners considered Winthrop's illegal actions. Winthrop argued his own case and was acquitted. The legal proceedings were extensive and complex, but the resolution was clear. Most of the deputies, fearful that their towns would have to share the court costs, conceded that the petition was erroneous and that "the Hingham militia company had mutinied against their legitimate commander," Eames.

The deputies had lost their fight against the magistrates and Winthrop. Hingham had lost, too. John Tower, who had been jailed in Boston for refusing to post bond for an appearance in court, had to finish his jail term. The other eighty petitioners were fined for court costs according to their "culpability." Hingham was enjoined from nominating its own militia officers. A pleading petition three years later secured an order that Allen be lieutenant and Joshua Hobart ensign, but a Weymouth man was made captain. Not until 1651 did Allen receive that office. When Allen left for Boston the following year, Joshua Hobart succeeded for his lifetime to this powerful post.

Luckily, for the first forty years, the militia's importance was mostly precautionary. Relative peace and security prevailed with the local tribes of the Algonquian nation. Even so, rumors of danger persisted, and vigilance remained the rule. By law, men were obliged to carry arms to a public meeting or when traveling more than a mile from home. Many Hingham town meeting actions concerned the trainband.

Plymouth and Massachusetts Bay lands had been hunting, fishing, and farming grounds of Native Americans for several thousand years. When the settlers first reached Bare Cove, today's North, South, and Fort Hill Streets were still aboriginal paths. A trail of the Massachuset skirted the town's southern boundary. The Massachuset under Chickatabut lived as far south as Marshfield; south of them, the Wampanoags under Massassoit; to their southwest, their enemies the Narragansetts. But in 1617, a "great plague" had emptied many of the coastal villages, leaving cleared planting fields ready for use, and so, land was not a source of conflict with the newcomers. Besides, Massassoit, needing allies against the Narragansetts, had made a durable treaty with Plymouth. In 1633, Chickatabut was succeeded by his grandson Josiah Wompatuck, and under Wompatuck peaceable relations were maintained for years.

Thus, the significance of the militia controversy of 1645 was not military but political. It was part of a struggle over the constitutional status of the colony. Peter Hobart claimed no law had been broken by the town's petitioning about its militia officers. The General Court, he declared, was "but as a corporation" under *English* law. This challenge, one scholar thinks, may have been part of a "carefully organized plot" to bring about "greater liberties to those who disagreed with the established order" in Boston, a plot masterminded by Winthrop's chief antagonist, William Vassall of Scituate, just over Hingham's border in Plymouth Colony.

This interpretation is confirmed by what happened a year later in 1646. Dr. Robert Child and six others, including Thomas Burton of Hingham, petitioned the General Court with complaints about the excessive and arbitrary use of power by the magistrates and the denial to many of the right to vote for "magistrates, captains, or other civil or military officers." Underlying this and future actions by some of the petitioners lay the threat to petition the Commission on Foreign Plantations *in England*, to appeal to the English parliament. Appeals to England were "not allowed" by the Colony's charter. Whatever dissatisfactions there were among Bay colonists, few wanted English intervention. Thirty-one of the thirty-six deputies voted against the petitioners. Among the five minority votes were those of Joshua Hobart and Bozoan Allen. With the exception of Thomas Fowle, who escaped to England, the petitioners refused to recant and were fined huge sums.

Winthrop suspected that not only Vassall, but also Peter Hobart, was instrumental in these events. Seeking advice, the General Court convened the mainly Congregational elders. Hobart was present. Denying any knowledge of the petition, he nonetheless sensed that opinion was against him and left the meeting. The General Court declared a "fast day." Fast days were the chief Puritan rituals of expiation of God's anger as expressed in natural disasters, in misfortunes, and in the central danger to Puritan community, dissension—in this case, the dissension and disruption surrounding the Child petition. "The pastor of Hingham, and others of his church," wrote Winthrop, disregarded the declared fast day.

One footnote to this story concerns a young Boston carpenter, his wife, and four children. Overheard making negative comments about the Court's decision, he was briefly imprisoned and put in irons. He confessed his involvement, was released, and moved to Hingham. He was Thomas Joy, who either built or enlarged the grist mill, the original site of which is now buried beneath Station Street.

The next year (1647), Hobart was forbidden by the Court to deliver a *sermon* at the Boston wedding of one of his parishioners. His opposition to the government was cited; he was a "bold man, and would speak his mind." And in a final episode of the 1640s, he was again at odds with Boston. The English parliament, now presbyterian, was trying to bring the churches of England and Scotland into conformity under the Westminster Confession. New England Congregational leaders resisted any attempt to "reform" their churches, to force them to accept Separatists, to tolerate all Protestants. A synod was held in Cambridge, Massachusetts, but those of "presbyterial" leanings refused to attend, Hobart among them. The "Cambridge Platform" that emerged was an assertion of Congregational polity. It was tantamount to a declaration of ecclesiastical independence from England. Hobart characteristically remained loyal to the English parliament.

For Hobart and Winthrop, this was the final clash; in 1649, Winthrop died. They were two strong-willed leaders with conflicting visions of how a good society should be governed. Both cherished localism, but they interpreted local control differently. Winthrop the Congregationalist believed that power within each church "society"— what would later be called a congregation—came from all members, but that membership should be severely limited. Until 1664, to vote in civic affairs, one had to be a church member, and so Winthrop's position denied the vote to many. From Winthrop's point of view, Hobart the presbyterian managed "all affairs without the church's advice." Presbyterianism did place greater power in the minister and elders; however, membership included "all except public sinners," and hence it granted a broader franchise. By 1640, Hobart's church included virtually all town families, whereas churches in Winthrop's Boston included fewer than half. This difference reflected a deep division in religious-political doctrine.

It also reflected the differences between Winthrop the idealistic utopian and Hobart the more pluralistic pragmatist. Hobart's practicality had led him to recognize early the difficulties that arose from restricting church membership to "visible saints." A "visible saint" was an adult who had made a public declaration of faith and had described a conversion experience. Only then could he or she participate in the communion service and be admitted to full membership. Such exclusive membership caused political problems. A town was entitled to elect one deputy for each forty male members. By 1647, the number of males in Hingham over twenty-one years of age was only seventy-nine, which would have denied Hingham its second deputy. Furthermore, the *children* of "visible saints," though usually baptized, were increasingly preoccupied with worldly matters and often did not seek full membership. To insure enough members to elect deputies, a kind of part-membership, a "halfway covenant," would be a practical necessity.

And what of *their* children, the grandchildren of the "saints"? Could they be baptized? These problems, both religious and political, were finally resolved by compromise in a 1662 synod. But Hobart had anticipated the compromise by about twenty years. He was widely known for his inclusive approach to baptism: "Parents who were not members of the established church, for whatever reason, brought their children to be baptized, some coming from as far distant as Lynn." At first, he had refused to baptize John Otis's granddaughter: her father, John Burton, was an Anglican; she was not the child of a "saint." But very soon we find this entry in Hobart's diary: "1641 May. Hannah Burton baptized." This departure from the strict Congregational Way was the first of Hobart's divisions with Winthrop, and it prepared the way for the other four. It was also prophetic of what became a theme of Hingham history: an act of accommodation, a tactic of assimilation.

That Hobart's spiritual and political leadership was pleasing to the majority of townsmen can be guessed from their liberality. Solomon Lincoln suggests that his unusually large salary of one hundred pounds was voted in 1651 to help pay Hobart's fines to the General Court. But the same amount was voted for nineteen years. So, while some recent scholars have contrived the picture of Hobart as an irascible fomenter of disputes, he was in fact in tune with forces that challenged and, much later, broke the Congregationalists' hold on Massachusetts. His policy of inclusiveness and assimilation was a force for local community and stability, as was his longevity. By no accident, he was succeeded by John Norton from presbyterian Ipswich, and Norton by presbyterian Ebenezer Gay from Dedham. Such leaders set their stamp early on the personality of Hingham.

CHAPTER TWO

Land of the Puritans' Children

IN the spring of 1676, old John Tower was sixty-seven. He could not have forgotten those days he spent in a Boston jail for his role in the defiance of Winthrop, but he remained stubbornly independent. Twelve years before, he had moved from Pear Tree Hill to a thirty-acre farm near Tower Brook. The fortified house of this "sturdy and resolute" man stood on Main Street two miles south of the meetinghouse with its palisade and powder storage and a mile from the fort at the Common. Two other forts also commanded the town's approaches and water supply, one on what later became the Hingham cemetery hill, the other on Fort Hill. Linking the forts was a network of garrison houses. Now, Tower declared his independence once more. He petitioned the government in Boston to prohibit Hingham from calling away his sons and his hired man to defend other fortifications, "my sons having deserted their own dwellings and brought their goods into my fortification." The town awaited attack by King Philip's Wampanoags. Three of Philip's men had been executed for killing an "Indian" friend of the English. In June, 1675, Philip had launched a war in which twelve or thirteen towns were destroyed, one thousand colonists killed, dwellings burned, and cattle slaughtered.

For months, Hingham prepared. Then, in April, 1676, half a mile south of Tower's house, young John Jacob, chasing a deer out of his wheatfield, was shot to death near Glad Tidings Rock. The terrifying news was spread by clanging bells, beating drums, and hurrying messengers. Citizens retreated to fortifications and officers Hobart, Smith, and Thaxter took command. The anxious night passed, but with the dawn, smoke rose from what had been the Jones and Sprague houses

The twelfth day of December, 1677, The Inhabitants of the Town of Hingham, drew their Lots for their Fourth Division of Land next Weymouth line, as followeth:

Lots.		Shares.
1	Thomas Hobart,	10
2	Joseph Jacob, 4 Shares, James Bates 6 Shares, and Clement Bates 3 Shares all in one Lot,	13
3	Serjant Daniel Lincoln,	08
4	Thomas Lincoln (husbandman) and his son Joshua Lincoln,	15
5	Josiah Loring, senior,	07
6	John Otis,	10
7	Francis James,	09
8	John Magoon,	02
9	Andrew Lane, for his fathers right and his own,	10
10	Simon Burr, senior,	06 h.
11	John Tucker,	10
12	Robert Jones,	05
13	Anthony Sprague, for his own right, and his fathers,	12
14	Thomas Lincoln, (carpenter)	10
15	Samuel Lincoln, senior, five Shares, and 4 Shares, that belong to the Heirs of his brother Thomas Lincoln, deceased, and four Shares of Will. Woodcock's were all drawn in one Lot, and entered into the said Samuel Lincoln's name,	16
16	Israel Fearing,	04 h.
17	Thomas Lincoln, Cooper,	05
18	William Hersey, senior,	17
19	Lieutenant John Smith,	15
20	Edmond Pitts,	10 h.
21	John Beale, senior, and his son John Beales drawn on Lot for both their Shares,	12
23	Cornelius Cantlebury, for his own right, and his mother Williams,	08 h.
24	George Lane, and his son Josiah Lane,	13
25	James Hersey,	07
26	Nathaniel Baker,	15
27	Ephraim Hewitt,	05
28	Henry Ware,	04
29	Ann Tucker's heirs,	05
22	Mr. Hobart,	25

Lots.		Shares.
30	Stephen Lincoln,	05
31	Simon Gross, bought of Josiah Hobart, five Shares,	05
32	George Bacon's heirs,	05
33	Moses Collier,	08
34	John Kinghs heirs,	02
35	Daniel Stodder,	03
36	John Skath,	04
37	Abraham Ripley,	05
38	John Tower, senior,	08
39	Caleb Beales, for his right and Thomas Hinly,	05
40	Samuel Stodder,	03
41	Benjamin Bates,	05
42	John Prince, 6 Shares, Joseph Joy, four Shares, Thomas Tayer, 5 Shares, of Henry Chamberlains drew all their Shares in one Lot,	15
43	Samuel Thaxter, 5 Shares, and five Shares of Joseph Churchs, drawn in one Lot,	10
44	Edward Wilder,	08
45	Thomas Nichols,	09
46	John Stodder, four Shares, that he bought of Michael Pearse, and three of his own, drawn in one Lot,	07
47	Joseph Church, as he is executor of his fathers Will,	08
48	John Langlee,	
49	Edmond Hobart and John Jacob, drew their Shares in one Lot,	20
50	Robert Waterman 3 Shares, that he bought of Onesiphorus Marsh,	03
51	Nathaniel Chubbuck,	04
52	Jacob Beale 4 Shares, that he bought of Margaret Burton's heirs and 2 of his own,	06
53	John Fearing,	06 h.
54	Matthew Cushing,	12

Lots.		Shares.
55	Michael Pearse,	08
56	Thomas Marsh's heirs,	08
57	John Lovell,	06
58	Benjamin Lincoln,	03
59	John Hansfield, 5 Shares, and four he bought of Simon Rick,	09
60	Thomas Gill, senior,	09
61	Daniel Cushing, senior,	35
62	Joseph Jones, senior,	06
63	John Ripley,	13
64	Deacon John Leavitt,	14 h.
65	Captain Joshua Hobart,	18
66	Nathaniel Beale, senior,	08
67	Matthew Hawke,	06
68	John Chubbuck, in his fathers right,	08
69	Samuel Stowell, 4 Shares, and three of Henry Gibbs,	07
70	Joshua Beales, 4 Shares, and two that he bought of Onesiphorus Marsh,	06
71	Joseph Bate, 6 Shares, and Samuel Bate 6 Shares, drew one Lot for both their Shares,	12
72	John Farrow senior, 5 Shares, and John Farrow, junior, 2 Shares, drew their Shares in one Lot,	07
73	Thomas Andrews, ten Shares, and Joseph Andrews 2, drew 1 Lot,	12
74	Nicholas Baker,	05
75	Ensign John Thaxter,	16 h.
76	James Witon, senior,	05
77	Thomas Fay,	04
78	Jeremiah Beale, senior,	09

This Fourth Division is entered and recorded in the Town's great Book of the records of their Lands — By Daniel Cushing, Town Clerk.

The seventy-eight proprietors as of 1677 from Hosea Sprague's early nineteenth century copy of the town clerk's records from 1635 to 1700.

over the Weir River, and Chubbuck, Hobart, and Whiton houses across the southern horizon. The attackers were gone. A second attack failed, and in August, King Philip was dead, shot by a "praying Indian." Native American power in eastern Massachusetts had ended.

In forty years, Hingham had spread perilously far from its first protective nuclei. Although Great Lots, planting lots, and fresh and salt meadow had been distributed to the first settlers, huge stretches of land remained held in common. Hingham was already cautious in its decisions, and so it is not surprising that talk of dividing "Conyhasset" on the East halted with two resolutions in 1663 and 1665 not to give this land to individuals. Then quite suddenly, in 1669, there was a decision to divide. Committees were chosen to determine which lands would still "lie common" and which would be divided. In less than a year, eleven town meetings were held to adjudicate the basis for division. Ultimately, the formula was based on the acreage of house lots already owned. This may explain why Peter Hobart twice reminded the town that his house lot had been taken by the "Court," "by law," and that he was due a replacement. In May, 1669, he was granted fifty acres on the Great Plain, and as a result, when the divisions began, he held twenty-five division shares. One share would represent more or less two additional acres.

How much agitation and controversy surrounded the dividing can be surmised from a directive to Town Clerk Daniel Cushing: no minutes or votes of null and void decisions were to be given out. But the "major part" of the one hundred voting inhabitants finally agreed in January, 1670, that "their common land . . . be cast into 700 shares . . . to enjoy to themselves & their heirs & assigns forever." With less difficulty, after King Philip's War, the town decided to divide land in the southwest along the Weymouth line. In the eight years 1670-77, over one third (7291 acres) of the land in the town was divided, made private property, with almost 25 percent going to Hobarts and Beals (intermarried) and to Daniel and Matthew Cushing in addition to what they owned already. By the conclusion of the divisions, the four Hobart brothers owned an additional 825 acres. Only Daniel and Matthew Cushing, with 493 acres, and the Beals, with 437, were close. Of the one hundred proprietors, twenty-six men held 317 of the 693½ shares recorded. Along the way, it was agreed that smaller shareholders could pool up to twenty shares. Thus, brothers, fathers and sons or sons-in-law such as Thomas Hobart and John Magoon, and even Cornelius Cantleberry and his widowed mother-in-law, combined. By 1677, there were only seventy-eight proprietors.

Why did these large divisions happen when they did? One explanation is the increasing size of each generation. Adult children needed land not just as an inheritance but as a means of support. Their fathers and grandfathers had left England at a time when land was increasingly scarce and property passed, by primogeniture, to the first son. Now, for generations of males, whatever their order of birth, to remain in Hingham, each would need land of his own. Perhaps to fulfill this need and to prevent piecemeal loss of parcels, no one was allowed to sell his part of the divisions to an outsider without selling "his whole seat . . . in the town." Thus, land came to belong to fewer, larger families.

The timing of the "Conyhasset" division suggests another explanation as well. It came just before the General Court *quadrupled* the property requirements for voting. In that year of 1670, Joshua Hobart was on the General Court's committee to revise laws. If this dramatic change was in the wind, he surely brought the news home. By the new requirements, only proprietors with sufficient property would remain freemen, allowed to vote for county officers, deputies, and jurymen, and to nominate magistrates. Political power was being consolidated, concentrated. To keep power, Hingham would have to depart from its tradition of public lands.

There was yet another pressure for change coming from the outside world. New England was becoming more like old England. Trade with the mother country was growing, especially after the restoration of the monarchy in 1660. Was there a new sense of urgency to establish land ownership more in line with English property law? Hingham had insured its legal ownership of its "plantation" in 1665, through the deed negotiated by Joshua Hobart and John Thaxter with Chief Sachem Wompatuck and other representatives of the Massachuset tribe. This deed legitimized ownership against any claims by the Massachuset, the Bay Colony, or the English king. The deed is cautious. It is dated the "seventeenth" year of the reign of Charles II, dating his ascent to the throne from the year (1649) of his father's beheading by Puritans, even though Charles was not restored until 1660. Worldly prudence was winning out against Puritan independence. A year after the deed, Hingham declared its fidelity to the king, despite the Bay Colony's policy of independence from England. The Peter Hobart who had confronted Winthrop on this issue was still in charge.

Legal ownership of the plantation had been secured prior to the divisions of land into private ownership. It is ironic that, with this partition into large family holdings and enclosures, Hingham was reverting to the village arrangements that had led many to leave England in the first place. The decision to divide was a crucial historic change.

There remains one more possible explanation for the timing. Common land fell into two categories. Most was held for future division. But some was held for community use, and its use was frequently and precisely defined, as in today's zoning. Trees on the "training ground" could not be cut at all. They shaded cattle in summer and provided the militia with a practice area similar to surroundings in which they might have to fight. No individual could take timber from such lands "out of town." No oaks were to be disturbed; white oaks would be valuable for shipbuilding and for barrels to hold molasses, wine, and olive oil as trade grew. Timber was already a major trading item, particularly the great white pines, "mast-trees" such as those on Mast Hill Plain, whose trunks were worth one hundred pounds when exported to England for a navy at war. The growing mercantile impulse triggered investment in vast stretches of timberland, an early form of "futures."

Restrictions on the uses of timber were an early version of town planning. The repeated strictures and heavy fines noted in town records suggest an urgent desire to protect timber at a time when the supply for private use was diminishing. For almost two generations, every house, barn, and fence, and all fuel had come from the town's richest resource—its timber. Historical geographers have estimated that an average colonial family needed fifteen to twenty cords of wood a year, the equivalent of about three-fifths of an acre of woodland. For Hingham's 130 families, this would total at least seventy-eight acres a year. The growing need for timber for private use was another compelling reason for assigning land to private ownership.

In the years of the divisions, the town's most powerful man was Joshua Hobart. It was not unusual for him to wear the three hats of selectman, deputy to the General Court, and militia captain. Hobart was appointed first to the committee to advise on which lands would remain common, then to another on what land to divide, and another to determine the most equitable basis for division. He received each inhabitant's list of house lots and was given a "letter of attorney" to answer suits about the divisions. As a militia officer, he was part of what would now be called a "small claims court," which settled minor disputes; as captain, he was warden with extensive powers to maintain order and to punish. In 1650, his name was presented to the General Court "to marry persons in the town"; so anxious were the Puritans about ecclesiastical domination that clergymen could not celebrate marriages until 1686. In a small town where voting was by a show of hands, Joshua

Hobart's influence would have to be carefully considered. He was the town's chief officer and also its "power broker." In thirty-eight years, he was elected deputy twenty-four times. While it was chiefly his brother Peter who had symbolized the challenge to Bay Colony authority, Joshua meanwhile had moved into the colonial government with the instincts of a politician. In their lifetimes, the brothers shaped the institutions of church, trainband, and town meeting.

In the 1670s, at the time of King Philip's War, the Hobarts presided over a town much changed. The population had climbed back to seven hundred, but the 130-odd homes were now divided among villages linked by rutted lanes. The first cohesive clusters of households had become a network of "well rooted and extended patriarchal families." Forty-seven families made up seven-eighths of the population; eighteen of them half; six of them one third; Hobarts-Beals and Lincolns one quarter. Some modern scholars conclude that town politics had also changed. A few men, they suggest, controlled local power as an "oligarchy" or "Town Street Clique." Oligarchies were not uncommon in Massachusetts towns, but the term may connote too much. True, a few men, Joshua Hobart, Daniel Cushing, Thomas Andrews, and John Smith, repeatedly held major offices. Yet, many men were elected selectmen, and many served only a year or two. The coalescing of power into what scholars call an "elite" did not occur until the next century.

At the same time, in the period from the 1660s to the 1720s, town life became more stable and orderly, with more laws and regulations. Rules were instituted to govern price-fixing, inn-holders and taverners, field drivers and packers, and fire safety. Every householder was required to have a ladder long enough to reach his roof and in good repair or pay a fine. Town membership grew more stable. Throughout the Bay colony, geographical mobility was limited. Newcomers to towns were not welcome. During this period, Hingham had "virtually no inmigration, low rates of outmigration . . . and a high degree of marital endogamy." In short, the town became extremely inbred.

Until 1691, its population growth resulted mostly from the impressive fertility of resident families, from the rate of survival, and from a life expectancy that would not become longer until the late 1800s. Births outnumbered deaths by three or four to one. Hingham women bore an average of 6.5 children each. Over 90 percent of women married, and fewer than 5 percent of marriages were barren. Over 80 percent of children lived past the age of twenty. In the generation after 1691, however, the births per married woman dropped to 4.6, and the population grew only from seven hundred to nine hundred. One likely explanation

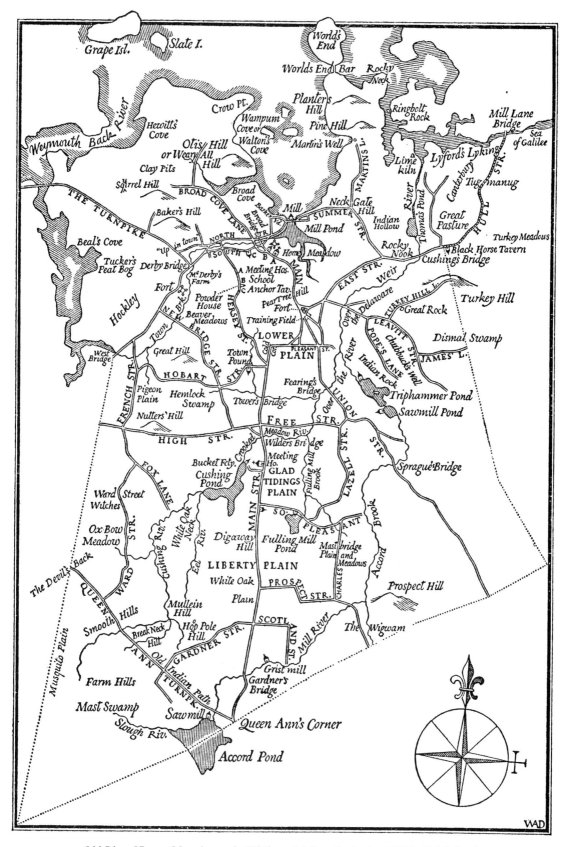

Old Place Names Map drawn by William Addison Dwiggins (1880–1956) for the
1935 tercentenary book HINGHAM OLD AND NEW.

HINGHAM, MASS. EST 1635

Line drawing collage by Barbara Menzies of Hingham's ancient houses and buildings.

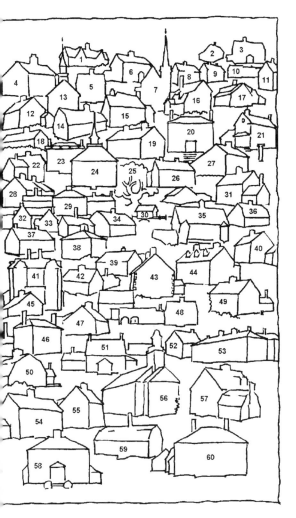

1. 53 Lincoln St. Benjamin Beal (1821).
2. 4 Green St. Court. "The littlest house."
3. 88 Summer St. John Barnes (1734).
4. 184 South St. John Beal.
5. 29 Pleasant St. Ebenezer Lincoln (1733).
6. 89 North St. Ebenezer Gay (1728).
7. St. Paul's Church (1871).
8. 79-81 North St. Cornelius Nye (1740).
9. 73 North St. Elijah Waters (1762).
10. 6-8 North St. Town Mill & Cobb's Paint Shop.
11. 44 North St. Daniel Bassett (moved from near Salem, c. 1817).
12. 185 North St. Israel Fearing (1673).
13. Methodist Church (1829; moved 1882).
14. 182 North St. Samuel Lincoln (part c. 1740).
15. 21 Lincoln St. Thomas Andrews (1688), later Francis Barker, Wilder's Tavern, Old Ordinary.
16. 28 South St. Water Co.
17. 40 Middle St. Ephraim Sprague (before 1758).
18. 99 Fort Hill St. Indian Fort House.
19. 181 North St. Benjamin Lincoln (part 1667?).
20. 34 Main St. Old Derby Academy (1818).
21. 294-298 Main St. William Fearing, 2nd stores.
22. 207-209 Main St. Daniel Cushing (1692).
23. 126 Main St. Isaac Hinckley (1811).
24. Old Meetinghouse (1681).
25. Buttonwood Tree, Hingham Centre.

26. 80-82 Leavitt St. Benjamin Loring (by 1752), later the Agricultural House.
27. 210 East St. Peter Cushing (1678).
28. 347 Main St. Nehemiah Ripley.
29. 303-309 Main St. Hawkes Fearing (1784).
30. Union St. Little covered bridge.
31. 133 Leavitt St. Hezekiah Leavitt (1751?).
32. 567 Main Street. Ezra Wilder.
33. 565 Main St. Daniel Bartlett.
34. 557 Main St. Jabez Wilder (1761?).
35. 171 Union St. Hornstra's barn. +
36. 61 Leavitt St. David Burr (1789).
37. 528 Main St. John Tower (1664).
38. 648 Main St. Deacon Peter Jacob (1752).
39. 650 Main St. Quincy Lane's store and post office.
40. 192 S. Pleasant St. Ebenezer Cushing (1752).
41. Wilder Memorial Hall (1879).
42. 479 Main St. Bela Sprague.
43. 757 Main St. Theophilus Cushing's tavern.

44. 36 Pleasant St. Thomas and John Fearing (1809).
45. 82 Gardner St. Elisha Whiton (1763).
46. 1029 Main St. Jesse Gardner (1816).
47. 1019 Main St. Daniel Whiton (1768).
48. 791 Main St. Elpalet Loring (with tannery, between 1825 and 1841).
49. 46 S. Pleasant St. Abel Cushing (1720).
50. 1035 Main St. Samuel Garnett (Gardner) (1738).
51. 1062 Main St. Warren Jacobs (1846).
52. 19 Elm St. Intermediate Schoolhouse (1878 -- today's Light Plant office).
53. 1220-1222 Main St. Nathaniel Damon, (1775) later Whiting Tavern.
54. 1083 Main St. Enoch Whiton (1680).
55. 692 Main St. Elisha Cushing (1753).
56. Second Parish meetinghouse (1742).
57. 771 Main St. Job Loring.
58. 1030 Main St. Anthony Gardner (1822).
59. 753 Main St. Theophilus Cushing (1687).
60. 768 Main St. Daniel Shute (1763?).

is that growth had reached the limits of land and economic opportunity. Here was a remarkable example of early family planning, a display, as one scholar observes, of how a traditional community controlled its fertility when circumstances dictated.

During the 1670s and 1680s, the town's inner stability and orderliness were strengthened by external dangers. King Philip's threat was followed by a threat from overseas. With its monarchy restored, England became more aggressively interested in its now prosperous mercantile colony in Massachusetts. Boston's aristocracy welcomed this incipient imperialism as a promise of wider markets. But England went too far. In 1685, New England was made a dominion of the Crown, and the colony's charter was overturned. In 1686, royal Governor Edmund Andros arrived. Here was a bigger threat by far to local autonomy than Governor Winthrop. Andros set aside the General Court, imposed taxes by fiat, and even forbade town meetings except for town elections. Colonial rebellion might have come eighty-five years before 1775, but the situation was saved when, in 1688, King James II was overthrown, and in 1691, Massachusetts negotiated a new charter with a more tolerant England.

The new charter brought changes. Hingham no longer stood on the boundary between two colonies, for Plymouth was absorbed into Massachusetts Bay. The charter mandated some religious tolerance, and Congregationalists lost exclusive control of political life. Hingham had a new minister for these new times. By 1678, old Peter Hobart could no longer carry the burden, and a young man with a different style replaced him. Of John Norton, said the 1893 *History*, "little is known" except that this quietly fervent, "faithful and beloved pastor" enjoyed a thirty-eight-year ministry "for the most part quiet and peaceable." More is known now. Norton was the son of a well-known orthodox minister of Ipswich, a town allied with Hobart. His doctrine deviated in subtle but important ways from the more austere and otherworldly religious beliefs of Puritan settlers. He believed "fallen man was not completely without light," "God's law is nature's law," and moral law is written in the hearts of all. He anticipated the new toleration by stressing "spiritual independence." New doctrine and style suited a town now peaceably stable in some ways, but restlessly mobile in others.

Mobility within the town was both geographical and socio-economic. As farming, trading, and early industries expanded, wealth concentrated. We can see both kinds of mobility in the rise and spread of the Cushings.

Old Matthew died in 1660. By the 1670s, his son Daniel, town leader and wealthy entrepreneur, presided over the homestead below Pear Tree Hill. Daniel's sons began the dispersal to the lane that would become East Street south of the Weir River and to South Hingham, where Theophilus bought property from Spragues, a Stodder, and "my brother [in-law] Samuel Thaxter" and willed the lands to several sons. The fourth generation included fourteen males. They married Fearings, Jacobs, Joneses, Lorings, Lincolns, and others, and a few, finding lands stretched to the limits, moved away. Brothers Abel and Theophilus, leaders of the clan in South Hingham, were wealthy farmers and mill-owners. Abel owned a fulling-mill on South Pleasant Street. Theophilus had taken over their cousin John Jacob's sawmill and fulling-mill and added a grist mill at what would be Cushing's Pond, connected beneath Main Street to Fulling Mill Pond by an "amazing underground aqueduct." A Cushing cousin, Matthew, operated a sawmill at what would become Triphammer Pond. Here he prepared boards, clapboards, and shingles from nearby woodland. One family controlled most of the growing mill industry.

During the late 1600s, the demand for finished lumber had increased with the rise of a new domestic architecture. With peace after 1676 and with the wealth of a few families, new and more commodious homes were built for the children of Puritans. The Cushing homestead at Rocky Nook (210 East Street) was built in 1678 or 1679. The Beal homestead beyond it over the Weir near the site of the later Black Horse Tavern (313 East Street) and two Cushing houses below Pear Tree Hill rose in the early 1690s. About 1688, Thomas Andrews erected what would expand into today's Old Ordinary.

The most impressive monument of this new era was a new meeting-house. In the Massachusetts Bay Colony, thirty meetinghouses were built between 1677 and 1683, most of them to replace aging, more primitive buildings. Only one of them, Hingham's, survives. In 1680, Hingham decided to follow the new trend and taste and to give its new minister a spacious building, forty-five by fifty-five feet, with a steep pitched roof and a "bell half as big again" as the old one. Inside, the "entire framework was visible to the upturned eye—the great [oak] beams and the carved struts and braces, smoothly chamfered and firmly pinned together, rising into the high, unceilinged loft," from the center of which the bell rope hung to the floor. The timbers of the loft gave the look of a ship's frame in reverse as if put together by local ships' carpenters. So ambitious was the structure that an expert mill-builder, Charles Stockbridge of Scituate, was hired to supervise.

What did it signify to those who saw it first? We can only guess. It may well have signaled a new time of peace and prosperity with new cultural priorities. Some scholars believe that colonial culture was undergoing basic changes in the late 1600s. They argue that the old Puritanism with its austere religious character was fading; that the children and grandchildren were far more interested in commercial advance and the good things of secular life; that the clergy were losing power and a merchant class was gaining it. If so, the handsome new meetinghouse expressed a new belief: the "legitimacy of wealth and personal possessions." Other scholars, using the same evidence, find little sign of the breakdown of old beliefs and values. Merchants and mill-owners were not necessarily any less religious than the original settlers. If so, then the new meetinghouse reaffirmed the traditions of church power and religious faith.

Why was it built? Was the old building, probably raised in haste, beyond repair? Was it too small? The population was about the same size as forty years earlier, and with the geographical spread of the population and the changes in religious life already suggested, church attendance may even have declined. The estimate of historian John Coolidge places the capacity of the 1681 meetinghouse at no more than five hundred when the population numbered about seven hundred. Another modern scholar thinks it was built in an effort to head off moves to establish separate parishes in Cohasset and South Hingham, but by 1681, the settlement of Cohasset had only begun, and such separatist moves were still a generation away. John Richardson believes "there must have been shortcomings in the old house. Otherwise, why would an overwhelming majority have voted to tear down the old meeting-house and build a new one on the same spot?"

Whatever the motives, in January, 1680 (N.S.), the town voted to proceed "with all convenient speed" and named a committee to look at what other towns were doing and to report on dimensions and costs. The eventual cost, £437, represented ten times that of an average dwelling and seven times the yearly cost of running the town. Taxpayers were assessed according to their wealth; 144 families paid from one to fifteen pounds, indicating the spread of wealth as of 1680–81.

On January 5, 1682 (N.S.), the house was ready for its first town meeting, and three days later, John Norton preached from his new pulpit. Over three hundred attended. They were seated according to a careful hierarchical plan: old leaders at the front, young leaders at the front of the galleries, 172 men and 161 women in separate sections, boys, girls, and servants in their places at the sides. The plan balanced geographical sections with degrees of wealth and prominence in an "intricate tapestry of social precedence." The tax status of occupants "gently declined along with the social status" of each row. "How many hurt feelings there must have," exclaims John Coolidge, "when a new 'pecking order' was officially decreed in that contentious and in-bred community!" His uncharitable assumption cannot be proved.

There had, however, been contention over the location of the new edifice. A majority had favored the original site near present-day Old Derby, but a minority of thirty-seven dissented. They included wealthy taxpayers to the south, and they fought for a more "convenient" central site in the spreading town. They appealed to Boston, and the colonial government prohibited construction until a "fair vote" was taken. A compromise was in order. After a year's controversy, Captain Joshua Hobart offered the town the fine hillside location where the meeting-house now stands, and the site was agreed upon. It was only a tenth of a mile closer to "the Plain" than the old site, hardly a geographical compromise. But some of Hingham's more remote villagers had begun their struggle against "Town Street" domination.

The struggle continued as the new century opened, first in the matter of schools. As early as 1661-62, a schoolhouse stood close to the first meetinghouse, and here from all parts of the town came any scholars who wanted instruction from a schoolmaster hired "as cheap as they can get one . . . not a man that have a family." But dissatisfaction grew with the "increase and spreading out of the inhabitants," and a vote of 1708 decided that the school would meet at different places in different seasons. In 1721, a schoolhouse was built on "the Plain," but the Cohasset district was far from satisfied. In fact, Cohasset had now been "in a state of virtual rebellion" for almost a decade, and had finally won its battle for separation as a second Hingham parish.

These growing geographical problems would enter a new phase. A time of relative stability was over. In 1716, John Norton died, and in 1718, a new young parson took over the pulpit and the moral leadership of a dividing town. In his years, stability would be repeatedly threatened, and the social mobility of the Puritans' children would harden into a class structure.

CHAPTER THREE

Parson Gay and His Times

FEW lived long enough to remember when old Ebenezer Gay came to Hingham in 1718, as a young man not yet twenty-two, and was ordained minister of the First Parish. When he died one Sunday in 1787, he was ninety, the meetinghouse was 105, the town was 152, and the new nation was on the eve of its constitutional convention. Much had changed, and so had Gay.

During his sixty-nine years as minister, the town tripled in population. The birthrate increased by half. Most of the growth was from within: of the 405 households in 1790, four-fifths were headed by descendants of early settlers. The economy was chiefly agricultural. Corn led the grain crops with over 11,000 bushels a year (about 466 acres); over 3000 sheep grazed; large crops of flax and hemp provided homemade clothing. By the 1770s, over 10,000 acres (almost sixteen square miles) were tillage, mowing, and pasture lands. One can imagine the disappearance of the forests.

In Massachusetts, a commerce based largely on timber and livestock had given way to one based on large-scale agriculture. The seaboard colonies had grown, and New England traders provided the South and the West Indies with food, bartering for tobacco and sugar, which in turn could be exchanged overseas. Hard currency was scarce; the economy worked chiefly through barter, neighbor trading with neighbor, potatoes for fish or nails, cheese for sugar.

The times were punctuated by wars, but periods of peace, especially the years 1725-44, allowed for progress, especially in southeast towns remote from attack. More surplus meant more trade, and in turn, more transportation. Daily packets plied between south shore towns and Boston carrying livestock, corn, salt pork, barrels, hoops, and staves, destined for faraway markets. New crops of the early 1700s, the potato, flax for linen and linseed oil, added to the produce. New seeds for grass and grain were imported and tried. As old, thin soil grew less fertile, it served as sheep pasture, while new land was put under cultivation. Tools remained simple, but more farmers owned ploughs, and oxen had assumed their special place as beasts of all labor:

> They moved heavily loaded drays in port towns. On the farm they pulled the plough, hauled grain to mill, delivered ship timber and logs, jockeyed boulders out of the grain field, and drew in hay, apples, and firewood.

Man's labor was not much lighter. One Hingham farmer left a diary of his work. Young Joseph Andrews, the sixth generation descendant of settler Thomas, would later be town treasurer and a selectman during the Revolution. But in the 1750s, his days were filled with farming. He was an only son; his father had died young, but he had several uncles to work with. The spelling is his.

Sept. 7, 1753: Helped Uncle And[rews] about carting some dung [by sled]

Oct. 30: Finisht Giting up my Potatoes and Helpt Uncle take up his Flax

Nov. 2: Helpt Uncle Sat fence . . . and Git Up Some Potatoes

Nov. 19: Killing my Beef. Simon Stoddard Helpt me Killed three

Jan. 3: Killed my Pigs today. Knight Sprage Helpt me.

Jan. 15: Threshing my Barly: Uncle And[rews] Helpt me.

Jan. 30: Spent the day in Reckoning with Uncle And[rews]

April 3, 1754: Down at Plan[ters] Hills Picking up Stones All Day, seven of us in all

May 3: Helpt Uncle And[rews] Plowing & Spreading Rock-weed [still a common fertilizer near salt water].

Labor was still chiefly dependent on neighborly and family cooperation, on children, a few indentured servants, and, on some large farms, African and Native American slaves.

Big farms demand big land ownership, and the more land owned by a few, the less—if any—owned by many. Down East Street to Rocky Nook stretched the farms of Joseph Cushing, Stephen Cushing, and Peter Cushing, who lived in the homestead built for his grandfather, Peter, in 1678-79. To stand here above the Weir River and look east across the meadows and uplands, sloping to the river and rising to Turkey Hill, is to sense the extent of some eighteenth-century Hingham farms and to realize why Peter Cushing owned slaves.

The Barneses, their homesteads on Neck Gate Hill (today's Summer Street), farmed at World's End. Farms stretched down Union Street "over the river" to the Lasell farm. Many fields of the Third Division (now Wompatuck State Park), John Richardson concludes, were at this time treeless agricultural land. On Prospect Street were the farms of Samuel Dunbar and Joshua Hersey (Codman farm in the twentieth century). Across the Great Plain on Gardner Street, Stephen Gardners, father and son, farmed Fourth Division lands, and on the uplands west of Accord was the farm of brothers Benjamin and Abel Whiton. Chubbuck, Garnet, and Loring farms stretched down Main Street from "the corners" (Queen Ann's), and in South Hingham, ancestor Daniel Cushing's "huge tract of land" was now covered by "the title deeds of many farms." At the Centre were Josiah Leavitt's (much later Kress's) and Benjamin King's, which passed down almost two centuries through his descendants, twin brothers James and George, to World War I. In World War II, as the Couperus farm, it was the site of military barracks. On Pleasant Street was farmer Ebenezer Lincoln, grandson of Thomas the husbandman; below Great Hill off Hobart Street were the farmer great-grandsons of the first Edmund Hobart. And almost bounding the Hobarts, north to South Street, were the one hundred-plus acres of Dr. Ezekiel Hersey and, later, of his widow Sarah Derby.

Land was still the basis of wealth. As in other old towns, the effect of growth was a shortage of land. Prices of land rose with its scarcity. The old practice of dividing among sons and sons-in-law reverted to the English custom of primogeniture—the first-born inherited—and younger sons sought opportunity elsewhere, when times of peace permitted frontiers to expand and new towns to form.

Two-thirds of the new towns were divisions of old towns, born out of local disputes. "Towns that would not, or could not, divide were thereby doomed to political divisiveness." This was Hingham's fate. When Gay arrived, Cohasset's struggle for its own parish had virtually been won, though its steps to full separation as a town took another half century. By no accident, its minister was Gay's classmate and affectionate ally, Nehemiah Hobart, grandson of the Rev. Peter. Cohasset had won its fight in 1721, and six years later, South Hingham Cushings and their friends opened their own campaign for separation from the First Parish. In 1742, they took the controversial step of building their own meetinghouse and, in 1746, after nineteen disputatious years, won their battle for separation. Approximately four hundred Hinghamites from Tower Bridge to Liberty Plain had their own church. The diplomatic skills of their opposer Ebenezer Gay must have been extraordinary, for they invited him to be their minister. When he declined, they turned to twenty-four-year-old Daniel Shute, who was, like Gay, a Harvard graduate. In Shute, Gay found a lifelong friend, ally, and theological disciple.

The political leaders of Hingham, centered at Broad Bridge, handled these disputes in a distinctively Hingham manner: they resisted, then compromised, and accommodated by expanding and dispersing power. They increased the number of selectmen from three to five and initiated sectional representation. Possibly for this reason, South Hingham never followed Cohasset into secession. Nonetheless, a few wealthy men had come to dominate local life. Their great wealth and new social status are key facts about the new century.

In Hingham, as generally in the western world, eighteenth-century society was stratified into a more rigid and unequal class structure than the earliest settlers could have dreamed of. By mid-century, the richest 10 percent owned 35 percent of the land; the poorest 20 percent, no land at all. Poverty grew; in 1747, the town instituted its Overseers of the Poor, and by 1785 it needed its first poor house. Socioeconomic mobility declined. Men were now much more fixed in one property ranking through their lifetimes, fathers and sons more likely to hold the same status. The new rigidity and inequality not only undermined communal solidarity, but also, here and elsewhere, generated the social and political upheavals of the next half-century.

The growing inequality is evident in the changing franchise before and during Gay's lifetime. The right to vote was closely tied to property ownership. In early colonial years, church membership and land ownership were roughly equivalent, and most adult males could vote. But by the late 1680s, with higher property qualifications for voting and with unequal land distribution, this had changed. Not all property owners ("proprietors") were "freemen," and only a "freeman" could vote for deputies and jurymen. Hingham men, like men in other towns, were divided into "freemen"—those who could vote in colony elections—

and "other inhabitants," who could vote only on town matters. The amount of property a man owned made the difference.

The franchise expanded and contracted in waves. The new 1691 *provincial* charter insured the vote to Protestant dissenters and reduced the property qualifications; so, for a time, the franchise was broadened. Town records began to refer to "free-holders" rather than "freemen." But what constituted a "free-holder"? If readers and historians find all this confusing, imagine how eighteenth-century townsmen felt. The difficulty began with a discrepancy between the charter's text in London and the copy sent to the colonies. The original said a forty shilling free-hold or £50 worth of property qualified one for the provincial vote; the copy said £40. Successive printings sometimes included one figure, sometimes the other. As for who could vote on local matters, the language was so imprecise and caused such dispute that in 1735 a law was passed to define it.

This muddle was worsened by the chaotic and fluctuating money situation. Qualifications for voting provincially were measured in English sterling; qualifications for voting locally were measured in Massachusetts paper money, bills of credit. These bills of credit went unredeemed in increasing numbers, and their values fluctuated. But when the legislature tried to stabilize the currency in the 1730s, inflation followed. To help pay off the bills of credit, Parliament finally voted to reimburse the colonies in coin ("specie") for the costs England's wars had imposed on them. A large shipment of specie arrived from London in 1749, and the legislature voted that thereafter all payments would be made in "coined silver." This policy did stabilize the currency, but in doing so, it also deflated values. With their property values lowered, many citizens lost the right to vote. Once more, the franchise was restricted.

Modern historians tend to agree that until about 1740 approximately three of four Massachusetts men could vote. But after 1740, owing to the confusion in money and an increasing inequality in the distribution of wealth, fewer and fewer men were enfranchised. The trend continued into the later years of Parson Gay's ministry. Some little noticed numbers illustrate this concentration of power. In 1778, a first state constitution was submitted to the towns to be ratified by their "freemen." Towns were obliged to record the votes. In Hingham, the vote was negative, fifty-six to zero. Fifty-six men were controlling major political decisions for a population of over two thousand. Hingham's vote in the first gubernatorial election (1780) was forty-four for John Hancock and twelve for James Bowdoin, an identical total of fifty-six. Not until 1821 did Massachusetts abolish the property requirement for voting.

The narrowing of the franchise was one expression of the widening gap between rich and poor. This differentiation was accompanied by the "emergence of a distinct social elite in Hingham," with its elegant houses, carriages, sedan chairs, imported luxuries, and in some cases, slaves.

The story of slavery in Hingham—indeed, of the almost invisible African-American community from the 1660s to the Civil War—can be recovered only in fragments. "Piecing together black history on a local level," writes James Deetz, "is a fascinating and often frustrating process of assembling fragments." Eighteenth-century record-keeping about African-American and Native American populations was haphazard and sometimes contradictory. The spread and acceptance of slavery, nevertheless, were undeniable facts about the century.

The colonists had carried on slave trading in the seventeenth century, but its size and status were limited and unclear. By 1700, however, Boston merchants were openly selling slaves, chiefly in trading ports. Before 1690, even though they were social outcasts, blacks were granted due process and were subject to the same laws as whites. Before 1707, the terms "slave" and "servant" were used interchangeably. The seating plan for the 1681 meetinghouse included twelve spaces for "Negro servants men and boys and also Indians." In the new century, the distinction was sharpened. The older law fining a ship's captain for carrying a black was past history, and it was no longer necessary for a trader to sneak in a few slaves by night at Nantasket. A 1698 declaration made the children of slaves slaves, too. Harsh regulations for the control of people of color began to accumulate. In 1733, Hingham ordered that "No Indian or mallate Servant or Slave may presume to be absent (from the families whereto they respectively belong in the evening after nine of the Clock) unless upon some busseness of their Respective Masters," and must carry a note if so engaged.

Between 1723 and 1727, ten "Negroes" and one "Indian" were described when they died as "belonging to" some of the forty or more "most respected as well as enterprising citizens of the town [who] were slave-holders." Of the slaves named Gregory and Billah, we know only that two of their three children died, that Gregory died in 1725, and that Billah had three more children between 1727 and 1732. We know that Jack and Dinah had six children between 1727 and 1738. In 1739, they and their children were willed by James Hersey to his wife, along with the rest of his "property." In 1743, Ebenezer Gay legitimized their common law marriage.

That year, Parson Gay began a separate list for "Negroes, Mulattoes, and Indians" whose life transitions touched his ministry. In his sixty-nine years, he baptized sixty-one adults, and of these, three were "Indians" and fourteen "Negroes"; four of the "Negroes" were admitted to full communion. From his and other extant records and from George Lincoln's later research, we can pick up the threads of a few lives. Such sources are all the more valuable in light of one record that is significantly missing. In 1754-55, Suffolk County towns—Hingham then belonged to Suffolk County—were asked to submit counts of their Negro inhabitants. Of all the towns in the county, only Hingham's count is missing. It is known, however, that at the time of the first colonial census in 1764, seventy-seven slaves were held in Hingham, one for every thirty-two persons, a high ratio relative to the ratio for the whole colony.

What became of Private "Primus Cobb, negro," who was on the rolls of a Hingham company in 1758, or of Private "Squire," Captain Peter Cushing's slave during the Revolution? When George Lincoln refers to Pompey and Phillis Barnes, married slaves, is this the "Philis" Barnes who entered the almshouse in 1810 and died there in 1819 at ninety-six? She had two sons, Ezekiel and Cromwell, who were familiarly known as "Zeke Pomp" and "Crom" and who lived on Fish (later Ship) Street. Zeke's wife Flora was remembered as a good nurse and servant. Their son Pete either "died away or was lost at sea." Then there was "Black Sam," remembered as "an expert mower, a superior hostler, and a most skilful farm hand." He was said to be the son of "Black Dick," Samuel Stodder's slave.

We can catch glimpses of two sets of lives. Before 1750, Hawkes Fearing sold a slave boy, "Prince." In 1783, Gay married a "Prince" to "Pate" or "Rate." Here the trail evaporates until 1803, when annual furloughs from the almshouse were voted for "Prince" and "Pat" or "Patty" to "the great plain." Periodically, the surname "Shute" is found next to their names on the list of the almshouse, where they lived almost continuously for twenty-five years until she died in 1827 and he two years later. Was Patty the "black Patty" who, while visiting an ancient herbal garden at Huet's Cove in 1818, mistook the first regular steamboat to Hingham, its stack billowing smoke and sparks, its paddles churning up the bay water, for a demonic appearance?

By 1735, Jack and Dinah had a fourth child, "Cesar." In 1767, Joseph Humphrey willed his "negro man Caesar his freedom," together with eleven acres of land, a horse and saddle, three steel traps, and a yoke of oxen. The following year, Gay married "Cesar" to "Candace Indian." Owing to a shortage of Native American men and African-American women, such marriages were not uncommon.

> Caesar was an athlete; muscular, tough, subtle, and quick of action mentally and physically . . . . He was especially expert with the scythe, and his services . . . were in constant demand from the neighboring farmers during the summer months.

He had a son, also Caesar, and it is to the son that the few surviving early nineteenth-century property records of black people refer. Son Caesar was born in the 1760s, and probably he was the eight-year-old child deeded to John Fearing in 1772. Born while his father was still a slave, he could be exchanged as property.

In 1808, son Caesar sold six acres of his father's land at "Nutty Hill," near High and Ward Streets. To "make one whole" of this transaction, he agreed to pay $4 a year either to Candace or to Chloe Ward or to both (the document is ambiguous). In a later document concerning the agreement, both women refer to the "estate of my late husband." Caesar the first, it seems, had not only a Native American wife, but also a much younger white consort, Chloe Ward, born the year he married Candace. Candace went on living on Humphrey property. She must have been poor, for in 1807, the committee for the almshouse voted "To allow Candice (Blackwoman) 1-1/2 cords of wood," and in the almshouse, 1815, "Candace an Indian woman" died.

The *un*told tales of these tiny minorities include those whose progeny were unrecorded, perhaps sold elsewhere, those who moved away, who never married, and who never needed the help of the town. Documents disappear; records are fragmentary. But one life spanned the eighteenth century. At Huet's Cove, a mysterious "Indian" woman gathered roots and herbs and sold them to townspeople. The place became known as Patience's Garden. She lived in a hut on what is now Green Street. She too came to the almshouse in 1799, and died there in 1803 at ninety-nine years. Much unrecorded local history died with Patience Pometuck.

By the time of the Revolution, the concept of "bondage" had become more and more repugnant in the North. In his name, one black child marked the change. Born in 1777, he was called Freedom Fearing. For a time, Freedom lived in a tenement behind Derby Hall. He had two sons. A hostler, he was especially pleased by the large tips given him by Daniel Webster when Webster went gunning at Nantasket.

The Massachusetts constitution of 1780 outlawed slavery, and by 1790 all New England states had followed suit. How long slaves were held unofficially is impossible to say, but it is meaningful that, when General Benjamin Lincoln and his friends raised their New North Church in 1806-7, they built "slave galleries" in it. Paradoxically, their church would become a center of Hingham's antislavery activity less than forty years later.

The first three quarters of the 1700s, a period when slave ownership was accepted, coincided with a time when extreme inequality was the rule. Based on his exhaustive study of eighteenth-century Hingham, Daniel Smith concludes that a small group of wealthy townsmen continually held power. He notes that 36.4 percent of selectmen whose fathers had been selectmen before them were followed in office by their sons. Lincoln followed Lincoln as selectman and town clerk, and Andrews followed Andrews as treasurer. Between 1718 and 1740, 53 percent of selectmen's terms were filled by Beals, Cushings, and Lincolns. Between 1740 and 1799, half of the new selectmen were among the richest 10 percent of townsmen. These incontrovertible facts depict a government by hereditary oligarchy. But like many facts, they have another side. Many selectmen were not "hereditary," and more than half were not of the richest 10 percent. Reelection was dependent on performance in office. Power was limited and accountable. Leaders were subject annually to town meeting disapproval.

During these decades, throughout Massachusetts, the power of town meetings grew as the dissident and the aggrieved turned to them for redress. The earlier political ideal had been to reach consensus or "accommodation" informally before meetings were held. In his study of New England towns as "peaceable kingdoms," Michael Zuckerman argues that this informal governing by "accommodative consensus" continued through much of the eighteenth century. But historian Benjamin Labaree finds that, "in town after town," the informal old way was replaced by majority votes in town meetings. This seems to have been the case in Hingham.

Consider how the recurrent issue of schools was handled. In the 1720s, Cohasset and Great Plain tried repeatedly to have the town's one school meet part of the year in their villages; or if not, to be given back part of their taxes to maintain schools of their own. Repeatedly, town meeting majorities refused or compromised. Finally, in 1734, the majority approved a plan to have school meet in three places. But not until 1752 were there two schools. Not until 1763 was each parish given back its full tax portion. Not until 1781 did the town fund three schools all year. Or recall a town meeting of 1741, a *special* meeting *called by* nineteen inhabitants—this became possible in the eighteenth century—to protest the fencing and enclosure of common lands. Twenty-five others challenged the legality of the meeting. The protesters were opposed by the town's political leaders. The protesters won by majority vote. This is not the "peaceable kingdom" picture.

What is striking, though, is that divisive issues were handled politically rather than legally. Lawsuits were unpopular; as late as 1768, there were only twenty-five barristers in the whole province. In Hingham, the *Salem Mercury* reported in 1789, there had been only one jury trial between 1740 and 1789, and only one law suit in the prior six years. In addition, the office of constable, that symbol of legal authority, was notoriously hard to fill. No one wanted it. Rich men bought their way out; others sought to be excused. This trend of avoiding the constable's job increased after 1720 and "leapt forward" after 1740. Why so?

Daniel Smith believes that this trend marked a weakening of community responsibility and solidarity. Together with other "indices," it tells us of the stresses and strains in the world Parson Gay tried to hold together. The "traditional rural community and its authority pattern"—that is, family and church control—were breaking down. By the 1740s, Smith finds, there were numerous signs of a "socio-demographic crisis" in Hingham.

It was seen in the election in 1723, after a lapse of years, of "tythingmen," guardians of town morality, and in new regulations and ordinances to curb drunkenness and disorderly conduct, to impose strict curfews. By 1763, the "alarming increase of drunkenness and moral decay" led to the forming of a committee, including Dr. Ezekiel Hersey, to recommend remedies. There were approximately fifteen inn-taverns in Hingham, and the committee argued for no more than three in the North, two in the East, and one in the South. The proposal was rejected by the town. The period was singularly short on sobriety and moral delicacy, and the harbor was a center of sea-faring men and a few "disreputable and stealthy" women. Many taverns were located nearby. North Street had several: Samuel Johnson's, Cornelius Nye's, and two owned by Elijah Waters; Seth Cushing had taken over Fearing's (185 North). Captain Francis Barker may have operated his tavern at today's Old Ordinary. On South Street (the present sites are 98 and 162) were the Anchor and the Pine Tree. The Centre boasted the Lewis Inn. Captain Ebenezer Beal ran the Black Horse near the end of East Street, and South Hingham had the Cushing Tavern.

The most notorious tavern belonged to Queen Ann's Corner. The John Whiton house stood on what was then the Scituate line, sometimes taxed by one town, sometimes by the other, a suitably marginal site. His daughter Ann was born in 1711 and died at eighty-eight in 1799, unmarried with three daughters. From 1730, she operated her inn and tavern for nearly half a century. She did "not have an enviable reputation for cleanliness and was given the name of 'Queen of Sluts,'" no doubt recalling as well the old English usage of "quean" as whore. She lived, so the story goes, with John Corthell, a tall, lank fellow known as "Long John." Peter Jacob once affixed this rhyme to her door:

> *Directions here for Plymouth way.*
> *Here's oats for horses, also hay.*
> *Here lives Long John and Ann the queen*
> *As great a slut as e'er was seen.*

Here, too, lived a shrewd matchmaker. Ann's tavern was a popular rendezvous during the Revolution. About 1777 she gave a ball to excel any other. One handsome young fellow, Abel Moulton, on foot from Plymouth to join the army, joined the party, proved himself the best dancer, and fell in love with his partner, Content Dunbar. Two years later, still on foot, he was back, wounded but "as chipper as ever." Where could he find his Content? Ann, at the bar making gin slings, gave directions, and two weeks later, she furnished the wedding supper. Such at least is the story.

The alarming number of taverns and the increase in drunkenness were one index of a "moral crisis" in mid eighteenth-century Hingham. There were other signs of the break-up of traditional controls. One is subtle: the steady drop in the use of Biblical or parental names for children. Equally subtle, an increasing number of daughters defied tradition and married out of their order of birth. Marriage, a "nearly universal" experience earlier, became more uncertain, as younger sons moved away and left spinsters and unremarried widows behind. Among those who married, the mid-century saw more "bridal pregnancy"—that is, evidence of premarital sex. In Smith's witticism, "the young people of the town . . . voted with their genitalia for autonomy." The South Parish faced this growing problem in 1764 and deliberated on what confessions to accept when a child was born within seven months of a marriage. The same parish had already seen another index of moral change: the sharp drop in new male church members. Of sixty-five who signed the covenant of the parish in 1746, only twenty-five were men; in its first ten years, only one third of new members were male.

Amid signs of moral crisis, the patriarchal powers of Ebenezer Gay, the town's spiritual leader, were increasingly tested. Numbers of Hingham people were now unchurched. Others were stirred by a powerful religious awakening which swept out of the Connecticut Valley in the 1730s. Itinerant preachers of this "New Light" called for a revival of Calvinist doctrine holding that man was innately sinful and in the "hands of an angry God." For Gay and other leaders of "rational religion," this movement seemed to go hand in hand with dangerous libertarian excess. The "error" of New Light doctrine, "enthusiasm," was a threat to the authority of established clergy and to social stability and community. It challenged the Enlightenment's belief in a rational universe and human reason. When the charismatic itinerant English preacher George Whitefield was "stirring up" eastern Massachusetts towns in 1744-45, Gay's diplomacy kept him out of Hingham. In Gay's middle years, such diplomacy was effective. But it could not forestall later outbreaks. In 1782, Gay was not entirely blameless in the "mobbing" of a visiting Baptist preacher at Hingham Centre. Such "mobbing" could only happen with widespread acceptance. It was the dark underside of an "age of reason."

Gay's religious and social attitudes present an important paradox. His new "liberal" religion was consistent with social conservatism. The New Light orthodoxy in religion engendered disorder and division. Gay and his religious allies worked towards what was harmonizing, unifying, and inclusive. Believing the innovation to be his own, Gay baptized many adults, bringing them into the "halfway covenant" promoted by his predecessor Peter Hobart. Inclusiveness was a way to social order, and social order was a way to piety.

During his long ministry, Gay moved cautiously into a new doctrine. A rational and benevolent deity offered salvation to "all intelligent beings." Through good works and the rational interpretation of the Gospel, all beings could prepare for "God's electing grace," and this preparation "became the mechanism of salvation." Through reason, man would understand and fulfill his moral obligations. This doctrine of "rational religion"—what was called at the time "Arminianism"—would later evolve into Unitarianism.

The new doctrine was especially congenial to the individualistic "intelligent beings" who were the self-confident merchant-traders, shipbuilders, and fishing magnates of New England's coastal towns. For these exemplars of initiative and worldly virtue, the doctrine provided justification of their lives and relieved them of complete dependence on Christ's atonement. In Hingham, Gay's chief friends and allies belonged to this class.

Among them were new entrepreneurs who controlled a newly bustling waterfront. Along the harbor and on Broad Cove, shipyards, wharves, warehouses, salt works, and vessels signaled the rise of maritime industries. Coopering grew by their side. Master mariners such as Elijah Whiton and Demerick Marble built their houses near the Cove. Captain Francis Barker enlarged his home at the old Andrews tavern (today's Old Ordinary). In 1750, Barker opened his shipyard near the north foot of Ship Street. In 1752, he joined with Dr. Ezekiel Hersey, Captain John Thaxter, tanner Solomon Cushing, and traders Hezekiah and Elisha Leavitt to form a fishing company. For their friend Ebenezer Gay, it was an easy stroll to the waterfront from his house on North Street (89). He was a familiar sight at the harbor in his black broadcloth, with his steely grey eyes and great gash of mouth visible under a wide brimmed hat.

The wealthiest and most notorious of the new magnates was Elisha Leavitt, known irreverently in local legend as Old Punk. Son of a Leavitt Street farmer, he began worklife as a blacksmith but shifted his sharp attention to coastal trading. He sailed on small schooners to and from the West Indies, growing richer by the trip. On one voyage he somehow acquired much treasure from a Spanish man-of-war in distress, sailed it back to Hingham, and hid it in the walls of his house, the old Thaxter mansion where St. Paul's Church now stands. Steadily he bought up land near the harbor adjoining Barker's shipyard, including dwellings to house the many seafaring folk in his and Barker's employ. John Souther, Jr., recalled in old age how much Old Punk owned when his father, John, Sr., bought the shipyard and much Leavitt land in 1790-91: "all the land east of Ship Street, east of father's except about an acre and the house of Elijah Waters." By the time of the Revolution, Leavitt's was the highest tax valuation in town. When he died in 1790, he owned about one thousand acres worth £9300, including several islands in the harbor and Quincy Bay.

Maritime trade and fishing were anything but safe and stable work in Gay's times. Massachusetts was virtually in a state of war for forty-six of the seventy-five years between 1689 and 1763. The wars were between her mother country and France or Spain, and they were often fought at sea by warships and privateers bent on disrupting the enemy's West Indian trade. Canada was still French, and France could threaten the coast from its bases in the Maritimes and on the Saint Lawrence. To defend its borders and harass English colonies, France made alliances with disaffected and dispossessed Indians.

Hingham men served up and down the coast and on the Canadian border. War dragged on from 1702 to 1713, and an uneasy truce was broken in the 1720s. In the 1740s, there was war with France in Canada, and Hingham men joined expeditions to Crown Point, Lake Champlain. They fought in the conquest of Acadia, which dispersed the wretched Acadians up and down the coast, bringing some to Hingham in 1755. War was again declared in 1756, the French and Indian or Seven Years War. Hingham's most famous soldier of the day, Major Samuel Thaxter, led Hingham men in the disastrous campaign at Fort William Henry. A French officer saved Thaxter from being roasted alive by Indians, and he returned to Hingham just after his own funeral to be greeted with, "Good God, Major, is that you? Why, we have just buried you!"

Walter Bouvé estimates that roughly 224 men served on the town quotas during the 1740s and 1750s at a time when adult males could not have numbered more than seven hundred. War finally ended with British victories at Quebec and Montreal, and the Treaty of Paris in 1763 established British control of North America. Hingham men had fought and died as loyal Englishmen. But abruptly there appeared a new enemy, a "foreign" attempt to control and tax New England trade. The new threat came from the mother country herself. The outcome would end the aristocratic era of Ebenezer Gay, place that loyalist and now aged parson in an unusually awkward position, and begin the labor pains of a new nation's birth.

CHAPTER FOUR

✖

More Than One Revolution

B ETWEEN 1775 and 1812, a variety of national and local
revolutions affected Hingham lives. First came the war for
national independence. Then followed a revolution both social
and moral, from the lively elegance of the old century to the middle-
class earnestness of the new. With this change came a revolution in local
political power, reflecting the onset of the industrial revolution as it first
touched Hingham's economic life.

In 1760, young George III, imbued with autocratic ideas of king-
ship, ascended the British throne. His ministers wanted more than loyalty from colonial Massachusetts; they wanted revenues. Each new af-
front from London increased the crisis atmosphere in Boston. The
enforcement of Navigation Acts menaced merchants' habits of smug-
gling to avoid paying tariffs; the Writs of Assistance permitted the search
of private houses; the Stamp Act placed duties on legal documents and
newspapers; and the Townshend Acts taxed such popular goods as tea.
Angry Bostonians organized a boycott of British goods. Riots broke
out. In 1770, one confrontation provoked the Boston Massacre, in
which guards of the Customs House fired on a Boston mob, killing five,
including the mulatto Crispus Attucks.

On a December night in 1773, 340 chests of taxed tea were uncere-
moniously dumped in Boston Harbor. Among the "Indians" from
Hingham that night were Jared Joy, Amos Lincoln, Samuel Sprague,
and Abraham Tower. Sprague recalled:

> That evening while on my way to visit the young woman I afterwards
> married, I met some lads hurrying along towards Griffin's Wharf who
> told me there was something going on there. I joined them, and on
> reaching the wharf found the "Indians" busy with the Tea Chests.

Wishing to have my share of the fun I looked about for the means of disguising myself. Spying a low building with a stove-pipe by way of the chimney I climbed the roof and obtained a quantity of soot with which I blackened my face. Joining the party, I recognized among them Mr. Etheridge, my master. We worked together, but neither of us ever afterwards alluded to each other's share in the proceedings.

Ebenezer Gay watched such mounting "irrationality" divide his friends. Some were Tories, loyal to the Crown; others were Whigs, opposed to British policies. Dr. Ezekiel Hersey led the Whig resistance until his death in 1770. The Rev. Daniel Shute, Gay's friend and ally, opposed him in politics. Gay formed his fellow Tories into a club and preached "passive obedience" to the king. His efforts and the influence of Tory merchants prevailed for a while. Hingham refused to join the boycott of British goods and ordered its representative to the General Court to work for "Loyalty to the King." Boston leaders called Gay a "rank Tory" and the town "tepid," lacking the patriotic zeal of other towns. Hingham's representative replied: "The present leaders in the Town of Boston are hurting the cause of liberty as well as the cause of Government." But following the Boston Massacre, local sentiment began to shift. The militia prepared. A new Whig leader emerged. Young Benjamin Lincoln would remain the "dominant figure in Hingham's public life" for almost forty years.

Early on the morning of April 19, 1775, the call "To arms!" was heard as a horseman from Boston reached the streets of Hingham. The sleepers were wakened by the ringing of meetinghouse bells, the roll of drums, and "the cheerful notes of the fifes." Men of the militia hurried to the training fields. Four companies, numbering 154 men, set out on the long march to Lexington under Lincoln, then a colonel. They were too late to join in the first battles, and ended up in Roxbury to await their role in the long siege of British-held Boston. At the battle of Bunker Hill, forty-one-year-old Joseph Bates gave his life.

Only a month after Lexington and Concord, Hingham had its own skirmish with British troops. Needing hay and other supplies, the British dispatched two sloops and an armed schooner to Grape Island off Huet's Cove. Here, the island's owner, Elisha Leavitt, a leading Hingham Tory, offered them good provisions. On that Sunday morning, May 21, Hingham was in an uproar at rumors of imminent invasion, and some townspeople packed their household effects, preparing to flee. Militia companies from Braintree, Scituate, and Weymouth headed for the scene. Captain James Lincoln's Hingham company marched from their camp near Crow Point. The tide was low, and the militiamen fired small arms in vain at the invaders. But once the tide was high, the militiamen crossed by boat to Grape Island, the British withdrew, and Leavitt's forage and cattle were burned or removed. Hingham's battle was won.

For the next ten months, Hingham companies joined in the siege of Boston. In March, 1776, three companies were summoned to man new fortifications on Dorchester Heights. On March 17, the commander of the British army, General Sir William Howe, gave up and evacuated his army. Hingham's "fighting parson," Joseph Thaxter, a young chaplain and the only townsman to reach Concord eleven months earlier for the battle at the bridge, left his own account of Dorchester Heights and the evacuation in lively doggerel:

> *In seventeen hundred and seventy six*
> *on march the eleventh the time was perfixed*
> *our forces marc'd on upon dorchester neck*
> *made fortifications against an attack*
>
> *The next morning following, as howe did espy*
> *the banks_____ cast up were so [corpine?] and high*
> *Said he three months all my men with their might*
> *Could not make two such forts as they've made in a night.*
>
> . . . .
>
> *Then hilter skilter they run in the street*
> *Sometimes on their head and sometimes on their feet*
> *Leaving cannon and mortar, pack saddles and wheat*
> *Being glad to escape with the skins of their teeth.*
>
> . . . .
>
> *Let em go let em go for what they will fetch*
> *I think their great howe is a miserable wretch*
> *And as for their men they are fools for their pains*
> *So let them return to old England again.*

The British Navy remained in Boston harbor. But in June, 1776, as crowds watched from hill and shore, the master plan of Benjamin Lincoln, now a general, unfolded. American artillery opened fire from harbor shores and islands, and the British retreated past the Nantasket peninsula to the open sea.

The tides of war from now on would flow at a distance from Hingham, but fears of attack from the sea persisted. Coastal defenses at Hingham and at the new Fort Independence on Telegraph Hill, Nantasket, remained on alert, manned chiefly by Hingham soldiers. For five years, local men served in home defense and in the Continental Army. They fought and died at Ticonderoga and Brandywine and suffered through the winter at Valley Forge. Regulars were away for years; others were called out for days and months at a time. Walter Bouvé estimated that "some six hundred different individuals performed military duty" during these years when the town's population numbered only about two thousand. Local farming, faced with extraordinary demands to clothe and provision the troops, was left to women, old men, and children. Normal life was suspended.

The town took on the look of a military camp. French officers stationed at nearby Fort Independence enjoyed the Anchor Tavern; General Lafayette slept there. Little Lydia Bates, later mother of historian Solomon Lincoln, remembered the arrival of General Lafayette in his cocked hat, knee breeches, sword and pistol. "Lafayette partook simply of bread and milk at his own request—as the family were in distress at the death of one of their children." Captured British officers on parole were housed in town. The poignant story of one Englishman survives because his daughter became one of America's most popular novelists before Harriet Beecher Stowe. Lieutenant William Haswell, Royal Navy and Customs officer, settled at Nantasket in 1763 with an American wife. Four years later, he brought the child of his first marriage to join his family. In her autobiographical novel, *Rebecca, or the Fille de Chambre*, Susanna Haswell Rowson recreated her idyllic childhood in Nantasket and the grim years that followed.

Her father seemed blind to his precarious situation as a loyalist. In 1775, a party of fifty men surrounded Haswell's home and his property was confiscated. The family was moved "under guard" to the Stephen Lincoln house at Broad Cove, and Hingham was ordered to provide food and firewood. The Massachusetts Council continued to suspect that Haswell was hostile to the patriot cause, and in 1777, the family was moved further inland. During a snowstorm, they were shifted to Abington to a three-room "hut" with dirt floors, broken windows, and no fuel. That evening, "the sons of two of their best friends" in Hingham, Peter Lane and John Barker, arrived with firewood and a tinderbox. In the darkness, a "cart" with furnishings, candles, and food followed. The young men stayed overnight and tightened the drafty place. Fifteen-year-old "Rebecca" (Susanna) faced the winter with a desolate father and his ailing wife. With the help of a half-sister, she collected firewood. The family subsisted mainly on "Indian bread and potatoes."

In her autobiographical preface to *Rebecca*, the author "begs leave to add to the names already mentioned, those of [Ebenezer] Gay, [Elisha] Levitt [sic], and [Samuel] Thaxter," the Haswells' Hingham benefactors and leading Tories. Their assistance was not without risk. A Committee of Correspondence kept watch on those loyal to England and procured "evidence against such persons as are suspected of being inimical to this and the United States of America." On one occasion, Leavitt averted mob violence at his Broad Bridge mansion by rolling out a barrel of rum and "dispensing its contents liberally." Even Parson Gay was "visited" to make sure his house hid no arms. His legendary rejoinder was in character: "Gentlemen," he said, laying a hand on his great Bible, "these are my arms, and I trust they will prove sufficient." Tales survive of fugitive Tories hidden in blind passages and smuggled away. War was no romance to townspeople living under the eyes of a Committee of Correspondence, fearing hidden enemies, attacks from the sea, and reports of casualties.

The costs in money were staggering. The new nation was a mere cluster of colonies, and localities had to pay, feed, clothe, and supply soldiers and aid their families. The value of money plummeted, and prices skyrocketed. In 1778, Hingham taxed itself £2370 for war costs; in 1779, £6000 to pay its soldiers in New York; in 1780, £30,000 for soldiers' pay and £4000 for their clothing. Seth Stowers received £63 for seven bushels of corn, and Bradford Hersey, £4 for a pair of soldier's shoes. When the war ended in 1781, the economy was in chaos. The nation entered its first years in financial crisis, and political crisis followed.

Farmers in western Massachusetts were especially hard hit. Their farms were taken for debt, and some went to debtors' prison. Was this the liberty they had fought for? During the eighteenth-century wars for the mother country, the least prosperous had suffered most. Called away from small farms or work as artisans, they had lost their most valuable assets, time and labor, and had come home to inflation and debt. In the Revolution, for service to their new country, they suffered again. In the winter of 1787, led by Daniel Shays, the poor farmers rebelled, attacking the Springfield arsenal. Weeks of guerrilla action followed. Over thirty of the rebels were killed or wounded, and most were cornered and captured by a militia moving up and down the Connecticut Valley. The militia commander, General Benjamin Lincoln, had ended a first threat to a fragile Union.

Hearing the news of the rebellion at Mount Vernon, George Washington wondered if the new republic would survive. In London, minister John Adams feared anarchy. "The response of the social and political elites to the rebellion," says historian James Burns, "was drastic: build a stronger national government." One leader opposed this policy: Thomas Jefferson, minister to France. Here were the seeds of factions that would soon divide the nation into hostile camps: the Federalists, who pushed for central government by the elite, for a national treasury, and tariffs; and the Jeffersonian Republicans, who feared and opposed them.

Benjamin Lincoln, a revolutionary Whig when young, was transformed into a conservative Federalist. He had come early into eminence. Born in January, 1733 (N.S.), he was only twenty-four when he followed his grandfather and father as town clerk. At thirty-two he became a selectman. After 1773, he represented Hingham in the General Court and the Provincial Congress. After serving on the vitally important committee to supply troops, he commanded a division in New York and was severely wounded at Saratoga. Recovering, he was sent by General Washington to command the Southern Continental Army, where, despite the ill-fated attack at Savannah and the hopeless defense of Charleston, he retained Washington's trust and later served as his secretary of war. According to a well-known story, he received the sword and surrender from General Cornwallis's deputy at Yorktown: "Washington, not willing as Commander-in-Chief to complete the ritual with the British second in command, pointed to his own deputy, General Lincoln . . . . Whether Lincoln accepted the sword . . . has been a disputed point."

Retiring to Hingham, he was a familiar figure being driven about by "Black Robert" in his "little low carriage, low on account of his lameness from wounds received in the war." He remained a leader in the governing group who lived close to Fountain Square. Yet, his last years were embittered by local conflict and by the rise of men who ended the power of his allies. The beginning of that end came, symbolically, while he was quelling Shays' Rebellion.

On May 8, 1787, preparing for Sunday services, Parson Gay died. The question of his successor had been of major concern and, in view of his liberal theology and conservative politics, controversial. One possible candidate was William Hazlitt. Hazlitt, the father of English essayist William and painter John, was an Anglo-Irish Unitarian minister of radical views in religion and politics. Unable to find a pulpit in Britain, he came with his family to the United States in 1783 and eventually settled in Weymouth. His Weymouth parishioners were not impressed. His personal style prompted a Boston observer to describe him as "the most conceited and imprudent man I have ever met with." In private, he was derisively referred to as "Paddy."

Nevertheless, while in Weymouth Hazlitt was invited on a number of occasions to preach at Hingham's meetinghouse, where he was well received by the "sacred circle" that included the Thaxters, Joshua Barker, Benjamin Lincoln, and Sarah Derby. Madame Derby "quite doted" on little William, Jr., who walked over from Weymouth with his father and stayed with him in the high pulpit during the sermon. Hazlitt preached Socinianism, whose central tenet was not Christ's divinity, but his perfect manhood. For him as for Ebenezer Gay, historians claim a pioneering role in the founding of Unitarianism.

Gay would not have agreed with Hazlitt's anti-Tory politics. But here nearby was a colleague with whom he was in agreement on religious doctrine. In his last years Gay was a lonely man: his wife Jerusha and seven of their eleven children had died; his Tory attitudes had strained old friendships. Hazlitt's daughter Margaret was persuaded that her father would have become minister of the First Parish had he not returned to England just before Gay's death. Instead, the "sacred circle" of Gay's friends, who still controlled the First Parish, turned to the Harvard with which Gay had so long been prominently connected, and from which his young theological disciples had been called to the parishes of several South Shore towns. Twenty-three-year-old Henry Ware was their choice as Gay's successor.

Born in 1764, this brilliant young scholar had graduated from Harvard in 1785, the valedictorian of his class. When Parson Gay, aged eighty-seven, visited Harvard in 1783 for a reunion with old friends, "their stately procession to the college chapel was watched by undergraduate Henry Ware, who would preside over the liberal theological revolution at Harvard in the early nineteenth century." But first, Ware would "steer the Old Ship into Unitarian waters."

Young Ware came to Hingham in the fall of 1787. Sarah Derby gave a grand ball after his ordination to celebrate the occasion. One guest, Ware's college roommate John Quincy Adams, recalled that dancing went on until between two and three in the morning. The next night, after more dancing and card-playing, "a number of the lads . . . went serenading all over the town till daylight." Three years later, Sarah Derby died, but her liberal spirit lived on in the new school she had endowed. And suitably, one policy at that school authorized student absences for dancing lessons. Madame Derby would have approved. Others did not. As the new century opened, social style and moral tone were changing, a new middle class was reaching for power, and what they thought of such a policy echoes in the remark of Henry Ware's successor, Joseph Richardson, who referred scornfully to the Derby school building as "that dancing hall."

The radical differences between two Hinghams—one of the eighteenth century and one of the nineteenth—are well represented by the personalities and lives of these two prominent Hinghamites, Sarah Derby and Joseph Richardson.

Madame Derby (1714-90) remains Hingham's legendary Cinderella, an elegant, whimsical figure surrounded by stories considered "too traditional" by some of the town's 1893 historians and "bosh" by George Lincoln. Sober history is unlikely to dispel completely the fable of the poor island fisherman's illiterate, ragged daughter, rowing ashore for the family water at Martin's Well, sighted there among buckets by the smitten young Ezekiel Hersey. The truth, however, is equally rich. Her father, John Langlee, ran a tavern and a small boatyard. Her great grandfather was John Otis; her cousin was John Hancock; her aunt had married William Hersey, so Ezekiel was a remote cousin. She was born and lived in the home-tavern at the corner of Ship and North Streets, and here came Dr. Hersey, the family physician, to treat and to court her. They married in 1738.

Her rise to enlightened patrician was a very eighteenth-century tale. As hostess of the large Hersey farm (the site of today's South Shore Country Club), she was noted as an astute and imperious manager. If

> she wanted a load of boards from "the cove," and no other means were at hand to fetch them, she would go for them herself. The boards she would have put through the carriage windows, after she had taken her place on the back seat. Of course, the people were obliged to give her a wide berth.

Her vitality is preserved in a story told by Edward Bouvé. Sitting one day "decidedly in dishabille" outdoors at her farm, she glimpsed a carriage of unexpectedly early guests approaching. "She jumped down from her perch, ran round to the back of the house, caught a brace of chickens on the way, twisted their necks and flung them to the cook," received her guests in the guise of her servant, hurried to her room to dress, and descended to the parlor as "Madame." Such earthy exuberance and grace were in tune with tastes in the world of Ebenezer Gay.

The farm became hers upon the death of Dr. Hersey in 1770. Widow Hersey soon married the wealthy Salem merchant Richard Derby. When he died in 1783, she came home. The moment was auspicious for the future of education in Hingham. New England's century-old tax-supported college preparatory schools had fallen on hard times. Taxpayers resented public funding for a few privileged boys, and Hingham's public academy had closed in 1779. Most worried by the consequences of this event was the Rev. Daniel Shute of South Hingham. When the wealthy widow returned from Salem, Gay brought Shute to meet her and to persuade her that Hingham's need for an independent academy was greater than Harvard Medical School's need for further bequests. When she died in 1790, her estate funded a trust to pay a preceptor to teach boys and girls in separate classrooms and a needlework mistress for the girls, to buy books and clothing for poor students, and to maintain the original Derby hall, which in 1818 would be replaced by the stately building familiar to later Hingham as Old Derby.

Derby School—it became an "academy" in 1797—opened in 1791 and survived to become the "oldest incorporated, independent, coeducational school in New England," the third oldest in the nation. By 1793, between eighty and ninety boys and girls were attending. Who they were is not known. There were no terms, no classes, no graduations. Enrollment books were not kept until the 1830s. By then, on an average day there were present thirty boys, average age 13½, all but four from Hingham, and twenty-one girls, average age twelve. Only one boy in school that day would attend college. No South Hinghamites were enrolled. The students came from artisan and commercial families; the academy was not, its historian concludes, the elitist institution its critics claimed. But neither was it the town-wide college preparatory academy envisioned in the eighteenth century by Daniel Shute and Sarah Derby.

By the 1830s, the local world of society, politics, and religion had undergone sometimes traumatic, even revolutionary change. The most dramatic phase of this change began in 1805, when Henry Ware, after eighteen years as minister of the First Parish, resigned to become Hollis Professor of Divinity at Harvard. One personal reason for Ware's departure was the toll taken on his wife by managing their life with an inadequate salary. He pleaded impoverishment, but no adjustment was made. Much later, historian George Lincoln asked, "Was it political?" The Wares had a large family of their own and also boarded young boys to supplement their income. The departure came too late for Mary Ware, who died shortly after their arrival in Cambridge.

Ware's Harvard appointment stirred controversy on the larger scene as bitter as the controversy over his successor in Hingham. Ware was already recognized as a leader in the evolution of Unitarian doctrine out of the liberal theology of Gay and his allies. Liberals now controlled

Harvard's Corporation and Board of Overseers. An alarmed "ortho-thodox"—that is, anti-Unitarian—minority claimed that the candidate Ware's

> particular religious principles . . . though often asked for, were not disclosed . . . . It was particularly asked by one of the honorable members of the Senate, whether the candidate was a believer in that important doctrine, the divinity of the Lord Jesus Christ? The reply conveyed no precise or satisfactory answer on that point.

Nor were his views on "the depravity of human nature, the impotency of man, the character of Jesus Christ, and the future of the wicked" any more satisfactory to the orthodox. The liberals prevailed. The orthodox left Harvard to form a more conservative school of theology at Andover. The battle over Ware's successor in Hingham had similar effects. The Andover group endorsed that successor.

The story of this battle cannot be fully reconstructed. Contemporary accounts are acrimonious. Nineteenth-century historians avoided it, either because it was too recent and could not be told coolly and fairly, or, later, because it was too far in the past and the wounds were now healed. But the event marked or precipitated a revolution in town history and is much too important to be slighted.

Young folks who sat beneath the pulpit of old Parson Joseph Richardson half a century later would not have believed how controversial he had been when, in 1805, he was nominated to succeed Ware. He was then a young Charlestown schoolmaster, a poor farm boy from Billerica, a graduate of far-off Dartmouth. He was nominated by Hawkes Fearing, the leader of a group of new industrialists centered chiefly in Hingham Centre, a group that would now make its bid to seize control of the First Parish from the old "sacred circle," the friends of Gay and Ware.

Hingham knew nothing about Richardson. The old leaders made inquiries and then launched a campaign of vilification: (1) he was being sued for breach of promise by a bitter young woman in Billerica; (2) he had betrayed the confidences of his mentor, a rabid anti-republican, to Jeffersonian friends; (3) he had been forced to leave his boardinghouse by fellow boarders, who thought him improper; (4) he had been seen outside of a house of ill repute; (5) he had been horsewhipped in a brawl. The first, second, and fifth seem to have been true, though variously interpreted.

Enemies claimed that the issue was moral: Richardson was a disputatious rake. Defenders charged "aristocratic usurpation," insisting that the "moral" charges were a cover-up for "old tory" politics; Richardson was an outspoken Jeffersonian, as were his defenders. Caucusing at Hawkes Fearing's tavern, they charged that the evidence was false or distorted and demanded that the accusers face Richardson with documents and witnesses. Enemies claimed they had tried to do so but had been outmaneuvered by a "secret committee." The enemies lost. When Richardson was installed in July, 1806, they had already walked out. They held services in Derby Hall, Henry Ware returning from Harvard to lead them, and built their church, the New North, across from General Lincoln's home. They exerted their influence to isolate Richardson from neighboring clergy; only Plympton and Middleboro in Plymouth County, to which Hingham had belonged since 1803, sent ministers to his ordination. He was refused the customary pulpit exchanges and a decade later was barred from the Bay Association of clergy.

However truth and justice are apportioned, this battle began the most lasting social conflict in Hingham history. As late as 1847, Richardson published a pamphlet urging an exchange of Hingham pulpits, and New North minister Oliver Stearns replied in some embarrassment: he was willing, but his congregation said no. Three years later, Stearns, as ever the Christian persuader and conciliator, took one service out of his church and conducted a "sylvan baptism" at Tranquillity Grove, in what is now Burns Memorial Park between Central and Hersey Streets. Richardson stood not far from him. It was "the first time since that stormy division" forty-four years earlier that pastor "met with pastor, and people with people in holy rite." Bitter feelings persisted. Hawkes Fearing's son Albert, later benefactor of the public library, had dared to court and marry a daughter of New North and met with considerable resistance within the parish twenty-five years after the split. Little boys would "get behind walls and throw stones at people going to the other church." The sick, early in the twentieth century, would call only doctors of their own parish.

Those who left Richardson's church in 1806 were, as Derby Academy historian Theodore Roscoe calls them, the "Derby family," and so the academy was embroiled in the conflict. The spokesman for Richardson's enemies was Abner Lincoln, the school's first preceptor and General Lincoln's son-in-law. The annual Derby Lecture was summarily removed from the old meetinghouse to New North Church. In 1817, complaints were lodged against this action and against the ordaining of Derby's preceptor at New North. "Quite possibly," thinks historian Roscoe, "it was feared that Derby, the town academy, with a clergyman-preceptor and five Unitarian ministers among the trustees, was leaning

Reverend Ebenezer Gay (1696–1787).
Pastel portrait sometime between 1784–1787,
by the English painter, John Hazlitt (1767–1837).

General Benjamin Lincoln (1733–1810).

Sarah Derby (1714–1790).

Reverend Joseph Richardson (1778–1871).

The Old Meetinghouse (1681) and to the left, Willard Hall (1831), a private academy and public hall. Used for manufacturing in the 1840s. At the rear, Baker and Sons twisted cord. This complex burned in 1847. An 1840s lithograph by painter, lithographer, and photographer William Hudson, Jr. (1820–1907).

Second Parish Meetinghouse (1742). The earliest image found of the church, a woodcut (1830) by Hosea Sprague (1779–1843), printer, publisher of a chronicle, and keeper of meteorological records.

New North Church (1807). Fountain Square is in the foreground. Burr, Brown's factory (1865) to the left rear. Obviously, the photograph was taken before or during the building of St. Paul's Church in 1871.

in the dangerous direction of becoming a parochial school for Unitarian New North Church." There was a "resurgence of orthodox"—that is, anti-Unitarian—"thinking in the town."

There is no clear evidence that the schism of 1806 was caused by a conflict in religious beliefs. Richardson, to be sure, was more cautious in his doctrine than the New North ministers, but he called himself a "liberal Christian." Rather, the causes were political and socioeconomic. The leaders of New North Church and of Derby Academy were Federalists, haters of the "atheistical," "Jacobin" Thomas Jefferson, fighters of a rearguard action to keep Jeffersonian Republicans out of power and professional influence. They lost, and a new socioeconomic group took political control of the town.

Thaxters and Andrews, friends of General Benjamin Lincoln, led the Federalist reaction; Fearings and Leavitts of the Centre led the revolt. Lincolns were divided, as were Cushings. Colonel Charles Cushing of School Street, farmer, state representative, and a strong Republican, was so vexed by Federalist power that he moved his family to Lunenberg in 1797. The Federalist group with their eighteenth-century professions included Nathan Rice, merchant, shipfitter, and "Old Punk's" son-in-law; merchant Thomas Loring, married to a Thaxter; trader-magistrate Samuel Norton, married to an Andrews; physicians, father and son Thomas and Robert Thaxter; physician Levi Lincoln; attorney Ebenezer Gay, grandson of the parson; trader-magistrate Jerom Cushing, a Thaxter son-in-law; shipmaster Luther Lincoln; John Barker, son of the shipbuilder Francis; and Thomas Andrews, "gentleman," of the class most hostile to Jefferson.

The new leaders, in Hingham as elsewhere, were predominantly farmers and artisans who would become the industrial entrepreneurs of the new century. Thomas Fearing, John Marsh, Solomon Jones, Isaac Cushing, and Solomon Lincoln, father of the historian, were farmers. Hawkes Fearing had begun his cordage works. Seth Lincoln and Laban Hersey were tanners; Jacob Leavitt was a wheelwright; John Leavitt, a pump and block maker; James Stephenson, a blacksmith. Such men dominated town offices after 1805. Solomon Jones remained town clerk for seventeen years. Fearings and Lincolns served continuously as town treasurer, state representative, and customs collector. Jeffersonian Solomon Lincoln, Jr., wrote the first town history in 1827 and became town moderator in the 1830s. Joseph Richardson himself, an astute politician, served two terms as state representative and two in the United States House of Representatives.

The local revolution epitomized on a small stage the birth pangs of a new industrial society and the struggle between Federalists and Republicans for the political soul of a new nation. No sooner had the republic established its constitutional government than it began its fragmentation into factions, a process aggravated by foreign wars. Jacobin France stirred sympathy for Britain among Federalists under John Adams. Republicans under Jefferson and Madison charged the "feds," as they called them, with seeking war against France. In 1800, Jefferson defeated Adams in a slanderous election, "howling atheist" against "would-be monarch." In 1804, Jefferson was easily reelected. It is ironic that his attorney general was a Lincoln, Levi, a native of Hingham, while his only entrenched opposition, the Supreme Court, included a descendant of Hingham Cushings.

The "feds" weakened and grew desperate. In these years, political tempers ran so high that "Hingham maintained rival Republican and Federalist lines of Boston packets; and if a Federalist missed his boat he would spend the night on Long Wharf rather than take the Jacobin sloop," thus avoiding the friends of Joseph Richardson.

During Jefferson's second term, war between Britain and France intensified and was often fought in North Atlantic shipping lanes. British warships seized and searched American traders. Seeking to avoid war and hurt British power, Jefferson signed an embargo in 1807. The embargo actually hurt not the British, but American trading ports; hundreds of ships and thousands of sailors were idle. The Massachusetts South Shore, already distressed economically by the Revolution, wore "the appearance of stillness and retirement." The embargo "set off paroxysms of rage in New England."

In Boston, General Benjamin Lincoln, customs collector of the port, refused to enforce the embargo. The old Federalist, now in his seventies, had weathered more than one revolution since his years as a revolutionary Whig. His appointment as collector had come from George Washington nearly twenty years before, in a world that was passing away. He had served the state as lieutenant governor, was honored with a degree by Harvard, and was prominent in learned societies. His preeminence among his fellow townsmen was undiminished by the battle that divided the First Parish; the Richardsonians carefully conceded that "the venerable age of a good man had been abused to sanctify, by the authority of great past services," the "indiscretions of friends." When he died in 1810, government officials joined the "long train of bereaved relatives and mourning friends" in the funeral march from New North to the family tomb on the hill just behind the old meetinghouse. Bells in Boston tolled, and the flags of vessels from Boston Harbor to Fort Independence hung at half mast.

We can only imagine what Benjamin Lincoln would have felt had he lived two years more to see that harbor at the onset of a second war with Britain. Alarms of expected invasion and news of British raids were heard again. Some Hingham ships were hauled up in the town dock or at Broad Cove. The packet *Rapid*, built in Hingham in 1811 by Daniel Bassett's father, was drawn up in the Back River and camouflaged with "green boughs." Others were captured and destroyed, and some of the shipowners were bankrupted. On June 1, 1813, local youngsters gained a memory to tell their grandchildren half a century later, when the nation would fight its bloodiest conflict. Hinghamites of all ages stood atop Turkey Hill, while off Scituate, one of America's legendary naval battles was fought. The *Chesapeake* responded reluctantly to challenges from the British *Shannon* and sailed south out of Boston Harbor. Broadsides and musket fire swept the *Chesapeake* from stem to stern. Her commander James Lawrence was mortally wounded, but before he died, he ordered, "Don't give up the ship." A divided new nation sought to follow his command.

CHAPTER FIVE

Entrepreneurs and Evangelicals

PEACE brought happier sights from the hilltops, peacetime fleets returning. Two- and three-sail schooners with high quarter decks and pink sterns dotted the bay, home with their loads of mackerel. Reuben Stodder, son of a mariner lost at sea, spent his boyhood in "the long green house" (later the site of Quinn's garage) near the Cove. Years later, as the famous poet who had changed his name to Richard Henry Stoddard, he recalled the bustling port:

Old homestead! in that old gray town
Thy vane is blowing seaward.

Thy slip of garden stretches down
To where the tide is flowing.

Below they lie, their sails all furled,
The ships that go about the world.

That teeming harbor would be fondly remembered after the Civil War, when mackerel boats were precious few, packed ships unloaded thousands of tourists, and some industries struggled to survive.

Peace after 1815 was the take-off moment for industry in New England towns large and small, and Hingham's industries grew prodigiously. The mackerel fishing fleet climbed to sixty-five vessels in 1831, the year when Hingham became a customs port. At the wharves that year, 50,000 barrels of fish were packed. Along the shore toward Otis Hill stretched the shallow vats and windmills of Scarlet Hudson's saltworks, processing the preservative. Shipyards were busy from Broad Cove to the Weir. Shipping required cordage, and the ropewalk grew.

Three factories made chairs and cabinetware. The Wilders opened their bucket factory. Hingham was renowned nationally as "Bucket Town." When Richard Henry Dana sailed two years before the mast in the 1830s, a young sailor on the ship, a native of Hingham, was immediately dubbed "Bucketmaker." On the ship's return from California in 1837, Dana saw Hingham at its peak of enterprise:

> The high land of Cape Ann and the rocks and shore of Cohasset were full in sight, the lighthouses standing like sentries in white before the harbours; and even the smoke from the chimneys cʌ ʌne plains of Hingham was seen rising slowly in the morning air. One of our boys was the son of a bucket-maker, and his face lighted up as he saw the tops of the well-known hills which surround his native place . . . . A firing was heard in the direction of Hingham, and the pilot said there was a review there. The Hingham boy got wind of this, and said if the ship had been twelve hours sooner he should have been down among the soldiers, and in the booths having a grand time.

Beneath those smoking chimneys industry was growing. Joseph Jacobs added steampower to his tool works; the blacksmith family of Stephensons made scales and balances, and their partner Charles Howard, prize-winning ploughs. Benjamin Thomas built a cast-iron foundry on the Weir. There followed at the Cove a copper and brass foundry, a tinware factory, and the Eagle Iron Foundry. Factories opened for tanning and currying and for making textiles, boots, and shoes. Trimmings, cords, and tassels were made at the corner of North and Main Streets. In 1837, the Umbrella Company produced over 18,000 umbrellas and parasols, and four manufacturers made 3422 hats. The most daring entrepreneur, Lincoln Jacob, tried to manufacture sewing silk from cocoons on his own mulberry plantation. The enterprise did not last. Indeed, most of this entrepreneurial energy did not survive a half-century. A later chapter will consider why it ended.

This restless generation fell in love with speed, and horsepower led the way. The stagecoach sounds ancient, but the fast stage was a marvel of the new century, along with breeds of fast horses. Once the elliptical spring was invented (1804) and suspension systems followed, the "flying coach" was ready to burn up new turnpikes. In 1803, privately owned pikes spanned the countryside from Boston. That year, the pike named for Queen Ann (today's Whiting Street) was laid out. Local thoroughfares followed. In 1831, the hill below Derby Hall—Hingham's first burial ground—was lowered to straighten and level Main Street. The same year, Summer Street, "from the mill dam around Cobbs Bank by the seaside," was built. A year later, "common convenience and necessity" required a road "from a point opposite the dwelling house of Abigail Thaxter on Main Street across the Mill Pond to the easterly end of the mill dam and Summer Street." By November, Water Street was "passable," and entrepreneur Charles Shute had sold nineteen house lots on land he bought in 1830. "Some of our enterprising mechanics"—keynote phrase for the new age—began building homes. In 1833, the "Great Rock" near Turkey Hill, on which Hosea Sprague had chiselled an inscription about the first settlers, was blown to bits for use in road building.

At various times in the late 1840s and early 1850s, North Street was leveled, widened, and straightened. Trees, including elms, ashes, and buttonwoods planted by General Lincoln himself, were not allowed to stand in the way of "progress." In 1847, Elm Street was approved: "A road to connect [Main and Hersey] has long been needed. The village of Hersey Street is a thriving place, the people well disposed, industrious, and enterprising. They have already labored under the great disadvantage of being so far removed from the business part of the town." In the 1850s, Rockland Street was laid out to Hull and Cohasset, Cushing to Derby Street, and Thaxter Street to Crow Point.

By 1812, coaches between Boston and Plymouth could cross the first drawbridges built by the new Hingham and Quincy Bridge and Turnpike Corporation over the Fore and Back Rivers. Abigail Adams of Quincy could lunch in Hingham and be home by three. After 1828, stage driver Abiel Wilder had rival "knights of the whip," and villagers thrilled as the Plymouth stage came in at full gallop, its horn sounding the arrival of the mail. Speed meant faster communications, more post, more papers and journals. Hingham's first newspaper appeared in 1827; in the 1830s, briefly, there were two. In the 1840s, there was *Hosea Sprague's Chronicle* and in the 1850s, *The Cabinet,* published by two precocious boys, who saluted the new bustle in galloping verses:

> *The town from which our paper hails*
> *Has won great notoriety*
> *For manufacturing wooden pails*
> *In wonderful variety . . . .*
>
> *Here churns and kits and tubs abound,*
> *Pill boxes and dumbetties;*
> *"The Hingham Journal" here is found,*
> *And here "The Cabinet" is . . . .*
>
> *Our hides we tan, our ropes we make,*
> *Our furniture we fashion,*

But still most pride in buckets take,
  For Buckets is our passion.

We forge our steel, you may have heard,
  Full many a shining hatchet,
Make tassels and twist silver cord,
  And then weave lace to match it . . . .

Our "balances" are famed afar,
  Our merchants enterprising,
Our Bank stock always quick at par,
  Our Rail Road stock is rising.

And when through fear of burning down
  We suffer past endurance,
We have conveniences in town
  To do our own Insurance . . . .

The age was precocious, with a passion for knowledge and invention. Two Hingham brothers represent it well, Joshua and Martin Wilder, two of the twenty-one children of Edward Wilder. Joshua, known as "Quaker" Wilder, was nationally renowned for his clocks—his specialty was the "Grandmother Clock." Martin, a blacksmith and wheelwright, worked in Boston, where he was reputed to be the inventor of "C" springs, which smoothed the ride of buggies and wagons in the city. Dying childless in 1854, Martin left most of his estate to constitute the Wilder Charitable Fund to assist young South Hingham mechanics in their education and apprenticeships. Another enterprising Hingham youth was James Hall. He was the son of an English immigrant, foreman of the Hapgood woolen factory on the Weir River. Young James attended the Centre grammar school, then studied at evening classes while working days as a manual laborer. Awakened to scientific curiosity, still in his teens, he walked over 220 miles to Troy, New York, to enroll in what became Rensselaer Polytechnic Institute. Graduating at age twenty in 1832, he later became Professor Hall, state geologist of New York, and president of the American Association for the Advancement of Science.

Perhaps the time's epitome in Hingham was the Rev. Charles Brooks, New North minister from 1821 to 1839. A pioneer with Horace Mann in promoting the free school movement, he introduced Hingham to the virtues of anthracite coal, helped start the temperance movement, initiated the project of the steamboat line, and promoted the establishment of the town's first savings bank.

[75]

Banking and insurance, two more industries, spread through the towns with the extraordinary growth of capital and speculation. The Hingham Bank (115 North Street) was built in 1833. When the Mutual Fire Insurance Company was incorporated in 1826, shopkeeper David Harding, Secretary, could transact its small business in Jotham Lincoln's store at the harbor (24 North Street). When the Institution for Savings came into being in 1834, Harding became treasurer. He was famous for conservative management of both until the Civil War.

Some conservatism was certainly needed in a time of reckless expansion and fearsome power. Poor Black Patty saw that power one day in 1818 when she fled at the sight of the steamboat *Eagle* entering the harbor. The eight-year-old child Helen Thomas saw another of its incarnations thirty years later. Already famous for calling and feeding her tame fishes and turtles, she watched as her lovely wilderness at Thomas's Pond was invaded. Surveyors "cut a broad swath through our beloved wood." After "the Weymouth ledges had been torn asunder and the floating meadow between West Hingham and Broad Bridge partially conquered" came construction trains with their "toot and rattle," their "streams of sparks." She watched the "trees ruthlessly cut," the cars pouring gravel into *her* pond, the "rough shanties on the meadow beyond" where railroad workers' families lived.

The South Shore Railroad of the Old Colony line opened in January, 1849, with grand festivities. In its first years, however, it did not live up to expectations. Timetables were unsatisfactory and fares were unpredictable. Financial losses were charged in part to mismanagement by its first president, Alfred C. Hersey, and he was replaced. This vain and irascible Hinghamite was not one to give up peaceably, and his uncontrollable tongue spread unkind words about his successor. One Monday in October, 1855,

> Broad Bridge was thrown into an unusual state of alarm . . . by the sound of a threshing machine, and the din of battle, in one of the passenger cars of the 5 1/2 o'clock train for Boston . . . . The difficulty was between Mr. Humphrey, President of the South Shore road, and Mr. Hersey, ex-President . . . . It commenced in the immediate vicinity of the Old Colony House station, by Mr. Humphrey requesting Mr. Hersey to sign a paper retracting a statement . . . not at all complimentary to the habits of the former.
>
> Mr. Hersey declined doing anything of the kind, when Mr. Humphrey drew a pair of pistols, one of which he offered to Mr. Hersey, and proposed settling matters on the spot. Mr. Hersey declined doing this, and succeeded in getting the pistols away from Mr. Humphrey,

whereupon the latter started on foot for the Hingham depot. Mr. Hersey followed him shortly after in the up-train, and upon the arrival of the cars at the Hingham depot, the two men met in the cars, Mr. Humphrey having a cowhide in his bosom, which Mr. Hersey seized and made to perform the work for which it was intended, over the person of Mr. Humphrey.

Some of the lady passengers were extremely frightened, and it was some time before quiet was restored, and the train enabled to proceed on.

The trains did proceed on, sounding the death knell of stagecoach and private turnpike. But Hingham was only on the Braintree-Cohasset branch. Later, the major freight lines went elsewhere and took with them Hingham's brief industrial glory.

But who could anticipate that decline in 1835, when the town celebrated its two hundredth birthday and young Solomon Lincoln delivered his oration, a salute to progress, prosperity, and enlightenment? The population was climbing fast. From 1776 to 1810, it had risen only from 2086 to 2382; between 1810 and 1830, it jumped by a thousand, and by 1855, another nine hundred to 4257. It rose even as the birthrate continued to drop, as childhood mortality almost doubled, as life expectancy fell. (The early industrial years were not good for human health.) It grew as Hingham attracted a workforce of new townspeople, and the villages grew with them.

Broad Bridge and the harbor, now "the business part of town," showed signs of mercantile expansion. The Barneses on Old Colony Hill had turned from farming to commerce. Luther Barnes grew wealthy on the wharves and shops at the harbor, and his neighbor Laban Hersey did, too. Their sons, Charles Barnes and Alfred Hersey, Boston merchants, were among the town's richest men by the Civil War. On Lincoln Street, not far from what was, in these years, a thriving Wilder's Tavern, merchants and bankers built new homes or rebuilt old ones. At Broad Cove House (66), Captain Barnabas Lincoln kept pace with the changing economy. Once a master mariner who had been captured by pirates, he became a manufacturer of upholstery trimmings as the age moved from seafaring to domestic commerce.

One story that began on South Pleasant Street signals the cycle of change. Here stood the fulling mill that gave the pond its name. It served farmers' families by carding wool into rolls for home-spinners, and "fulling"—that is, scouring and shrinking loose home-woven cloth. By the 1830s, this cloth was being replaced by factory woven fabrics, and the business faded. Elijah Cushing gave up and worked for years on the Hingham Station packet in Boston. In the 1850s, she sank at her mooring, and Elijah followed a typical nineteenth-century pattern: he retired to farming. His brother Laban had turned the fulling mill into a shoe peg factory, until a fire in 1845 brought that to a close.

Stories from other villages sound similar messages of change. Captain Elijah Corthell of Hersey Street (194), like many Hersey villagers, began as an apprentice box-cooper, then went as mate on a trading vessel, later commanding his own. He left the sea intending to return to box-making. But entrepreneurs such as his neighbor Edmund Hersey had discovered that fewer workers could produce more as machinery superseded hand manufacture. So Elijah Corthell became a retail grocer in a town that produced less food and bought more of it.

Captain Solomon Dyer recalled a similar career. Dyer lived on North Street (56) in one of the few old houses on the mill pond side—new ones went up in the boom of the 1830s-40s.

> In 1835-37, when the fishing and other business was at its height in Hingham . . . I sailed three years with Captain Thaxter, and our freights were principally Hingham woodenware, fish, bait nells, cordage, castings from the foundries in Hingham, and an immense amount of anchors which were made in Halifax and Hanover . . . brought to Hingham by teams,

and no doubt spurring the demand for new roads. After Dyer gave up the sea, he worked as a pilot to Boston. He then turned to shoemaking. In old age, when fire destroyed his shop, he helped his son Frank in his grocery store. It was a nineteenth-century pattern: from mariner to shoemaker to grocer.

Across North Street from Dyer in the peak years of Hingham enterprise, an equally characteristic but different story was lived out. Jotham Lincoln learned the trade of chairmaker. After a serious accident left him lame, he turned to teaching school. His story is continued in an anonymous note that dramatically illustrates the political turmoil after the First Parish's split and after the formation of competing church societies:

> The division of the parish taking place and he remaining of the old Society, and that being a majority of the town, and he being qualified, he could have any office in the gift of the town. For more than twenty-five years he was Justice of the Peace, Town Clerk, Representative . . . and many other offices till the Universalist Society was set up which, with the other [religious] societies of the town, changed the majority of the town, since which time the offices have been among all the societies.

*Abigail Smith Thaxter (1722–1807),
wife of Major Samuel Thaxter and great-great
grandmother of Susan Barker Willard. In later
life, the widowed Abigail lived in the home built
in 1788 by her son, Thomas Thaxter. The house
is now St. John's rectory.*

*"Girl with a Dog,"
drawn by Hannah Cushing Andrews
(1811–1835) at about age twelve. Hannah
was the daughter of Thomas Andrews, one of
the founders of the New North Church.
Hannah's sister married a stalwart
of the Old Ship, Albert Fearing.*

The barque SAXONY. Built in Hingham (1841) by William Hall for James Huckins and Alfred C. Hersey, commanded by Nelson Scudder in 1842. Sold to the British in 1864.

The woodburning sidewheeler EAGLE, first steamboat between Boston and Hingham. Ran on a regular schedule 1819 and 1820. The EAGLE could carry two hundred passengers.

BOSTON,
Plymouth & Sandwich
MAIL STAGE,

CONTINUES TO RUN AS FOLLOWS:

LEAVES Boston every Tuesday, Thursday, and Saturday mornings at 5 o'clock, breakfast at Leonard's, Scituate; dine at Bradford's, Plymouth; and arrive in Sandwich the same evening. Leaves Sandwich every Monday, Wednesday and Friday mornings; breakfast at Bradford's, Plymouth; dine at Leonard's, Scituate, and arrive in Boston the same evening.

Passing through Dorchester, Quincy, Wyemouth, Hingham, Scituate, Hanover, Pembroke, Duxbury, Kingston, Plymouth to Sandwich. *Fare,* from Boston to Scituate, 1 doll. 25 cts. From Boston to Plymouth, 2 dolls. 50 cts. From Boston to Sandwich, 3 dolls. 63 cts.

Leonard and Woodward's stagecoach schedule, November 1810.

Village post offices were moved about according to the convenience of their postmasters. In 1849, Seth S. Hersey, farmer, was appointed South Hingham's postmaster and moved the post office to the building next to his home at 632 Main Street.

Woodburning locomotive at Thaxter's Bridge. By 1860, Old Colony Railroad engines had been converted to coal.

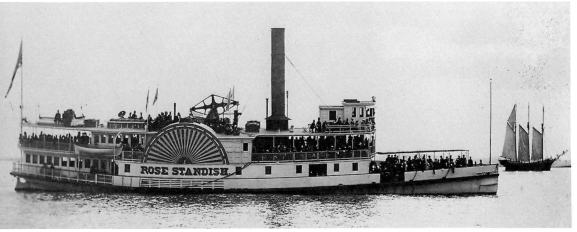

An excursion party on the first ROSE STANDISH, built 1863. Used briefly by the U.S. government during the Civil War to exchange prisoners. Destroyed by fire in Calais, Maine, in 1900.

Souther's shipyard. A rare photographic image by William Hudson, Jr. (1820–1907), much of whose work was destroyed by fire shortly after his death. The yard was below the north end of Fish (now Ship) Street.

Packing barrels at the harbor, c. 1867.

Hingham woodenware. Left to right: a piggin, a pail, and the distinctive Hingham bucket. This design in different sizes was used for storing and shipping foodstuffs. The staves were tongue and grooved to prevent leakage, the lids were fitted, and the broad bottoms were recessed inside the staves so that the buckets could be stacked.

Handmade parquetry pail, lid, and stand made by William S. Tower (1824–1898), founder of the Tower Toy Guild, probably over a ten-year period. The herringbone pattern and star ornaments were created by alternating over 47,500 pieces of red and white cedar. This ensemble was purchased by the Agricultural and Horticultural Society in 1865 for $50.

Nineteenth-century photograph taken for Selectman Seth Sprague's son, Anthony J. Sprague, who manufactured woodenware, along with Crocker Wilder and Son, at Cushing Pond.

Joshua Wilder (1786-1860), clockmaker.

Martin Wilder (1790–1854), carriage smith, a younger brother of Joshua. His will established what was originally called The Wilder Charitable Fund. Through the initiative of the trustees, Wilder Memorial Hall was built in 1879.

Tall clock (95"). On the face, the name of the maker of the brass movement, "Joshua Wilder, Hingham." An example (c. 1840s) of the Roxbury style case, particularly characterized by the fret along the top of the hood. Mahogany and mahogany veneer. The case was probably the work of Reuben Tower. South Hingham neighbors, Wilder and Tower (1795–1881) were prominent American clockmakers and noted for rare dwarf tall clocks (average height 41") nicknamed "grandmother clocks."

Methodist Church (1828) in its original location facing west on the southeast corner of North and Thaxter Streets, photograph c. 1865.

Methodist Church in 1885. Moved (1882) to its present location. To the right, the house of the Thaxter sisters, demolished in 1906 by Ira G. Hersey.

First Baptist Church (1828) in 1885. To the rear is the larger of two Elm Street schoolhouses, in use until new schoolhouses were built in 1894. It later became Eagle Hall.

First Universalist Church (1829) in 1885. The society disbanded in 1927. The building was purchased by Oddfellows Old Colony Lodge 108 and the Revere cast bell by Henry Ford in 1930. Today, 196 North Street.

Evangelical Congregational Church (1849) in 1885. The latest of the evangelical churches built in Hingham, it was interchangeably referred to as "Orthodox" or "Calvinist" throughout the later nineteenth century.

By 1818, he had built a large house (57-59 North Street) and accumulated much land. But with the election of Andrew Jackson as President (1828), he lost his customs office, his position as town clerk, and his popularity. He went into the lumber business, lost heavily, and had to sell house and lands. He "removed to a small tenement in the west part of town, where, after a few years, he died, April 16, 1844." Of Jotham's ten children, only Thomas, a carpenter on Elm Street, stayed in Hingham. Ironically, Jotham Lincoln's house became the home of Oliver Stearns, pastor of New North, the rival parish.

Jotham Lincoln's political allies at the Centre were more fortunate. In these years of hectic enterprise, several events spurred the proud growth of this village: the expansion of its political power through domination of the First Parish, its new factories, and its victorious struggle of 1844 to locate (at 373 Main Street) Hingham's first "town hall." Old artisans were new entrepreneurs, and Justin Ripley, Justin, Jr., and Samuel Bailey built them commodious dwellings. A mere count of houses raised between the turn of the century and the Civil War testifies to the growth: seventy-one, and of these, roughly two-thirds were built after 1830.

A crucial event in the history of land opened up space for homes. Until 1744, the training field extended over an area bounded by Main, Leavitt, School, Pleasant, and Pond Streets. But that year, the town decided to distribute much of it among heirs of early settlers. Ebenezer Lincoln, grandson of Thomas the husbandman, received a large piece and sold part to his neighbor John Fearing. So the land remained for almost a century. Then, in 1841, Ebenezer's grandson Ebenezer died childless. His heirs, now living in Maine, sold the land in lots, to add to the growing residential enclave.

The Centre, "Little Plain," was a self-sufficient village of homes, shops, factories, and farms. Farmers, manufacturers, and shopkeepers lived close to work and to each other. Here, as in Dickens's England of the 1820s and 1830s, the most distinctive new class was the *petit bourgeois*, small shopkeepers. With the growth of industrialism, the old self-sufficient farm, often including a small artisan workshop, where domestic needs were satisfied, was giving way to retail trade. What is remembered as the "old country store" was a creation of the early 1800s.

Shops multiplied all over Hingham. The first grocery store at Queen Ann's Corner had opened in 1815. At Magoon's Bridge in the 1830s and 1840s were "Lane's new store" and Greenleaf's tobacco factory, selling that revolting new fad, chewing tobacco. At Broad Bridge, George Lincoln, John Todd, D. H. Abbot, and Elihu Thayer opened their businesses. Shops for lumber and coal dealers, carpenters, house painters, and blacksmiths multiplied. Nine horses supplied the power for the North Street bakery of George Hunt. Here, seven to nine "hands" produced white and brown bread, sponge cake, crackers, gingerbread, even "election cake" to be munched during town meeting days, for homes where the homebaker had decided to hang up her apron. In West Hingham in 1845, George Hersey opened his grocery (211 South Street). At Little Plain were shopkeepers Sprague, Hersey, and M. & F. Burr; in South Hingham were Ezra Wilder's store at Friend Street (still there as the Cracker Barrel), Josiah Lane's grocery north of the Wilder Hall site, and two Cushings, who retailed across from each other on Main Street. On Liberty Plain, Daniel Wilder's shop (1011 Main) was built in 1836, and Johnny Wilder's under Liberty Hall (1040) in 1857.

Shopkeepers and small industrialists played a new role in town politics and changed it accordingly. Change is seen in a sequence of new names and new occupations. After the rise of the town's Jefferson-Madison majority in 1805-08, no more Thaxters, Beals, or Andrews held office. Cushings remained strong, but Ned was a cabinetmaker and Oliver a painter. The first-ever Gardner selectman was a shoemaker; the first Lane since the seventeenth century, a dealer in fishing outfits; the first Marble, a carriage maker; three Gills were a carpenter, a silversmith, and a shopkeeper. Most striking was the political rise of Fearings and Spragues, from Centre and South. Trader Martin Fearing was town treasurer from the 1820s to the 1850s, and in 1858, shopkeeper William Fearing 2nd became treasurer for half a century. The Spragues, eclipsed in the eighteenth century, produced three selectmen, two boxmakers and farmer Seth, who served continuously from 1857 to 1895. The leading Lincoln was Solomon, a lawyer and banker, born in 1804, town historian in 1827, state representative, then state senator, and moderator by 1833, serving often and in alternation with scale-maker Luther Stephenson and civil engineer Charles Seymour.

Such men dominated the local association of National Republicans, successors of the Jeffersonians and forerunners of the Whigs. Joseph Richardson had laid the groundwork as a United States Representative in the 1820s. When his parish called him home in 1829, he went to Quincy and helped persuade John Quincy Adams, the former President, to succeed him. A letter from Solomon Lincoln to a political ally in 1830 captures the local political atmosphere at the moment of Adams's first campaign:

> We think him a good rallying point for those who wish to throw off the incubus of Jacksonism . . . . With our federalism of the old-fash-

ioned kind, clannish, selfish, and monopolizing, with our old-fashioned republicanism, mingled with Jacksonism, with our anti-tariff and anti-Masonic parties to season the medley, we have in the Old Colony but little hope of being able to bring any of our politicians who have had much to do with parties recently, into the field for Congress, who can succeed.

Richardson and the *Hingham Gazette* spearheaded the campaign, and from 1830 until his death in the chambers of the Speaker of the House in 1848, the grand old man of National Republicanism was Hingham's congressman. To Adams and the local attachments to Senator Daniel Webster—"godlike Daniel," the "great cannon loaded to the lip"—can be credited the steady string of National Republican and Whig victories in Plymouth County.

Webster almost became a Hingham resident. John Richardson recalls:

According to George Lincoln, Webster evidently considered purchasing the Otis Hill region for his farm, but ended up in Marshfield. The old [coach] route between Marshfield and Boston ran along North Street and over the Beal Street turnpike. Webster sometimes stopped en route at Wilder's tavern [today's Old Ordinary] and visited with his good friends the Soules at their house on North Street [Talbots store, 164]. Mrs. Soule was the granddaughter of the Captain Thomas from whom Webster had bought his Marshfield farm.

For many years until the 1940s, a wooden statue of Webster stood on a mound beside the Soule house, "looking out from under its heavy brows at the passing trains, or in winter carefully wrapped and tied in straw like some huge, rather shapeless umbrella."

Webster's career as a powerful but frustrated national leader spanned decades when the nation was struggling through the youth of an institution the founding fathers had dreaded: political parties. Under Madison and Monroe, the Jeffersonian faction had grown moderate, and during Monroe's presidency (1817-25), there was virtually no opposition. Then rebellion stirred, led by the greatest of polarizers, Andrew Jackson of Tennessee, who won the presidency in 1828 and 1832. The Jacksonians called themselves Democrats; the new anti-Jackson coalition called themselves Whigs. Hingham gave Jackson only thirty-three votes in 1828 and forty-eight in 1832.

By the late 1840s, the Whigs were moribund nationally but not in Plymouth County. In 1836 and 1840, Hingham voted two to one against the masterly Democratic party-builder Martin Van Buren, and in the 1840s, three to one against Democrats James Polk and Lewis Cass. But by 1848, the pattern of politics, of changing labels and one-issue third parties, had been further confused by the heating up of national sectional strife.

To the growing political ferment of these decades was added a new ferment in religious life. "Liberty" was now the battle-cry of the Republic, and religious liberty would no longer be denied. A period of feverish economic enterprise and political turmoil was also a time of ardent evangelical revival and division. Before the Revolution, a single church congregation or "society" had controlled local power in most towns. Conflicts could be resolved informally within the "society" by political-social means. But increasingly after 1775, such conflicts were resolved instead through litigation. A chief cause of this change, one scholar concludes, was the proliferation of "dissenting" churches. As townsmen divided into more and more sectarian congregations, they had to seek resolution of conflict through the legal system.

Elsewhere in Plymouth County, the proliferation of sects began earlier than in Hingham, with an alarming impact on the social fabric. Middleboro acquired three separate Baptist parishes. In 1802, a schism occurred between Trinitarians and Unitarians in Plymouth, and 1803, between Unitarians and Congregationalists in Pembroke. Abington's minister was fired for teaching the Swedish visionary Swedenborg. By 1812, "discord and contention," Kingston's minister lamented, had disrupted a town "remarkable for peace, unanimity and concord." In the 1820s, the Bridgewaters were "witness to a religious cacophony."

Hingham had striven to insulate itself against such upheavals, and it did succeed in delaying them. Its ancient meetinghouse had long stood as the religious and political center of North Hingham. Even after the painful division of 1806, it would hold its unique power as the locus of loving memory, from its velvet cushion at the pulpit "soft as feathers could make it, and sending up, when pounded by a sacred eloquence, clouds of sacred dust"; to its square pews, whose cushionless seats were "hung on hinges, and raised in prayer-time, and which followed up the amen with a loud, rattling, running report, like an old-fashioned militia fire"; to the "discordant sounds" of the double bass, violin, flute, and clarinet players, tuning "their instruments in the porch during the first prayer." But henceforth it would share power with numerous other church "societies." By the 1820s, "the discordant sounds" of other sects would no longer be silenced. In 1829, John Lane of the First Parish confided to his journal that "the state of this town as it respects religion is the most lamentable that it has ever been for twenty years."

The establishment of four new denominations in the decades between 1820 and 1850 suggests the rapid rise of a population heterogeneous in background and belief. It also expresses a variety of reactions against the religious dominance of the three Unitarian parishes: the First and Second Parishes and New North Church. At the time, such reactions were almost interchangeably identified as "evangelical" and "orthodox," as opposed to "rational" and "liberal," the terms Unitarians used to describe themselves in doctrine.

"Orthodox" in this new usage did not necessarily carry its old connotation of "Calvinist," although the new *Evangelical* Congregational Church of the 1840s was identified for the remainder of the century as "Orthodox" and "Calvinist." Baptists, Methodists, and Orthodox Congregationalists shared a belief in the Trinity—they were "Trinitarian" as opposed to "Unitarian." They also shared a faith in the dependence of sinful human nature for salvation on the grace and mercy of God, as distinct from the Unitarian faith in the power of individual human reason and enterprise to earn salvation.

Universalists differed from Unitarians in a more subtle way. Both were "liberal," in that both rejected Calvinism's emphasis on man's sinfulness and expectation of damnation, and both believed in universal redemption. But for Unitarians, damnation was unreasonable; for Universalists, it was unjust. Nonetheless, Universalists in these early years remained more "orthodox" than Unitarians: they still held to the Trinity and to the divinity of Christ. Thus, it is accurate to say that all four new churches, together with the Trinitarian Episcopalians, represented a "resurgence of orthodox thinking in the town." That all of these new congregations were late in establishing themselves testified to the continuing strength of Hingham's Unitarian—that is, rational and liberal—religious tradition.

In 1827, Solomon Lincoln wishfully celebrated Hingham's "utmost harmony in the churches, unanimity among the people." His son Francis claimed, in 1893, that "there was not in this town any division of the churches on denominational lines, as was common in other places." Such a claim would have surprised some groups early in the nineteenth century.

Records for the early years of these new sects are sparse. But it is known that they had common difficulties, with small memberships and little money or influence, and that some met appreciable opposition. Laymen gathered in each other's homes. Of the five denominations, only the Episcopalians had a secure hall, on North Street, owned by the "devoted churchman" Daniel Bassett, and there a first service was held in 1824. Yet, interest waxed and waned, and the strong revival of Episcopalianism came only after the Civil War.

In 1809, in order to join the Episcopal Society of Scituate, Captain Charles W. Cushing and thirteen other South Hingham men had asked to be set off from the Unitarian Second Parish. But such was the growing religious pluralism and instability that fourteen years later, Cushing was instrumental, at a meeting at his home, in the organizing of a local Universalist Society.

Methodist meetings, too, were held in homes, those of Moses Tower, Robert Goold, and others, sometimes with sermons by circuit preachers, the first in 1807. In 1818, a "class" of seven Methodists, mostly Goolds, was formed. During their meetings, acts of harassment from outside were not uncommon.

For the Baptists, such opposition had come earlier. In 1782, late in Ebenezer Gay's pastorate, some Hingham Centre families such as the Spragues had "formed the nucleus of a small underground Baptist community." When they invited a preacher to speak, he was threatened by a mob with clubs and staves. After cow dung was thrown in his face, he was forcibly ejected from town. The same mob promised to burn any home in which Baptist meetings were held. So it was not until 1818 that the handful of Baptists organized a prayer group, formed the town's first Sunday school, and heard a Baptist preacher in Hingham. Like those of the Methodists, their meetings were marred by disturbances. In a hall they rented for a year at the Cove, as they sat on their board seats, the group was once locked inside and "no officer of the law intervened." Curious townsmen watched the first adult baptisms by immersion in the harbor at the north foot of Ship Street in 1820. A story about one of these occasions persisted in local memory. As "the congregation watched from the shore and joined in hymns led by a cornet," the cornetist "inadvertently burst into a rousing 'Pull for the shore, boys!' instead of the expected hymn. For a long time after, the village boys were likely to whistle 'Pull for the shore' when a member of the congregation passed."

The persistent fervor of these little groups was finally manifest in the appearance, within two years, of three meetinghouses. The house of the Universalists on North Street (196), with its sixty-four pews on the floor and twenty-two in the gallery, was built in 1829. The First Parish's John Lane was indignant:

Feb. 2, 1830. Much is doing by the enemies of truth to entangle the careless in that soule destroying doctrin [sic] Universalism.

April 28, 1830. Ordination at the Universalist this day. What is the state of the church coming to? Is false doctrine triumphant? O maluncholly! Maluncholly!

The meetinghouse later became the Odd Fellows Hall, and it remains in its place today, unrecognizable as a church.

Also in 1829, the Baptists built their church at Main and Elm Streets. The Methodists' at Goold's Bridge (West Hingham crossing) was built and financed in 1828 with funds provided by the Rev. and Mrs. Stephen Puffer, who then sold pews to cover the costs. Here was entrepreneurial enterprise at its most devout, even if the building did not stop tricksters from re-harnessing horses so their heads faced the wagons while their Methodist owners worshipped inside. Undiscouraged, they had seventy members within a few years, and the Baptists had fifty-one, though these numbers rose and fell over time.

Understandably, the Orthodox Congregationalists were slower to break away from their originally Congregational, now Unitarian parishes. In the years prior to 1847, "desiring," in Robert Edson's words, "to have a trinitarian congregational presence" in the town, dissatisfied Congregationalists met for services in the town house. In the summer of 1847, the Rev. E. Porter Dyer visited Hingham, was engaged to preach, and set about organizing a congregation. Dyer was a graduate of the Andover Theological Seminary, the center in Massachusetts of anti-Unitarian training. By the end of 1847, his congregation numbered only eleven members. With financial help from the Norfolk Conference of Churches, however, a church was built the following year at the junction of Main and Pleasant Streets and dedicated on January 4, 1849. Dyer remained pastor for sixteen years, was active in town affairs, and played a leading role in the anti-slavery movement. But the congregation's small numbers and lean budget made it impossible to pay him an adequate salary, and in the early 1860s he was obliged to resign.

The generation of Hinghamites who were adults between the coming of peace in 1815 and the 1840s had lived during the turbulent adolescence of the American republic. They lived through times of industrial and commercial expansion. They struggled with confusion and change in politics. They splintered into new religious sects. But the conflicts they had known so far were nothing to what would follow, as a single moral and political issue dominated national life, and a deeply divided Union came of age under fire.

⊠

CHAPTER SIX

"The Great Principle of the Age"

The great principle of the age is human freedom.

Before a man can be educated, he must be a free man.

HORACE MANN
Hingham's Congressman
Eighth District, 1848–1852

IN 1835, about a dozen women met in the vestry of the Baptist Church. So began the Hingham Female Anti-Slavery Society, tiny seed of a cause which became a consuming issue for the next twenty-five years. The women pledged themselves "to use all Christian and pacific means for the abolition of American slavery."

The town, like the nation, was divided on the "means." The *Hingham Gazette* (1827-38), the *Hingham Patriot* (1838-48), and, after 1850, the *Hingham Journal* were filled with letters. Sentiments expressed in them ranged widely. The Anti-Slavery Society put its faith in "moral suasion." William Lloyd Garrison, the militant editor of America's first abolitionist newspaper, advocated immediate national emancipation. Hingham's Universalist minister, A. A. Folsom, argued that liberation should occur through state legislative action. Albert Fearing believed the only solution was to buy the freedom of slaves and send them to colonize Liberia. Others thought that slavery would die away if the 1808 law prohibiting further importation of slaves was enforced and if slavery could be excluded from new territories. Instead, an illegal external trade by way of Texas and an increasing internal trade invalidated such optimism. Meanwhile, slavery remained constitutional in that "fatal drop of Prussic acid" whereby a slave represented three-fifths of a "person" and counted as such in determining southern representation to the United States Congress.

Some of the women in the original Female Anti-Slavery group joined the Hingham Anti-Slavery Society, formed in January, 1838. Meetings were held in the homes of its founding members and officers: Derby preceptor Increase Smith, Baptist pastor Waterman Burlingame, Jairus Lincoln, Rufus Lane, Louisa Beal, Joanna Humphrey, Peter Cushing, Royal Whiton, and the Thaxter sisters. Here they discussed the thorny problems associated with slavery. Did public "conveyance companies" have the right to exclude blacks? What could be done to stop the building of American ships specifically designed for Spanish slavers and the fraudulent use of the American flag to protect slave ships from British search and seizure? Should Southern cotton, rice, and tobacco, the products of slave labor, be boycotted? What legal protection should be afforded slaves? What were the obligations of Northern freemen to fugitives? Did the Bible justify slavery? Should churches exclude clergy and communicants who sanctioned slavery by passivity and silence? What of the "second table communion," for blacks after whites?

In these years, the fugitive Frederick Douglass spoke often at antislavery gatherings, including those in Hingham. Without condoning conditions in the South, he pointed to forms of prejudice in the North, particularly in churches with "Jim Crow pews up aloft." Such practices, charged a writer to the *Patriot,* were found "within . . . the town of Hingham."

The town population of "coloureds" shrank from forty-five to twenty-five between 1820 and 1855. Most of them lived in the Ward Street neighborhood known as Tuttleville. But in the North Ward lived a single mulatto woman named Lucretia Leonard. Different sources say she was born in Marshfield, was brought from North Carolina by Mary Elizabeth Hobart Stringer, or was the daughter of a Thaxter slave. She was a domestic who lived with three spinster Thaxter sisters, Eliza, Katy, and Anna. Active in the antislavery movement, they became fast friends of Oliver Stearns, settled as New North pastor in 1840. Each Sunday, the sisters sat in the corner pew at the right front, and a solitary Lucretia sat in the slave/negro gallery for women in the rear, to the left of the choir loft. To the right was a gallery for "coloured" men.

In 1841, at a Hingham meeting of the Plymouth County Anti-Slavery Society, Stearns engineered the *unanimous* passage of a resolution against the use of architectural segregation. As a result, Lucretia Leonard was invited down from the gallery. According to one of many versions of this story, the event caused a "great catouse." One parishioner threatened to withdraw from the congregation. The Thaxter sisters insisted that if Lucretia could not sit with them, they would hear the service from the church porch. They prevailed, and Lucretia sat in the Thaxter pew, with and without the sisters, for over half a century.

"Miss Eliza" died in 1869; Katy in 1870. Anna's mind failed, and their brother, Norton Quincy Thaxter, moved into their house (now gone) next to today's location of the Methodist Church. Early one winter morning in 1873, after he had shoveled snow, Lucretia discovered him in a kitchen chair, his feet crossed, his life expired, his customary pipe still hot on the floor. Now, Lucretia was left to care for Anna. In 1878, Anna died, the last of this line of an ancient family. But several more traces of Lucretia survive. In 1886, she appeared on the rolls of the "out of the almshouse poor" and received assistance from ladies of New North. In 1887, she was a guest at a surprise party for eighty-eight-year-old Lincoln Goold of Thaxter Street. In 1894, when Mrs. Increase Smith was interred in Hingham Cemetery, one of the three people who came to pay their respects was an "old colored woman" who had lived as "help" in a family with whom Evelina Smith "became intimately connected" during her years in Hingham. We are sure this was Lucretia. Finally, in 1903, someone, perhaps Susan B. Willard or a member of the Stringer family, arranged for a photographic portrait of Lucretia.

Eight months later, Lucretia Leonard was buried by her many friends from New North Church, and she joined Eliza, Katy, and Anna in their plot behind the old meetinghouse. Her local memory endured. Her portrait became a Hingham icon, a symbol of painful and divisive history, but also of brotherhood and reconciliation.

Was she present at Willard and Derby Halls, at New North, Baptist, Universalist, and Second Parish meetinghouses, to hear the speakers of historic stature who came to Hingham: Frederick Douglass, the Rev. Samuel May, Edmund Quincy, the Misses Angelina and Sarah Grimké, Harriet Martineau, William Lloyd Garrison, Theodore Parker, and Wendell Phillips? According to the *Patriot*, the sentiments they advanced were "much at variance with the general sense of the community." Antislavery activists were a minority. At a citizens' meeting held over a series of nights at Derby Hall in 1842, hostile feelings exploded. Given an evening to rebut Nantucket abolitionist George Bradburn, a "Mr. [William] Stringer of [Raleigh] North Carolina," husband of Mary Hobart, accused Bradburn of serious "misrepresentations and misstatements." Stringer challenged anyone in the crowded hall to refute what he said, but when some tried to do so, they were shouted and hissed back to their seats. This "mobocratic spirit," the *Patriot* editorialized, was "unworthy of a civilized community." Years later, Jairus Lincoln wrote that "Derby Hall will long be remembered by those who congregated there . . . when a man's foes were often those of his household."

Some Hingham women ignored the sneers that met their petitions, the suggestions that their behavior was unseemly, the pressure of their husbands. Antislavery positions hardened: parties and candidates not directly opposed to slavery could not be supported. The staunchly Whig *Patriot*, though sympathetic to antislavery, began to object to the growing political influence of abolitionist positions. Whigs viewed the Liberty (1842) and Free Soil (1848) parties as spoilers, handing Massachusetts elections to Democratic "loco-focos" such as Governor Marcus Morton. State and nation grew belligerent. Rancorous and threatening debate was common in legislatures. The attitudes, resolutions, fiery language, and sometimes injudicious behavior of abolitionists provoked charges of fanaticism, of worsening the slaves' situation by increasing Southern fears of rebellion, and of "sowing disunion." Many wondered about the aftermath of freeing slaves. "Our almshouse," wrote a Hinghamite, "would be filled."

This belligerent mood caused the tragic death of Hingham's Melzar Gardner. He had moved to Virginia in 1841. As a newspaper editor, he protested the use of slaves hired out by their owners for public works in Norfolk. The "wages" were so low that they discriminated against poor white workers. Gardner refused to back down, and in 1843, horrified witnesses saw him shot and killed on a wharf by a member of one of Virginia's wealthiest and most influential families. The banner carried among the almost one thousand mourners in Gardner's funeral cortege read, "The Working Man's Friend—murdered in defending their rights." *Patriot* editor William W. Wilder mourned "the playmate of our boyhood, our companion at school, and an apprentice in the office of this paper."

The town's early antislavery movement reached a spectacular climax in August, 1844. Hingham was the site for the annual celebration of abolition in the British West Indies (1833). With Jairus Lincoln as marshal, celebrants from Plymouth and Norfolk Counties assembled in front of Stearns's New North Church and went to greet others from Essex and Suffolk Counties at the wharf. Years afterwards, Andrew J. Clark recalled "Hingham's Great Day." Two steamboats discharged their passengers onto a long wooden walk to the landing with its red-spiked gates. Accompanied by bands and banners, the procession moved along North, South, and Main Streets and a "private passageway", later Elm Street, to Tranquillity Grove. A "monster picnic" awaited; "roped off tables [were] loaded with food." There was plenty, too, for those outside the ropes, along with mugs of coffee and lemonade.

Oliver Stearns gave the opening prayer. A letter was read from aging, infirm John Quincy Adams to Anna Quincy Thaxter, signed "Your faithful friend and kinsman." "A Hymn for the 1st of August," composed by teacher and poet and Hingham native Almira Seymour, was sung by Barnabas Lincoln's son Nathan. Hingham pastors John Lewis Russell (Second Parish), Sereno Howe (Baptist), and Levi Daggett (Methodist) spoke, along with Douglass, Garrison, Phillips, and James Freeman Clarke, minister of the Unitarian Church of the Disciples in Boston. White cloth banners, tacked on the evergreens, bore black-lettered sentiments such as

> *True Freedom is to be*
> *Earnest to make OTHERS free*
>
> *True Freedom is to share*
> *All the chains our Brothers wear*
>
> *They are slaves who fear to speak*
> *For the fallen and the weak.*

This was the last "tea party" held in Tranquillity Grove for many years. Brothers Edward and Henry Thaxter, the owners, found that the "mass gathering . . . had ravaged and almost ruined the choice retreat."

Some antislavery leaders moved away. Derby preceptor Increase Smith took with him his "indefatigable" reformer/wife Evelina. Sidney Howard Gay, great grandson of the pastor, had already left to become a lecture agent and then editor of the *Anti-Slavery Standard* in New York. Trained as a lawyer, he found he could not take the required oath to uphold a Constitution that sanctioned slavery. He became instead a distinguished journalist, editor of the *New York Tribune*, and historian. Jairus Lincoln offered for sale his shares in the Hingham Bank, Pew Number 16 in New North, and home and acres at 182 Main Street. He had offended local Whig leaders by refusing to endorse candidates until they made clear their position on slavery. He had led in the minority antislavery cause. He had ignored the advice given him when he came to Hingham in the 1820s:

> If you wish to be *popular*, I advise you never to disapprove of anything that the leading men of the town may say or do. Let them have their own way for a time. If they differ from you on any subject, *ap-*

pear to agree with them, but when they are found *to agree with you,* then express your own views as freely as you please.

This descendant of Stephen Lincoln, Henry Ware's son-in-law, Derby trustee, teacher, and musician, resettled his family in Northborough. No longer would his daughter Ann, with her intimate friend Eliza Hersey, later Mrs. John Andrew, walk through Tranquillity Grove or to Nantasket, or play around the little bathhouse her father had built by the creek which came winding through Home Meadows to their back garden.

A new issue now forced deeper rents in a torn nation: the annexation of the slave-holding territory of Texas. One local leader remained prominent on the national scene: Hingham's congressman, former President John Quincy Adams. First a Federalist, then a National Republican, later a Whig, Adams remained consistent in principle. He knew that only a constitutional amendment, impossible because of the combined power of the South and many Northern Democrats, could abolish slavery. But his position was clear. This "old man eloquent" offered a witheringly sarcastic "memorial" in the House in 1839. He called for the formation of a "White Washing Committee" which would expel any member whose pedigree had a tinge of "African blood." He "prayed that the notoriously false assumption contained in the Declaration of Independence . . . that 'all men are created equal' be expunged." The House overwhelmingly refused to receive his memorial. "There is a humiliating confession of wrong," Adams wrote his constituents, "in the refusal to *discuss* the question of slavery." Slavery was a "cancer."

He received hundreds of petitions, but his struggles to present them met with parliamentary maneuvers and gag resolutions. He remained undaunted in the face of personal assaults, accusations of high treason, threats of censure and assassination, and the exploitation of his views by "immediate abolitionists," whose schemes he thought as impractical as those of the Liberian colonizers. Most of his petitioners were women. At a meeting in Tranquillity Grove, he said he considered the women in his district as much his constituents as the men who actually voted. Word of their petitions against slavery, especially in Washington where a market selling manacled slaves stood within sight of Congress, filtered to blacks and gave them hope. So said Frederick Douglass in Hingham's Baptist Church. Women also petitioned against efforts to annex Texas. In a letter to a Hingham friend, Adams wrote, "it was mainly owing . . . to the petitions of women in the free states that Texas had not been admitted," and "if ever slavery is peaceably abolished, it must be done by the women." Neither hope was to be realized.

[91]

It is difficult, almost 150 years later, to grasp how profoundly the Texas issue affected a small New England town, unless we recall the impact, much later, of the Vietnam War. When Whig President William Henry Harrison died in 1841 within weeks of taking office, he was succeeded by Vice President John Tyler, a slave-holding Virginian whom Adams scorned as having infiltrated the Whig camp. Adams predicted that Texas would be admitted by "the back door." Before he left office, the lame duck Tyler advanced the annexation process by means of joint resolutions of simple majorities in the Congress. By mid-summer, 1845, Texas voted in favor of annexation. According to the annexation decree, the huge Texas territory could divide into five states.

The fearsome possibility of annexing a huge slave-holding territory briefly consolidated Hingham factions. In January, 1845, the town sent delegates to the "great Texas meeting" at Faneuil Hall, where people from all parts of the state and of every political persuasion opposed annexation as unconstitutional and designed to uphold and extend slavery. Ten months later, Oliver Stearns preached against the proposed Texas constitution. It not only supported slavery, he charged, but perpetuated it, since it deprived "its own legislature of the power ever to pass laws of emancipation." There were now more slaves, he noted, than the country's total population at the time of the Revolution. He called for a protest meeting. It was held at the old meetinghouse with Pastor Joseph Richardson as chairman. With a solidarity that was only temporary, a forty-member committee to collect signatures for a remonstrance to Congress included clergy, Whigs, Democrats, and antislavery activists. Almost 40 percent of the town—1422—signed. Nevertheless, in late December, 1845, Texas became a state.

The new President James Polk had already sent military support to Texas. The country was in an undeclared state of war with Mexico. Many Hinghamites held that the war was unjustified, an evil for which "the sanctifying cause is *wanting*." It was "murder," wrote lawyer John W. Browne in a scathing open letter to President Polk.

The Texas issue and the Mexican War formed the epicenter of a firestorm that spread through all social, religious, political, and economic life. In the South, white labor saw work lost to hired-out slaves; in the North, white labor felt economically threatened by black artisans. Southern merchants began black-listing Northern manufacturers who expressed antislavery sympathies. Political parties were thrown into a chaos of realignment. Whigs and Democrats divided within, sometimes on slavery extension, sometimes on the loss, especially to Massachusetts commercial and manufacturing interests, of Southern markets. In its first fifty-two years, the nation had had only eight Presidents; between 1840 and 1860, no President served more than one term.

In 1848, there were four candidates for President. Hingham Whigs were jubilant when Mexican war hero General Zachary Taylor won. A cadre of marshals from Hingham Centre, representing some of the town's most important manufacturers, led several hundred in a spirited torchlight procession which "surpassed in novelty and brilliancy any public parade which has ever been seen in this town." But it was the last Whig parade. The party had just lost Adams, Taylor died halfway through his term, and its long-time leaders, Senators Daniel Webster and Henry Clay, were growing old.

As Southern "ultras" threatened secession and Northern idealists scorned the "scarecrow of disunion," Webster and Clay tried to mitigate the peril with the Great Compromise of 1850. One of its most controversial parts was a harsh Fugitive Slave Bill. It held that a runaway slave had stolen his master's "property," could be returned by his master's simple declaration, and could give no evidence in a hearing before a United States Commissioner. Persons aiding a "fugitive" or obstructing his return could be imprisoned for six months and fined up to $1000. Horace Mann, who followed Adams as Hingham's congressman, wrote his constituents: "This bill derides the trial by jury secured by the Constitution. A man may not lose a *horse* without a right to this trial; but he may [lose] his *freedom*." With one exception, the Massachusetts delegation voted against the bill, but it passed both houses. Jairus Lincoln, visiting in Washington, wrote that the danger was in the North, where some legislators and citizens, in their general indifference to slavery and its extension, were giving the "100 slaveholder" representatives additional power in the national legislature.

Crowded, excited meetings were held in Boston at Faneuil Hall and Tremont Temple. Fugitive slaves were arrested, and disorder followed the "rescue trials" of those who intervened. In two years, the flow of runaway slaves following the North Star to Canada grew to six thousand. And in 1852, the runaway best-selling novel, *Uncle Tom's Cabin*, sold 400,000 copies.

Galvanized by outrage, antislavery leaders spoke again in Hingham. Theodore Parker suggested that violence was inevitable. Parker, Samuel May, and Jairus Lincoln publicly declared that they would aid fugitive slaves. Although Hingham was not on the routes of the Underground Railroad, unconfirmed stories persist that there was a "station" under Andrew Cushing's house at 710 Main Street and that Peter Cushing and others also hid runaways.

In a sermon on the Fugitive Slave Law in March, 1851, Oliver
Stearns asserted that to condone it was "radically unChristian and in-
iquitous." His recourse would be civil disobedience: "I advise no one
to resist it by force; but I cannot obey it." Caught up in the controversy, townsmen interpreted and reinterpreted Stearns's words, as well
as the cautious sermon of Joseph Richardson, "Christian Obedience to
Civil Government." They debated the "higher law" of God invoked by
activists and questioned by what authority humans could presume to
know it.

One of those asking that Stearns's electrifying sermon on the Fugitive
Slave Law be published was a young new townsman named John
Albion Andrew. On Christmas Eve, 1848, at New North Church,
Oliver Stearns had married this native of Maine and little-known Boston
lawyer to Eliza Hersey of Hingham. It was a moment when local and
national history intersected.

CHAPTER SEVEN

John Albion Andrew

FOR ten years before marrying Eliza Hersey, John Andrew had studied and practiced law in Boston. Among the antislavery activists who became his friends, two were most important to him. One was John W. Browne of Hingham, son-in-law of Barnabas Lincoln, whom Andrew called the most intimate friend of his life. The other, George Thompson, was the English member of Parliament most instrumental in the emancipation of the slaves in the British West Indies. Thompson had visited America in the 1830s. Before being mobbed and forced to flee to Nova Scotia, Thompson spoke at Bowdoin College. Sophomore John Andrew fell under the spell of his oratory and his argument that slavery was "the worst institution in the world." With a talent for accent and mimicry, Andrew could recreate that "prism" scene of his youth almost perfectly.

The message would profoundly affect Andrew's response to two events years later in 1854. He sat quietly in his Boston office as a milling crowd and a clanking military cavalcade escorted fugitive slave Anthony Burns back to a ship and his owner. Although Andrew had not joined in the rioting and illegal attempts to rescue Burns, he could not accept the fact that Massachusetts Judge Edward G. Loring, who was also a United States Commissioner, had ordered the return. Within a week, Andrew warned a Boston audience that no Massachusetts law prevented a state officer from rendering up a fugitive.

The other event was the passage by Congress in 1854 of the Kansas-Nebraska Act. This replaced the 36 degree 30 minute latitude boundary between slave and free states, set by the Missouri Compromise of 1820, with the principle of "popular sovereignty." Territories could now decide before applying for statehood whether to be slave or free. In September, 1854, Andrew advertised in the *Hingham Journal* for a meeting of anyone, whatever his party, interested in "uniting to repel the alarming aggressions of the Slave Power." The immediate aim of the meeting was to select delegates to the first state convention of a new "Republican" Party. At the convention, John Andrew and Thomas Loring, also of Hingham, were elected permanent officers. They, together with Thomas Bouvé, Samuel Downer, Ebenezer Gay, Marshall Lincoln, Joseph Sprague, and Joseph Thaxter, Jr., had bolted the Whigs to the Free Soil Party (1848), then to the Free Democratic Party (1853), and now to the new Republican Party. The demise of Hingham Whiggism was at hand.

Out of its death was born a lively, meaningful Hingham Centre tradition. As their party was decimated by the antislavery coalition, Hingham Centre Whigs turned disappointment into broad, topical comedy. They published "The Spunkville Chronicle," a spoofing account of several July Fourths. They invented an "anti-hero," a presidential candidate named Ensign Jeheil Stebbings of Aroostook County, Maine. On July 4, 1854, clad in a "motley array" of costumes including mismatched old uniforms with clam shell epaulettes, the Stebbings Life Guard under General Hawkes Fearing, Jr., and the Spunkville Artillery led by Colonel John Stephenson marched to mock-battle with the "hosts of disloyalists and anti-annexationists" at Fountain Square. In 1858, Ensign Stebbings, "the greatest hero the world never saw," was killed off. The "body" of Jeheil was found drowned, or perhaps murdered, in Fulling Mill Pond. When a blacksmith's bellows failed to revive him, "thirty-nine grotesque-looking mediums . . . chanted the *taedium*":

> *Bellow, ye bulls, and barol, ye bats,*
> *Encore, Encore, ye amorous cats;*
> *Boreas, the news spread far around*
> *That Ensign Stebbings has been drowned.*

By then, local Republican strength was irresistible. Oliver Stearns had left New North, but other religious leaders, William T. Clarke of the Second Parish, John Cargill of the Universalists, and E. Porter Dyer of the new Congregationalists, had taken up the cause. In 1856, they practiced what Clarke defended as "pulpit politics" and endorsed Republican John C. Fremont for President. Fremont lost the presidency, but Massachusetts Republicans won the governorship and placed majorities in the General Court. Hingham elected Republican William Whiton as representative.

Die-hard Whigs still feared that disunion and civil war were worse than slavery itself. Why shouldn't states determine whether they would be slave or free? What did it matter that the Missouri Compromise had been nullified? As Republican power grew, such Whigs joined the Constitutional Union Party. Clutches of Stephensons and Fearings at the Centre, together with Albert Fearing in the North Ward and Charles W. Cushing in South Hingham, were its stalwarts. In 1860, in his fifty-fourth year as First Parish pastor, Joseph Richardson sent his "sentiment" for the national candidates of the Constitutional Unionists, John Bell and Edward Everett.

In late 1858, their political hegemony gone, local Constitutional Unionists, particularly Albert Fearing and Charles Cushing, took a momentous step. They led in founding the Agricultural and Horticultural Society. Here, the rancor of politics was forgotten. Members discussed scientific farming and the aesthetic and environmental importance of trees, and displayed their harvests and manufactured products. It would be a social institution of tremendous healing power.

Meanwhile, John and Eliza Andrew had purchased a small winter home on Charles Street in Boston. He took cases other lawyers rejected, representing women in divorce cases, defending prisoners. Every Sunday afternoon he visited prisons. At the same time, he was gaining a remarkable understanding of constitutional and slavery law. He wrote later: "All the victories of life have to be won before the battle itself begins. A man must *see* a thing in his mind, before he can *do* it with his hand; and unless he has seen every step of the process, he has not seen it at all."

During this preparation, Andrew watched some dismal events. The Kansas territory had become an armed and bloody camp of warring anti- and pro-slavery factions. Northern opponents of slavery such as Hingham's Thomas Bouvé and his Boston pastor Theodore Parker funded arms and supplies for free-soil settlers in Kansas. When a vote was held in 1856 on a free-state constitution, "border ruffians" from Missouri threatened election officers, blocked polling places, and smashed ballot boxes. Charles Sumner, Senator from Massachusetts, responded with an excoriating personal attack on the South and was savagely beaten at his Senate desk by a South Carolina congressman. Thus, the voice of one of Andrew's most articulate allies was stilled for several years.

In 1857, the Supreme Court handed down its Dred Scott decision, which found the Missouri Compromise unconstitutional and ruled that no black, slave or free, could be a citizen. And in the Massachusetts legislature, a bill intended to remove from office Judge Loring, the man who had ordered the return of Anthony Burns to slavery, had been stalled for three years. It was time for Andrew to act.

In 1858, he won a seat in the General Court. The Goliath of the Massachusetts House of Representatives was Caleb Cushing of Newburyport, a powerful Northern Democrat with Southern sympathies. When Andrew spoke against the Dred Scott decision, an infuriated Cushing accused him of trying to "establish the equality of the black and white races." When the bill to remove Loring passed, Cushing delivered a defiant speech, blaming "black" Republicans. A stunned silence fell on the House. Then its startled members saw Andrew take the floor. He had a habit of turning up his coat sleeve when he warmed to a subject. That day, he turned up his sleeve and answered the intimidating Cushing point by point in a speech of spellbinding eloquence. When he sat down,

> there was a storm of applause. The radical men had found their prophet. The House was wild with excitement. For a moment, the Speaker was unable to preserve order; some members cried for joy; others cheered, waved their handkerchiefs and threw whatever they could find in the air.

"That infernal statute," the Fugitive Slave Law, could no longer be enforced in Massachusetts.

Andrew returned to private practice the following fall. But by now, he was prominent in the state Republican Party. He was second only to Wendell Phillips as an orator and had stepped into Sumner's shoes as an organizer. The physical contrast was amusing: he was as rotund and short as they were lanky and tall. But the three shared a commitment. For Andrew, it came from an intense religious belief in the worth of every human being. This belief prevented him from ever making personal attacks. He refused an invitation to join Garrison on a rally platform because he had heard too many men he respected abused on such occasions. His integrity, said Sumner, passed into proverb.

Andrew would need it. On October 16, 1859, abolitionist John Brown and a small band of followers took possession of the arsenal at Harper's Ferry, resolved to establish a stronghold for insurgent slaves. First a crowd, then the militia and Marines, surrounded the arsenal. Two of Brown's sons were killed, and Brown himself was jailed, summarily tried, and hanged. Some of Andrew's friends had helped fund Brown in Kansas and later. Andrew had not; he had met Brown once and sent him a small gift. But he criticized the haste of the trial, publicly solicited funds for the defense, offered legal advice, and spoke at a meeting to raise money for Brown's family. There he used a phrase which, for Andrew, became a verbal trap. Brown's enterprise, he said, may have been right or wrong, but that was not the issue; "John Brown himself is right." The phrase bedeviled Andrew for months. His enemies chose to interpret it as the statement of a radical abolitionist. Subpoenaed by a Senate committee, he was hostilely questioned by Virginian James Mason and Mississippian Jefferson Davis. Brown, he replied, was worthy of sympathy and admiration, but possessed by a monomania. Andrew had intervened only because of the "judicial outrage" of haste.

While the committee in Washington viewed him with suspicion and dislike, in Massachusetts his popular support grew. In May, 1860, he was the overwhelming choice to lead the delegation to the Republican convention in Chicago. By fall, he was stumping the state as nominee for governor, avowing his conformity to the party platform: slavery must not be extended; the Union must be preserved. He won by the largest majority any candidate for the office had ever received. In Hingham, torches flared and tar barrels blazed as a victory procession of several thousand greeted the governor-elect at Fountain Square. Two months earlier he had said, "Here . . . dear friends, I have found the home of my heart."

Although Hingham did not yet know of Abraham Lincoln's ancestry, it had a dual interest in that election. In 1858, that little-known Illinois lawyer had campaigned unsuccessfully for the Senate, but his debates with Stephen Douglas had moved him to the center of the national stage. In 1860, the hopelessly split opposition offered three candidates for President, and Lincoln won. The Hingham returns were Democrats 31, Douglas Democrats 45, Constitutional Unionists 206, and Abrasham Lincoln 467. The great, great, great, great grandson of Samuel Lincoln, weaver, of early Hingham was elected President. Hearing of his election, South Carolina seceded from the Union, other states followed, and the Confederacy chose its own leaders. Lincoln and Jefferson Davis left for their respective capitals in February, 1861, and in April, Fort Sumter was attacked.

The outbreak of war was no surprise to Andrew. In December, 1860, before his inauguration, he had encountered Senator Mason in Washington. Mason suggested that dissolution was inevitable, that a reconstructed union would require the northern states to repeal all antislavery laws. Andrew sensed conciliation was hopeless and war almost a certainty.

As fledgling governor, he immediately began to invigorate the militia. The General Court voted an emergency fund. The Adjutant General made a requisition list: 2000 overcoats, 2000 blankets, 2000 knapsacks. Wealthy Boston merchant John Forbes, an Andrew admirer, made discreet inquiries about steamers to transport troops. In less than three months, despite the scoffing of his detractors, Andrew had a prepared militia. On April 17, five days after Fort Sumter was bombarded, the Massachusetts 6th Regiment was the first to leave for the South and the only one to reach Washington before the capital was cut off. Fourteen years later, standing beside the newly erected Andrew statue in Hingham Cemetery, his senior aide Horace Sargent recalled the governor in those feverish days:

> the memory of his witty words, laughter that was almost articulate with mirth, and his cheery shout of merriment at some pronounced absurdity, reminds me of how much his sunshine lightened labor in these early days of the Rebellion; when matters were so hurried that the aides would follow the soldiers of moving regiments down the steps, to tighten some buckle of belt or knapsack, or to thrust percussion-caps into the pocket! . . . . There were sutlers seeking an outfit, and saints with bandages and lint; . . . inventors of new-fangled guns, pistols, and sabres, only dangerous to their possessor, and which the inventors, to our great joy, threatened to sell to the Confederacy if we did not buy them; . . . gentlemen far gone into consumption, desiring gentle horseback exercise in the cavalry; ladies offering to sew for us . . . philanthropists telling us that Confederate workmen in our arsenals were making up cartridges with black sand instead of powder; . . . bands of sweet-eyed, blushing girls bringing in nice long nightgowns "for the poor soldiers," or more imaginative garments, "fearfully and wonderfully made," redolent of patriotism and innocence, embroidered with the stars and stripes, and too big for Goliath.

Andrew would need all his humor, tolerance, and patience in the years ahead.

If his Massachusetts was ready, Washington was not. No answers came, no orders, in response to his telegraphed inquiries, suggestions, offers of regiments. Yet those Massachusetts troops which had already departed had to be maintained in the field. Andrew authorized his longtime friend Samuel Gridley Howe to investigate stories of privation. Exasperated by well-intended but impractical contributions such as ice and

Oolong tea, Howe reported that the soldiers needed health officers more than chaplains, washerwomen more than nurses, and "Soap! Soap! Soap!"

In November, John and Eliza Andrew went to Washington with Howe, his wife Julia Ward Howe, and James Freeman Clarke. Andrew fondly remembered this trip as "the ladies' expedition." Mixing pleasure with the official duties of war, they called on a discouraged President Lincoln, visited hospitals and encampments, and attended troop reviews. A review across the Potomac ended abruptly when Confederate troops attacked. Union troops and coaches jammed the narrow road back to Washington. To pass the time, Andrew's party sang army songs, one of which was an old camp meeting tune. A composer had set new words to it when John Brown was hanged. As they sang "John Brown's body lies a-moldering in the grave," soldiers alongside the carriage in "the evening dews and damps" responded with the chorus, "Glory, glory, hallelujah!" "Mrs. Howe," said the Rev. Clarke, "why do you not write some good words for that stirring tune?" In "the grey dawn of the morning twilight" at the Willard Hotel, as troops marched in the streets below, Julia Ward Howe awakened, lay musing, and got up to scribble "The Battle Hymn of the Republic," an anthem for a nation at war.

Andrew was frustrated by the less than energetic early prosecution of the war. He also had to endure persistent conflicts at every level over the commissioning of officers. Except when quotas were not filled, this was the prerogative of governors. Militias, in their jealous localism, grew truculent when elected officers were replaced by scions of old Boston families or by leaders with military training. Not all had changed since the conflicts of the 1640s, when a militia member who was a partisan of Bozoan Allen shouted that he'd rather die than not pick his own officers. But Andrew's reasons were pragmatic. He wanted powerful families to remain involved in the cause, and he felt that good leadership was due the humblest soldier, that it would save lives.

The greatest challenge came from a man Andrew himself had commissioned in the first rush of 1861, Brigadier General Benjamin F. Butler. Butler would later become the bane, as well, of Hingham's other governor, John D. Long. Butler's military achievements were remarkable: the rescue of Washington, the quelling of rebellion in Maryland, and the capture of New Orleans, where, as military governor, he became known as "Beast Butler." In politics, however, Butler was unreliable and dangerous. He persuaded President Lincoln that he could raise "regiments of Democrats" and gained the power to choose officers. An adamant Andrew refused to sign commissions and repeatedly protested. In Washington, Butler began a smear campaign against Andrew. The controversy became a scandal which ended only when the new War Secretary, Edwin Stanton, shut down Butler's "Department of New England."

Disappointed that the war would not be quick and decisive, dismayed by Lincoln's failure to support him, Andrew also shared with many others an additional anxiety. What were the President's intentions regarding emancipation? Andrew himself had remained silent on the slavery issue during his first year as governor; this was a war for union. When popular feeling intensified that it was also a war for freedom, Lincoln continued to consider the slavery issue only as it affected the Union. Lincoln the cautious strategist was biding his time, even though Lincoln the moralist must have seen the irony so clear to Andrew. Growing discomfort with the uncertainty was defused when Lincoln issued a preliminary emancipation order in September, 1862. The Union victory at Antietam had provided the occasion he had been waiting for. Constitutionally, he justified it as a war measure. But on January 1, 1863, a permanent proclamation was signed.

Within days of the proclamation, Governor Andrew secured an order from Secretary of War Stanton to enlist and organize black troops. Andrew was convinced that if blacks took no part in the war, they would remain "a poor, despised, subordinated body of human beings, neither strangers, nor citizens." Stanton insisted there be white officers for the segregated regiment. Pay, however, was to be equal. By the summer of 1863, the Massachusetts 54th Regiment was ready.

The colonel of the 54th, selected by Andrew, was Robert Gould Shaw, son of a wealthy, influential abolitionist family who were neighbors of the Sidney Howard Gays on Staten Island. Shaw wanted black freed men as soldiers, and recruiting proceeded carefully. Two sons of Frederick Douglass enlisted. After weeks of training, the 54th was ready. With the band playing "John Brown's Body," it marched along State Street, Boston, the way where Crispus Attucks had been killed in the Boston Massacre, the way by which Anthony Burns had been returned to bondage. It continued its march to Battery Wharf and a deadly destiny in the attack on Fort Wagner, South Carolina. Leading his troops in the assault on July 18, 1863, Shaw was killed on the battery and cast by the Confederates into a mass grave with his men.

Later that year, two Hingham black men enlisted in the 54th: David Henry Champlin, a laborer, and Louis Leonard Simpson, a shoemaker. A second black regiment, the Massachusetts 55th, which Andrew sent off in July, included white officers, Alphonso Marsh as a lieutenant, Lieutenant (later Captain) Peter Sprague, and Private John Talbot. After the War Department followed Andrew's initiative and formed national black regiments with white officers, Hingham's Thaddeus Churchill served as lieutenant in the 3rd and Benjamin Curtis Lincoln, who died of a battle wound, as a major in the 2nd. To the 5th (Black) Cavalry Regiment, Hingham sent five enlisted men.

Andrew's task was not finished. Amazed by the news in Colonel Shaw's last letters that the War Department was paying his troops as laborers, Andrew battled doggedly with Washington during the next year trying to correct this injustice. When there was still no federal action, he persuaded the Massachusetts legislature to make up the $6 monthly difference. The troops refused it on principle. Three times Andrew wrote directly to Lincoln. He cited the case of a black soldier who had deserted and been shot. The government's breach of faith, Andrew argued, had released the soldier from his contract: "the Government, which found no law to pay him except *as a nondescript or a contraband*, nevertheless found law enough to *shoot* him as a *soldier*." In September, 1864, the black regiments finally received their full pay of $13 a month retroactive to enlistment.

At the war's end, Andrew went to Washington for the grand review of the armies of Grant and Sherman. His friend John Forbes remembered

> a comic incident which marks the Governor's perfect indifference to appearances, or to the supposed requirements of his high position as to personal dignity . . . . When he arrived . . . the whole city was so much absorbed by the coming spectacle that a seat in a carriage could only be found for Mrs. Andrew; but the Governor, nothing daunted, hired a dark brother with a cart, and, depositing their baggage in it, appeared in due course of time at my house, perched on the top of it.

His wife, Eliza Hersey of Hingham, would also have found this amusing. She, too, as Andrew described her before their marriage, was a "hater of seemings, governed very little by forms or customs." His letters reveal their warm affection. He particularly loved small children and delighted in his own. One of the maids recalled that his first and last stop, whether in Hingham or in Boston, was invariably at the nursery. If the weather changed during the night, he would check and reposition the children's blankets. Now at last, in 1866, the public man could escape from "my mill," leave his larger family, and return to private life.

He had worked, wrote his old pastor, like Goethe's star, "without haste, without rest."

> He worked like the great engine in the heart of the steamship. The vessel may be rolling and pitching amid frightful seas, her decks swept by successive waves, but there, in the centre of the ship, the engine works steadily on, with tranquil accuracy but enormous power. Such force, so steadily exercised, was his. There was no jar, no strain, no hurry, no repose; but constant equable motion, on and on, through all those weary years, to their triumphal end.

> One secret of this great working-power was the natural equanimity of his temper. He was always cheerful, sunny, full of anecdotes and pleasant mirth, with infinite good nature, with none of the corrosive element of irritable self-love. If we keep to our image of an engine, this oil of kindness was the lubricating medium which prevented all waste of power by friction.

To spare party division, Andrew announced early that he would not run again. His five years in office had exhausted his financial resources and sent his clients elsewhere. He seriously considered an offer to become president of Antioch College, whose first president, Horace Mann, had been his mentor. To the relief of his friends, he remained in Boston. His admirers' efforts to see him placed nationally failed. He resisted any move to put him in contest with Sumner or Henry Wilson for the Cabinet or the Senate. He refused a federal judgeship, a seat on the state supreme court, and Lincoln's offer of the Port of Boston customs collectorship, the most lucrative public post in New England. As war governor, he felt he had held a "sacrificial office," had sent the blood of New England to battle, and no sinecure should compromise that.

Andrew inspired friendship, honoring everyone with a candor tempered by magnanimity and fairness. His partisans sometimes shuddered at his feckless honesty, his frankness in defending unpopular positions. When Sumner once questioned the political wisdom of some action, Andrew serenely responded that the people of Massachusetts had the annual option of choosing another governor. To call him "principled" might have troubled him, for he believed

> Principles are of GOD. That is they are founded in the Eternal fitness, harmony, and reality of the Universe over which he presides. Measures . . . are human devices by which men attempt to actualize in human affairs the principles they perceive and believe in.

He believed leadership, the capacity to cause things to happen, was a gift. But no man ever worked with more passion, prepared more carefully, and then persisted.

He described his "radical" positions as conservative, aimed at getting to the root causes of evil. He was persuaded that if there had been a system of free schools in the South, there would never have been a Civil War. As for black people, much as he wished them to be enfranchised, he wanted them to be, for a brief time, relieved of being "the subject of political controversy," so that they might grow in knowledge of "the political function of citizenship." He defined that function in an address: "The first duty of a citizen is to regard himself as made for his country, not to regard his country as made for him."

His insight into the tension between individual liberty and constitutional government radiates from his legal writing. The mind stored with poetry and the Bible, the man who loved singing hymns, was also capable of the most translucent and cogent legal argument. In court he was spectacular. His valedictory on Reconstruction, on the constitutional status of the Confederate States, is the work of a political philosopher. He was in sharp disagreement with more radical Republicans who would punish the South. Not long before he died, Andrew voiced concern over the distracted state of a Congress thinking of impeaching a President:

> my only anxiety is that the Republican party may have an inadequate sense of the grandeur of its position, and the responsibilities it carries. We are working for the ages, not merely for an election campaign. If we show ourselves broad-minded, true-hearted, patient, hopeful, and statesmenlike, the people will not allow the Election to go against us . . . . We can be beaten only by ourselves.

His law practice flourished, and he enjoyed trips with his family and friends. But the governor was as much a casualty of the war as any soldier. In the fall of 1867, he refused several invitations from his friend John Forbes, writing that he was not feeling well. A journalist noted:

> there were periods during the War when the Governor's friends feared he would break down. He had a worn, absent, "flabby" look and had to go off for a few days to recover himself. I saw that same look on him . . . an uncertainty of gait, so it seemed to me—the last time I met him, perhaps ten days ago, on Tremont Street.

At age forty-nine, on October 30, 1867, Andrew collapsed from a stroke. The following evening he died.

Tributes flowed in, but the one he would most have appreciated was wordless. As he lay dying, black citizens gathered quietly in front of the Boston home of the man who had once said that, whatever faults he might have, he was "never mean enough to despise any man because he was ignorant, or because he was poor, or because he was black." They stood respectfully at the back of the church and outside during his funeral services. Then they followed the cortege on foot all the way from Boston to Mount Auburn Cemetery, where he was first buried.

Two years later, Governor Andrew finally returned to "the home of my heart." His remains were escorted to their final resting place on the Hingham Cemetery hill by superintendent John Todd. But controversy and factionalism followed Andrew even in death, and six years more would pass before his Carrara marble statue, by sculptor Thomas Gould, was erected. It stands looking away from the town, with its back to another monument, a plain obelisk that honors other Hingham men who gave their lives and preceded him home.

With the dedication in 1870 of that other monument, the story of modern Hingham appropriately begins.

Page from a song book (1843) prepared by Jairus Lincoln for the local antislavery society. Contributors included Mary L. Gardner, Almira Seymour, Reverend Henry Ware, Jr., Reverend Samuel Willard, and lyricist for this song, James H. Wilder, who resurrected the defunct town paper in 1850 and renamed it THE HINGHAM JOURNAL.

*Lucretia Leonard
(born between 1818 and 1821, died 1904).*

*Reverend Oliver Stearns (1807–1885),
pastor of New North Church (1839–1856),
president of Meadville Theological School,
professor of theology and dean of Harvard
Divinity School (1863–1877).*

*John Quincy Adams (1767–1848), sixth president
of the United States, Hingham's congressman (1830–
1848). Adams' friend and cousin, Thomas Loring,
brought William Hudson, Jr. (1820–1907) to paint
this portrait (1844). Hudson felt he could not paint
hands, so he asked Adams to put one hand inside his
vest and to hold his spyglass in the other.*

*John Albion Andrew (1818–1867),
Civil War governor of Massachusetts.*

PART TWO

The Sociable Island

(1865 - 1896)

CHAPTER EIGHT

✠

A Changing Hingham

ONE Friday in June, 1870, George Lincoln, a busy, sociable shop-keeper at Broad Bridge, climbed with other townspeople up the hill behind the old meetinghouse. This was a great day for Hingham. Oldtimers had never seen "such a splendid military display," the streets filled with uniforms, the air with martial music. On the hilltop, awaiting dedication, rose a monument to Hingham's Civil War dead. From here, Lincoln could see much of the north of a town already very old, showing signs of change and renewal. Already he saw it with the eye of one who would become the town's most diligent and dedicated historian.

We will come to know the man George Lincoln in a later chapter. But first, we should try to visualize the town he lived in as he would have known it in those years just after the Civil War. To do so, we need a double act of imagination. We must see what is no longer visible and not see much of what surrounds us now. We must not see most of the luxuriant cover of trees that canopy and hide so much of the view from the hilltop eye. In the 1870s, it was easier than now to see stretches of meadow, scattered villages, bare hills, bridges, and water.

Below the cemetery hill, the Town Brook emptied into the wide tidal mill pond, and four or five trains puffed by daily over a trestle along its southerly bank. Lincoln probably smelled the brook and the pond, for they served as dumping places and sewers. Along the harborside beyond tenements lay old wharves, some in disrepair. Near the north foot of Ship Street lay the gaunt skeleton of an old sailing ship, where once had been Souther's busy shipyard. East of the Cove were signs of new life: two steamboat wharves where rival lines unloaded crowds of summer visitors and colorful horse-drawn "barges" picked them up. From here,

Summer Street climbed Old Colony Hill to meet the busy highway of Rockland Street, running through the empty, ancient heronry to the rapidly expanding resort of Nantasket. When George Lincoln walked to "the Beach" there in the 1870s, he noticed "many changes," "almost like a work of magic," new cottages with "high-sounding names: 'Spray Cottage', 'Valley Lane Cottage', 'Dewdrop Inn'." Quaintness was giving way to fashion.

He often walked from his Broad Bridge shop up Pear Tree Hill to Little Plain (Hingham Centre) for tea and talk with Fearing Burr. On Main Street he saw both the old and the new, colonial homes and merchants' mansions. Past the Baptist Church and Bassett's livery stable (93 Main) rose the ornate villa (1867) of merchant Thomas Whiton, later the First Parish hall (107), across from the Federal Isaac Hinckley house (126), a striking contrast. Old Thaxter homes had become post war estates. Past Water Street on the left stood the Thomas Thaxter house (1788), lately the home of George Lincoln's mentor, historian Solomon Lincoln, in our day the rectory of St. John's Episcopal Church (176). Across Main from the new Winter Street, old parson Joseph Richardson lay impoverished and dying in his Justin Ripley mansion (1817, 197), soon to become a Bostonian's summer place.

Starting up the steep hill, Lincoln saw a striking image of change. On his right stood the 1690 homestead (209) of Daniel Cushing, the wealthiest townsman of his day. In 1870, it was the estate of John Keeshan, an iron moulder at Howard's foundry, who had come from Tipperary in 1849. He had worked hard, saved money, and bought and renovated the old place. He would marry one of his daughters to young shopkeeper William Hennessy, to whom the estate passed.

At the top of the hill, the line of homes on the right was followed by a cluster of shops much patronized in these years—a wheelwright's, a harness maker's, a carriage painter's, and a blacksmith's, where 247 Main is today. Beyond them on the right were a general store, on the site of John Smith's seventeenth-century garrison house (at the corner of today's Garrison Road), and the home (289) and shop of Fearing Burr (285—torn down in 1918) where George Lincoln often visited. Across the street lived their fellow antiquary, Leavitt Sprague, next to the old Lewis Inn at the corner of Leavitt Street. In front of the inn stood, as it stands today against a different background, the buttonwood tree said to have been set out by Hosea Sprague in 1793.

No other Hingham village could have so struck George Lincoln with its mix of continuity and change as Little Plain. Eighteenth-century homesteads stood where they still stand: on Leavitt Street, the homes of Burrs, Leavitts, and Southers; on Pleasant Street, those of Lorings and Fearings, and of Jacob Cushing, reputed to be the first house in town with square window glass. On Pond Street (2), the third Peter Sprague in a row lived in the house of his box-cooper grandfather. On School Street were the old Cushing (74) and King (48) farmhouses. When Captain Thomas King built his in 1786-87, Colonel Charles Cushing "wanted to know why he did not build larger" and was told that King "preferred a small house well filled to a large one with nothing in it." Such facts were alive in the minds of Fearing Burr and George Lincoln. For them, "a house isn't just a house. A house is a story."

Among the old families and homes at Little Plain stood newer houses, shops, and factories. On the right side of Main Street, heading south, was the fire station, the Niagara Hose House, with a fine social hall for dances upstairs. Beyond "Niagara" was Stephenson's Scale and Balance factory, and alongside, a drive led to the short-lived Jute and Bagging factory, adjoining the thousand-foot-long ropewalk of the Cordage Company, stretching across the later site of the Central Playground. South of Stephenson's on Main Street still stood the derelict Folsom house (c. 1654), shortly to be torn down over the heads of its poor occupants to make way for the first of a line of elegant post-war mansions. On the other side of Main Street were the Cloudman shoe factory and the new public library of 1869, on the site of the present day War Memorial. Diagonally across from where the G.A.R. hall would appear in 1889 was the 1844 town house. Town meetings were held here until 1872, and here were gathered the first agricultural fairs. In 1869, the fairs had moved to the most imposing of the new buildings, Agricultural Hall, at the corner of East and Leavitt Streets.

All of this was within George Lincoln's customary walking range, and he was a brave walker in all weathers. To venture further, he would hire a carriage. He enjoyed visiting kinfolk at the southern end of town. On one pleasant outing in the autumn of 1873, he started out from Cushing's stable behind the hotel at Broad Bridge and detoured up Old Colony Hill to pick up his son. A Summer Street steeper than ours passed by the mansions of wealthy Charles Barnes (59), Alfred C. Hersey (104), and Hersey's brother Henry (110). Henry Hersey's house would soon become the summer home of his niece, Eliza, Governor Andrew's widow.

As Lincoln drove past the Blake summer estate (83 Summer), he may well have felt strange emotions. It had known mixed fortunes as a public and boarding house since his father, the old sailmaker, had lived here. George was born in the house in 1822. Here, too, his father-in-law, shipbuilder William Hall, had lived when George courted and married Mercy in 1844. Up the hill was George and Mercy's first home, "the neatest little cottage" with "the neatest little fence."

Where Summer Street turns right at the hilltop were the charred ruins of the Old Colony House, which had burned the year before, in 1872. This steamboat hotel, built in 1832, had prospered before the Civil War, before the rise of Nantasket as a resort, when summer visitors stayed in Hingham and traveled by carriage to "the Beach" for excursions. From this point, George Lincoln and his son "took the back roads," Summer and Kilby Streets, East and Back Streets, "and on past David Whiton's farm" on Union Street, "through Lazell Street and Prospect Street past Welch's halfway house" in what was then West Scituate. The "back roads" still ran through farming country. Farms surrounded the grounds of the Agricultural Society, where the library and town offices stand today. Farms extended along both sides of Union Street: on the right, the long, rich fields of David Whiton (later Jordan's, later Hornstra's farm); on the left, the farms of Reuben Thomas, Abel Fearing, and Israel Whitcomb. Whitcomb's had special interest. On the traditional site of Anthony Sprague's homestead, burned by King Philip's warriors in 1676, Whitcomb grew his famous acres of asters. He was an ardent horticulturist and an enthusiastic musician, a fit ally for George Lincoln. More farms, owned by Fearings, lay along Lazell Street, and at the far end of Prospect Street were the old Dunbar (208) and Hersey (215) farms.

Having reached West Scituate, the Lincolns headed west to the still wild shores of Accord Pond. Above the pond, on the farm (427 Gardner Street) of her father Joseph Whiting, lived Salome Lincoln, George's widowed stepmother, with his young half-brothers Joe and Wilbur. Long afterwards, Joe Lincoln would be famous as a maker of hunting decoys, still living in the old house above the pond "where the only noises" he heard were "the soughing of the winds through the pines and the pipings of wild duck and geese." When Joe was a boy in 1873, the shores of Accord were still open for fishing and watering livestock. Near the farm was a grove among the trees, and

> the people coming up from the Cape with a herd of cattle driving them through to Brighton used to stop here overnight, and when they came back next day or two from Brighton they'd have another herd going back and they'd stop there. And a wagon load of gypsies used to come every year and stay a week. They never disturbed anybody. Course they never had a very good reputation.

[112]

George Lincoln tarried at Accord an hour, "gathering meanwhile a basket of autumn leaves and a bag of walnuts," then set out down Main Street through the village of Liberty Plain to call on "Uncle Alfred" Loring at his large tannery on the southwest corner of Main and Cushing Streets. Liberty Plainers had recently made their own "quiet village" survey and found, among other things, that they had 72 dwellings, 314 inhabitants, 31 horses, 64 sheep, 411 "female hens," 39 carriages, and 21 wheelbarrows. In some ways they felt closer to their neighbors in East Abington (Rockland) and South Scituate (Norwell) than to far-off Hingham. In times of bitterness, they wondered if Hingham remembered them at all. They were chiefly small farmers and shoemakers; their names, Whiting (the spelling had taken hold in the 1820s), Gardner, and Loring, with a few Herseys, Spragues, Dunbars, and Wilders. Their rich man was the retired toolmaker Amasa Whiting. Whiting lived in what is now called the Whiton House (restaurant) built by his great grandfather Witon in 1757.

Old Witon-Wyton land stretched down Main Street. The Enoch Whiton house (1680, 1083) is half a mile north of Queen Ann's Corner. Still further north, Liberty Plain's most influential farmer, Seth Sprague, selectman from 1857 to his death in 1895, lived in the Elijah Whiton house (1764) on what, in the 1930s, would be Fletcher Wason's farm, and later, the grounds of Resurrection Church and Notre Dame Academy. Across Main Street from Sprague's farm stood the social center of the village, Liberty Hall (1857, 1040), with Johnny Wilder's store downstairs. Liberty Hall served its village half a century for religious services, sabbath school, and social events until it burned in 1911. North of the hall was the mixed schoolhouse (1843-95), where students of "grades" one through nine studied together.

Houses were sparse along here; of about eighty buildings now between Queen Ann's Corner and Liberty Pole Hill, only about one-third were there during George Lincoln's ride in the 1870s. The hill was so high and bare that—but let Nettie Loring give her memory of it. Her husband's

> grandfather in Hull was the first one that ever was on Telegraph Hill that used that uh thing that saw when the boats and things were coming in, you know. A telescope. And it was so powerful that—he had a white horse and Grandma Pope used to come over and visit Mother, and when she started down Libty [sic] Pole Hill, he could see her from Hull on Telegraph Hill.

When George Lincoln rode down the hill, he entered the village of South Hingham.

At the foot on the left was Uncle Alfred's tannery, and across Main and down South Pleasant Street were Cushing farms. Newer homes reflected the continued prosperity of this farming-milling clan, and the old Main Street homesteads of Theophilus (1687, 753), Pyam (1748, 707), and John (1753, 692) recalled their prosperous past. North of the Cushings lived Wilders and Jacobs, close to the industries of South Hingham: on Mill Lane the busy Wilder bucket factory; beside it, the Jacobs hatchet factory and the new Tower toy factory; and on Friend Street, the Whitman Whitcomb shoe factory "in full blast." There was ample employment for the villagers of South Hingham.

At High Street, George Lincoln was entering the old domain of the Towers. He had reasons to detour up High. He cared about old cemeteries, and the High Street Cemetery, like other ancient burial places in town, was being beautified. Further along High Street were similar signs of new tastes, the Rockdale Nursery (67) and the Bates (101-03) greenhouse. Beyond these he had town business to look into. In 1873, the new chapel of Second Adventists was built near the corner of High and Ward Streets (312). Lincoln, a member of a town committee to approve the project, called on Mr. John Tuttle, "a respectable colored man" and a leader of "the colored people of that locality."

From Tuttleville, the Lincolns could head home, by way of French and Fort Hill Streets, through two more separate villages. Fort Hill was the ancestral place of their forebears stretching back over six generations to Sergeant Daniel. Lincolns and Cains had long worked as shoemakers, and some of them now traveled to work in Weymouth. Marshes, Stodders, Frenches, Humphreys, and Remingtons were now shoemakers, carpenters, and masons; Hobarts were butchers. West Hingham village, too, was now a working class neighborhood of old families, sharing close ties to the Fort Hill Ladies Circle and to the Universalist, Baptist, and Methodist churches. They had their factories for making soap, furniture, and shoes, and through their midst ran the often noisome Town Brook and the noisy, often dangerous railroad.

The Methodist Church still stood facing west, across North Street from its present location. On the corner of North and Thaxter Streets, one old Thaxter sister lived with her devoted caretaker, Lucretia Leonard. Returning to "*the* village" on North Street, the Lincolns passed other old houses occupied by spinsters, old mariners, and widows, relics of past times. Broad Bridge must have seemed as crowded and busy as the "square" seems today. It had changed much, but not all had changed, and with his historian's eye, George Lincoln saw a multilayered reality.

At Fountain Square, ancient dwellings were hidden in altered mansions. Albert Fearing lived in what had begun life as the Andrews house (1685), today St. Paul's Rectory, and his farm stretched to Broad Cove. Timbers of the eighteenth-century Enoch Lincoln house remained in Widow Soule's mansion, the Talbots of today. And in the house whose oldest part had been built in the mid 1600s (possibly in 1667) lived the granddaughter of General Benjamin Lincoln with her husband, jeweler Samuel Crosby. The Benjamin Lincoln house would pass down by the distaff side from Crosby to Beveridge.

The site of the house (73 North) of old packet captain Elijah Beal (1805-72), George Lincoln's late neighbor at the corner of North and Ship Streets, had been a part of Hingham's history since it began. Here, legend said, Peter Hobart landed in 1635, and here, in 1636, John Otis and Thomas Loring built houses. Both burned in 1646, and by the 1760s, the third houses had been raised on the corners of Ship Street. In the seafaring years of the early nineteenth century, 73 North Street belonged to Captains Demerick and James Marble, both lost at sea. After Elijah Beal's death, it would pass to Thomas Magner, son of one of the first patriarchs to come to Hingham from Ireland. In the early twentieth century, it went to Raymond Barba, an Italian fruitdealer. A house may be a history in miniature.

The most imposing new structures at Broad Bridge in 1873 loomed over the rest. Across the south leg of Cottage Street (today Fearing Road) from the disreputable old Union Hotel rose Hingham's newest church, St. Paul's, with its lofty slate steeple. Behind the church appeared the four-story mass of the Burr Brown cord and tassel factory. The work of William Nelson, also the builder of Agricultural Hall, Burr Brown's had opened grandly in January, 1866, with a promenade concert and ball. Here worked almost two hundred townspeople, many of them young women of the new Irish citizenry. The cornerstone of the church was laid, in George Lincoln's presence, just five days before the Civil War Monument was dedicated in 1870. The three structures, church, factory, and monument, symbolize essential features of changing Hingham after the Civil War.

In 1865, Burr Brown had needed room for expansion. They bought the old "Thaxter-Leavitt" place (147 North). The decaying and vacant mansion was sold at auction for $165 and torn down, its materials sold "second hand, cheap." Behind it, on the hillside, Burr Brown built their factory. The front lot was advertised for a "manufacturing property," but no offers came, and in 1866, they sold it to "the Catholic Society of this town." "The Society is quite large," evidently close to five hundred strong, "and has long felt the need of suitable accommodations," having failed in earlier attempts and having held services in the town house. Thus, mundane circumstances led to the siting of St. Paul's in an imposing position that dominates Hingham's busiest intersection.

After four years of planning and fund-raising, the church was built, and in July, 1871, it was dedicated. The ceremony was attended by a "numerous throng." The steamer *John Romer* brought a "host of our city friends," and George Lincoln confided to his diary, "A very large number of strangers—mostly Irish—are consequently in town." When he stood at the war monument the year before, had he appreciated how suitable was the timing? The war dead included not only old Hingham names, but also new ones: Breen, Corcoran, Farrell, Fee, Fitzgerald, and Murphy. Irishmen had fought and some had died for their place in Hingham history. And when, twenty years later, Lincoln completed his genealogy, he included more than eighty Irish family names.

Most of these families had come to Hingham between the 1850s and the 1870s, the time of the Irish post-famine diaspora. They emigrated from all over Ireland: Breen from Kilkenny; Dunn from Limerick; Crowe and Keeshan from Tipperary; the Fee clan, six brothers and two sisters, from Leitrim. There were Crehan from Galway, Brassel from Kerry, Barry and Dower from Waterford, Murray from Clare, Fanning from Monaghan, and Gorman from Donegal. The largest number were from Cork: the Buttimer brothers, Carnes, Casey, Corcoran, Daley, Donovan, Magner, Noonan, O'Connell, and the Pynes.

The Irish founded their neighborhoods in various parts of town where land and work were available to them. Some had clustered at the Cove. Cedar Street, laid out by 1850, was the enclave of the Fees. Thomas, a farmer who had come that year without a dollar, worked, bought Whiton land, and built his house in 1851. Near the north end of Hersey Street was the land of John Crowe, an iron moulder like his fellow Tipperarian Keeshan. By the 1870s, Crowe's Lane, Hersey near Elm Street, upper Elm, Emerald Street, and Bates Court were an Irish village, close to the industries of North and West Hingham. The brothers Michael and John Burns lived on Emerald Street. Much of their property is now the Burns Memorial Park off Hersey Street. Near South Hingham's industries on Friend Street settled the families of Barry, Coughlan, Daley, and Dunn. Irish farm families lived on far-off Prospect Street and on Cross Street. At the north end of Thaxter Street lived Irish iron moulders, masons, teamsters, and laborers, close to the farms of Jeremiah Murphy, David Breen, and Edward Sweeney off Lincoln Street. They were all making their places in a changing town.

The nature and extent of the change can be measured. Between 1800 and the Civil War, Hingham's population grew steadily, doubling from about 2100 to about 4300. The first half of the century had been a time of enterprise and expansion. Post-Civil War townsmen remembered it with nostalgia, when the growth faltered and the numbers sometimes went down. Between 1865 and 1895, the town averaged about 4500 people, and they lived in an average of about 1000 dwellings. But averages can be misleading. The reality was ups and downs. The decade 1865-75 was a time of growth, from 4176 to 4654, a gain of 478. From the mid-1870s to the mid-1880s, the population shrank to 4375, and local leaders were alarmed and argued about what to do.

Economics always plays a major role in human movement. The year 1875 was the midpoint in a four-year national depression, and 1875-85 was a time of decline for Hingham, when the town felt and acted poorer than before or after. In 1865-75, the town had spent money with bravado; appropriations climbed from $36,000 to $74,000. Nervous frugality then took over, and they dropped to $46,000 in 1876 and to $26,000 in 1885. The impact on the town work force can be imagined. The tax rate in 1875 was $14; in 1885, it was down to $9.50. Then came a new rise in appropriations to $56,000 in 1895 and a tax rate of $16.

The population accompanied the economy upwards, climbing from 4375 in 1885 to 4815 in 1895. But these numbers tell only part of the story. They do not say how many new people there were, how many old people had disappeared, how much the population was changing in identity. One fact is easy to compute: if we count names of early settlers, obviously only male lines, we find that their numbers remained about the same, their percentage of the population about 10 percent. The real proportional decline of old Hingham families would come in the next century. But their numbers were *not growing*. They were having fewer children, and many of their children were moving away. The town's population was growing older. In the decade of decline, 1875-85, the total population dropped about 6 percent, but the drop in children from five to fifteen years old was 17 percent. In 1885-95, the population grew by 10 percent, but the number of children still declined until 1890.

In fact, the birth rate remained at about twenty per thousand people, and so did the death rate. In the three decades 1865 to 1895, the difference between births and deaths accounted for only 25 percent of the total change. The other 75 percent must be explained in terms of people coming and people moving away. Most of the rise in 1865-75 meant people were coming in hope of work; most of the decline in 1875-85 meant people were going away for the same reason. The decade 1885-95 saw something new and different: a first wave of affluent suburbanites.

Who were the newcomers? In 1865-75, there was a net gain of 478 people, and of these, 200 were foreign-born, 119 from Ireland. The number of foreign-born living here rose from 508 to 706. In 1875-85, this number dropped only slightly, so most of those who moved away in these hard times must have been native-born. In 1885-95, the number of foreign-born jumped again. The new foreign-born were chiefly Canadians of non-French origins. After 1895, the largest new foreign group was Italian.

What can we guess about people who immigrate to a foreign land? They are younger; they are childless or have young families. As Hingham's population grew older, it did so chiefly among old families, while more and more children were children of new immigrants. Here are the percentages of children born to at least one foreign-born parent: in 1865-75, 43 percent of all births; in 1875-85, 37 percent; in 1885-95, 43 percent. Of the 2747 children born in Hingham during these thirty years, 1126 were born to at least one foreign-born parent, 41 percent of Hingham youth. Notice, too, the low birth rate among native-born parents: the yearly ratio was one child to sixty or more people. Births to foreign-born parents were three to four times higher in ratio. The percentages of newlyweds tell the same story.

The story is of a growing non-native population that was younger and of a static native population that was older. This is the picture of human change in 1865-95. It had not been so before, and it would not be so again in our times. Change is always with us, but change itself *changes* from time to time. In this as in other ways, the later nineteenth century was a unique chapter in the story of Hingham.

CHAPTER NINE

✠

A Half-Century of Work

In that building, long and low,
With its windows all a-row
　　Like the port-holes of a hulk,
Human spiders spin and spin,
Backward down their threads so thin
　　Dropping, each a hempen bulk.

At the end, an open door;
Squares of sunshine on the floor
　　Light the long and dusky lane;
And the whirring of a wheel,
Dull and drowsy, makes me feel
　　All its spokes are in my brain.

As the spinners to the end
Downward go and reascend,
　　Gleam the long threads in the sun;
While within this brain of mine
Cobwebs brighter and more fine
　　By the busy wheel are spun.
　　　. . . . .

Then a homestead among farms,
And a woman with bare arms
　　Drawing water from a well;
As the bucket mounts apace,
With it mounts her own fair face,
　　As at some magician's spell.

Then an old man in a tower,
Ringing loud the noontide hour,
　　While the rope coils round and round
Like a serpent at his feet,
And again, in swift retreat,
　　Nearly lifts him from the ground.
　　　. . . . .

Ships rejoicing in the breeze,
Wrecks that float o'er unknown seas,
　　Anchors dragged through faithless sand;
Sea fog drifting overhead,
And with lessening line and lead,
　　Sailors feeling for the land.

LONGFELLOW, "The Ropewalk"

THE changes that made the most concrete and relentless impact on Hingham lives were economic. For almost half a century since the 1820s, the town had depended on its numerous and varied small industries. By the end of the nineteenth century, almost all of them had vanished. So too had the rope-spinners, the sailors, and the bucketmakers suggested by Longfellow's evocative poem.

For George Lincoln, looking back from the 1890s, "Fate seems to have put her seal of disapproval . . . upon the town as a permanent manufacturing or commercial center." He lamented this "fate." But the first suburban wave of wealthy townspeople welcomed the end of the bustle and din of industry and the new bucolic peace of a pastoral re-

[119]

treat. The decline of local industry inexorably changed how Hingham's workers earned their living. Livelihoods were changing, and so were the ways in which people thought about and described their occupations.

In 1865, the occupations of over three-fifths of the town's male workers fell into the categories of shoemaking, barrel and woodenware manufacturing, ropemaking, trading (merchants), cabinetmaking, blacksmithing and other metal work, leather working, seafaring, "labor," and farming. The development of farming as an occupation was so fluid that it will be treated separately in the next chapter.

Life was still local. The home was still a relatively self-contained operation, often including a home industry. Most food and supplies were raised or purchased locally; heat came from fireplaces or stoves, water from wells, artificial light from oil or kerosene lamps. Transport within the town was by horse carriage or wagon, or on foot. However rustic this picture may seem, the period was one of tremendous expansion and "rising expectations" and of centralized industry and specialized labor. Textile, paper, and shoe towns, with their large new, cheap labor force, had access to major railroad freight lines. In 1869, the transcontinental railroad opened up the whole continent to commerce and migration. Speculation and optimism escalated, and manic expansion aggravated the cycles of boom and bust.

With war inflation, prices more than doubled. Wages did not begin to keep pace, and sales of goods were slow. By 1867, prices began to fall, business improved, and six years of euphoria produced both public and private spending sprees. Businesses began or expanded. But expansion required newer, bigger buildings and machinery, and a patent mania in inventions engendered new machines. To build, to replace old machinery with bigger, better, faster machines, more capital was needed. Otherwise, one could not compete with larger companies for growing markets. Much capital was going where profits were most promising: big industry, railroads, large banks, whose directors colluded with railroad monopolists to manipulate the national economy. The economic climate was unstable in the extreme. In the spring of 1872, "capitalist dragon" and railroad monopolist Jay Gould made a million dollars on the stock market in just ten days.

Panic came in September, 1873. It began in the banks, spread to the railroads, then to city business, and inevitably to the towns. In December, George Lincoln noted that "dealers in the country towns are beginning to feel the effect of the great panic." Severe depression persisted for almost five years. Hingham bankruptcies were numerous. Unemployment grew, and town expenditures and employment shrank.

"Tramps" from the desperate city roamed the towns and villages; robberies and incendiary fires increased.

Such shocks could be absorbed by companies with large capitalization, but small businesses found it difficult to pay loans and to adjust to alternately growing and shrinking markets. If overinventoried, they simply laid off "hands." Some Hinghamites, committed to the idea of an economy of small manufacturers, watched Plymouth County towns grow in population by a rate of 8 to 20 percent, while Hingham's increase during the same generation after the Civil War was under 2 percent. Hinghamites lamented that "other towns in our vicinity . . . have advanced beyond us in population, wealth, and importance, as the result of activity in their manufacturing interests."

The 1867 County Directory illustrates this contrast. Of six forging companies advertising, four were in the Bridgewaters. The largest of these made everything from steamship and railroad supplies to nail and tack machinery. It had telegraph connections to its offices in Boston and New York. Two railroad lines ran through the Bridgewaters. The size of such companies, their access to transportation, and their growing labor pool had precipitated, prior to the Civil War, what became a slow decline of small foundries, such as the two in Hingham. The heavy industry to make engines, furnaces, farm implements, boilers, presses, water wheels, and shoemaking machinery was elsewhere in Plymouth County.

The decline of shoemaking in Hingham, by contrast, ran its course after the war. It was this loss that most mystified and discouraged George Lincoln, for he saw the shoe industry as beneficial to the stability and prosperity of communities. In 1872, *The Shoe and Leather Record* described the industry in Hingham as "flourishing," particularly at Whitman and Whitcomb's, where sixty "hands" were at work manufacturing for southern and western markets. Plans were made to enlarge the building, add more machinery, and double production and employees. How quickly this changed after the panic is suggested by a poignant entry in Lincoln's diary at the end of 1877:

> Charles A. Coolidge died suddenly at South Hingham, 29th inst., aged 29 years 9 months. He had been employed by Whitcomb's shoe factory . . . . Being in destitute circumstances at the time of his death, the residents of the neighborhood made up a purse of about $100 for his widow. Mr. Coolidge bore a good name for industry and frugality, but had been out of work for some time.

Shoemaking had become big industry, increasingly specialized and fragmented. A pair of boots or shoes involved as many as thirty-three operations. When Elijah Burr made shoes half a century earlier in his little shop at Broad Bridge, men and boys crowded around to watch

> every incision of the awl and every motion by which the stitch was faithfully jerked into its place, their faces reflecting the light of a single lamp, struggling with difficulty through the [tobacco] smoke.

They could "witness the whole process of making their boots and shoes from beginning to end." But now, Whitman and Whitcomb's ran assembly line style, with different workers stripping, sizing, rolling, cutting, lasting, stitching, edge trimming, crimping, pasting, heeling, burnishing, and more. Even so, neither they nor the small Hingham shoemakers could sustain the 230 Hinghamites who described themselves as "shoeworkers" in 1865. Of 179 boot and shoe manufacturers listed in the county in 1867, seventy-three were in the Abingtons and sixty-nine in the Bridgewaters. Whitman and Whitcomb were competing as well with East and North Weymouth, where, in one month of 1870, eight manufacturers produced over 24,000 pairs. Doubling production at Whitcomb's would have reached a maximum of 6800 pairs a month.

Start ups and lay offs continued, but by 1885 business was so poor that Whitcomb's closed, and in 1887 the building was sold for a shoe-jobbing operation, where heel-making machines turned out 16,000 heels daily. The drift of labor had already begun. By 1880, over a third of Hingham's 150 shoeworkers left every morning for Weymouth. The same year, twenty-five families left Hingham permanently to seek work elsewhere. By 1889, Brockton had eighty shoe factories.

What Hingham—and only Hingham among county towns—still had were small companies specializing in precision metal-casting and the industries for which it was uniquely famous: coopering and cordage-making. The Jacobs, edge-tool makers, and the Stephensons, scale and balance makers, came from a tradition of blacksmithing, but they made specialized equipment still needed in an emerging world. Their loss to Hingham was not due to competition. When his father retired in 1884, Henry Stephenson's business tripled. Scales and scale beams were needed in factories, and in the South and West for measuring crops such as sugar, cotton, and wool. After Henry died unexpectedly, full orders still came to the new owner, George A. Loring. But in 1889, the business was sold to interests in Lowell.

Something similar happened to the edge-tool company. Three generations of South Hingham Jacobs had been blacksmiths when, in the 1830s, an entrepreneurial cousin came from Scituate and began making hammers by hand. In a year, he added horsepower, and in eight more, steampower. Production expanded to include hatchets. In fifteen years, a one-man shop had become a factory of about twenty-five. The products became world-famous, reaching markets as far away as Australia. Needing "additional power and facilities," the plant moved in 1860 to Wilder's Mill. Two sons joined the business. Despite a large fire, Joseph Sr.'s retirement, and Joseph Jr.'s leaving the work to sell investment mortgages for farms in the West, and despite the distance from the railroad, the plant continued to run at full capacity. But in 1883, the other son sold his interest and all the machinery to a firm in Nashua, New Hampshire, joined it as assistant superintendent, and invited all who wished to come with him. We do not know how many accepted the invitation, but Hingham had lost a stable industry which employed twenty men at an annual payroll of $12,000. No longer could the child who grew up to be Mrs. Henry Cushing watch delightedly as "the hatchets in a crude state were withdrawn from the fiery forges . . . the sparks . . . fly out . . . the men working so quickly to temper them [that it] seemed uncanny to me."

Older still were the industries of coopering and cordage. Early in the century, "Bucket Town's" reputation for well-made buckets, barrels, and boxes extended to the Caribbean and to Chicago, where a transplanted Hinghamite saw boxes identified by local names in a store. Part of coopering's complex history was tied to the diminution of fish harvests. The problem worsened with the introduction of seine netting in the early 1850s. Seine nets trapped everything, including "tinkers," fish too young to have spawned. With the decline in fish, the need for barrels, fish kits, and salt in which to pack them also declined. Hingham's saltworks closed in 1862. The need for rope lessened as the fishing fleet vanished. In 1865, only eighteen men described themselves as ship captains, mariners, and fishermen. Only five were under fifty years old. Twenty years later, three of the younger men had disappeared from the directory, and the two who remained had become a spinner and a shoemaker.

Between 1855 and 1865, the number of "coopers" fell from seventy-one to forty-nine. Their self-descriptions included specializations such as box, bucket, and toy makers. Three-quarters of this group were over fifty years of age. Would their skills and knowledge be passed on to the young? "A lot of young go elsewhere for their worklife," wrote a former Hinghamite in 1856. During a visit home, he found few of his old schoolmates. When Arthur D. Marble was a child during and after the Civil War, he pegged boxes by hand. Long afterwards, he remembered the attic floorboards over Fearing Burr's store groaning with the weight of woodenware that customers had bartered for other supplies. The assortment was astonishing: pails, tubs, and churns—for drawing well water, washing clothes, making butter, storing staples—and every sort of container box. Country store proprietors, who called themselves "traders" with accuracy, had shipped woodenware to Boston for decades. Before 1840, it was sold out of the Hingham Station packets moored at Long Wharf. Sometimes a trader with a bulging inventory would transport his supply to Boston by wagon, exchanging woodenware along the way to supply his general store.

Making woodenware was a cottage industry throughout the town. But most of what survived was mechanized bucketmaking, dependent upon specialization, innovation, and large-scale production. Brothers Crocker and Alden Wilder had organized a bucket factory in 1845 on the site of the old grist and sawmill at Cushing Pond. Here, buckets were made by steam power. It was only after Crocker's son William died in 1891 that the factory's future became uncertain. A man from Winchenden bought it, planned an additional building, and installed new machinery. Seventeen-year-old Elwin Fearing worked there: "This felluh was an awful crank, oh boy! He was the hardest man to work for that I ever worked for. And I guess business was pretty bad, and he had to take a mortgage on his machinery to pay for movin' it down here." He also bought the now defunct Cordage Company's hydrants. But hydrants and mill pumps were not enough when, on Easter Sunday, 1902, Hinghamites in churchgoing garb watched from every promontory as the bucket factory turned into an "inferno." Fifty workers, producing a thousand buckets a day, were jobless.

Hersey boxmakers had long worked on Hersey Street. Edmund Hersey, who had begun in the old tradition of hand manufacture, introduced steam in 1851, established a factory, and designed machinery to make wooden containers for pills, salt, figs, and strawberries. By the late 1860s, he had thirty to forty workers. One year, it was reported, he sold a million and a half boxes. Edmund retired in 1877 to become an experimental farmer and instructor, and his factory was taken over by Seymour and Cain. Aged practitioner Nelson Corthell worked on into the 1890s still making boxes and buckets by hand. In a year, he sold no more than six dozen. His entry in the 1894 directory includes the melancholy phrase, "last of the many small shops."

Other Hersey specialists included Caleb and Samuel, who were not only box makers, but also the only listed toy makers in the county in 1867. Samuel exhibited handmade wooden toys at the agricultural fairs.

But in an era when a new interest in childhood took hold, toys became big business, and the industrial toyman became king. In Hingham, the king was William S. Tower. Former "wood turner," "cooper," and "bucket maker," he moved into Woodenware Company buildings at Cushing Pond in 1869 and began a steam-powered toy factory. Tower won a Bronze Medal in Paris in 1878. He had a Boston agent for distant markets and stores at Downer Landing and Nantasket Beach. Among his 125 wooden toys were pails and shovels, log cabins, grist mills, and spinning wheels.

By the early 1890s, his successor F. W. Burrell needed "a quarter of a million lumber" annually, three tons of metal for hoops, twenty-five miles of wire, and a thousand pounds of nails and tacks. Three South Hingham factories were not enough, and additional space was used at the old Whitcomb factory. In 1896, the operation moved to Hersey Street, where Burrell added a "steam job shop and planing mill." By 1899, "Mr. F. W. Burrell's shrill little whistle morning, noon, and night [was] a pleasant reminder that something in the way of business [was] being done in Hingham." But something went wrong here, too. Elwin Fearing and "two other felluhs" worked at the turn of the century in the

> little machine shop down there, and we made the punches and dies and one thing or another . . . . And just before Christmas, they loaded up a box car just for Christmas and some big concern bought 'em. And he got the check and was *gone* with it. And that put them out of business . . . . Every doggone place I went to went out o' business!

We do not know what "he" Fearing refers to. But Burrell reappeared as a foreman in Boston in 1908. Soon, the only toy makers left in Hingham, such as William B. Luce, Loring Jacob, and the elderly, fragile George W. Fearing, produced colonial toys by hand.

Parallel to the long fading history of coopering is the story of cordage making, especially the making of cables for rigging, mooring, and towing ships. The business created by Hawkes Fearing was carried on by his sons. In 1853, it incorporated as the Hingham Cordage Company with a capitalization of $50,000. Its only competitor in the county, Plymouth Cordage, had a capitalization four times larger. In 1855, fifty-two men worked at the ropewalk. During the war, all cordage manufacturers prospered. In 1865, the ropewalk, now almost a thousand feet long, was destroyed by fire and about "eighty hands" were out of work. It was quickly rebuilt and was doing well in 1873 with "seventy-five hands." In the early 1880s, there was still plenty of work, and the plant had been repeatedly upgraded, with a sprinkler system, hydrants, an added wing with a steam elevator, and new jennies.

What happened thereafter was tied to the story of the national industry. It had tried for over two decades to fix prices and set monthly quotas for all manufacturers. Every pound over the quota was penalized, and a bonus was awarded for staying under it. This system was replaced in 1887 by a real trust, which controlled production even more tightly until 1893. During these years, Hingham's ropewalk was idle. It paid dividends and taxes but offered no jobs. In 1885, only a dozen and a half men described themselves as associated with rope making. Their trail became increasingly difficult to follow as they were forced to find other work, and as the trend became to identify oneself simply as an "employee," a symptom of the bureaucratization of labor.

The Hingham Cordage Company had one last gasp in 1894. New machinery and boilers were put in place, bales of hemp and tar were received, and workers were hired. It was too late. Within six months, the men were discharged for "lack of orders." The industry was in chaos. Cordage manufacturers sprouted inland, close to where cord was needed for baling crops. Larger ships used wire cable or required even heavier, longer cable, which the ropewalk did not make. Bigness was the order of the day. In 1902, the works were sold to a Boston-Montreal firm.

The largest, most stable manufacturing operation in postwar Hingham had little to do with practical needs for shoes, containers, or rope, but satisfied a new market for the Victorian love of ornament. Carriages, uniforms, upholstery, shades, and curtains were decorated with trimmings: fringe, tassels, and gimp. Burr Brown produced them. The company had evolved out of several small industries and partnerships, and by 1866, was located in its large new factory. "An army" of young women made tassels on the first floor; men made trimmings and cord on the second and fourth; a weaving room was on the third. The dye house stood across North Street where Hennessy's store is today. Burr Brown employed almost two hundred and, on occasion, ran day and night to fill orders, which also included draperies and canopies for windows, doors, mantels, and beds.

The company gave "steady employment to a host of operatives" for half a century. Its generous policies included giving barrels of flour to the poor, Thanksgiving turkeys to all employees, and annual beach picnics for their families. It prospered in national markets, surviving depression and deaths of partners. But E. Waters Burr, its guiding genius, died in 1897, and the plant closed the following January. The

RULES AND REGULATIONS
OF THIS ESTABLISHMENT.

1st.   On and after January 1st, 1860, work will com-
mence at 7 1-2 o'clock, A. M., and close at 6 o'clock, P. M.   Dinner hour from 12 to
1. On Saturdays work will be suspended at 3 o'clock, P. M.

2d.   Each person to have a proper place assigned them,
and all moving about from place to place is positively forbidden.

3d.   All reading, singing, loud talking, laughing, hair
dressing, or any thing not relating to the work of this Establishment is strictly
forbidden.

4th.   Diligent attention to business during working
hours will be required.   Any person wishing to be absent part of the day or more, will
report themselves to the foreman of their respective department, in order that he may
govern their work accordingly.

5th.   A disregard to the above indispensable rules, will
be considered as indicating a willingness to leave the Establishment.

BURR, BROWN & CO.

in addition to the above all Talking from one table to another will not be allowed under any circumstances.

No Employee will be allowed to invite or receive visitors on the premises during working Hours.   *Burr Brown & Co*

Burr, Brown's amended work rules, 1860. The signatures of employees are appended to these orders.

building was eventually sold to the Boston Spiral Tagging Company and became known in local memory as the "shoestring factory." Burr's death occurred at the time when the taste for excessive ornament and the heavily draped house was rapidly giving way to a new taste for sunny, well-ventilated, simpler homes. Lecturing in 1894, Mrs. A. P. Soule advised that houses be kept healthful by a "simplicity and adaptability" of furnishings, and recommended one set only of curtains and shades at windows. Even the stablest and wealthiest of managements could not have reversed such trends.

Less stable ventures foundered in cycles of hirings, layoffs, bankruptcies, fits and starts. In 1868, Frederick Long and a partner opened a woolen goods plant on Main Street, and within a year, they were supplying some of the "largest dry goods houses in the country." Growth and competition demanded new space and machinery, and in 1872 Long moved into a new four-story building on Elm Street (located where numbers 70 and 74 are today). Next year came panic and depression, and by 1874, Long's plight called for new investors. The Hingham Manufacturing Company was formed; directors David Whiton, Andrew Cushing, and Charles Strauss claimed to have paid $100,000 for shares. In fact, they only claimed to have paid in order to improve the company's credit. In September, 1875, the sickening news broke: they had failed. Other prominent townsmen would fail, too, for signing their notes. The company was bankrupt, its hundred operatives among the unpaid creditors, its officers arraigned for fraud. The factory had two subsequent owners and was renamed South Shore Mills, but to no avail. Boston was now the nation's largest producer of medium-priced ready-to-wear clothing. By 1888, the factory was closed, its machinery sold. Its erratic career had lasted exactly twenty years.

Similar stories could be told of other ventures in this perilous time: of a jute and bagging company, for example, which, at its peak, employed seventy, produced half a million yards of cloth in a year, and was dissolved in ten years. The competition came from the "spindle cities" of Fall River and New Bedford, which became the largest textile towns in the country.

Any analysis of why Hingham manufacturing died out will inevitably distort, for the causes were as complex as the time itself. Competition and economic instability ended the shoe, textile, and garment industries. Buyouts took away the precision metal industries. Corporate collusion, new technologies, and changed markets ended the Cordage Company. Steel cable and steel drums replaced rope and wooden barrels. Paper replaced wood; Francis Overton, local ice cream manufacturer, now sold his product in "pasteboard" cartons. In currying and tanning, chemical processes and chrome-dyeing replaced natural materials. When Alfred Loring died in 1882, a Quincy bank foreclosed on the large tannery at Main and Cushing Streets; he had been forced to take a loan during the depression of the 1870s.

Many Hingham factories were located far from fire engines and, later, from hydrants, and were especially vulnerable to fires. They were far from the railroad depot, too, and were penalized if they shipped small loads, since the cost of freight was prorated only on shipments of over one hundred pounds. Many young artisans worked out of town or moved away; some went West where opportunity beckoned. Those with most capital tended to invest it more profitably elsewhere. The visions of Charles W. S. Seymour and Edmund Hersey that the town could support small industries such as charcoal and brick-making and apple-drying were mere visions. Incentives to encourage industry, such as tax abatements, came later than such strategies in other towns. Hingham, once a port, was no longer exporting, but importing goods in huge quantities, some of which it had once supplied itself: hay, lumber, grain, bricks. A long era of manufacturing history had come to a close. Some influential townsmen felt no regrets and preferred the "hum of the bee" to that of industry.

As the region became more corporate and technological, the need grew for supervisors, specialists, and service workers. Locally, some citizens adapted well. Charles W. S. Seymour, a carpenter at twenty-five, then an "overseer" of a box factory, was a "civil engineer" by the mid-1880s and first superintendent of the Water Company. Wallace Corthell, grocer, wood-engraver and painter, was manager of the Light Plant in the 1890s.

This period marks the growth of "professions" in American work life. Hingham had increasing numbers of resident lawyers, physicians, dentists, even clergy. Bankers and brokers in this time of speculation were more numerous. New job designations included engineers—civil, marine, mechanical, electrical; architects; draughtsmen; electricians. The time of the generalist, when a man kept his own records, bartered, repaired his fences and buildings, dug his ditches, and tended his livestock, had almost passed. "Business" was becoming a "profession." And more citizens in business and the professions, among them new summer residents, commuted to the city.

By the 1890s, when the weather was fair, it was a familiar sight to see Charles B. Barnes, who walked to the wharf he owned, greeting clothing manufacturer Ebed L. Ripley, reputedly the town's richest man, as he alighted from his carriage for the steamboat. Shortly after the Civil War, there were about forty-five commuters, a mix of prosperous businessmen, professionals, brokers, agents, and clerks. By 1885, they numbered about seventy-five, and a decade later, about 115, including more clerks, salesmen, bookkeepers, and stationers. Levi Hersey had more company on the train when he commuted to Boston. By 1897, he had made pianofortes for Hallet and Davis for fifty years and held a railroad season ticket longer than anyone else on the South Shore.

As the town grew more residential and its social and commercial life expanded, the largest occupational increase occurred in the building trades. In the three postwar decades, the growth was from under fifty to 160, counting only carpenter-builders and painters and not including masons or laborers. They had built or renovated houses, summer "cottages," social halls, stores, churches, hotels at "the Beach," and Melville Garden. These projects did not include work on the town's infrastructure: more roads, brick sidewalks, drains, rail lines and bridges, a waterworks, electric service.

Many laborers worked for the town. In the road mania of the early 1870s, the town payroll for road work ranged between two and three hundred persons per year. Many had familiar old names. They did occasional work and received small payments as part of a traditional worklife that included multiple jobs. But this was changing. The percentage of Irish names was growing, and some Irish families were becoming part of a town labor force: three Dalys were paid $903; three Fees, $808. The category of "laborer" had been established as an occupation, and by the 1890s, on the eve of the "electrics" and the arrival of Italian work crews, the Irish labor force had reached its peak.

Five men recorded on the town payroll of that time provide a vignette of labor on public works in the 1890s. What they earned as well from nonpublic sources—water, electric, railway, steamship, construction, farming, ice-harvesting, gardening—we cannot know. They worked a six-day week, a nine-hour day, and were paid $1.75 or $2 a day, no "benefits" or vacations. For comparison's sake, in Hingham, a female teacher was paid $350 to $400 a year, a male teacher $600, a clergyman $1500, a wealthy industrialist $10,000. In 1890, Jerry Corcoran cleared the Town Brook, repaired highways, worked on a new sidewalk, and for 54 1/3 days received $95.17. In 1891, Bart O'Connell and Tim Osborn were busy on similar jobs: brook clearing, road repair, drain digging, altering South, North, and Pleasant Streets, and rebuilding a wall. O'Connell worked 190 days for $384; Osborn, 209 days for $417. In 1893, a stretch of the brook was covered, and sidewalks were ordered for several streets; Water and East were altered, Emerald was graded, and a ledge was removed from Fort Hill. For such work, Michael Joyce was paid $335.

The work, always unpredictable, dropped off sharply in 1894. Patrick Griffin was paid only $200. He had done much better in 1892-93, but his horse was working then, and a laborer's horse made $1.50 a day. What had happened to his horse? Of such uncertainties a laborer's life was made. Luckily, Patrick Griffin also worked on the grounds of houses at Little Plain. They were an easy walk from his home across from the ropewalk, the first to be built on Central Street (241) in 1880. As the 1900s opened, his was a full house with nine family "boarders," most of them Griffin's unmarried working daughters.

Public works projects in the town were partially justified as needed to attract a new class of residents and to support a new social life. A service economy grew in response to the same needs and generated new occupations. The clientele were vacationers and local people seeking entertainment. For them, there were the Cushing House and the hotels in Nantasket, the Rose Standish House, and the amusement park at Melville Garden, Crow Point, with all their employees and ancillary providers. Ice cream and oyster saloons were popular, and ice crops became big business. In 1894, one dealer built an ice house so large that it took three freezings of Foundry Pond to fill it. Francis Overton's ice cream business expanded so much, as he supplied nearby resorts as well as the town, that he used his whole ice crop for his own ice cream business.

With the phenomenal growth in seasonal services and consumer goods, transportation, too, became a "growth industry" in Hingham. In 1865, those directly or indirectly involved—expressmen, coach drivers, carriage and stable men, harnessmakers, blacksmiths—numbered about forty. Thirty years later, they had increased to over ninety, not including three dozen workers on steamships and the railroad. Expressmen, who were especially busy, had a troubled relationship with the railroad, which tried to set prices and control freight. Informed by the railroad that her late husband's contract was no longer in force, Mary Howe, the plucky widow of James H. Howe, determined to carry on the service by road. A lawsuit restored her rights to use the railroad. In 1894, she sold the business to William McKee.

Mary Howe reminds us of all those hard-pressed working women who struggled to keep the tenuous threads of life together. Pre-Civil-War census data omit their occupations; afterwards, they are included, suggesting their growing role in the labor force outside the home. In 1893, George Lincoln gave two clues that women were at paid work before 1865: fifty-three nameless "females" worked at the umbrella company in 1837 and thirty-one in shoemaking in 1855. The 1865 census lists thirty-five tasselmakers at Burr Brown, forty-nine vestmakers, and seventeen dressmakers. We also know of the "girls" who pasted "uppers" at Whitman and Whitcomb's and the fifty women at the woolen mill when it was running. As social life and fashion grew, numbers of dressmakers and milliners doubled in thirty years. Their work was expedited by the marvel of the sewing machine, electrified in the 1890s. They worked at home, as did others who sewed flags for Allen Lincoln, finished worsted garments for Frederick Long, and made mattress tufts on strange devices loaned out by Burr Brown.

If not working, paid or unpaid, in their own homes, many women worked in others' homes as domestics. By 1865, the "Bridgets," so called because most of them came from Ireland, already numbered eighty strong. Others nursed the sick and cared for infants. With the population not growing, the number of nurses did not increase significantly, but the numbers of those they cared for were incredible. In 1883, nurse Mary E. Patterson was recognized in a celebration at the Methodist Church. When she died eight years later at seventy-seven, the *Journal* recorded her service. She had

> begun her professional career in Hingham in 1833, caring for the twin children of Mr. and Mrs. Zebulon Davis, and more than fifty-seven years afterward filled her last engagement in the fourth generation of the same family by again caring for the twin children of Mr. and Mrs. Herbert W. Hersey. She had cared for 398 children.

As the number of wealthy townspeople increased, so did the need for such serving women. But many of them began to move up the economic ladder. By the century's end, a few older women ran boarding houses, others were "housekeepers," and some had disappeared into factories. Younger ones, with new commercial offerings at the high school, stayed to graduate and became bookkeepers and accountants, stenographers and clerks. A frequent *Journal* advertisement of the 1890s reflected a shortage: "A capable girl wanted for general housework."

This story of work would not be complete if we forgot those who found no work or worked in poverty. How did they live? The town's system of poor relief was traditional and modest, handled by the Overseers of the Poor. A small part of the system consisted of the poor farm and almshouse, the old brick building of 1833 off Beal Street near the Back River, today's Project Turnabout. Those in total poverty, often elderly, some with incapacitating illnesses, were admitted here, along with thieves, incendiaries, and town drunks, until the Lock-Up opened in 1874. Few could work on the farm "owing to extreme old age and infirmity." The almshouse averaged fifteen to eighteen occupants.

The only description of almshouse life at that time is found in the 1881 report of the Board of Health. At a time of awakening social consciousness, the board reminded the town of this remote, almost invisible institution and its antiquated heating. One small coal stove stood in one room on the female side. The only other heat came from old cylinder stoves. Except for two female rooms, the rooms were not heated.

> The women pass their days either in the kitchen or in one of the heated rooms. The men generally by day occupy a room in the basement heated by a cylinder stove. To expect men and women of an advanced age and consequent feeble circulation and many of them

weakened by pulmonary disease to sleep in a room which in the most severe weather is never even tempered by a fire, that too on the north side of a house in a very exposed situation, is not, to say the least, in accordance with the humanitarian principles of the age.

Quincy, Weymouth, and Randolph had already installed steam heat. That year, the town was shamed into approving $1000.

The same years saw a gradual rise in the annual budget for the poor, from about $3000 in 1870 to $4000 in 1880, and, from the mid-1880s on, a fixed $6500. From this sum, the Overseers also assisted the "deserving poor" living "out of the Almshouse." To do so judiciously was "the most difficult duty the Overseers of the Poor have to perform." The burden was growing. During the 1870s, the town assisted about thirty persons or families with payments ranging from $4 to $156 a year according to need. In the 1880s, the number doubled and payments rose. A widow with young children might receive $300 a year, and poor widows were numerous. Stories of a few of them remind us that "the annals of the poor" are often neither "short" nor "simple."

The widow of Robert Beal, a farm laborer, had borne ten children and lost five of them, one as a result of the war. In 1876, Jacob Stodder, a West Hingham shoemaker, died, leaving a widow of seventy. Benjamin Wilder, son of a South Hingham farmer, constable, and military captain, detoured far from such roots to become a hairdresser at the Cove. After he died in 1850, his third wife, Pamelia, survived on town aid until she died in 1879. In 1882, a disabled veteran and shoemaker died at thirty-nine, leaving a widow and five young children, and the entry "Widow Otis Lincoln Battles and Family" appeared annually for $270 or $300. Widow Donovan's husband Michael died in 1871 at twenty-four, leaving her with two children under two. And in 1886— the last of her charges, the Thaxter sisters, having died in 1878— Lucretia Leonard began receiving small payments from the town.

Finally, there was another group of Hingham working men sometimes forgotten by history. In the 1893 *History*, they were somehow deemed not worthy of record, even though one of them, George Lincoln, chaired the whole enterprise. They were local merchants, shopkeepers, and "traders," about forty of them as of 1867, who carried a wide choice of merchandise in their shops. That broad offering would soon decline as specialties grew and tastes changed. The days of William Tower's South Hingham "country store," "where one could buy anything from a penny whistle to a church organ, from a box of pills to a feather bed," were ending. By the mid-1880s and 1890s, there were almost sixty local merchants. Thirteen sold only dry and fancy goods; others, only groceries and provisions, or watches and jewelry, or periodicals, pharmaceuticals, or hardware, or clothing, boots and shoes, or ice and coal. Several had delivery wagons. Enterprising Edmund Hobart, combining the old tradition of the variety store with the new expectation of convenience, put his store on wheels:

> he had a covered wagon, and he had everything in it from a spool of thread or I don't know what, brooms and mops and one thing and another hanging on the side, a ten gallon can of kerosene, everything. Drive all over town. That's what he did.

This group included new arrivals and successors but also long-time survivors who had adapted to change. In 1891, George W. Burr needed a new coal wagon. He turned to a surviving coterie of craftsmen at Little Plain. Blacksmith Henry Merritt did the iron work, William A. Tower painted it, Henry W. Cushing made the brass-mounted harnesses. Bela Whiton and Demerick Marble, carriage-makers and wheelwrights, assembled the wagon. Whiton and Marble died in 1898, the year the first automobile was sold in the United States. But the same George Burr, whose old-fashioned logo for many years had been a capped and knickered boy, was also an entrepreneur for new times. He ran front-page advertisements for his "Boston prices," with discounts for cash. In 1896, one of his coal cargoes weighed one thousand tons. The next year, appeals to the federal government for harbor dredging having failed, he arranged privately for dredgers to widen the channel to the coal wharf.

Among the oldest survivors were two businessmen at "the Bridge." One icy winter's Saturday morning in 1893, at age eighty and seventy-two, merchant-tailor John Todd and tinware maker Enos Loring showed what brave survivors they were. Stepping out of their houses (45 and 38) over the top of the rise on Lincoln Street, they accepted the offer of some boys for a sled ride down the slope to their shops. They coasted past Wilder's Tavern, New North Church, and Fountain Square and slowed at Thaxter's Bridge. On their right in Ford's Block, dry goods dealer Suzie Gates and watchmaker Thomas Margetts were "taking down" their shutters. On their left was the railroad depot.

Todd and Loring alighted, and carefully treading around icy patches, passed the new (1889) Anthes Building on the corner and turned left onto South Street. They bid good morning to a third survivor, Frank Overton, at the door of his cafe under Oasis Hall in the old Abbot's Building. As Loring opened the door of his hardware shop in the Lincoln Building, Todd continued around the corner onto Broad

TRADE CARDS

CUSHING HOUSE
HAIR-DRESSING SALOON,
HINGHAM, MASS.,
W. H. HENNESSY, Prop.

COMPLIMENTS OF
LORING JACOB,
HINGHAM CENTRE.

JOHN TODD,
MERCHANT TAILOR
AND DEALER IN
Ready-Made Clothing & Gent's Furnishing Goods,
No. 1 Lincoln Building, Hingham, Mass.

AFTER THE RACE-OFF CITY POINT, BOSTON HARBOR.
DAVID COBB,
Painter and Glazier,
HINGHAM HARBOR, - MASS.

Bridge, with a wave to his new neighbor William Hennessy. Hennessy had recently taken over the shop of a fourth long-time survivor, George Lincoln. Lincoln was probably home on Ship Street that morning, putting the final touches to the proof of his monumental genealogies for the 1893 town history. With so much change, so much irretrievably fading away, he had worked steadily on his unmatchable gift to Hingham, a record of its people.

Todd, Loring, Overton, and Lincoln had survived the rampant inflation and low sales of the 1860s, the depression of the 1870s, and the precipitous drop in prices during the fourteen years after the war when bleached cotton fell from 55 cents to 10 cents a yard, sugar from 39 cents to 9 cents a pound. They had survived the onset of advertising and the blandishments of discount stores in Weymouth. They had survived the growing trend of shopping in Boston, with the help of local boosters such "Quilp," the novelist and journalist, who proudly announced that

> The crown of the head and the soles of the feet are covered by hat and shoes purchased of Mr. Elijah L. Whiton . . . . The stove which heats his writing room came from E. and I. W. Loring . . . . Coal from Caleb B. Marsh . . . the table cloth covering his writing table came from George Lincoln . . . . George Hersey and Co. supply his groceries . . . when ill he immediately calls in Dr. H. E. Spalding . . . and the distinguished tonsorial artist Clary still survives the honor of having cut the distinguished novelist's hair.

"Quilp" ridiculed those who thought they could find no "assortment" at Todd the tailor's and those who

> will go to Boston and buy a lamp, on which they may or may not save a few cents, saying nothing of their fare and other expenses, and when their lamp gets out of order . . . they think it very strange if Mr. Loring can't accommodate them at once, and go around telling, "You can't ever get anything you want down here."

Though they had survived, the four old traders had also sensed the loss of continuity and of self-sufficiency in their community as it entered the early stages of becoming what many feared: a "suburb." They had seen old occupations fade away and had mourned the deaths of artisan friends who took their skills with them. They had wondered at the demise of manufacturing in Hingham. From the too-close perspective of the 1890s, George Lincoln felt that these changes had been fated. But they were also the result of human decisions, of choices. "Choices," wrote a historian a century later, "are the essence of history."

Burr, Brown factory (1865–1935) on Cottage Street (the section later renamed Fearing Road), remembered as "the shoestring factory," present site of St. Paul's parochial school.

Hingham Cordage Company and Ropewalk, on the east side of Central Street, now the site of Central Playground. Only the head house remains.

Wilder's bucket and woodenware, Jacobs' edge tool, and Tower's toy factories at Cushing Pond, the site of Theophilus Cushing's saw and grist mills in the 1730s.

St. Paul's Catolic Church (1871) and North Street in 1885. Beyond it, the Cushing House, the Perez Lincoln garrison house (the original part, according to George Lincoln, built c. 1640; moved to Chatham, 1941), the Hingham National Bank (1833) and residence of its cashier. On the right: the Railroad Depot (1849-1949), the Thayer Building, and beyond it, the tall chimney of the Burr, Brown dye house.

Corner of South Street and Broad Bridge in 1885, looking into George Lincoln's dry goods store in the Lincoln Building (1859). John Todd's tailor shop on the right. Enos Loring's stoves and tinware shop to the left, facing South street. In the abutting small building (Abbot's Hall) was Overton's ice cream "saloon." Beyond the vacant lot (Anthes Building, 1889—now Noble's)and beyond Thaxter's Bridge is the Whiton Building (1879) with shops on the street level, the Second District Court of Plymouth on the second floor, and on the third (destroyed by fire), the meeting rooms of the Oddfellows.

✠

CHAPTER TEN

The New Agriculturalists and Their Society

If fish refuse to be caught, sheep and poultry may be more submissive; flocks may prove as good an investment as fleets. When mackerel won't fill our barrels, perhaps apples and potatoes will; and the hoe may take the place of the hook . . . . The hills may be ploughed to as much advantage as the waves . . . and the rope which has become useless for rigging may serve to bind a load of hay . . . . The shop may give as profitable employment as the ship. It may be as well to pound on the lapstone . . . . The hammer may be handled instead of the marlin-spike, the splitting knife give way to the sickle, the anchor be transformed to the anvil, and the branding iron beat into the spade.

James C. Wilder, 1860

During the same half-century of declining industries and changing occupations, many Hingham people still worked the land. It is difficult to estimate how many or to measure precisely how farming had declined in Hingham since the heyday of agriculture in the eighteenth century. In 1820, Solomon Lincoln calculated, 279 of Hingham's 819 working men, 34 percent, were "engaged in agriculture." The modern scholar D. S. Smith counted only 20.3 percent as of 1840, and by 1895, counting only *native-born* males, he found only 6.45 percent engaged in agriculture. He concluded that Hingham was a leader in Massachusetts' early, steady, and irreversible decline in farming. But his shifting categories make precise comparisons impossible. Many "engaged in agriculture" after the Civil War were not native-born. Many were artisans who farmed part-time at home. Some were gentlemen with other occupations. Nor did the actual number of those "engaged in agriculture" indicate the extent of farming. Agriculture had been revolutionized by new machinery and scientific methods. Fewer men could produce more.

A striking fact about post-colonial farming in Hingham is how little is known and how little has been written. Edmund Hersey's brief chapter in the 1893 *History* describes farming in the town's first 150 years, but offers only a general sketch of what came later. Thomas T. Bouvé's chapters on natural history say nothing of soils, livestock, or crops. Edward, his son, guides us to "ancient landmarks" as if farms were invisible, except to note in the far south corner "a country now extensively covered with woods where formerly were farms." Father and son were in love with trees and forests, and where forests grow, farms cannot.

Other writers dwell on flower gardens, rustic idyls, and the old agricultural fairs with no mention of the agriculture that occasioned them. Mason Foley makes one brief, suggestive remark: "Although the yeoman farmer was the backbone of the town's economic prosperity" in the early nineteenth century, the town was much influenced by the "somewhat too logical conception of Henry Clay's American System, in which the North was to confine itself to manufacturing." Of the later part of the century, Foley writes only that it was a "time of declining industry and agriculture."

This stereotype of steady and irreversible decline would have astonished several large farmers and numerous smaller ones, some of them Irish, who built up a dairy, poultry, and pork industry, in part to feed a growing summer colony. And it would have dismayed the founders of Hingham's most influential nineteenth-century institution, the Agricultural and Horticultural Society.

Its first president and chief sponsor was Albert Fearing, one of Hingham's most generous benefactors. Fearing was a childless Boston shipchandler of enormous wealth who made a vocation of charity. He presided over Seaman's Aid, the Children's Mission, and the Home for Aged Men. He worked for the colonization of Liberia and once bought the freedom of twenty Tennessee slaves to be sent there. His father, Hawkes, the Hingham cordage pioneer, had been a leading Richardsonian at the First Parish, and Albert was a loyal son of the old meetinghouse. This fact proved troublesome when he courted and won Catherine Andrews, a daughter of the "other" parish. "Although," as George Lincoln told his diary, "there was great opposition with certain people of the New North society, they became man and wife and lived happily together." Ironically, when Fearing died in 1875, his home in Hingham Square passed to a nephew whose father-in-law, Henry Miles, became New North minister and lived in the house. So, as Lincoln remarks, "the late Hon. Albert Fearing's house is to become the New North parsonage. What would Mr. Fearing say if he could look down upon us and speak?" And what would he say if he could have seen it become St. Paul's rectory?

On the eve of the Civil War, Fearing was one of a group of wealthy Boston men who gave up the city and turned to agricultural life. In 1858, he left his "small farm" in Boston and bought a large one in his native town. It stretched northeast of Lincoln Street across the later sites of Miles Road and Burditt Avenue to Broad Cove. He was not the first to return home. In 1849, young Charles W. Cushing, already a successful city contractor, came home to Main and South Pleasant Streets to prove that farming could be a science. And one day in Boston in 1855, John Brewer's father told his wealthy merchant son about ten Hingham acres for sale. The son bought them. A house was built; a "yoke of oxen, a cow and a calf, and some hens and roosters were purchased, and the farming commenced." In 1864, Brewer bought World's End, with its three solitary elms, from Norton Quincy Thaxter and Solomon Lincoln, and by the early 1880s his land stretched to Porter's Cove. During the same period, entrepreneur David Whiton acquired the farm one later expert called "the best in the state," 220 acres on the west side of Union Street. At the end of 1858, these new gentlemen farmers, together with experimentalists Edmund Hersey, Fearing Burr, and others, formed the Hingham Agricultural and Horticultural Society.

An earlier Agricultural Society had existed from 1814 to 1831, but, in the town's brief era of fishing and frenetic industrialism, it disappeared. In the 1850s, that era seemed to be ending, and the new agriculture held the promise of renewed prosperity. New England agriculture was in a time of scientific advance, of new inventions and improved implements. Journals for farmers proliferated and agricultural education was born. As cities and industrial towns mushroomed, a decline in general farming was counterbalanced by the growth of market gardening and poultry and dairy farming to provide town and city people with fresh fruits and vegetables, chicken, eggs, and milk. Experiments yielded new seeds and varieties; selective breeding and special feeds produced high-yield dairy cattle. Just before the Civil War, chemical fertilizers came into widespread use; the growth of this industry could be seen during the war at Weymouth Neck in Bradley's mammoth phosphate works.

The new scientific farming required a lot of capital.

In a farming town, only one son, obviously, could take over the ancestral homestead. A second or third son would need considerable capital in order to buy and stock a local farm, assuming that he could find a good one for sale.

In Hingham, finding a good farm to buy had been inhibited by what one observer called "hereditary rust." Owners of ancestral lands had been reluctant to part with them even though their farming was inefficient, often producing large but mediocre crops. But in the depressed years before the Civil War, these owners were "land-poor," some of their sons joined the trek westward, and the reluctance faded. Gentlemen farmers had the needed capital, could hire labor, and had leisure to attend meetings where the science was disseminated. It was not mere coincidence that men such as Fearing, Cushing, Brewer, and Whiton set about large-scale farming and established their new Society at this time.

The aims of the Society were in part scientific and economic. They included "encouraging and improving the Science and Practice of Agriculture and Horticulture, [and] of promoting the amelioration of the various species of animals, grain, fruits, and vegetables." The aims were also social: the physical improvement of the town and the fostering of a new social atmosphere, wherein "all political and sectarian matters" were "excluded" from meetings. In a broad and conservative sense, the aims were also moral and educational: to restore the traditional self-reliance of town life; to develop "the minds, genius, taste and skill of all the inhabitants"; to revitalize "in these days of public schools and sewing machines," the old domestic arts.

In September, 1859, the first annual fair was held in temporary quarters. E. P. Dyer, the Congregational minister, later reminisced:

> The old vegetable tent by the town house, where we proudly exhibited our mammoth squashes . . . has given way to the splendid Agricultural Hall; and Yale's mammoth tent on the Common is superseded by a magnificent dining saloon.

Down Main Street that first year, led by Charles Cushing, came fifty yoke of oxen drawing a vehicle full of young misses representing the seasons. After a dinner for six hundred, Quincy Bicknell celebrated the new departure in lively verse:

> *Adieu to buckets and to pails!*
> *Adieu to boxes eke!*
> *No more the hammer and the nails*
> *Old Hingham's craft shall speak . . . .*
>
> *No more shall saw-mills whiz and whir,*
> *Nor tanyards scent the gale,*
> *The ancient town is all astir*
> *To bid the ploughshare hail . . . .*

And he who owned, a year ago,
A cow or two at most,
Now hies him to a cattle show
And buys a goodly host . . . .

Now CUSHING talks of monstrous yields,
And crops that he shall reap,
HOBART reclaims his barren fields,
And shows his flocks of sheep . . . .

The women, too, with zeal are fired,
And seize the hoe and rake,
All with a farming rage inspired,
Gay flower beds to make . . . .

A more prosaic speaker then cited two obstacles to local farming: first, the belief that farming was not respectable; second, the belief that it was not profitable. The Agricultural Society set out to disprove both beliefs. It had better luck with the first.

The members began with experimental methods of growing grain, but profitability was menaced when, after the war, new railroads opened up the great grain fields of the West. By 1870, Peter Whiton's grain store at the harbor was getting corn and oats "by cars direct from the West." As for livestock, Charles Cushing predicted that beef prices would remain high; ironically, as Boston prices began to fall in 1866-67, meat prices led the way down. The stock most popular in eighteenth-century Hingham had been sheep, and in the Society's first years, sheepraising increased sharply. In the 1860s, Hingham led Plymouth County in sheepfarming; the numbers of sheep pastured in Hingham climbed from 598 in 1861 to 1232 in 1865. But the numbers soon declined. Why so? One answer often heard was dogs. On World's End, roving dogs killed many of Brewer's sheep. Sheepdogs, roaming afar from their duties on Union Street, became savage attackers among Cushing's flock on South Pleasant Street. But the main cause for the decline was, paradoxically, the growth of woolen factories, which required larger quantities of wool at cheaper prices than New England farms could offer. These factories imported wool from the West and from overseas.

More reliable and lasting were pig and dairy farming. However offensive to local noses—and by the 1880s to the new Board of Health—"piggeries" multiplied. Herds of purebred cows came to town. The new summer colony added to a growing hunger for poultry and eggs. But "whether it is profitable to raise hens" filled many a newspaper column with debate, some of it good for a wry laugh. One poor experimentalist

tried raising chickens with six roosters and reported his disaster. The
roosters

> got into a political or some other kind of quarrel, and they kept up
> the fight until four of them were killed outright, and two died from
> exhaustion . . . . Of the four chickens remaining, the rats got two,
> one died of the *pip*, and the fourth one is now pining in solitude, has
> a bad cough, and is evidently fast going with consumption.

Judged by their original aim to improve farming, the annual fairs of
the Agricultural Society peaked early. A list of participants in 1869 indicates the magnitude of the local effort:

OUTDOORS

18	exhibitors	showed	247 sheep and lambs
12	"	"	111 swine
10	"	"	10 bulls
23	"	"	109 poultry
10	"	won prizes for	19 cows
19	"	"	23 heifers
8	"	showed	14 yokes of oxen & steers
20	"	won prizes for	horses
11	"	showed	26 calves
8	"	won prizes for	11 beef cattle
8		competed in	ploughing matches
3		competed in	spading matches

INDOORS

113	children	showed	140 articles
80	exhibitors	showed	134 useful & fancy articles
40	"	"	110 plates of apples
36	"	"	170 plates of pears
29	"	"	116 plates of grapes (42 varieties)
25	"	"	27 displays of peaches, quinces, cranberries
36	"	"	57 displays of honey, pickles, etc.
14	"	"	70 displays of grain and garden seeds
6	"	"	8 displays of butter and cheese
60	exhibitors	showed	field & garden vegetables
33	"	"	flowers
15	"	"	bread
26	"	"	manufactured & agricultural articles

Changes, however, were soon to come. The outdoor "Cattle Show," as it was called, decreased in size, and the indoor show grew. Hingham began to lose prizes to yokes of oxen from Bridgewater and Scituate, and Charles Cushing warned, "The committee cannot but feel much anxiety for the future of that noble animal, the ox." Family and driving horses began to displace steers and oxen, and a new social tone was set in 1876 when prizes were awarded for horses driven by "ladies and gentlemen."

Market and home gardening began to replace general farming. Fearing Burr's pioneering *Field and Garden Vegetables of America* had appeared in 1863. In 1867, the Society began to promote the raising of vegetables and fruits for a healthier diet, a shift away from the traditional emphasis on meat, bread, potatoes and other root crops. With the discovery in 1872 of the vacuum method of canning, foods could more safely be stored for future use. Market gardening of perishables for the city began to pay. By the mid-1870s, Moses Leavitt expected to sell 40,000 boxes of strawberries in a season.

At the fairs, flower exhibits betokened another change. By 1874, Hingham had two commercial greenhouses. It had become fashionable for ladies to work in flower gardens. In 1878, an unnamed observer recalled that "thirty years ago, flowers, shrubs, fruit trees, and highly cultivated lawns were rarely seen." Now in 1878, "we cultivate every inch and fill our grounds with fertilizers, and so we contaminate the very water we drink." Not all is changed. In 1881, George Lincoln estimated that "more than 2000 rose bushes were cultivated in Hingham by members of the Society." Next year, he gave a talk titled "Autobiography of a Chrysanthemum." And in 1885, when his wife Mercy realized that the first of five buds on a night-blooming cereus was beginning to open, she invited neighbors, and almost forty stopped by to see what George had started from a single slip three years before. Trees also were becoming objects of cultivation. In 1879, Charles Shimmin invited inspection of his tree nursery of twelve to fifteen hundred seedlings, and in 1880, the Tree Club was established.

Its relations with the Agricultural and Horticultural Society were carefully amicable; the Society's president was made vice president of the new club. The dominant social position of the Society discouraged the forming of any new society that might seem competitive. In 1865-66, the town had short-lived Natural History and Historical Societies. In 1869, Fearing Burr tried to form a "Hingham Institute" for the "acquisition and dissemination of knowledge concerning the natural history, the aboriginal inhabitants, the settlement and history of this town and vicinity"—in short, a Hingham Historical Society. It came to nought. Some felt that "it might injure this [Agricultural] Society, by diverting some interest." The Agricultural Society's dominant role had the effect of a monopoly, in a way analogous to the earlier impact of the Unitarian churches on efforts to form other religious groups. It sought to embrace every facet of the town's social and economic life. Its exhibitions included the arts and crafts and the products of industry and commerce. And as its attention broadened, its original focus on agriculture narrowed.

Albert Fearing died in 1875, and his farm was inherited by the son of his brother-in-law, H. W. Burditt. Burditt's dairy so pleased summer customers that they convinced him to supply their winter homes in the city. The year of Fearing's death was also the year of David Whiton's financial ruin. Whiton's 220 acres were sold for $15,000 to pay off his creditors, and they went first to a horse and stock farmer, then to Charles Shimmin for his trees, and then to seedsman Aaron Low. On World's End, John Brewer completed his land purchases and continued farming until his death in 1893. In South Hingham, Charles Cushing persisted in his campaign to make farming into a science. His stock as of 1877—oxen, cows, horses, sheep, swine—were fed almost wholly from his own land. The manure was recycled. The milk was so rich that butter was made in ten minutes. His barn was loaded with hundreds of bushels of turnips, parsnips, carrots, and beets, and his orchards produced one hundred barrels of apples in an autumn.

But in 1882, Cushing sounded the alarm and identified the trends that would gradually undermine Hingham farming during the next half-century:

> The writer of this report remembers well when the Thaxters, Herseys, Lincolns, Lorings, Bateses, Remingtons, Barneses, and others of the middle district, the Hobarts, Herseys, Lanes, Cushings, Lorings, Whitons, Gardners, Shutes, Towers, and others, in the south district, each raised and kept from one to six yoke of oxen and steers, and thousands of sheep, and raised the hay, grain, and fodder to feed them in winter, and had abundance of clear, well-fenced pasture to summer them.

> Now it is almost impossible to get a decent pasture for a cow, at any price. This looks to me as though the present generation had greatly degenerated from the example of their ancestors, or that our greatly increased facilities for education have given much higher ideas of life to them than tilling the soil and earning their bread by the sweat of their brow.

It was becoming more appealing and profitable for the young to "keep books" in Boston than to work on the farm. Boys were joining girls in the high school to prepare for business. For many of them, farm life would soon become only a fond childhood memory.

Elwin Fearing, born in 1883, reminisced eighty-six years later about the self-sufficiency of a farm family with little money. His father Edwin farmed in the Cushing country of South Pleasant Street (192). At the close of summer pasture, large farmers would sell off old cows, and one year, his father bought one for $11. Fed with a "couple of bags of meal and all the good hay she could eat," the cow was "dressed off," and the sides of beef were hung up on "them things there on both ends of the house, and she'd freeze up and stay froze all winter long, lest you want some steak for breakfast, it'd be so froze up you'd have to saw it off."

> Most everybody had a couple of pigs and 'd have them dressed off. My father used to make sweet pickles for the hams and shoulders. Boy, they were nice, too! And the rest of it—for fresh pork and salted. I got a couple o' stone crocks down cellar now that they used to put that in. Cut it up in strips 'bout that wide. Cover the bottom with coarse salt, then put a layer o' that in, then another layer o' salt, another layer o' pork, another layer o' salt, then fill it up with water, and a board to put on top of it, a big rock on it, and there's salt pork all winter.

With late spring and summer came strawberries, raspberries ("thimble-berries"), currants, gooseberries. "My father made me peddle them strawberries along Main Street. He built shelves in one of those old wicker baby carriages which I had to push from house to house." "Then when the garden thing come along, we'd have sweet corn and summer squash and that stuff, you know. Gawd, we'd have probably fifteen twenty bushel of potatoes and turnips, and carrots, parsnips, beets, oh gosh, we'd have vegetables to go all winter."

Born six years earlier than Elwin Fearing, Nettie Gardner Loring re-membered in 1969 the life of the 1880s on a family farm near the junc-tion of Whiting and Gardner Streets:

> Oh golly. I always went with my father and I used to go with him wherever he went and I used to ride the horse and cultivate and plough and do all those things. We had cows and sheep, and we had turkeys at one time, oh yes, and we had lots of hens. Always had a pig. Cellar was always full of preserves that my mother had canned all summer. We had *every* kind of fruit that grew. Fruit trees and rasp-berries and currants and gooseberries and all those things. We just *lived* off of the products of the place there . . . . We had plenty to eat, but we didn't have a lot of money . . . . Think of it. [Under her breath:] Golly! You *live*. That's what I think.

When they grew up, Nettie became a schoolteacher and Elwin an auto mechanic.

The fondest memory of childhood in these years, however, was not farming, but the old agricultural fairs. What a wonderful sight it was to watch Charles Cushing leading his great team of oxen down Main Street. How crowded and amusing were the pens of livestock, hens, ducks, and rabbits. But even more amusing were the multiplying attractions that had nothing to do with agriculture and horticulture. For the Society's sponsors, the fairs were becoming a problem; the "Cattle Show" was becoming a carnival. As early as 1868, the Committee on Rural Sports was finding it hard to come up with novelties, hard to compete with other fairs for performers. Refreshment stands multiplied, and so did sideshows, swings, flying horses, fire engine musters, parades, band concerts, bicycle races, high-wire acts, balloon ascensions, and baseball games. Some asked, "What should be the aim and object of the society? Certainly not for social entertainments, yearly holidays, an annual dinner, side-shows, or local pride."

Others disagreed. From its start, the Society had had a strongly social flavor. Its grand Agricultural Hall, one hundred by sixty feet, with an exhibition hall on the main floor and dining hall for six hundred above, was built in 1867 and soon became the town's social center. In 1883, Governor John D. Long reviewed the Society's first quarter century. Appropriately for this eminently sociable man, he saw its chief contributions as social. Its

> true results are to be found in its unseen, unmeasured, undemonstrative contributions to the character of the public sentiment of the community . . . . It has been general in its influence for the refinement of our people and home surroundings . . . the betterment of taste in living . . . . Its annual festivals have brought us together, harmonizing our relations, and softening our differences.

✠

CHAPTER ELEVEN

The Sociable Life of George Lincoln and His Neighbors

T HE Agricultural and Horticultural Society had played a role in initiating and nurturing a new era in the town's history, an era uniquely "social." During the mid nineteenth century, a powerful new idea of the *social* displaced old codes of religious and political sectarianism: the idea that social life, harmonious and pleasurable, is of fundamental value. Signs of a new sociability appeared in Hingham in the 1850s. Ladies promoted the creation of social halls, and ladies of Fort Hill began their annual fairs. At the Centre, the Agricultural and Horticultural Society was born, and so were the yearly suppers of the Clams, Oysters, and Plum Pudding Corporation (C.O. & P.P.). These lapsed for a dark decade and when, in 1866, the officers called the next meeting, they explained the long hiatus. The financial panic of 1857-58 had paralyzed business, credit was not to be found, and garments were threadbare.

> Then came years of desolating war bringing seasons of darkness and gloom. Welcome peace next succeeded. Under its genial influence, grand schemes for public accommodation and improvement are being devised and carried out. Palatial private residences are being erected. Manufacturers are elated by rapid sales . . .

and so on, in the droll, exaggerated style of C.O. & P.P. ritual. In fact, business was slow and postwar inflation monstrous. But gloom was giving way to gleeful relief.

The symbolic monuments of this era were three large social halls, Loring, Agricultural, and Wilder. Its individual epitome was George Lincoln, whose voluminous diaries picture Hingham at the peak time of a rich, dense public life. As a Broad Bridge shopkeeper, he had an ideal looking and listening post. Meticulous secretary of organizations and events, he was also a Pepysian chronicler of life's changes. He played his social role the more effectively by avoiding controversy. In his humane practicality, he was something of an eighteenth-century man. His faith was in the rational enjoyments of social harmony, and at its core was his abiding love of music. We look first at his own style of life and then at the town's social life, in which he shared enthusiastically.

A descendant of Sergeant Daniel, George Lincoln was born in 1822. His father, for many years a sailmaker at the harbor, was one of Hingham's first Methodists—in this, a more "nineteenth-century man" than his son—and late in life, he became a lay preacher. George's mother was a Loring, sister of tanner "Uncle Alfred." Enos and Isaiah Loring, stovemakers and tinsmiths, were his cousins. Another cousin was the wife of Major Benjamin Meservey, George's neighbor on Ship Street and a leading town Democrat. General Luther Stephenson, the other Democratic leader, was a friend. George, a loyal Republican, avoided politics in society.

He was also a loyal Derby alumnus. At fourteen, he finished school to work in a Boston store, and by 1839, he was managing a shop in Provincetown. Memories of four years there give rare glimpses of a romantic side:

> Hingham Harbor is open below Button Island, and the miniature seas and white caps remind me of the scenes of my youth at Provincetown . . . . It was a custom then for young men and women when they were courting to bundle. The passage between Boston and Provincetown was almost exclusively by sailing vessels.

Such odd juxtapositions are one of the charms of his diaries.

In 1843, he came home for a wife and, like Albert Fearing, chose a daughter of the "other" parish, New North. Between 1846 and 1869, Mercy Hall and George Lincoln had nine children, three of whom died in early childhood. In 1869, he began his diaries.

They trace the daily routines of a village shopkeeper. He raised his shutters at eight, closed at noon for a dinner break at home, when he enjoyed visitors or worked in his garden, orchard, or "glass house." The shop reopened until eight or eight-thirty, and many an evening was spent at social entertainments or visits to fellow antiquaries. Early Saturday mornings, he traveled to Boston by steamboat or "cars"—the train—to order goods and pay social calls. On these trips, he relished one of his keenest pleasures, "pleasant conversations" or "agreeable interviews" with fellow townsmen. On Sundays, again like clockwork, he attended two services at the old meetinghouse, although other family members might be at New North.

Coloring the diaries' bland fabric of daily dry-goods are bright patches of life, his own, but also the town's.

Jan. 8, 1871: Baby Alfred, known as Lo-Lo, "got at the kerosene filler after tea and swallowed some." Dr. Spalding was called. Quite feverish overnight, Lo-Lo improved on Sunday, but "his breath and discharges still have a kerosene-ish odour."

Oct. 3, 1871: "The well at my house is so low that I have discontinued drawing water from it to drink for fear that the health of my family may be injured."

Nov. 29, 1871: "John Beal brought a load of manure for my glass house border this afternoon. It was pretty poor stuff, but I paid him at the rate of $10 per cord for it nevertheless."

Dec. 8, 1871: Old Charles Ray, who had died at the almshouse, once "followed the occupation of boat fishing, eeling, clamming, etc. He frequently furnished our table with these eatables . . . . One would think after hearing his statements that clams weren't worth eating if they were taken in any other locality than Goose Point; and then his teeth would rattle and shake and another statement would be made relating to the dangers experienced at a certain time in navigating through Hull Gut, etc."

Jan. 15, 1872: A late evening at Fearing Burr's, working on the Civil War history. "It was about half past 11 when I left for home. The dancing school assembly at Loring . . . was not out when I passed, so I listened to the music for a few minutes. The scene was one of youthful vigor, grace, and beauty."

July 22, 1872: "Julia our servant girl went out visiting last evening and has not yet returned."

Aug. 15, 1872: At 1 a.m., there was such a violent thunderstorm that said Julia was "invited into the front chambers with our children, where she passed the remainder of the night."

Oct. 18-25, 1872: "Wild geese flew over today." "Herman and I gathered the Bicar pears, and the Garrigues, and Clinton grapes this noon." "Mercy and I mixed a keg of grape juice, sugar and water, for making wine this evening."

Feb. 18, 1874: "Mr. Seth L. Hobart, our surveyor of highways in the North Ward, has an ox sled with a snow plough attached to the side, which is drawn by six cattle through the streets, clearing a track from three to four feet wide at each passing."

April 17, 1874: "Herman and I raked up the rubbish about the yard this morning, and burnt it."

Aug. 3, 1874: "I paid my town tax this morning of $60.50, less the discount of $3.02, making $57.48."

April 11, 1875: George and Herman did their annual chore of moving the stove into the back room from the dining room. It would be moved back in October.

April 20, 1877: Walking home after midnight, "I stopped for a few minutes at Loring Hall to see the children dance."

Aug. 9-10, 1877: "Willie Easterbrook, who is boarding with his parents at the Cushing House, and Alfred, have built a boat in our yard mostly from a large packing box, rigged it into a sloop and painted it two coats. The name 'Flirt' is painted on the stern." (Alas, next day: "The 'Flirt' was stolen last night and broken up by some Irish boys.")

Nov. 12, 1877: "All my leisure mornings and noons, at home, is devoted to the trimming of grape vines."

Oct. 20, 1879: "This noon I potted lemon verbenas, heliotropes, three varieties of variegated leaf plants, tea roses, etc. etc. . . . . Wild geese flew over us, going south this afternoon."

But there were no winter trips for George, no vacations. Through the severest of winter storms, he kept his shop open and walked the streets, empty of all but driving snow. Few winters could match 1875. His son Herman had Washington's Birthday off, skated to Hull and back, then skated to Dorchester Bay, "where after remaining to see the trial of ice boats, he took the cars" home. Soon after the holiday came the town meeting. March 8, 1875: "I was present all day, and enjoyed the proceedings as much as I should a play at the theatre." Spring was heralded in April by Fast Day, an old Puritan holiday now secularized. On Fast Day, 1878, George attended a *Union* service at New North; in the afternoon he went to an *entertainment* at the Orthodox Congregational Church; in the evening, he was at Loring for the annual concert and ball of the Hingham Brass Brand.

To the new holiday, Memorial Day, George made a special contribution. People delivered cut flowers to his store, and daughter Sara and her friends arranged bouquets for the G.A.R.'s grave decorations. On one occasion, "we furnished them with 170 bouquets." George shared

The major attraction at the 1876 fair was the Madawaska Cavalry of the Commonwealth of Spunkville, Ebed L. Ripley, commander-in-chief. This burlesque assemblage of about 150 paraded, drilled, and fought a sham battle. The men were fantastically outfitted in attic rummagings. Boys became Indian scouts, whose make-up artist was Franklin W. Rogers.

Agricultural Hall (1867–1965).

Seedsman Aaron Low's display wagon for an 1880s agricultural fair. The initials of the society and the year of its founding (1858) are outlined with flowers.

Albert Fearing (1798–1875).

John Reed Brewer (1818–1893).

Charles W. Cushing (1811–1898).

Edmund Hersey, Jr. (1823–1909).

Mercy Lincoln (1824–1916).

George Lincoln (1822–1909).

*Samuel Downer
(1807–1881).*

Alfred C. Hersey (1804–1888).

General Luther Stephenson (1830–1921).

Bird's Eye View of Melville Garden in 1881. Beneath Otis Hill, left to right: Lincoln Hall, the Café, the Music Hall. Crow Point Bridge over Downer Avenue to slightly south of today's Kilmer Road. West of Downer Avenue, the ice cream pavilion with the rounded hexagonal roof. Facing each other across Walton's Pond: the Clam Bake house and the band stand. Parallel to Downer Avenue running northeast: the bowling alley, Foley Hall, a second bowling alley, and the entrance to the Garden at the water's edge of Alice Walk. Bathhouses are visible along the beach. The GOVERNOR ANDREW is steaming towards the Rose Standish House (not pictured), near the site of the Yacht Club today.

with tailor John Todd the duties of supervising and beautifying Hingham Cemetery.

June brought the annual Derby Academy exhibition, procession and lecture; George's children all went to Derby. July Fourth was not yet the formal celebration of the twentieth century, but children celebrated in their noisy ways. In 1875, Nelly Whiting spent the night with Sara, and they "were out firing crackers and torpedoes at 3 o'clock. The other children were equally patriotic by 5 o'clock."

> Sara J., Helen S., Alfred L., and Nelly Whiting, went with [nephew] Walter and I on a boating excursion, carrying our lunch, etc. We went in one of David Cobb's rowboats. After proceeding a short distance, we made a temporary sail of some cottoncloth we had taken with us for an awning . . . . At home we dined on green peas, new potatoes, etc., from Uncle Alfred's. Strawberries and ice creams for supper.

Summer was also a time of picnics, and the Lincolns joined the First Parish festivities at Melville Garden. Late summer focused on preparations for the fair. For eight years (1867-74), George worked busily as secretary of the exhibition as well as readying his own prize exhibits of grapes and pears.

In October, politics heated up, but George avoided party caucuses, fearing the sort of thing that happened on October 3, 1874.

> Alfred C. Hersey made a blank of himself, by boldly stating at the meeting that "A man cannot get an office in this town unless he is a member of the Agricultural Society, or belongs to the Old Ship." He called the meeting "a cliquey affair," and told some of the officials at the meeting to "shut up," etc.

On the first Tuesday in November, George invariably "rode up to the town house", later to "Ag Hall," "and deposited my vote for the regular Republican ticket." But whoever won, the prudent shopkeeper decorated for political parades. Only in the acrimonious election of 1876 did his tolerance run short. The Democrats' torchlight parade

> was a hard-looking procession, numbering 175 torches, mostly from Weymouth and Braintree, and composed mostly of Irishmen. There was a great deal of noise and carousing about the Bridge during the first part of the night. Herman, on his way home from Abington, saw several of these "Dimicrats", with their torches, piled up by the wayside, apparently drunk, and sleeping with their torches burning [Nov. 13, 1876].

The big family holiday was Thanksgiving. In good years, there were roast turkey and plum pudding noon and night, and "we breakfasted on roast pork and baked potatoes" from Uncle Alfred's. In hard times, "Herman brought us a splendid Thanksgiving turkey tonight when he came from Boston. It weighed 11 1/2 lbs. and cost 21 cents per lb." Christmas, for these descendants of Puritans, was not yet a holiday: "On Christmas Day I was at the store for most of the day and did a good business although I only took the door shutters down." But on Christmas night, the family were all present for the First Parish party, the big tree, the exchange of gifts, Colonel Spring as Santa Claus, the blessing, the banquet, and dancing till 1 a.m. And so, the year closed, and George Lincoln began a characteristic task: each year's diary was exhaustively indexed.

He was the ideal clerk, on his way to becoming the town's historian. The committees on which he served were legion, his reports voluminous. He and Fearing Burr labored for years on the Civil War history. Almost every Thursday he wrote an article or an obituary for Friday's *Journal.* In 1872, an added job opened up new sources of local human information: he became Justice of the Peace, hearing oaths, filling out pension applications, and certifying contracts. For each action he received twenty-five cents; in hard times, those quarters helped. When his appointment expired in 1879, he was glad to have it renewed by a Cottage Street neighbor, John D. Long. He called on the governor-elect at the State House, and "Mr. Long paid the whole expense, $7, not-withstanding that I tendered him the money; said he wished to do so for my personal benefit, and for which, of course, I expressed my sincere thanks" [Nov. 29, 1879].

He was par excellence the tolerant preserver of local changes and characters. What he disliked is summed up in his one bête noire:

> Alfred C. Hersey Esq. called and relieved himself of considerable bombastic talk . . . . He is certainly one of the most self-conceited men I ever knew; and yet he has many good qualities, and would be a valuable man in society if he could but bridle his tongue [Aug. 23 and Oct. 3, 1873].

> Captain Alfred C. Hersey and Gen. Luther Stephenson, Jr., [the town's other most outspoken man] had a disgraceful battle of words in my store this morning. Their conversation became personal, and the language used by each towards the other, was blasphemous in the extreme [Oct. 19, 1875].

What he liked shines through his words on the death of a neighbor, old packet captain Elijah Beal: "a fair-minded and kind-hearted man. He was always pleasant and agreeable in his conversation; in fine—*he was a good man*; and a Christian if there ever was one" [May 12, 1872]. Between these two extremes, George chronicled the small scandals of life with his own private blend of the chaste and the tolerant.

On illegitimacy, for example:

July 27, 1874: William Hersey Senior died this morning, aged 75 years 9 mos. 11 days. He was an illegitimate son of Mary Hersey, the daughter of Jonathan Hersey. His father was a Mr. Brown—a temporary resident here . . . . Mary the mother of William had two children of illegitimate birth. She afts. m. a Dill.

April 12, 1879: William Tower was an original character, a great collector of old furniture, pamphlets, musical instruments, etc. He kept a variety store where one could buy anything from a penny whistle to a church organ; from a box of pills to a featherbed, and notwithstanding, he had a little, peculiarly feminine, squeaking voice, he was a man of more than ordinary talent—especially in his line of business. He was an illegitimate son of Jotham Jacobs. His mother was Jotham Jacobs' wife's sister.

Infidelities, however ancient, were told to his diary with propriety.

Drunkenness was another unfortunate fact of life for one who, in times of temperance fervor, made and enjoyed in moderation his currant and blackberry wines. The Committee on Pickles, Preserves, and Jellies at the 1860 fair felt unqualified to judge them and "would by no means advocate the use even of home-made wines as a beverage; yet, when needed for invalids," they would be more beneficial than Port, Madeira, or Sherry. This was very different from: "Bill Drew, the present landlord of the hotel in this village, is drunk today, and has been so for the last week" [September 27, 1871].

Brutal facts of life included epidemic diseases, high infant mortality, and tragic deaths. George's octogenarian friend, retired minister Henry Hersey, brother of the bombastic Alfred, was manhandled during a robbery and ten weeks later hanged himself. George's compassion was stronger than his sense of the sinfulness of suicide:

Sept. 23, 1877: I think he has been a great sufferer both mentally and physically since he was gagged and roughly handled . . . . He has frequently told me since the "shaking up", as he expressed himself after the attack, that he would rather the ruffians would have shot him than to have treated him as they did. I therefore have a great deal of charity for this last act of my aged friend.

Two months later began what was for George Lincoln the saddest tragedy of all. Herman was nineteen when, on December 4, 1877, his father noted: "Herman had an ill turn in Boston this afternoon." We know that Herman died nine months later and can only read on with anguish. No illness was named. There was one visit to a Boston specialist. In spring and summer, Herman kept up a frantic pace of visits and outings. "I fear," wrote George, "it is too much for Herman." In September, his strength ran out.

Sept. 7, 1878: Herman had a serious talk with his mother and I after I came home from the store at night. He seems to realize that he is to remain with us but a short while longer. The dear boy.

Sept. 12: The dear boy is failing, but is patient and resigned.

Sept. 25: Herman had a very sick day. He wanted his mother or [sister] Mercy W. with him all the time; and yet he was interested to learn about the Fair when I came home.

Sept. 27: Our dear Herman (precious boy) died this noon at about five minutes of two o'clock. He would have been 20 years old tomorrow. His last words to me—taking my hand in his—were "Dear Papa." In answer to his mother's question—"Are you suffering, Hermy?" he replied—"Dear Mama, God is good." He retained his mental faculties to the very last moment, and died without a struggle. He was perfectly willing to go.

Two days later, on a mild and pleasant Sunday, by a grave on the hilltop across from the Civil War Monument, "beautifully embellished with evergreen and choice flowers, the work of my neighbor, Mr. John Todd," they said goodbye.

One thing helped George Lincoln through the months that followed: his music. As a boy he played violin, and later he studied the flute and singing. In the bad business times of the 1870s, he took on violin students, including a young man from Downer Landing named "W. James," later chief of police. In the hectic spring of 1875, he rehearsed with New North musicians, played at Mary Lincoln's while she tried out her new Chickering, and played with the *kinder* symphony.

His son George M. was a professional violinist. He had debuted at eight in the early years of Loring Hall, playing an Amati. Concerts featuring "Master George" drew full houses; at one, his father accompanied him on the flute. For the father, these were solace for many losses in the 1850s: his grandmother, mother, and three small children. In the 1870s, George M. led the oratorio orchestra at Clapp's Hall, Weymouth, and his father gave up Sunday evening church to play first flute. Daughter Sara began playing the piano in public at age ten, and citizens stopped by to congratulate the proud father. In February, 1877, she first played in Boston, to warm reviews. In the sad weeks after Hermy's death, she and her father played many a Haydn duet at home.

The air was filled with music. A visit from George M.'s Boston friends launched a musical orgy, the only kind of orgy that we know George enjoyed. No telephone was needed to set up a last-minute home concert. Once in July, 1877, about seventy attended a Ship Street gathering, and the music went on until 1 a.m. George missed church next morning. In October, the orgy was repeated. "We have had music in the morning, noon, and at night; and from 9 to 11 o'clock this evening," interrupted only by a long walk to Triphammer Pond, where, in an open field, "the 'boys' practiced a little hopping and jumping."

He was also an eager spectator of amateur theatricals, farces and tableaux at Loring Hall, and of pantomimes under the auspices of the Orthodox Congregational Church. Old orthodoxies were giving way. In May, 1875, George noted with surprise: "The Baptist Society of this town have a sale this afternoon and a concert at Loring Hall this evening. I think it is the first time a public exhibition was ever given under their auspices." Hingham was buzzing with entertainments and social gatherings at hall and home. A new social ethic prevailed. George Lincoln expressed it best in December, 1876. In a centennial year marred by depression, dispute, bankruptcies, and diphtheria, he inaugurated a "course" of Ship Street entertainments at his home and opened the occasion with a little speech:

> Our entertainment this evening is intended as an introductory one to a course which we hope will follow during the winter months, in this street. The object we have in view is to bring the different families together for social enjoyment . . . a pleasant time in which we may spend an hour or two socially together [Dec. 14, 1876].

After a concert, the company was invited to view a burlesque art exhibit "which we had arranged in our dining room," twenty-eight items climaxing with "Relics from the Garden of Eden." Burlesque or not, it was his idea of the Garden of Eden. He was an eighteenth-century man who believed in cultivating his garden and sharing it with his neighbors.

In the social life of George Lincoln's Hingham, solemnity seems to have gone out of fashion. Nowhere is this more evident than in the transformation of holidays, following the Civil War, from a few religious and patriotic observances to an array of social celebrations. The old Puritan Fast Day now began with a Torrent Engine Company parade, after which the "fast" was thoroughly broken with one of Zenas

Loring's famous chowders. Thanksgiving evening was filled with "balls, parties, and friendly gatherings"—our "forefathers would scarcely recognize their bequest." Washington's Birthday was observed with "grand calico balls" at Loring Hall, followed in March by growingly popular St. Patrick's Day. July Fourth took on festive airs, and lively parties marked Christmas night.

A favorite event was the "surprise raid," quite like the traditional surprise party except that the gentlemen, rather than the ladies, sent the invitations and brought the "collation" and celebrants to the home of the "guest." Everyone was set on having "a very lively time," and everyone was to "contribute something towards the success of the entertainment." On the Silver Anniversary, in 1872, of the Dunbars of Thaxter Street, over 150 persons "filled the parlor, sitting room, and dining room, and even took possession of the kitchen." The Rev. Jonathan Tilson offered prayer. Levi Hersey presented the gifts. A letter from Dunbar's fellow Boston junk-dealers, accompanied by a pair of rag pantaloons, was read "amid roars of laughter." Cakes and ice cream followed, and

> singing, conversation, and lots of laughter occupied the time . . . .
> And as the hands of the clock upon the sitting room mantel piece
> pointed very near the hour of twelve, a few of the remaining guests
> struck up "Auld Lang Syne" and "Home Sweet Home."

There was neither liquor nor dancing: this jovial multitude was Baptist.

The times were hungry for ever more "novel entertainments," new "manias" and "rages." First came the Pedestrian Mania, which began when E. P. Weston lost an election bet, walked from Boston to Washington, and enjoyed it so much that he made a profession of walking against time. He was paid to walk at the Hingham fair in 1868. This rage was quickly followed by the Velocipede Madness. The two-wheeled bike appeared in America in the 1860s. The *Journal* advised:

> All you have got to do is to keep the velocipede up and keep it going.
> You can't do either of these separately, you have to do both at once.
> Which makes the difficulty, because if the velocipede stops it falls
> down. At the same time if it falls down, it will stop . . . . The rule for
> riding is, "Straddle, paddle and skedaddle."

The "mania" reached Hingham in 1869, when young George Cushing, stablekeeper at the Union Hotel, gave a demonstration of velocipedic skills in the railroad depot hall.

The most lasting new mania was baseball. The game had been invented in 1839 or 1845—depending on which historian you believe—and its first national association was formed in 1858. Hingham's first recorded games took place at the 1860 fair, when two town teams played. Peter N. Sprague was high scorer with seven "tallies." After the war, "baseball fever" spread rapidly, and Hingham's Bay State Club was playing by 1867. The mania inspired comic verse, another new fashion:

> *"Now stop this game," the old man said.*
> *"The second base has smashed his head.*
> *The pitcher, too, has sprained his wrist.*
> *The umpire's brain is in a mist."*
>   *Base Ball.*

By 1871 in Hingham, "this healthful game has become exceedingly popular . . . . It is a game indulged in now by all classes . . . even little fellows no bigger than a tadpole." Indeed, the "tadpoles" challenged old sabbatarian laws, and on a Sunday in 1873, some were arrested. But the erosion of such laws was inevitable in a time dedicated to entertainment and sport. A small but momentous transition took place in 1879. Some bicyclists were convicted of riding on Sunday, appealed to the Superior Court in Plymouth, and had their conviction thrown out.

The new social code decreed wholesome "entertainment" and "amusement." A chief function of public institutions was to promote good fellowship through fun. The Agricultural Society "deserves our gratitude" for the "series of agreeable entertainments which have been presented at Loring Hall." The new high school will "tend to promote, what all towns need, a more homogeneous social life, the art of friendly and genial entertainment." When a Catholic Youth Association was formed, "We trust that . . . our citizens will encourage these young people in their praiseworthy endeavor to cater for their amusement." Universalist pastor Phebe Hanaford applied the new morality to childhood: "The desire to give pleasure to childhood is ever an indication of a noble and benevolent nature, and parents and guardians cannot but feel grateful as they see their children happy." Entertainment was the best antidote to the partisan and the antisocial: "Few things tend more strongly or more directly to banish crime from a community than plenty of cheap and proper amusements." South Hingham reported, "a parish that cannot unite in having a good time at least once a year is in a sad plight. Party and sect are to be here unknown." As we will see, such a faith led to Samuel Downer's philanthropic creation at Melville Garden, the "amusement park."

Loring Hall was always busy and crowded, so packed in 1879 for the "grand dramatic entertainment" of the G.A.R. Humphrey Post, itself a major postwar social organization, that two hundred were turned away. Fortunately, Agricultural Hall had risen in 1867. South Hingham needed its own large hall. The trustees of the Wilder Charitable and Educational Fund secured permission to use their surplus funds to build Wilder Hall. Ground was broken on June 10, 1879, and the hall was dedicated on December 18. By February, 1880, Wilder Hall was "bringing South Hingham to life." It opened its career with a "big glittering masquerade ball" for a town that had fallen in love with dances.

Music was everywhere. At "the Bridge", Jernegan's periodical shop sold canaries, and many passers-by "loafed" at the door to hear them. Two bands were formed in 1866, the Hingham Brass and the South Hingham Cornet, and the next year a music stand was built on the Common and a bandstand at Fountain Square. The bands played for all kinds of occasions. "Nothing so tends to harmonize the feelings of a town or neighborhood so much as the cultivation and encouragement of music." Music became part of the school program. General Stephenson, chorister of the First Parish, called it "beneficial to the moral condition of the children," "making them happier and better," "soothing the passions." Concerts, singing classes, and piano teachers multiplied. In 1873, George Lincoln made a list of the town's piano owners and found there were seventy-two. At Loring Hall, for twenty-five or thirty-five cents, you might hear the Misses Cushing sing "Come to the Forest!", Master Remington play Mendelssohn, Serena Long play "The Last Rose of Summer," or a quartet of Rametti, Bassett, Lincoln, and Whiton sing "The Sea Hath Its Pearls." All were outshone by pianist Sara Lincoln. The names tell of a wealth of local talent. The town was making its own entertainment.

Local talent also fostered the rise of amateur theatricals, truly the deathknell of the old Puritan spirit. The prevailing taste was for "roaring farces," "side-splitting comicalities." The very titles of long-forgotten Victorian farces evoke the echo of boisterous laughter: "The Swiss Cottage; or, Why Don't She Marry?" "Farmed Out; or, Nursy Chickweed." At a Universalist ladies tea "the announcement was made that a few friends had prepared themselves to entertain the audience with a dramatic performance, and that the farce known as 'Smashington Go It' had been selected . . . . The farce was followed by a charade." Minstrel shows were also the rage, and no one worried that the rich comic potentiality, as was said, of the Negro Character might be demeaning. A company from Hingham Centre, the "Who Dar Minstrels," "fairly took down the house." The dramatic reading, popularized internationally by Dickens, became a local favorite when New North pastor John Snyder illustrated his readings with "tableaux vivants," "poses plastiques."

The social spirit had its intellectual side. If George Lincoln did not have a concert, play, or dance to attend, he had a lecture to hear. The town had "long felt the need" for the Lyceum series begun at Loring in 1871, and in 1874, the Agricultural Society offered its own series, seven or eight lectures for $2. Depression interrupted; prices and support fell. By 1877, a series cost only fifty cents, and topics such as "Hard Times" suggest the chief preoccupation. A more modest "home" version, the Monday Night Club, was launched in 1878.

In the 1880s, as prosperity returned, a new tone was heard, a call for refinement. "Fun" and "Phunnigraphiana" were challenged by "taste." The western world had entered its Aesthetic Decade, and Hingham was affected. The "Amateur Orchestra" was renamed the "Philharmonic." The baseball club became the "Aesthetics"! The fashionable First Corps Cadets, formed from Boston's "Codfish Aristocracy," chose 1882 as the year to shift their summer base from Nahant to Hingham. In 1884, they bought grounds on the Fearing farm, and here, high society followers visited them.

One village declined to surrender completely to the new refinement. Little Plain refused to take itself too seriously and persisted in its lively tradition of parodic humor. Hilarious, spoofing reports to the *Journal* included the description of an imaginary Leap Year Ball, sponsored by the "Podville" maidens. The middle names of female floor managers were breeds of hens: Minnie Formosa Spellum, Lotti Brahma Smith. Guests included General Stickum, Major Shootem, Colonel Killum, Captain Lancem. The caterers were Stuffem and Bustem.

A still political, but now strongly Republican Centre organized the mock trial of Democratic postmaster, hotelier, and fire chief George Cushing. He was "charged with stealing Ebed L. Ripley's rooster." A scruffy cock in a dilapidated crate advertised the event. An often-convulsed audience of six hundred at Agricultural Hall watched the trial and heard the jury's twenty-seven-second verdict: Cushing was found *not* guilty and instructed *not* to do it again. And in a Fourth of July celebration, Centerites Charles Burr and "Charlie" Howard, the latter in drag, impersonated Democratic President Grover Cleveland and his wife and were driven about in a four-horse landau. The sense of fun had been handed down from previous generations of Centerite fathers, who initially called themselves the "Scribes and Pharisees," and then reformed as the "Phoenix Club," as if to signify that this genius for the ridiculous would survive and rise again. The same old family names appear and reappear, along with others, in reports of the Centre's unique clubs: The Phoenix, Ombre, Croquet, and Clams, Oysters, and Plum Pudding.

Yet in the midst of the fun, townspeople also had a bittersweet sense that the old, unrefined, home-grown social life was slipping away. A writer to the *Journal* in 1885 expressed this sense. It was easy

> to slip up to Boston not only for shopping, but to make calls, to take dinner or tea, to attend a concert or the theatre. *We are only a suburb.* Good entertainment and home pleasures are less prized. We lean to a centre a dozen miles off.

The old life seemed small, inelegant, remote:

> I have heard too much about the old days in Hingham to doubt that they abounded in enjoyment. The large parties, the practical jokes, the games, the forfeits, the dances, the bountiful suppers, the merry sleigh rides home . . . . Those days are not gone from Hingham alone, but from all the towns around our metropolis . . . . What used to grow in sunlight is now dwarfed . . . . Is not something going on here already far better than those large parties and late suppers? . . . . Where hearts and minds are touched to finer issues, there will be here in time a more enjoyable social life.

Perhaps so. Perhaps not. Perhaps the writer's fatalism, with its *fin de siècle* tone, merely rationalized what the writer wanted to believe. The fact is that, by the mid-1880s, a time of communal, self-sustaining social exuberance seemed drawing to a close. That it came at all was remarkable. It *could* come partly because of a revolution of a technological kind: the revolution in transportation, in ways of "moving about," that also helped bring its demise. Each period of history sows the seeds of its own passing.

CHAPTER TWELVE

✠

Revolutions in Moving About

IN the forty-three years before the Civil War, a lineage of single, small steam packets, chiefly for freight, plied the waters between Hingham and Boston, with occasional lapses owing to lack of patronage. Following the side-wheeler *Eagle* and the smaller *Lafayette* were the *General Lincoln*, which could make the trip in an hour and a half, and the *Mayflower*, a quarter of an hour faster. In 1858, the *Mayflower* was replaced by the *Nantasket*, "fastest boat in Boston Harbor." The war intervened, and the *Nantasket* went temporarily into federal service.

With peace, the "neat little Rose Standish" of the Boston and Hingham Line reappeared, "looking as gay and trim as a Washington Street belle." A Boston writer calling himself "Hawkeye" left a fine picture of her arrival:

the water has nearly run out of Hingham Harbor; we are to go up that crooked channel. See how beautifully she sheers from one side to the other, how gracefully she rounds that point near the old landing. The pilot says the tide is very low and we must run slow, or else we cannot get to the wharf. With how much apparent chagrin the Rose Standish hears the bell to slow her down, when she has made almost the quickest trip on record.

By 1867, the *Rose* had a rival. In Boston, other "hawkeyes" were eyeing possibilities. They bought the *Nantasket* and Cushing's Wharf, which soon bore the name of the guiding spirit of the new People's Line, Harvey T. Litchfield, an East Boston entrepreneur and the son of Samuel, a large landowner in Hingham. The new line bought land on the Weir River, built a wharf, dredged the channel, and the

Nantasket reappeared as the *Emmeline*. She had mechanical troubles from the start, however, and was replaced by "the magnificent William Harrison."

The duel of rival lines thus joined was the start of the South Shore's transformation. Litchfield had his hawkeye not only on steamboats, but also on the summer resort possibilities of Hingham and Nantasket, which, it was predicted, would become a "second Newport." He bought land at Strawberry Hill, Hull, negotiated for a new railroad station, and purchased about forty acres near the Old Colony House for a "shady grove." After the hurricane of September 8, 1869, his crew cleared the land, built a dance hall, dug wells, and mounted swings. A week after the storm, eight hundred members of Charlestown's St. Francis Catholic Society inaugurated Litchfield's Grove. First a hurricane of wind and rain, then a storm of building, then a flood of city visitors. The summer boom had begun.

Litchfield was touted as the magician who had "inaugurated the new line of steamers, reduced the fare, and thus has brought thousands of people to Hingham," transported townsfolk to Boston at a trifling cost, and revived local business. Thanks to him, "multitudes can escape the heat, dust, and turmoil of the city." He had created a populist summer dream:

> *Sheltered beneath a large marquee*
> *With a beautiful breeze right from the sea*
> *You can get good chowder, coffee or tea*
> *And watch the white seagulls, Sir.*
>
> *CHORUS. Laughing, singing, all the way,*
> *Joking, dancing, all the way*
> *As we sail down Boston Bay*
> *On board the Harrison steamer.*

The alarm of the directors of the Boston and Hingham line can be imagined. They cut fares on the *Rose* and increased the frequency of her trips. In 1869, their larger, faster boat, the *John Romer*, was ready. That summer saw four boats where there had been one.

For five years, the rivalry raged, and the "steamboat excitement" was "the chief topic of conversation in hotels, stores, and other places." The fare war grew absurd: ten cents, five cents, free! Steamboats sometimes raced, passengers cheering them on. The jealous little *Rose* "came up dutifully to the Wm. either for the purpose of giving a kiss or receiving an embrace . . . and received such a smack as to leave the print of the Harrison's lip deeply indented upon her paddle box." To outrace her rival, the *Rose's* pilot passed too near a buoy, and a state inspection ensued. Local partisans practiced what looked like sabotage: as the *Harrison* sought to return through the harbor, a fishing smack anchored in the channel stopped her for half an hour. Old line directors waxed indignant at their rivals. David Whiton, president of the old line, was so annoyed one day by the "bummers" of the new line, "who stand at the foot of Pearl St., and at the head of the old company's wharf, enticing passengers," that he pushed the "bummer" into the street or slapped his face. The president ended up in Boston Police Court.

The rivalry had its gentler moments. The channel was so narrow that casks of water were rolled to one side of the steamboats to "careen" them for the turn between Langley and Sarah Islands. But boats still got stuck in the mud; as one wag put it, "There is one good thing in all of this—an enemy's fleet could never shell Hingham unless they brought a mud-digger with them." The *Romer* ran aground on the channel edge, and the *Harrison* risked the same fate to remove passengers. The *Rose* went aground in thick fog, and the *Harrison's* offer of aid "was respectfully declined." On yet another occasion, the *Harrison* went on the flats, and the *Romer* broke a hawser trying to pull her off.

By 1872, the Boston and Hingham was winning its aggressive battle. The *Harrison* was withdrawn for want of patronage. Litchfield was not one to cling to a losing investment. Consider his whale. The poor beast had been captured in Boston Harbor, and Litchfield charged admission to view it. When it died, he had it preserved and chartered a rail car for an exhibition tour. Then he displayed it in a building on Dartmouth Street. When the Boston Board of Health ordered the nuisance removed, he gave it to the Natural History Society. When Hingham, to use the idiom of colonial days, "warned him out," he turned full attention to Nantasket.

But the trend he had started took hold of Hingham imaginations. War profits and unbridled speculation had produced new fortunes. Summer resorts were the fashion, and summer homes were in much demand and low supply. The

> beautiful hills on both sides of Hingham harbor . . . with the pleasant coves, inlets, and islands, should be brought to the notice of persons desirous of attractive situations for residences. In a few years, the whole of this region will probably become dotted with picturesque cottages and villas.

Not for the first time, and not for the last, the town was urged to redefine itself. One resident attacked the town's "Rip Van Winkle sleep":

"Why is it that the thousands seeking relief from toil and new scenes for the mind, fail to turn their attention where so much invites? . . . Hingham, with ordinary enterprise, should have been long ere this the most popular summer resort in the world!" "Arouse yourselves!" Drive back "to that puritannical source . . . the spirit of opposition to all and every innovation offered!" The dream was tempting, the optimism at one with its expansive age. The call was heard by a most unlikely developer.

Samuel Downer was born in the same Dorchester house where he died at seventy-four in 1881. A boyhood friend remembered him as "a genius . . . and an eccentric," a "benevolent eccentric." His great wealth was made in the manufacture of kerosene, but his deeper interests were political and social. In the 1840s, he was a New England organizer of the antislavery Free Soil Party. In his youth, he was an intimate of the educational pioneer, Horace Mann. Others among those he called his "prophets" included Samuel Gridley Howe, for his work on the Underground Railway; radical theologian and humanitarian Theodore Parker; and abolitionist U.S. Senator Charles Sumner, the great grandson of farmer Joshua Hersey of Hingham. In the last of the lay sermons he preached in Hingham, Downer eloquently expressed his humanitarian faith: "In these thoughts of mine there are no ologies or isms, but only those sympathies and feelings innate in the human heart, that well up and gush out in every consciousness and meet a common sympathy." He was something of a philosopher-king, a benevolent patriarch, whose final creation was his own little kingdom on Crow Point.

Here he named streets after his "prophets," Howe, Mann, Sumner, and Parker, and after beloved family and friends, Malcolm, Marion, Merrill, and Scudder. Crow Point hill became "Mount Gertrude" after his daughter, and Mann Street was on "Mount de Wolfe," after his wife's father, "Nor'west John," an old clipper captain and the first American to cross Siberia to Europe by land.

Downer's little kingdom arose as if by magic. Since settlers first used it, Crow Point had been hay, pasture, and farm land, joined to distant Hingham only by a narrow cartway sometimes under water. In the 1850s, Downer bought forty-three acres from entrepreneurs as the site for a kerosene factory, a might-have-been to trouble the sleep of zoning boards. After the Civil War, he had a better idea.

In the autumn of 1869, young newcomer John D. Long wandered the Crow Point hills and mused in blank verse:

> *The furrows of the earth just ploughed and fresh*
> *With all the fragrance of the new-turned sod;*
> *The sheep that herded closer when we came,*

Stand picturesquely grouped upon the ledge
And scan us with grave eyes; the cattle love
The sun, and saunter feeding here and there,
Unconscious that they grace the hillsides now . . . .

Twenty months later, sheep and cows had new marvels to scan, and so did George Lincoln when he and old Leavitt Sprague rode over in Fearing Burr's carriage on June 23, 1871, to see the fantastic rise of "Downersville." Work had begun in the fall of 1870, with the constructing of a new wharf, the laying out of streets, and the building of Downer Avenue. Downer had an agreement with farmer Charles Cushing, who owned eight acres, now Cushing Avenue, to develop their adjacent lands. Downer dug wells, laid stone drains, and built a sea wall. By June, 1871, cottages were "springing up like mushrooms," and at the end of the Point rose a resort hotel.

The chief marvel materialized on the small peninsula northeast of Walton Cove, where buildings were "being erected near the grove for the accommodation of pleasure parties." It was named Melville Garden, after the family of Downer's mother-in-law. Mrs. Downer's cousin was the novelist Herman Melville. Their grandfather was Major Thomas Melvill, a member of the Boston Tea Party and a Revolutionary War soldier. The Garden opened in July, 1871—admission ten cents—open to the public every day but Mondays and Thursdays, which were reserved for large picnic parties. Each spring, new structures were eagerly greeted. The Rose Standish House, the hotel, was too small from the start. In 1873, there were cots in the halls, and in 1874, the capacity was doubled to eighty rooms, with a dining hall for 150, a billiard hall, laundry, and "Vue de L'Eau Cafe" on the wharf. Next year, undeterred by the depression, Downer added a playroom and gym for children— some would remember him as "Papa Downer"—and a piazza for their elders. No wonder the Rose Standish House became the "select family resort of Boston Bay."

A short walk under a canopied walkway known as "the shades" brought guests to Melville Garden. New buildings sprang up for the flying horses of the merry-go-round, a bowling alley, shooting gallery, and dining saloon; a floating wharf served boating parties. When Downer managed to buy land on the other side of Walton Cove, he built a fenced dam that also served as a covered bridge at the mouth of the Cove to improve swimming and boating. On the southwest side rose three immense buildings: a cafe-dining hall with a clocktower, a music hall for dining and dancing to be used by private parties, and a clambake pavilion. By 1875, the Garden covered six acres, and every foot of the ground is decked off most pleasingly with tents, houses, retreats, bowling alleys, lunch stands, shaded bowers, rocks, hills, flowery dales, a huge dance hall, with Edmands' Band daily, and a grand dining hall that will easily seat one thousand. At the latter a fish dinner consisting of clam chowder, steamed clams, fried and battered clams, bluefish etc. is given at 12 and 4 each day Sundays included for 50 cents . . . . The past week from 1500 to 2000 per day have visited this magnificent resort . . . . Steamers leave Rowe's Wharf six times daily for Downer Landing, fare 25 cents.

In 1876, Downer bought Ragged Island. A side-wheeled, hand-propelled boat, the *Melville*, connected the Garden with a cafe and pavilion on the island. Then he added land across Downer Avenue, and visitors could cross by an elaborate overhead footbridge to the monkey house, duck pond, ice cream saloon, and bear house, and to "rural woodland" for escapist picknickers. In all, Downer spent as much as $250,000 on land and another $160,000 on the Garden.

MELVILLE GARDEN,

DOWNER LANDING, . . . BOSTON HARBOR.
OPEN EVERY DAY EXCEPT MONDAY.
One of the Finest Harbor Resorts in New England.

The Garden contains First-class Restaurant, Bowling and Shooting Alleys, Billiard Tables, Patent Swings, Flying Horses, Camera Obscura, Menagerie, Bear Pit, &c. Row Boats and Yachts to let.

RHODE ISLAND CLAM BAKE at 12, 4 and 6.30 o'clock. DINNER TICKETS, 50c.
EDMANDS' BAND, DAY AND EVENING.
The Garden will be Illuminated Every Evening with 20 Electric Lights
Grand Concert by Edmands' Band Every Sunday Afternoon and Evening.

HINGHAM STEAMERS LEAVE ROWE'S WHARF at 5.45, 9 15, 10.30, 11 30, 12.30, 2.30, 3.30, 5.30, 6.30, 7.45 and *9.30. RETURNING, LEAVE DOWNER LANDING at 7, 7.35, 9.45, 10.35, 12.15, 1.15, 4, 5.15, 6.45, †8.30. †9 30. CROSS TRIPS to and from NANTASKET BEACH. Leave Downer Landing at 11.20, 12.20, 1.20 and 4.20. Leave Nantasket Beach at 9.30, 12, 1, and 4.50. SUNDAYS. Boston to Downer Landing at 10.15, 2.15, 4.45, and 7.15. Downer Landing to Boston at 12, 3.30, 6, 9.30. † Mondays excepted. * Saturdays excepted.
☞ BUY THE EXCURSION TICKET at Rowe's Wharf, 60 Cents. ☜ (over)

A Melville Garden trade card listing the Garden's amenities and schedules in 1880.

The crowds came, by steamer or by gaily painted pleasure wagons, "barges." In 1877, steamers touched at the Landing twelve times daily, and eighty thousand people visited. On the evening of July 4, 1879, with more than four thousand on hand, Melville Garden reached a peak of fantasy. Gas lamps on the avenue and in the Garden gave a "brilliant light and very beautiful effect through the foliage of the trees," lighting up the rocks and waters of cove and harbor "like a scene of fairyland." So it must have seemed to the countless organizations that came: religious groups, lodges, and workingmen's associations. And to the youngsters!

One youngster remembered at ninety-five the long-ago days when she, Mrs. Nellie Fee Kelly, was a "holy terror":

> There were ten children in our family, and we all had chores to do. I remember that the Garden opened early in July and Father used to say, "If you get all the hay in, I'll give you each a quarter and you can go over to the Garden." [One day at eight or nine, she] found the door of the monkey house ajar. I climbed in and the door slammed shut behind me. Apparently the monkeys were as scared of me as I was of them, for they made no attempt to harm me . . . . When, after a frantic search, someone finally found me, my father's only comment was, "too bad you didn't keep her in there."

A somewhat older Nellie put on her sister's stockings and dress to look grown-up, and from a spot near the bandstand she watched the players in Edmands' band. Finding the one she liked, she married him.

The fortunes of her clan were tied to Downer. Her father, James Fee, owned a farm on Planter's Field Lane; her uncle, Cornelius Foley, managed the Downer farm, where Mrs. Foley ran the dairy that supplied the Garden. Foley was a trusted manager; Downer named the entrance building after him. Foley's daughter married the Garden's assistant superintendent, a brave young man from Hull named Washington Irving James. After the wedding at St. Paul's and a reception at Foley's home on Downer Avenue, Samuel Downer threw the lucky slipper at the happy couple as they departed for the cottage at Melville and Alice Walks, the Garden entrance, where they would live. Wash James received good training for his later life as chief of police by controlling rowdyism at the Garden. Downer's superintendent, his son-in-law James Scudder, was well-known as a keeper of tight control. Hingham citizens were regularly assured of his efficient management, part of Downer's persistent efforts to stay on good terms with the town.

When Downer died in 1881, his marvel lived on. Under Scudder's direction, it flourished for another fifteen years, attracting even greater numbers. As a financial investment, so Downer's old friend claimed, the venture was unsuccessful, probably because Downer had subsidized it so heavily. He had built a fantasy park and playground for people of small means, kept prices low, and sustained it through years of depression. But "in the light of the intentions of its projector," it was "a decidedly humanitarian success," and it lived on as a "monument to his philanthropy" through the season of 1896.

For Hingham, Melville Garden was a profitable and cheap investment, most of all for the Boston and Hingham Steamboat Company. The company's stock paid a 10 percent dividend in 1881. But the directors had bigger markets in view. In July, 1880, their new *Nantasket* carried eighty thousand round-trippers to Nantasket Beach. In the 1880s there were again two steamboat lines. As more excursion steamers were built, they grew larger and even more elegant. The *Miles Standish* (1895) had a feather bucket wheel and 160 electric lights. On July 4, 1894, twenty-five thousand celebrated at "Boston's Coney Island," Nantasket. They had come by steamer, but also by railroad.

By then, the summer vacation world had reached far beyond Hingham and Nantasket. The conjurer responsible was the railroad. Steamboats had churned into the quagmire of postwar financial speculation, where railroad was king. As early as 1870, plans were afoot to extend the coastal track south from Cohasset. Between 1871 and 1874, the line leapt to Greenbush, Marshfield, Duxbury, Kingston, and Plymouth. The fast growth beyond Hingham is sadly symbolized by what happened on October 7, 1872. The ninety-room Old Colony House, relic of earlier local ambitions, was wrapped in flames, its walls and roof fell in, and in two hours nothing remained but smoldering ruins. A newly delivered mother, her children, and the clerk were alone and got out safely. The proprietor and others were away, off to Duxbury for a celebration on the new rail line.

By 1875, Cape Cod travel had assumed enormous proportions. By 1879, the Old Colony owned all South Shore Rail stock and the Narragansett Steamship Company, and a new resort world was opening: Oak Bluffs, Wood's Hole, and Martha's Vineyard. Hingham would not become the world's "most popular summer resort."

The South Shore saga was a chapter in a national epic. In the summer of 1867, while rival steamers raced for Hingham, thousands of laborers—Chinese "coolies," Irish immigrants, Civil War veterans—raced from California and the Great Plains to link the Central Pacific and Union Pacific Railroads and join a nation coast to coast. In May, 1869, the telegraph flashed the news: they had met in the Utah desert. Local imaginations followed the trail. WESTWARD HO! was the cry, and ARE YOU GOING WEST? was the question when New England economies sagged. The *Journal* printed letters from "The West," enticing offers of railroad bonds, ads for millions of acres of cheap farmland. Former Universalist pastor John Cargill wrote from Kansas, where he farmed for a living and preached when he had a chance. From west of Denver came shocking news that Jotham Lincoln, Jr., had been killed by "Indians" on his ranch. In June, 1869, Rev. Calvin Lincoln of the First Parish was welcomed home from a five-thousand-mile railroad vacation in the South, Midwest, and Canada. As the Republic closed its first century, Charles Cushing decided to see for himself. He took the train to California and back.

Locally, the railroad grew and prospered. The "iron monster" had become part of Hingham life before the war, but then its noisy invasions had belied the small size of its business. In 1867, one car attached to the passenger train brought all of Hingham's freight. Ten years later, a daily freight train left carloads for South Shore distribution at the new freight yard on South Street. By 1883, two freight trains left their "dumps" at the yard. In 1867, two or three passenger cars sufficed on the busiest trains. By 1879, some had six or eight, and in summers of the mid-1880s, there were eighteen daily passenger trains to and from Boston.

The trip, however, was slow and circuitous: from Cohasset via three Hingham stops, through East Weymouth to Braintree, and a wait there to be drawn into Boston on the main line. For some villages, it was even worse. A glance at county maps of 1867 and 1884 shows that South Hingham, in spite of its industrial activity, was in a large area utterly without rail service. How were such places expected to compete in a cutthroat age without equal access? South villagers demanded their rights. When a new line was proposed from South Scituate, Liberty Plainers applauded. "We'll have a railroad of our own, and when . . . the iron horse comes whizzing up to the Depot, located in the vicinity of Queen Ann's corner, we can just . . . snap our fingers in the direction of your Depot." They were tired of "cruising about at right angles," being obliged to "*wiggle* themselves to Boston." The new line, originating in South Scituate (Norwell), would follow Main Street north from Queen Ann's Corner, cross over near the ropewalk (on Central Street), travel west to Fort Hill and north along the Beal Street turnpike to Beal's Cove, and cross the Back River, North Weymouth, and Quincy Point to Wollaston. Capital was needed from investors in the towns to be served. Only Hingham capitalists refused to go along.

Meetings began in 1869 and continued for five acrimonious years. Old Colony Railroad supporters attacked the idea as "most chimerical." Advocates attacked "avaricious stockholders" and found it "most horrible to contemplate" that the project "should be strangled to death in the home of its friends." Would the *town* buy stock? Deeply divided meetings voted NO. Opposition was directed at the very precedent of a town's taxing itself for large public enterprises. Thus, the groundwork was laid for rejecting a public water company. Opposition also revealed a new defensive posture of the town. Closer links to Boston might "destroy the wholesome, ancient, and independent character of our good old town, and merge it into a common-place suburb, new and tawdry with the cheap show and close admixture of a lodging house for the overflow of the city."

The politics of transportation had reared its ugly head, as it would again at the time of the "electrics." It was doing so already over that most local means of moving about, roads. In 1870, it made sense from the perspective of North Hingham to extend Lincoln Street from Crow Point Lane to Back River, and Cottage Street to the Cove, where business was growing. It made sense, when Agricultural Hall became a social center, to lay out Winter Street along the Home Meadows. But when south villagers argued their need for a straight road from Cold Corner to South Street, controversy over its costs ensued. Embattled, they reduced their request to a road ending at Elm Street, where the South Street estates of Royal Whiton and Norton Quincy Thaxter stood in the path. Finally, the town voted to share the cost with the county, and in mid-1872 work was underway on Central Street. Three and a half years later, Ellen, last of the Thaxter heirs, died young and the estate was "soon to be sold." But the matter rested for almost twenty years until the coming of the "electrics" on Main Street made it urgent to complete Central Street.

In 1877, another plea was heard. Samuel Downer had built a road below Otis Hill to Broad Cove and sought town funds to carry it across the mouth of Broad Cove estuary to Ship Street, a handsome harbor drive. Would Hingham, he cajoled, benefit, or would the current of progress turn to Nantasket with its "more active enterprise"? The town was charmed again by this siren song, but hesitated. Finally, funds were voted to add to the private subscription. Broad Cove was bridged and partially dammed, Otis Street was laid to Ship Street, and the town had its shore drive for under $3000.

In these years of "rages" and "manias," the "road mania" was the most costly. Who were the roads for, anyway? many Hinghamites asked. For us? For wealthy summer people? For hordes on their way to nearby resorts? People saw the traffic increase and lamented "the town's nearness to a great summer resort, and the constant traffic to which our streets are subjected." By July, 1880, 117 carriages passed the junction of Water and Summer in forty-five minutes. On a July Sunday, 174 teams passed the Cushing House in an hour. Roads were neither safe nor convenient. Wind down East Street or along Hersey Street in 1990 and imagine roads narrower, more winding, less level, covered only with gravel (if, after a storm, at all), with rocks as the glacier had left them, obtruding ledges, tree limbs, mud puddles, ice patches, and dust clouds. At the "sharp rise" on East Street, two vehicles could barely pass. Down Hersey Street, loaded with woodenware, came David Cushing's express. The driver heard the train, couldn't stop, and turned sharply and disastrously onto South Street. Frightened runaway horses were common. The congestion of teams forced pedestrians to dodge horses' heads and risk being tangled in carriage wheels. Faulty roads brought damage suits. Safety and prudence demanded repairs and alterations.

The problems grew, and so did the costs. In 1870, eight of thirty-three town meeting articles concerned road work; the next year, fifteen of thirty-nine. In 1876, it took four sessions to wrestle through sixty-eight articles, twenty-nine about roads, many instigated by citizen petition. The system of supervising roads kept changing; some charged there *was* no system. Up to 1868, men were allowed to "work off" their highway taxes by doing repairs themselves; one can imagine the "dumping," "smoothing," "tinkering up dangerous places." The selectmen were supervisors of roads, paying themselves to do some of the work. In 1871, supervisors were elected, but they spent huge sums and were investigated.

Citizen revolt against this "mania of road-straightening" was inevitable. "Reckless extravagance" would "repel new inhabitants, if indeed it does not drive out some of our heaviest tax-payers and best citizens." But weren't such expenditures needed to *attract* new inhabitants? The dilemma forced soul-searching but could not be resolved. In 1876, a year of rebellion, when citizens created a Board of Auditors to check extravagance and when cuts in school funds threatened payments for fuel and teachers' salaries, the town still voted money to lower the grade of Pear Tree Hill.

Opposition orator Luther Stephenson, Jr., warned that a town "constantly burdened with schemes for straightening roads, erecting bank walls, and demolishing old landmarks is building not to delight, but to disgust, the people of the future." But then, everybody knew General Stephenson was a "Conservative," a Democrat. The battle went to the heart of public policy:

> The plea of public good is made to cover a multitude of sins . . . . And what does the public good amount to? Frequently only the saving of a few rods of travel to a small number of people . . . . Men are always ready to pray for a new road. They may be remiss about praying for their daily bread and for the forgiveness of their sins, but are always willing to pray for a new street.

Roads were only one of the divisive political issues of these years. There were others. That the town held together as well as it did was due, in part, to the new social spirit and to the influence, in particular, of one political townsman.

CHAPTER THIRTEEN

The Political World of John Davis Long

I N Hingham, as in other old New England towns, the arena in which political issues and choices were thrashed out was still the town meeting. Town meetings were still all-day, all-male affairs. First in the morning came the election of town officers, and then, after a lunch break, remaining articles were debated all afternoon. The attendance grew so large that in 1872 meetings were moved from the town house to Agricultural Hall, and here too, in the fall, voters—all male—came to vote for state and national officials. The occasional unpleasantness of town meetings is hinted at in a *Journal* appeal of March, 1872: "We trust that the meeting will be characterized by a spirit of harmony, that all will act in good faith and for the best interests of the town, and that nothing will transpire to cause us shame, or regret." Political realities sometimes made this ideal of harmony, so desirable for a sociable era, impossible to realize.

At the meeting of 1879, rebellion flared. In highly unusual moves, the selectmen were contested for reelection and removed as Overseers of the Poor, and three School Committee members were replaced. A Board of Engineers was created to manage the costly and inefficient Fire Department. Efforts were made to cut officers' salaries. The report of the selectmen was torn apart. Charles Strauss, Democratic leader (and later mayor of Tucson, Arizona), took the floor, and

> then the storm really burst, as he had the town book in his hand, and in a voice heard in every part of the hall, he commenced to comment . . . until the report of the selectmen was pretty well riddled with the speaker's small shot.

The report was sent for investigation to the recently created Board of Auditors. Business was finished by five o'clock. Astonishingly, we are assured by the *Journal* of the "almost universal opinion . . . that it was in every respect the best town meeting we have had for years, and . . . entirely free from politics." This miracle was credited to the moderator, unanimously elected and serving his seventh year.

He was lieutenant governor of the Commonwealth, and before the year ended, he was governor-elect. On November 5, 1879, a large procession, led by brass band and drum corps, marched up Cottage Street past illuminated houses. Bonfires burned, rockets and Roman candles flared in the darkness, guns fired from Powderhouse Hill. Cheers rent the air as the host welcomed one thousand celebrants. Hingham had found its hero, John Davis Long.

We can know him well because, like George Lincoln, he was a diligent diarist, starting at age nine. John D. Long's journal reveals a private, poetic lad hiding behind a jovial toastmaster. His journal was a place far from the "Chinese gong-beating" of political life, safe from being "harassed by demands," "badgered for my influence." Its fullest revelation was written in Hingham on Sunday, November 9, 1882, when he was completing his third term as governor.

> I enjoyed the absolute privacy—even the loneliness and dismal stillness of the house. I thought of . . . my boyhood and youth. I looked out on the snow-covered land—and saw the cold, clear afternoon light stream from the shining West across the hills. It recalled days when, alone and homesick in college or despairing in later youth of ever winning success, I dreamed dreams, and longed for companionship, for a divine love, for achievement and force in the world. Ah! those days of intense, interior life! Who would believe I ever lived them! I pause in a career of the most absorbing activity, excitement and labor, and wonder if it is I, who am this creature of popular interest, this football of the mob. How little the world knows me; how little it suspects that the old dreams are still hanging like mists on the hilltops—that I am still a dreaming youth!

For John D. Long, Hingham was a retreat like his journal. Yet, for forty-five years he played a dominant role in the town's life, and his style perfectly fitted the town's need. His devotion to everything unifying, everything harmonizing, is plain from his earliest political models to his final religious priorities.

He was born in Buckfield, Maine, in 1838. When just nine years old, he chose Daniel Webster as his model because he saw Webster as a reconciler against disunion. He favored Democrat James Buchanan in

1856 as a President who would "inspire harmony and good will." In 1859, he heard abolitionist Wendell Phillips speak and hated the "radical, abusive tirade" to stir up "unkind feelings and prejudices." In 1860, he supported Abraham Lincoln, whom his father did not like, in the hope that under Lincoln the Republicans would become a "conservative party" and heal national divisions. When Long was only twenty-three, his native town elected him moderator, and he found himself, as he often would later, caught in the middle. Buckfield Republicans found him too conservative; Democrats, too radical.

He thought himself a conservative, yet he would come to support causes that at the time appeared radical: women's suffrage, total abstinence from alcohol, opposition to the death penalty, and anti-imperialism. His life-long ideal of moderation can be seen in his daydream of a daughter brought up on "that perfect line between the right amount of latitude and freedom, and that of error and hazard, a woman of unbounded liberty and yet pure-minded and principled."

This man of harmony loved poetry and music. At nineteen, he wrote, "Sometimes, I have an ambition to be a poet. But I am going to be a lawyer. I don't think I am capable of being a poet." But later he would publish three books of poems, and during hectic months as speaker of the Massachusetts House of Representatives, he began a translation of Virgil's *Aeneid* and finished it in a year. He played guitar and piano, violin and flute. He sang bass in the New North choir, and his home above Hingham harbor was "filled with canaries."

Initially, it was the harbor that brought him to Hingham. He loved the sea. When he came to Harvard as a lonely, precocious boy of fifteen, he could gaze on the ocean from his sister's windows in East Boston. Nearby, as a law apprentice, he rented a fifth floor overlooking the "water far and near." In 1867, he and a friend sailed to Hingham on the *Rose Standish* and engaged board for the summer in "Mrs. Johnson's attic on Lincoln Street" (50) looking east to the harbor. After another summer, he wanted a "home in the village." In 1869, he bought seven and a half acres off Cottage Street, a house was built, and in September, 1870, he and Mary Glover, another summer resident, were married and moved in.

Within a year, town Democrats tried to nominate him for state representative, but he clung to his "independency." By 1872, he was the orator of choice at town occasions, and in 1873, at thirty-four, he became moderator. A year later, he went to the state legislature as a Republican, and his fellow lawmakers soon made him their speaker. He was famous for "push, energy, and verve"; he got business done early, yet was always "faithful, impartial, courteous, affable."

Each year in April, the Long family closed its winter house in Boston and was "carried down with our bundles, our nurse and servants and dear Baby to little Hingham." Until autumn, he commuted daily:

> Get up at six, start for Boston at seven, get there at eight, work in the office till nine. Attend Supreme Court in Waters and Waters till 10 1/2. Go to the House of Representatives and preside till one. Dine with Nelson and Julia. At two, preside again till after five. Return at 6 1/2 and get home at 7 1/2.

His father, who lived with them in these early years, imagines John hurrying to "take the cars for Hingham," walking to the house, and, "I hear your pleasant voice saying, 'Halloo, Father,' as you enter the door." In his years as governor, he sometimes came home at midnight, met by his coachman at Quincy.

Long had run for governor in 1879 against the pugnacious divider Benjamin Butler. "My campaign," he wrote, "vindictive, personal, bitter beyond example in Massachusetts, and the terrible strain of work, anxiety, and leadership has left me nervously prostrate and weak." Such conflict distressed him deeply. Yet he served for three terms before going to the United States House of Representatives in 1884. After six years there, he resisted pressure to run again, finally feeling as free as "an uncaged bird."

The saddest irony of this peaceable moderate's career came at the end. Called out of retirement by his friend President William McKinley, he returned to Washington in 1897 as Secretary of the Navy. The next year he persuaded the President to send a U.S. battleship to Havana "in a friendly way" to "exchange civilities and courtesies," a perfect Long gesture. "Remember the *Maine*"? It was blown up there. Long had to ponder "the horrors and costs and miseries" of war with Spain and to send Admiral Dewey to the Philippines. He also had the task of reining in his assistant secretary, Theodore Roosevelt, an adventurous activist totally different from Long in manner and policy. To his wife, Long wrote, "I wouldn't have had the war, and I wouldn't have been burdened with Puerto Rico or Cuba or the Philippines. They are an elephant, just as everything is an elephant that disturbs the even tenor of our national life."

Two momentous accidents shaped his last years. McKinley's first term was nearing its close when, in April, 1900, Long noted, "The Vice President business is in full swing . . . . I have told everybody when

asked that . . . I should be entirely content whether it came or not."
McKinley wanted Long. But McKinley's manager Mark Hanna had
offended the Pennsylvania and New York delegates. They blocked
Long, and Theodore Roosevelt became Vice President. The next fall,
McKinley was assassinated. Long reflected, "The slightest turn in fortune would have nominated me for Vice President, with McKinley . . .
in which case I should have succeeded him, but a miss is as good as a
mile." Hingham was not to become a President's home.

The year 1901 brought two great sorrows. His friend McKinley was
killed. And his younger daughter Helen, having lost her fight against
tuberculosis like her mother, Mary Glover, before her, was brought
home to die "in the loved Hingham home." Beside this sorrow, the
lost presidency paled. And when, on Saturday, August 28, 1915, John
D. Long died at home at the hour of Helen's death, he was remembered as "Governor Long."

Like his great predecessor Governor John Andrew, Long was a man
who cared little for appearances. But in his case, the unconcern extended to public life. His indifference to the sartorial was a subject of
affectionate fun in the press. He was teased for his straw hat on a raw,
chilly day at the agricultural fair and for poorly fitting plaid suits and
"shocking bad hats." Everyone wore hats. They indicated occupations
and subtle gradations in social status. John D. Long did not care. But
the teasers admired the man beneath:

> One could but notice the difference between mind and matter as seen
> on Tremont Street one day last week [reported the Boston *Times*].
> Hon. John D. Long, short and chubby as ever, was hurrying down
> the street. He had on an ulster which evidently was new some years
> ago. It was rusty in appearance, and the binding on it had faded
> badly. The genial ex-governor's shapely head was surmounted by a
> tall beaver hat, which had long since lost its gloss, and well corre-
> sponded with the ulster . . . . A short distance behind him was a
> young man, faultlessly dressed . . . . It was a striking contrast which
> was thus presented, but one which did the young man no good. He
> had the matter and his tailor's bills; the ex-governor had the mind and
> the bank account.

Like Andrew, too, he had an unforced congeniality and a genius for
public diplomacy. When the Hingham veterans of the G.A.R. invited
the chaplain of the U.S. Congress to speak at a memorial service in
1891, they did not discover until past the point of retreat that their
honored guest had fought as a Confederate under Robert E. Lee.
Peacemaker John D. Long sprang into the breach with a characteristi-

cally affable introduction. The ex-Confederate was warmly received. Part of Long's diplomacy was an extraordinary recall of names and faces, and when it lapsed, of graciously feigning. "And how is the old white horse?" he asked a constituent one day. "How did you happen to remember about the old white horse?" a friend asked later. "Didn't you notice the white hairs upon the farmer's coat?" Long replied.

In Congress, he was comfortable on both sides of the aisle.

> Long is a small man with short legs and a great big round bald head [observed the Louisville *Courier-Journal*] . . . . He has a great many friends on both sides of the House, and it is a not uncommon thing to see him spend hours on the Democratic side.

But his Republican principles remained intact. After joining the liberal Republican revolt led by Horace Greeley in 1872, he remained a strict party loyalist. When, in 1886, Republican Congressman John F. Andrew, the governor's son, accepted the Democratic nomination for governor, Long called it a "travesty." In an uncharacteristically acrimonious speech, he referred to young Andrew as a chip off the old block, but "only a chip." Here was state politics at its most local: Cottage Street facing off against Martin's Lane.

Finally, like Governor Andrew, Long had found in Hingham the home of his heart. It was always "such a happy, dear, sweet return to my home" for one who had said of himself, "I have a constitutional love of home." Retired from Congress, he had "such a merry walk to the Brewers' . . . on the opposite side of Hingham Harbor," with second wife Agnes, dragging their little Peirce on his sled. Agnes had been a "country girl" of refinement teaching at the high school when they met, and some would remember that "long ago evening in Loring Hall when our attention was centered upon a slender, dark-haired, vivid figure in gypsy costume, an evening when everybody noted the growing interest in the eyes of our guest of honor, the Governor of the Commonwealth."

He loved the walks through the square and over Turkey Hill, the drives with Agnes along Jerusalem Road, the "clustering in the vestibule" of New North Church, the "friendly meeting and greeting." His essential sociability found a home here in church. In his view, "the social element in religious societies is the one thing that holds them together, if, indeed, the term 'religious' is not synonymous with 'social' in its best sense . . . the mutual obligations and dependencies which constitute the brotherhood of man." And he believed in a brotherhood without exclusion. On St. Patrick's Day, 1906, he spoke to a meeting of Hingham "Hibernians":

> The generation of the Irishmen who came here, sixty or seventy years ago, were a good stock—just as good as our pilgrim ancestry, and very much like them, in some ways . . . . There is no longer any one race among us, not even the native. It is an amalgam of all nationalities, slowly compositing into the American citizen of the twentieth century.

The harmonizing influence of such a man at such a time in the history of Hingham would be hard to exaggerate.

The political world in which Long exerted this influence was a discord of issues and personalities, local, state, and national. All politics, we are reminded by "Tip" O'Neill, former speaker of the U. S. House of Representatives, is local. Regional and national politics is played out on a local stage, and local politics colors larger struggles. Moreover, politics is never merely political, but becomes entangled in moral, economic, and sociological issues.

In national politics, Long's career covered the slow and confused change from the "dance of factions" that had characterized pre-Civil-War parties to the two-party system of the twentieth century. The radical new Republican Party of the 1850s grew into a majority coalition that was dominant with few lapses for a half century or more. After the Civil War, its opposition, in shambles, was still the "Old Democracy" of states' rights and agrarian values.

Hingham Democrats called themselves "the conservative ticket." Local Democrats who ran against Long had old family names: Cushing, Hersey, and Lincoln. The irate Democrat who, in 1879, intended to burn Long's house and vented his frustration by breaking fingers off the statue of Governor Andrew, was alleged to be a Leavitt. Hingham's new Irish citizens, forerunners of a later Democratic electorate, could hardly have found a political home in a town party led by Luther Stephenson, Jr., the most outspoken of conservatives. Not until 1884, when Massachusetts had just sent its first Irish Catholic to Congress and Boston elected its first Irish Catholic mayor, were there clear signs in the state of a new Democratic Party. Not until the twentieth century was its influence marked in Hingham.

In a now strongly Republican state, Plymouth County was becoming the "prize Republican County." Among county towns, Hingham was not unusual; even Weymouth sometimes "went more Republican." Hingham's loyalties were manifest in the results of five presidential elections following the war.

1868		1872		1876	
Grant (R)	506	Grant (R)	431	Hayes (R)	591
Seymour (D)	230	Greeley (D)	129	Tilden (D)	268

1880		1884			
Garfield (R)	581	Blaine (R)	449	Butler (Pop)	11
Hancock (D)	186	Cleveland (D)	296	Prohibitionist	61

It is not possible to determine the impact on these votes of John D. Long's popularity. But the complex results of 1884 hint at its strength. Republican James Blaine, the tainted "plumed knight," was opposed by a resurgent Democratic Party under Grover Cleveland. Boston "Mugwumps," liberal Republican cross-overs to the Democrats, worked in vain for Long's allegiance. He refused. Cleveland came within a hair of winning Massachusetts, but Hingham remained loyal. The small third-party vote for Benjamin Butler is also suggestive. Butler, who was the antithesis in style and the political *bête noire* of Long, had been a radical supporter of Grant, had then split Massachusetts Republicans, and was now a Democrat. In 1884, he bolted the Cleveland party to seek the new Irish ethnic vote. In the state at large, his success was enough to lose Massachusetts for Cleveland. In Hingham, even with its sizable Irish electorate, he failed markedly. One likely cause was Long's bipartisan popularity.

On the local stage of Long's political world, town, state, and national issues vied for attention. In town affairs, Hingham was wrestling with new ideas of public policy, of what a town should do and pay for. In addition to the hosts of other issues confronting the town, two symbolic national issues were dominant in local politics. Both of them were of cardinal importance to Long, and for him, both became lost causes. These were temperance and the rights of women.

The campaign for temperance in America during these decades has been called a "symbolic crusade" of symbolic politics, much as the crusades for and against abortion rights became a century later. On its negative side, the temperance campaign had a Nativist bias against the immigrant Irish; it was an anti-tavern drive that "bullies a poor man and toadies to wealth." On its positive side, as we will see, it served as an umbrella for progressive causes. In any case, for three decades after the Civil War, it dominated state and local politics.

Should the state try to enforce its prohibition law or grant towns the local option to issue licenses? Until 1875, this question surfaced annually in the Massachusetts legislature, and annually the answer veered back and forth. Should the town issue liquor licenses? As state law kept changing, Hingham debated this question in alternate years until 1875, and thereafter, every year. John D. Long stood firmly in support of legal prohibition. A majority of townsmen disagreed. Characteristically in favor of local control, they nonetheless joined Long in voting through the 1860s and 1870s not to grant liquor licenses. Nearby towns usually did the same. In 1872, for example, only Quincy voted to license, and briefly the futility of local control became evident. Weymouth beer peddlers simply set up their shack on the Quincy side of the bridge.

Constables periodically raided illegal stills and home taverns. Enterprising Mrs. Caroline Williams won notoriety for her "groggery at the Cove." Edward Margetts and Francis Overton, keepers of ice cream and oyster saloons, were convicted of selling cider and beer. Overton sold out and moved to Waltham, but two years later he was back, and Hingham kept its "ice cream autocrat" for half a century. Apothecary J. L. Hunt lost his appointment as town liquor agent, but continued to sell "patent medicines" such as 90 proof alcoholic Jamaican ginger and Lydia E. Pinkham's Vegetable Compound, alcoholic content 21 percent.

The old hotel at Broad Bridge had a checkered career in these difficult times. Built in 1770, the house had served as the private residence of Col. Nathan Rice, son-in-law, shipping partner, and next-door neighbor of Elisha Leavitt. By 1821, it was the home of Jairus Lincoln; his son Henry Ware Lincoln, a Hingham pharmacist half a century later, was born in the room where he would stay as a hotel guest in 1874. In the 1830s, the house was the tavern of coaching partners Isaac Little and Thomas Morey. When taverns came under attack, they turned it into the Union Hotel. By 1864, Little was dead, Morey had moved away, prohibition made its survival precarious, and it changed hands often. As Drew's Hotel, it was "pressed too hard for selling rum," and in 1872, Drew sold out to his young stable-keeper George Cushing.

The respectable sighed with relief. "Mr. Cushing believed that a hotel in Hingham could be supported without making it a nuisance and a curse." He set a model of stylish renovation at "the Bridge" by adding a mansard roof, Italian awnings, a laundry, billiard room, and piazza. The space where stage coaches had once driven under the buttonwood trees was replaced by a lawn. But even Cushing had his troubles. He was no teetotaler, but in the great "reform" year of 1876, when the "temperance tidal wave" swept over Hingham and other towns, he took the pledge. A fellow arrived to stay overnight and needed a drink. George kept a little "in case of sickness." Next day, the fellow was

[181]

joined by "friends" with the same need. They were witnesses, of course, and Cushing paid his fine.

In 1876, Hingham men organized a Reform Club, and Hingham women formed a branch of the Women's Christian Temperance Union (the W.C.T.U.) to oppose licensing. Until 1880, the town repeatedly rejected licensing. But from 1880 on, the debates grew more complex, and the town's ambivalence is seen in a see-saw of votes: *yes* to licensing in 1880, 1884, 1886, 1887, 1889, 1891, 1893; *no* to licensing in 1881, 1882, 1883, 1885, 1888, 1890, 1892, and 1894.

In licensing years, advocates of temperance, this "greatest of all reforms," believed that drunkenness and disorder increased. In 1883, the town having voted two to one against licensing, a law and order meeting was held at Loring Hall to insist that the selectmen bring their "full weight" against the illegal sale of "intoxicating liquors." The speakers included Governor Long. At Wilder Hall, South Hinghamites started their own temperance society. Temperance members of the Congregational Church met with the Reform Club. Reform Club members opened a room in Abbot's Hall on South Street, where coffee could be purchased on any evening at a moderate price. But such societies were controversial and divisive. Reform Club meetings were disrupted, just as Baptist and Methodist meetings had been earlier in the century. The zeal of temperance groups aroused hostility. The proprietors of some of the town's prize assets, the Cushing House, the Rose Standish House, Melville Garden, and Overton's, licensed from time to time, were targets of this zeal. "Spotters" testified to violations in court, but even many temperance advocates saw "spotting" as entrapment, harmful to their cause and sometimes an act of hypocrisy or spite, and cases were quickly discharged.

In 1887, almost 80 percent of the towns in the Commonwealth voted not to license, and the next year, Hingham followed suit by only three votes. On the following Sunday, H. Price Collier, minister of the First Parish, Republican, and temperance advocate, gave an electrifying speech at Loring Hall. This man for all seasons had himself voted against licensing, but he opposed prohibition and rejected as "pure silliness" the notion that a clergyman not supporting prohibition was like a fly in a bowl of milk. Prohibition, he said, was "the gigantic lie of our politics," a weapon antithetical to true reform, used to injure fellow townsmen. Looking to the balcony he declared, "Those Irishmen in the gallery, I dare swear, are no more inclined to break the laws of this country than were their ancestors, some of whom died to save it." There are "other devils than the wine cup." But let the selectmen and constables now enforce the law, citizens abide by it, its real authors give it truth. Not to be law-abiding is worse than being a "sot." Collier and two others of the town's most admired clergymen, Henry Miles and E. A. Horton, Unitarians all, published statements: this complex moral problem would not be cured by legislation and law enforcement, and certainly not by way of hairsplitting over what constituted an alcoholic beverage or debates over fermented cider.

The debates did not stop. The town could not make up its mind. On one issue, however, it did not waver: local control. In 1889, the town voted two to one against a state constitutional amendment for prohibition. It did so despite John D. Long's support and despite the efforts of many women, who appeared for the first time at the polls to distribute ballots though they could not vote.

The alliance of Long with women reformers reminds us that the issue of temperance was linked to the other great issue of the day, the rights of women. The Women's Christian Temperance Union had a national agenda far broader than its name implies. It "studied and agitated on issues of labor reform, prostitution, health and hygiene, prison reform, the needs of black women, drug use, international arbitration, and world peace." Its national leader Frances Willard "saw the possibility of harnessing women's newly released energies in a multi-purpose organization which might work, not for temperance alone, but for a broad welfare program appealing to women, including women's suffrage."

The two issues of temperance and suffrage had been linked since early in the century, when married women still could not sign contracts, own their own property, or retain custody of their children. The abolitionist movement gave women their first training in organized public action. The struggle for "Negro" rights intensified the campaign for women's rights. In 1848, Elizabeth Cady Stanton and Lucretia Mott called the Seneca Falls convention, and an organized women's movement was underway. State laws began to change, but at a snail's pace. Without the vote, reform would be small and slow. Susan B. Anthony decided to launch a drive for a suffrage amendment to the United States Constitution.

Then came the Civil War. A manpower shortage brought American women out of the home. War relief work drew thousands into national organizations. After the war, a "veritable domestic revolution" began to free middle-class women to enter public life:

> gas-lighting, municipal water systems, domestic plumbing, canning, the commercial production of ice, the improvement of furnaces, stoves, and washtubs, and the popularization of the sewing machine

.... Increased immigration threw large numbers of unskilled women on the labor market as cooks and nursemaids.

But suffrage leaders were soon disillusioned when Congress excluded women from the Fourteenth and Fifteenth Amendments.

The national organization split over issues of marriage and divorce, over whether suffrage would be expedited best by federal constitutional amendment or by state legislative action, and over whether to link suffrage to the temperance movement. Some leaders feared—rightly, as it turned out—that linkage would arouse further male opposition. The radical wing, the National Association, went its way with Stanton and Anthony; the more conservative wing, the American Association, joined forces with Willard's W.C.T.U. and worked state by state for suffrage and temperance. The struggle came to Hingham in the presences of three remarkable women.

First came Mrs. Phebe [*sic*] Ann Hanaford, author and editor, as temporary preacher to the Universalists. After three months of "great acceptance," she was reengaged. In February, 1868, the meetinghouse on North Street was the scene of an historic event. Ten Universalist ministers took part in the ordination service of Phebe Hanaford. The sermon was preached by Weymouth minister Olympia Brown, the first woman to be ordained in the United States and already a national suffrage crusader. Many years later, Phebe Hanaford wrote, "I was the first woman ordained in New England. I was also the third in the Universalist Church and the fourth in the world."

Mrs. Hanaford was in her mid-thirties, "neatly molded," with dark eyes set in an "amiable face." Each Saturday she traveled to Hingham from Boston. Reminiscing about those trips, she recalled one weekend in which expressman Eli Kenerson made a desperate forty-five mile drive to and from Boston via Hull to find her misplaced baggage. It contained not only the black pulpit dress to replace her grey traveling suit, but "of far more consequence . . . the sermon over which I had spent some long and weary hours." An eyewitness of her preaching described her as having "a good, sound, Baptist Christian experience"—actually she was raised as a Quaker on Nantucket—"with a bud of Universalism grafted upon it." She spoke "an earnest appeal from an earnest heart to sinners to be reconciled to God in thought, in purpose, in spirit, and in life."

> Her enunciation is full, clear, and distinct, the tones of the voice sweet and well-managed, her style rich and flowing, but not gaudy. Her gestures easy, natural, and yet forceful. As a writer her rank would be good; as an orator, high; as a Christian, highest.

She served over three years in Hingham, lecturing on temperance, fostering sabbath school outings and entertainments, gently preaching the early feminist gospel, and anticipating "the day when the ballot is given to woman and her place as a citizen is fully acknowledged." In 1870, she left to go to a parish in New Haven, where she also became the first woman chaplain to the Connecticut legislature.

The Hingham ministry of Anna Howard Shaw was briefer and, for her congregation, somewhat ignominious. She was born in England, but her father emigrated to work in Lawrence, Massachusetts, then settled his family in the Michigan woods, where Anna grew up a "young pioneer." Feeling called to become a preacher, she was the sole woman in her theology class at Boston University in 1875-78, so poor that she often lived on crackers and milk. During her last year as a student, Hingham's Methodist congregation was also poor. Unable to attract a male minister, it accepted Anna Howard Shaw's application.

> The year in the pulpit at Hingham had been merely tentative, and though I had succeeded in building up the church membership to four times what it had been when I took charge, I was not reappointed. I had paid off a small church debt, and had the building repaired, painted, and carpeted. Now that it was out of difficulties it offered some advantages to the occupant of its pulpit, and of these my successor, a man, received the benefit. I, however, had small ground for complaint, for I was at once offered and accepted the pastorate of a church at East Dennis, Cape Cod.

There, doubling as Congregationalist pastor of Dennis, she spent seven years. In the 1880s, she made several trips back to Hingham, speaking in church or at Loring Hall on behalf of women's suffrage. Finding her Cape Cod ministries too "comfortable," she earned an M.D. and worked with Boston's poor women as minister and physician. Then, through the W.C.T.U. and the National Suffrage Association, she went on to become America's unmatched woman orator late in the century, Susan Anthony's closest associate, and president of the association. For her work in World War I, she received the Distinguished Service Cross.

The older woman who had first inspired young pioneer Anna Shaw in the Midwest was the third of Hingham's feminist constellation. When Daniel Livermore replaced Phebe Hanaford as Universalist minister, it was announced that his famous wife would "sometimes preach." Soon no Hingham lecture series was complete without Mary Ashton Livermore, "one of the foremost feminists of the late nineteenth century."

[185]

A nationally known speaker, Mary Livermore was also a writer and an editor. She had begun as an abolitionist, and during the Civil War, she was a leader of the United States Sanitary Commission, forerunner of the American Red Cross. She visited hospitals and in one year wrote 1700 letters for sick and wounded soldiers. She would take down the last messages of dying men to their families and then add her own words of comfort. Almost twenty-five years later, the old mother of one of those soldiers showed Mary Livermore a tattered letter. She and her daughter-in-law had found great solace in this last letter with Livermore's added message. They had shared it with so many others that it finally had to be stitched together. Her daughter-in-law's dying request was that Mary Livermore be given her wedding ring, and the old woman had come to fulfill that promise. The solemn melancholy of the moment left the usually eloquent Mary Livermore speechless.

Part of her persuasive power lay in the fact that she was a living refutation of harsh caricatures of early suffragists. Devoted wife and mother, ardent celebrator of marriage, she was proof, said Lucy Stone, that women's suffrage would not divide families. Anna Howard Shaw preserved a fine story about the Livermore marriage, from the days when she and the Livermores shared their neighboring parishes on Hingham's North Street. Before preaching one day, Mrs. Livermore dropped her bonnet and coat on a chair. Mr. Livermore, below the pulpit with "adoring eyes," held them on his lap during her sermon. One church member asked sarcastically, "How does it feel to be merely 'Mrs. Livermore's husband'?" "In reply, Mr. Livermore flashed on him one of his charming smiles. 'Why, I'm very proud of it,' he said, with the utmost cheerfulness. 'You see, I'm the only man in the world who has that distinction.'"

The adoring eyes were not his alone. Hingham listened with rapt attention as she spoke, sometimes from the same platform with her ally in temperance and suffrage causes, John D. Long. She asked, "What shall we do with our daughters?" and lamented "Superfluous Women." She mourned a nation where taverns outnumbered schools and churches ten to one, attacked unjust property laws, and argued for job training and educational reform. One listener heard her speak for two hours without notes, displaying "exhaustive knowledge of history, philosophical research, invention . . . . It all sparkled with brilliant points and glowed with wit and illustration." At South Hingham in December, 1873, people crowded the hall to hear her treat "'the woman question' with so much delicacy and yet such firmness, that none but a bigot could object either to her presence on the platform or her argument."

However much enthusiasm Hingham may have felt for the presences and messages of its constellation of Hanaford, Shaw, and Livermore, the linkage of temperance with women's suffrage injured the latter cause severely in Massachusetts. Powerful liquor and beer lobbies influenced legislators, and the legislature repeatedly defeated a broad suffrage law.

In the 1880s, the chief public energies of Hingham women were invested in a new social outreach through their churches. The outreach included work for temperance. But the more politically complicated and explosive issue of women's right to vote lay dormant much of the time. In 1884, the Massachusetts Women's Suffrage Association met at Loring Hall, with star speakers Anna Shaw and John D. Long, and two hundred attended. Four years later, however, when Cora Scott Pond came to organize a Hingham League, a mere twenty-six, including some men, enrolled.

By 1890, Massachusetts was one of nineteen states that granted women the right to vote for school committee members. But to register, women in Hingham had to present to the selectmen every year in person a receipted bill for property or poll tax. Later, they could register for this small privilege if they signed their names next to their husbands'. Hingham records give no indication that women exercised this limited franchise.

In 1895, the legislature posed a referendum question as to whether women should be given the municipal vote, and the issue was debated before the Hingham Women's Alliance, formed out of the three Unitarian parishes. It was absurd, argued Mrs. Alice Fessenden Peterson, to think that voting would make women vulgar or less feminine. "Women who believe in the justice of women suffrage are not a sisterhood of unsexed shriekers-for-rights." Why think it is

> better to gambol meekly in our old "sphere" and be content to darn stockings cheerfully and rear children to the end of the chapter and confine our interests in the affairs of the nation to such home discussions as our lords and masters will vouchsafe us, trusting to our gentle restraining influence to assist them in voting for the right?

In reply, a "remonstrant" warned that blocks of immigrant women posed grave political dangers if they voted, and that "prejudices" and "jealousies" among women would aggravate feelings between capital and labor. The old laws of property, child custody, and equal pay, she claimed, had already been righted by "noble men." Was not woman's influence "more powerful now than it will be when she steps down from the pinnacle where man has placed her into the turmoil of politics?" A vote was taken, and two-thirds of the Women's Alliance favored the position of the remonstrant. Most of the "angels of the house" refused to come down from their pinnacles.

The following fall, just seventeen women registered to vote on the proposed law. On election day, 355 men voted "no," 163 men left blanks, and 154 men and twelve women voted "yes." All of the twelve lived in North Hingham. Three represented different kinds of feminism. Martha A. L. Lane, vice president of the Alliance, was a traditionalist who opposed commercial courses in the high school and delighted that Hingham's days of "commercial activity" had ended. But with a "brave liberalism in thought," she voted "yes." The second was a woman of property of a different sort, eccentric shopkeeper and Universalist Miss Susan R. Gates. Third, Alice Fessenden Peterson, who protested the common abuse of horses and abjured the "unlovely" new electric streetcars, said of suffrage, "it will come."

It did come, but not until a quarter of a century later. Susan B. Anthony's constitutional amendment, which had been introduced annually in the U.S. Congress, virtually disappeared between 1896 and 1913. Of the four principals of our story, John D. Long and Mary Livermore died well before the Nineteenth Amendment passed Congress in June, 1919. It passed just days before Anna Shaw, who had carried on Anthony's crusade, died in July. Of the four, only Phebe Hanaford lived long enough to know that the amendment was ratified in August, 1920.

Governor John D. Long (1838–1915).

Reverend Phebe A. Hanaford (1829–1921).

Reverend Anna Howard Shaw (1847–1919).

Mary A. Livermore (1820–1905).

Yellow warbler on a dogwood spray: watercolor, Isaac Sprague (1811–1894). Sprague's botanic art is closely associated with two renowned naturalists. Sprague accompanied J. J. Audubon on his last wilderness journey, along the Missouri River (1843), painting backgrounds and plants. For forty years, Sprague also illustrated the works of botanist Asa Gray. The first edition of Sprague's WILDFLOWERS OF AMERICA was published in 1882.

"Hingham Pastures": oil, Winckworth Allan Gay (1821–1910). Gay studied, lived, and traveled far from his South Street home over his long and prolific career as a landscape painter. He was a great-grandson of Reverend Ebenezer and brother of Sidney Howard Gay. W. A. Gay was long remembered for his introduction to Hingham of the legendary Forget-Me-Nots.

"The Scottish Gentleman": oil, Franklin W. Rogers (1854–1917). Rogers was a well-known painter of animals who, late in his artistic career, produced an even greater number of subtle and masterful Hingham landscapes.

"Trout Fishing": oil, 1943, Frank Vining Smith (1879–1967). A South Hingham resident and skilled sailor, Smith was a nationally known painter of clipper ships and seascapes who began his career as a newspaper artist and cartoonist and who also contributed to magazines such as FIELD AND STREAM, YACHTING, and OUTDOORS. Trained at the Museum of Fine Arts, Boston, the Toronto Art Institute, and the Art Students League, New York, his prizewinning works were widely and frequently exhibited and installed in yacht clubs.

Left: Drew's Hotel prior to 1872, when it was purchased by (right) George Cushing (1841–1920), fire chief, postmaster, and hotelier. Periodically enlarged and remodeled, most notably with a mansard roof and a veranda, the Cushing House was a popular family South Shore hotel for over three-quarters of a century.

The old West School (1857) survives at 36 Thaxter Street, having been moved forward when the new West School was built in 1894.

Derby Academy classroom in 1889, now the F. Morton Smith room of Old Derby Hall.

CHAPTER FOURTEEN

Transforming the Schools

ONE issue of paramount importance to women was childhood education. In the late nineteenth century, the only political office open to Hingham women was membership on the School Committee. In a single year, male voters actually elected Ellen Thaxter and Adeline Whiton to the committee, making them the first women to hold elective office in the town's history. The year was 1874, a crucial moment in the transformation of Hingham's schools.

Three other women lived long enough to record in 1969 and 1971 in their own voices their memories of school in the Hingham of the 1880s. Like many schoolchildren, they remembered chiefly the teachers they loved or feared, subjects they hated, wrongs they suffered. Helen Thomas was born in 1875.

> I first went to a little private school taught by Miss Elizabeth Bates, and it was in one part of a store, the same location where Charlie Cushing's is now. Her father was one of the Select Men in Hingham. Then I went to the *old* Centre School. The grammar school was upstairs and the primary school downstairs, and back of that was another building with the intermediate school. The primary school teacher was Miss Irene Lincoln . . . we all loved her. We used to watch for her when she was coming up the street . . . . Then I went over to the intermediate school . . . and I was there for three years. Then I went to the grammar school upstairs. I had two different teachers—a Mr. Andrews, he was a nice teacher but he had an awful temper . . . . After he went, we had a Mr. Litchfield . . . . He was awfully nice. He and I used to play piano duets.

Nettie Gardner Loring, born in 1877, had her troubles at South Mixed School, where all ages met together and one teacher "taught the whole thing, just as I did when I was teaching . . . . I had forty-three students."

> Don't write this down, but I was a very bad acting child. Always was stood in a corner. And I was expelled from school. The superintendent was a classmate of my aunt's at Bridgewater Normal School, and he says, "You know, she isn't bad. They don't give her enough to do." . . . Isn't that awful? . . . Mary Lane's the one that expelled me. I did dressmaking years after, and I always used to sew for her, and . . . she says, "Well, you know, Nettie, sometimes the ones that act the worst when they're young are the smartest when they grow up." I never made a murmur or changed my expression.

Hattie Shute Wilder, born in 1879, went to the "new" old South School.

> Oh, I hated to go to school . . . . I hate to tell you, but we were awfully *active* . . . . I remember we were taking a test on music and we had to sing—La Do Sol See So Fa, and then backwards. And I'd get halfway through and "I can't do it," I said three four times, and the teacher was pinching me all the time . . . . Never forget her. Fannie Oscar Cushing . . . she was a holy terror! She'd as soon slap your face . . . . And she did that to my sister the first day she went to school 'cause she didn't know the word *fan* . . . . We used to have a habit of saying, "McClellan *he*" [the Civil War general], and then we'd get a call-down. "You don't need both." I hated that worse than anything. I liked the "way back" history . . . . Sargie Cushing and I went to school together . . . . He sat up back there and he didn't care whether he learned anything at all.

Like them or not, schools were the most important social institution of the later nineteenth century. As church and home began to lose their traditional roles, schools were expected to develop citizenship, cultivate character, and prepare for life. At mid-century, the public schools were far from ready. American orators sang their praises as the bulwark of democracy, but the bulwark was flimsy. Only twenty weeks of school attendance per year were required by Massachusetts law, and the law was weakly enforced. In Hingham, as elsewhere, some children worked in factories or stayed home for chores.

Anyone sentimental about the old one-room schoolhouse would be shocked by a time-warp visit to Hingham schools in the 1860s. There were thirteen "schools"—that is, schoolrooms—in eight buildings, one school to a story. On Thaxter Street was a two-school building (still there next to Thaxter Park), and on South Street a one-school. At Elm and Main Streets was a three-school house, and at Friend and Main Streets, a two-school. At School and "Back" Streets stood the two houses remembered by Helen Thomas; the larger survives as the Tree and Park building. At the town's far ends, at Main and Gardner Streets and on Canterbury Street, were the "mixed schools." Here all children met in one room. The other schools were beginning to be "graded," but a grade covered three years, Primary one to three, Intermediate four to six, Grammar seven to nine. With the grammar grade, public school years ended.

The curriculum was a traditionalist's dream: reading, copy-writing, grammar rules, spelling, arithmetic, geography. A few subjects were added in the grammar grade: Latin, algebra, and a "little natural philosophy" (science). All subjects were taught by *the* teacher; the teacher, if male, was paid a bit over $500 a year; if female, from $250 to $382. Former teacher Jairus Lincoln remembered the old system of examination. For weeks, each student was coached in one paragraph to read, one word to spell, one problem to solve. If, on the day the examiners came, one student was absent, the whole sequence was thrown off and the "cat was out of the bag."

Try to imagine all those pupils in a single room, poorly lit and ventilated, with one "schoolkeeper" to teach all subjects. Or hear what the 1871 School Committee said: "It is *shameful* to pack more than fifty active, restless children into an ill-ventilated room, 26' long and 18' wide." No wonder that the Centre primary teacher believed, "Order is Heaven's first law," or that the West Grammar School's teacher had for a motto, "Work—constant, hard work." Rote memorization and drill dominated the pedagogy; one school committee called it "the teaching of idle minutiae," the "mechanical impress of stereotyped forms." Attendance was poor. Many students came and went as jobs and parents dictated, two or three days a week, two or three weeks a term. Teachers could not know whom to expect and had little time to notice who came. The awakening of Hingham's pride in its schools was far in the future. In the proportional funding of education, it was 198th among Massachusetts towns, in part, of course, because Derby Academy was privately funded.

But the situation statewide was also dismal. The Common School movement had been born in Massachusetts in 1837, thanks to leaders such as Horace Mann and Charles Brooks, a former pastor of New North Church. In 1852, Massachusetts had led the states in making attendance compulsory. The idea was romanticized; as one historian comments, "the idealist notions of the Common School seemed to border on the absurd." By the end of the Civil War, enthusiasm had waned, and critics began to discover how ineffectual the schools were. Some segments of the Catholic Church were starting a campaign for a parochial alternative, and to fuel the drive, they disparaged the public schools. It was not hard to do so. Towns gave meager financial support; parents and physicians feared for the health of schoolchildren; truancy was rife. Without child labor laws, compulsory attendance was a "sham." The state reacted slowly, but in the 1880s the parochial challenge provoked efforts to regulate and improve. By the 1890s, a "new spirit" was abroad.

The spirit had first come to Hingham twenty years earlier. For a brief, inspiring time, the town was a leader in school reform.

The first step was taken in 1871: the town at last established a high school. We know where and when it was built: on new Central Street near what was still known as Cold Corner, dedicated in May, 1872, and opened in September. The interesting question is why. Familiar answers fail to tell the real story. In 1855, when Hingham reached four thousand in population, state law required a "school for the entire town" to teach advanced "classical" subjects. By 1871, the town had failed to comply for sixteen years, but so had almost forty other towns. As of 1865, the state denied to noncompliant towns their share of state school aid, but as the School Committee noted, the aid was a mere "pittance" anyway. There seems little reason to suppose that after sixteen years the town abruptly suffered qualms about illegality, or that the "pittance" made a difference, or that forty to forty-five students constituted a significant need, especially since a bare handful went on to higher education.

The usual explanation for the delay is that Derby Academy had served since its opening the purposes of a high school. We read that the town tried twice to "ascertain whether" Derby could be used to satisfy the law, and that when both efforts failed, the town reluctantly went ahead. When the first effort was made in 1855, the Derby trustees sought legal counsel. They were advised that, under the terms of their trust and incorporation, they could not surrender control of the academy to the town. The answer seemed final. Who reopened the question, and why?

The 1893 *History* was diplomatically vague. The trustees "in a friendly and liberal spirit" were "desirous of taking any consistent action which would bring the Academy into harmony and concert with the town schools." School Committee reports of the 1860s give a livelier picture. They allude to "that institution, which has often been regarded as a disturbing force to the prosperity of the public schools," and criticize it for lowering standards to draw off students from North and West Grammar Schools. Town and academy were competing for students to the detriment of already poorly supported public schools. Would making Derby a "high school" further erode that support?

Derby, too, was in trouble. Its endowment was drastically devalued by war inflation. It was having trouble hiring and keeping teachers. Its drive for students was making it a mixed school of limited quality. Its trustees feared that the opening of a public high school would threaten its very survival. As feared, the high school took away most of Derby's advanced students. In the late 1880s, it graduated ten; in 1899, only one. The academy survived by opening an intermediate, and then a primary, school, and went on to flourish in the twentieth century in its distinguished new identity, no longer a "town academy."

The renewed negotiations of 1870-71, then, must have been somewhat desperate. What happened next was fully reported in the *Journal*, though reporters on both sides were angrily biased. In February, 1871, the School Committee published its recommendations, assuring the town that Derby would answer all the purposes of a high school and that the trustees had agreed to a plan whereby it would be overseen by the town. The town in turn would pay $1500 toward Derby's costs; the trustees, $2000. Conceding that the plan would leave South Hingham children unprovided for, the School Committee proposed adding one woman teacher to the South Grammar School. She would receive $600; the Derby teacher, $1800.

Signs of a storm were seen at once. One critic charged that Derby was "far behind the times" and would not serve as a high school. It was a grammar school with younger pupils unqualified for advanced studies. The plan was "utterly unfair" to South Hingham, and the academy "should not be allowed longer to stand in the way." In South Hingham, a group of irate citizens plotted their strategy. The town meeting of 1871 was one of the most surprising on record.

The group moved to substitute for the whole School Committee report a motion establishing a high school and appropriating $20,000 for a building. What ensued was indignantly reported months later by John Snyder, New North minister, committee member, and Derby trustee. The School Committee's report

> certainly deserved more dignified treatment than the unceremonious dismissal it received . . . but the South part of the town had been stung to the quick . . . and [the report] was hustled out of doors . . . followed by the jeers of the southern members . . . . A printed set of

resolutions [appeared] . . . no man knew whence they came . . . . We were expected to act on the spot . . . . In a few moments the town had agreed to assume a debt of $20,000 . . . . All deliberations seemed paralyzed . . . a large number of gentlemen stood by in amazement and disgusted silence while this offspring of a caucus was hurried to a vote, with as much dignity as would be consistent with the establishment of a town pump!

John Cushing, leader of the South Hinghamites, remembered things differently. They had waited for years. The resolutions had been shown ahead of time to "several persons." The committee plan provided for only part of the town. Snyder responded, and while his tone was unpleasant, his concessions were revealing: "I am no better satisfied with the Derby Academy than you are. I believe it has outlasted its usefulness and is a hindrance rather than a help to our school system . . . . In good faith, with no hidden purposes," the trustees had "offered the town the use of their fund and their building." If Snyder is accurate, Derby trustees were ready to give up the academy. It is an irony of history that they were prevented from doing so, and Derby survived to become the school we know.

The high school was built, but "sectional prejudices and local jealousies" had been "wrought upon," and bitterness persisted over the "High School Folly." Other upcoming projects, such as a public water system, were jeopardized or doomed. One townsman went so far as to oppose the local subscription for the John Andrew monument because the town's citizens already had "one elephant on their shoulders." At the dedication of the school, peacemaker John D. Long did his best to celebrate it as a victory for the whole town. The keys were then handed to John Snyder, unanimously chosen first school superintendent, a fine stroke of Hingham diplomacy. But by the year's end, he had moved to his new parish in St. Louis.

The compelling argument for a high school had nothing to do with sectional jealousy. Nor did it have much to do with student demand. For the first dozen years, attendance ranged in the sixties and annual graduates numbered between eight and twelve. The first real growth came after 1885, but by then, curricular changes had been made. In 1879, the school was judged deficient in preparation both for college and for business, and practical studies and teachers were added. By 1886, one-seventh of Hingham's students were in high school, an average unsurpassed in the state. But its more pressing initial aim was different. It was needed, the School Committee argued in 1870, for its "tonic effect" on the lower schools. It would be a first step in revitalizing and standardizing the system. This aim was implicit in an action taken as the high school was being built. Hingham became one of the first towns in the state to appoint a superintendent of schools. In 1870, only seventeen towns had them. In 1872, the second superintendent, Allen G. Jennings, launched his drive for coordination and change and published his program.

Jennings had come in 1870, age twenty-seven, from Meadville Seminary, to become minister of the South Hingham parish. Meadville apparently attracted and produced men willing to challenge and change old institutions and habits. Its tie to Hingham was established in 1856, when the Rev. Oliver Stearns left the New North Church to become Meadville's president. Stearns had led in the local struggle against slavery; Jennings would lead in the struggle for educational transformation.

Jennings admitted, "There are many who shudder at the very idea of anything new . . . . It is hard to break up old customs and methods, particularly in the school room, and it can only be done by persistent and well-directed attacks." Critics found his attacks redolent of "absolute power" and Jennings himself a "well-disposed young man," but a "scandalizer" who had not been in town long. The young man persisted in his efforts to improve the staff. Teachers were required by contract to attend monthly meetings, and their attendance was reported in the *Journal*. Teachers were reappointed annually. But Jennings was not only a manager. He was an educational visionary in touch with a new spirit among reformers. The new spirit has been called "the progressive impulse," the first phase in progressive education.

Three years after Jennings took office, Francis W. Parker, the man John Dewey called "the father of Progressive Education," was named superintendent of schools in Quincy. Parker abandoned the set curriculum and introduced a new emphasis on observing, describing, drawing, and understanding. So remarkable were the effects that Quincy drew national and international attention. But by the time (1875) Parker arrived, Jennings' new program for Hingham had been published, and the supply of copies exhausted by requests from other towns and cities. It is probable that a copy awaited Parker on his new desk. He would have found it prophetic.

The Hingham School Committee evidently knew what it wanted. Before Jennings was appointed, it had taken strong stands. The mere study of grammar rules was useless for children. Geography ought to stress the world nearby, so a "scholar" would not "cite South America when asked to name a peninsula near to Hingham." The old teaching of reading had failed because it sought "mere facility in pronouncing the words." Teaching should develop children's faculties, not simply store their memories. Jennings carried on in the same vein. He attacked the "slavish use of textbooks," the teaching of spelling in isolation, the teaching of geography as mere "place names" with no ideas. His key terms were "practical" and "useful." Declaring himself a "progressive," he urged teaching "principles instead of rules, examples instead of theories," and he anticipated the Parker-Quincy emphasis: cultivate first the "perceptive faculties," second, the memory, and third, reasoning, the sequence according to a revolutionary idea: the natural mental development of children. "We complain because our scholars do not *think*, when in reality they are *not old enough to think*." He ridiculed the growing list of state-required subjects: we "cover too much"; our aim has been "not to develop the mind, but fill it up." Not all is changed.

Slowly his innovations took effect. Visitors and students from other towns indicated that Hingham schools "compare more than favorably." Teachers were learning to emphasize essentials. Attendance was improving. By 1880, Jennings began to see what he hoped for:

> a class of bright, animated faces, each eager to speak first, as an idea is awakened in the mind . . . [not as before,] an uneasy, uninterrupted row of little ones, to whom reading is a mystery, and school life a drudge from which escape, even through a truant's course, is hardly blameworthy.

The memories of Nettie Gardner and Hattie Shute remind us that there was still a long way to go, but a beginning had been made.

Truancy remained a stubborn problem. Jennings could not force the state to adopt new laws, but he would try to enforce the local ordinance that fined factory employers who hired children without their twenty-week school certificates. Ironically, his efforts were aided by the long depression of the 1870s, when a scarcity of jobs kept more children in school. But the depression also took its toll on his ambitious work. No innovative program could go far with low morale and poor support. With cutbacks in appropriations, with noncompetitive teachers' salaries, there began the annual litany of teacher turnover. In 1881, Jennings himself resigned his superintendency and his parish, and Hingham's educational pioneer moved away.

The terms of his successors, John Turgeon, William Bates, and Allen Soule, were brief, as were those of many Hingham teachers. By 1885, the town was becoming "a training school for our wealthier sister towns." In the five years 1885 through 1889, each of the four grammar schools had five young principals. School budgets were austere. In 1888, 153 Massachusetts towns spent a higher percentage of the value of their taxable property on schools than Hingham.

The number of "school-age children," from five to fifteen years old, declined. At the same time, total enrollments held relatively steady, and the high school population grew.

	age 5-15	total enrollment	high school	appropriations
1875	803	703	62	$15,000
1880	696	775	58	13,000
1885	666	713	78	14,300
1890	597	718	106	15,000

Children were staying in school longer than before. They did so for several reasons—among them, (1) the town offered them fewer factory jobs; (2) child labor laws in the state stiffened; (3) the traditional education of home, shop, and farm declined; and (4) schools were expected, even mandated, to meet increasing demands for vocational training.

"The great trouble with the present," complained the School Committee in 1881,

> is that our schools, which were founded as auxiliaries to home training in morals and manners as well as in intellectual development, are now left in too many instances to do the whole work.

The committee's frustration was apparent:

> At no recent period have so many fermenting and transitional ideas filled the Commonwealth on educational subjects. The legislature is invoked to pass aggressive laws; public opinion is violently stirred; novel projects are attempted under sensational watchwords.

The prevailing "watchword" of the 1880s was heard in the repeated challenge: "Do our schools meet the demands of practical life?" While innovators, following Jennings, pursued new goals of intellectual and moral development, some "carping critics" charged that "our common school system" was "leading our youth away from honorable paths of manly labor in the vain pursuit of a livelihood without real work"—that is, to jobs in the city as clerks and bookkeepers. These critics fought for manual training. Other critics pushed for additional commercial courses for those potential clerks and bookkeepers. In prescriptions for the teaching of arithmetic we see their thrust: students should learn to measure the *cost* of building walls and excavating cellars, to "make out bills, notes, checks, and receipts"—that is, to become bookkeepers, not carpenters. The critics agreed, however, that a male student should go forth "with a thorough mastery of some trade or calling."

Superintendent Louis Nash (1887-93) took a moderate stance. Manual training, he conceded, was a good trend. A girl could now learn sewing and cooking better at school than at home; a fourteen-year-old girl should "learn to make a good biscuit as much as she should be able to draw a correct map of Africa." Nevertheless, it was *not* "the business of any system of public education to teach to boys and girls the particular means by which they shall get a living." His successor in 1893, Elmer Curtiss, attacked the "vocational attitude" more aggressively, dismissing the expectation that "a boy or girl just out of school should be able to step into a business house or shop and pick up the work as though he had been training for that alone."

As we will see, Curtiss presided in the 1890s over fundamental physical and structural changes in Hingham education. But his new curricular emphasis came first. He noted with satisfaction a shift from "the concrete and practical vocational" to the cultural. Too much emphasis had been placed on the useful and too little on the beautiful.

The conflict between these ideals had begun in the 1880s. It had been waged over broad and complex issues of public policy. It had been waged in years when public institutions other than schools, and when new marvels of utility, began to transform the life of the town.

CHAPTER FIFTEEN

The Rise of Convenience and Safety

THE 1880s gave birth to conflicts of taste and policy which persist to the present day. Could a love of the useful coexist with a love of the beautiful? Could a new taste for unspoiled nature survive the onslaught of technologies of utility and convenience? Did a new demand for public convenience and safety warrant the restricting of private rights? Should new systems of public convenience and safety be publicly or privately owned?

The years after the Civil War abounded in inventions which would revolutionize daily life. A prodigious number of patents were granted. People came to expect safety, comfort, and convenience. The more they received, the more they expected. In Hingham during the 1880s, a safe and reliable water system was constructed. A new Board of Health struggled to control pollution and contagious diseases. The demand for safety in the streets was met with the arrival of electric lighting, but it also stirred debates over the hiring of policemen. The miracle of the telephone brought not only convenience, but also the added safety of rapid communication. And a newly efficient Fire Department, aided by hydrants and electric alarms, made some progress in the control of fires. All of these systems came to Hingham between 1880 and 1889. All were linked to each other, and frequently they impinged on each other's efficiency.

The first, a water system, was in place by the summer of 1880. Town ownership had been discussed for ten years, but the town was not the owner. In 1875, Quincy Bicknell, spokesman for a committee to investigate the feasibility, costs, and safety of Accord Pond water, offered an interesting argument. He computed the increased productivity, in dollar value, based on the assumption that a pure water supply would add a year's life for every resident. It was a new equation of human and economic value. He included quality of life and safety as goals. A water system would provide a safe supply, protect against drought, increase fire protection. Wells were often empty and sometimes contaminated by inadequate drainage and by the accelerating use of fertilizers. In dry weather, dust clouds billowed from gravel used to dress roads. Fires caused by incendiaries, lightning, or sparks from trains were a constant hazard. Combustibles such as kerosene, hay, sawdust, and straw were everywhere. A water system would alleviate such dangers and nuisances and reassure potential newcomers.

The year of Bicknell's arguments was, however, a year of depression and fiscal retrenchment, a year when the state put a cap on town debt of 5 percent of property valuation. This did not augur well for a town-owned water system. Nor did recent town conflicts. Some voters were still angry at the "High School Folly," South Hingham was smoldering at the town's refusal to invest in its railroad project, and Liberty Plainers felt "Cod Pond" was theirs.

> *Hingham, spare that pond*
> *Touch not a single drop*
> *We gun, and fish, and bathe there,*
> *And we don't want to stop.*

They had even held boat races on the pond. Between 1876 and 1878, townsmen voted five times on the issue of a town-owned water company. Each time, the vote grew more negative. At the largest meeting in the town's history to that date, the fifth vote was 323 opposed to 182 yeas.

Consequently, the Hingham Water Company was privately financed. A small group of wealthy Hingham men was free to incorporate when the governor signed the enabling law in March, 1879. The driving force was George P. Hayward. He had made extensive inquiries in towns which already had waterworks and was especially interested in the materials for mains. Over the ensuing years, the grounds of the Agricultural Society sometimes presented the unusual scene of men spreading cement on the inner and outer sides of sheet iron cylinders.

In the spring of 1880, cement barrels and pipe lined the streets in South Hingham, where trenches were being excavated. On June 23, Water Company President Ebed L. Ripley, contractor C. L. Goodhue, Fire Chief George Cushing, and George Hayward opened the water service from Accord Pond to Liberty Hall. Two days later, at 700 Main Street, John Cushing opened his faucet and became the first customer.

Within a week, gravitational flow from the South was providing the central corridor of town with its first, albeit cementy-tasting, domestic water. There was new fire protection as well, in the form of fifty hydrants, only one of them, it should be noted, on Liberty Plain. On July 4, Hingham officially received its first hose carriage, named for Isaac Little, teamster, hotelier, and first captain of "Torrent No. 4." The carriage's thousand feet of linen hose was tested at the hydrant in front of St. Paul's. The stream reached six feet above Burr Brown's flagstaff.

"Cod Pond" water supplied the Cushing House and every room at the Rose Standish House. Samuel Downer had a standpipe, hydrant, and hose carriage in place for fire emergencies. On Ship Street, George Lincoln watched a "water gang" digging a trench in front of his house, ending those anxious times when his well was either dry or polluted. The service also provided a new convenience for travelers. No public water had been available between South Hingham and Broad Bridge. Now, drinking fountains were set at the junction of Main and Friend Streets, near the Public Library, and at Fountain Square, the last a gift from John D. Long. The communal dippers, an object of concern only when they disappeared, seemed not to trouble anyone as a public health issue. Only when there was an epidemic of glanders among horses were owners warned not to let their animals drink from the horse troughs.

Accord Pond had been low in the months before service began. The pond, however, measured one-half by three-quarters of a mile and in some places was seventy feet deep. As if to disarm the skeptics, who prophesied that when the service was ready there wouldn't be any water, it rained six inches in July.

At Nantasket, by contrast, wells and cisterns were drying up, and water cost fifty cents a barrel. Some Water Company investors held interests in the Boston and Hingham Steamboat Company and in the restaurants and hotels at Nantasket. In 1881, one hundred tons of mains were laid to Nantasket pier and "the Beach." Hull and Jerusalem Road also tapped into the supply. To protect these distant places in the event of an emergency at Accord, a water tower, a steam pump, and a conduit from Weston's (now Foundry) Pond were installed. The new infrastructure took its toll of wildlife. When Fulling Mill Pond was drained and cleared for a receiving basin, an ancient turtle, weighing thirty-five pounds on a hay scale, was homeless.

In his new South Street office, from 1882 through the rest of the decade, Superintendent Charles W. S. Seymour was busily directing the installation of mains on old streets such as Hersey (1883) and new ones such as Jarvis and Burditt (1884), where faucet water was an appealing new convenience for builders and buyers. By 1890, pipes went up Thaxter Street, where the Bradleys, father and son, were creating their family compounds. Israel Whitcomb, innovative farmer and aster-grower, supervised the preparation of High Street for mains (1894), using lots of dynamite to blast granite ledge. The three hundred sub-scribers of 1881 grew to nine hundred in six years. By 1892, there were fifteen hundred customers and forty-three miles of mains. Charges were based on the number of faucets, and sharing may have been common. Every day, George Melcher reminisced, two Derby boys were sent across Main Street to Henry Harding's house to fill two buckets.

At its 250th anniversary, Hingham's favorite toastmaster, John D. Long, glowingly introduced George Hayward as the man who had given the town pure water. It had been a bold and benevolent act, and it paid off handsomely. The stock of the Water Company was among the strongest in the state and paid a $3 dividend in 1883. Soon, the twelve hundred shares were selling above par, and finally they could not be purchased. The company was stable under Seymour's management; its directors remained essentially unchanged. Debate over town owner-ship, however, continued. The charter of the company included the proviso that the town could buy the company at any time by a two-thirds vote at a meeting called for that purpose. The town could pay the initial cost of $80,000 at 10 percent interest minus dividends. It had already paid the Water Company $3000 to purchase and pay the cost of hooking up hydrants. Annually it paid the company $1500 for service to hydrants and for the water itself. The failure to purchase would haunt the town's future.

Despite the pride of "little," "backward" Hingham in having water works before Weymouth, Quincy, and other nearby towns, this first great convenience created some inconvenience. In years when rain was plentiful, run-off from marshlands around Accord Pond caused the water to taste like a "newly-shingled roof." In drought conditions, wa-tering of lawns, gardens, and newly planted trees—popular contempo-rary trends—was limited to two hours a day, with the threat of a cut-off if the rule was violated. This was an early lesson in the tension between public good and individual liberty; previously, only nature or neglect had dried up a private well. New kinds of accidents required new ad-justments: a thirty-foot stream of water shot into the air when lightning struck the road above a Summer Street main; a faucet was left open for a week in the home of Mrs. J. Sturgis Nye; during severe winters and spring thaws, pipes froze and then burst. The new convenience gave birth to a new local service occupation: plumbing. It also tore up streets. During the 1880s, the twelve-inch main which ran under the tracks at Broad Bridge had to be lowered twice. It was causing the Town Brook conduit to back up, creating a hazard to the very public health that it had been installed to safeguard and improve.

Public health was a new national priority of post-Civil-War years. Complaints about public health and amenity grew frequent in Hingham. Just after the war, the town discovered that its large and expanding new industrial neighbor on Weymouth Neck, William Bradley's fertilizer works, driven out of Roxbury as an offense to "nice-nosed people," was a mixed blessing, especially in warm weather when windows were open. As the town's visions of a summer colony took hold, town meetings were asked to take action on the "bone nuisance"—fish bones were part of the plant's raw materials. Annually, the problem was referred to a special committee. As the phosphate works grew, Bradley bought land on the Hingham side of Back River, and controversy escalated. Some scoffed at the idea that the "effluvia" were unhealthy. After all, Mr. Bradley was a "live man, as well as a perfect gentleman," and his works were running day and night to meet national demand. But a group of citizens led by John Brewer insisted that they either run harmlessly or be closed.

The problem was solved by an internal system of covered blow pipes and furnaces. But the Brewer group, in their protest, had offered perhaps the first local enunciation of a public health philosophy, of the principle of human and ecological interdependency. "Every individual," they proclaimed, "has a free heritage in the purity of air, light, and water." This was in 1870. It sounded the keynote for a growing awareness of public health in the years to follow.

One of the actions of the tumultuous town meeting of 1879 eliminated the duty of the selectmen to serve on a committee on health and created an elected Board of Health. Recent state law granted such local boards substantial powers to investigate and control health and safety hazards. Over the next fifteen years, however, the work of Hingham's board scarcely improved the two most glaring: the conditions of the mill pond and of the Town Brook. Of the members of the first five-man board, four were physicians. Their first report expressed the opinion that the conditions were not demonstrable causes of disease, although they might become so in the future. Yet there had been epidemics of diphtheria and infant cholera (a form of dysentery) in the 1870s. Complaints persisted through the 1880s. After flood tide on the mill pond, Main Street residents looked over offensive smelling de-

bris on the Home Meadows. In 1883, the state gave the town authority to take and fill the pond. This solution, however, involved complex
legal problems of "rights and privileges," the expense of damages, and
the cost of the project. Officials of the railroad, whose tracks ran on a
trestle across the pond, rejected a mutual effort. Over fifty years would
pass before the problem of the mill pond was "solved."

The pond was used to dispose of trash and garbage and to receive
run-off from households, some of them with livestock. So was the
Town Brook. Heavy rains caused the brook to overflow, turning flood-
plain meadows in West Hingham into ponds. Exceptionally heavy rains
in 1886 left four feet of water in front of Rufus Lane's house on South
Street and three feet in the basements of stores at Broad Bridge. Sidewalks caved in. Train service came to a standstill. Muskrats swam in the
brook. Such natural catastrophes were made far worse by the pollution
of the brook and the pond.

The brook's already sluggish flow was impeded in the 1870s by scum
from a West Hingham soap factory; by the washing into it, after storms,
of gravel and sand used to repair streets; and by the "cast-off hoop
skirts, tin cans, old bottles and our semi-annual increase of the feline
race." The annual reports of the new Board of Health in the 1880s
provide lurid images of the problem. The "surface wash" into the
brook "carries with it . . . a greater or less amount of contaminating
matter from buildings somewhat remote from the stream itself. Drains
emptying into it have been constructed to carry off such waters from
natural basins in the midst of the village." The board urged "immediate
cessation of all drainage from privies and water closets" and the forbidding of "pig-stys near the brook." Letters of complaint in the *Journal*
described the brook as "an open sewer" and the mill pond as "worse"
and singled out such often concealed but not unnoticed facilities as
"the piggery behind the house at the corner of North and Cottage
Street."

In 1887, a committee urged that the brook be cleared of rocks and
debris and widened and straightened by changing its course from the
north to the south side of the railroad track. Dr. Henry Spalding, physician to most of the families on North Street, objected. He felt his
records proved that these families had few medical problems; eighty-six
people who lived along the brook had survived past the age of seventy.
If the stream bed was moved to the south side, the meadows there
would not drain at all. Spalding, perhaps inconsistently with his earlier
argument, then echoed a plea, heard throughout the 1880s, for sewers.
Despite some improvement in the regulation of piggeries, the stench

and other problems continued. The 1890s brought more complaints and more committee work. Townsmen continued to reject any large or long-term solution and instead voted money for much-needed schools and authorized the treasurer to borrow $50,000 to purchase the light plant. The growth of public institutions had bred the dilemma, familiar to us now, of fiscal priorities.

The Board of Health did, however, have a positive impact. It brought health to prominence in local consciousness; its detailed reports, together with tables of illnesses provided by the town clerk, made health and illness a part of public information. It awakened the town's conscience to improve heating in the almshouse and ventilation in schools. It increased disease control, enforcing new state regulations which compelled householders to report contagious diseases and barred from school the children of infected households. Smallpox had been almost eliminated, and typhoid cases were few. The most feared childhood diseases were diphtheria and scarlet fever. In 1894, there appeared the yellow Board of Health placards which placed houses infected with these ailments in quarantine.

Except in epidemic years, the board's assessments were positive. As of 1885, "Hingham still continued to be one of the most healthful towns in the state," its rate of mortality declining. The largest numbers of victims were claimed by consumption and the "various lung diseases," but these were still seen less as contagions than as effects of poor living conditions and hygiene. Only old age and accidents caused more deaths, and over these, the board and town physicians had no control.

Physicians seem to have been less busy caring for the sick than tending the wounded. The interconnectedness, during these years, of health and safety is most pointed in the high incidence of street accidents. They were caused chiefly by the poor condition of the roads after the long years of "tinkering up dangerous places." The town passed stringent new bylaws to restrict hazards and prohibit obstructions. Many rocky obstacles were cleared, primarily out of a fear of suits. Town meeting warrants abounded with articles to fill holes, change grades, widen and straighten streets, improve surface drainage, and repair and maintain sidewalks. Such improvements were needed to accommodate what was by now a busy day and night street life, to ameliorate the flow of traffic to Nantasket, and to lure newcomers who would augment the tax base, reduced by the loss of manufacturing. But each article came up against cost.

Entry from the west to "our beautiful town" still ran along the malodorous Town Brook. North Street from the Cushing House to the

Cove was dangerous and narrow, only twenty feet wide in one section. There, an unnamed single abutter continued to obstruct change. After rainstorms, pedestrians were forced to walk in the middle of Main Street. At Broad Bridge, they competed for sidewalks with carts, cows, and bicyclists. Trains often blocked both Broad and Thaxter's Bridges. Ladies' heels and horses' hoofs caught in the tracks. From West Hingham station to Water Street, a distance of about a mile, twelve railroad crossings were gateless. To reach the trains, every passenger had to use the streets, either on foot or in wheeled vehicles. The amount of railroad traffic can be summed up by one figure: in August, 1889, 7200 tickets to all points were sold in the depot at Broad Bridge.

That year, however, streets began to improve. The state mandated that towns have either a commissioner of roads or a street superintendent, and a caucus of citizens prodded the selectmen into hiring Alonzo H. Kimball of Concord as street superintendent. Kimball began his road work on North Street between Cottage and Ship. His crews excavated a proper bed, laid large stones and pipes to carry off surface water, and installed catch basins. At his quarry on Side Hill Road, John Beal blasted a fourteen-ton rock, which, when crushed, supplied half of the material to "dress" North Street. Eight two-horse teams formed a steady supply caravan from the quarry.

Sounds of blasting and clouds of stone dust now entered the town's atmospherics. Dynamite blew away land along the Weir River, exploited by Beal as a source of rock. Dynamite blasted ledge in the path of water mains, gas lines, new roads, and old ones in need of straightening. Some of the town's old contours disappeared forever, and some of its archaeology, too. Removing a gravel knoll in the way of his spur railroad track, Beal unearthed seven skeletons. The site, on Hingham's far eastern edge, had been the burial ground of smallpox victims who died in the eighteenth-century "pest house."

Quarrying operations grew rapidly. Beal's South Shore Quarries already supplied Cohasset with crushed stone for its roads and later would supply all the stone used instead of wooden planks for the crossings of the Nantasket "Electric Road." By 1896, Beal's spur track accommodated thirteen freight cars, and he shipped all over the state. His three crushers could demolish 450 tons of rock a day. An "endless bucket" then fed the material into a cylindrical "sieve," which sorted it into four sizes. Beal also owned a steamroller for building streets, and Superintendent Kimball rented it, offering Hingham's street spectators a giant symbol of a townscape being transformed in the interests of convenience.

In 1883, the county had ordered a road bridge to connect North and Summer Streets. Now, Otis, Summer, and Rockland Streets required constant attention because of the high volume of day-trippers to "the Beach." For those seeking summer retreats, new streets were needed for houselots. In 1897, town meeting voted to extend Cottage Street to Burditt Avenue. The road from North Street, at St. Paul's, to a stump at the first corner was part of Cottage Street until, with the extension, the entire stretch from North to Burditt was named Fearing Road. Two years earlier, a short but much more important stretch of road had been added between Elm and South Streets: the Central Street extension. The old Quincy Thaxter house, now almost touching the corner, would become the Wompatuck Club. The extension opened a throughway parallel to Main Street just six months before tracks were laid for the "electrics." Carriages and teams would not have to travel the same route and could arrive directly at the depot and the freight yard.

As a public employee, Street Superintendent Kimball's situation was vastly different from that of wealthy private citizens such as Samuel Downer, the Bradleys, Henry Burditt, and John Brewer, who built and extended their own roads, bought their own materials, and hired stone crushers, horse-drawn steamrollers, and many laborers. By contrast, Kimball was given no flexibility in the use of appropriations. If money for a specific project ran out, work ceased until more funds were provided. Appropriations were small for ever larger needs. During Kimball's first year, the selectmen decided that his salary of $1100 would come out of the $3900 appropriated for streets. A few years later, they delayed so long on his reappointment that he began looking elsewhere, and only an additional $100 kept him in Hingham. In the 1890s, he was forced to watch new work torn up again and again for more water lines, leaks in mains, changes in railroad tracks, and poles for new utilities. He was also expected to confine and clean up unregulated dumping. Nevertheless, he worked energetically and with general approval through 1897 on the town's sixty miles of roads.

Better street surfaces alone could not untangle two knotty problems associated with the town's nightlife: darkness and human behavior. New expectations of safety and convenience included an improved code of deportment, but some deportment grew worse: "loafing" at Broad Bridge, nude bathing in the mill pond, vandalism in the North Ward—unhinging and destroying gates, trampling gardens, throwing stones at the windows of houses, storefronts, and factories, damaging street signs and lanterns, stealing fruit and hens, and burglarizing homes and stores. "Young roughs" broke up a Reform Club meeting, a Baptist prayer meeting, and, with whistling and dancing and stone-throwing, a peaceful evening service at Zion Hill Chapel. Even the town safe and the safe at the depot, which had its door blown off, were not exempt. Baptist minister Edward Ufford preached on "The Callous Young Men of Hingham, What Will Become of Them?" On July 4, 1887, at the Common, H. Price Collier spoke about unruly public conduct. Among the floats in that year's parade was one titled "The Hingham Burglars" with a banner that read, "There are no flies on Hingham Burglars." There certainly were not. When a great quantity of silver was stolen from John D. Long's house, three spoons that he most prized were returned a few weeks later signed "B. F. Butler." General Butler had acquired the nickname "Spoons" for allegedly filching silver during the occupation of New Orleans.

Much of this disorder was blamed on the unsettled policy about the hiring of night police. On this issue, the town was not ready to pay for safety. In 1880, two policemen were on duty almost full-time, their pay $2.50 a night. Then, the treasurer of the savings bank, even though his bank had been burgled twice, moved to reduce their pay to $1.50. In 1885, when a South Hingham resident's motion was approved, the town found itself with no night police; letters from South Hingham suggested that Broad Bridge businessmen should hire their own. Failure to provide police meant that as women workers walked home from the new manufacturing firm of Lahee and Eady (on the Elm Street site of the Long factory and later of Rhodes Ripley), they were insulted. Homeward-bound domestics were also accosted. In 1886, the town was persuaded to spend $26 on police, and the following year, the selectmen were authorized to hire four policemen. Public funding for police came slowly and controversially. But by the 1890s there were eight paid policemen. Among them was Washington Irving James, who, in 1907, became Hingham's first chief of police.

One new technology helped most in the campaign to make life safer and a police presence more visible. Just as the marvels of steam power and faucet water had filtered into towns, so would the harnessing and application of electricity. One corner of Hingham was electrified early, when Samuel Downer had Western Electric set up a generating plant on Crow Point in 1880. An arc lamp, its two electrodes producing six thousand candlepower, was placed on "Mount Gertrude" (Merrill Street), another at the wharf, a third at the music hall, with smaller ones elsewhere in Melville Garden. But arc lamps were only a beginning. At Menlo Park, New Jersey, a telegrapher named Thomas Edison was convinced that "somewhere in God Almighty's workshop" was a fila-ment to make continuous incandescent light. In 1879, he found it, and in 1889, the filament came to Hingham.

Morris Whiton was seen that year escorting "parties" interested in street lighting through the town. The selectmen gave permission to the new Weymouth Light and Power Company to put up street poles, with the proviso that the top arm be reserved for a fire alarm system. By October, 1889, ten lights were in place on Main Street. Street lighting followed on North, Otis, Summer, and Rockland. Street lights stayed on all night for the second annual Firemen's Ball in 1890. The Gamewell Fire Alarm Company loaned an immense gong for the occasion. At the press of a button, the gong signalled the forming of dance sets. Loring Hall and the Congregational and New North Churches were wired. By 1892, the town had about three hundred street lights, and the selectmen were deluged with requests for more. The following year, perhaps regretting its failure to purchase the Water Company, the town voted to have its own electric plant and appointed Wallace Corthell manager. By 1894, the bonds it had issued at 4 percent were fully subscribed.

Despite a general feeling that this clean, heat-free form of light had its dangers, electricity began to move indoors to private customers. It went first into Broad Bridge businesses—the *Journal*, Hennessy's, Breen's, and the shop of Miss Suzie Gates—and into the homes of the wealthy. The trend accelerated. Manufacturers were so flooded with orders for light bulbs that they could not keep up with demand. By 1900, two hundred Hingham houses were wired, and seven years later, the number had doubled. Service expanded. In the early years, power was provided only at night and sometimes erratically: street lights were often on when the moon was full and off when the sky was cloudy. But when customers began to realize the potential of daytime power and the company began to provide it, a domestic revolution began. The Light Company sold coffee pots, chafing dishes, water heaters, electric fans, and curling irons.

The toxic emissions and other dangers of gaslight and kerosene lamps were going the way of the broken pump and the polluted well. However, the new pollution-free technology of electricity created some pollution of its own. The manufacture of light poles involved scraping bark from the logs. The scrapings necessitated great bonfires at the dump near the freight yard on South Street, and several hours of over-powering smoke ensued.

The convenience of electric power compromised another new marvel of convenience, the telephone. Telephone wires ran along light poles in Quincy, with the result that connections were abysmal, characterized by a constant hum. Not that there were many telephones in Hingham yet—only about twenty by 1890. Their locations, however, were an important new component in the perception of public safety. In 1878, just two years after Alexander Graham Bell shouted his momentous message to "Mr. Watson" two rooms away, William Fearing, 2nd, had Hingham's first connection. It ran between his home and his store nearby at Hingham Centre. Later, he installed a public phone. In 1880, Fire Chief Cushing could be reached by phone from the Rose Standish House, and in turn, he could use a connection between the Broad Bridge depot and the Cordage Company. Now, in the event of a fire, Crow Point, Broad Bridge, and the Centre were linked by phone. The Water Company installed a telephone at the Rockland Street pumping station to serve in emergencies. The ordinary citizen's emergencies were also provided for. He could use a pay station in front of Beal's Fish Market at the Cove to reach Dr. James Robbins, the first local physician with a phone.

How the new conveniences depended on each other, interfered with each other, and sometimes failed is seen in two stories. When the first incandescent street lights illuminated Main Street in October, 1889, Gamewell Fire Alarm Company installed twenty boxes and more than fifteen miles of wire along the top arms of the poles. A disastrous fire in Ebed Ripley's mansion six months before had prompted calls for fire alarms. But a conflict of interests soon emerged. Weymouth Light and Power Company blamed a blackout in Hingham on the fire alarm wires. W. T. Litchfield, superintendent of the fire alarm system, replied that the alarm system would be much improved "if Supt. Brydges [of the Light Company] would order *his* men not to cut *our* wires." And even when not inadvertently sabotaged, the new systems were fragile. As ledge near the Old Colony depot was being dynamited, a piece of rock broke a pole, splitting and crossing the fire alarm and telephone wires. All the "strikers" of the Fire Department rang simultaneously, and volunteer firemen came scrambling from everywhere.

The town's oldest system of public safety, fire protection, had undergone radical change. In the decade following 1879, it had entered and become dependent on a new network of conveniences: hydrant water, improved roads, new regulations, electricity, and telephones. It could use new and improved equipment. A brief glance backwards will suggest the many ways in which firefighting had evolved from a private obligation to a public institution.

In Hingham's first 167 years as a town, fire protection had been an individual responsibility. Town law required only that a householder keep a sound ladder long enough to reach his roof. He was expected to assist his neighbors in a traditional covenant of mutual aid. Then, in 1802, two large groups of citizens decided to own fire engines. These engines were tubs filled by bucket brigades from the closest water source. Men "manned the brakes"—that is, long wooden bars, seesawed up and down by hand in order to rock a metal beam that moved a piston. The piston in turn pumped water through a hose and nozzle called a "pipe."

The earliest of these "bucket tubs," named "Precedent No. 1" because it was the first ready in 1802, was made entirely, except for the brass work, by craftsmen at Little Plain, and was privately owned by citizens of that village. The second, "Centre No. 2," belonged to citizens at Broad Bridge. The town assumed only the obligation to provide housing for these tubs, as it would also do for South Hingham's "Constitution No. 3" in 1805 and West Hingham's "Torrent No. 4" in 1826. But when, in 1830, the "Hingham" was purchased to protect the Cove, the town paid not only for a building, but also for the first suction apparatus and a hose carriage.

Early firemen, though volunteer, expected some compensation. The early nineteenth century's most memorable fire was a disaster because firemen were in rebellion; the town had refused to waive their poll taxes. As a result, Madame Derby's old mansion at the west end of South Street, then occupied by Widow Hannah Bourne, was totally lost in 1835. In 1843, the town agreed to the waiver of poll taxes, and regular companies were formed, twenty volunteers for each engine, forty for the tub at the Cove. Three years later, the town voted to buy three new suction engines and "Hingham No. 5" from its private owners. The town now owned the engines and four stations, at the Cove, West Hingham, Little Plain, and South Hingham.

With the exception of a hook and ladder company formed in 1874, this was the system until that climactic year of 1879, when the Board of Auditors published the mounting expense of firefighting and urged more uniform accounting. Adopting a new state law, Hingham organized its first fire department. It was governed by a Board of Fire Engineers, who were chosen by and accountable to the selectmen. George Cushing would be chief for forty years.

The change was linked to the advent of the Water Company. Once fifty hydrants were in place, the old "hand-engines" were obsolete, except for "Constitution" and "Torrent" in the south and west, so far without hydrants. The old engines were decommissioned; some were sold, and others would be seen only in the nostalgic "Hingham Vet musters" that were started in 1893. New hose carriages were purchased, new companies formed.

In the 1880s, response to fires became faster and more efficient. When a roof on Cottage Street caught fire in 1885, the Isaac Little hose was attached within five minutes to a hydrant with adequate pressure. When William Fearing noticed smoke coming out of the roof of Stephenson's scale factory in 1886, a call brought the hook and ladder truck along with the new "Niagara" hose carriage. On both occasions damages were minimal. But when, in the spring of 1889, there was an explosion in Ebed Ripley's gas furnace and fire got into the walls of his immense house, the Fire Department had never faced such a problem and could do nothing. New systems could go only so far in coping with the risks of new conveniences.

State fire laws became more stringent. As of 1888, all fires had to be reported and investigated. Departments had to have a chute, a jumping net, and an arrow gun for throwing a rope up to a roof. The town modernized its equipment. It bought an extension ladder (1891) after a fire at Agricultural Hall, since the old one reached only to the windows of the mansard roof. With new equipment, hydrants, telephones, and alarms, there was a temporary sense of security. But South Hingham was not so carefully protected: it lacked hydrants, was short of hose, and had no telephone in the 1880s. Liberty Plain did not receive an alarm box until 1894.

By 1895, the old anxiety had reawakened. The danger of fire at Broad Bridge was much discussed: buildings there were so close that a fire could be catastrophic. By now, water pressure was inadequate for firefighting, and the Board of Engineers recommended buying a "steamer" because of the "condition of our water service." Chief Cushing installed his own hydrant and hoses to serve his hotel and stable. Public policy had not yet replaced private initiative.

In winter, Chief Cushing removed the hoses from the carriages and put them on large sleds, "pungs," for faster response through the snow. But big winter fires, especially in places without nearby mains and hydrants, were almost uncontrollable. On a January night in 1897, three huge barns on the Samuel Whittemore farm, filled with eighty tons of hay and fodder, burned to the ground. An earlier spectacular fire (1890) caused by lightning destroyed a hay storage barn on Summer Street owned by Messrs. Barnes, Blake, Bouvé, and Brewer. The blaze was seen for miles.

In this instance, it would not have mattered, but there were complaints about the delayed response of the Fire Department. The cause of the delay was significant: the alarm wires were in contact with the limbs of trees. Trees, it seems, had become an inconvenience, a threat to public safety. The new utilities were in conflict with another kind of change: a new taste for the beautiful.

CHAPTER SIXTEEN

The Wider World Touches the Island Community

WHEN the Rev. Henry Miles spoke in 1885 of "hearts and minds . . . touched to finer issues," he connoted another kind of change that took place in the 1880s and 1890s. As marvels of convenience began to transform the look and the life of Hingham, other influences from the wider world also were felt. The conveniences, together with these other influences, would eventually end Hingham's long history as a traditional, self-contained town—what has been called an "island community."

In the cultural history of the western world, the 1880s and 1890s are sometimes called "the aesthetic period." Aestheticism's most prominent English spokesman, Walter Pater, set forth the "epicurean" belief that a love of the beautiful was the most powerful stimulus toward a fuller and higher human life. A love of the beautiful expressed itself in many ways, artistic, but also moral, social, and religious. It touched minds and hearts to "finer issues."

In Hingham, there were many signs of the wider world's touch. It was seen in a changing townscape, natural and manmade. It was seen in styles, in the ways people looked and behaved, their fashions and leisure activities. It was seen in the impact of women's tastes and values and in a new sense of the beauty of childhood. It was seen in a changing religious life and a new taste for the "beauty of holiness." It was seen most obviously in new public buildings. They were designed in exotic and eclectic styles that made them appear strikingly different from the plainly handsome, horizontal, direct, and usually square buildings that remain Hingham's pride.

The second "Torrent," at Marsh's Bridge, West Hingham, in 1862. It was one of four suction fire engines purchased by the town in 1846.

First trolley of the Hingham Street Railway Company, 1896. Summer cars had open sides.

Snow plough on Short Street. Wires for lights and a public telephone lead into the foreground building (1858), once the store of William Fearing, 2nd, occupied at the time of the photograph (1898) by pharmacist Reuben Sprague. Today, Dependable Cleaners.

John Beal's stone crusher on Side Hill Road.

A view of the 1886 flood, looking west to South Street from Lafayette Avenue. In less than thirty-six hours, George Cushing had twelve horse barges available as alternate transport to the trains.

Wreckage at the harbor after the northeaster, November, 1898.

The bucket mill fire (1902) began in the drying attic, consumed the whole building, and caused the first fatality —J. Arthur Batchelder, Hose 4—in Fire Department history. What were the thoughts of the solitary figure? Who was the photographer whose holders were loaded with glass plates to record this instant?

Wilder Hall (1879) in 1885.

Stained glass angel medallion from the sanctuary window of St. John's Episcopal Mission Chapel and Church (1883-1920).

Architect J. Sumner Fowler's sketch of the Hingham Cemetery Chapel (1886).

The second Public Library (1879-1966). Today, the site of Hawke Park with its memorial boulders.

LEFT: *Truly the "boys of summer." All lived on Summer Street in the summer during the 1890s. Left to right, front row: Roger Scaife, Charles T. Sprague; second row: Charles White, Charles B. Barnes, Jr., (Hingham's Town Moderator, 1907–1928), William O. Blake; third row: Donald E. White, Lauriston I. Scaife, Frederick A. Turner, Dr. Benjamin S. Blanchard, Charles Jeffries.* RIGHT: *Michael "King" Kelly (Hall of Famer, 1945). An authorized re-issue of a tobacco card of 1888.*

A Vet Firemen's Muster at the fairgrounds, 1895.

Hingham Centre croquet players on the court built on Charles Marble's Irving Street land in 1894. The clubhouse to the right, "The Parthenon," was built in 1895.

Most widely visible was a new passion for landscape. Trees, which for over two centuries had been a commodity for coopering, building, fuel, and industry, were now relatively few. Photographs of 1880s Hingham show barren stretches. These treeless expanses were not uncommon in New England towns. The modern leafy canopy that covers metropolitan Boston did not yet exist. Then, rather suddenly, many people began to prize trees as beautiful objects, "priceless ornaments." The change was due in part to the influence of Charles Sprague Sargent and Frederick Law Olmsted, who began collaborating in 1878 on plans for the Arnold Arboretum, both as a park and as a museum of trees. Olmsted had designed New York's Central Park, and he would initiate Boston's "emerald necklace" park system.

The scarcity of mature old trees, those priceless ornaments, also occasioned an awareness of their vulnerability. Many huge buttonwoods, planted in the eighteenth century, had died off from disease in the 1840s. Storms, drought, age, and insects—the canker worm, beetle, and tent caterpillar—menaced Hingham's historic elms. Techniques for their care were a common topic. The elegant row set out by Bela Tower in the eighteenth century still flourished near Ebed Hobart's store on Main Street near Tower Brook. But thirty-seven elms at the Gay mansion (262 South Street) in West Hingham wore special protective collars.

Many elms had been cut down since the Civil War. Horses, too, took their toll, pulling leaves and chewing bark. New conveniences were an added threat. Trees were removed to facilitate railroad turnouts, to accommodate a second track, and to make room for wider, straighter roads and safer sidewalks. The common practice of moving buildings left roughly amputated branches. When utility poles were installed, roots were injured and limbs lopped off. Men of the Weymouth Light and Power Company, though expressly forbidden to do so, topped the maples of Oliver Stoddard in West Hingham, removing ten years' growth.

In 1880, Francis W. Brewer suggested the forming of a Tree Club. Within weeks, a Hingham Tree Association was setting out rock maples on Pear Tree Hill and Cottage Street. The following spring, lindens and Norway and rock maples were planted on Summer, Green, North, and Lincoln Streets. Replacement maples were furnished for the grounds of the Agricultural Society, for schoolyards, and for homeowners, too, if they would furnish holes, loam, and care. Interested homeowners could obtain information at the stores of tree enthusiasts Fearing Burr, George Lincoln, and John Todd, who, as superintendent of the Hingham Cemetery, had labored to bring the beauty of trees and landscaping to that ancient burial ground. Members of the Tree Association loved the beauty of trees, but they were also persuaded of their value in preventing erosion and serving as watersheds. They saw trees as a gift to the future, too, and so, in 1884, they established a nursery at Hobart and New Bridge Streets with about four hundred young trees and shrubs.

Private landscaping was now prized as a public benefit. In 1880, the year of his son Francis's initiative, John Brewer began his ambitious program of planting on World's End. By fall, nine hundred trees were in place. Later, European and native varieties were set doubly and closely along curving roads planned by Olmsted, and more were planted on Langley and Sarah Islands, which Brewer owned. Of all of Olmsted's monumental achievements in landscape architecture, he was least involved in the development at World's End. Yet it remains the conservancy that is most faithful to his aesthetic. He believed in working, insofar as possible, with the existing topography, using native plants, particularly grasses, with an artful simplicity to create restful vistas and open spaces. The "country park," he felt, was restorative in its pastoral beauty. Because it did not include active recreation, it reduced competitiveness and stress and brought human beings into harmony with the natural world. World's End was Hingham's first "country park," and the public, if well behaved, was welcome there.

Elsewhere in town, lawns were well-tended, and the sale of hand-pushed rotary mowers, newly affordable in the 1880s, was brisk. "Unsightly fences" were removed. Leather hoses were replaced by garden hoses of rubber—vulcanizing was a new technology—hooked up to the new convenience of faucet water. Trees, shrubs, gardens and "hot houses" became fashionable on estates. Flower exhibits multiplied at annual fairs and shows. There was a pool of available workers to care for gardens; in the 1890s, new Italian immigrants augmented the labor force for pick and shovel work, while more established workers, chiefly Irish, tended estates.

People, as they moved about in this changing townscape, expressed a new ideal and love of visual beauty. This was a self-conscious time, a time intensely aware of appearances. Fashion columns filled the *Journal*. Fussy, stolid Victorian styles were giving way to feathered hats and furs, to the theatrical styles soon to be called Edwardian. A leisured outdoor life indulged the love of spectacle. From their new verandas, a feature of domestic architecture introduced about 1885, some townspeople looked on, and they in turn became part of the outdoor spectacle for spectators on the sidewalk.

Imagine a thousand people listening to a concert at the fair, hundreds disembarking at Melville Garden, the Cadet Corps marching off their steamer to their Burditt Avenue grounds, the "procession of family, carriage, saddle horses and ponies escorted by the band" around the fairgrounds, the parade of "fashionables" at Peter Bradley's polo grounds near Huet's Cove, the Crow Point Yacht Club's end-of-season sail of boats hung with Chinese lanterns. Imagine excursion steamers on race days, "basket" parties to the islands, rose and strawberry festivals, cotillions, croquet and tennis games, and bicycle races—all set against a backdrop of fireworks and music. Public life was filled with style and color.

Color, in the art and life of the period, was valued in itself. A newly picturesque townscape was rich in decorated and painted surfaces. By 1880, the factory-made paints of Sherwin and Williams were on the market, making it no longer necessary to mix white lead base, linseed oil, turpentine, and pigment. Ornament and color such as are seen in Blue Willow china and Oriental rugs were prized in homes. On the streets, George Cushing's barges grew more brilliant by the year, and signs of spring featured freshly painted carriages carrying furniture to "cottages" where wealth and leisure fostered a type of life beyond the practical, and where "stereopticon views" nourished a taste for the wider world, faraway places, Italian art, and ancient cultures.

As part of life became exotic spectacle, people became spectators more than participants, and as spectators, they wanted a visual record. Near the bandstand at Melville Garden, a photographer stayed for the season, and professional photographers with glass negatives and darkroom equipment periodically set up a mobile shop near Broad Bridge. Notable Hingham photographers included William Hudson, Charles A. Lane, William B. Luce, Charles Marble, and Frank Reed. In 1888, Kodak marketed a revolutionary hand-held hobbyist's camera, making every person a potential photographer. Its unique feature was an already-loaded flexible film of one hundred frames. Once the film was exposed, the camera was sent to Rochester, where the photo-finishing was done, and prints and a freshly loaded camera were returned by mail. That year, Hingham formed a Camera Club.

The camera froze visual moments for the spectator, images of the instant, exactly as seen in the viewfinder, not subject to the vagaries of memory or to the electronic manipulation of images we know today.

The camera offered a distinct new form of historical record. The past could be preserved with visual immediacy.

The love of beautiful spectacle also embraced an increasingly "refined" passion for the theatrical and the musical. While one ladies' Chautauqua Circle studied the French Revolution, another arranged a Greek evening of pure theatre: the ladies dressed themselves and their hair in classical style, ate supper on little couches, crowned the winner of a Greek game with a wreath, and read from Lucian. Theatre trains, the brasswork on their engines gleaming, their conductors in gold-buttoned frock coats, carried spectators to Boston and home again. Visiting companies came to Hingham. The popular "tableaux vivants" of earlier decades gave way to livelier forms, especially operetta. Children rehearsed "Red Riding Hood" and "The Berry Pickers." Adults performed "Patience," "Pinafore," "Iolanthe," and "Daughter of the Regiment." Gilbert and Sullivan operetta was the vogue.

Another favorite musical form was oratorio. Under the chairmanship of George Lincoln and the conducting of Morris Whiton, a seventy-member Hingham Choral Society sprang up almost overnight in 1885. The oratorio form could not have been better suited to the musical resources of a small town. It required no costumes, action, or scenery. The number of players and singers was flexible; if one soloist was not available, another singer or part of the oratorio could be substituted. The society's favorites were Handel and Haydn oratorios. Their themes appealed to a new confluence of tastes and beliefs: the love of natural beauty ("The Seasons"), the faith in redemption ("Messiah"), and divine origins. In a jammed Loring Hall in 1888, one hundred members of the choral societies of Hingham and Weymouth sang Haydn's "The Creation."

The Hingham Centre Amateur Orchestra, refined into the Hingham Philharmonic, held open rehearsals under conductor Reuben Sprague, apothecary. Morris Whiton borrowed some of its members to form a string orchestra. George Cushing's barges carried instrumentalists and singers to the Cohasset Musical Association and Weymouth's Clapp Hall. The tiny Clarion Social Orchestra rehearsed weekly and gave parlor concerts. Parlor evenings of song, accompanied by the piano, itself a sign of refinement, were arranged by women, increasingly the arbiters of taste.

In the belief of the times, music was not simply beautiful. Music evoked the spiritual and uplifted human nature. It was an essential component of the "beauty of holiness." A *Journal* editorial of 1888 praising the Choral Society declared: "Music preaches better sermons than most men. There are more ways than one of serving God on Sunday, and more ways than one of being and helping others to be good citizens." Religious life, too, was being touched by the wider world. It was evolving, Henry Miles suggested, toward something "not yet clearly seen," perhaps, he hoped, toward a "new crystallization."

Three new religious buildings expressed contemporary influences in religious life. As part of the altered townscape, their initial impact was visual. Together with three prominent new secular structures, they were designed in forms and textures that appeared exotic among the stately simplicities of old Hingham architecture. Though they were still made of wood, they looked distinctly different, neoclassic or neogothic, whether with pedimented windows or with high angular gables. Their surfaces were paneled, then painted in contrasting colors or heavily ornamented along their edges with wooden "lace" or iron filigree. The overall effect was of bas-relief carving.

The first new secular building, Wilder Hall (1879), with its lofty paired pilasters, its tall and slender windows and high mansard roof, was "Hingham's finest building in the French academic style" of the Second Empire. Wilder was enthusiastically greeted as "an ornament to the town." The second public library, dedicated a few months later in 1880, did not evoke the same enthusiasm. Some criticized its "narrow" appearance, its wooden instead of granite stairs and portico, its iron instead of slate roof. Money had been "wasted" on excessive ornament when what was needed was a card catalogue. The second floor rooms, one of them a tower, seemed cramped and wasteful of space. The third secular structure, G.A.R. Hall (1889), was designed by a young architect of the Centre, Henry Merritt, in a simpler neogothic style.

The three religious buildings adopted variations of the same late Victorian gothic. St. John's Episcopal Mission (1882) signaled the Anglican and Anglophile revival of the period and the late growth of Episcopalianism in Hingham. Support for a chapel's construction on Main Street opposite the present site of St. John's came from wealthy summer residents who had traveled to England and brought back images of gothic churches, of luxuriant gardens set against long green stretches, of architectural richness and color. St. John's Chapel (1883) was painted in two shades of red; the roof, moss green. Inside, the light from two memorial stained glass windows was filtered onto brilliant blue, red, and oak. One, of a mother and two children, was designed by that staunch Unitarian John D. Long and given by him and his mother-in-law, Mrs. George Glover, in memory of Long's first wife. Not everyone in town was pleased with the chapel as a vivid emblem of the beauty of holiness. As rector James Coolidge recalled, "The people of Hingham have nearly always considered that an Episcopalian was in many respects a Roman Catholic." For a time, there were mutterings about Catholic vestments and rituals. But other churches soon felt the aesthetic influence. Congregationalists and Baptists added stained glass windows. Abundant flowers and the increased celebration of Holy Week expressed a growing taste for religious ceremony.

The first Episcopal chapel is long gone. The Hingham Cemetery Chapel remains, though time has not been kind to it. Described in its original state, with high gables and a tower, as a "beautiful gothic chapel," it is prized by modern interpreters for "Queen Anne" detail: "decorated barge boards, roof brackets, pointed dormers." In its southwest end is a large stained glass window in memory of Mrs. Annie P. Ames. Built by subscription through the efforts of the trustees, the chapel was consecrated in 1887. Many who had moved far away from the town were still returned for burial in the Hingham Cemetery, and the chapel was needed for their services. The need declined. Though the exterior, now very changed, was finally repainted in the late 1980s, the interior and its fittings lay unusable and neglected for lack of funds.

A third religious building, also now gone, was dedicated in 1891. The first hall of the First Parish stood between Loring Hall and the Baptist Church until 1977. While its style signified the same aesthetic impulse as the two chapels, in function it represented a new dimension in religious life. It was needed to provide "a living, working church" space for a growing number of extra-liturgical activities: Sunday school, lectures and public meetings, and weekday classes. It stood for a changing idea of the role of church and clergy in the social world.

This idea can be seen in the brief but conspicuous presence in Hingham of H. Price Collier, minister of the First Parish. Collier remained for only six years (1882-88), but he left a strong impression. His ecumenism embraced liturgical freedom; his compassion, all social groups. He coached and promoted athletics. He preached to the First Corps of Cadets and joined in union services with fundamentalist churches. In the old meetinghouse, he participated with two other Unitarian ministers in the sacrament of the Lord's Supper, complete with the very Anglican element of a boys' choir. He celebrated the marriage of Charles Barnes's daughter according to Episcopal rite. At Mount Zion chapel in Tuttleville, during a blinding snowstorm, he conducted the funeral of twenty-eight-year-old John Edward Simpson, George Cushing's black assistant, clerk, and friend, and a familiar, well-liked presence at the hotel. Johnnie's pallbearers were all members of the recently formed Catholic young men's Hingham Social Club, to which Johnnie also belonged. The announcement of his death included these words: "No one who knew him will deny that no whiter man for character ever lived and died in Hingham."

The new religious ecumenism promoted the redeeming value of brotherhood at a time when attitudes toward black people, in Hingham as elsewhere, were in a shifting and contradictory state. Popular minstrel shows and costume balls caricatured "the Coloreds." It was "fun" at agricultural fairs to throw ripe tomatoes at the woolly head of "the African dodger." Yet, when a local barber refused to cut the hair of a black employee at Downer Landing, he was fined by Judge Walter Bouvé. When negative comments were made in 1886 about the "coloreds" of Tuttleville using Wilder Hall, the trustees rebuked the critics and reminded them that the village was part of the parish and "entitled to all the rights of anyone in South Hingham." And when, in 1887, black Civil War veterans of the 54th and 55th Regiments came with their wives and children to decorate Governor Andrew's grave, the G.A.R. Post greeted them at the steamboat and escorted them to a collation at Loring Hall, where Centre postmaster Peter Sprague, once an officer in the 55th, reminisced to great laughter and applause.

A Melville Garden trade card advertising the Clam Bake in 1880.

The new social outreach of religious life was also seen in another religious building. It was built in the same year (1891) as the First Parish house, at the corner of Gardner and Derby Streets. The name of its sponsoring group expressed its aim: the United Social Society. Liberty Plain still felt isolated, and its children had too far to go to Sunday school. Sisters Annie Belcher and Sara Chubbuck discovered that adults nearby also wanted a place for regular services. Land was given by Lewis Gardner, and within twelve months, through the efforts of only twenty-two members, the Gardner Street chapel was completed. (It can still be seen in altered form and new location at 319 Gardner Street.) Ministers from other Hingham churches and nearby towns were its preachers. The society seemed to have no strict denominational bent. Most meaningful in its name is the word "social"; most significant about its creation is that it arose through the initiative of two *women* out of concern for *children*.

Hingham women were still barred from politics, but they played active roles in the outreach of the churches and in campaigns for reform associated with the temperance movement. Two notable Hingham women took their humanitarian energies to the wider world. They were daughters of Hingham's governors. Elizabeth Loring Andrew, a modest person with "daring opinions," an advocate of suffrage and a skilled linguist, was well known for her social work among the Italian immigrants of Boston's North End before her death in 1897. Margaret Long served as a military nurse at Brooklyn Naval Hospital during the Spanish-American War, worked in settlement houses in East Coast cities, and graduated from the Johns Hopkins Medical School. As a physician she became, as far as can be ascertained, the town's first woman professional. These two were forerunners of women of the Progressive movement, who would influence the life of Hingham early in the twentieth century. In the late nineteenth century, however, most Hingham women stayed at home and channeled their energies into efforts on behalf of children.

The child was no longer viewed as an adult in miniature. The child was a unique and developing individual, and childhood was prized as beautiful. Children were often the focus of parish activities. Local clergy wrote sermons for children, while literary artists of the wider world produced classics for them. Edmund Hersey, 2nd, a long-time superintendent of the Universalist Sunday School, took great pride in his school and its annual "Floral Sunday." This was a joint service of children and adults, one which Phebe Hanaford had inaugurated. The church was filled with flowers, and canaries in cages were "suspended from the gallery." Children, flowers, and song: who would not be spiritually improved by the innocent, the beautiful, and the shared joy of music?

The outward missionary impulse and the inward impulse for a more refined and orderly life—the seedbed of the Progressive era—were applied with clear-eyed practicality by some of the town's children. A few little girls formed the Mustard Seed Society and arranged a fair to benefit the Universalist Sunday School. John D. Long's daughters held a sale of handmade items to help the City Missionary Society's Fresh Air Fund. In the summer of 1888, twenty-eight working girls enjoyed a two-week vacation, board not over $2 a week, in a Cottage Street house rented with funds raised by the Girls Friendly Society.

The initiative which led to the most lasting program was taken by six young girls who called themselves the Hexagon Club. They decided that Hingham should participate in the Boston YMCA's "Country Week," and it did so from 1887 until well after the turn of the century. The central adult in this story was Mrs. Samuel Souther. "Nursey Souther" cared for the city children at the farm on Hobart Street (101). Almost ninety stayed there the first summer, and

> One could not tell which was more delighted, the good woman or the children, when the latter stowed away under their jackets the abundance of fresh vegetables she put on the table at dinner time. Her largest milk-can full of green peas disappeared in about one-tenth of the time it took her to shell them. A large hay wagon was kept for the purpose of giving the children rides. They all sat on the floor of the wagon, packed in like sardines, and as they started off for the beach received her parting injunction to "make all the noise you want."

Other adults helped the Hexagon Club with fundraising events. Sara Lincoln played Mother Goose at a party held at Loring Hall. Dr. Henry Spalding, father of one of the six girls, offered his beautiful flower-filled grounds on South Street for a day-long fair, complete with tent, Chinese lanterns, a concert by the Hingham Philharmonic, and the usual "tables." There were games, a grab bag, and "Betsey Bobbitt," the figure of an old lady in a rocking chair. Five cents bought three chances to knock the pipe out of her mouth. The proceeds brought city children for their healthy, happy weeks with Nursey Souther. They were invited to a fish dinner at Nantasket Beach and a day at Melville Garden. As they stopped, laughing and singing, at Broad Bridge, Thomas Margetts gave them bags of "goodies" and others offered fresh fruits.

The love of childhood exerted its influence on the new ecumenism of religious life, sometimes reducing divisions or crossing wide boundaries. Representatives of "other religious societies" were present at St. Paul's Church in 1888, when Archbishop John Williams confirmed seventy children. The Rev. Henry Miles of New North Church expressed the new spirit when he urged more social interaction among denominations, praised the Catholic Church as "of great service among us," and said it should make Protestants ashamed of their divisiveness.

But Miles also identified a growing problem in Hingham's churches. With a population of 4500 in 1885, the town, he estimated, had no more than 1500 worshippers on Sundays, the largest number at St. Paul's. More denominations also meant that each would have a smaller membership, and small memberships found it hard to keep their ministers. The tradition of long or lifetime pastorates had ended. In 1888, the departure of two young ministers, Collier and Edward A. Robinson of the Congregational Church, to urban parishes, and of aging James Coolidge from St. John's, left eight of Hingham's ten churches without settled clergy. The churches were facing difficulties like those of the town in general. There were too few communicants to support so many societies.

The problem showed itself, ironically, in an area of cultural life that seems remote from religion: sports and games. Sports had not yet become the "religion" that they would be for many Americans by the mid twentieth century, but in the new outdoor life of the 1880s and 1890s, they were increasingly important. Fresh air and physical well-being were powerful themes of the public health movement. The picnic was one popular expression of these themes. Another, field games and sports, was featured at the annual fairs. Women now rode horseback, played tennis, and biked. Among the bestsellers of W. W. Hersey's 1500 selections of sheet music were "A Bicycle Built for Two" and "Take Me Out to the Ball Game." A shop on North Street sold the new "Indian" or safety bike (1885), with wheels of the same size, less bone-jarring than its predecessor the "velocipede." Behind Fearing Burr's store at Little Plain, the Croquet Club played their favorite game. Charles Marble, successor to club president Ebed Ripley, built a new court in 1895 at his Irving Street home and installed electric lights, ending the era of moonlit croquet. The court's new clubhouse, "the Parthenon," was dedicated with characteristically parodic Centre ceremony, including a thunderous salute by the "Croquet Club artillery, stationed on the brow of the Acropolis."

But the current rage was "the old ball game." Baseball bats were for sale on Breen's counters. Hennessy offered a private room next to his billiard hall for meetings of the "Hinghams." Home games were played on Saturdays at the fairgrounds against the Braintree "Trimountains," Cohasset's "Black Rocks," and "picked nines" from Weymouth. Opposite the music hall on Otis Street was a diamond for Melville Garden visitors. Derby Academy and the high school had teams; the "Hingham

Juniors" appealed for games with other juniors. Even grammar school girls formed teams, the "Conquerors" of the Centre, the "Vultures" of South Hingham. The "Hinghams" had town stars such as brothers Matt and Fred Townsend. "No doubt," the *Journal* boasted, " we have several future Mike Kellys now developing."

The name of that celebrity of the wider world suggests what would go wrong. As with churches and other societies, there were too many clubs to support. Late in the 1880s, the town had three teams besides the "Hinghams," the gate receipts of the "Hinghams" (fifteen cents a person) dropped, and income was not enough to pay expenses or hire players. Some local stars switched to other towns. Hingham's amateur teams struggled on in the 1890s, but the front pages of the *Journal* gradually reported less local baseball and more "brilliant" society events. Town interest was shifting to the Big League, the wider world.

The Music Hall in Boston, with a capacity of four thousand, could somehow reproduce by telegraph the distant ball games of the Boston "Beaneaters." Their star and manager was the flamboyant Michael "King" Kelly, whose local admirers were passionate. In 1890, in a grand gesture and with much fanfare, friends and admirers gave the "King" and his bride a Hingham homestead, the late Dr. Harlow's house at 507 Main Street. "A few months later, a local group also presented Kelly with a coach and matched pair of white horses." The same group, the Hingham Social Club, of which Kelly was a member, added a holly wood riding whip with an ivory handle and a gold mount to complete the ensemble. Such gestures capture the time's fascination with far-off celebrities. Hingham now had its resident celebrity.

His reign, unfortunately, was brief. "Heavy drinking and high living" took their toll. Gambling losses brought him near bankruptcy. Kelly's place in baseball history was not fixed until much later; he was finally admitted to the Hall of Fame in 1945. His demise came early, at the age of thirty-seven, in 1894. He had been famous not only as a catcher and a hitter, but also as a slider; "Slide, Kelly, Slide" was a popular song. As he was dying of pneumonia, the "King" fell or was dropped from his stretcher. He is said to have whispered, "This is my last slide."

In 1893, Kelly's Hingham home had been sold for nonpayment of taxes. The year of his death, far to the north at 156 East Street, a more respectable celebrity joined the community. Gertrude Edmands was the daughter of Melville Garden's bandmaster, T. O. Edmands. To be a singer in the "Gilded Age" was one of the few acceptable careers for women. These were years when Toulouse Lautrec was immortalizing Yvette Guilbert, and Nellie Melba was singing her way around the world. Gertrude Edmands toured the nation, sang with the Maritana English Opera Company, the Boston Symphony, and the Handel & Haydn Society. She sang at Arlington Street Church, where she was Boston's highest paid woman singer at $700 a year. Music-loving Hingham was charmed when she sang at Loring Hall or the Rose Standish House. A summer resident, in 1894 she bought the "ancient homestead" of Stephen Cushing. Her purchase was greeted with enthusiasm.

The arrivals of Hingham's celebrities were, of course, isolated instances. But they betoken what was happening to the ancient town as the nineteenth century closed. For two decades after the Civil War, most of America was still composed of "island communities." They still felt a strong sense of local autonomy, a "jealous localism," and "enjoyed an inner stability." Then, in the 1880s and 1890s, many changes—technological, economic, social, even aesthetic—"shattered this relative isolation and stability . . . . The great casualty of America's turmoil late in the century was the island community." Hingham's "island community" had responded to the wider world.

Amid the exciting spectacle and exotic color, some felt a sense of loss and a desire to commemorate what was passing. The building of G.A.R. Hall and of the cemetery chapel were acts of commemoration. The raising of St. John's chapel renewed ancient ties with Hingham, England: from St. Andrew's Church came gifts of a lectern, an ancient oak bishop's chair, and a silver and gilt chalice and paten. In many ways, some direct, some oblique or subtle, the town was connecting with its past and absorbing it into present life. The camera was capturing images of departed personalities and also of sites and buildings later lost: the steamboat landing, the Anchor Tavern, Burr Brown's factory, the rope works, the bucket mill, and Melville Garden. Signboards in photos, when readable, show exactly where merchants had their shops and what they saw from their windows. Such records mark a watershed in images of the past.

William Taylor, the "photo artist" near the railroad depot, advertised: "Secure the Shadow e'er the Substance Fade." Inadvertently, he expressed a new mood, commemorative and elegiac.

✠

CHAPTER SEVENTEEN

The Old, the Young, and the End of an Epoch

A s an epoch draws to a close, the past and the future meet and mingle. For old people, the past seems to be ending; for the young, the future opens with new horizons. In the life history of Hingham, the 1890s seemed to be such a time. A single year, 1896, marked a watershed between past and future. For the old, the mood was elegiac; for the young, it was a mixture of regret and anticipation.

What did old townspeople feel as they made their way to one memorial ceremony after another, along new sidewalks and altered streets, where hydrants sprouted, new poles grew, and rows of overhead wires vied with green files of young trees? A commemorative passion had been born at the end of the Civil War with its monuments and new holiday, Memorial Day. In 1876, the nation commemorated the end of its first century. In 1881, Hingham marked with rich ceremony the two hundredth anniversary of its meetinghouse, and four years later, the 250th of its founding. Plans were made for a monumental town history. As the century grew old, the old grew ever more conscious of the "lost" past. Newness awakened a fascination with Oldness. A vision of the "ancient town" took hold. The nineteenth century's watchword was Progress, but its romance was with the Past.

In the depression year of 1876, the town wondered if it could afford a centennial celebration; but by June, plans were underway. July Fourth was observed with a grand parade. The old and the young shared the honors. In one carriage rode fourteen gentlemen whose years totaled 1055; in two others, young ladies decked in costumes of Ye Ancient Maiden or in red, white, and blue portrayed the thirteen colonies and thirty-nine states. In sixteen carriages rode five hundred schoolchildren, among them Americans with no ancestral tie to 1776.

The next solemn commemoration came in 1881. Aged guests arrived by boat and train as August skies cleared. Outside the old meetinghouse, grounds were green; inside, memories were nostalgic. Decorations were simple so that "the quaint architecture of the building might be more easily seen"—or could have been, were it not for Victorian "refinements." The morning was filled with psalm and anthem, prayer and poem, and a condescending oration by Harvard's Charles Eliot Norton, who derided all things "Puritan" and expressed relief at "how widely parted we are" from narrow-minded ancestors. After lunch at Loring Hall, the multitude returned to hear speeches until six o'clock, when they reluctantly, we are assured, went home.

The speeches are fascinating for what they express of a potent new attitude toward the past. They make a striking contrast with Solomon Lincoln's oration at the town's two hundredth birthday in 1835. Young Lincoln spoke then with exhilaration of the prosperous present and with prophetic confidence in the future. He celebrated the "heroism and piety of our pilgrim fathers" as living models of civic virtue. By contrast, the elderly speakers of 1881 dwelt on the remoteness of the past, its "quaintness." The future was dim; the past was "shadowy" and picturesque. These heirs of early settlers summoned up ancestors in fanciful whimsy, as if enjoying a final reunion in the face of irresistible "progress." They could afford to be playful. Their past was a quaint preserve shared by fewer and fewer.

"Does it not seem," asked a descendant of Lorings and Jameses, "as if more than two centuries had elapsed?" What would ancestors say to "the crowds that throng to Nantasket in the summer on Sundays?" Another told anecdotes with amused embarrassment at "the grave and sedate character" of one's forebears. Some evoked childhood visions of "good old Parson Richardson" and sabbaths spent puzzling over why the bells stopped ringing when he reached the pulpit and whether the sounding board would fall on his head. Their tones said, "The past is dead." A Wilder spoke "for the last time in good old historic Hingham." Governor Long prophesied, "The nineteenth century will not see again such an anniversary as this." Pastor Calvin Lincoln, at eighty-one, offered the prayer. A month later in the same place, he prayed for the recovery of President Garfield, mortally wounded by an assassin's bullet. As he did, he became ill and was taken home, where he suffered a lethal stroke, another melancholy note of closure.

In a strange elegiac mood, Hingham prepared for another poignant finale, its 250th anniversary in 1885. This was a day for the "Old Boys," fittingly the "fairest of autumn days," when surviving flowers mingled with autumnal tints. Trains and boats "brought to their former homes the returning sons of Hingham," now scattered far and wide. Church bells rang at dawn; enthusiasts fired cannon; houses wore "sentimental and historic mottoes" to welcome "the returning wanderers." Streets filled, and "here an old man welcomes his former schoolmate with a warm clasp of the hand, and recalls some youthful frolic." The day's anthem was "Home Sweet Home." Home was the past, boyhood (evidently not girlhood), an ancient place to revisit one last time. "I have felt, sir, today," said a speaker, "as if I must be asked as a representative of the past and not of the present at all." "There attaches to the old town," said Solomon Lincoln's son, "an indescribable quaintness."

An "old boy" came home to see "the fields that I used to run about in," not to confront the present or salute the future. Speakers made vague bows to posterity, but only John D. Long conceded the present, in that note of fatalism so prevalent in these years: "The most boastful son of Hingham must admit that the town has fallen off in some respects. Our fisheries are not what they used to be, with the exception of the smelts. Our buckets are no longer our jewels." The town's jewels were now its surviving ancients. They were tallied as living "institutions." George Lincoln recorded stories of these "ties between the last century and the present," noted twenty-three townsmen born before the turn of the century, and told of the few surviving celebrants of 1835: Jotham Burrell, New North sexton, and Levi Hersey, Baptist piano-maker, had rung the bells of their churches for both anniversaries.

Those of great age became the focus of enormous interest. The *Boston Globe* printed a list of Hingham's eighty octogenarians, and there were lists of war veterans, lists of graves decorated on Memorial Day. Elderlies were surprised by birthday parties and honored at special services where they sang old hymns accompanied by "bass viol and violins as of old." Old dress was unearthed for antiquarian teas and balls. The marvel of the camera fixed for all time an image of four generations. Anxiety lest the record of the past be lost prompted the History Committee to provide a fireproof safe at the store of George Lincoln, whose genealogies were finished five years before the 1893 *History* was published.

The imaginative grip of the past persisted in this impressive monument. Every book of history is written by and for its own present, recreating the past as seen by that present. In its achievements, in its biases, the 1893 *History* tells us much about its own time, a time when other South Shore towns also produced histories. The decision to devote two of four volumes to genealogy is symptomatic. Genealogy had grown popular; it was the democratizing of the idea of ancient lineage, a personal link to the past. The same emphasis prevails in the historical volumes. Institutions are recounted primarily in terms of individual men. Population groups are barely visible; population numbers are hidden at the end in "miscellaneous matters." Four groups are noticeably absent: women (except for Madame Derby), the Irish (a substantial minority for forty years), most politicians (controversial topics are avoided), and the poor. Genealogist Lincoln made no such omissions; he was an unusual member of the team. The team, nevertheless, did prodigious work. Most of the history proper was written by three Bouvés and Francis Lincoln, two merchants, a lawyer, and a real estate broker. All four represented the nineteenth-century middle-class intelligentsia, a remarkable class. All four, devoted to their vision of Hingham as a postindustrial retreat, kept strong metropolitan connections. Naturally, their chapters reflect their priorities.

The elder Bouvé's chapters portray an unimaginably old setting of natural history, endangered by human progress, not a human environment. Son Walter had learned well from Scott and Macaulay; his military history fills almost half a volume with massive amounts of information and images of old wars. Francis Lincoln, an exhaustive researcher, lets documents speak mostly for themselves, setting a model of caution. Edward Bouvé is less cautious, more personal, and because of these qualities, his "Ancient Landmarks" remains most readable. But all were, in the times' social spirit, anxious not to open old wounds or divisions. Better to dwell on the remote past. For them, the past had ended fifty years "since," followed by change and decline.

In his autumnal elegy, Edward Bouvé takes us in search of "ancient landmarks," and "ancient" means everything older than half a century. Fifty years "since," his father saw porpoises sporting off the steamboat, but along with deer, wolf, otter, and beaver, they are gone. Ancient flowers and shrubs hide in forgotten places, and wine glass elms stand alone in wet meadows. The ancient heronry has been destroyed by Rockland Street, and in "quaint" little Tugmanug, "all is now 'spick and span,' tidy and humdrum." Along the harbor, decaying wharves and rotting warehouses are "sad reminders." "Alas, alas! how the mercantile, manufacturing, and maritime enterprises of Hingham have faded away, never [thankfully?] to return." More matter-of-fact George

Lincoln parades the line of ancient industries and laments the fatality that has doomed them during the past fifty years.

Like any history, this one had messages for its own present. First was the integrity of traditional local character, heir of "earnest and sober country farmers and mechanics and sailors" of long ago. John D. Long recalled

> that sturdy, educating, self-reliant New England town life which till forty or fifty years ago was so unique, but which since then has gradually been disintegrated and changed by the tremendous influence of the railroad, the wide scattering of the New England seed, the influx of foreign elements, the rapid growth of large cities.

Second, somewhat at odds with this ethnocentric message, was the thesis of traditional Hingham tolerance. Francis Lincoln fancied that the First Parish obstructed the founding of separate parishes because "perhaps like a fond mother, she could not bear the thought of trusting her children alone," and that Hingham's evangelical churches were latecoming (not because they were warned out, but) because the town did not need them. The third message was the "one central and pervading principle" of local independence, of distance from and defiance of Boston. This message was heard even in the voices of writers for whom such distance and independence seemed doomed.

The first edition of this monument for its times sold out, and a second was prepared. Its guiding spirit, George Lincoln, also wrote fifty-five "Historical Notes" and countless obituaries as elders died away. Perhaps the hardest for him to write was the 1897 obituary of his long-time friend and fellow historian, Fearing Burr. Lincoln compiled a list of everyone since the town's settlement who lived "Eighty Years and Upwards" and catalogued almost five hundred historic artifacts in an exhibit sponsored by the Women's Alliance. It was the last big project in a life given to memorializing Hingham. Only some of his priceless records—the remainder were water damaged beyond recovery—were rescued from a leaky barn in the 1950s by Mason Foley.

In 1888, after an illness, George Lincoln had sold his corner shop to William Hennessy. Lincoln was sixty-six, had worked since he was fourteen, and had been a dry goods dealer for forty-five years. He continued to supervise the *History*, but his two appeals for the forming of a Hingham Historical Society were to no avail. It would be born only five years after his death. When he died at the end of September, 1909, a short obituary was almost hidden on the *Journal's* fourth page.

[231]

For young townspeople, there was momentous change as well, but for them, new horizons opened as old joys disappeared. They had new schools to travel to. They had a new way to get there, an exciting new kind of transportation that made moving about town cheap and easy. But when it arrived, they had two fewer favorite places to go.

While the *History* was circulating in 1894, new monuments arose to youth: two large central schoolhouses. They had long been needed. As Superintendent Louis Nash complained in 1889, our buildings were "in pitiable contrast to those now being erected in some towns." He took the opportunity to urge an economy that would be a hallmark of change in the 1890s: centralization. He proposed more "departmental"—that is, more specialized—instruction, which centralization would allow.

Small old schoolhouses were closed and auctioned off. Some were moved and are now homes, in such places as 222 South, 64 Thaxter, 26 Friend, and 56 Fort Hill Streets. Two six-room buildings rose on Thaxter and School Streets, and South School was renovated and enlarged. By October, 1894, the buildings were ready. They reflected a new era in education. They also fostered a basic social change: the town, so long a network of separate villages, would be brought closer together. This change was furthered by the arrival, in 1896, of a new convenience, a new wonder for the young, "the electrics."

In 1889 in urban America, electricity was applied to street railways, and trolleys became "lords of the streets." They sped along "at twelve miles an hour, about twice as fast as the horses' pace." Fifty cities had trolleys by 1890, and before the decade ended, "the clanging of the streetcars was heard . . . far beyond the city limits." Small-town America, its sense of distance changed forever, could connect for everywhere.

In Hingham, the story of the electrics opened with the failure of south villagers to secure their railroad. They felt slighted in schools, fire protection, and streetlights, and the Water Company had taken their pond. "Perhaps," Henry Miles suggested, "the only remedy is to give that village, in some future time, a separate existence, sorry as we should be to part with it." But the stepchild strove to reinforce its connectedness with the North and also with Weymouth. In 1889, Articles of Association for a Weymouth and Hingham Street Railway were announced. The eight-man board included two South Hingham Cushings, and of fourteen Hinghamites buying a symbolic one share, ten lived in South Hingham. The first stretch of rail was laid in 1891 from Weymouth village to East Weymouth, close to Hingham's western boundary line. There was still no connection between Weymouth and South Hingham.

There the matter lay until 1894. Then, directors of an association for the forming of a new company, the "Hingham Street Railway," petitioned for a hearing with the selectmen. They proposed an "electric road" along Main Street from Queen Ann's Corner to Broad Bridge. At Hingham's town lines, other "electric roads" would connect, and at Broad Bridge, three Hingham lines would meet. Passengers could transfer from the Main Street "car" to trolleys running east to Nantasket and west along Lincoln Street to the Back River and Weymouth-Quincy-Boston lines. A spur track up Downer Avenue would lead to Melville Garden and the boat wharf at Downer Landing.

The hearing with the selectmen was the most acrimonious since meetings about the Water Company. After Walter B. Foster read the proposal of 850 petitioners—621 of them registered voters, almost two-thirds of the voting list—there was wild applause. The strongest objections came from some of the town's most influential men, Ebed Ripley, Charles Barnes, Walter Bouvé, and John D. Long. Long challenged the competence of the contractor and asked how many shares he held in the new company. The propriety of his questions was questioned, a difficult moment for this man of harmony, and he withdrew. That summer, he rented his house and went to Maine. Rumor followed that he would stay there, but in September he returned, and later he accepted the inevitable coming of the electrics.

Opponents feared the danger to pedestrians, especially children, and the loss of the beauty of the streets. But the high school principal thought the electrics would be a convenience and did not mind their running in front of his property. William Fearing, though he owned a horse and carriage himself, said the electrics would benefit those who did not. Banker Joseph Jacobs argued that they would enhance South Hingham real estate. In a few weeks, the selectmen granted the petition of the Hingham Street Railway. The legislature granted its charter. Local capital was insufficient, and so began the process typical of the electrics' thirty-year life: merger and outside capitalization. Hingham had what investors wanted, access to Nantasket Beach, and by the beginning of 1896, a Philadelphia engineering firm and a Newton investor held controlling interest.

The owners promised electrics by the first of July. The Cove and harbor became a human scene of unimaginable busy-ness. From Cobb's Bank (the mound on the site of today's Fruit Center), "sidewalk supervisors" watched as four months quickly passed. While men cleared grounds and buildings around the old Howard foundry, the foundry shell served as a stable for horses and mules shipped in by freight train. Other men were inside the shell, using it for protection while they were framing for the powerhouse. Work gangs at the waterfront unloaded from barge and schooner the thousands of bricks to build it. Carpenters, masons, brick tenders, and cement carriers were hired. Riggers came from East Boston to bolt together and then hoist the huge iron chimney, towering to ninety-six feet. Over six hundred tons of coal arrived at Thompson's Wharf to fuel the powerhouse. Wilder and Kimball's received cargoes of lumber from Maine for the car barn's trussed roof, six tracks, and repair pits. Carloads of rails sixty feet long were shipped in, together with fifty Italian laborers, who dug the trenches for those rails and their cedar ties and holes for the power poles. From tower wagons, cross pieces were placed for wires. The Water Company complained that the electrics would corrode their pipes but laid pipe to the powerhouse anyway.

In June, 1896, the boilers and engines began to bubble and hum for "the cars". Celebrations began with a trial run by the engineers in pouring rain. Then came the first run south with a summer trolley full of officials and invited guests:

> Car number 32 left Broad Bridge at about 7:30 o'clock in charge of motorman John Brinks and conductor William Moore . . . decorated in the national colors . . . . At Hingham Centre, the National Brass Band helped to fill the car, which immediately proceeded southward. The arrival . . . at Meetinghouse hill was the signal for a demonstration such as South Hingham has seldom witnessed. Bonfires lighted the scene, the bell in the church rung out joyously, cannon fireworks roared and screeched, and this was added to by the cheers of the multitude on the church green. With music by the band, the car made its triumphal way through this babel of sounds,

and after a derailment, proceeded to Queen Ann's Corner, then returned to Wilder Hall for a concert and collation. Liberty Plainers, feeling left out as they had often felt before, had their own celebration with Norwell.

However unattractive some found the street railway, Hingham was saved from the grid pattern of Boston's "streetcar suburbs." Its villages were ancient, and the tracks followed old roads between them. The impact, however, was tremendous. Southernmost villagers could arrive at the depot and Broad Bridge in about twenty minutes. They could ride to Nantasket or reach the Weymouths via High or Lincoln Street. A fare of eighteen cents took commuters and shoppers into Boston by way of Lincoln Street to the Quincy-Boston line. By the turn of the century, when all rails south of Boston were consolidated into the Old Colony Street Railway, a five cent fare with transfers took the passenger anywhere in town; school children paid half. Cars could be chartered for evening events. Members from all villages could attend central organizations such as the new Wompatuck Club. The Gun Club moved to easily accessible grounds in South Hingham. The town was hooked into a network of rails for commuters, excursionists, and workers. Derrah's *Official Street Railway Guide* ran into numerous editions. Riders could leave Brockton, connect at Queen Ann's Corner, and be at Nantasket in an hour and a half. In six months of 1896, Hingham's twenty cars carried over 450 thousand passengers.

Like others, this new convenience bred difficulties. Initially, the rail was a single track with turnouts, but double tracks would be laid on Rockland Street and at Broad Bridge. There were many serious accidents. The noisy trolleys ran too fast, their thirty-foot lengths blocked the view at Broad Bridge, their whistles annoyed Main Street residents, and their careless maintenance, claimed Wallace Corthell, interfered with street lighting. In 1900, the First Parish held a mock town meeting. People had not lost their sense of humor despite the confusion. Article Twelve read:

> Will the town appoint a committee to ascertain whether the Water Company, the Philadelphia Syndicate, the Telephone Company, the Electric Light Commission, or the townspeople own the highways, and which, if any, have the right to hack the trees, with a view of finding out where we are at?

"Where we are at" must have been perplexing for the old. For the young, it was exhilarating to "be at" more places.

In that watershed year of 1896, however, a favorite event and a favorite place vanished. With their disappearance, even the young may have sensed the close of an epoch. The last of the annual outdoor agricultural fairs was held, and Melville Garden closed forever. Their simultaneous passings reflected the same changing tastes—indeed, seem to have been caused by them.

The old fairs had continued to change from "cattle shows" to indoor exhibits and outdoor carnivals. Pleased by the exhibits and increasingly dismayed by the carnivals, the Agricultural and Horticultural Society struggled to recapture its original aims by holding Farmers' Institutes, but the schedule for 1896 illustrates what "farmers" were supposed to care about: Spraying Trees and Shrubs, Among the Ferns, Fertilizers,

Market Gardening, and Ladies' Night. In 1893, a lady, Mrs. Charles Marble, edited the annual *Transactions*, and her sentimental vision relegated farming to the past:

> How eagerly, when farming was the principal occupation in our vicinity, would our grandfathers have studied the pages of these reports, as after the day's work and chores were all done, they sat in the old roundabout with feet incased in home-knit socks . . . before the open fireplace on which the logs were briskly burning.

Nonetheless, through 1896 "everyone" came to the fair. Fifteen-year-old Dennis Gibbon observed, in 1894, with a social novelist's eye:

> The rich man is there because he desires to patronize the Society; the poor man is there for the reason that he has a holiday and wants to enjoy it; the farmer and his wife, both in their antiquated go-to-meeting best, are there, the former to compare his vegetables and cattle with his brother farmers and to discuss "craps" with them, the latter to examine the pastry and fancy work, and to see what her neighbors wear. The fashionable young woman is there, dressed in the latest style. You will know her by the involuntary motion of her hands to see if her hat is on straight, and her self-conscious appearance. And the small boy is there in full force, haunting the peanut and ice cream stands, and maybe if he is real naughty, smoking a two-for-a-cent cigar in the woods beyond.

Next year, the Society offered prizes for essays by high school students. The winners were more diplomatic than Dennis in their essays. As the first day dawned, recalled Margaret Griffin,

> Wagons of vegetables and fruits were being unloaded at the door of the Hall, men were running in and out bearing huge squashes, watermelons, etc., while the women were hurrying along laden with preserves . . . regular prize-catching loaves . . . neat rolls of butter . . . . The young lady sends some delicate needlework, or if she is skillful, a fine painting, while her older brothers send pianos and organs, or stylish, inviting buggies from their respective factories.

Early that same morning, wrote Edward Gibbons,

> you could hear the hammers as the fakir stands went up, just in front of the cattle pens, and they do a brisk trade in eatables and everything else . . . and that very sober and much abused dog Toby had his hat pulled off by Punch and chewed up Judy at frequent intervals.

Helena Kimball remembered that

the bicycle racing and horse trotting kept a crowd on the hill overlooking the track . . . . What a crowd of little folks was present! . . . The many small boys who dodged the aides, and who feasted on "double-jointed, hump-backed peanuts," "chocolate squares," and "candies ten for a cent!" . . . the village beau . . . distinguished himself by throwing three ripe red tomatoes at the woolly head of the African dodger.

Margaret Griffin managed to visit the lower end of the grounds to find

savage bulls, mooing cows and calves, big pigs, great pigs, huge pigs, and small pigs, smaller pigs, and tiny pigs, sheep of all size and goats of both sex . . . loving bantam families, doves continually billing and cooing, fighting roosters, tough old hens and speckled guinea hens . . . timid, bashful rabbits, and not far away the noisy, boisterous ducks.

The children did not notice how the pens were shrinking. It did not bother them that fakir tents and horse races had turned the fair into something the Society had long resisted.

Imagine the shock when, in 1896, the Society announced there would be no more outdoor fairs. One grand revival would be held in 1900, but otherwise there would be only indoor exhibits intended to teach those who came—they came in diminished numbers—"how to improve the products of their orchards and gardens, how to make useful household articles, and also to hold social intercourse with neighbors and friends." The Society promised that "no effort will be spared to meet and gratify public taste." Clearly, the Society was not referring to the old taste for fakir tents, horse trotting, hump-backed peanuts, and boisterous ducks.

The same changes of taste were working at Melville Garden in 1896. In the early 1890s, the old amusement park still flourished. Attendance was larger than ever. Steamer access had to be increased, and a new wharf, landings, and buildings were proposed. The Rose Standish House had grown to 150 "apartments". The flower beds, tended by the same Savin Hill man for seventeen years, grew more glorious each summer. Special police, the "Jolly Seven," and Assistant Superintendent Wash James kept order. When unruly members of the fashionable Cadet Corps scaled the fence, they were promptly collared and made to pay twenty-five cents admission. Harder to rectify were their other offenses—nude bathing in front of Otis Street homes; the theft of a sign, "Swings 5 cents," which reappeared at the Cadet camp as "Swigs 5 cents." Also hard to control was the swigging place, the notorious "Pig and Whistle," run by a disreputable Fee in the woods beyond the monkeys and bears. Would the cheap, easy access by electric make matters worse?

The Garden, in Downer's dream, was for everyman, the "Favorite Resort of the Pleasure Seeker and the Refuge of the Weary Worker." Prices were kept low. In four sittings at the Clambake Pavilion, a thousand people still feasted for fifty cents. Black organizations were welcome; black and white employees were domiciled near the Garden. At her home on Whiton Avenue, the wife of Francis Brewer, architect of Melville Garden, heard the beautiful singing of black waiters, after their day's work, floating across Walton Cove. But Downer Landing was growing fashionable. Expensive homes were owned or rented by people who wished to escape the city and with it, no doubt, the city crowds who came to the Garden. Four of Downer's daughters had summer cottages. Their neighbors were wealthy friends. They were among the "fashionables" at Saturday afternoon polo games; they played lawn tennis on a new court and joined in the weekly regattas of the Crow Point Yacht Club. It is surprising that they coexisted with Melville Garden as long as they did.

In May, 1896, Downer's son-in-law James Scudder died unexpectedly. He had managed the Garden strictly since its start. The Scudders wintered at the Cushing House, then moved to Jarvis Avenue for summers. He was often seen about town with his grandson and his bay gelding, riding and sleighing. When he died, there was no trusted local gentleman to carry on Downer's expensive dream. The decision to close was soon made.

Other reasons for the decision can be guessed from what happened at two new houses on Otis Street. Bandmaster T. O. Edmands had built them, and each summer he and his family returned here from the city. But by the 1890s, there was an Otis Street entrance to the Garden, and the neighborhood was scarcely the place for a summer retreat. For his last two seasons, Edmands rented the cottages, and he, his wife, and daughter Gertrude retreated to Rocky Nook (East Street). Looking back, his tenants agreed that "the removal of Melville Garden" was "a great benefit to Downer Landing as a residential locality." The Landing would be free of city hordes, just as the fairs would be free of naughty boys.

In the fall of 1896, the town accepted the hydrants and made "public highways" of Merrill and Malcolm Streets. Garden buildings were moved elsewhere in town or razed for secondhand building materials. The Rose Standish House vanished in six weeks. George Cushing bought the equipage and opened a summer stable; Cornelius Foley bought the ice business; Liba Studley moved an octagonal building to renovate into a laundry for Tom Sing. The "pleasure seekers and weary workers" would have to go elsewhere. The cottagers formed a Crow Point Improvement Association, their retreat from the city secured.

What had the city come to mean to those so anxious to retreat from it? The menacing spread of the "great grey metropolis" caused widespread alarm. Boston had long engaged in a campaign of "annexation" as it spread erratically from an isolated peninsula to "several isolated districts, divided by rivers, tidal estuaries, or ocean." In mid-century, pressures for expansion and annexation increased as the city changed from a trading port to a manufacturing center, with a new immigrant labor force squeezed into every alley. Pressure on space and resources precipitated successful forays to annex the "streetcar suburbs," Roxbury (1868), Dorchester (1870), and Brighton, West Roxbury, and Charlestown (1874). Alarmed, the surrounding towns united to resist.

But their "fierce localism" was soon compromised by a growing need for regional services. In 1889, rising worries over public health and polluted rivers led to the creation of a Metropolitan Sewerage Board. In 1892, increased desires for open space and recreation brought into being a Board of Metropolitan Park Commissioners. "Metropolitan" authorities—the very concept of "metropolitan" was new and threatening to towns—seemed to be gobbling up thousands of acres of park and wetlands. In 1895, a Metropolitan Water District was established, with plans for a reservoir and delivery system. Hingham's geography placed it just beyond the bounds of expansion, but who could guess how far the expansion would go?

Old towns wondered fatalistically when they would become "mere suburbs." The very idea of the "suburb" was antipathetic to their idea of community. The suburbs they saw were designed on a grid plan, and the grid plan "did not concern itself with public life." Grid suburbs made no accommodation for villages. The term "village" carried crucial positive connotations in local minds. The village was a center of public life; without that public life, there was no true community. This was what the spread of the "great grey metropolis" had come to mean.

The alarm climaxed in January, 1896. A legislative committee in Boston endorsed a proposal to consolidate all the new authorities into one Metropolitan District Commission. In Hingham, the report caused a "sensation." Its past as an "island community" seemed to be ending.

Finally, 1896 was a "watershed year" in national politics. Here, too, the local impact was dramatic. The story began in 1884. Following

Grover Cleveland's victory and "Beast" Butler's appeal to ethnic voters, the atmosphere grew ugly. Republicans had labeled their opponents the party of "Rum, Romanism, and Rebellion," but they could not ignore new voters. "Unless we can break this compact foreign vote," wrote Senator George Hoar to Henry Cabot Lodge, "we are gone." To "break" meant to divide the new immigrants politically from the established Irish. Yankee and Irish politicians strengthened their defenses. The late 1880s saw a resurgence of religious bigotry, a politicized anti-liquor lobby, and an overt hostility to parochial schools.

In 1888, the strategy seemed to work. Benjamin Harrison defeated Cleveland, and Boston elected a Republican mayor. In Hingham, the margin remained more than two to one Republican. Hattie Shute (Wilder), a South Hingham child, remembered long afterwards:

> We was all Republicans. We always thought nothing was Democrats but the drunks and no-goods . . . . I remember one night—I think Cleveland was running for Democrat. I don't remember who the Republican was. And of course, after the other felluh got in, then they had a sort of march down the street to see the illuminations . . . . And up in the house next to the Hall [Wilder], there was another Josiah Lane lived, and he was a Democrat—oh a red hot terrible one! And we went up by his house, and he had a picture of Grover Cleveland on the piano with a candle back of it so you could just see, and the rest of the house was pitch dark. Of course, we was tickled to death and we didn't know why.

But Democratic hopes were rising. In 1892, Republican tactics backfired, and the Democratic percentage in Massachusetts and the nation reached its high mark of the half-century. Butlerites returned to the Democratic fold, and many Republicans crossed over. Cleveland won the state and the presidency. Harrison won Hingham, but the Democratic vote increased.

In 1895, for the first time, Hingham Democrats nominated a townsman of Irish descent for state office. Thomas H. Buttimer, Jr., School Committee member and attorney, was their choice for state representative. The *Journal* reassured its readers: "Although of Irish parentage, Mr. Buttimer is thoroughly American in his ideas, and is a gentleman of refinement and intellectuality." Buttimer lost, but the margin was only three to two. Were the trend to continue, given the town's demographics, Hingham Democrats might become a majority.

But "Showdown 1896" changed all that. The national Democratic Party was captured by rising populist forces in the West and South. The spectacular Nebraskan William Jennings Bryan mesmerized its convention with his "Cross of Gold" speech. To the defamatory label "Rum, Romanism, and Rebellion" was now added "Radicalism." But "Romanism" wanted no part of Bryan. Conservative Irish Democrats were less alienated by Yankee Nativist slurs than by Bryan's fundamentalist rhetoric and radical policies. Massachusetts voted overwhelmingly for McKinley; even Boston "went Republican." Democratic hopes were dashed for years to come. The decision of Irish voters to bolt "their" party in conservative reaction is seen in the Hingham results. Bryan received only forty-five votes to McKinley's six hundred.

We know already the effect on the town of McKinley's election. His friend John D. Long went to Washington as Navy Secretary. We know the terrible irony of Long's tenure, inadvertently touching off the powder keg in Havana harbor and directing the naval arm of the nation's first imperialist venture. We know how deeply troubled he was by the new foreign policy. America was moving onto the world stage as a major power. As Long retired in 1902 to "little Hingham," he must have sensed how the place had become a refuge, how the greater world would impinge on "the even tenor of our life," and how this ancient town, with its increasingly fragile and precious local life, would be affected.

"Not all is changed," he wrote later. But much had changed. An epoch had ended.

PART THREE

The Island Community Fades

(1897-1928)

A last glimpse of a favorite childhood pastime, pung riding, photographed by Frances Cooke Macgregor in 1938. The driver has been identified by William Antoine as "Mr. Marshall."

ABOVE: Boy Scout Troop 1 at Prospect Hill Farm in 1911. Reverend Robinson (dark suit) of the Congregational Church was scoutmaster. The hatted boy on the ground to the right, looking directly at the camera, is Julian Loring.

Joseph Lincoln (1859–1938), American decoy maker of distinction. He captured "the essence of a duck." Clockwise from the upper left of his armload: merganser, golden eye, canvas body Canada goose, wood duck, Canada goose.

"The Blacksmith Shop, Water Street, 1940": drawing, Edgar T. P. Walker (1889–1965). A Harvard-trained architect, Walker's Hingham buildings include the Old Colony Lodge, the three fire stations, and Foster School. He was consultant for the enlargement of St. John's Church and for the 1930s restoration of Old Ship. He also produced watercolors and many fine drawings of national historic sites and of Hingham scenes.

"Houses Along the Old Mill Pond": drawing, Louis Ruyl (1871-1951). A specialist in drawings for newspapers, Ruyl covered the Spanish-American War and, after he moved to Hingham (1906), recorded New England street scenes. Here, he has captured a vanished piece of Hingham from the perspective of Water Street, looking across the pond to lower North Street.

"Train Time at Sunset at Hingham Square—1910": watercolor, Howard Leavitt Horton (1904-1983). Horton was famous for "ragging" the Baptist Church organ. He was known in Boston and around the South Shore as "the dream melody pianist" during the 1920s. His notes to this memory of the Square state that the white horse was an Arabian from Peter Bradley's stable and the horse and buggy to the left were John D. Long's.

Smelt fishing at Beal's float, Hingham harbor, 1908.

Hingham Society of Arts and Crafts
(1901–1922) paper label.

"Oriole" basket (c. 1903) made by Harriet Blanche Thayer.
Coiled raffia, dyed yellow, dark blue, and red from natural
materials. Though the red is now faded, the paper label
remains firmly attached.

Susan Barker Willard (1856–1925).
A photographic post card that Miss
Willard sent as a New Year's greeting
in 1913.

Doll's house, furnishings,
and photograph by
William B. Luce
(1860–1924), toy-
maker and
photographer.

CHAPTER EIGHTEEN

❊

Memories of Childhood and Youth

As the twentieth century opened, the attention of adults was ever more focused on children, their lives and development. But every child has his own agenda and point of view. Some of the most vivid of childhood memories grow out of the times when the child is having a private life. Paradoxically, the locus of a child's private life is often very public and out of doors. Through the public images and private lives of several Hinghamites who lived to reminisce in the 1970s and 1980s, we can rediscover the town at the start of the new century. Hingham was undergoing historic changes. For the child, however, change has little to do with history and much to do with daily sights, sounds, and smells, and with the rhythms of the seasons.

For much of the year, a child saw Hingham life on the way to school and home again. Louise Wilder had only to scramble under the fence from home to Old Derby. Myron Ray Clark, who lived next door to his school on Thaxter Street, found himself a little too close. One day he felt bored and ambled home; it was a short trek back under his mother's guidance, his earlobe between her thumb and forefinger. For Alma Tinsley, the stretch between home on Leavitt Street and Centre School allowed for some innocent "deviltry." There were a "few dumps to play in"; the informal refuse heaps around town were fun.

Some children traveled by "electrics." The cars were endlessly interesting in their most ordinary operations, such as reversing the direction of the trolley. The conductor, Myron Clark remembered, would carry the cord reel box and,

> tugging the trolley arm from the overhead wire, he would swing the arm in a wide arc . . . aim it at the live wire overhead. His objective

was to fit it into the groove in the pulley at the end of the trolley arm. It usually took several tries. When he would miss and the arm banged into the wire, there would be a series of very satisfactory big sparks and flashes. At night, these pyrotechnics would be even more spectacular. Some conductors were more adept than others. When one would make it on the first try, he would rate a little round of applause from the passengers.

When Myron's family moved to Main Street opposite Wilder Hall, he would take the trolley to Centre School for some subjects. From Mullein Hill off Cushing Street, Professor Dallas Lore Sharp's boys had a long hike through the woods before hopping on the electric. From nearby at the corner of Gardner and Whiting Streets, Nettie Gardner rode down to the high school in the early morning electric "mail car."

> If we had fifty cents, we could ride down the five mornings to school down at Cold Corner. That's where the high school was then. And we had to walk home. Think of it, five miles, four years in succession . . . . Rain, snow, whatever it was . . . . And in the morning, I used to walk that mile [to Main]. And in Gardner Street the sides of the street are all big pine trees. Then they were scrubby little pines, you know. And it was dark practically at seven in the morning. I was scared to death. If ever I started to run as I entered this woodsy place, I ran clear the whole length of the street, scared to death for fear somebody would bob out of the trees at me.

Wilmon Brewer and his sisters had no such fears. They were delivered to school from Great Hill in Father's "Pope-Robinson," and later, when Father gave up that dangerous new "automobile," in the elegant horse-drawn "Democrat." Wilmon faced his own challenges. On his first day, he confronted black Billy Tuttle on his fatness and was warned that Billy might fall on and squash him. Later, Wilmon was dared to fight by John Breen, did so, and won.

After school, ethnic tensions and territorial instincts made some home-goings less than peaceable. In the North Ward, neighborhood boys had such tribal names as "Covers" and "Red Doggers." A later "Covuh," Bill Quinn, remembered the panicky run home of one Waspish lad, chased by those terrors, the Magner boys, all the way to Fountain Square from West School.

For the more leisurely child homeward bound from Thaxter Street to the Cove, there were many things to notice and stops to make. She set out down North Street, past the smells of Olson's fish market, across the street from the smells of Amos Humphrey's butcher shop and meat-processing plant. She passed the bustling new emporium of Greenfield's. As she passed Fountain Square, on her right was the old Soule mansion, not yet fashionable Talbots. Next to it was an old commercial building, Ford's Block. From upstairs came the sound of the *Journal*'s presses running. Downstairs was Margetts' "lovely candy store" and the dry goods shop run by that odd character, Miss Suzie Gates. No telling what gossip the child might overhear in that shop or what pranks might be played. "My brother and I," recalled Bertha Stringer,

> did an awful thing once. My sister had a game and it had little silver things that looked like ten cent pieces. So we gathered them up one day and went down to Miss Gates' and bought some spools of thread and all this, and paid for them. They looked like ten cent pieces.

Across from Miss Gates' at the railroad depot, a Boston train blocked Thaxter's Bridge. Horse-drawn buggies and teams, trolleys, bicycles, even a few new "autos", were waiting in a muddle. The train pulled out. Rolls of Boston newspapers had been dropped off, and boys were scurrying to carry them to the newsdealers, Hennessy's and Breen's. Kitty Hennessy, John McKee remembered, rewarded the boys with free penny candy.

Across Central Street, in the corner cellar of the Anthes Building (Noble's Camera Store today), was the laundry of Quong Hing. The homeward bound stroller might peek in, but "there's rats in there," so she probably hurried down South Street, past Frank Overton's ice cream parlor, to the corner of Main Street. Here, if the year happened to be 1912, she could stop in front of Hennessy's (7 Main) with its new ice-less soda fountain and watch the old Acadian house, the "Hollis place," being torn down to make way for the new town office building (today the School Department offices). Then, jay-walking across to the corner of North Street, she would pass Barba's fruit stand with its whistling peanut roaster and stop next door to peer into the shiny display of Bickford's hardware window. Across North from Bickford's stood the old Cushing House. If the weather was warm, little old ladies sat on the veranda rocking and fanning themselves.

The next point of interest was the fire station, the Isaac Little Hose House, at Magoon's Bridge (the junction of North and South Streets), and beyond that, at 70 North, was the "lock-up," the new police station (1901). The town's first chief of police, Wash James, remembered by petite Anna Calvi as "that itty bitty thing," might be returning from some scene of accident or crime in his fringed buggy with his dog beside him. On, then, the child went, past the blacksmith shop with its coal fire, glowing iron, steamy sizzle as it hit water, pungent smell of

[247]

pared hoof as it burned, smell of straw, manure and horses. Past the mill she went, stooping

> to pat the cat on the doorsill and to look into the soft shadows . . . where even the cobwebs were hung with flour dust . . . the sound of running water . . . through the floorboards . . . the building [was] shaking and groaning to the sullen rumble of the millstones . . . the fine corn meal . . . fanning out into the bins, yellow in the yellow dust.

Then past Anderson's grocery (later, the site of Page's, then Stars restaurant) and across from it, the paint shop (now Ye Olde Mill Grille), where "crusty old Yankee" David Cobb was "daubing the brushes."

Reaching the harborside, the child saw no waterfront park, no highway. A narrow "harbor street" wound from Otis to Summer Street through decaying tenements that had once been ship stores, sail lofts, and fish houses. On the waterside were Thompson's tall coal silos, full of pigeons when empty, Kimball's lumber yard, and the Yacht Club with its two-masted schooner, *Otranto*, near today's Iron Horse. On a lucky day, the child might see a schooner unloading lumber at Kimball's, but that was a rare sight in these years.

> The lumber used to come in on small ships, sailing vessels, and they had a channel where they marked that—they cut birch trees and left just a bunch of branches on the top and they'd go out and stick them down in the mud, and that was the channel. And the coal coming in in barges, and a tug boat'd push 'em up to the wharf there.

Her walk finished, the child turned into "Kickapoo," Green Street and the Court, the little Irish neighborhood where she lived.

The streets were fascinating places for the attentive child in the new century's early years. Streets were always changing. Stacks of materials lay here and there for the endless street work. Hastily laid trolley tracks needed repair. Ditches were being dug for gas and water pipes. Poles were being planted for electricity and telephones. Wires stretched everywhere—pretty stuff in a snowstorm—for electrics, fire alarms, lights, and phones. The street superintendent and his men were busy improving streets, covering dusty surfaces with oily, smelly "Tarvia" and building "granolithic" sidewalks.

It was hard for a child not to stare at the work gangs. To Myron Clark, they talked in "staccato bursts" that sounded like "gibberish." "They laughed a lot and shouted at each other—all the time with picks flying and long handled shovels scooping the earth . . . . At noon, work would stop on a whistle signal from the red-faced foreman," a "brawny, sunburned and freckled Irishman." From a bandanna in the folds of a shirt came a "large chunk of crusty bread and either sausage or cheese or sometimes both. This they would chew with their strong white teeth, washed down by copious drafts of water, dipped from a pail brought around by a boy." Another boy, Howie Horton, watched these Italian men coming up the street after work, waving their hands in the air, to their boarding house off Elm Street. Howie sneaked up after supper to watch them sitting in the doorway, one playing an accordion, another singing Italian folksongs, bone-tired, dreaming of home.

Even more exciting street scenes erupted with the ringing of the fire bell. At Broad Bridge, volunteer firemen would appear out of nowhere, stop at George Cushing's stable behind the Cushing House for a pair of horses, then dash down to the fire engine house at Magoon's Bridge and hitch the horses to "the steamer." They would "wheel out of the firehouse with all the children . . . running after them." Elders threw open their windows and called out excitedly, "Where's the fire?" as the "mad mob" raced past "accompanied by the barking of all the mongrel dogs."

There were terrible fires. Myron Clark remembered the one at Jordan farm, on Union Street near Pleasant, in 1901.

> The farm buildings had been reduced to a pile of blackened embers. A big wooden silo, partially burned, had split open and spilled out its load of chopped corn stalks in a slimy and odorous mound. There was another pervading scent in the air . . . the partially consumed carcasses of scores of cows.

The old bucket mill burned in 1902, watched from every hilltop by children and adults in their Easter finery. In 1910, one of Hayward's ice houses caught fire from the spark of a passing locomotive, a not uncommon accident in spite of "spark arresters" on the trains. In 1913, the steamship lay-out burned at Crow Point, and an inferno at Bradley's fertilizer works on the Back River could be seen for miles. In 1916, Paragon Park burned, and in 1917, the old ropewalk off Central Street. "The smell of the fire," John McKee recalled, "lasted for a year."

Fires could happen at any time of year. Other events and activities, favorites of childhood and youth, came at their regular times in the long rhythm of the seasons. The child's year began with school in the autumn and crawled toward summer with highpoints along the way.

Autumn's event was still the fair, but it was all indoors now with children playing their orderly parts as exhibitors of crafts. Some could remember the fair of 1900, the one-year revival of the outdoor spectacles of yore, with livestock exhibits and ponies and draft horses. Two ball games were played, one between Hinghams and Norfolks and another between lawyers and doctors-and-clergymen. Broad bats were in order; "clothes baskets for flyballs were handy in case of need." The highlight was a spontaneous cakewalk by Mr. Burdett and Dr. Hersey to ragtime music by the National Brass Band.

One popular event at that 1900 fair would long be a favorite of outdoor celebrations: the "Vet Muster." On these occasions, veteran volunteer firemen would bring back out of storage some of the old "bucket tubs" and compete according to the old methods. Warren Lincoln remembered the hats, wide belts, and red shirts of the "Vets," the filling of the "tubs" by a bucket brigade, and then, the "play-out" as the men labored to get water up a line of hose and through a long nozzle with a small bore. "Break her down, boys," shouted the captain. "Break her down!" The length of the stream was measured in feet *and* inches, on paper, from one hundred fifty to well over two hundred feet. "They'd take that last drop as their measure." The musters would make any child wish to be a fireman.

October brought sights of wealthy summer people closing up houses and of McKee's express moving them to city winter quarters. It brought sounds of hunting: "considerable fusilading" was "heard in the neighborhood." At Accord and Triphammer Ponds, in the Third Division Woods, and on Back River, fishing and sporting camps were busy places. But hunters in North Hingham read the handwriting on the wall. After 1914, a bird sanctuary extended from Lincoln Street at Broad Cove across the hills to the Back River; no shooting was permitted near the Navy's new powder magazine "up town in Hockley" after 1909. Children whose families raised poultry on Beal Street heard plenty of talk about foxes round the hen house. Like children, the foxes had an instinct for open, unguarded territory.

What would the storms of November and December bring? Grown-ups measured every storm by the violent Nor'easter, the Portland Gale of Thanksgiving Saturday, 1898. Fallen and uprooted trees and broken poles lay criss-crossed everywhere. Wires "coated with frozen snow . . . hung in festoons in the streets." Tides reached almost to Green Street. The carbarn floor sank, leaving trolleys at a dangerous angle. Railroad tracks were in ruins. The steamer *Hingham* was impaled on its pilings, its wharf lifted off the quay, and so ended the harbor's days on the steamboat line. Bathhouses, boats, sheds, lumber, and coal lay scattered across the landscape. Droves of spectators came to view the disaster scene. Bertha Stringer was eight: "I sort of vaguely remember the storm of 1898 because electric cars went by here [15-17 Lincoln Street] to go to Nantasket, loaded down with people . . . . You had to change at the Square." Children could not hope for such another storm, but February, 1911, delivered the biggest gale "since." It raised a new Main Street house off of its foundations, damaged the Second Parish steeple, and blew over Ervin Horton's mail wagon.

Winter meant sledding, but in the new spirit of safety, Chief James prohibited sledding on dangerously hilly streets. Never again would a boy coast from the top of Ship Street almost to Button Island. Self-professed tomboy Bertha Stringer remembered:

> We used to coast from the top of Ship Street across onto the harbor before Otis Street was cut through as a highway. They used to put the plough down Ship Street . . . . We used to put water down so's it would be faster . . . . We used to do it down Winter Street and down Fearing Road from the top and up the next hill. It was quite nice . . . . And down Lafayette Avenue there was a photography shop at the bottom, and a sign said, "Walk In." We never made the curve on our Flexible Flyer, so we went right into the door.

She challenged the boys at "punging" too:

> They used to deliver groceries in long carts with two runners, and we used to just go punging to get a ride . . . . Sometimes the drivers weren't so nice to us . . . . We used to spend Saturdays punging, go from one end of the town to the other.

Pungs, as Myron Clark remembered them, were "conversions of wheeled wagons and carts to runners . . . . The sled frames were equipped with heavy-steel-capped runners . . . . Most pungs were open-topped with flat-bed bodies . . . . The low flat-bed varieties were ideal for small boys seeking to 'hook' a ride." Street Superintendent Clifford's new snowroller made streets ideal for punging. "As the pungs went by, the kids would run along and jump on the runners or into the back. Those who couldn't make it on the pung itself might tie their sleds on behind, but this made them vulnerable to snowball broadsides from their cronies already in the pung." This was perilous sport.

Skating was safer. "We loved to go skating at [Cushing Pond] . . . . We stayed half the night, and listened to Cy Cushing's brother play the harmonica." Skaters could follow the Weir River upstream to Triphammer Pond to watch a striking young woman do figures on the ice to music from a tiny wind-up Victrola, and "could she skate!" The skater, first and long-time captain of the Girl Scouts, Bertha Stringer, remained an immortal image in the childhood mind of those times. An equally lovely winter image was the sleighing. "The atmosphere," one child remembered, "was sometimes filled with the tinkling of many sleigh bells." "We would sit in this cozy place," said another, "all covered up with buffalo robes . . . . The bells were hospitable, and if you passed another sleigh you'd wave and say hello . . . . People were more full of one another then." A good snow made a "speedway" for sleighs and trotting races between Derby and Pear Tree Hill. "Main Street presented quite a spirited scene . . . when the trotters were out in their sleighs, and the spectators lined the sidewalks, watching their favorites."

Ice-harvesting was eagerly awaited. With the hard freeze after New Year's, George Hayward's gangs were out on the ponds with their chisels and bars, cutting big sections, dividing them into blocks, and loading these onto wagons to go into sawdusty storage in cavernous ice houses to insure a summer's supply. The ice wagon was a familiar sight among the town's assorted wagons and teams.

Winter also had its indoor pastimes and spectacles. With the new marvel, the Victrola, there were lots of dances for the young, with country dancing, the waltz, the fashionable "Duchess," and the two-step to "Oh You Beautiful Doll!" Ruth Marsh fondly recalled the annual Christmas dance at Wilder: the girls wore long skirts, and the boys, white gloves to protect the girls' sashes. "You always had a fan, and the boys would fan you after a dance . . . . If you missed the last street-car, you had to walk home."

The era of silent film had opened. "Way back," remembered John McKee from childhood, "Bob Rich would show movies in the G.A.R. Hall." In 1912, the trustees of Loring Hall took the step of renting their hall for films, and clubs began sponsoring evening movie parties. For a while, young Howie Horton provided piano accompaniment, daring to practice at the Baptist Church, where his stern grandfather, a deacon, let him try out the organ. "As soon as Grandfather would leave, I'd play moving picture music and ragtime. Boy did I rag that organ— the whole church would sway back and forth. Then Grandfather would come back and yell, 'Howard, stop that wicked music!'"

Out of sight of the children, men played cards all winter, some at clubs and lodges, Italians in the powerhouse at the Cove. Sam Cassidy and his friends played nearby at the lumber yard in the middle of a pile, but the kids saw them and picked up their empty bottles to collect the two-cent deposit. Pool was in vogue; "We were all great pool players," remembered Louise Wilder (Cobleigh). The Wompatuck Club had ten teams, and others could play at Frank Buttimer's pool room upstairs in the Anthes Building. Ice hockey was becoming popular, and the splendid new armory, opened in 1910, offered a better place than Loring Hall for basketball. In 1916, Hingham's "Fearless Five" were South Shore champions.

With the coming of spring, baseball returned, and its revived popularity again put Hingham on the sports map. The great "Breezy Hills" were responsible. Their local stars, "Ace" Bergan, Heffernan, "Doll" Breen, "Tup" Tinsley, Fee, two Wallaces, Mause, Bjorklund, and Markham the Great at shortstop, challenged comparison with the Hingham greats of the late 1800s. By 1915, the "Breezies" had taken on Boston's best. But their real competition was subtler. Major League scores were posted at Buttimer's, and the *Journal* reported those games. The decline of the 1890s repeated itself. After the Great War, which took Breezy Hills and Fearless Five together "Over There," it again became an annual struggle to subsidize a good local team.

Bergan Fanned Three In a Row
in the Seventh

W. Wallace Slid Safely into the Plate
with Hingham's Lone Tally

In warm weather, marbles, skip ropes, and bean shooters were drawn out of childrens' pockets. Kites wobbled skyward and then glided on thermals. Games such as "Tap on the Back," "Prisoner's Base," "Hoist the Green Sail," and "Run Sheep Run" held a special magic in the dusky hours before bedtime. Boys still burned pitch and swung birches. When Elwin Fearing went with his family to picnic on the top of Prospect Hill,

A favorite game was to walk along the walls—there was lots of walls on the hill—and from the top all you could see is walls and fields with cows and sheep. Some of the fields had open sheds or other little buildings which we explored. Father had an old telescope he took up

[253]

the hill. It had belonged to my Grandfather Perez Fearing. Father would set me on the wall and hold the telescope while I looked at the steamers and sails goin' in and out of Boston. When I look back at it now, it was a beautiful sight. I wish I could do it again but the last time I went up the hill, about 1938 after the hurricane, it had all grown up to brush except at the top . . . . I remember one huge "ole white oak" with limbs that stretched out low to the hillside. Each limb was as long and thick as a tree. One limb came down so low we kids could step onto it and walk right up to the trunk which was so big that we used to form a circle around it and dance around hold'n' hands.

"On Sundays, when kids made their own entertainment," said Ruth Marsh, "we always walked somewhere . . . to Turkey Hill for picnics [or] along the railroad track as a short cut to Nantasket." Some families would travel south by electric and come home with pails full of blueberries and whortleberries. When Susie Belding Eldredge was very young, "Kitty Hennessy had a niece, Rita, and when Rita came to visit, she would take the three little Beldings and Rita to Nantasket for the day . . . or we'd get on the streetcar across the way and go for a picnic at Accord Pond. That was a big deal! That was a whole day trip." For Mason Foley, too, "The long trolley ride my three brothers and I used to take from West's Corner to play with four boys [the Sharps] on Mullein Hill was an all day adventure." West's Corner took its name from Charlie West, an early twentieth-century grocer who owned considerable land thereabouts. Mullein Hill was named for the wild flowers abundant there, the velvety plants with "thick fuzzy leaves" and "tall spikes of yellow flowers." In Howie Horton's vivid memory, they mingled with the long-ago sights of the little Sharp boys, "all dressed alike running down the hill with their long hair flying out behind them in the breezes," of the red farmhouse roof "seen for miles around," and of a nearby country store, where little old Miss Rozine Gardner asked in her squeaky voice of boys in quest of penny candy, "Well boys, whatchagunnahave?"

With summer coming, the "whole world" awaited the opening of George Dodge's 1905 brainchild, the huge amusement park, truly a Paragon, with its 50,000 electric lights, music of the carousel, click and roar of the roller coaster, aroma of hot dogs. One boyhood Saturday, Alma Tinsley's nephew reached Nantasket by a wonderfully circular route. First he traveled into Boston to meet his father for an afternoon at Fenway Park. After the game, they took the steamer to Nantasket, then home by electric to the Centre, where they stopped at Seth

Sprague's store to buy "the best bag of peanuts in town." In 1987, a frail, ancient Alma Tinsley sat in a hospital bed and cupped her hands around those remembered peanuts. "They were still warm."

One day, Myron Clark and his cousin went up a little brook:

> We both carried buckets . . . . We were bound for the "herring run."
> . . . . The little bridge was crowded and the banks were lined with people. The stream was swarming with silvery herring fighting to get into fresh water for spawning. Catching them was simple. You just dipped your pail or bucket into the water and brought it up full of flopping, wiggling fish.

"Oh yes, we fished," said Ruth Marsh. "I remember shooting frogs from the little island in the middle of Triphammer Pond, for the frogs' legs." Anna Calvi went "down there" to fish. "Turtles—big! Smelts galore!" In Hingham, smelts were legendary. When they were running, families rented boats and anchored in the harbor. In those days, John McKee recalled, "you could swim and clam and drop a line over the water and catch smelts." Louise Wilder and her brother "started out at 5:30 A.M. and sailed from Kimball's Wharf. On bad days I used my slicker as a sail. My father was hysterical. We would get thirty dozen on a good day. My mother did all the fish cleaning. We'd have fish chowder with salt pork." Every now and then there'd be a great year. In 1917, Arthur Hersey took home forty-two dozen after five hours, Johnny Barba topped him with fifty-two, and Fred Smith claimed sixty-two plus four. But already, this idyl was threatened. Illegal seiners came out from Boston. Harbors were contaminated by sewage. Dead fish were found along the shores.

A state inspector checked the water around the bathing beach for swimming, and the beach added a special officer and a lifeguard. Times had changed since the days when Thompson's owned much of the waterfront and everything was covered with coal dust. Bertha Stringer

> used to swim from the bathing beach and try to dive off the lumber schooner, which was not supposed to be done . . . down at the corner of Burditt Avenue and Otis Street . . . . The houses were built into the bank. It was awful dirty through there, all coal dust.

There were, Horton remembered, "bathhouses in irregular rows, red or green or yellow, like a little Bohemian village in itself, and beyond that the Lincoln Boathouse, with a little jetty out into the harbor, and next to the boathouse a few cottages," and beyond them, Otis Hill, where he and a friend picked ox-eyed daisies.

Some boys were too busy for much swimming. As legendary as the smelts are Hingham's forget-me-nots. Brought from Fontainebleau, France, in the mid nineteenth century by Hingham artist W. Allan Gay, they flourished in and along the Town Brook. By June, local teenagers braved the noisome brook, picked the flowers, and sold bouquets. Myron Clark pictured "the youngsters lining the tracks alongside a train stopped at the station, holding up their flowers for sale—small bunch ten cents, large bunch a quarter—and the passengers leaning out opened car windows to make a purchase." In 1910, someone estimated the boys' gross at more than $2000. In 1913, one enterprising lad took out an ad in the *Journal*: "Will deliver." In those summers, the square turned into a steady stream of autos, thousands on Sunday. In the stall and crawl, some motorists complained of boys climbing on running boards, scratching their shiny machines with shoes, and when no sale was made, using profane language. After the war, the commerce subsided. Eddie Long's flower shop at the depot sold forget-me-nots packed for shipping.

Summer band concerts were crowded, but their heyday came later. Later, too, was the organized July Fourth; publicly funded patriotism grew out of World War I. Old Fourths were unplanned and unsafe. Thompson's shop was open all night for the sale of flags, horns, revolvers, cartridges, and fireworks. There were numerous injuries and many a runaway horse. The Centre had its huge midnight bonfire.

A few days later came summer's crowning glory. Every July between 1882 and World War I, a special train arrived from Boston with as many as four hundred cadets, the First Corps of the Massachusetts Militia. They climbed off the train, formed in parade, and marched up Fearing Road to their grounds on Broad Cove. Myron Clark was "much impressed by these men in their dark blue flannel shirts, neckerchiefs, khaki trousers and campaign hats . . . the First Corps Cadets was an elite outfit and . . . its ranks boasted many scions of Boston's Back Bay 'codfish' aristocracy." They held dress parades every day, and every evening a band concert. There were maneuvers around town. Clark recalled a sham battle up the slope of Broad Cove, with much waving of swords and shooting of blanks. When the real war began and the "boulevard" was being cut through the marshes across the Cadets' firing range, boys made good money salvaging empty casings.

"We used to go over Fearing Road," said Horton, "to watch the soldiers parade." "We" stood along the picket fence, and

> munched popcorn and candy which was purchased from one of the balloon men with a basket on his arm, laden with candy and brightly

colored pinwheels, spinning in the breezes . . . and balloons fluttering
. . . . Just then the bugle would sound, and the air was tense with
excitement as the soldiers hurried into place, the band started to play
and the parade was on . . . . Finally, the colors were lowered, and the
crowd dispersed.

After 1916, the crowd dispersed forever. In the early 1920s, the camp-
grounds were taken over by Boston developers, but Derby Academy
managed to save the old parade grounds from Hingham's first housing
boom.

August brought the lovely sight offshore of the Hingham Yacht
Club's annual regatta. Between forty and fifty yachts, "all with a reef
down, many with two, started off Crow Point, had a run to the Peddocks Island mark, a reach to the Strawberry Hill mark, a beat to the
Sheep Island mark, a run to Peddocks again, a reach to Strawberry Hill,
a beat to the Bumpkin Island shoal buoy, and a close lay to the finish
line." Hingham had become a town for avid sailors. In August, 1910,
when George Lincoln's son Alfred—the little "Lo Lo" who had built
his own "Flirt"—was second commodore, the Yacht Club held its first
Open Race Day for all townspeople. Smaller boats raced in the harbor,
larger ones off Crow Point, and for non-sailors there were swimming
and tub races, canoe tiltings and the like, while onlookers lined the
shore, the old Yacht Club piazza near the Cove, and Thompson's
wharf.

After that, summer's end came too quickly. The Italian organ grinder
was long a memory, and the basket-weaving Penobscots had vanished
from their annual campsites on "Fearing Hill" or along the Weir River.
The *Journal* announced, "Only ten more days til Labor Day and then
the bottom will drop out of the summer business." At Hennessy's shoe
shop appeared the dire portent: tennis and yachting shoes were replaced by school shoes. The seasonal rhythm of life in the young
century began again.

CHAPTER NINETEEN

Years of Improvement

IN America between the turn of the century and World War I, many ideas and programs of social reform were afloat. A generation of reformers, in politics and elsewhere, committed their organized energies to address the human wants and needs that had been neglected or aggravated by the growth of industrial cities. The reformers were activist and optimistic; their ideas were an "intriguing interplay" of new and old. Their impact on the nation during these years gave a name to the era: "Progressive." Historians usually portray "progressivism" as a phenomenon of the cities, but its influence was also felt in towns near to the cities, which were on the verge of becoming suburbs.

In Hingham, as in other towns, the watchword of this progressive impulse was "improvement." In the first years of the 1900s, "improvement societies" were springing up across the country. The idea of improvement reflected in these societies had several aspects: aesthetically, it promoted more refined tastes; morally, it promoted more elevated and humane behavior; socially, it promoted a more orderly and secure community life; and economically, it promoted better resources and facilities. The improvers, to be sure, in their idealistic zeal, were not always sensitive to the values and feelings of those in traditional communities with less money and with little desire to have their established worlds and ways improved. Nevertheless, improvement was institutionalized in Hingham in 1910 with the founding of the Village Improvement Society, the "V.I.S.," one of several symbolic new organizations coming to the fore in that year.

The society was formed on May 31 at a large meeting at Loring Hall with John D. Long presiding and with over one hundred original members. Its broad aims were exemplified by the various projects it initiated in its first years. The first was to plan a "safe and sane" Fourth of July. The dangerous old Fourths are well pictured in a journal entry of 1892 by Charles A. Lane. Lane and his son Chester

> after breakfast began firing crackers. Chester fired the crackers. I got them ready. I also fired for Chester's amusement the little iron cannon my Mother gave me when a small boy. We had three large cannon crackers, that we fired, one each, morning, noon, and night as a salute. I never saw a boy have a happier time than Chester. He fired crackers all day, on the ground, in the air, and under a tin pail and the best part was he didn't get a burn all day.

Planned safety was a major aim of the improvers.

One keynote of improvement was the new idea of childhood: the child should be protected and nurtured; his life should be planned. Columns in the *Journal* now included "Tips for Mothers," prescribing tolerant and attentive childrearing. In part of a house at the Cove, rented in 1901 by Governor Long and his wife, a progressive preschool opened with kindergarten teacher Elizabeth Bates in charge. Soon there was another at Derby. In the summer, organized play was initiated. An incident of the summer of 1910 nicely exemplifies the new idea. Boys had long regarded the Common at the Centre as their playground. Suddenly that summer they came in conflict with the aesthetic priorities of the improvers, in the form of a new flower garden. Hingham's solution was to appoint a committee to study the problem and accommodate both parties. Two years later, Central Playground was created. And in an incident of October, 1910, the Village Improvement Society furthered its program for an organized childhood. Just two years earlier in England, General Baden-Powell had founded the Boy Scouts to train boys in citizenship, character, self-reliance, and social responsibility. In 1910, the movement came to America and the Boy Scouts were organized in Hingham. Suitably, the organizing meeting was sponsored by the Village Improvement Society.

The society's agenda gradually expanded to include trash receptacles (marked "V.I.S."), systematic waste disposal in a town of informal village dumps, a cleaner Town Brook, a clean bathing beach, and the protection of song birds. In 1911, its plan for a more orderly life led to the improvement—that is, the regularizing—of the erstwhile casual stops of the electrics, in the interests of getting businessmen to the Boston train on time. The same year, the society assumed its role in the improvement of public health with a war against the fly. It would pay a child twenty-five cents a quart for flies to be delivered and measured at West School. The contents of the quart must be dry and dead *and* caught in Hing-

[259]

ham! As these activities expanded, an interesting pattern emerged: the society would initiate a project; often, once it took hold, it assumed public status and was adopted as policy by the town.

By 1912, the "wave of improvement" was "sweeping the country." In Hingham, this was a year of combat against dust and puddles, of street-paving and sidewalks. The street superintendent and his men moved from site to site with their rock-crushing machine and cement. The tree warden's men were all over town trimming dead wood and spraying for gypsy and brown tail moths and elm bark beetles. Improvement had its environmental dangers. After the spraying, Dallas Lore Sharp's "valuable" cow became sick from eating the roadside grass. Many birds, especially robins, were found dead under trees. Nonetheless, improvement was on the march.

It was not simply a result of progressive trends in the world outside. It was also, and perhaps more urgently, a result of vexing local dilemmas which the town found itself facing. In the first decade of the new century, Hingham felt small and poor. Between the Civil War and 1900, it had grown in population by only five hundred, and as of 1905, it had begun to shrink once more. The following figures suggest the problems it faced and the timing of drastic remedies it applied.

year	population	real estate valuation	no. of dwellings assessed	tax rate
1890	4564	2,675,415	1079	12.00
1895	4819	2,971,544	1119	16.00
1900	5059	3,109,586	1179	15.00
1905	4819	3,255,363	1233	17.70
1910	4965	4,902,740	1288	12.80
1915	5264	5,480,375	1435	18.00

First, the population. It went up a little, then dropped back to the 1895 figure, started up again, and then jumped significantly. Second, real estate valuation crept up until 1905 then took an upward leap. Between 1915 and 1925, it would more than double. Third, the number of homes grew by only eight to twelve a year until 1910, then picked up momentum; by 1925, it would be increasing even faster. Fourth, the tax rate. Between the Civil War and 1890, it had held close to $13. Then it moved up and wavered between $15 and $18.

In 1905, people reflected, we are small and growing smaller. How can we afford our increasing expenses? Our real estate is undervalued and not valued fairly. In 1908, we vote for revaluation and hire assistant assessors to do it. They do; see the jump in 1910. We have brought our tax rate down, but with higher valuations, we are paying as much, and our state and county taxes rise. We need *more people*, and they must be "desirable," wealthy people in expensive "estate" houses. Such people are beginning to flee the city. Ours is a beautiful town. Why not entice them here? To entice them, we must make improvements, and we cannot make improvements without paying for them. We are not gamblers, but we must gamble.

The year of the big gamble was 1912. The Village Improvement Society had paved the way. In Hingham that year, there were seventy-one articles on the warrant for the town meeting, some of them traditional and familiar, others comprising an agenda of improvement: the improvement of drainage; historic "guide boards"; the purchase of land for town departments and a playground; the furnishing of the new town office building; the addition of fire alarm boxes and street lights; the suppression of the moth. The most ambitious and costly project was the building of Lincoln School, the town's first junior high, for grades seven through nine.

This investment had long been needed and long delayed. The grade schools, new in 1894, were overcrowded, and the problem of their overcrowding was aggravated by poor ventilation and the malodorous old "dry" toilet facilities. Extra school space for primary classes had to be rented in the North Ward. Aged primary buildings on Elm (today's Light Plant office) and Fort Hill Streets were kept in use, and the mixed school in Canterbury village near Kilby Street had to be repurchased. In the years just after 1900, the high school was bulging with its four grades. New business programs, mandated by the town in 1898, had persuaded almost all grade school graduates to go to high school, where three out of four studied bookkeeping, typing, and stenography. In 1902, the high school building was enlarged, while students shivered in temporary class space in Agricultural Hall. The situation was only briefly ameliorated.

In 1910, the School Committee proposed to buy two acres at the corner of Central and Elm Streets, land which Morris Whiton had offered as a dump site eleven years before. Here, a school building would be built, its estimated cost $34,000. Town meeting of 1911 was not ready for such an "extravagance" and "indefinitely postponed." But by 1912, the fiscal atmosphere had changed dramatically, the motion passed, bids were let, and handsome new Lincoln School opened its doors in 1913.

The same meeting of 1912 also reversed earlier delays and voted funds for playground space. Much of the old Cordage Company land on Central Street was purchased, and the Central Playground was opened. The voices of the improvers were heard in the argument that "the role of play in social progress" was vital. The advocates described a significant and historic change:

> When fields situated in all parts of the town were common and un-used, the question of where our boys and girls could play was not raised, but as the central parts of the town became more thickly set-tled, available playground was greatly restricted, and what fields were left became too valuable for other uses to allow boys to roam over them at will.

A key phrase is "too valuable for other uses." Planned and central facilities would replace the old, informal uses of land. Planned childhood activity would foster a healthier and more orderly town life.

The costliness of such improvements was clear. Between 1906 and 1916, town appropriations doubled. A committee was formed to examine "why the expenses of the town have increased to such an alarming extent." The answer, of course, was obvious. But the improvers ran into resistance. Grocer-butcher Amos Humphrey became legendary for repeatedly questioning quorums at town meetings when the remaining item was money for two hydrants, or for haggling over the distinction between "miscellaneous" and "incidentals". The proposed improvement of home mail delivery was put off for many years because many people refused to number their houses, buy letter boxes, or cut slots in their doors. When Daylight Savings Time began (1918), a "few 'set fellers' vowed they won't push their watches ahead."

But the days of the "set fellers" were numbered. The gamble had been taken. Realtors began seductive advertisements. The "desirables" came in increasing numbers.

At first, they were summer residents. In spring and fall, McKee's trucks made three trips a day between Hingham and Boston, moving furniture and pianos. Servants came ahead to prepare mansions and "cottages." Across the brow of the first hill on Crow Point stretched a family compound of four mansions. Palatial new residences arose on the edge of the Crow Point golf course and on the northeast bluff of Pleasant Hill. The golf course opened stretching from Pleasant Hill (now the Bel Air subdivision) toward Foley Beach. Hammocks were in place on lawns and piazzas, and "garden fetes" animated the town. Commercial town directories included separate listings of summer people whose winter addresses were mostly in Boston and Brookline. By 1920, there were eighty-eight summer listings on Crow Point alone.

Many visitors rented for the season, and some old-timers capitalized. On Summer Street were "Hersey's Cottages"; on Pleasant View Beach, Litchfield's. Cornelius Foley developed his colony at Foley Beach. In 1912, Joseph Newhall, longtime cabinetmaker and at ninety the town's oldest man, was fatally stricken while supervising repairs to his "cottages at the Beach." Even local residents moved to summer homes: the Reuben Herseys and the Wash Jameses from Hersey and Water Streets to Otis Street and Downer Avenue. Fire Chief George Cushing entertained friends at his summer camp on the Back River.

"Now is the time to sell!" one realtor exhorted old Hinghamites, and many did. A number of old homesteads became summer "estates." Wealthy new owners, fleeing the city to a green retreat with "improved" comforts, brought their expectations with them: pure water, good drainage, dust-free streets, sidewalks, good street lighting, night police and fire protection, telephones, and of course a serving class. They demanded pastoral peace and security, but also modern conveniences. A typical advertisement of 1913 summed up their desires:

> Modern Hingham estate reduced for quick sale—5 minutes from electrics, 12 from station, 1¼ acres of fine vegetable and poultry land, fruit in variety, 2½ stories, 9 rooms, bath, electric lights, piazza, heat, etc., surrounded by lawns studded with shrubs and shade trees, near best of neighbors—$5,500, part cash.

The fugitives brought their style of relaxed elegance and costly simplicity. For gentlemen, new fashions included the "sack suit," a softly structured tweed; for ladies, the loose-waisted Empire style, the kirtle and the kimono, the practical "tub" dress. The style was suited to a late Romantic vision of Nature. What this means is implicit throughout a description of the Home Meadows by Mary C. Robbins in 1911 in *Hingham*, a collection of essays that well articulates the town's new image. "This lovely scene lies in ever-changing beauty, unvexed by the restless men who come and go beside it," imparting "the blessing of quiet Nature to the anxious mind." Daubs of human life are small motifs in her word-painting: little houses at the cove; mowers at autumn, their scythes filling horse-drawn ricks with hay; winter eel fishermen and skaters. Occasionally, shrieking trains "fill the air with rolling clouds of smoke and umber." The Boston Light "glows like a great star on the distant horizon"—where the city belongs.

The ideals of pastoral quiet and beauty, well-kept houses and lavish gardens and antiques, evoked a "village memory." The loss of manufacturing and commerce was no matter for regret. Moneymaking should take place elsewhere. As Dallas Lore Sharp wrote from his farm at Mullein Hill, "I have no quarrel with the city as a place to work in. Cities are as necessary as wheatfields and as lovely, too—from twenty miles away . . . . The city is necessary; city work is necessary; but less and less is city living necessary."

Sharp was expressing an important motive of improvers in the Progressive era. They were deeply disturbed by what had become of life in the industrial cities. By 1900, its industries crowded into a dense city with a huge immigrant labor force, Boston had become the nation's fourth largest manufacturer. From 1850, with a population of 137,000, 47,000 of them immigrants, it grew by 1910 to 671,000, of which 241,000 were foreign-born. Nightmarish slums dramatized the effects of degradation: disease, pauperism, prostitution, alcoholism, crime. Escape for the fortunate had begun in the inner "streetcar suburbs" of Dorchester, Roxbury, and Hyde Park. Then refuge was sought in surrounding towns.

Boston, the "grey octopus," was still threatening to follow. As the new century opened, the Filene Commission was pursuing the "metropolitan" visions and programs of the late nineteenth century. In every renewed effort to define a "Greater Boston," the leaders of towns found hidden the threat of "annexation." In 1916, a fearsome plan was proposed: a municipality to include Hingham, Hull, Cohasset, Braintree, Weymouth, Quincy, and Milton, circled by a highway, with a target population of half a million. Nothing came of the alarm, but such suggestions served to strengthen a village bastion mentality against Boston and its politics.

The same mentality now envisioned a Boston controlled politically by corrupt Irish Democratic "machines." Leaders of the Progressive era were Republican, many of them from old Republican families. Hingham's improvers and its new "desirables" were, too. Yet, as the years of improvement opened in the small town, the old Republican population was shrinking and the percentage of the Irish Democratic electorate was rising. In 1902, for the first time, the Catholic Democrat Thomas H. Buttimer, Jr., was elected state representative. The surprising history of his bids for this office suggests a nervous and diminished old Republican electorate. In 1901, after a recount, Buttimer's opponent had won the district by only three votes. In 1902, a recount revealed that the announced victor had actually lost and Buttimer had won by forty-nine votes. The mistake was suspicious. "The ballots," explained *Journal* editor and Town Clerk Fred Miller, "were carefully counted, but it would seem, were not as carefully tabulated by the town clerk, who, although not entirely authorized, made it his duty. No one else is to blame." In 1903, after another recount, Buttimer's opponent had won by only five votes, and in 1905, Buttimer won again.

As late as 1912, close votes remained the rule. Democratic Governor Eugene Foss lost in the town by only 344 to 364; David I. Walsh, candidate for lieutenant governor, by 310 to 397. (Both won statewide by pluralities.) Shopkeeper William Hennessy came within thirty votes of defeating a Republican Hersey for state representative. Had Hingham remained small and relatively poor, the Irish Democratic vote might well have become a majority, especially with the rise of David Walsh in state politics as a stimulus to the local party. The population grew and changed, however, and newcomers were chiefly well-to-do Republicans. By 1915 and 1916, Republican majorities were growing and the town's Democratic organization was weakening.

The results in the presidential election of 1912 are interesting in another way. The town's voters divided as follows: Taft (Republican) 361; Wilson (Democrat) 309; Roosevelt (Progressive) 216. In the town as in the nation, Republicans split between Taft and Roosevelt. The size in Hingham of the third party vote for Theodore Roosevelt, in the face of John D. Long's strong opposition, indicated the strength of a new Progressive faction in the town.

It would, however, remain a minority in *local* politics for years to come. In town offices, incumbency was still the norm and would remain so for another generation. Francis Lincoln, son of Solomon, the first historian and longtime moderator, remained moderator from the 1880s to his retirement in 1906. Charles Barnes took his place until 1928. William Fearing, 2nd, was treasurer from 1858 to his death in 1905. When Selectmen Seth Sprague and DeWitt Bates died just before and after the turn of the century, Walter Jones and William L. Foster joined Walter W. Hersey on the board. Hersey died in 1915, to be succeeded by George Marsh, who resigned after many years to be replaced by Walter Bouvé. Foster would serve until 1945. Charles Marsh was town clerk for almost forty-five years until his death in 1900, and then Fred Miller served until he died sixteen years later.

Such men seldom ran unopposed, but their opponents, often Irish, received few votes. Some suspected it was a case of "Irish need not apply," but other challengers, including women running for School Committee, met the same fate. A few Irish townsmen did move closer to power. James Dower, son of the oldest ropemaker, joined the Board of Assessors; Timothy Murphy was annually reelected tree warden; and Thomas Buttimer, Jr., was a schoolcommitteeman for thirty years. The first citizen of Irish descent to hold a major town office, however, was a woman. That story belongs to the 1920s.

As a few Irish citizens entered town affairs and local commerce, the old immigrant-patriarchs passed on. Thomas Buttimer, Sr., for many years an estate caretaker, died in his ninetieth year in 1916. John Magner, another Cork patriarch, died in 1910 at eighty-seven; six grandsons, Magners, Dalys, a McKee, were his pallbearers. Daniel Daly, father of Postmaster Edmund, died in 1911 in his eighty-seventh year, having worked fifty-eight years for the Barnes family. At the same age, Cornelius Foley, another of "the old school of Irish gentlemen," died in 1914. Collectively, these four had lived in Hingham almost 240 years.

Other passings were also reminders of a life gone by: in 1910, at eighty-eight, Edwin Tower, in early years a shoemaker, then a cooper at the bucket factory; in 1913, Wallace Corthell, grocer, secretary of the Agricultural and Horticultural Society, manager of the Light Plant, Past Master of the Masons; in 1914, William Jernegan, the town's, perhaps the nation's, oldest newsdealer, active through his eighty-sixth year; in 1915, at seventy-eight, Francis Overton, whose worklife spanned many transitions—shoemaker, mackerel fisher, railroad engineer, and "ice cream autocrat"; and at eighty-seven Loring Jacob, hand-maker of toy colonial furniture, known nationwide through the Society of Arts and Crafts.

The most momentous death was that of "the governor," John D. Long, in August, 1915, at his beloved "large, plain, red-roofed house" on the hill between Cottage and Otis Streets. Characteristically modest, he left orders to refuse a state funeral. The town hearse moved him to New North Church, and here he lay in state while the Company K Honor Guard stood at attention and seven hundred people filed by in an hour. Shops closed at noon, doors were locked, shades drawn, and trolleys, horse vehicles, and autos "joined in the peace desired." Not quite all. Police Chief Wash James, directing traffic outside the church, was struck by a horse shying at an auto, knocked down, and shaken up.

The indomitable chief was back on duty by evening. But in that same week, two bandits were arrested trying to break into Huntley's garage. Leaving the "Lock-Up" on North Street to take them to court, Wash let the men use the washstand. While his back was turned, he was knocked down and beaten about the head with a hammer. The bandits fled on foot. The conductor and motorman on a passing electric saw the men running and heard cries. At that moment, Dr. Charles Whelan drove by in his auto. The chief and others jumped in and chased the fugitives up Lincoln Street. Though seriously injured, James leaned from the window and fired his gun. One bandit was killed; the other was captured. After a month's recovery on Crow Point, James returned to duty.

The heroic exploits of Chief James reveal a growing new problem which was much too large for the Village Improvement Society to solve. The automobile was adding its own menace to the fearful situation on improved streets. With autos joining in the mix and tangle of pedestrians, cyclists, buggies, barges, trains, and electrics, transportation was at best an adventure. There were growing complaints about reckless bikers and fast trains. An elderly crossing tender was hit and killed. Streetcar conductors, as they worked their way around the running board collecting fares, sometimes collided with poles and tree limbs. Train whistles and the clanging bells of electrics startled many a horse into a runaway, throwing passengers and cargoes from buggies and wagons onto the street. William Fearing's frightened horse crashed into the window of Suzie Gates's store; another, into the hydrant in front of St. Paul's, flooding the square. As electrics waited in front of Southworth's Drug Store (now Conte's dress shop), they blocked the view. An auto heading up South Street from the harbor would collide with another heading south on Main.

One awful accident vividly pictures the confusion. Two teamsters were driving home to Hull. An electric bound for "the Beach" was bearing down on the wagon and its young horse. Two autos were speeding up from "the Beach." Seeing no space between electric and autos, the teamsters tried to cross over, only to be struck by the electric. A sign of the escalating trouble was a 1904 advertisement for a horse: "not afraid of automobiles."

In 1902, Wilmon Brewer's father Francis had bought an auto, a "Pope Robinson," and garaged it two hundred feet from his house in case its engine exploded. He did not like it and relinquished the honor of sole auto-owner to Atkins S. Rich. Most unusual was Hingham's fifth auto, assembled and constructed by E. L. Lane, who had carriage painter Joseph Sprague of the Centre paint it black and yellow—old clothes for a new age. In 1905, Lane was local agent for Cadillacs, Fords, and Marions; and James Kemp opened the first garage in the powerhouse, whose days of supplying the electrics had ended early in 1899; by then, their electricity was imported from Braintree and Abington. Kemp's account book for 1908 includes such items as the following: in July, John D. Long used 168 gallons of gas, and W. H. Canterbury of Crow Point needed four Reliance plugs, six new batteries, a valve spring, and a coil, and had his inner tubes patched; in September, Ed Jones had his "Ford car" in Kemp's three times, requiring twenty-eight hours of labor at a cost of $63.90.

By 1910, the new monster was "here to stay." Police had the added duty of hauling speeders into court, and their names—all from out of town—were published. State regulations increased, and Chief James insisted on compliance. Autos were required to blow their horns when approaching *any* intersection, and a few irritated wags filled the square with their honkings and tootings. One angry motorist complained that the police would do better to direct traffic in the square than to man speed traps on the Nantasket road. A motorists' lobby was forming. By May, 1910, there was a Hingham Automobile Club.

The new club could not be of much help to busy, unlucky Doctor Charles Whelan, whose saga summed up the new menace. In 1910, he wrecked his new auto trying not to hit a cyclist and had to visit patients by electric or on his "pedal extremities." In a new car three months later, he was seriously injured when he tried to avoid an indecisive teamster and struck a twenty-inch water pipe by the side of the road. Next year, he had a new Packard; in March, 1912, a "new auto"; and another in October, a coupe with sides of glass to protect against the elements. Next month, en route to visit a patient, he collided on a double curve with the son of his patient. In 1915, "while endeavoring to crank his machine," he broke his wrist. Physician, heal thyself.

Despite such hazards, auto tourism grew. Cushing added a taxi to his stable; Roy Litchfield had a Buick for hire; David Cobb conducted auto tours of Jerusalem Road for $5. On the Fourth of July, 1911, Hingham witnessed its first auto parade. Auto prices dropped: in 1912, the Model T arrived—a "Torpedo" cost $590; a touring car, $690. That year, the town bought its first motor-driven fire engine for $12,000. In 1913, the selectmen held hearings on licensing eleven gasoline dealers, and the *Journal* admonished:

> the most dangerous spot in the world is the railroad station of a small town. Within a stone's throw are three grade crossings and a junction of three electric street railway lines, and along the narrow streets in summer there is a constant and swift procession of automobiles, more in number, probably, than in any other place in the Commonwealth.

They drove through that crowded square to the harbor and over Summer and Rockland Streets to Nantasket Beach or points south. On a

July Sunday in 1914, upwards of 3200 "machines" went through the square to see a hydroplane exhibition at Nantasket. In one hour on a June Sunday in 1916, 1026 cars drove through, and on a July Sunday, eight thousand in a day. The policeman could do very little but count.

What seemed at the time the only sensible remedy had been promoted by John D. Long and others. In May, 1915, a Hingham "boulevard" bill passed the legislature. By the summer of 1917, a steam shovel was progressing about twenty feet per day "through Otis Hill," and the "boulevard" was moving over the Broad Cove marshes from Thaxter Street and Downer Avenue to the harbor. The Cove took on a bare look: "Many of the old landmark houses near the coalyards are in the course of being torn down to make way for the new state highway." This first leg opened in August, 1918. The rest would wait for peacetime, but Hingham Square had been saved from gridlock.

The Automobile Club, like the Village Improvement Society, established the same year, was just one more addition to a long and growing list of social organizations, old and new, which channeled Hingham's social energies in the years of improvement. Between 1890 and World War I, a town of no more than five thousand people sustained over sixty-five organizations, not including many church groups. The organizations were of many different types: historical, political, cultural, and occupational. There were clubs and lodges for men and women, children, sportsmen and hobbyists, and a number of new and old service organizations.

The rapid proliferation of social organizations was a major national phenomenon of this period. Many have speculated on why it occurred when it did. Some would agree with Peter Kropotkin that such associations were simply "a manifestation of the same ever-working tendency" for "Mutual Aid." A keen foreign observer, British Ambassador James Bryce, who, incidentally, visited Hingham in this period, saw the "habit of forming associations" as pervasive in American life. He was confirming what Alexis de Tocqueville had suggested in the 1830s. But whatever its causes, "in the late nineteenth and early twentieth centuries, organizational activity engulfed America." Historians Charles and Mary Beard called it a "general mania." The "mania" was fostered by greater leisure and mobility, but it reflected a new social fragmentation. Some associations offered the group insurance necessitated by a growing instability in economic and social life. Immigrant groups formed protective associations in a strange land, and Nativist groups organized in reaction. Some associations reflected the weakening of church influence and of moral and social traditions at a time when traditional community was in peril. They represented an effort to recreate community in new ways. Like other aspects of life in the Progressive era, they brought together old ideas and traditions with new ideas and programs. Three Hingham societies in particular reveal this conjunction of the old and the new. One extraordinary woman, whose leadership links all three together, is a perfect example of this conjunction.

Susan Barker Willard was a living tie between Hingham's eighteenth and twentieth centuries. Though she was born in Deerfield in 1856, her forebears were rooted in Hingham history, her ancestors a roll call of New North aristocracy, including Barkers and Thaxters. Her grandfather Samuel Willard conducted Willard Academy for six or seven years in the hall (it burned in 1847) just north of the old meetinghouse and was active in the antislavery movement. By the early 1880s, she had returned from Deerfield to Hingham permanently. She lived with her mother and father at Tranquillity Lodge (137 Main Street), the house of her grandfather Henry Thaxter.

When she died in 1925, two of her successors to women's leadership, Mrs. Elizabeth Emmons and Mrs. Amy Howard, publicly shared their feelings. Susan B. Willard was "symbolic of the best that New England tradition holds—kindly, courteous, proud, brave, reticent, loyal . . . strong in her feelings, having intense likes and dislikes" [Emmons]. "Often I have heard her say, 'When I have once made up my mind that a thing is right, no matter how difficult or unpopular it may be, I am willing to work for it'" [Howard]. "I seldom met her without her little basket filled with delicacies made by her own hands for someone of the many she was forever remembering. She loved life, gaiety, beauty, music, color, flowers, laughter" [Emmons]. "When a child, who knew of her love and work for the community, heard of her death, she said, 'Miss Willard was the real citizen of Hingham'" [Howard]. Ruth Marsh recalled that "her hands were old," but her clothes "too youthful." Old hands and young clothes characterize her well. For her, the colonial past was alive, but her unique influence and energy were contemporary.

Susan Willard was prime mover in the formation, in 1901, of Hingham's Society of Arts and Crafts, the third in the state. The first had been formed in Deerfield, her birthplace. The movement had begun in England as a reaction against the mechanization, mass production, and alienated labor of the industrial revolution. Its goals were to restore pleasure and pride in individual craftsmanship, to revive "home industries," and to return to honesty and simplicity in work and life. Its philosopher and practitioner was the socialist William Morris; in an essay on the Hingham society, Susan Willard repeated his credo: "Have nothing in your house which you do not know to be useful or believe to be beautiful." The Victorian love of bric-a-brac and clutter was rejected, but not the Victorian ideal of the home. The home remained the center of life, where true values are preserved and exposure to the beautiful develops a disciplined eye, good taste, and character. At the close of her essay, Miss Willard echoed the slogan of the Progressive era: "Plain living, high thinking."

Miss Willard was consistent: craft work should create what is useful. And what are more useful than rugs and baskets? Twenty women began making baskets of raffia and palm leaf. They studied Indian baskets at the Peabody Museum in Salem and old work retrieved from dusty attic corners, then worked to their own designs. Mrs. E. J. Picanco experimented with natural dyes for the raffia work and the rags used in woven rugs. Her colors included madder and indigo, onion skin and barberry root yellows, and "fustic" green. She became the society's official dyer and was invited to lecture about her work at Hampton Institute, the internationally known black college in Virginia. The activities were not carried on only by women. William B. Luce was the almost exclusive creator of beautiful burned reed baskets, and Matthew Townsend was the weaver of mats and rugs. The Hingham Historical Society possesses an artfully executed rag rug made between 1905 and 1910. It is unusually large, consisting of three loom widths carefully matched and sewn together.

Unfortunately, the principle of the Arts and Crafts movement—that art can be democratized; that everyone can be educated to the beautiful—was flawed. Good craftsmanship is rarely cheap, and, it became clear, not everyone is capable of it. C. Chester Lane described how these problems beset the Hingham society:

> It was determined that a high standard of excellence should be set up . . . . The committees . . . do not hesitate to reject inferior or inartistic productions. This was a point which at first there was some difficulty in making plain. If a worker made a . . . basket which she was confident would sell, she could not understand why the committee should reject it. On the other hand, if a needy and deserving person offered inferior or unsuitable work, it was not always easy to make the decisions seem just and equitable.

Only after the committee of review determined the high quality and suitability and resolved problems of equity did the society affix its small paper label with its round logo of a bucket and the society's name to an item for exhibition and sale.

The first annual exhibition and sale was held in August, 1902; the 1903 exhibit was ecstatically reviewed in the *New York Sun*. By 1905, the society's fifteen "departments" included not only baskets and woven and braided rugs, but also beaded and tooled leatherwork; brass, copper, and tinware; pastels, watercolors, oils, and photographs; the woodenware and toy furniture of George W. Fearing; rush-bottomed colonial chairs; ironwork; limited editions from Frederic and Bertha Goudy's Village Press, set up in 1904 in the Job Lincoln house at 45 Lincoln Street; and, most important, needlework of every description. All could be found at the salesroom on South Street, with its swinging sign created by society members: lettering by Goudy, at the time America's foremost designer of typefaces; design by Clarence Hoyt; and ironwork by M. K. Huntley.

Dearest to Susan Willard's heart was "the old *white* embroidery of our grandmothers . . . [adapted to] modern uses, keeping as closely as possible to the spirit of the colonial needlewoman." In many ways, white embroidery expressed best the ideals of the arts and crafts movement. It was a return to old methods, to skilled work with the simplest tools, to produce items that were both useful and beautiful. Its ideals are implicit in a scene recreated by Elizabeth Coatsworth of her visit to Roseneath Cottage, Susan Willard's later home, "with its cage of love-birds usually quarreling in a sunny window."

> Miss Willard goes to a drawer and brings out a small compass, a pair of silver knee buckles, and white knee breeches of the finest doeskin, still soft and delicate to the touch. "Do feel them," urges Miss Willard. "See how white they have kept . . . . They belonged to my great-great-great-grandfather Major Samuel Thaxter, whose house stood where the Catholic Church now stands."

The tale takes us from the French and Indian Wars to the present feel and look of those knee breeches, made entirely by hand, still so white and uncorrupt, so carefully conserved as treasures and models from the past.

The ideals of the arts and crafts movement fostered a renewed appreciation in Hingham of colonial homes and furniture, which in their sturdy construction and straightforward lines fitted the movement's standards. House styles varied enormously, but there were constants of wrought iron, stone walls, gardens with evergreens, fruit trees, roses, lilacs, and mock orange. Indoors, the spinning wheel became a favorite ornament, pairing the chief practitioners of arts and crafts in an industrial age, women, with their pre-industrial counterparts.

The movement's broad influence also significantly affected program-matic goals for children. In an industrial society, they no longer learned the manual and domestic arts at home. "The public school," wrote Miss Willard, "is the place to which we should turn chief attention in our effort to promote a more beautiful public life in America." As a young woman in the 1880s, she had held a kindergarten in her home, but as her interest in education broadened, she became a self-appointed preceptress to the town. Grammar school children were asked to write essays about "How to Make Our Town More Beautiful." The high school was presented with a reproduction of Phidias's frieze on the Parthenon as a model for free drawing.

The arts and crafts impulse was echoed in the eloquent pleas of School Superintendent Nelson C. Howard for training in sloyd, a pro-gram that began as a discipline in woodcarving and joinery but soon expanded to include the making of useful, beautiful objects by hand out of other materials as well. Sloyd, he argued, would encourage eye-hand coordination, good work habits, resourcefulness, and joy in work, and diminish class prejudice. Town meetings between 1900 and 1910 were scattered with discussions and appropriations for extra room and equipment for sloyd. Just as initiatives of the Village Improvement Soci-ety were eventually adopted as town programs, so too was manual training. The Rev. George Weld had begun a Free Sloyd School in a building behind St. John's Church in 1904. In 1907, all the tools and benches, almost half the total needed, were donated to and accepted for the public schools. They went first to West and Centre Schools and soon would be installed in Hingham's first junior high, the Lincoln School.

The most important and lasting part of this gift was the teacher, Annie B. Whidden. For forty years, through many of which Hingham teachers' salaries were low and their annual turnover high, Annie B. Whidden taught sloyd to the town's junior high school classes. Ann Tolman still recalls her "cheerful style" and her interest in all the stu-dents. She stood by the shop door greeting them as they passed. "I wasn't very good at sewing. She taught me copper work." Herbert Hirsch delightedly remembers her as white-haired, "short and a little stocky." She "always wore a floral print smock—could have been any-one's grandmother." Unruly students were led by an earlobe down the hall and placed in the wire cage where finished projects were stored until the year ended. "We'd tease them a little." In her eighth grade class, Hirsch "finished three good projects, including a nice gumwood table." In high school, without her, he made only the too-familiar hexagonal plant stand. Annie B. Whidden taught this expert carpenter "how to use hand tools." Many a boy remembered her instructions for the jack plane: "Steady, straight, and up!" There is no evidence that Annie B. Whidden and Susan Willard knew each other personally, but the Whidden command was another suitable motto for Susan Willard's society.

In 1911, Miss Willard's essay on the Hingham Arts and Crafts Society appeared in the collection *Hingham*, published by the Daughters of the American Revolution as part of the celebration of the town's 275th anniversary. Other contributors included Dallas Lore Sharp; Louis Cornish, Old Ship pastor and first president of the Arts and Crafts Society; Francis Lincoln and Walter Bouvé, 1893 historians; Martin Gay, descendant of the Reverend Ebenezer; and Governor Long. The group exemplifies the cultural elite of Hingham at the time—a mix of intelligentsia, clergy, professionals with Brahmin attitudes, and descendants of old families.

The Old Colony Chapter of the D.A.R. had been founded in 1894. Its efforts to preserve the past began with authentically costumed colonial teas. One was held in Tranquillity Lodge, amid Miss Willard's antiques, to promote sales of a cookbook assembled by the Women's Alliance. Miss Willard became regent of the D.A.R. in 1905 and served through nineteen years of change, conflict, and world war. Under her leadership, the chapter joined Louis Cornish in a drive to erect the Hingham Memorial Belltower, monument to the first settlers, beside the old meetinghouse. The tower was dedicated with pomp and circumstance in 1912, its lovely bells sending competing sounds among the din of electrics and horns of autos at intersections. It holds one of only twenty sets of change-ringing bells on the North American continent, whose peals would have been familiar to the first settlers. Some of the first settlers would also have recognized the old flintblock from the market place in Hingham, England, which was sent for the cornerstone. Because of its irregular shape, it could not be so used and was placed inside.

Two events of 1913 recall the influence of Miss Willard and the D.A.R.'s efforts to awaken and preserve local memory. When the Society of Arts and Crafts held its exhibition at Derby Hall, it included a large exhibit of loaned antiques. And at the Shute house in South Hingham, the D.A.R.'s colonial tea included a guided tour of the house. The idea of locally sponsored historic house tours had been born. It is not surprising that the year following, the Hingham Historical Society was organized. Among its founders were, of course, Susan

Willard, Louis Cornish, and John D. Long as first president. It began its collecting and receiving of antiques and artifacts and its study of old houses. At the close of 1919, Wilmon Brewer bought the Old Ordinary, and he and his wife gave it to the new Historical Society in 1922. In 1925, Susan Willard left the society her estate.

By then, members of the D.A.R. and the Historical Society had been overtaken by world turmoil and disruption. The patriotic fervor in the air was congenial to Miss Willard. The state G.A.R.'s past commander could not remember the American flag ever passing without her salute. Under her leadership, chapter meetings of the D.A.R. always opened with the salute and the pledge, and flags were presented to the schools.

But what had become of the glorious Fourth of July? In 1916, the uncertain state of international affairs renewed enthusiasm for an organized celebration. Big plans were made, but most were abruptly canceled. Was it really wise, people asked, to spend over $1000 on the Fourth when, ten days earlier, Company K had left the armory to go to war?

CHAPTER TWENTY

Years of War

NOT "Over There," but "Down There" to the Mexican border. Hingham's entry into European war took a circuitous route. Wealthy Hinghamites returned from abroad at summer's end with their old-world tales and lantern slides. In the fall of 1914, they had other tales to tell. Early that year had come rumblings of "Balkan troubles." Spring brought news of naval build-ups. In May, a grand spectacle may have struck some as ominous: twelve hundred army regulars, stationed all over Boston harbor, rendezvoused at Hull, paraded to Hingham Square, ate their noon rations, marched to the new "Magazine" at the Back River, camped overnight, and marched back to Hull. Nonetheless, a festive air prevailed, and Memorial Day speakers talked confidently of peace. One hundred twenty thousand Americans went on European tours.

Suddenly, in August, 1914, "WAR FEVER GRIPS ALL OF EUROPE AS LITTLE SERVIA FLAUNTS AUSTRIA." In five days, Germany declared war on Russia, German troops invaded Belgium to attack France, Germany declared war on France, Belgium called for help, Britain declared war on Germany, and Austria declared war on Russia. In the White House, a distraught President Woodrow Wilson sat by the bed of his dying wife. All over Europe, borders were closed, passenger ships were canceled, and banks refused to cash checks. Americans panicked, fled when they could to London, and awaited ways to get home.

Trickle home they did in the weeks ahead, and once more, Europe seemed safely distant. Newspapers began their romantic columns: "Eyewitness Accounts," "Gripping Tales," "Picturesque and Thrilling Scenes." Experts predicted "staggering costs" in lives and money and prophesied that such "insensate war" could not last. On October 4, Hingham churches observed Peace Sunday, but peace did not come. Belgium was overrun. Czarist forces crumbled, France invaded Germany, and a British blockade threatened the continent with starvation. Nineteen fifteen settled into bloody trench stalemate. Nineteen sixteen brought the awful epic battles of Verdun and the Somme, of Russia with the Central Powers, of the world's greatest navies at Jutland. Other nations joined in.

Many Americans felt horror, pity, and contempt for the belligerents and struggled to stay neutral. The *Journal's* reports sedulously avoided anti-German propaganda, and John D. Long pleaded for sympathy for "our German fellow citizens." But neutrality was precarious. Neutral shipping carried munitions to both sides, as America discovered the huge profits to be made on war markets. Orders from Europe put the country on the brink of unprecedented prosperity. The Fore River Shipyard in Quincy was making submarines. There were many new workers in Hingham, and they earned better wages. Bradley's fertilizer plant closed, but workers did not have far to go for new jobs: up the Back River to the burgeoning new Naval Magazine.

The greatest threat to neutrality came in May, 1915, off the Irish coast, when the *Lusitania*—"no safer ship afloat"—was torpedoed by a German submarine. The crisis united the nation behind Wilson, and, with anxious energy, the preparedness campaign was launched. In late 1915 and 1916, many Hinghamites, led by the Special Aid Society for American Preparedness, were caught up in the campaign. The aim, they insisted, was preparedness for *peace* and against *invasion*. If invasion came, what more logical target than a town with a large ammunition depot?

Focus then shifted to the Mexican border, where a war scare had started in 1913. The Mexican president was assassinated, and his rival, Victoriano Huerta, took power. Wilson allowed shipments to anti-Huerta forces and seized the port of Veracruz. Huerta was overthrown, but the rebellion continued under the peasant "Robin Hood," Pancho Villa. When Villa began incursions over the border in 1916, U.S. troops were sent to pursue him across northern Mexico, and National Guard regiments went to protect the border. And so, Company K went to war, an odd war, patrolling the border, skirmishing with fly-by-night bandits, playing company baseball at Camp Cotton, discovering the delights of "watermelon feasts" in southern Texas. They left Hingham in June, 1916, for the long train ride and were home in late October. Some who welcomed them could remember a far-off July fifty-five years before, when the Lincoln Light Infantry had come home from Virginia. Then, too, it had seemed that a brief war had ended.

In the first weeks of 1917, America's posture turned around. War seemed imminent. President Wilson had won reelection in 1916 largely on the hope of staying out of war. Then Germany made a desperate move: it revoked its pledge that its submarines would respect neutral shipping and started an all-out campaign to cut off supplies to Britain. American ships were sunk in the English Channel. The famous "Zimmerman Telegram" was intercepted: Germany had proposed a secret alliance with Mexico. Wilson broke off relations with Germany, and on April 2, 1917, he asked Congress to declare a state of war.

Hingham's town meeting had unanimously passed a resolution in March supporting the President. A Public Safety Committee was formed and a mass recruiting rally planned. "Your country needs you! Come to the Armory March 25th." The country "entered the greatest struggle in the history of the world," Democracy Against Autocracy. "The country is at war," said the *Journal*. "A good time to practice calmness of speech and action."

It was good traditional Hingham advice. The town was not to be stampeded into patriotic frenzy by the sudden turn of events or the nation's new propaganda machinery. There was understandable reluctance to volunteer. Ireland was in open revolt, and numbers of Irish-American townsmen had good reason to be anti-British. Company K remained short of even peacetime strength. The *Journal* changed its tone: "Is there no way that the ambition and patriotism of the young men of this town can be aroused? . . . When all other places are alive with the spirit of preparedness, have they so deteriorated from the courage and bravery of their ancestors?" Recruits trickled in from Rockland, Abington, Braintree, but "the Hingham boys, where oh where are they?" A Home Guard of older men was recruited, but a similar reluctance was evident. Only three flags appeared on Main Street. Indignantly, some people remembered the flags of the Spanish-American War: Ira Hersey's ten-by-eighteen foot barn-roof flag; General Blackmar's at World's End, visible for miles at sea; Amos Humphrey's over his store in West Hingham.

In events that followed, a shrewd strategy was obvious. On a cold, rainy Sunday in April, a public flag-raising took place, and "to the local Aerie of Eagles," an Irish Catholic lodge, "deservingly fell the honor." Townspeople filled the sidewalk up Main Street to Elm and along Central, under the pin oaks and maples that Tree Warden Arthur Young had planted years before. A band paraded with schoolchildren, and

Captain Ernest Lincoln's old father, a veteran of 1861, raised the flag. Private Justin Hennigan of the First Corps Cadets appealed to Hingham's young men to do their "little bit" and urged their mothers to encourage them. Soon, patriotic sermons filled the churches. The curate of St. Paul's pulled out all the stops: the shirker was unChristian; "the various races of this land are one now. We are all Americans by birth or choice."

Nine days later came national draft registration, and local reluctance faded. Buddies joined buddies. The following weeks brought funny, inspiriting stories from the Draft Board. "How's your feet, young man?" "Flat but not cold" was the reply. A Centerite youth was told, "Sorry, my friend, but I can't pass you." "Ain't I fit? What's the trouble?" "Teeth." "But I want to fight 'em, not bite 'em."

Company K, first mustered in 1903, was mobilized in July, 1917, as part of the Army, in the Fifth Regiment, 101st Infantry Battalion, and later in the new 26th or "Yankee" Division. It bivouacked in tents at Central Playground, anxiously awaiting orders. Once orders came, the town would hear twenty-five strokes on the fire alarm. After a long wait, on August 17, 1917, the alarm sounded. Crowds assembled at the railroad depot. Selectman William L. Foster spoke feelingly about "Pilgrim ideals" and the desire for peace. Mothers and sweethearts remained calm, so the report tells us, with "moist eyes and full hearts." Company K departed.

Terrible storms broke out ominously over their camp in Framingham, and back at Broad Bridge the buildings were surrounded by water. Lightning struck a tree in front of the Wompatuck Club and brought a card party of Odd Fellows across the street in the Whiton Building to their feet. Three days later, another storm struck six houses on Main Street, threw the town into darkness, and killed two of George Hayward's horses in their barn.

By late September, most of Company K had reached France and begun training. In letters home, the boys told their story. Harry Fekkes described boarding the transport: "We scrambled for bunks and I got a middle one with Jack Barnes of Cohasset and Albion Bjorklund of Hingham in the lower bunk . . . . It has been mighty hard work to satisfy the fellows with the bum place we have to eat in and the way the food is cooked." Stanley Lane tried bravely to comfort his folks: "There is one thing that is worrying me," he wrote his mother, "and that is that you are worrying yourself too much." James Parker assured the home front: "Every man is fighting an individual fight with dogmatic determination . . . . 'Kaiserism' must be done away with."

Parker was an ex-Marine and policeman. The others were mostly boys, untouched by battle and amused by their new role. Ralph Stevens drew a funny picture for his sister of "me promenading along through the deep, sticky mud, with my heavy, homely, cumbersome knee-high trench shoes on, a gas mask over my face, and topped with a khaki-colored steel helmet. Some sight, believe me!" But boyish amusement could not survive "the long, dismal marches, the muddy, wet fields, the bitter, bitter cold nights sleeping rolled up in our blankets." Homesickness seeped through. Lester Dill's thoughts

> often wander back to Hingham Square . . . . I can imagine a crowd collecting there now with Wash James the cynosure of all eyes, and his able assistant, Patrolman Stevens, who no doubt is giving his views on modern warfare. I suppose Chief Cushing is still on the job waiting for the old bell to peal out to put him in action, Bert Kimball the unconquerable fire king dashing down Main Street, striving his best to beat out Combination 1 Boys.

The months of training ended early; the Americans were urgently needed at the front. In February, 1918, John Tower vaguely warned his father, "By the time you get this letter, I will have moved again. You will not hear from me for a couple of weeks, but never mind everything will be all right, no need to worry."

At home, the northwest corner of little Hingham was turning into a war center. Along both shores of the Back River stretched the "Magazine." It had opened in 1909. The Navy had decided that its ammunition storage facility in Chelsea needed to be replaced and relocated. A board of officers surveyed the New England coast. In the old area of Hingham called "Hockley," they found what they wanted, a sheltered coastal flat terrain surrounded by hills. In 1906, they began the purchase of 697 acres on the Hingham side and 208 in Weymouth. Marine guards arrived in 1909. Weymouth children could see a sentry on the hill as they swam in the marsh grass at high tide. Barracks and utility buildings were built by 1911. The Magazine was to serve the Boston and Portsmouth Navy Yards, to store and provide ammunition—"powder," mines, torpedoes for the North Atlantic fleet.

The new "Depot" brought jobs in ordnance and construction and, coincidentally, a protected boundary for the new bird sanctuary. It was the "home of high explosives." The complement of guards expanded every few weeks as the war began, and by its end, civilian workers numbered about five hundred. Wages rose and overtime fattened pay envelopes. Labor was drained from town businesses, placing some shopkeepers on the verge of closing. The town was jammed with workers;

men were boarding in shifts of three, four, five to a room. It was "Hingham's Klondike."

Another naval invasion had taken over the south end of old Hockley. Five hundred sailors were stationed at "Camp Hingham." The "jackies" invited Hinghamites to their camp on Sunday. Town families walked in from Fort Hill Street, along hilly Clifford Court past the cedars to the cluster of barracks in Hockley hollow. The Navy band enlivened the square, and the newcomers danced in their "whites and blues" at the armory. Their reception was cordial but cautious. A YWCA speaker came to talk to "the women and girls" about "problems arising out of the presence of camps in our neighborhood." Still, hospitality prevailed, and many a sailor far from home was included in holiday dinners.

Cooks did not have an easy time. Food shortages were a challenge. Sugar disappeared first, and meatless and wheatless days followed. Planting a backyard garden became a patriotic duty. Many celebrated "the quietest Fourth of July ever" by eating their own peas. Father McCall of St. Paul's offered ploughed and harrowed land to anyone willing to plant it. On Bradley Hill there were "billowing acres." Women took classes in home canning. The 1917 fair was a harking-back to communal thrift and husbandry.

Home front mobilization made for an atmosphere of frenzied fellowship. Benefit dances, drives, and patriotic rallies were frequent. The Home Guard drilled. Children threw fruit pits, needed for gas masks, into a collection barrel and proudly compared their war stamp books. Ladies made bandages, knit garments, and packed Christmas boxes for Over There. One Hingham lady in particular, Elizabeth Emmons, was known as "The Angel" for her work in building the Red Cross chapter and for the "lawn parties and festivals for servicemen" at her beautiful Main Street home.

Angels such as Elizabeth Emmons were much needed in Hingham in the winter of 1917-18. Coal supplies were acutely short. Customers who had yielded to blandishments to convert to gas fretted over high prices. One of the severest, coldest winters ever on the New England coast added more hardship. The waterfront was "one mass of ice and the outlook . . . as barren as an Arctic region." January school openings were delayed, and the high school shared half-day shifts with Lincoln pupils. Public buildings and places of entertainment closed or went on limited hours. The Firemen's Ball was canceled. People cut firewood and fished through thick ice for smelts. The smelts were patriotically plentiful.

The draft news was incessant and upsetting. Families waited anxiously for postcards: report for physical, for induction, for the train from Rockland to Camp Devens, for exemption hearings. Town Clerk Arthur Burr had trouble keeping track of men in service, since recruiting went on all over the Boston area. In the fall of 1917, he estimated 110; by the war's end, his estimate topped 280. The names reflected a changing town: men with old names were there—Burr, Cushing, Hersey, Lincoln, Loring, Souther, Thaxter, Whiton, Wilder—but they were less than 10 percent of the Hingham men in service. Irish names outnumbered them three to one, and new names appeared on the draft lists, such as Abbadessa, Calvi, Infusino, and Scioscia, taxing the *Journal's* orthographic powers. Some Italian Hinghamites were already citizens, and nine served. In 1918, married men were called up, and registration included all men between eighteen and forty-five. The need Over There was increasingly urgent.

Grim winter and early spring brought dreaded reports of casualties. The first death "brought the war closer home than any event since it began." In December, 1917, a submarine sank the destroyer *Jacob Jones*, and one of those lost was Coit Rogers, artist son of the late Hingham artist Franklin Rogers. Soon, ex-policeman Parker lost his war against Kaiserism and died of pneumonia in France. Seaman Albert Ross died when his destroyer collided with a British ship. Colin Campbell died of meningitis contracted in the trenches; a carpenter, he was better remembered as the popular pin boy at the Wompatuck alleys. Home from Bumpkin Island to visit his folks, Harold Crehan Barrett died of pneumonia. Still, the terrible trench warfare had scarcely begun for Hingham boys.

On the Western Front, both sides were nearing exhaustion. The French had suffered great losses, followed by mutinies, and the offensives in Flanders had drained British manpower. Germany, blockaded for three years, had also experienced heavy losses, but in the autumn of 1917, the Russian army collapsed, and with Russia no longer a threat, German divisions shifted to the West. As 1918 began, Germany had more than 3.5 million men on a front stretching in an arc fifty-odd miles from Paris. German commander Ludendorff trained his shock troops and prepared a series of five spring offensives. Would enough Americans arrive in time?

Ludendorff's offensives stalled. In July, Marshal Foch launched a heavy counter-offensive, and by summer's end, the Germans were in retreat, their leaders negotiating for peace. A turning point came with the costly victory of American Marines at Belleau Wood. Major Edward

Cole, the Hingham native for whom the American Legion post would be named, was mortally wounded when he tried to protect his men by throwing back a German grenade.

When the war was over, John Knowles of Hull, later Hingham's popular state representative, wrote the calendar of Company K's nine months of almost ceaseless combat, beginning with

> that day in August when I marched from the Centre with the old Company K. . . . The company entered the trenches in the cold days of last winter, February, 1918. We held several sectors on the Soissons front in the months of February and March . . . . The Huns must have known our identity for they began a heavy barrage at dusk on the 16th and continued it for the long period of thirty-six hours. From that front we were sent to the Toul sector and remained there until the middle of June . . . we made things lively for the Germans. Our division made history there in two engagements [Apremont and Scheisprey] . . . . As the summer time advanced the Germans were causing undue pleasantness in the region of Chateau Thierry. So the next trip was across the country again to that section. We entered there and took part in the second battle of the Marne, which drove the Germans from the entry to Paris. After a breathing spell of ten days we were sent to the Argonne and Verdun region. At that district the company caught it. Terrific bombardment marked the entire day's record. However, the Bosches were driven back and it was at this point we were when the whistle blew announcing to the whole world that the Bosch had thrown up his hands.

So it seemed afterwards. But while the boys were "in it," they could not name places and had no hindsight. Their letters evoke the mixture of war life: adventure, absurdity, horror, heroism. Frank Damon went on patrol with a "Poilu" (Frenchman). With no French, Frank trudged along "mum as the proverbial clam," until the "Poilu" broke into laughter, asked in perfect English, "Why don't you say something?" and recounted his ten years as a waiter at Boston's Hotel Touraine. Lawrence Kibby grew so used to sleeping underground that he warned his mother to keep the cellar doors locked when he came home. As John Tower looked out over a field torn by shell holes, he thought of home and "the sea on a windy day" and likened the whistle of a shell to "the siren on the Hingham fire engine only faster."

On May 31, 1918, Company K boys went "over the top" and spent a night in a gassed dug-out. Four days later, Bjorklund, Damon, Fekkes, Roger Borland, Al Hall, and Jack Mackenzie were in the hospital. Borland's vivid account of the raid is an epitome of World War I.

One Sunday morning our lieutenant came to us and said the Colonel wants so many men to go on a raid. How many will volunteer? Well, a lot of us did and he said he had enough, so next morning we started training and after a week, day and night training, the *fatal* night, as we call it, came . . . .

We got to our front line long after dark and soon was crawling over to Fritz's side of No-Man's-Land. After getting as close to his wires as we dared we lay waiting for the minute that is set for the jumping-off moment, so everyone will work together; well it came; 2:30 and bang out of the cool stillness of the night, about twenty batteries of artillery started our barrage and we all up and started on our first crack at the Bosch, our engineers blew up a whole lot of their wire and then like a pack of wild Indians, hollering, the fellows went through the gap and into their front line, over it and on to the next one, cleaning them up as we went along, then over the third line and part way to the fourth, all this time the din and noise was something terrible, there was artillery, machine guns, automatic pistols, grenades and dug-outs blowing up, and all combined to make one glorious Fourth of July. This din went on for about ten or fifteen minutes and then out we came. It was on the road out that we ran into the gas . . . .

I had the pistol to shoot the lights to tell the Major we had reached our objectives successfully so he wouldn't need to send reserves, well, I shot the light up all right but some wild bloodthirsty American thought I was a Bosch signaling for help and he fired about a dozen shots at me and lucky for me he was a poor shot. But right on top of that a shell came over and landed close to me and bowled me over into a trench and when I got up all mud and looking right at a Bosch, I still had my automatic in my fist and I just up and let him have it. Now, believe me, he took about fifteen fellows' dose. Gee, I everlastingly pasted him. I made up my mind somebody had to pay for all this trouble of coming to France.

From such grotesque nightmares were boys made heroes.

Not many miles away, Hingham's woman at war, Red Cross worker Emma Stringer, heard the guns of the advancing Germans. She had first served at a plant in St. Didier where volunteers made bandages by day. The knowledge she had gained as a potter about the temperatures of kilns served well as she heat-sterilized the bandages at night with one French helper. Now, working at a Paris railroad station, she watched refugees stream in from the war-torn countryside. As allied forces moved up and down the front, she helped feed "four or five trainloads a morning," "something like slinging food at Child's." Finally, on July

26, as the counteroffensive turned the tide, she could exclaim, "Isn't the news wonderful?"

Company K boys were part of it. Folks at home read of them in columns by Hingham's Frank Sibley, decorated war correspondent for the *Globe*. One attack in the "second Marne," he wrote, turned into a Hingham "festivity." The South Shore's best athlete, Douglas Ross, took over a machine gun position, and "for the rest of that merry morning . . . pranced through that fight like a boy at a picnic." Also at the "picnic" were Reginald Beal, son of the West's Corner policeman, and Arthur Irwin, Francis Krause, and James Cresswell. In the same drive, Alfred Hall, one of Hingham basketball's "Fearless Five," was cited for bravery. When his group surrounded a railroad station, Al climbed up a line with an automatic rifle, and "every time one or two Bosches tried to make a run for it, Hall's automatic rifle would remark briefly, PUT PUT PUT." For Al Hall, the war never ended. Afterwards, he was in and out of hospitals for the lasting damage of gas and shell-shock.

In a moving letter of August 15, 1918, James Cresswell summed up what the "boys" were learning:

> Although I'm only a kid yet, I think that these years of the army has been quite enough for me. I've seen about all the adventure and real war I care to. I said that when I came back from the [Mexican] Border, but when I come back this time I'll say it again . . . . Do you remember when I came home from the Armory that night and told you that I had enlisted? I guess it will turn out better, though, as I will settle down sooner.

> I'll say this though, Pa, the army has taught me more than ten years of knocking around in civil life could teach me. I've learned that there are all kinds of people and that they all have different ways of thinking and doing things; that one man is no better than the next; that to do what you're told is the best way to get along with your superiors; that war is serious, grim business, and not what it is pictured in paintings and stories, and that to get the other guy before he gets you you have to be wide awake and not afraid.

His philosophy would be triumphantly tested a few weeks later. On the heights of the Meuse north of Verdun, platoon commander Cresswell personally led an attack that wiped out four machine gun nests and captured and held the last heights. For this, he was awarded the Distinguished Service Cross.

Company K had already made its final move. In September, 1918, Roger Borland wrote to Ma, Pa, and brothers, "Fritz took a run and we ran after him . . . . We chased the Deutsch over hills and dales all that day and night until the next day and they ran so fast we had hard work catching up to them." A month later, Roger Borland was killed in action. Home in Hingham a few weeks later, Eddie Collins told of his fall, of staying by his side and dressing his wounds as he lay dying. Borland, twenty-two, left a young wife, his parents, and two brothers. He would not come back to work with his Pa at the grocery store on Weir Street. In all, twelve Hingham men died.

On November 7, 1918, the false report of an armistice reached Hingham. Horns began to blow, flags to fly, smiles to broaden, bells to ring, and a spontaneous auto parade erupted. A bigger celebration greeted the real armistice four days later. One by one, the men came home. Marines were discharged from the Magazine; civilian workers were furloughed. Local planners prepared for a monumental welcome but kept postponing the celebration until they could be certain that everyone had returned. A shipload of troops reached Boston harbor in early April, 1919, and at the invitation of the Nantasket Steamship Company, more than five hundred local people sailed in to welcome old Company K. The giant transport came in view. The boats surrounded her, all a-wave. No one could catch familiar eyes up on the transport's deck, no one but Frank Damon, who had come home earlier. Frank cleared a space on the steamer and "went through a series of dancing steps, his sole copyright, witnessed by every K boy . . . just weeks before Over There. Instantly a score of voices megaphoned from the transport's decks: 'That's Damon! Oh, you Mussy!'"

At 1:55 in the morning, April 8, 1919, a truck from Camp Devens pulled into Hingham Square with eleven "K boys" aboard. Hastily the Fire Department was summoned, and the "apparatus set forth a mechanical howl that brought a few hundred people to the spot. A bonfire of good proportions was started . . . . Corporal Hall of machine gun fame asked to be pinched to see if he was among the living." In the dead of night, a line of autos formed to escort each hero home.

The Great War had ended.

Hingham Square around the turn of the century.

Nantasket Beach, July Fourth, early 1920s. Most of this traffic came through Hingham.

*Washington Irving James (1851–1928),
Hingham's first police chief (1907–1927).*

*Thomas H. Buttimer, Jr. (1868–1933), state
representative, school committeeman, and
superintendent of St. Paul's Sunday School.*

*Amos C. Humphrey (1858–1942) in 1941,
grocer-butcher, "Mr. Town Meeting," and
"Guardian of the Warrant."*

*William W. Melcher (1881–1936), harbormaster,
early 1930s, where he was happiest, in the Yacht
Club tender, the DOLLY MADISON.*

Bertha Stringer (1890–1978), first Girl Scout captain, in uniform.

Anna Taurasi Calvi (born 1906), just before beginning her teaching career on Peddock's Island.

Hattie Shute Wilder (1879–1977), in her dining room, age 75, using a hand-operated addressograph for a Second Parish mailing.

Margaret McSweeney (1897–1990), a founder of Wilder Nursery School, a humane and witty social commentator.

Amy Rand Howard (1880–1958), first woman on the Planning Board, planner of the town forest and the Girl Scout house.

Major Edward Cole (1879–June, 1918), World War I. The American Legion Post was named in his honor.

Coit Rogers (1888–December, 1917), first Hingham casualty, World War I.

William Rhodes (1918–December 7, 1941), first Hingham casualty, Pearl Harbor, World War II.

Allan Rogers (1920–August, 1941), first Hingham man killed in 1939–1945 war, Coit's nephew.

Victor Rhodes (1926–June, 1951), first Hingham casualty of Korean War, William's brother.

Curtis Chase (1943–May, 1967), first Hingham casualty of Vietnam War.

CHAPTER TWENTY-ONE

❈

Years of Anxiety

P EACE did not bring the desired return to normalcy. The "Welcome Home" plans, already postponed several times, were delayed again by a police strike in Boston. Some ex-servicemen, now in Hingham's State Guard Company, found themselves back in tents, in Boston's Ronan Park, Jamaica Plain, and Roxbury, where the Guard had been called for police duty by Governor Calvin Coolidge.

The strike was symptomatic of unrest across the nation. Coal strikes caused shortages reminiscent of the war years. By 1921-22, industries nationwide were depressed. Unemployment was massive. Shoe and textile industries in New England entered their long period of decline and closings. In the factories of Brockton and surrounding towns, 21,000 workers took a 10 percent pay cut. Some industrialists used the situation to engage in union-busting and to establish "open shops."

Hingham, despite its many commuting workers and few remaining industries, was affected. It took satisfaction in the fact that "trouble-makers" were "outsiders." The Rhodes and Ripley factory on Elm Street closed in August, 1920, and reopened six months later as an open shop. Union pickets arrived in March, 1921, set up headquarters at Eagle Hall, and started efforts to turn workers away. Chief James marshaled his forces with help from Hull and Cohasset; the Fire Department had hoses ready. Against "outside forces," cheered the *Journal,*

Hingham maintained her reputation as being a peaceful, law-abiding community, where the rights of individuals are still respected . . . . Without going into the merits of an open or closed shop . . . . Every man and woman has a right to do what he sees fit in such a matter. From a town standpoint the invaders were unwelcome, but they were

[287]

allowed their rights and no more, and the public and property were protected to the letter. Good for Hingham!

Two years later, local telephone operators were applauded for sticking to their posts in spite of "loafers" from out of town.

The economic impact was severe as the war machine wound down. At the Magazine, the work force was cut back to two hundred. Camp Hingham was closed, and seventy-two buildings were put up for sale. Hard times were worsened by high prices. Even though prices declined during the depression of 1921-22, the cost of living still averaged 55 percent higher than eight years before. In April, 1920, a West Hingham family got out their old grocery receipts of 1895 and discovered that what $15 had bought then now cost $35, even though food prices were falling. The opening "specials" of the Hingham Cash Market included roaster chickens at 49¢ a pound in a town where poultry raising was common. Foley farm delivered a quart of milk for 15¢; eggs were about 60¢ a dozen, potatoes 39¢ a peck, at the new A & P on North Street. The "famous" One Cent sales at Dykeman Brothers Pharmacy and "Mighty Slaughter Sales" at Greenfield's helped. A haircut at Merlino's, Rizzotto's, Zona's, or Testa's cost 35¢. Coal, when available, cost $16 a ton.

Some of the economic gloom was dispelled by the automobile. A plain Model T cost just over $300 at Litchfield's in 1922. By 1924, there were 980 cars in Hingham, one for every six-plus people. Autos opened up new kinds of entertainment. The auto freed people from the worry of "missing the last electric" and having to walk home—from Nantasket, for example, where the immortals of the silent screen, Pickford and Fairbanks, Keaton and Chaplin, Valentino and Swanson, gave an evening's entertainment for 35¢. The auto took one to Loring Hall, where 50¢ bought a full show of movies and five acts of "Vodeville," and allowed one to dance until closing time at Herbert Kearns's Broad Cove Ballroom on the new "boulevard" at 7¢ a dance, ladies free.

The newest entertainment rage was radio. Richard Pratt at the Centre welcomed one and all to hear news bulletins and Wednesday night concerts from Medford. At clubs, members gathered hopefully for programs. "Ssh," said a West Hingham female fan to a husband arriving home, "I'm going to get Schenectady." "Immense," he replied, "but who's going to get my dinner?" People with nerve and wherewithal could stop in at Hunt's Auto Supply for wireless parts. The directions were not for the faint of heart: "Don't place the tickler or plate variometer tight against the grid coil or a change in the plate circuit will detune the grid circuit." The air was full of "music and speech" and advertising. The *Journal* whimsically sketched the new blessings advertising brought to Hingham lives.

> It has made the Victrola dog famous. It has put Castoria down your throat. It left bristles in your gums, and then came along with a rubberset that took them out. It has put SOZODONT, PEBECO, and PEPSODENT on your teeth. It has put a Gillette against your hayfield. It has put Arrow collars around your neck, and Ingersolls around your wrist. It has jammed your feet in holeproof socks, put Paris garters on your legs, and Tiffany rings on your fingers. It has worn out your jaws on Wrigley's, and posted you on what to buy to cure corns, warts, bunions, and in-growing toenails.

All you needed were money and work.

Unemployment was persistent, especially among ex-servicemen, and some were bitter. In 1922, Timothy Murphy was running again for tree warden, but this year he was opposed by another Murphy, Thomas F., whose political advertisement read as follows:

> Entering this election mainly to secure employment to provide bread and butter for my children, and not do as your present Warden has for several years, employ . . . a man who is *not* a citizen of the United States. How many of the boys would have taken this position since their return from the service? How many of their fathers would have taken the same while their sons were in the war? Remember 100% American is the protection of your country.

Timothy won, but Thomas received over two hundred votes, a sizable protest on behalf of unemployed veterans and against aliens, with that new battle cry "100% American." Before the war, America had seen the greatest flood of immigration in its history. One fruit of war hysteria was a patriotic jingoism aimed at immigrants, aliens, radicals, and pacifists, all lumped together in an anxious Nativist mythology. New immigrants were "hyphenates," their loyalties divided between old country and new. President Wilson's idealistic approach to the postwar treaty stirred their hopes that smaller nations would be protected. The Treaty of Versailles betrayed such hopes.

The frustration of the older immigrant Irish-Americans, themselves still somewhat "hyphenated," was deepened by the state of Ireland. Sinn Fein was fighting to make Ireland a republic. In 1919, Irish Hinghamites formed the Phil Sheridan Branch of the Friends of Irish Freedom, the life of which was short but vigorous. It met in St. Paul's new Guild Hall, with Timothy Murphy as president and curate Father Foley as treasurer. Speakers came to plead the cause of righting "wrongs inflicted on Ireland." Garden parties raised funds, a drive for Irish Republic Bonds went over the top in five days, and a house-to-house canvass raised over $2000 for Irish relief. At Loring Hall, Hingham was introduced to "the Poetic Beauty of the Irish Soul" in song, dance, and story. One outspoken local leader, J. Frank Crehan, spoke of "undying nationalism."

Irish-American solidarity in Democratic politics fluctuated as the Republican majority grew. In Hingham's votes for governor in 1914, David Walsh had received 325 votes to a Republican's 464, and in 1918, the Democratic vote had been 320 to Calvin Coolidge's 465. But in 1920, Hingham voted three to one for a Republican governor and for Warren G. Harding. Ethnic Democrats had lost faith in the party of Wilson and the League of Nations. In the 1920 primary, only seventeen Democrats voted; in 1922, only fifty-three; in 1924, with Walsh running for the U.S. Senate, only thirty. In 1926, however, the Walsh "miracle" was revitalized, and by 1928, to the surprise of many, it had prepared the way for the Al Smith "miracle," and Massachusetts politics changed permanently. That year, Hingham Democrats elected a town committee of ten, almost all with Irish names, and about four hundred people attended a Smith rally. The Hingham-Hull Smith Club rented quarters and held a "monster torch light parade." Smith carried the state, the first Democrat to do so since the Civil War. In Hingham, to be sure, he received only 36 percent of the vote, but the change in presidential voting was remarkable:

	1920	1924	1928
Democratic	471	424	1046
Republican	1398	1562	1878

Democratic Irish solidarity had revived after generations of "assimilation" into the old Republican town.

At the time of World War I, three new immigrant groups were being assimilated into Hingham, two of them with some difficulty. The third was not really a "group" so much as a series of north Europeans, later described by Elizabeth Coatsworth as "Hollanders who came . . . more than a generation ago and took up dairying . . . [and who] deliver their excellent milk and cream every day from door to door . . . . Hingham takes an especial pride in them." They had come singly and had never formed an enclave because the large amounts of rich farmland needed for dairying precluded it. They were scattered throughout the town.

The earliest, Joseph Threlfall, Levi Unangst, and Sytze Damstra, were in Hingham by 1908. Threlfall's cows pastured on South Pleasant Street, near Lazell, on part of what had been Cushing farmland. Further southeast on Prospect Street, on former Joshua Hersey land, was Levi Unangst. And in West Hingham, near the intersection of North and West Streets, were the cows and the meadow of Sytze Damstra. Between the time of their arrivals and World War I, Yentze De Young bought the Souther farm on Leavitt Street over the Weir River next to Albert Kress's dairy. South on Union Street, with the purchase of the Jordan farm in 1917, began the life of Hingham's most long-lived and familiar dairy operation, Hornstra's farm. On High Street, Karl Winquist, a quarryman in 1910, was running a dairy by the war's end. And in the early 1920s, Melius Couperus bought what had been the farm of twin brothers James and George King on School Street.

By contrast, the other two groups remained isolated, even geographically, from the community. "I have only a very vague idea," wrote Coatsworth, "of what share the Finns take in the community life." For a time, they remained marginal, almost invisible. They had unusual names—Ivonen, Jaakola, Salenius, Ovaska, Torvi, Wanakainen, Wirkala —and they made their community in the woods along Cushing Street. Like other immigrant groups, they came where the work was, and the work was at Plymouth Quarries on Whiting Street, a major local industry. Margaret McSweeney, the daughter of engineer John Rooney, who "came out to supervise the quarries," described the granite, unique to the area, as "Weymouth-Hingham Seam Face." Its grey, tan, and yellow blocks are filled with iron oxides, turned by water and rain into red and lavender. It was shipped all over the eastern United States and was used in the building of St. John's Church, Hingham, in 1920-21.

After their arrival in 1911-12, the Finns worked at the quarries. They were hard-working and ambitious, branching out into other occupations and sending their sons to high school and college. By the late 1920s, a Kartunen was a bleacher and another was a shoeworker, two Ovaskas and a Salenius were shipfitters, a female Wanakainen was a stenographer, a Walkpraa and a Weijanen were carpenters, and four Wirkalas were shoeworkers. When Harold Newcombe took over management of the Thayer farm at the start of the Great Depression, he had a Finnish helper, a "good worker who knew how to do everything." Warren Lincoln remembered the Nissulas as excellent high school athletes. John McKee recalled the Finns as good people with saunas in their backyards. Coatsworth pictured them

[291]

among the groves of birches or in the clearings in the pine woods. Their houses are usually new, and they are not afraid of rocky soil or of ponds, stumps, and the second growth of woodland. Often they build cabins, like modern pioneers, but a few years later the cabins have been replaced by substantial houses and the rough clearing shows lawns and flower beds.

Closer to the reality of the 1920s was the account of a Cushing Street neighbor, Dallas Lore Sharp's son Waitstill. He wrote in anger at a touchy time when the ardent patriotism of 1919-20 was obsessed with "Americanizing" immigrants already here and barring those who were not.

> This town's attitude toward the foreigner is of the worst kind, for Hingham despises its foreign class . . . . About 1850 the town began to realize the menace of the vile "foreigner" and discouraged all manufacture until the mills were abandoned and Hingham became a select residential town . . . . The immigrant avoided this pleasant place until by occupation he had to live here. Then he came, fought and stayed . . . . In 1911, the Finns bought a few acres on Cushing Street at $35 per acre. They felled trees, drained meadows, removed stumps, besides fighting pneumonia, typhoid fever and starvation.

Now they were making prosperous homes of "wrecks such as the old Chester Hobart place, the C. L. Danforth estate, and Goddins' truck farm." Every one of these sixty people, Sharp insisted, did "all his business in Weymouth and Quincy," feeling little attachment to Hingham.

The Finns, Margaret McSweeney believed, had peculiar difficulties learning English, and the problem was mutual. Pity the poor postman George Magner as he struggled with the names. One day in despair he tossed all of the Finnish mail into one postal box, and the postmaster received many complaints. Perhaps the language problem helps explain why "they were very clannish people . . . . The Finns looked after each other." So did another new group.

Like the Finns, Italians had come where the work was, hard work once done by old Yankees and, after them, by Irish laborers. Work gangs of Italians had appeared in Hingham in the 1890s, imported by labor brokers whom they called "padroni." In 1895, William Nelson was building dormitory housing along the Weir River for Italians working on the railroad. Others lived in cheap West Hingham boarding houses beside the railroad tracks and in tents on Reuben Hersey's land off Hersey Street. When a job was done, "the Italian Colony . . . like the Arabs, folded their tents and as silently stole away." They lived at a subsistence level and saved what they could to send home to wives and families in Italy. The saddest Hingham story of this custom, reported some years later, concerned a "son of sunny Italy" who was arrested and fined $50 for carrying a concealed weapon. He had gone to Boston to send his wife his savings of $300 and believed he needed the protection. The $50 his wife did not receive represented more than a month's labor.

In 1895, the census takers found eighty "foreign born" Italians in Hingham; in 1905, the number was the same, and, in a new category, there were also ninety-two of "foreign stock," the children of Italian immigrants. Almost all of these must have been transients, for the residential directory of 1902 lists no Italian names. By 1908, fourteen Italian families were resident, among them names later familiar: Barba, Barillaro, and Calabro. The 1915 census recorded a big increase to 178 foreign-born and 211 of foreign stock. The 1920 directory reflected this increase: there were eighty-three resident adult *males* with Italian names, many of them family names that would become part of Hingham history: Abbadessa, Amonte, Calvi, Condito, Conte, DeLuca, Dominello, Fuda, Galuzzo, Lombardo, Pagliccia, Rinella, Rizzotto, Saporito, Silipo, and Zona. The 1928 directory added Barbuto, Merlino, Nardo, Nese, Rando, Taurasi, and Testa. Apparently, growth slowed in the 1920s because of immigration bans and restrictions. In sum, Hingham's Italian community, mostly clustered on Kilby, Rockland, and Hull Streets, gathered chiefly between 1908 and 1915. Neighborhood memory suggests that a number of families came here together about 1913 from a coalmining region of Pennsylvania. Others came via Boston from southern Italy.

Most of the men were laborers. Theirs were years of "pick and shovel" work. They shoveled coal at the power station and snow off the tracks, changed railroad ties for a dollar a day, loaded lumber at Whitney's and fifty-pound blocks of ice for Hayward. They unloaded cargoes at the harbor, dug ditches for water and gas lines, labored on big farms, cut hay on the Bradley estate, and gardened for summer residents. At Lane's quarry east of Foundry Pond, they loaded stone onto freight cars. Rocks were a theme of their worklife: "All they did was move rocks rocks rocks," recalled Anna Calvi; "they killed themselves working by hand. Their backs were killed." Their sons, when their fortunes improved, became land contractors. No one could better understand the value of mechanized heavy equipment.

Their wives and daughters often worked at Greenfield's clothing factory and at the laundry on the corner of Kilby and Rockland Streets.

Several of Paolo Taurasi's daughters became bookkeepers, and one, later Mrs. Anna Calvi, became a teacher. From the old high school, where she starred in field hockey and earned her "H", she went on to Hyannis Normal School. Then, she commuted daily by boat to teach school on Peddocks Island. But it was rare then for Italian children to finish high school: they were needed at home for work and wages. Some parents distrusted further education and knew that their children were encountering the same prejudice that they did. Hingham did not escape the tensions between old Irish and new Italian immigrant cultures. Italians sometimes worked at non-union rates. Postwar scarcity of jobs aggravated the tensions, as we have seen in Thomas Murphy's campaign. Italians were also suspect as "birds of passage," who came and worked to save money with the aim of returning to Italy.

Some did cross and recross the Atlantic, sometimes returning with a wife and family. Peter Rando was born in Boston, but when he was only three, his father took the family back to Italy. In the early 1930s, age seventeen, Pete returned alone to Hingham. He worked for two uncles at their barber shop and on their poultry farm. The uncles had bought a home from nurseryman James Thom on Pleasant Street. A neighbor, away on business at the time, had a nervous call from his wife: "Some Italians are buying the house next door." He rushed home and built a high fence. Later, both families laughed together over that panicky prejudice.

The immigrant experience of the *contadino* was harsh. His cheap labor was needed for the "building of America," but his presence was ignored or despised:

> The indignant Irish, the superior and alarmed "American," the avaricious and scheming *padroni*, the uncertain employment, the inevitable job accidents, the long hours spent bending over pick and shovel listening to the snarling voice of the boss, the ethnic jokes and curses . . . the sick children, the children returning home from school wishing to know why it was bad to be a "guinea".

Since the first Americans they had to cope with were Irish, the overt prejudice, unlike the subtler "old stock" variety, seemed to come from them. That cheerful fighter Mrs. Calvi wonders about it still:

> The Irish wouldn't accept us . . . . They'd call us guinea or something. I'd pull their hair or kick . . . . We came from Hull to school in Hingham by bus. Hingham people resented it. The kids would pick on us and tell us to go back to Hull. If they knew you were Italian, they'd pick on you terrible . . . "Get out of the way, you guinea." I said, "what did you say? I'm an American. I was born right here on

K Street." I kicked her right off the bus at the last stop. . . . The Irish were running us. It seemed, in the clubs, if there was an Irish girl and an Italian was coming in, they didn't like you to look at them.

On Kilby Street, in pre-war years, Italian families created the only kind of village they knew, self-contained and self-sufficient. They grew vegetables and cultivated grapes for wine. "You could buy the most delicious asparagus there," said Ruth Marsh. There was milk from cows and goats for drinking and cheese-making. They had hens, eggs, and chickens. Each year a family would slaughter a pig or call in "Charlie the butch" Henningsen, Danish father of Mrs. Oscar Beck, to do it. The Weir yielded fish and turtles. Wherever the Italians live, Coatsworth wrote,

> the country comes to life. Paint appears on the houses, new terrace walls are built, and the vines begin to grow on the trellises. Children run about, a bright laundry flaps on the line, a goat and her kids feed on the green grass.

Early school days were spent at the old school house near Canterbury village. Not many went to church at St. Paul's. When children went to Sunday school, someone in authority called them "guineas." Southern Italian men had long been suspicious of clergy, and the American—that is, "Irish"—church seemed strangely austere. The real religious life took place in Boston's North End, where children were baptized and "festas" were shared with friends and kin. Once a month, though, an old priest would come to Kilby Street from St. Paul's and say mass in a barn with Frank Calvi as translator. The Italians worked each other's gardens, sharing dinner at the last house of the day's work. They cared for each other when they were sick or disabled, and the need was great when, in the influenza epidemic of 1918, most of those who died in Hingham had lived on Kilby Street. Neighborliness was their code.

Most townspeople knew little of this. They knew respectable barbers or the assimilated family who bought a house on North Street, operated a fruit market, and purchased their building, the Barba Block. Raymond Barba and his wife "removed to Elena, Italy," in 1928, leaving son Johnny to run the store, but they reappeared on Hingham street lists in the years following. Much of Hingham knew only the stereotypes in the newspaper. All over America, "The Italian still bore as vividly as ever the stigma of impassioned crime . . . . Headlines . . . trumpeted the tale of Italian bloodlust incessantly." Hingham grew accustomed to lurid *Journal* items: "Italian Shooting Affair," "Fatal Shooting, Kilby Street," "Melee at East End." Chief James, with his dog in his canopied buggy, would, after a prudent delay, visit the village and sometimes make an arrest.

Cultural analysts tell us that for many Italians, *La Famiglia e tutta; Lo Stato non e nulla;* family is all; government is nothing. Semi-feudal life had taught poor southern Italians to place no trust in legal authority, to vest all values in family and family honor. All this underlay two Hingham stories. Had Shakespeare dramatized them—and he dramatized several like them—they would be called tragedies. So they were. They live on in several distorted forms. They are also matters of public record. The names need not be recorded, and those who recount these stories do not wish to be quoted. To retell them, we conflate several versions.

A man came from Italy in 1920, leaving his wife behind. Another man, a war veteran, received a letter from Italy reporting ill of the lonely wife's behavior. He spread the gossip. The angry husband confronted him, and they fought. The husband was fatally shot. The war veteran went to prison for several years. On Memorial Day, 1927, the dead man's son was decorating his father's grave. Across the grave, he saw his father's killer, as he thought, leering at him. He pulled a gun and chased the killer away. The son was arrested. A year later, the decomposed body of the killer was found in the woods near Canterbury. A woman witness stepped forward, and three men were arrested, one a hired gunman from New York. The killer, who had come home unscathed from months in a German prison camp, had been executed. Justice had been done.

There was a powerful man; some called him the King of Kilby Street. In the Italian patriarchal tradition, he disciplined his children strictly but let no one else do so. One of his neighbors was a difficult, angry man; four years earlier, his own wife had wounded him for things he had said to her. One of the King's sons pushed the son of the angry man into the Weir River, and the angry man disciplined the boy by pushing him in, too. The King's son caught cold and told his father what had happened. The King confronted the other father and there were angry words. Early next morning, the angry man came to the King's house and beat him to death. The killer, after three weeks of hiding, gave himself up, was sentenced for manslaughter, imprisoned for several years, and pardoned on Christmas day, 1932.

He was warned to stay away from Kilby Street, but in the spring of 1933, he went anyway. As he was chatting by the roadside, he stood too far out in the road and was run down and fatally injured near the place where he had killed the King. The truck was driven by a son of the

King. An investigation ruled the incident accidental. Perhaps it was. Perhaps honor had been upheld.

Such stories inflamed stereotypes in years when Nativist resentment of immigrants intensified and when some citizens grew so anxious that they donned white sheets at night and burned crosses. Hingham, too, was affected. Nativism had waxed and waned since the Know Nothing days before the Civil War. It waxed anew after World War I. The patriotism that had fueled the war effort turned to a militant creed of "America First," a slogan of Warren G. Harding's campaign. General Luther Stephenson, Jr., summed up the anxieties in a speech in 1914; after the war, the same attitudes were resurgent:

> We are living in an age of unrest and passion, and dark clouds appear on our national horizon. The influx of hordes of ignorance and crime, of men and women who do not understand the difference between true and unrestrained liberty, who are constant violators of necessary laws for the protection of life and property. We feel the effects of the tyranny of greed and selfishness in the action of the so-called "trusts" and combinations in business and the more dangerous tyranny of labor, led by unscrupulous demagogues, some of whom are leading the ignorant and vicious with arguments of socialism, anarchy, and infidelity.

Nationally, the first impact of Nativism was the passage of laws restricting immigration. Each annual renewal brought reports of a "flood" of immigrants racing for the American gates before quotas were filled. In Hingham in 1924, the Timely Topics Club listened to warnings about anarchists, "Reds", "so-called pacifists," and "Wobblies"—the International Workers of the World. People read and talked about the Sacco and Vanzetti case and its prejudiced reviews by the Supreme Judicial Court and the Lowell committee. The crime, the robbery and murder of a factory paymaster and a guard, had happened in Braintree in 1920. Only after Sacco and Vanzetti were executed in 1927 did the *Journal* risk informing Hingham that Nicola Sacco had spent a season in town cutting ice for Hayward. Were there others?

Nativism's second impact was a concerted program of "Americanizing" aliens. In some parts of America, this went to ugly extremes. Hingham sought with apparent success to avoid such extremes. Its public measures were moderate. The new American Legion post joined local clergy in promoting assimilation, and Hingham's D.A.R. formed an Americanization Committee, but its tone was conciliatory. Americanization, it declared in 1919, does not mean forcefully seizing the newcomer and compelling him to adopt the American viewpoint without thoroughly understanding our motives. It does not mean compelling him to forget his native tongue and the traditions of his homeland . . . . We shall honor and respect their innate love for their homeland and its customs, but by processes of education and by friendly contact we shall establish in their minds an entirely new conception of their adopted country.

That year, a committee surveyed the town's aliens and estimated about three hundred, "not a large number . . . to assimilate." The committee urged every English-speaking family "to become acquainted in neighborly fashion with one or more Finnish and Italian families." Village centers were set up to facilitate this work and to offer "helpfulness and advice." Hingham Centre led off with a Halloween party for the children. Free night classes were offered in English, civics, and American history. In 1924, the American Legion sponsored a revival of Hingham's Fourth of July, with a children's parade, sports, concerts, fireworks, and the traditional great bonfire of railroad ties and tar barrels at the playground. The town thought this form of Americanizing a worthy idea, and the next year it voted the money and took over the celebration.

Not everyone was satisfied, and other fires burned in Hingham in the mid-1920s. The Ku Klux Klan, spawned in the South after the Civil War, was resurgent amid the Nativist anxiety and spread over the country. The Klan's efforts were aimed now not just at black people, but at all immigrant groups and the Catholic Church. In 1922, KKK groups met in Massachusetts; in 1923, they rallied in Worcester. On an April Saturday evening in 1924, crosses burned in over a dozen communities. One of our interviewees, an old gentleman of precise memory, remembers the man (unnamed) who headed the Klan in Hingham. At the peak of primary season in 1924, when James M. Curley campaigned for governor on a platform that attacked the KKK, rumors of a rally spread. The *Journal* was defensively satiric:

Hingham was all agog Monday evening. Someone started the story that there was to be a big outdoor meeting of the KKK on the border lying between Hingham and Weymouth with all the fixings. The traffic up that way was said to be very brisk. So far as we know not even a scarecrow was in evidence. It seems almost ridiculous that men, otherwise perfectly sane, should have a form of dementia that forces them to concoct these stories.

However, between 1924 and 1927, the *Journal* was obliged to report four fiery crosses: one behind Lovell's greenhouse, one at the back of Linscott Road, one in the Damstra meadow, and one atop Otis Hill.

Another symptom of social dislocation and breakdown in the same years was a large increase in break-ins and vandalism. A week seldom went by without reports of a store robbery or a highway holdup. In response, the town added streetlights to more remote sections and funded all-night lighting. Burglar alarms and theft insurance became popular. Tensions were increased by a frightening number of fires, allegedly set by youth gangs. By 1928, the gangs had turned to vandalism, breaking windows even in the Memorial Bell Tower and lights in the bathing beach house.

Historians link this breakdown in legal authority to Prohibition, one effect of which was the flaunting of an unpopular law by the respectable and affluent. The politics of Prohibition became entangled with the politics of Americanization: "wets," immigrants, and Irish politicians were tied together in Nativist propaganda. From 1896 through 1918, Hingham voted annually more than two to one to remain "dry." A local lodge, the Grand Temple of Honor, promoted the pledge of total abstinence, and Methodist and Baptist churches were scenes of mass rallies. Irreverent wit James Kimball, disguised as Carrie Nation, convulsed a 1916 "Vet shindig" with an "effective although somewhat qualified lecture on the temperance question."

A federal prohibition amendment, the Eighteenth, was ratified in 1919, and would remain in effect until it was repealed by the Twenty-First Amendment in 1933. At town meeting in 1919, Hingham characteristically declared its independence, surprising even itself, and voted to go "wet."

> *Oh listen, have you heard the news*
> *That comes from Hingham town?*
> *The "wets" at last will have their booze,*
> *The "drys" were voted down.*
>
> *Nantasket now has lost its charm,*
> *No more the beach we'll roam,*
> *Goodbye, the Garden of the Palm,*
> *We'll buy our rum at home . . . .*
>
> *Large cities in our Nation,*
> *On booze are shutting down,*
> *But we'll show all creation*
> *A grand, wide-open town.*

The surprise was short-lived. In 1920, Congress passed the Volstead (enforcing) Act and Prohibition became law.

Locally, it started out with jokes. *Rumor:* "quantities of bayrum are being used hereabouts, not for tonsorial purposes." *Warning:* "Get the wet goods into your basement before Saturday night"—not meaning laundry. *Hope:* "a patient will be limited to two cases of beer a month, but there is nothing in the Volstead Act that limits the patient to one physician." *Hideous mistake:* woe befell the skipper of a long, low, rakish-looking motor yacht maneuvering in darkness between Button Island and the Yacht Club, who drew a crowd and a police ambush, but was only coping with engine trouble. A folklore grew up about "men in blue" who looked away as trucks sped their "booze" through town or even peddled "alky" themselves. But there was little to joke about at the time, and Chief James, battle-weary and already in his seventies, had his hands full. Local stills were raided. The "police station looked like a storehouse of the old fashioned saloon." For a time, the rumrunners hung safely off the Scituate coast, sending small boats ashore to load trucks, "booze ships," which then sped through Hingham and were sometimes caught by James and his men on Lincoln or Whiting Street.

Later, the rumrunners anchored out in Weymouth bay. Boats ferried cans ashore, and these were collected at low tide and stashed under hay in nearby barns, awaiting distribution trucks. Chief James's big raid came on Tuesday night, December 11, 1923. His men had found four hundred cases, worth $80,000, in a barn owned by the well-known truckfarmer Patrick Murphy near the Back River. Officer McKey tailed a Lynn truck to the dark barn, where other out-of-town trucks were lurking. Notified at midnight, Wash called the "Feds" at Rockland, and the truckers were promptly arrested. All, interestingly enough, had Anglo-Saxon names. Farmer Murphy "disclaimed all knowledge" of the incident.

The town was divided over whether Prohibition was working. In the public debate over its effectiveness, new voices were heard. In the years of the temperance movement, women had traditionally exerted their social influence in behalf of restriction or prohibition. But in the early 1920s, Mrs. Elizabeth Emmons, president of a new organization called the Women's Republican Club, declared in an advertisement that the Volstead Act simply meant "higher taxes, corruption, graft, increase in crime, lawlessness and disorder." Progressive women such as Mrs. Emmons had concerns about public order and morality in politics that outweighed their belief in temperance. And such women now held political power. In the very year of the Volstead Act (1920), they had finally won the vote.

In Hingham as elsewhere, the last years of their struggle for suffrage had been divisive. At the turn of the century, suffragist leaders "had to confess failure in their campaign for the vote, save in a handful of states." In 1913, the movement again picked up momentum. In January, a "monster mass rally" was held at Tremont Temple, Boston, and in February, local meetings began at the Main Street home of Mrs. Joseph Lovejoy, historian of the D.A.R. The next year, a Hingham Equal Suffrage League became active, and a booth at the fair distributed suffrage literature. Chief James had yet another tense situation to manage. A "plucky little woman," suffragist Mrs. Claiborne Catlin, was riding through the state on her "little mare Diana," seeking converts. She addressed a large gathering at the railroad depot, while James and an assistant insured that she was not harmed.

Nineteen fifteen was the target year for a state referendum, and as the suffrage forces gathered, their foes, including other women, mobilized. An antisuffrage rally was held at the home of Mrs. J. W. Spooner with Miss Abby Bradley in the chair. Why, they asked, add more voters to an already "clumsy, unwilling electorate?" As November approached, both sides were confident. It is merciful that suffragist John D. Long, who had died three months before, did not live to see how badly his cause lost.

War came, and the energies of activist women were needed elsewhere, but after the war, they were not to be denied. In May, 1919, Congress overwhelmingly adopted the Nineteenth (Woman's Suffrage) Amendment. On August 16, 1920, in Tennessee, ratification was completed, and the *Journal* burst into verse:

> *So I'll stay and change the "dydies"*
> *When Mother goes to vote—*
> *If I have to wash the dishes,*
> *It sure will get my goat.*
> *For a feller from the mountains*
> *Down in Eastern Tennessee*
> *Voted "aye" on women's suffrage,*
> *So it's Home Sweet Home for me.*

But would women vote? As of the last Hingham town election before ratification, an estimated sixty-five women were registered, but of 304 ballots cast, all were by males. It took energetic political education to overcome the reluctance of women to vote. Suffrage leaders were chiefly Hingham's new women, Republican and well-to-do. Women of old families and immigrant families may well have shared a reluctance, possibly a fear. The new women's Republican town committee went to work, and on one evening in late August, 1920, 174 women were added to the voting rolls. In the primary that fall, 50 percent of registered women cast ballots, contrasted with only 20 percent of registered men. By October, the voting list had climbed in six months from 1250 to 2183, 40 percent of them women. In November, spirits ran so high that some of both sexes electioneered improperly on the steps of the town office building. A Republican landslide ensued; even Boston went Republican, with disillusioned ethnic Democrats staying home. A West Hingham man lost his bet, and on Saturday evening was expected to climb a telephone pole in pink pajamas.

Women were slow, however, to elect each other to office. In 1921, three ran for School Committee, but male candidates beat them two to one. The radical change came by accident in July, 1922, when Town Clerk Arthur Burr died suddenly, and the selectmen named his woman assistant to serve. She sat *ex officio* on the Board of Registrars and was soon elected to the Board of Health. Her accession was confirmed at the 1923 election when she defeated her male opponent for the clerk's office 953 to 404. It may have reassured some old Hinghamites that her name was Mrs. Mary G. Lincoln; in fact, she was a daughter of James Buckley and a parishioner of St. Paul's.

Three other women soon followed Mary Lincoln into town office. In 1924, Amy Howard was elected to the Planning Board, and Sarah Bates became an Overseer of the Poor. In 1926, the new Hingham Women's Club persuaded Louise J. Root to run for School Committee, and she won. Henceforth, women would exert strong influence in Hingham's political life.

It is wrong to suggest that they had not been influential before, but their influence was subtler. In the late nineteenth century, married women, the "angels in the house," had economic power; it was they who supported the growing market in consumer goods. But they stayed at home to raise children, and their social world was essentially limited to church groups and neighborhood circles. In Hingham, until the turn of the century, there were not many women at paid jobs, with the exception of teachers, domestic servants, nurses, milliners, dressmakers, and seamstresses. A few entrepreneurial sorts ran boarding houses or dry and fancy goods shops.

The change came between 1900 and 1910, in response to the growth of commerce, health services, education, and new technologies. By 1908, of a total Hingham workforce, male and female, of about

1750, over ninety women worked as clerks, bookkeepers, accountants, and stenographers. Seventeen of them commuted to Boston. One was Annie Griffin, a clerk. In the Central Street household of her father, Patrick Griffin, the old laborer and estate gardener, she "boarded" with six other women of the same surname. Their occupations were a catalogue of available jobs: a dressmaker, two milliners, two stenographers, and a bookkeeper. One new occupation depended entirely on women: "manning" the switchboard. By 1908, there were twelve telephone operators at "Fort Hill 7600." Most of these positions were held by single women of Irish families, who generally lived at home as "boarders." Other women worked at the Rhodes and Ripley factory stitching wholesale clothing for the Boston market and, later, on the knitting machines at Greenfield's.

Some of the working women came from old Hingham families. Hattie Shute Wilder began her work life around the turn of the century. She recalled it long afterwards at the age of ninety in her house at 605 Main Street. Here is what she said, transcribed in a phonetic approximation of her classic old Hingham accent:

My faathuh—Oi dunno what he deeud, he wuhked in a shoe shop. Thayuh was a factry down back heeyuh. He wuhked thayuh a long toime. An' he used to wuhk ovuh to Weymouth. An' this one buhnt down. Oi was thayuh when it buhned. We nevuh missed a foyuh. Roight in back o' that stowuh. My husband and his faathuh were runnin that stowuh at the toime. Oi wasn't married then . . . . My husband Fred Woilduh was a stitchuh. That was *the* job those days yuh know . . . . When we fuhst married, we lived down ovuh the stowuh. We hoiyud it, paid eight dolluhs a month. Oh it was beautiful! We were down ovuh the stowuh for twelve yeeyuhs. An' Oi had the most beautiful flowuhs. An' then we had to come up heeyuh and take cayuh o' the old folks, an' Oi thought Oi would doie! But Oi lived through it. Oi wuhked so haad—Oi wuhked in the shoe string factry thuhteen yeeyuhs. Walked back and fawth or rode a bicycle, or went in "the caahs." It used to be on Elm Street. Do you know what they call Rhodes Ripley's? Seems to me thayuh was a candy factry thayuh at one toime. We wuhked thayuh a long toime, an' then they moved down in back o' the Catholic Church . . . . Oi used to have to get up an' leave at half past six in the mawnin. Get home at six at noight, an' then wuhk at home for faathuh an' mothuh. Oi wuhked so haad an' then Oi'd come home and bake poies. An' when Oi had a vaycation, Oi'd clean house, which Oi *don't do no mowuh.*

It was not unusual for working women to marry late, a trend that substantially affected the birthrate. Louise Wilder wanted to go, via

Vesper George art school, into art teaching, but her family sent her to Burdett business school. From there, she went to work for the Hingham Institution for Savings at $5 a week, and later, for her dentist-brother. In her thirty-sixth year, she and Mr. Cobleigh decided they had enough money "to get by on" and married. Anna Calvi's story is similar. At her one-room school on Peddocks Island, she worked "like a beaver" with forty pupils in eight grades for $27.50 a week. Except for her boat fare, "momma took every bit of that money. They needed it." She, too, married in her thirties.

A few women became legendary in local business. Miss Margaret Crehan served twenty-five years as assistant postmistress, and after her death in 1919, Miss Nellie Brassil succeeded her. Mrs. and Miss Cushing presided over the Cushing House. On Hersey Street, an old Cape Cod couple, B. R. Rich and his wife, ran their little side-by-side shops for almost half a century. Down at the railroad depot, that "slightly chubby woman with white hair," Kitty Hennessy, managed her father's "Waiting Room" and its penny candy counter. Also "famous" was the "stout, bustling, and talkative" Miss Elsie Pratt, who, with her "lean, tall and silent" sister, Miss Millie, took over Walter Hersey's dry goods shop in 1911. Their business moved often, finally to "an old building with a tin roof" in West Hingham. Here, in her store with its old lending library and casual, word-of-mouth employment agency, Coatsworth remembered Elsie Pratt amid her "dust, cobwebs, and disorder," thimbles behind the penny candy and bolts of cotton buried under pots and pans. One day, Coatsworth's brother-in-law F. Morton Smith stopped by when Miss Elsie was rebuilding her coal fire and watched in horror as she shoveled the hot ashes into a paper carton.

Most renowned was the perdurable Miss Susie Gates, whose dry goods shop stood at the corner of North Street and Thaxter's Bridge. She was best remembered for her outlandish appearance: "Long before women cut their hair, she cut hers right off. And she wore shirtwaists and black skirts, very no-nonsense. She'd have worn pants if there had been any for women." This proto-feminist, Universalist personage was born in 1846 and carried on into her eightieth year.

As wealthy newcomers arrived, the number of Hingham women in custodial service grew. By 1928, there were eighty-six maids, fifty-four housekeepers, and twenty-seven nurses. One record survives as a clue to the wants of the affluent and the work women did for them. In an advertisement of February, 1928,

> Miss Coatsworth takes pleasure in recommending Miss Mary Doie as general seamstress, maker of slip covers, and accommodater. Southern

dinners for Thursday and Sunday nights [cook's time off] a specialty. Telephone Hingham 0470. Mary Doie will also come in evenings to care for children. References: Mrs. F. Morton Smith, Miss Emma Stringer.

What could traditional homemakers have thought of such a notice? Many had survived into this strange new world. In 1903, Mrs. Ellen Callahan of North Street died at the age of 102. Born in County Cork in 1800, she had outlived all but two of her eight children. In 1913, Miss Mary F. Hersey Corthell, a descendant of Peter Hobart's father, died in her ninety-sixth year. Mrs. Deborah Marble, descended from Hawkes, Burrs, and Groces, lived long enough to ride in an automobile in her ninetieth year. "Essentially a homemaker, devoted to her family, she did not mingle much in the general activities of the town." "Grandma Lane" spent her ninety years in that quiet old enclave the Centre, and "Grandma Pyne" died on Emerald Street, having come from Ireland at age eleven in 1854. Amos Humphrey's mother, who died at ninety-three, had come as a bride to Hingham and lived in the same house for seventy-seven years. At her death the oldest First Baptist, she had been an ardent temperance worker, a charter member of the W.C.T.U. Miss Mary Bonner Cazneau, the oldest Methodist at her death, first president of the W.C.T.U., died at ninety-five in the house where she was born.

In their modest lives, such women might not have sensed their own importance, but they were the "little black knots holding the web of history together." They had significant unofficial influence: a reminiscence at the time of the centenary of the Methodist Church noted that, "although the women have no say in the church business, a common custom during the Board meeting was to say, 'Hold on until I can go over and see Miss Cazneau.'" Now their roles were evolving even within traditional associations. As Hingham joined in the national growth of men's fraternal societies, women followed suit with their own: the Order of the Eastern Star in 1913, the Rebekahs in 1915, the women's auxiliary of the American Legion post in 1920, and in the same year, the Pythian Sisters. The Pythian Sisters sponsored a gala benefit for disabled veterans in 1922. What traditional women, chiefly of working class and lower middle class stock, worried about in the early 1920s is whimsically revealed in conversations overheard at that benefit:

I hear he's a drinking man—They've forbidden digging clams at Hough's Neck—Just two more payments on the old car—The Assessors' Book gives her as just 38—Huh!—I've got two ton, one of Pea, the other of Stove—At her age bobbing her hair!—There's Maria going to get a new dress for the primaries.

The collective power and experience of organizational management had come earlier to women of a more affluent and Progressive class. Some of their priorities can be learned from the work of one summer resident, Isabel Hyams. Miss Hyams, the daughter of wealthy Dorchester parents, a graduate of M.I.T., worked for years in public health research, and in 1895 founded and financed the Louisa M. Alcott Club for children in Boston's South End. These were the years in American cities of the settlement house movement and of summer camps for poor children. In 1901, Miss Hyams bought "Orchard House," the John Fearing homestead of 1809 at 36 Pleasant Street, and invited club members here for two-week vacations. The children remembered those holidays all their lives: the delicious meals, the daily rides in the surry, the chores, the berry-picking picnics, the playhouse and masquerades, and most of all the trips by "electric" to Nantasket Beach.

Isabel Hyams' "camp" was no simple charity, but a carefully conceived program of childhood development, domestic science, and progressive education. Her agenda paralleled those of other women moving into public life. The turn-of-the-century scares about the "white plague" of tuberculosis, and about influenza, infantile paralysis, and diphtheria had strengthened concern for public health. For several years, Miss Abby Bradley made it a personal charity to pay a district nurse. In her absence in 1912, a group of ladies instituted a District Nurse League, only to disband in embarrassment when she returned and refused to share the burden. The next year, the town appointed an inspector of milk, and in 1914, a medical examiner. In 1919, monies for a district nurse were included in the town budget, and in 1920, a District Nurse Association, later the Hingham Visiting Nurse Association, was formed. Mrs. Ethel Cherry succeeded Visiting Nurse Emily Poulin, who had become public health and school nurse.

The expanding role of the HVNA is seen in its report for 1925: 2918 bedside visits, 249 medical and 45 surgical cases, and 132 babies examined at the new baby clinic. As public consciousness grew, so did the town's public health budget. In 1927, the police got their first ambulance, and parents were asked to allow public health doctors to examine their children. A few citizens, led by Dr. Charles Howard, began a hospital movement in 1923, inspired perhaps by the South Shore Hospital's opening the year before. The Hingham Memorial Hospital Corporation received donations, but progress was slow, and fruition was still several years away.

The John A. Andrew House on North Street was the symbolic structure of this period when the public policy of the town expanded to include multiple social service functions. It was built in 1915 through the generosity of Mrs. Charles Mason and named in honor of her grandfather, the Civil War governor. First to move in was the school for small children from the rented house at the Cove, with Elizabeth Bates still as teacher-supervisor. Within a decade, the Andrew House had become a beehive of activity—not just for the HVNA and its clinics, but for the Mothers Club, Teachers Club, Women's Club, and W.C.T.U. The Glee Club, directed by Gertrude Edmands, and theatrical groups rehearsed there. The place was so busy that two or three committees, if they forgot to reserve ahead, might turn up at the same time.

The Girl Scouts met at the Andrew House until 1928, the eleventh anniversary of their founding. They had organized in Hingham on the eve of America's entry into World War I; indeed, the initiative had been taken by the Special Aid Society for American Preparedness. The organizational meeting took place at New North Church on March 10, 1917. On March 19, twenty-four girls formed the "Holly Troop," and later that year, Bertha Stringer became its captain. By 1927, they had expanded and outgrown their space at the Andrew House and had launched a drive for a home of their own. Amy Howard, Emma Stringer, and Beatrice Ruyl researched, produced, and sold an historical map of Hingham. A little pony named "Midget Bartlett" did her part in the fundraising, giving ten-cent rides around the Common. Isabel Hyams, feeling reservations about the "militaristic" origins and overtones of Scouting, donated anonymously to this project of her friend and neighbor Amy Howard. By June, 1928, the Girl Scouts had purchased land on Burr Road, and that autumn, they picnicked on their own grounds.

The Progressive women active in such organizations as the Hingham Visiting Nurse Association, the Andrew House, the Hospital Association, and the Girl Scouts belonged to a newly enfranchised force in the town's public life. Many of them were part of a large influx of suburbanites who moved to Hingham shortly after World War I. In the early 1920s, they led in the forming of organizations that expressed their concerns: the Hingham Women's Republican Club and the Hingham Women's Club. In 1922, the new Women's Club held a mock town meeting. Among the items on their "warrant" were these: subsidizing the electrics; building a new high school; establishing a town forest; and appointing a town manager or adopting a limited town meeting. Together, the items hint at what was happening in the town to which these women had moved and in which they wielded new power.

As it wrestled with its own versions of national problems, immigration, ethnic tensions, Prohibition, and women's political roles, Hingham also faced critical problems of its own. It faced new fiscal challenges. It weighed for the first time radical ideas of land use, public policy, and town planning. It faced a crisis as to its very identity. The gamble of improvement, initiated in the first decade of the century, had succeeded to such a degree that the town could scarcely recognize its rapidly changing face, environmental and human.

CHAPTER TWENTY-TWO

Boom and Identity Crisis

IN the 1920s, old Hingham committed itself irrevocably to a new life. The pattern of change, as we have seen, began in the late nineteenth century, when local industry had almost faded away, and a small number of wealthy people discovered the delights of the town as a summer resort. As the new century opened, the national "wave of improvement" washed over Hingham. "Improvement," the thinking went, would pay for itself by attracting more desirable residents. The idea of growth caught on, and smallness was no longer a value but a problem. In 1912, William Codman called for a new spirit:

> It is very obvious that the Hingham population has not grown as it should. The increase in fifty years from 1860 to 1910 was the smallest of any city or town in the Metropolitan District. The Hingham spirit, which is so well known, of "Let us alone, we are satisfied" will no longer do.

We need, said Codman, a town planning commission.

Following the war, growth accelerated to such a degree that the need for planning was urgent. By 1919, some Hingham rents had risen by 40 percent. A severe housing shortage in 1920 produced anecdotes such as this: a West Hingham woman took down her draperies for spring cleaning, and three desperate passers-by rang her bell to ask when she was moving out.

After the new "boulevard" opened from Lincoln Street to the harbor, Boston developers saw in the land from the "boulevard" across Otis Hill to the bay the chance for "big doings." In 1920, the firm of Brown and Stackpole bought fifty-six acres on both sides of Broad Cove, including Otis Hill, and in 1921, they purchased another sixty acres between Downer Avenue and the bay and named it "Wompatuck." In nine months, they built twenty-one bungalows. Most owners were "Boston professional or business men of high standing, and the balance are retired."

Near World's End, "Cedar Gables" opened, and in 1925 off Rockland Street, "Bonnie Brier Cliff" joined the boom. Not to be outdone, local investors purchased the parade grounds on Burditt Avenue for 20,000-foot lots. James Kimball, now a partner at Kimball's Lumber, was soon known as the designer of luxury homes on Burditt, and his reputation made him the logical broker for precious old estates: the Hawkes Fearing house at the Centre, the Whiton house on Pear Tree Hill, the Henry Hersey estate on South Street. Near Cold Corner, Leonard Linscott offered thirty-six house lots; in the northwest, a Boston developer bought from the Downer estate a 225,000-foot tract on Downer, Jarvis, and Whiton Avenues and Howe Street; and the Whiton and Paige estates sold their adjoining Crow Point properties. Another ambitious local entrepreneur was Henry Crehan. In 1912, he was a clerk boarding on Thaxter Street; in 1920, a teacher boarding on Elm. But in 1923, he saw his chance in the boom and began buying tracts, starting with the old Willard property, and announced that he would "open up Central Street for subdivision."

The quickening pace can be seen in numbers of dwellings: from a total of 1233 in 1905, they grew to only 1435 by 1915; then to 1811 by 1925 and to 2146 by 1930. Crehan summed up the "boom" mentality as of 1923: the Hingham population *ought* to reach ten thousand in a "few years"—it was then less than six thousand—if only "those who admire our beautiful elms, our bathing beach, our beautiful climate, etc., would, through a concerted movement, induce others to move into the town. Can the memory of the oldest inhabitants tell us the date when the last project was launched . . . to 'boom' the town of which we all claim to be proud?" *Everyone*, he insisted, benefits from suburban growth. Why not have a board of trade?

Trade was growing and expanding. There was continuity, to be sure. In his eighties, David Cobb still spent every day at his paint store; the Grain Mill carried on, helped by the demand for poultry feed; Anderson's grocery and Bickford's hardware survived, as did the stores of Elsie Pratt and Susie Gates. Hayward still provided the ice, and Connell, the gents' tailor, was "old reliable." But some merchants could afford to expand. Eddie Long built a new florist shop, and Herbert Kearns added a bakery to his luncheonette. Reuben Griggs tore down buildings on North Street at West Hingham crossing to erect a block of brick shops, and Barba bought the Thayer Building. Frank Buttimer needed more space for his insurance business, and George Hunt tore down the old blacksmith shop near the mill on North Street for an addition to his auto parts store. Roy Litchfield expanded his agency at Water and Summer Streets to make "the largest Ford plant south of Boston." Auto agencies, garages, and fuel stations multiplied, and so did antique and gift shops, candy stores, and tea rooms. Naturally, there were more realtors.

These were years when Boston "chain stores" began their suburban invasions, with oddly impersonal, non-local names: the "A & P" in 1922 on North Street, joined by "Rose Tea Company," "Economy Grocery Stores," and the "First National" on Main Street (later Baker's and Granite). Such names suggest much about change. Was change the unmixed blessing Henry Crehan claimed?

Hingham had entered a crisis of identity. A *Journal* editorial of 1923 attempted to define the crisis:

> Hingham—what is it—and what does it want to be? No town can succeed without a definite goal ahead any more than an individual. By the almost unanimous [?] opinion of its residents it does not aspire to be a manufacturing town. Geographically and otherwise, it is impossible to make Hingham a bounding success as a summer resort. The thing that is left, and what the town seems best fitted for, is a residential town. You hear it said that for that purpose it is second to none in the state . . . . If we are to be known as a first-rate residential town let's make it one in fact. It will cost us some effort and more money . . . but we can well afford . . . . Get behind . . . . Don't be a doubter or a kicker.

The identity crisis was fought out in the traditional place, town meeting.

There, a battle about the survival of the "electrics" opened the 1920s. Those wonders of childhood memory had a brief career, and by war's end their days were numbered. Tracks on Crow Point were taken up in 1920; Hingham-Nantasket electrics stopped in 1921, and "jitneys", motorbuses, plied the boulevard, which was continued in 1921-22 to West (or West's) Corner. Queen Ann's Corner was on another new boulevard between Boston and Plymouth. The auto was winning. Unless Hingham and Hull would subsidize an estimated deficit of almost $46,000, the electrics would be discontinued.

Town meetings of 1920-24 were badly split. In 1920, jeweler C. F. Godfrey derided the idea of subsidy, and some threatened to boycott his store. Deficits grew. The lines were kept open by semi-annual, increasingly grudging town grants. South Hingham workers depended on the Queen Ann-East Weymouth line, and because of their pressure, the line was subsidized for a while. In 1924, unused for several years, the tracks between the harbor and the depot were taken up. "Little by little the street railway tracks are disappearing from Hingham streets."

On June 14, 1926, a public hearing considered licensing the Eastern Massachusetts Street Railway to operate "jitneys" on town streets. Only seventy-five people attended. The last electric ran its last trip on the East Weymouth line three months later. An era was over, and few thought further about the "end-hogs" on the summer cars or missed the rapid-fire "bell-tattoo" of the conductor ringing up fares.

Other costly issues sustained a crisis mood. Every summer, the town waited anxiously for an announcement of the new tax-rate, and with each rise, the justification was the same: "we must pay for new needs." Appropriations increased by approximately 75 percent between 1920 and 1926; property valuation almost tripled; the tax rate wavered between $25 and $30. All this happened in a non-inflationary time, partly as a result of new obligations, brought on by the town's new self-image.

A single new undertaking was quite free of controversy: the establishing of a town forest. It was almost cost free and was a matter of pride. Hingham was the eighth community in Massachusetts to have one. The project was launched in 1922 with the gift of fifty acres at the corner of Charles and South Pleasant Streets from William Codman. A year later, John J. Moore bequeathed fourteen acres on Long Bridge Lane, now part of Wompatuck State Park. In 1929, an additional sixty acres were purchased from O. O. Smith. In 1932, the entire preserve would be named the George Washington Forest.

The forest took shape in the 1920s through the able leadership of Francis Lincoln, president of the Garden Club, and Amy Howard; and most especially through "the foresight and enthusiasm" of Tree Warden Timothy Murphy. By 1928, fifty acres had been planted with 60,000 trees, mostly white and red pine and spruce.

By contrast, proposals for a new high school provoked more than three years of controversy. The arguments began in 1922-23, when some favored a union school with Cohasset and Hull, some wanted only repair of the old building, and some spread "propaganda" for a new building with "popular features." In 1922, the town was not ready to approve the estimated cost of $275,879. Finally, in 1926, the bitter pill was swallowed, and the lowest bid was accepted. Completion was projected for August, 1927. That autumn, at 4 A.M. one October morning, neighbors of the old high school heard explosions, and by 5

A.M. the building was engulfed in flames. The loss was total, and the town used the insurance to provide furnishings for the new school. Old-timers long remembered 1927-28 as the year of a two-platoon system at Lincoln School: high-schoolers in the morning, junior high-schoolers in the afternoon. The new high school—later Central Junior High—opened in September, 1928, a costly and some felt debatable luxury.

A less expensive change offered itself in 1925. Thompson's Coal Company went out of business. A few citizens sat in the town offices and dreamed of a waterfront park. Hingham's fourteen miles of beaches were already dotted with "No Trespassing" signs. Here was perhaps the "last chance." At a special town meeting in October, "that old bugbear taxes" reared its head, and the familiar rejoinder was heard—the park would increase property values—but with a new twist: "If we don't get it we will probably have a straight business development." The motion passed, and by January, 1926, the town owned Thompson's.

The *Journal*, long a booster, now moderated its tone. March is "the one time of year to assert yourself regarding the expenditures . . . . Don't stay away, and then kick all the year." In 1928, developers bought from the Masonic Lodge the Loring-Sprague house at the corner of South and Main Streets, to be replaced by the Sprague Building. But when selectmen asked for about $30,000 to alter and widen the intersection for parking, their request caused fireworks. Everyone seemed pleased with the new waterfront park, but when, in 1928, most of the adjoining beach property northwest of Thompson's changed hands and the "last chance" voices moved to buy it, the move failed. Finally, as the year ended, rumors spread that a New York syndicate wanted to buy the Water Company. The "last chance" advocates proposed purchase by the town. As usual, the timing was wrong. This perennial issue, born amid the depression of the 1870s, would surface again in the depression of the 1930s.

With such expensive and competing possibilities, the time of establishing priorities had come, and the idea of town planning appeared. In a town long fiercely protective of private liberties, the idea was bound to be controversial. Beginning in 1922, Selectman William L. Foster gave speeches on town planning and even dared to advocate something called "zoning." The D.A.R. and the Village Improvement Society came together in a joint committee on planning, and two of its members, Susan Willard and Amy Howard, reported on the benefits of "zoning." In 1923, the town meeting established a Planning Board, and over the next two years, zoning became the major issue at meetings. Advocates mounted a promotional campaign, but to no avail. A zoning bylaw was "thoroughly threshed out" and indefinitely postponed in 1926. Hingham was not ready to surrender its character entirely to the new suburban mentality. Fifteen years would pass before that step was taken. Not all was changed.

But much was changing. Hingham was beginning to look like "our town" of sixty-five years later. The boulevard stretched to West's Corner; old houses had vanished in its wake; new ones and a harbor park lay beside it. Derby Academy seized its "last chance" when the cadet grounds succumbed to development, and in the fall of 1923, six new buildings on Burditt Avenue awaited the arrival of the middle and upper schools. In 1924-25, the town forest and the South Shore Country Club together joined the townscape. In 1927, the Universalists disbanded, and the Odd Fellows moved to their empty meetinghouse; and in 1928, the Masons built their temple on Central Street.

That year, the Hingham Yacht Club was forced to move. It had grown and prospered since its founding in 1895 by six Harvard undergraduates, with Charles B. Barnes, Jr., as first commodore. In its early races, only the girls were left to do the judging, and Dave Cobb, with "little attention to accurate timing," fired the starting shotgun. By 1910, it had 125 members and a long waiting list. By 1914, the small clubhouse of 1905 at the Cove was too small, and a full-rigged, two-masted schooner was purchased as an "annex" and anchored off the floats. The *Otranto* proved a "first-rate headache" and ended her days in the harbor mud. By 1928, the clubhouse at the site of today's "Iron Horse" was throttled by the boulevard and the waterfront park. Members raised $5000 to buy the Crow Point steamboat landing from the Nantasket Steamboat Company, and construction began in June on the club's new home.

The same month brought the sound of the steam shovel in the square as the Sprague Block began its sixty-year life. The stately old Loring-Sprague mansion, which stood on its site, was dismantled and moved to Falmouth. Other casualties included the Society of Arts and Crafts; it had died in 1922, the victim of Water Company growth—no more room in the building—and prohibitive rents. Agricultural fairs were supplanted by the activities of the new Garden Club, founded in 1924, with a membership of about fifty men and women and Robert Brewer as first president. Traditional local sports were in difficulty. Every spring brought efforts to return the town to "the baseball map," but every summer's end heard complaints of poor attendance and insufficient funds. Organized play was now a childhood affair; organized summer activity at the playgrounds began in 1925.

Individual passings also signaled lost connections with the past. Three disappearances were perhaps most momentous. George Cushing, hotel owner, postmaster for twenty-three years, and fire chief for forty, died in 1920. Susan Barker Willard died in 1925. And on Memorial Day, 1928, Washington Irving James, the town's first police chief, died. Two more of the seemingly ageless and spry oldsters at the Centre were gone: pharmacist Reuben Sprague, founder of the old Philharmonic, and George King, who died in the farmhouse where he had lived his ninety-two years:

> In the little one-room building on the grounds, the men of Hingham Centre, forty years ago, used to gather on winter evenings with the King brothers for their chats and discussions of affairs of state and nation, as well as local topics. It was called "the smoke house" and many a peaceful pipe was smoked there by a group of noted citizens.

By 1928, that world seemed increasingly peaceful and distant.

The town's dramatic changes during the 1920s were not so much in numbers. When the century opened, its population stood at just over five thousand, and after twenty-eight years, it had risen only to sixty-five hundred. The meaningful changes were in the identities of those who made up the numbers. The Rev. Donald Robinson places side by side two lists of names in the Second Parish Membership Book. By 1928, the new residents, the "out-of-town population . . . was the largest proportion of the general population." In 1921, a state law mandated the listing of men and women twenty and older, and Hingham's annual street lists reported the information. Now, every year the town was confronted with a measure of its changes. What is striking are the numbers of names *lost* since the previous list, of those *added*, and of the sum of the two, the actual change in identities. The "lost" include not just deaths, but movings away; the "gained" include not just comings of age, but new arrivals.

The case of the Robinsons themselves reminds us that family names can be a misleading index of change. Until recently, the ancestral names of wives were invariably lost when they married. Young males were far more likely to move away in search of jobs than young females. Some old Hingham families have stayed on with changed names. For example, Carol Robinson and her sisters, Helen Chamberlain and Nancy Howard, are great-granddaughters of Hannah Leavitt. The ancient Leavitt family played prominent roles in town affairs during the 1600s. In the

1700s, a grandson of John Leavitt, Hezekiah, and a great-grandson, Elisha, Jr., were among the wealthiest and most powerful Tory allies of Gay, Barker, and Thaxter. The 1893 *History* is notably silent about Leavitts after 1800. Before and just after the Civil War, the Leavitt homestead and farm were occupied by Martin Leavitt and his son Martin. In 1889, the homestead became the summer place of a Boston physician. What is striking is the number of Leavitt women who married into many other old Centre families: Burr, Howard, Lane, Souther, Sprague, Thomas, Whitcomb, and Whiton, and the resulting number of Centerite men who have had Leavitt as a first or middle name.

Nonetheless, the total changes of the 1920s are surprising: in 1921, 922 changes; in 1923, 887; in 1925, 959; in 1927, 947. With an average population of about six thousand, this meant a change of as much as *15 percent per year*. Of course, some of those who moved away were recent arrivals. But such short-term residency only strengthened the sense of change. As Susie Eldredge recalled from childhood, "The only people we were suspicious of were ones who came and didn't stay long."

Slowly but inexorably fading was the traditional memory of an "island community," a memory rich in continuity and recognition of who lived where and how everyone was related, a storehouse of "character" good and bad, of stories humorous and pathetic. Perhaps the richest surviving example of this kind of fading memory was captured many years later when its possessor was ninety years old.

Mrs. Hattie Shute Wilder's long local past was still vividly alive for her.

> I been around here ninety years [heeyuh nointy yeuhs]. I was born in 1879 in a snow storm. So they say. My grandmother broke her wrist coming up to see me, *that's how I know*. . . . And my great-great-grandfather was the first minister up here in the church and he lived *up where the Tweedys do*. And my father—they handed down the name "Danl" way down till they got to my brother, *and then they stopped it*.

> Grandfather was born—you know where Helen Burns lives, across from the church? And my aunt lived and died there all her life [doid thayuh all her loif] like I'm living and dying here all *my* life. I could go up the street. I *could go in their houses and put things back where they belong* . . . . Never lived anywhere below here nor above Liberty [Libty] Pole Hill. And I've been to church when I was so little I used to *set and feel my aunt's kid gloves*. I can remember everything [rmembuh evehthn].

And I'll tell you another thing I never forgot. Up here next to this red building, used to be the post office. Well that was a pretty little house *till they fixed it all over* [ovuh] *and ruined it,* I think. And there was the nicest couple lived there, Josiah Lane and Mary Lane. *Used to call her "Mary Josiah" in those days.* Well anyway, she had a turkey all stuffed and she was all dressed up—she was a very pretty, lovely woman. And she went upstairs for something and she fell down and broke her neck. I never forget it as long as I live. I was a little kid but those things stick in your mind. *And we knew 'em all then. I could take you up the street and show you them all.* Ayuh.

My grandmother Souther [Sohthuh] came from near Turkey Hill. They lived on Leavitt Street past the Agricultural Hall on the right. The Kresses had a farm right next to my Grandmother Souther. Oh dear. That's where they lived over there. And there was a little brook just two or three houses before you get to my grandparents' house. And my aunt used to drive her team through it, buggy and—I remember that very plain. *And they were all relations over there.* All my grandfather's sisters and all relations . . . . Hingham is ruined, I'm telling you [Oim tellin yuh]. It isn't what it used to be when the horses [hosses] trotted up and down the street and *you knew everybody and waved to them when they went by.* Now they go by and you don't know whether they are what they are or who they are.

My aunt, my mother's sister Ella, she had a horse and buggy and she used to come up and get us and take us down [to Melville Garden] and we used to have wonderful times. My sister and me dressed just alike. And my aunt furnished the hats always, and I remember we had great big blue and white plaid. In fact, we looked just alike standing back to, you couldn't tell us . . . twins. And then we had great big wide brimmed hats. I think they were brown with a white band on the edge with streamers down the back, so I must have been pretty little.

I forgot, my grandmother Hannah Shute had another sister Sarah and after they all died she lived down there, and she went kinda daffy in the head, you know. I aint laughin at it. No fun either. Anyway, I know my mother took us down there one day to see her. And she said, "Wait a minute, I got to go out and feed the children crying out on the door step." So she put out a dish of food. *There were nuthin out thayuh.* Ayuh.

Haunted by lost children, lost past, lost community.

The 1920s marked the beginning of the end of Hattie Wilder's Hingham. No one then could have guessed what turbulent decades were to follow or what global forces would invade the life of the town.

FOREWORD

THERE is never a time when town life is not touched by the larger world. But in some periods, the local is almost overwhelmed by the world's pressures. The four decades from 1929 through the 1960s were such a period.

As the past comes closer, the historian's lens grows myopic. With a past of sixty years, given our new longevity, we enter the space of living memory. Memories differ; each is wedded to its own version of what happened or should have happened. Making sense of the recent past is walking on eggshells. Historians must expect charges of breakage, even vandalism.

As a precaution, we now work in smaller segments, close-up views. We follow the recent fashion of "decades," trying nevertheless to avoid the stereotype exploited by the media that each decade is unique. This notion is specious. Much does not change, except on the surface. If modern consciousness is seduced into living on the surfaces of change, so much the worse for its historical understanding.

Decades do not begin conveniently according to the calendar. The decade of severe and lasting depression began in 1929. The decade of total war, with its disproportionate impact on Hingham, began in 1939. The decade of numbers, of suburban explosion and transformation, opened with the housing boom of the late 1940s. The decade of shocks, of social and political upheaval that rocked the town as it did the nation, began in 1959, when changes in transportation turned Hingham's historical geography upside down.

CHAPTER TWENTY-THREE

✠

"A Tough, Tough Time"

A HALF-TRUTH lingers in local memory: Hingham weathered the Great Depression better than most and can take retrospective pride in having stayed solvent. The town did remain "in the black." Whether that was wise public policy was debated later. Meanwhile, many townspeople suffered severe hardships.

What was American life like when President Herbert Hoover took office in 1929? No home had a freezer, a television, or a computer. If there were no drug or AIDS epidemics, neither were there antibiotics or vaccines, except for smallpox and diphtheria. Still in the future were nuclear plants, atomic weapons, space missions and probes. Industry worked on the assembly line, but it was still a cranks and levers technology without silicon chips, robotic arms, or remote guidance systems.

However primitive that technology seems now, the economy it fueled roared along. Corporate business, mostly unregulated, dominated national life. In 1929, the Gross National Product was $103.1 billion. Of a total population of 122 million, only 1.5 million were out of work. The national income was $81 billion. On Wall Street, the volume of transactions had risen phenomenally. Manufacturers, rather than reinvesting in their enterprises or in pay hikes, found the 12 percent return on stock speculation irresistible. So did the bankers. Stockbrokers sold on margin, requiring only from 10 to 20 percent from buyers. Profits did not represent real wealth, but only a pyramiding of paper. It was one grand casino.

Six months after Hoover's inauguration, an ominous reversal took place. Many big traders began selling off. The spiral careened downward. The market went into final collapse on "Black Tuesday," October 29, 1929. In one week, forty-four million shares were dumped at a "loss" of $14 billion. In three years, with no Federal Deposit Insurance Corporation to protect them, "nine million savings accounts were wiped out," and eighty-five thousand businesses failed. For a crisis of such magnitude, traditional corrections and adjustments were ineffective. Hoover, moreover, was basically opposed to a managed economy, to the use of federal funds for labor or "the dole" to the unemployed. He believed that if the economic engine was restarted, everything would fall into place. All that was needed was consumer confidence. Prosperity was just around the corner. Nothing improved, however, and by the end of Hoover's one term, the Gross National Product had sunk to $58 billion and twelve million were unemployed.

This profound and unyielding economic contraction was reflected in Hingham. Net business revenues fell from $2,995,267 in 1929 to $1,877,000 by 1935; $841,000 of the revenues in 1935 was the income of the town's twenty-five food stores, almost 45 percent. In depressions, people pay a high percentage of their income for food. Except for Safety Fumigant, which employed a few men in the old Rhodes Ripley factory on Elm Street, the only real manufacturing operation was the Old Colony Knitting Mills, begun by the Greenfields as a branch of their retail operation. They employed only eighteen to twenty-two workers. By 1930, without other industry, the "beautiful town" had to acknowledge an alarming problem of unemployment. Remedies were piece-work, make-work. Social agencies and the Board of Public Welfare gave direct relief, interpreting "need" according to their own informal criteria.

The desperation was obvious. Shortly after the Crash, twenty applied for a single policeman's job. It went to ex-marine Oscar Beck, later chief of police and selectman. When dump caretaker Odell Smith died in 1931, dozens applied for his place. In 1936, two dozen applied for a temporary janitor's job at Centre School. One hundred twenty men took the Civil Service exam for six letter carrier positions. Few with jobs gave them up. A school system that had been plagued by resignations lost only four teachers in 1933. Pupils were affected, too. The school doctor reported that seven entering children were seriously undernourished. The per capita consumption of milk per day was less than a pint. Susie Eldredge remembered the home of a childhood acquaintance where electricity was available only if a quarter could be spared for a metered coin box.

Anything heard about the depression, said Margaret McSweeney, was probably true: "It was a tough, tough time. Heart-breaking." One man "lived in a cave up in the woods and that wasn't so astounding, but he had a brass bed in the cave." Some whose homes were foreclosed moved into the Cushing House. Augmenting their income by knitting sweaters, wives of once-prosperous brokers collected their yarn at the post office. Regularly, Polly Thayer asked her Weir River farm manager Harold Newcombe to deliver two or three bushels of vegetables to St. John's parishioners who "had lost all their money." Scanty food supplies were augmented by digging the allowed bushel of clams per week—that is, when the state hadn't declared the shoreline too polluted by summer households. On Free Street, fifty unemployed tended their allotted 3200 square feet on land loaned for a "potato patch." The wrecked schooner *Nancy* on Nantasket Beach was offered for firewood to any who would take it.

Other signs of Hoover's "self-help" doctrine were manifest in many *Journal* ads, for "any kind of odd job," yard work, washing, mending for thirty-five to forty cents an hour. Many offered rooms in their homes: "Wanted: an elderly lady to board." One man asked householders to save fat; he was making soap. One survival strategy was to alternate between short-term labor and time at the infirmary (the renamed almshouse). In 1930, the "aggregate number of weeks of persons cared for" there was 331. By 1933, it was 509. Aid "outside" of the infirmary increased spectacularly. In 1930, aid went to 46 families with 105 dependents; by the end of 1933, 132 families with 404 dependents received aid. A new state law mandated assistance, averaging $8 a week, to the impoverished over seventy years old. In 1931, it went to 26 people; in 1933, to 47; by 1936, to 89.

Applying the self-help concept, the town employed as many as it could. Hinghamites did most of the work in repairing the infirmary and enlarging the town office building. But such construction required costly materials and skilled labor. Labor intensive projects were needed for the unskilled. Seemingly least important in a time of catastrophe, tree work and widening and straightening streets became prime activities. With eight fewer men in the Highway Department than in 1928, there was room for "temporaries."

In addition to self-help, Hoover's other tactic for recovery was volunteerism. Every organization from the Chamber of Commerce to the American Legion, from social clubs to parent-teacher organizations and teachers groups, tried to help. In 1931, in a town still dotted with small farms and dairies, Hingham Grange #299 marked its twentieth anniversary. In 1934, a new lodge was formed—the Independent Order of Sons of Italy—to carry on as a benevolent and charitable association. Church women repaired secondhand clothing and sponsored canning projects. The Welfare Board appealed for desperately needed second-hand shoes. William L. Foster, selectman and chairman of the Welfare Board, supervised the distribution of a thousand twenty-four-pound bags of flour made available through the Red Cross and $100 of groceries given by First National employees. He spent a Saturday evening and Sunday morning delivering 175 loaves of bread, donated by the A & P manager, from the "sensational" silence of his electric car. Benefits for the "needy" were countless, but proceeds were tiny. A huge concert ball and entertainment at the armory produced $540. Though well-intended, these laudable deeds of voluntary service were bandaids on a gaping wound.

It was a time, nevertheless, of quiet heroism by those who tried to make a difference, and a shining hour for the Hingham Visiting Nurse Association and the Red Cross. Hingham's "angel" of World War I, Elizabeth Emmons, carried on as chairman of the local Red Cross, even after the death of her husband Nathaniel, stockbroker and yachtsman, at age forty-seven, just six months after the Crash. In 1932 she resigned. Fate was not kind to Mrs. Emmons. Her estate gone, she moved away temporarily, then suffered an illness, a fire in her South Hingham home, a serious accident, and major surgery. Some years later, H. Leavitt Horton visited her "in a rest home far from Hingham propped up against her pillows":

> she pointed to her crutches and a birdcage containing her pet canary and said, "I shall get up again when spring comes. I am going to settle down in a little dream house by the sea." . . . . Somewhere in a quiet little corner of Heaven I am sure there is a LITTLE DREAM HOUSE BY THE SEA and seated at the window, an angel in a Red Cross uniform with two white dogs and a canary beside her.

Others carried on in the Emmons tradition. The Red Cross had set up an emergency closet at the John A. Andrew House, whose clean old linens, bedding, and nightwear were of "invaluable" help to Dr. John A. Peterson and Nurse Caroline Burns during periodic flare-ups of communicable diseases and especially during the extreme winter cold of 1933-34. Once federal money and supplies were available, Red Cross workers made one thousand cotton garments to add to the twenty-eight hundred ready-made items and two hundred blankets for local distribution.

The Andrew House, given to the Hingham Visiting Nurse Association by Mrs. Charles Mason in 1929, became a center of critical importance, especially for its children's clinics. The Thrift Shop, already an institution, brought in some revenue. The Garden Club sponsored tours to benefit the HVNA. At her home on Irving Street, HVNA president Mabel Dwiggins—with flower beds so luxuriant her husband advised tying a string around her so she could be found among the plants—raised seedlings to sell to benefit the HVNA.

Reduced fees at the Country Club, Derby's pay-what-you-can tuition policy, the loss of members from the four-year-old Chamber of Commerce, the canceling of the 1933 Firemen's Ball—all testified to the shrunken economy. Tax Collector Charles L. Keyes discovered that over 20 percent of town taxes could not be collected. Many public projects were postponed. Committees would outline needs; then, citing the "current economic situation," recommend "no action." The plot at the harbor surrounding a new war memorial, "Victory," for which the town had paid $23,000, remained barren, and the statue itself was soon referred to as the "Iron Horse." Appropriations for Memorial Day and the Fourth of July were halved. Assembling enough material for the annual bonfire was a problem.

Small farmers suffered, too. Agriculture was still a way of life; Hingham had seventeen poultry farms and twenty-five dairies—any operation with three or more cows was classified as a "dairy." About one in nine acres were planted in hay for cattle, from the far corner of Liberty Plain to World's End. A few large farmers did well. Harry Michelson was not only a dairyman, but also the biggest cattle trader in New England. Fletcher Wason sold his eggs in Brockton. Byron Linscott sold his garden produce in Boston. Now in his seventies, Linscott, famous for winning prizes at the fairs, continued to plough with his horse "Napoleon" like a small farmer, and not until Napoleon died did he switch to a tractor. But there his similarity to the small farmer ended. Small farmers depending on local markets found that eggs brought only about three cents each, cucumbers and ears of corn no more than a penny. When asked if it was true that the market for corn-poppers was booming, grocer Tom Howe replied, "Seems as though it ought to be. A corn-popper is about the only thing now-a-days you can put something into and see it grow bigger."

One anonymous townsman found his perspective restored by such lean times. He had learned how to live once more, enjoy "ordinary" food, have real friends. He had time to walk, visit with people, go to church, fall in love with his wife again. Such good feelings were probably not shared by the 170 "laborers", with names chiefly Italian and Irish, paid by the town in 1932. Only eight earned over $100. Despite some part-time work, a state census in 1933 found 381 men and sixty-eight women unemployed in Hingham, 17.7 percent of the labor force.

One in every five or six was out of work. The national average was about one in four.

On Saturday, March 4, 1933, an exhausted Herbert Hoover looked on as Chief Justice Hughes swore in the thirty-second President, Franklin D. Roosevelt. He had won all but six states. Hingham had remained loyally Republican, voting two to one for Hoover. Of 3403 registered voters, 3111 cast ballots.

Sending his wife Eleanor to represent him at the festivities, Roosevelt went directly to the White House to meet with advisers. His first concern was the imminent collapse of the banks. On the day before his inaugural, bank reserves were $6 billion, while deposit liabilities were $41 billion. All banks were ordered closed immediately. A week-long bank holiday followed. Town Treasurer William Lunt discovered that town employees would have to wait a week for their pay. Banks were graded and reopened sequentially according to their financial condition. The Hingham Trust Company, the Institution for Savings, and the Cooperative Bank, to their credit, opened when the holiday ended. They had survived other panics and depressions by conservative management. To complaints about the scarcity of loans to builders, one banker explained that the banks would not loan money they didn't have and, further, that many jobless were living on their savings. Mortgage foreclosures generally involved out of town banks; Hingham banks showed forbearance until later in the decade.

One week after the inaugural, the President gave his first Fireside Chat. It was an event of historic importance, the first deliberate political use of radio. Ostensibly explaining the bank crisis, this master political psychologist used the chat to rouse the country from its lethargy and hopelessness. He repeated his inaugural line: "The only thing we have to fear is fear itself." Hingham had twelve hundred radios, so his message could be heard in over half of its homes.

In the next three months, an eager Congress passed at least fifteen major pieces of crisis legislation initiated by Roosevelt and his "brain trust." They gave the President unprecedented power. Much of this legislation was hastily and badly written and would later be declared unconstitutional. It was then rewritten and the programs were renamed, adding to the confusing array of "alphabet agencies" created during FDR's first two terms. Several of these programs were instrumental in helping Hingham's unemployed, but not without difficulties.

Local governments in sound fiscal condition were expected to pay for project materials while the federal government paid for labor. There was grumbling that Hingham was being penalized for thrift; after all, Fall

LEFT: W.P.A. workers preparing cement at the Naval Ammunition Depot, 1937. RIGHT: Greenfield's, 1941. The woman is identified by William Antoine as Mildred Stoddard. BELOW LEFT: Main Street shoppers, 1941. Beyond the First National were the post office and Dykeman's drugstore. BELOW RIGHT: Movies at Loring Hall. The movie, I WANTED WINGS, was released in 1941.

HINGHAM
TERCENTENARY
PAGEANT
A LAND *and* WATER SPECTACLE
PERCY JEWETT BURRELL, DIRECTOR

OFFICIAL CELEBRATION *by the* TOWNSPEOPLE

1000 Actors, Riders, Dancers, Choristers
Extraordinary Lighting Effects

Thurs., Fri., Sat., JUNE 27th, 28th, 29th
PROMPTLY AT 7:50 O'CLOCK IN THE EVENING

PAGEANT FIELD, HUIT'S COVE, ROUTE 3A

FREE PARKING SPACE
1635   *Tickets*   1935
50 *cents* to 2 *dollars*, plus tax

Hingham Tercentenary Pageant poster, 1935. A graduate of the School of the Museum of Fine Arts, Boston, commercial artist George Marsh (1894–1978) designed not only this huge poster, 45" x 30", but also the forty-page pageant program and stamps of Hingham buildings. BELOW RIGHT: Charles H. Marble as the pageant patriarch.
BELOW LEFT: pageant Indians.

River did not have to pay for materials. There were also bitter moments and cries of foul when the Advisory Board, Board of Selectmen, and/or Welfare Board recommended against funds for materials, or when proposals for projects were delayed, killing hopes for federal money. The involuntarily unemployed heard humiliating comments, "it was easier to be on the dole," and town employees heard unpleasant talk about reducing their salaries. A financially solvent town which took satisfaction in 1931 that no "special appropriations" for relief had been called for, that the year's tax rate had been reduced by $4.15, and that the reserve fund was ample, found it difficult to acknowledge that more was needed than self-help, volunteerism, and frugality.

The earliest effect of the welter of legislation sent twenty-six young, unmarried Hingham men from welfare families off to camp at the "Mount Blue Section," to clear brush and remove currant and gooseberry bushes, which were hosts to pine blister rust. They were part of the Civilian Conservation Corps, one of the most successful and least controversial of New Deal programs. By the fall of 1933, as local director for the Civil Works Administration, William L. Foster had on hand $15,000 allotted the town for public works. Over the next thirteen months, the total received by Hingham through this agency and the Federal Emergency Relief Administration was $70,311. One hundred nine men graded land at the school yards, widened and straightened streets, drained swamp areas, and removed grass at the bathing beach. Another twenty were painting Agricultural and G.A.R. Halls, the infirmary, Lincoln School, and the interiors of the old library and the police station. The unskilled received fifty cents an hour for a thirty-hour week. Skilled workers were paid $1.20. Of these, some began numbering Hingham homes. The fifteen hundred boxes at the post office would be replaced by twice-a-day home delivery in 1936.

Federal money financed a health survey, barn sanitation, and renovations at the armory. The Works Progress Administration funded a land-survey by Lewis Perkins, intended to end the ancient and continuing confusion about land titles and thus regularize assessing. The National Housing Act (1934) guaranteed bank loans at 5 percent for home repairs, generating about 831 short-term projects, mostly for painters, carpenters, and roofers. Almost one-third of the town's houses were repaired, while its infrastructure was largely neglected. The biggest project, the extensive rehabilitation of the Ammunition Depot, also provided temporary work for the unemployed. And in 1936, two hundred war veterans received by registered mail close to $100,000 in Bonus Bonds. All were picked up from Postmaster George Magner within forty-eight hours to be turned quickly into cash for paying bills. Eighty-five percent of the men had already borrowed on their certificates. They had been among those "Half a million boots . . . sloggin thru Hell" in World War I, just eighteen years before.

However, each time federal funds ran out and workers were laid off, it was another emergency. The short-term projects were chiefly cosmetic, involving no real capital investment. Meanwhile, serious decisions were put off and long-term needs were unmet. One major potential investment was again postponed during the depression, the purchase of the Water Company. Water rates were high, and it was thought that they could eventually be lowered if the town owned the company. In 1936, a committee recommended that the system be purchased for $1.1 million, a price far below the holding company's estimate of its value. For two years, hundreds of hours were spent trying to amend by legislative action the original charter of 1879. But when the Supreme Judicial Court ruled that this amendment would violate the property rights of the company, it was "deemed prudent on the part of the town not to proceed further in the matter for the present."

Among serious long-term needs, only one, the desperate need for an adequate police station, was met late in the decade. The long delay was due chiefly to disagreement over a site. Not all is changed. At one point, the town even took by eminent domain the homestead lot on Central Street of E. Everett Whitney, leaving him little but the land *under* his house. A mild man, Whitney opined at town meeting he would rather this didn't happen. Others were more forthright: Howard P. Hersey called the taking "preposterous." Within six weeks, the town recovered its senses and rescinded the vote. Apparently lumber merchant Whitney excused the town: in 1937, he left a $30,000 bequest to pay for the bronze statue of Abraham Lincoln in Fountain Square.

At a mock town meeting, at which Dr. Charles Howard presided with a fifty-pound sledgehammer, a heavily ironic article asked if the town would appropriate for a *mobile* police station. Four policemen could ride around in it playing bridge. The dummy hand would direct traffic. Coffee and doughnuts would be sold on the side.

Architectural plans for a real station languished until the estate of Peter Bradley donated the triangle at Lincoln Street and Broad Cove Road. In the spring of 1937, Chief Harold MacFarlane and his men moved into their new home, with a recently purchased ambulance, motorcycles, and two-way radio-equipped cruisers.

By contrast, the School Committee continued to advise against any new "accommodations," despite Hingham's ranking of seventy-first among eighty-three similar towns in school expenditures and despite a 13 percent rise in enrollment from 1930 to 1932. Change came when, in 1933, Thomas Buttimer, Jr., chairman of the committee for fourteen years, died unexpectedly and was replaced by Dr. David Belding. Faced with 1556 pupils and a capacity of 1500, the committee urged that a new junior high school be built on the site of the old high school. The proposal was defeated in 1935.

The depression helped to "stabilize" the problem. In Hingham, as elsewhere, the birthrate dropped. With fewer loans and thus less building, houses for young families, if they could afford them, were scarce. Raising the entry age by two months reduced the first grade by twenty children. Teachers were aided by young college graduates, unable to find jobs, who were hired as "building assistants" for $5 a week. Any proposed changes in the curriculum were rejected by the town. The school superintendent and committee advocated vocational training; the state Department of Education would have paid half the cost of salaries, supplies, and maintenance to set up a program in sheetmetal and wood working, printing, and auto mechanics. But the town government resisted accepting outside assistance. A surface planer, a mortizing machine, and a band saw were added to the high school's manual training room to give it "shop flavor." Having been trained in eighth grade by the legendary Annie B. Whidden, vocational students, low on the town's priority list, went to Weymouth and Quincy as they do today.

Dr. Belding resigned from the School Committee in 1936. In 1938, his wife died, and with two daughters in college, he enrolled the third in a school in Virginia and moved to Boston, closer to his work as professor of pathology and biology at Boston University. His house below Pear Tree Hill was rented. During the depression, the stone wall in front had been marked with an "X" by beggars, a sign to the next that food would be given.

Of all the needs "indefinitely postponed," those concerning public health were most serious: the needs to control communicable diseases, protect the supply of milk and water, construct sewers, clear the Town Brook and the mill pond, dispose of refuse and garbage, and reduce the plague of mosquitoes. They remained postponed for the most part, despite all the efforts of depression Hingham's most controversial "boat-rocker," Mayo Tolman. Trained in epidemiology and public health, Tolman was elected in 1931 to the Board of Health and appointed in 1933 as Hingham's salaried executive public health officer. Indefatigable and abrasive, he was also efficient and dedicated. The member-physicians of the board pointed out that his first year's salary of $971 was offset many times by actions he had already taken.

How much money Tolman saved the town in preventing illnesses cannot be calculated. During a scarlet fever outbreak in 1932, he and Dr. John Peterson kept the fifty-four patients at home instead of hospitalizing them. Tolman prepared a chart tracing the outbreak to a single milk source. The following year, scarlet fever was limited to three cases. He pressed for the immunizing of all children against diphtheria, by then a preventable disease. In 1929, diphtheria had struck thirty-three homes; while Tolman served, there were no cases. At Andrew House clinics, one of Tolman's allies, Public Health Nurse Caroline Burns, gave free diphtheria shots to children whose parents could not afford them, in addition to making three thousand house calls in 1933 alone. Another Tolman ally, Dr. Henry Robinson, school physician, would not readmit children with apparent "colds," too often the unrecognized beginning of measles. Tolman also addressed aggressively the problem of tuberculosis. He urged responsible reporting and preventive measures. Every week, three different advertisements in the *Journal* advised on how to protect the young, and a clinic evaluated schoolchildren to find those with incipient or early tuberculosis.

By 1933, Tolman's initiatives had resulted in the forming of an association of local dairymen, all of whom were classified as small producers. With Albert Kress as president, they resisted a powerful state milk trust and regional producers who could sell milk at several cents less a quart. Most stopped squabbling among themselves and worked cooperatively. Tolman prodded them into pasteurizing in order to prevent scarlet fever, undulant fever, and tuberculosis, which could be transmitted by drinking raw milk. Anske Hornstra, Melius Couperus, and Harry Michelson installed pasteurizing plants, which also served other dairymen. As well as being a partisan and booster of this local industry, Tolman was also a diligent supervisor. Of 388 cows he inspected in 1933, 151 were found to be tubercular and were slaughtered. The selectmen, slow to face this problem, applied too late for the federal funds that would have compensated the dairymen for their losses.

Tolman also met resistance in his advocacy of a metered water service. Customers were still charged by the "fixture" or faucet. This, Tolman argued, discouraged conservation: who would bother to repair a leaking faucet when the wasted water cost nothing? It took a direct order, in 1934, from the Massachusetts Public Utilities Commission to institute metering in Hingham. Some homeowners, moreover, illegally connected new wells to the town water system. Tolman pointed out that such wells, easily polluted by raw sewage, would back flow through these connections and expose everyone to the risk of typhoid and dysentery. The Board of Health had no power to deal with these violators, and the Water Company itself had to sever their pipes.

Tolman was also controversial and ahead of his time in promoting a sewer system. The only extant system had been built on Crow Point in the late nineteenth century without any engineering plan. Tolman tried insofar as he could to schematize the maze of pipes which ran under private property and supervised the clearing and repair of these sewer lines. He discovered, for example, that an ancient check valve in an outfall pipe at North Beach had failed and allowed a huge discharge from an officially "non-existent" sewer on Cushing Avenue to be carried with the incoming tide around through the Yacht Club channel to the bathing beach, where the "visits" averaged twelve to sixteen thousand a season. But in the depths of depression (1934), the selectmen decided that the Crow Point sewer problem was too complex and expensive to remedy.

On North and South Streets, water closets still emptied into the Town Brook, and there, Tolman pressed for sewers. But not until 1936, the year he was forced to resign, did a committee recommend the creation of a sewer system as an "ideal combination of work relief and highly desirable improvement." As for the brook itself, a committee was charged in 1933 to secure plans for a more efficient flow and for the filling of the mill pond. They asked counsel Thomas Buttimer to define what they were legally empowered to do with their $500 appropriation and were told they could only "secure" plans. Only the selectmen, said Buttimer, had authority to make changes. But the selectmen held that improvement of the brook would benefit only a limited group, who should be assessed for "betterments." Tolman rejoined that every abutter from Hobart's to Thaxter's Bridge had offered a strip of land if the town would "fix that brook," and that abutters should not have to pay for the conduited section under railroad property in the square where clogging was greatest. But again, he was disappointed. At town meeting in 1934, on a motion of Walter Bouvé, those present voted to indefinitely postpone. As Bouvé said: "the Town Brook was there, and was there to stay."

Tolman's Weir River project was similarly derailed. The work, he argued, whether soundly or not, would have reduced mosquitoes, corrected severe flooding, and created a deep cool stream for fish. It would give nine months of employment to twenty-two men. The state was unusually interested, and federal funds were assured. Without naming names, Tolman strongly implied that this proposal by the Board of Health had been killed by local opposition.

Finally, the controversial health officer made proposals for the proper handling of trash and garbage and did his best to manage the dump on Hersey Street. The dump was spreading far beyond its original limits. Rats, cats, and flies were a serious nuisance to those living nearby. Garbage was often tossed in the dump when the caretaker was off duty. Roadside dumping was investigated. But when the investigations turned up bits of paper traceable to "some of our 'best families,'" they were discontinued. Each year, a new committee studied the problems. Finally, in 1938, the town voted $2500 for garbage collection, but the need for a new dump site was ignored until 1945, when the state ordered the dump closed.

Many of these urgent, important, but less than glamorous projects would have conformed beautifully to post-1933 guidelines for federal assistance, especially those of the Public Works Administration under Harold Ickes. But town officers clearly opposed such funding and repeatedly resisted Tolman's efforts. In 1936, his duties were reduced. His request for $50 to maintain mosquito-control ditches, already dug with state and federal funds, lost by four votes. His medical allies David Belding and David G. Underwood had recently resigned from the Board of Health, and the new members forced Tolman out. The official explanation read:

> Due to lack of cooperation the Board of Health found it necessary to re-organize the Department for the best interests of the town. Since the appointment of the new Health Officer, there has been a marked improvement in the routine of the Department.

It was a curious dismissal of the fastidious man who insisted on the proper care and handling of food in stores, of the energetic man who unhesitatingly opened manholes and entered culverts, where workers sometimes hesitated to follow him.

The account of Mayo Tolman is far more than the story of the difficulties of a pioneer. It is also an account of depression Hingham, whose "leading men" resisted change, deplored projects not locally funded and controlled, and preferred short-term solvency to long-term investment. Tolman had openly offended their priorities when he wrote, "good roads, beautiful trees, and a Ship Church" were not enough for a modern community. He had declared that long-range planning went far beyond dealing with the nuisance of a "pole cat that met its end in a private water supply." He had warned that sooner or later, the "fetish" of a low tax-rate, of which the town was "so unwisely proud," would have to be abandoned. These messages were prophetic but unwelcome. After his removal, letters charged that the Health Department was a "political football," that Tolman had offended some members of the Advisory Board and had faced "mysterious opposition," and that he had been forced to resign because he "dare[d] to tell the truth."

The truth was more easily borne, in such depressing years, when cloaked in kindliness and humor. More than any other man at that time, William Melcher provided both. Whenever he rose to speak at town meetings, he received a round of applause. An enthusiastic amateur actor, Melcher often played leading roles in theatrical benefits whose proceeds went to the Welfare Board and the Red Cross. But in his favorite role, that of town jester, he punctured the absurd and the hypocritical. In his humor, Melcher left a picture of a more agreeable side of Hingham during the depression.

As harbormaster, Melcher published his "annual reports" from the "Navy Department." Unsalaried, he offered to make a "noble gesture" of donating 50 percent of his salary "to be added to the fund for the unemployed, on condition that all other Town Officers . . . subscribe an equal amount." Asking for a $50 appropriation, he pointed out that "the entire equipment of his department . . . consisted of a pair of water wings and a typewriter." When he took office, he had "purchased my own badge." The harbor "not being popular for the landing of cargoes by night"—that is, bootleg liquor—he had yet "to derive any income from my official position."

What he really wanted was a "fast speed boat with the town seal painted on the bow . . . a sea-going chauffeur to operate it . . . [and] a uniform with plenty of gold braid." How much more suitable this would have been, he wrote, when he saved the first-ever majority of Democrats on the Board of Selectmen by rescuing "its Clerk," George A. Cole, "from possible death by thirst and starvation as his boat drifted towards Hull Gut." This was Melcher's genius for having fun. Everyone knew George Cole was an expert sailor.

In a speech to the Chamber of Commerce after one of the Cushing House's famous chicken pie dinners, "Harbormaster Bill" proposed some novel ideas for creating employment and industry from the harbor. Gondolas could provide taxi service to Crow Point; scows with "comfortable roosts" could collect guano from the northeast side of Ragged Island and then be towed to the Bradley plant; seals could herd herring into Walton Cove to a sardine factory built over the water. There was plenty of waste oil from Cities Service in which to pack them.

If anyone was interested, he suggested "we incorporate after this meeting."

During the unusually cold winter of 1933, the harbormaster wondered whether, if the accountant couldn't legally approve a fur-lined uniform, the Board of Health might not provide a few skins. "Kindly let me know if a few skunks would be acceptable," replied Mayo Tolman. "We could procure a goat skin for you but it is probable you would find it necessary to return it to the Town Accountant (to whom it properly belongs)."

When the casting committee was matching roles and people for the historical pageant to celebrate the town's three hundredth anniversary

William W. Melcher's Christmas card at the depth of the depression, 1932. The Harbormaster is playing the hurdy-gurdy. His wife, Elizabeth Bates Melcher, is knitting a sock. Their daughter, Elizabeth, in her new Troop 1 scout uniform, accompanies on the concertina. The family pet was a cocker spaniel named Princess, called "Prinnie."

in 1935, they gave the part of Seth Stowers to William Melcher. Stowers had escaped the massacre at Fort William Henry in 1756 by taking clothing from the military stores and throwing pieces behind him as his Indian pursuers got uncomfortably close. In the 1930s, instead of throwing out clothing, the harbormaster threw out funny lines.

The pageant for Hingham's three hundredth anniversary was the grand climax of years rich in anniversaries and restoration. Even during the depression, Hingham did have causes for celebration. Between

1932 and 1935, the Trust Company and the Institution for Savings marked their one hundredth years, the fairs (in revised form) their seventy-fifth, the old meetinghouse its two hundred fiftieth, and the First Parish and the town their three hundredth.

The great restoration of the 1930s was made inside the meetinghouse and was funded by Eben Howard Gay, the Rev. Ebenezer's great-great-grandson. The labor began in the spring of 1930, under the supervision of Hingham Centre architect Edgar T. P. Walker. The two-hundred-year-old ceiling was removed to reveal once more the interior's most distinctive feature: the arching, hand-hewn oak beams under the roof. In addition to a number of the original box-style pews, which had been reinstalled earlier, twelve more pews and thirty pew doors were discovered in private hands and set back in place. "Faithful copies" replaced those which had disappeared forever. The pulpit was raised and, as in the past, was reached by a single stair. Old customs were resumed: the minister turned the hour-glass, and the congregation faced the rear during the final hymn. In one of several dedicatory services, five living Old Ship ministers and the town's three Unitarian congregations sang the "Hingham Hymn," composed by Henry Ware, Jr., for the town's two hundredth anniversary. At another, the huge old bass viol, played from 1801 to 1867, once more resonated against the walls.

Efforts to reunite Old Ship with New North were less successful. In the end, the First Parish rejected a proposal to alternate Sunday morning worship between the buildings. It was feared this would jeopardize the reputation and heritage of "the Cathedral Church of American Unitarianism." At New North itself, however, the rare old organ was beautifully restored. The Congregational Church's interior was returned to its first appearance. Old Derby and the Old Ordinary were renovated. The eighteenth-century Harding-Whidden house, displaced by a block of stores south of the Sprague Building, was removed and meticulously reconstructed on Fearing Road.

Looking backward also reignited the impulse to celebrate one's progenitors. The First Parish sponsored an elaborate ceremonial: "Ancestors' Sunday." A shared ancestor gave rise to family reunions. The descendants of John Leavitt gathered for the first time in 1934; 154 were present. The next year, the Leavitts formed a national association at G.A.R. Hall. At the same time, one hundred members of the Tower Society, which had met for years, were assembled nearby at the Congregational Church, and on Main Street, descendants of James Wyton gathered at David Whiton's home.

Numerous other acts of recovering the past included a flurry of talks, articles, and events such as the "Old Timers'" baseball game against aging Breezy Hill immortals Townsend, Tinsley, Breen, and Bjorklund, a South Hingham street fair with scenes from its history, and the clearing of Revolutionary War graves at Fort Hill Cemetery by Herbert L. Foss. Hingham's sole Congressional Medal of Honor winner, Foss had been one of a team which cut the only communications cable between Havana and Spain during the Spanish-American War. The Wompatuck Club celebrated his heroism and honored him with a dinner. Along with the four hundred guests, he listened to a broadcast of his own story over WEEI.

All of these smaller commemorative acts prepared the way for the town's most lavish and restorative celebration of the decade, the pageant of 1935. At the depths of the depression, such a celebration was needed. The communal past was a place free of the corrosive and discouraging elements of present reality; it was a rich, apolitical, and endlessly absorbing mental retreat. In 1934, 266 town meeting attendants voted $14,000 from the sacrosanct reserve fund for a tercentenary celebration. A large committee had already been at work for months. They picked a site, the immense natural amphitheatre at Huet's Cove, and the dates, June 27-29, 1935. They chose a professional director, Percy Jewitt Burrell. Hingham's three-hundredth year pageant was also the three-hundredth he had staged. Using the research of Willis Rich, Edward Gibbons, Martha Lane, Mrs. Walter Shute, and Emma Stringer, Burrell prepared a huge spectacle on land and water. From headquarters in the Sprague Building, Mrs. Ruth Anderson coordinated all aspects of the production.

For over three months, the town bustled enthusiastically with preparation and promotion. Resident George Marsh, a commercial artist, designed immense color posters, with woodsman, farmer and ox-team ploughing, and the promise of one thousand actors, riders, dancers, and choristers. Hundreds of these posters were pasted up in Boston subways. The gas company distributed twelve-page promotional folders, with a cover design by artist Louis Ruyl. The *Journal* published a column, "Pageant News," every week. Tea shops, cafes, and three new guest houses opened. A Chamber of Commerce information booth was set up at the harbor. Banners were hung at main route junctions, and through nearby towns rolled a float portraying General Lincoln receiving the sword of Cornwallis.

In the upper room of Agricultural Hall, Mrs. George A. Cole supervised one hundred women volunteers, who stitched together 575 costumes, over half of the needed costumes, mostly from cheesecloth, in nine weeks, at a cost of less than a dollar apiece. Downstairs, Eleanor Holt, coach of the championship girls hockey team, rehearsed the "rhythmic divisions" of massed dancers and mimists. Elsewhere, an "enlistment" program matched Hinghamites to dramatic roles, including one hundred speaking parts. At Wilder Hall, music director Mayo Shattuck was training the chorus of over one hundred members, which would survive the pageant as the Hingham Community Chorus.

At Huet's Cove, the pageant grounds were being created. Stands and two stages were built by local labor for audience, band, and choruses. The National Guard strung three and a half miles of telephone wire to carry Burrell's five hundred cues during the four-hour performance. The "No School" signal sounded promptly at 6:15 P.M. if weather forced rehearsals indoors. All participants were given written instructions. Props and beautiful costumes appeared out of barns and attics. A "Distress Call" went out for horses, now in short supply—"educated equines" for inexperienced riders, preferably—but any kind, "saw horses excluded," would be welcome.

In the performance, everything went "like clockwork." As the pageant opened, trumpets heralded four young horsewomen. Peter Hobart's arrival was heightened by the twilight. Of the ten episodes recreated from Hingham's past, all but one had occurred before 1800. The ancient and the picturesque were combined. Drills of militia, Revolutionary soldiers, and Lincoln Light Infantry added authentic ritual. A husking party of close to one hundred, with corn donated by Anske Hornstra, displayed the simple pleasures of provincial life. English songs, country dances with a fiddler, and the reenactment of Madame Derby's lively ball for Henry Ware's ordination illustrated social tastes. A procession of artisans symbolized industry and labor. Dudley Alleman, "Governor Thomas Dudley," had persuaded newcomer Frederick Cheney to play "Richard Russell." In his red periwig, laughed Cheney's wife Evelyn years later, he looked just like Harpo Marx. Cheney's own memories included "all those little Indians slapping mosquitoes." The favorite of the pageant was the littlest Indian, George Silipo, Jr. Its most striking presence was Charles Hawke Marble at seventy-six, descendant of Matthew Hawke, as "Patriarch." With his shock of white hair and equally large Old Testament beard, on an illuminated dais, he narrated bits of Hingham history from "The Golden Book of Ancient Record."

In the long epilogue, torchbearers led all the actors up the slope to a great fire on a hearthstone. The symbolic groups, including goddess of the hearth and vestal maidens, portrayed Hingham "as a town of the

Family and the Home." Over the hundreds of kneeling figures, the Tercentenary Chorus sang a new "Hymn to Hingham" composed by Governor Long's son, Peirce.

The pageant would endure, wrote Peirce Long, as a memory of increasing "tenderness," teaching the "uncalculably valuable lesson of what loyal and whole-hearted coming together in common enterprise of life may achieve." The town's senior clergyman, Daniel Magruder of St. John's Church, who played Deputy Governor Winthrop, declared that, "No enterprise was ever accomplished with more eager cooperation and spirit of good feelings . . . . It was great fun, too." Increased fellowship and new friendships were the harvest. The town had created its own massive folk festival, with the therapeutic effect of inspiriting and binding itself together. Of the population of 7330, between thirteen and fourteen hundred, old and young, ancient and new families, had participated. It was a triumph of community.

Before the pageant, two years of effort by one woman for the tercentary had already come to fruition. Amy Howard had planned and organized the production of a small, tasteful souvenir book, *Hingham Old and New*, written by Mason Foley, antiquarian bookman, Derby teacher, and later selectman. In literary quality, Foley's writing about Hingham is matchless. It was also in perfect consonance with the pageant.

He presented the past through an act of imagination; the reader is invited to "Imagine Hingham." Like the pageant, his book is a celebration, with only the slightest reference to flaw or conflict. His pages hold together a community, past and present, animated against the backdrop of Hingham's natural beauty, which Foley loved most of all. His phrasing is cadenced; the language is song-like; word choice is as felicitous as the notes of a singer with perfect pitch. Past and present tenses sometimes play a kind of polyphony, then fuse harmonically. The *Old and New* of the title perfectly fit the intent to blend old and new into a single reality. That which is past is not gone but metamorphosed into new forms: "The watering troughs are filling stations where eighty horses drink at once. The young men are batting balls, instead of salting fish." Nothing could be more different than this from the elegiac language of the orators and historians of the 1880s and 1890s, by whom the past was commemorated from a melancholy distance.

In Foley's book, there was no room, as there was none in the pageant, for the prosaic explanations and verifications of historians. The factual is fused with the imagined: "As Dr. Shute stops to chat with the Tower girls, fishing at Wilder's Bridge, the staccato whine of the saw mill at Cushing's Pond comes down the Crooked Meadow River valley." Those who complained of "inaccuracies" in the book, as in the pageant, were missing the point.

The very scale of the book is appropriate. It captures essentials of the past in eleven brief segments. Historical time is foreshortened almost out of existence. The book's physical properties are a subtle accompaniment of great artistry to Foley's prose-poem. The book is slender, with small, elegant pages, a miniaturizing of past and present so that they can easily be held together in one hand.

The book design was the work of William Addison Dwiggins. Dwiggins had come to Hingham with his wife Mabel in 1904, to work with Frederic Goudy at the Village Press, and adopted the Centre as his home. By the 1930s, he enjoyed a national reputation for his typefaces and his many original and distinguished book designs. *Hingham Old and New* displays features that Dwiggins felt were essential. It has paper of good quality and a sewn binding, so the pages are comfortable to handle and lie flat. The type is easy to read. Dwiggins enhanced Foley's text with an "Old Names" map and redrawings of extant maps, beautiful examples of his calligraphy and stencil work. Dwiggins was partial to paper labels and die-stamping, even though he recognized that they were too expensive for most commercial publishing. The title on the paper label of *Hingham Old and New* is his calligraphy; the unique ornament, distinctively his own. The title on the extremely narrow spine, as fresh today as it was over fifty years ago, has the sculpted quality he liked. The pressure of the metal die causes the gold to glint off the letter edges. Both the label and the die-stamped title highlight Dwiggins' craft, the "thick and thin" of the pen, the effect of being carved.

The middle third of the book represented the visible present of the 1930s, in forty-seven photographs of buildings and sites taken by George W. Stetson. The final third, written by Foley and based on Amy Howard's many hours of consultation with town departments, outlined possibilities of future planning. Some of these proposals came to fruition, but often in altered forms, indirectly, almost by accident, or many years later. The ownership of the harbor islands (the town owned only Ragged at the time) came through bequests in later decades. A *private* airport (the prediction was that one family in five would eventually own a light plane) did materialize at Huet's Cove, but disappeared in 1939. A municipal golf course came into being half a century later. A new police station and a new county courthouse were built, playgrounds were acquired or improved, and a sewer system was begun. One acquisition was made in 1945, when the town voted unanimously to acquire Triphammer Pond and its shores. This would be the permanent memorial of the three hundredth anniversary.

Hingham Old and New went on sale for Christmas, 1934, at a price appropriate to the times, $1.00. Amy Howard directed that five hundred copies be set aside for the town's 350th, by which time the price had appreciated by 2500 percent. Copies were also placed in the time capsule buried in 1985. Amy Howard had reached further into the future than she could realize.

Persistence and collaborative skill enhanced the many efforts of this practical visionary and gifted planner. Her work with five other women resulted in Hingham's Girl Scout house (built in 1929), the first in New England, and a Scout program that filled it every day. She arranged rummage sales, a Christmas market, and a summer pet show to augment Scout revenues. Two entries in one of the shows were marionettes "Rat" and "Rover," the latter created by Dwiggins for "Billy Brown's Bravery," the first marionette show performed in his garage at "0.5 Irving Street" in 1932-33.

Another focus of her persistence and collaboration was the town forest. She and Tree Warden Murphy shared the confidence that small increments could bring about large accomplishments. Year after year, with meagre appropriations and private gifts, Murphy planted a variety of conifers, hardwoods, flowering evergreens, and deciduous trees. By 1937, the forest was fully planted. During the depression, firewood from pruning and thinning was available to those who needed it for heating and cooking. Murphy also tended the town nursery he had started in 1919, one of the first in the state, adding rescued stray saplings and seedlings. Wherever he saw an ugly patch, he landscaped with what was at hand. In addition to his regular duties, he cared for the town's little parks without compensation. Tree Warden Murphy was unfailingly supported and appreciated by Amy Howard.

She invited townspeople to the town forest as cordially as if it were her own living room and described in town reports what progress was being made there. She personally acknowledged every contribution. A superb diplomat, she stepped around the landmines of personalities and political divisions. At town meetings, she was memorable for the rich "contralto" of her dignified responses to the booming Dudley Alleman. Postmaster John McKee remembered her as "a beautiful person." When her postman retired, she thanked him for his service in a letter to the *Journal.* "I think of her," said Evelyn Cheney, "as I think of Mrs. Thayer, with her tiny waist, followed by her chauffeur with a basket over his arm, going into the A & P—as women escaped from an English novel." But Amy Howard's patrician dignity should not overshadow the person who planned a street fair at the Centre to include fortune-tellers and tea-leaf readers, bridge games, pingpong and horse shoes, a balloon man and a popcorn lady, a marshmallow bonfire, a midway with booths, street dancing, and her favorite, pony rides.

The patrician lady did not avoid politics. She was involved in two major political events that closed out the decade. For some years, she, her husband Dr. Charles Howard, and many others had actively sponsored the establishment of a Hingham hospital. In the building just above the later site of St. Paul's School on Fearing Road, a registered nurse, Marie Storm, had operated a convalescent home. Here, in 1932, there opened a small, well-equipped general hospital with Storm as director. During its brief five-year life, it received many accident cases, performed surgeries, and, for a blanket fee of $35 ($25 if paid in cash), offered pregnancy, delivery, and postpartum care to over two hundred mothers and their newborns. Powerful but anonymous resistance to the hospital began early. Many welfare cases were sent to other hospitals, even though the Hingham hospital charged less. In 1935, on a petition of five or six persons whose names we have not found, a seventy-year-old bylaw restricting the location of hospitals was resurrected. The hospital was ordered to close within two weeks. Director Storm held out but was unable to secure a site elsewhere in Hingham. In 1937, the town won its suit against the Hingham Memorial Hospital. Storm abruptly moved to Quincy, where she established another hospital.

Amy Howard's second political defeat came a year later. A renewed attempt was made to pass a zoning bylaw, supported by members of the Planning Board, Amy Howard, Francis Lincoln, Winthrop Cushing, Eben Hersey, and F. Morton Smith. In long and persuasive letters, Mayo Shattuck, an influential South Hingham lawyer, disputed the opinion of some that zoning was a class issue. He responded to the fears of those opposed to zoning: the town would not become a suburb for the rich; all non-conforming uses would be protected; lot sizes and setbacks would not be nearly as restrictive as in Dover and Weston; the law was strictly "our own" put together by "our own people." What newcomers had been drawn to, and what needed preservation, was the "absence of ugliness," of triple-deckers, junkyards, and trailer camps.

The article for the town meeting of 1938 was comprehensibly written, but the accompanying map was startling. Business was restricted to the existent area at the square, tiny blocks at the Centre and the northeast corner, and a wedge near the intersection of Beal and Lincoln

Streets. The only non-restricted area was a large triangle bounded by Whiting and Gardner Streets and the Weymouth line, including the three hundred acres that were once Joshua Hobart's. All the rest was residential.

Agricultural Hall was crammed with an estimated 1400 voters for the town meeting that Amos Humphrey, now seventy-nine, called the "most exciting" he could remember. Action on zoning took a bizarre twist. Following Francis Lincoln's supporting speech, there immediately came a motion for indefinite postponement. The vote as recorded in the town book was 717 to postpone, 449 against. Challenged on how the vote should be counted, Moderator Arthur Russell ordered a vocal and protesting "highly respected citizen," J. Frank Crehan, ejected. Saying "No! No!" the crowd moved forward. It was mollified only by the action of Crehan himself and Officer Edward McKee. An explosive situation had been quelled. What was later described as a fight between "old timers" and "invaders," whom the town had so assiduously courted for its salvation in the 1920s, ended in a temporary victory for the "old timers." The light of "the illumined circle where past and future meet," which Mason Foley thought so special to the town, was for the moment extinguished.

Familiar presences departed from that circle in the 1930s. Amy Howard lost her Scouting collaborators: Grace Richards, Mary Downer, Emma Stringer, and Isabel Belding. Walter Jones, selectman for thirty-two years, counsel Thomas Buttimer, author Dallas Lore Sharp, and the beloved William Melcher passed away. The business community lost some of its oldest members: Peter Bradley, fatally injured by a "jalopy" on Lincoln Street; newsdealer William Hennessy; Richard McKee, expressman for fifty-two years; manufacturer Abraham Greenfield; and shopkeeper Suzie Gates. In West Hingham, Millie and Elsie Pratt closed their store; the Village Improvement Society disbanded; and the G.A.R. Humphrey Post was voted out of existence by its two surviving members. Two familiar buildings, the Burr Brown/shoestring factory and Cushing's stable, opposite each other on Fearing Road, disappeared.

Nature added its own punishments to the decade of depression, saving its greatest violence for last. It had delivered frequent droughts, frigid winters, eighteen-inch ice, and snowdrifts so deep that the snow tractor had to be shoveled out. Flooding had caused the Weir River to rise eight feet and made fifty feet of the "boulevard" impassable; in the coal yards, water was waist-high. The final fierce punch was a hurricane that hit the East Coast on Wednesday, September 21, 1938. Storm tides inundated south-facing New England shores, destroying thousands of buildings and covering whole forests. Swollen rivers and streams swept away factories and homes. About six hundred people died.

In Hingham, at Huet's Cove, scene of the pageant, Bayside Flying Service moved its five planes out of the swaying old barn that served as a hangar. As seven men tried to anchor a seaplane, its gyrations carried them with it. At the Yacht Club, the forty-eight-footer *Malay*, its mooring snapped, rammed boat after boat before they sank or were swept away. Winds, gusting over one hundred miles an hour, lifted slates from St. Paul's steeple, sliced off roofs on Crow Point, blew away Fletcher Wason's henhouse, and toppled a thousand trees. As the trees fell, they buckled roofs and collapsed power and telephone lines into streets full of still-green leaves and debris. The town was in darkness.

With Foster away, Selectmen George Cole and Fletcher Wason declared a state of emergency. Line crews, police, firemen, highway and tree departments worked without sleep for thirty-six hours. Power was restored first to the police station, the Water Company, and the pasteurizing plants. Supplies in the stores of axes, batteries, flashlights, and candles were quickly depleted. Realizing the historic scale of the disaster, many bought film to record the wasteland. Great pines lay across Gardner Street; and along Main Street the roots of many elms made craters as they tore up sidewalks and curbing. "Hingham's noble trees," said Timothy Murphy, "have suffered as never before." Miraculously, no human lives were lost in Hingham.

The "circle where past and future meet" remained. Charlie Marble, the pageant patriarch, wintered in St. Petersburg now, but when he came north, he headed for the Wompatuck croquet courts. Elmer Curtiss, once town moderator and president of the Hingham Trust Company, always with a supply of biscuits, was still the favorite of the town's dogs. There were seven hundred of them, and they were still allowed to roam free if they were licensed and had rabies shots. For the young, Ethel Studley still made candy with "lots of butter and rich chocolate." For the sprightly, ballroom dancing was in its heyday; Warren Lincoln and John McKee still remember "Ag Hall" as having the best dance floor anywhere, "smooth as glass." One piece of land was set aside to remain forever untouched, except by nature, which changes its loveliness with every season. In 1937, F. Morton Smith gave the town Broad Cove Park.

Across Lincoln Street from the peaceful park, however, at the Smiths' home, there was anxious talk. A local branch, founded in 1932, of the

League of Women Voters met there to discuss the alarming state of world affairs. The men of the local Rotary Club, chartered in 1933, did likewise at the Cushing House. International instability became more frightening as the decade passed. Hitler threatened peace in Europe; Mussolini invaded Ethiopia; Japan invaded China; Stalin carried out purges in the Soviet Union; and Spain was torn by civil war. In the United States, the New Deal was in trouble as isolationism was resurgent. Hingham, like the nation, was headed into more than a hurricane. The small town was about to face the maelstrom of global war.

CHAPTER TWENTY-FOUR

✠

Small Town and Total War

As 1939 opened, William L. Foster, in his seventies, still chaired the Board of Selectmen, and in his eighties, William Lunt was still treasurer. Timothy Murphy was in his twenty-eighth year as tree warden. Octogenarian Amos Humphrey kept his front row seat at town meetings and wanted to know why the public welfare agent got a raise or why the town included school lunches in the budget. Signs of depression lingered. The number of school-age children still declined. Warren Baker expanded his thrifty 5¢ to $1 emporium; ladies visited the "Thrift Beauty Shop"; and high schoolers held a "poverty dance," jitterbugging in patched clothes.

There were also signs of returning prosperity. Subdivisions sprouted, "nifty little Cape Cods" with their extending "els" and garage breezeways. The numbers of people and homes were on the rise:

	1930	1935	1940
People	6657	7330	8002
Homes	2146	2290	2566

"Since 1929," said the *Journal*, "what few real estaters dared to hang on, grimly, till better times, have nearly starved to death." But in 1939, with the growth of Quincy Point at the Fore River Shipyard, the *Journal* predicted new growth with a marked difference: small homes at moderate prices—$6000 to $7000; families with public school children, newcomers different in status and style.

In 1939, on the eve of cataclysm, social status and style in Hingham were a mixture of old and new. Seventy-five percent of high school students still finished their schooling with grade twelve. Hingham High was still a power in football, toppling mighty North Quincy and routing Milton. An eight-team Twilight Baseball League was formed; a sixteen-team bowling league crowded Roy's alleys at the harbor. In the winter, the Skating Club opened its rink on Smith's Pond off East Street for the new rage, hockey; in the summer, the Fourth of July celebrations still began with a huge midnight bonfire. "Eating out" grew popular, from Peter Zounis's seventy-five cent Sirloin Special at the Colonial to Bert and May Brown's Rathskeller at the old Cushing House, and up the social ladder to Viola's at Downer Avenue and the new Country Fare at Queen Ann's Corner.

Crow Point remained a well-to-do summer colony. For the fashionable, golf, yachting regattas, tennis tournaments, benefit fashion shows, home weddings, and pre-dance dinners were in style. The children of many of the year-round wealthy went to Derby Academy, then prep school, then private college.

The year had its new local celebrities: Fred B. Cole became a popular Boston radio announcer, and star golfer Bunny Wilson joined the ranks of the famous. Its new monument was the Abraham Lincoln statue, endowed by ex-Hinghamite Everett Whitney, a copy of the statue by Charles Keck in Illinois. The new Christian Science Church was completed on Main Street. The WBZ towers rose at "the Beach." The year's chief worry was whether the bankrupt New York, New Haven, and Hartford Railroad would end passenger service and, if so, what four hundred Hingham commuters would do. The chief hope was that the Chamber of Commerce's trade show at the armory would persuade more people to BUY IN HINGHAM. The chief suspense: what would expert surveys say about the deplorable condition of the schools? In the year's worst accidents, thirteen-year-old Catherine Breen was killed by a baseball bat, and World War I veteran John Tower died of a heart attack after seeing the launching at Fore River of the aircraft carrier *Wasp* and watching as two Navy planes locked wings and crashed. His shattered body and shocked mind had never recovered from 1918. His Legion Post was just twenty years old. So recent was "the war to end all wars."

Danny Murphy's Loring Hall changed its double feature three times a week, with a galaxy of Bennetts and Benny, Garland and Garfield, Fairbanks and Fonda, Hope, Crosby, and glamorous Lamour. One film was titled "Good Girls Go to Paris." In August, 1939, Randall Lincoln's daughters sailed for a European tour. Cynthia Harrison sailed for a year of study at the Sorbonne, but world events kept her from Paris. On September 4, the *Queen Mary* reached New York from England with seven hundred passengers over its limit, including Mrs. Ralph

Haigh of Hingham with baby daughter. The giant liner had crossed without lights. Word reached William Weir that his mother's ship had been sunk off the Hebrides but that she was safe. Harry Shaw arrived home on North Street with an eyewitness story of the British bombing of a German submarine. They were all safely home in Fortress America.

Faced with newly elected isolationist opponents in Congress, President Roosevelt had entered 1939 cautiously. Then, with spring came disasters: the crushing of Czechoslovakia, the collapse of anti-Fascist Spain, Germany's demands for Danzig. In August, Hitler and Stalin signed a pact. In September, Germany invaded Poland, Britain and France declared war on Germany, and shortly afterward, Russia invaded Finland. Hingham's first war effort was a Finnish Relief drive led by Mrs. George Wirkala. Finland's heroic resistance convinced some that there could be a "just war."

Spring, 1940, came beautifully to town. Election day in March was "gorgeous, a harbinger of spring." Far away in Europe, Denmark and Norway fell before the Nazi blitzkrieg, and on May 10, the Low Countries were overrun. Hingham looked forward to its first Tulip Show on May 23. By May 25, the Germans had divided French and British forces, and only the miracle of Dunkirk prevented disaster. Preparing to invade, Hitler launched the Luftwaffe against British cities. The reality of Britain's plight was soon embodied locally in the refugee children, thirteen by Christmas, who came to Hingham and attended Derby tuition-free. In November, ex-townsman Waitstill Sharp and his wife Martha went through Lisbon into occupied France and gathered up twenty-seven children to bring to the United States. Pledges from relatives and friends guaranteed their care.

A week after the Tulip Show, Hinghamites convened to form a Committee of National Defense and wired the President their urgent pleas to repeal the Neutrality Act and send aid to Britain. Those who attacked such "intervention" found themselves in a sensitive position. Methodist Pastor Omar Hartzler became a "mild storm center of criticism" when he declared himself a pacifist. Law required aliens to register, and Hingham's four hundred were slow to comply. A Hingham policeman ordered a hitchhiker out of his car for "fifth column talk," and the Wompatuck Club barely averted a riot over a "quasi-Benito propagandist." The town's mood was mobilizing.

In the presidential election of 1940, Wendell Wilkie won Hingham (69 percent to 31 percent) but lost the nation. On the eve of his third term, Roosevelt declared America to be "the arsenal of democracy." A still-depressed nation had begun to recover through the expansion of war-related industries. In Hingham, as 1940 opened, the employment situation was still precarious; but by September, conditions had changed dramatically. The Fore River Shipyard in Quincy and the Hingham Ammunition Depot had received $800 million worth of contracts, and the workers at the Depot were "busy as beavers up to their necks filling ammunition orders for some of those fifty destroyers which the U.S. has turned over to Britain." Hingham's "real estaters" were "running ragged." Where would workers, Navy personnel, and executives live? In the late fall of 1940, there came the astounding announcement of plans for Bradley Woods: a "medium-priced American home community" of small, six-room houses, four to an acre, one hundred immediately, and perhaps a thousand in ten years.

The town, still unzoned after two previous attempts, was aghast. The reaction this time was dramatically different. Meetings were called and warnings heard of "tenement developments," of poor sewage and water supply. A zoning law, little different from the one routed by parliamentary maneuver just three years before, was proposed. In a crisis atmosphere, town meeting approved the law on March 9, 1941, with a record crowd of 1364 jamming the armory. Dudley Alleman spoke against the law and was booed. The vote was 1004 to 3. For the moment, what had seemed a class issue in the 1930s looked like an overwhelming consensus. Even Amos Humphrey spoke for the law and suffered a fainting fit afterward. It was the last of the old warhorse's sixty-one annual meetings. One year later, Moderator Arthur Whittemore opened the meeting by asking the hundreds to stand: "the one man in Hingham to whom town meeting meant more than anything else" had died that very day. How perverse of fate that his final joust had ended in a law that would change his old Hingham forever.

The partial futility of this grand gesture of local control came home with a thud four months later. The Navy announced that it would take seven square miles in Hingham and adjacent towns for a "mammoth ammunition storage depot" annex. Streets would be closed and families evicted. The *Journal* envisioned a "vast underground storage space for munitions of war" and expressed what others must have feared: "Most of us are certainly in the midst of a potential inferno." Depth charges, bombs, and other high explosives would be stored here. But what could be done? Agitations, hearings, and negotiations took place. "We had an extraordinarily interesting meeting," remembered Margaret McSweeney, "and oh, Brass from Washington, medals all over their chests, came down to the meeting and the Best of Hingham were there and spoke." Triphammer Pond and some homes were saved. But in

November, 1941, as some families moved into Bradley Woods, others departed their homes in Third Division Woods, later to become Wompatuck State Park.

> They took the property from the poor people . . . they had saved perhaps $50 (I don't know how much they paid, but they paid very little), for an acre of land, and they did most of the construction on a house for themselves, and they were suddenly asked to give it up.

Some were black families. One father stationed himself on his roof with a shotgun and told his friend Tom McSweeney, who "had a little more education and was more in touch with how you remedied things," "I'm getting so I don't believe in God." And McSweeney replied, "Well, look, my advice to you is, whether or not you believe in God, act as if you believe in God and come down off the roof. You have one shotgun and the U.S. can blast you right into the next world."

Years later, when McSweeney was serving as a liaison with Washington, he met one of the admirals who had participated in the hearings and was told, "If you people had protested just a little more, we would have yielded." The town had been handicapped by an unwillingness to appear unpatriotic. "Sure," was the sentiment; "it's tough to lose your home and such, but if Uncle Sam feels he needs this spot for national defense, it's okay with me." The 3744 acres, known as "the Cohasset Annex," were mostly in Hingham. Twenty-five miles of fence went up, and "stalwart guards" patrolled the borders.

Uncle Sam had other needs as well. When the nation's first peacetime draft took effect in the fall of 1940, the town numbered about eight thousand. By June, 1942, the *Journal*'s service Honor Roll held 212 names. Three years later, the roll had climbed to over nine hundred, 10 percent of the town. It kept its name of "Men in Service" even though, by the end of 1944, the roll included forty-four women. By December, 1944, almost a dozen men had died. By the end of the war and the time of homecomings, when John Macpherson died in a veterans' hospital and Ralph Young, South Hingham bus driver, died on a homeward bound transport, the total had reached thirty. Final victories were costly.

In November, 1940, the first two Hingham draftees were inducted, and one shop in the square was a gloomy place: Charlie O'Connell and Thaddeus Yonika were both clerks at Donovan's Drug Store. By a sad irony, the town's first casualty was kin to the first of World War I: Coit Rogers' nephew Allan was killed in a crash off Virginia Beach in August, 1941. In November, Lawrence Ripley died in an accident on maneuvers in the Carolinas. Then, early one Sunday morning in December, at Pearl Harbor, naval commander Admiral Kimmel was dressing for a golf game when his phone rang. Stepping out on his lawn, he saw Japanese dive bombers overhead and heard the first explosions. In two hours, much of the Pacific Fleet was left in smoking ruins, and thousands were dead. Hingham's William Rhodes was killed at nearby Hickham Field. Willard Beal was aboard the *Oklahoma* when she capsized, but he survived. On December 8, Hingham awakened to see convoys rolling through its streets. Troops were taking up guard duty in a small town transformed into a munitions center.

Nineteen forty-two was a year of grim desperation and unprecedented mobilization. By May, the Japanese had overrun southeast Asia and the island chains of the western Pacific. George Pickering, captured at Wake Island, was Hingham's first prisoner of war, and Franklin Bachelor and Mason Foley's brother George, minister of a Manila church, were POWs in the conquered Philippines. Across the world in the Atlantic, American merchant ships were sunk in growing numbers by German submarines. In North Africa, German general Erwin Rommel prepared a drive to push the British back to Suez; and in Russia, a German spring offensive threatened to knock America's new ally out of the war. The only hopeful note was that the heroic, outnumbered RAF had won its battle over Britain.

In April came America's equivalent to that resistance. In the Battle of the Coral Sea, what was left of the Pacific Fleet stopped the Japanese advance. Now, America was determined to hold its central Pacific base at Midway Island. In June, Japan attacked, suffered a disastrous defeat, and would henceforth have to fight a defensive war. In August, America opened its island-hopping counteroffensive with the bloody invasion of Guadalcanal.

Marine pilot Albert Tweedy, Jr., son of a selectman, was killed at the Battle of Midway. Lester Bruggemann and George Antoine were at Guadalcanal. Other Hingham men were harder to locate. On air and naval missions so farflung, men reported missing sometimes remained so for months or years before some of them reappeared. Paul Barrett was reported missing when the *Colhoun* went down near the Solomons, but he was home for Christmas. Army bombardier Nate Prince was reported killed, then missing, then a prisoner, but he turned up in Australia. Amy Howard received a letter from her son Edward saying he had "seen and talked to Nate." Edward himself was later lost on a flight between New Guinea and Australia. The mountainous crash site was not found until years after his mother's death.

[350]

While men and women were spread around the globe, their small town was changing utterly. By happy accident, on the eve of transformation, its pre-war humanity was captured in unique photographs. Frances Cooke Macgregor came to Hingham in 1936. During the next few years, while her husband was away on archeological trips, she lived at the home of his sister on Stoddard Road. Already an anthropological photographer of America's Southwest, she conceived of a book about Hingham that would be a pictorial equivalent of the sociological classic *Middletown.* Following the trend of 1930s woman photographers such as Margaret Bourke-White and Dorothea Lange, she photographed the town, not through its topography or architecture, but through its representative people in their social roles. Macgregor's was a distanced vision. As a Democrat from California, she found Hingham strange in its eastern formality and ardent Republicanism and behaved like a Westerner. She canoed and fished for trout near Triphammer and biked about town in slacks. "I felt," she said, "like a zebra!"

Under intense pressure from their common publisher, she agreed to collaborate with another woman. Eleanor Roosevelt would write the text for the book, which was to be titled *This Is America.* And so, what Mrs. Macgregor had conceived as her own sociological document became what Alexander Macmillan aptly calls "a handsome piece of propaganda," intended to awaken Americans to their communal values on the eve of world war. Mrs. Roosevelt's text misrepresents Hingham as a "typical American town" with healthy ethnic diversity and tolerance. Mrs. Macgregor's stunning portraits catch an old human Hingham at its last moment.

Mrs. Macgregor insisted that the President's wife visit the town, and so, Eleanor Roosevelt paid a surprise call on Hingham one icy January day in 1942. She was driven about, called Main Street "the prettiest Main Street in America," signed the register at the old meetinghouse, listened to sexton Frank Reed tell its history, and dropped in on a meeting of startled lady Republicans. Hurried back to Stoddard Road for lunch, she drank her bouillon while listening to "Franklin" on the radio delivering his State of the Union address.

The very week of Eleanor's visit brought news from Washington of plans for the further transformation of Hingham. Approximately 150 more acres would be taken. A Bethlehem Steel shipyard, known as "Beth Hingham," would build convoy ships, Destroyer Escorts, "DEs", sixteen at a time on sixteen "ways." The site would be Huet's Cove, once the scene of polo games and horse races by Peter Bradley's Arabians, then of the three hundredth anniversary pageant, of the Bayside

Airport until 1939, and briefly of Don Rand's Dude Ranch. The town was assured that "Beth Hingham" would be only a wartime industry. The local response was numb resignation. "If the Navy feels that this spot is what they want, well, Hingham will lose its individuality and become just another Navy workyard." So much for the zoning victory of a mere ten months before.

A 1943 Louis Ruyl drawing of DE91, the HMS Reynolds. Samuel Wakeman, the young general manager of the shipyard, overtook his father's record-time ship building in World War I with this DE 91. The 1300 ton ship was built in a total of forty-four days and was transferred to the British Navy immediately for anti U-boat and convoy duty in the Atlantic. Called the terriers of the seas, these ships had ready fire power and speed.

Construction began in February, 1942. Shops and warehouses seemed to rise overnight. The largest building, a steel plant, covered almost ten acres. A bridge was built to carry Route 3A over the connecting road across the highway. The Back River drawbridge was replaced by a high fixed bridge. In June, the first keel was laid, and in September, the first "DE" slid down its "way."

Town meeting, 1941. On the platform, left to right: Alice de Young, Town Clerk William Leavitt Howard, Moderator Arthur Whittemore, Selectmen William L. Foster, Fletcher Wason, and George B. Cole.

Backfilling an underground high explosive magazine at the Naval Ammunition Depot. A W.P.A. project, 1941.

Eleanor Roosevelt, following luncheon on Stoddard Road, Hingham, January 6, 1942. The United States was already at war and Winston Churchill was at the White House. The First Lady said afterwards that her day in Hingham was the most restful she could remember.

ABOVE: *One of the series of drawings by Edgar T. P. Walker (1889–1965) in which he depicted the process of building a ship until it was launched. Here, 1943, a section of a Destroyer Escort is being prefabricated at the steel mill.* BELOW: *Aerial view of Bethlehem-Hingham Shipyard (1942–1945), looking east: Lincoln Street (3A) is at the right. The largest building, still standing, was the prefabricating area and steel mill. Jutting into Huet's Cove on the left were the eight outfitting piers (nearest) and the eight shipways for building the ships.*

Employment skyrocketed. A federal housing project for workers was started off High Street. By December, 1942, close to 15,000 were working at the yard; at the peak time in late 1943, approximately 24,000. Workers parked their cars in fours along Route 3A or in huge parking lots. The Hingham Trust Company cashed 1466 workers' checks weekly. By August, 1943, a "DE" was launched in 119 hours. In December, under floodlights, the one hundredth was launched. In 1944, with the submarine menace over and allied invasions underway, Beth-Hingham turned from "DEs" to "LSTs" (Landing Ship Tanks).

The town was a vital defense area. Troops were everywhere, at the Ammunition Depot, at Camp Hingham on Prospect Street, in barracks at the Centre. A civil defense network included air watchers, wardens, a twenty-four-hour phone center, Motor Corps, demolition squads, first-aid teams, and auxiliary police and firemen. A Coast Guard auxiliary of yachtsmen patrolled the bay and the beaches day and night. Security was tight. Most of the town was in a "dim-out area" or a "sky-glow" area; "Bert Beal has dimmed out the square. It gives a fellow a creepy feeling." In periodic blackouts, Hingham was "shrouded in darkness," marred only by lanterns on railroad crossings or a beam from the town office door. Top halves of auto headlights were painted black, driving was dangerous, and servicemen walking the streets were near-casualties.

Gasoline was scarce, car production was cut, and "we can't buy tires" was a common complaint. Fashionable ladies were seen peddling bicycles to dinner dances. In March, 1942, ration cards appeared. With gas rationing came a litany of complaints: "So-and-So got an X card—lots of gas—and he uses it for pleasure drives; I hope those 'gestapo' inspectors of the OPA [Office of Price Administration] on the Boulevard to the Beach catch him." Sugar was added to the ration list. Victory suits appeared minus cuffs. With fuel oil rationed, some people closed off rooms; some switched back to coal, but then the miners went on strike. At the Ration Board at 1 Short Street, Ed Anderson wondered "what he will have to ration next." In 1943, shoes, canned foods, coffee, and meat were added, and a "point system" for purchases was established. There was little to buy and much to do.

If people were not busy working at the shipyard or the Depot, making clothes and bandages, drilling with Home Defense, patrolling beaches, the bay, the woods for fires, standing a watch at the Control Center, driving in the Motor Corps, planting a Victory Garden, or working at the Home Canning Center—why, then, people were conducting a "drive" or collecting stuff to donate. There were Red Cross drives, relief drives, bond and stamp drives. ALUMINUM FOR DE-

FENSE was collected, and "pots and pans" were tossed into the "cages" beside Loring Hall. Next came OLD NUMBER PLATES—Charlie Marble was "champ" with sixty-six—then WASTE PAPER, RAGS, OLD METAL, RUBBER, TIN CANS, JUNK—until, "This savings business is getting me goggle-eyed, for I'm afraid to throw anything away, with the result that my cellar looks like a junkyard."

No one who did not live through it can quite imagine the mood of exhilaration, desperation, and commitment, or the speed and magnitude of change. The *Journal* columnist "Prowler" reminisced:

> For many years I have enjoyed hiking about the hills of this beautiful town, but I am afraid that my wanderings will be fewer now. The spot off Lazell Street is closed to me, for the hills are laden with missiles to destroy my fellow men.—Huet's Beach, where I became an actor to portray one of the early settlers in the pageant, will soon be a thing of the past. Bradley's old place on Lincoln Street, where I saw some of the finest horses do their stuff, is now the location of an enormous building of concrete and steel. The field . . . that used to harvest the finest crop of daisies I ever saw is being filled with barracks. All these and more, all used for one purpose, to build machines, boats, or more stuff for one purpose—to kill and maim.

And the killing and maiming had just begun.

The end of 1942, said Winston Churchill, was "the end of the beginning." In 1943, the tide turned. Stalingrad became a disaster for the Germans. Rommel's Africa Corps was trapped between the British and the Americans, directed by a new leader named Dwight D. Eisenhower. At home, hearts and minds dreaded the invasions to come. In July, 1943, Sicily was overrun, Mussolini was forced from office, and Italy left the war and was occupied by German troops. In September, the Americans and British invaded southern Italy. Americans died in scores at Salerno, north of Naples, and later, when the allied advance bogged down, on another beachhead at Anzio, south of Rome.

Anzio was Hell. Across the world, Tarawa was equally hellish. Hingham men were at both. Milt Ingram wrote of Tarawa: "a beautiful green spot when we first saw it, but after our bombs and big ship guns finished, it was a desolate-looking place . . . . I had a chance to get ashore . . . found the place nothing but a shambles with dead Japs here and there." Milt's brother John, a veteran of North Africa, survived Anzio, only to die in a jeep accident near Florence after the war ended. Charlie Kearns was killed in a crash in Louisiana, and Parker Hatch died when the ship he commanded collided with a tanker off Cape May, New Jersey.

Early in 1944, casualties mounted. Wilbur Waldron died in submarine action in the Sea of Japan; Robert Laurie's flying fortress went down over New Guinea; Harry Trainor was killed near Monte Cassino. Arthur Snyder, severely wounded near Palestrina, directed his tanks from a stretcher. The Road to Rome was finally opened, and by June 4, American troops were in the Italian capital. Two days later came "D-Day," the long awaited and dreaded "greatest amphibious operation in the history of the world."

Through the spring of 1944, troops had massed in English fields; airstrips were jammed with planes, ports with invasion ships. At dawn on June 6, they hit the Normandy beaches. News reached Hingham at 3:32 A.M. as nightshift workers and insomniacs huddled by radios. Tom Kelly saw the beaches from the deck of a minesweeper, and Chaplain Curtis Spence, formerly minister of New North, went ashore with the invaders. Anselm Beal spent his eighteenth birthday on the beachhead. Hersey brothers Reuben and John met on the Normandy front after chasing each other all over England. John Root was killed over Normandy on D-Day. Lester Hutchinson, waist gunner on a flying fortress, was reported missing, but turned up weeks later with tales of hiding three months with the Belgian underground. Frank Tower, John's son, turned up in a German prison camp. William Chase and Sherrard Billings did not.

By late July, 1944, a million allied soldiers were in Normandy. Under Omar Bradley, an American blitzkrieg advanced, while George Patton's flying armored columns swept through Brittany, and a second invasion force moved up the Rhone. In late August, Paris was liberated. Then, the Germans held, and hopes for a quick ending to the war were dashed.

Older townspeople can remember the strange atmosphere at home in 1943-44. Americans were in mass migration from one war center to another, through a world of transients and strangers. In Hingham, "Things are going so fast . . . you can scarcely catch your breath . . . . The whole town is changing." Having barely survived the depression, workers now had more money than they had ever dreamed of, but little to spend it on except entertainment and war bonds. One young fellow asked, "What's the sense of going [to school]? I can get fifty bucks over here at the shipyard and that will give me a lot of fun." Another shrugged, "Why should I worry how long the war lasts, I'm sitting on top of the world." Said one woman to another, a stranger, on the Quincy-Hingham bus, "My husband and I are both working in defense plants, we never had so much money in our lives . . . . So far as I am concerned, it can go on indefinitely." The other, leaving the bus, hit her full in the face with a purse: "I give you that for my son who laid down his life at Pearl Harbor." War profiteering had been democratized, a danger signal for the future.

So huge was the demand for labor that local businesses and town departments were hard pressed. Harry Michelson had to sell most of his cattle. Lester Lovell the florist was "short of gas, short of tires, short of help." Winifred Mahoney, waitress at the Old Ship Galley, was home with the mumps and could not be replaced. Women, told for so long that their place was at home, were now told their patriotic duty was to work. After the war, when the old message was heard again, many would reject it.

Hingham women served in countless ways. Charlotte Prouty directed the Red Cross, and Mary Hoyt, its fifty-member Motor Corps. Mrs. Frank Donaldson supervised the sewing unit. Women of the Garden Club contributed to horticultural therapy programs at army, navy, and veterans hospitals, delivering hundreds of small bouquets for bedsides and flowers to decorate chapels and recreation rooms. Mrs. Seth Sprague was responsible for Hingham's Recreation Center (first located opposite the central fire station, later at 165 North Street) where, between September, 1942, and December, 1945, over 22,000 servicemen registered. Bill Quinn's wife, her three sons Bill, Jack, and Bob away in service, made a home for other boys day and night. There was always a welcome at "Mother Quinn's."

The town was bereft of nurses since so many had joined the services. Anna Schultz and Mary Talbot let the way to the Waves, Mary Amonte to the Air WAC, Sally and Ruth Brewer to the Marines, and

> *Nellie Calvi is a WAC.*
> *She's marching off to war,*
> *The light of battle in her eye,*
> *A firm set to her jaw.*

Mary Rizzotto served with the Red Cross in North Africa and Italy, and when the war ended, she founded the World Children's Foundation to care for illegitimate foreign children of G.I.s. Helen Gleason supervised nursing after the war at German camps for the displaced. Home front heroines were less well known: Jenny Ferraro, town canning champion; the nameless woman who made 101 pairs of socks; West Hingham's lady railroad crossing tender; and the women riveters called the "Rosies":

I watched one of the lassies over at the shipyard . . . and was I amazed. Her job was to lift boxes, the weight was around forty pounds, she pushed them around like feathers, so I beat a hasty retreat. I enjoyed watching a lady riveter, for she was the nearest thing to perpetual motion I had seen for years.

There were nameless legions of hostesses. There were also teenage girls whose poignantly blended hunger for romance and sense of duty led them into the arms of lonely, strange servicemen.

Familiar streets were filled with strangers. Most exotic were the gypsies—as many as two hundred—who settled "down Litchfield Beach way" (Wompatuck Road). The men worked as tin or coppersmiths at the shipyard. Coatsworth recalled the "women sauntering down the street, two or three abreast, talking in a strange tongue and laughing, while New England sunlight fell on their wide skirts of scarlet, orange, green, and watermelon pink." Crow Point kids would sneak over the golf course to spy on them, and one remembered seeing some "robbing Johnny Barba blind." They arrived in the spring of 1943, and by fall, they were gone. Such was the war.

Coming and going, too, were British and French sailors, awaiting their ships. A more lasting presence were hundreds of black soldiers and sailors—"fine colored boys," they were called then—segregated in the services and segregated in Hingham as well. They were not welcome at the Recreation Center. They "know," the *Journal* assured, "that segregation to a certain degree is mandatory," but "what to do to make them feel at home?" Mabel Diggs headed a Recreation Subcommittee to plan dances and parties with out-of-town "dusky ladies as hostesses"; after the war her group would grow into the South Shore Citizens Club. The men organized a band and played for their own dances at "Ag" Hall, and on July 4, 1944, Hingham saw the stirring spectacle of a parade led by an African-American band and two detachments.

Hundreds of married servicemen and war workers tramped the streets seeking homes. Rooms were found, but seldom apartments, for Hingham had zoned itself almost out of apartments. Hingham men were far away—who knew where? Letters home were limited to two pages, with no reference to location. "These censors," wrote Luis Merlino, "must have eyes like hawks, a razor on each finger nail, and descended from a long line of paper doll cutters." But they didn't cut his clever parody:

We left where we were about the same length of time before we got here . . . you could see the same sky overhead, even the same stars sometimes . . . . We have weather here too . . . . The sun shines in the daytime, if it is clear, and at night it gets dark. Sometimes I wish I was where I thought I was going when I was where I was before . . . . P.S. If anyone knows where I am, please write to me because I am lost.

Tight lip was the rule at home, too. "ON YOUR LIP KEEP A LAP. NO NEWS FOR THE JAP." "Watch out for the summer saboteur." "Report immediately any information or suspicions concerning espionage, sabotage, subversive activities, or statements to the FBI." A propaganda of anxiety, inevitable in total war, was sowing the seeds of postwar paranoia.

Indeed, the thought of postwar made people anxious. Veterans of 1917-18 remembered the dismal economy that "welcomed" them home and worried about how ten to twelve million men would be employed, housed, and rehabilitated. A town committee began planning, and the federal government enacted G.I. Bills. But each sign of the end—the closing of Camp Hingham, the return of night lights—added anxiety. War contracts were being canceled, and at Beth-Hingham, layoffs began after D-Day. Some worried whether the boys would even return to Hingham and if they did, whether they would even recognize it: "It will be no surprise," wrote one, "if I, on my return home, have to hire a guide to find such once familiar places as Dykeman's Drug Store, Pete's Barber Shop, or even the *Journal* office."

The winter of 1945 was cruel. Eight-below-zero temperatures closed schools, and a Nor'easter buried the town under snow. News came that the shipyard would close in August. Hitler's last offensive began. The terrible Battle of the Bulge went on for weeks, and Hingham was all too well represented in "the Luxembourg area." George Shute and Herbert Loring died there; Everett Studley died on the Belgian front, and Bob Brennan and Boris Demko over Germany. On January 3, the allied counteroffensive began. Seth Sprague, Jr., died leading his armored platoon against the village of Hatten. "Anzio lasted longer," recalled an observer, "but for sheer bloody vicious tenseness, hour after hour and day after day, Hatten was the worst." Russel Carnes, North Street grocer, died in Germany. Gordon Cushing, veteran of North Africa, Sicily, France, Belgium, Holland, and Germany, was killed one black night near the Elbe. It is little wonder that VE Day failed to cause much enthusiasm in Hingham. At 9 A.M., Tuesday, May 8, one long blast of the fire whistle signaled the German surrender. Downtown remained quiet. A long sea road lay ahead in the Pacific.

There, in 1944, America had won a string of costly island victories. Frederick Gordon got "plenty of grey hairs" at New Georgia, New

Britain, Bougainville, the Gilberts and Carolines. Charles Robison pushed his landing craft through the "shell-shattered, reef-bound pass" to the Saipan beachhead. Marines Reginald MacDonald and James Buckner died at Peleliu. On Guam it took two rifle bullets, three grenades, and two mortar shells to put John Wise temporarily out of action. Albert Reynolds bailed out over the Bonins and fell five thousand feet before his chute opened. Gordon Sears and Foster Trainor met on Iwo Jima to see the raising of the flag. Edward Keenan was killed off Okinawa when Kamikaze planes turned the *Bunker Hill* into a blazing cauldron.

A second Asian front opened. Bob Wesselhoeft caught polio in Tibet and had to be evacuated by mule. In India, Francis Disnard's malaria kept him off his bomber when it crashed with its entire crew. George Disnard, turret gunner on a Mitchell bomber and perhaps Hingham's most decorated warrior, saw seventy-three missions in Burma. But no Hingham man saw more of global war than the *Journal* editor's son, Signalman Frank Maclean, from Iceland to Casablanca, the Mediterranean, Sicily, Norway, the Caribbean, to the major battles of the Pacific. In June, 1945, Frank was "in the thick of it in Okinawa." By September, he was in conquered Tokyo. "Dad," he had written, "it's a far different war than you were in in 1918."

In April, 1945, an old President had died, and a new President made the awesome decision to use the Bomb. At 7:02 P.M., on August 14, an excited announcer broadcast the news of Japan's surrender, and sexton Frank Reed took only two minutes to reach the belltower. Streets "suddenly became as if by magic a bedlam . . . . Fire crackers, tin cans tied to the rear of autos, shrieking horns, torn paper that looked like New York's Broadway." Eighty-seven-year-old Patriarch Charlie Marble rode about town ringing a cow bell.

Victory's euphoria, however, was short-lived. Visions of the future were haunted by the Bomb. Moderator Arthur Whittemore, addressing high school students, used the incredible phrase, "possible Third World War." America and the U.S.S.R. clashed in the United Nations, and Soviet expansion in the Balkans confronted the Truman Doctrine. Labor unions, having reached their brief zenith of power, made 1946-47 the worst years for strikes in American history, bringing retribution in the form of the Taft-Hartley Act. In Hingham, it was grand once more to "see the lights on the boats off the town wharf," but the future lay in shadow.

In the summer of 1946, columnist "Prowler" approached a veteran in the square. He had a faraway look. What was troubling him?

[359]

I just don't know. I've waited for this day when I could get home, and now I miss the gang so much I want to go back. Everybody is swell to me, my old job is waiting for me, I have a nice home, but somehow things seem so dull, the excitement is gone, so I'm like a fish out of water, just floundering around . . . . I know the war's over and I'm supposed to take my place in the community as of yore. See that Honor Roll over there? Well, most of those boys' names in gold I knew. They were swell kids, and didn't deserve to die the way they did. Oh, heck, I'm going to get in the First National line and see if I can get some butter.

What had become of the "community of yore"? It was in a mood of denial. The "Welcome Home" sign atop the town office building was "sagging a bit," and few cared. The American Legion's effort to get town land at the harbor for its home and memorial was blocked. A young veteran told the town meeting in 1946 not to waste money on welcoming ceremonies and a plaque. In 1948, a request for only $500 for a plaque and boulder received an emphatic NO. The secretary of the Veterans Council reflected:

It is less than three years since the end of hostilities, and already Hingham's war dead are a forgotten issue . . . . The townspeople by their votes and their emphatic yells of NO have convinced us that their memories of these men are also dead . . . . Our faith in their integrity and sincerity has been seriously shaken.

On Memorial Day, 1948, one observer wondered "why it is that the younger men, those vets of World War II, who could and should parade, don't want any part of it." Perhaps they thought war best forgotten and would tolerate no more hollow rituals. Perhaps the denial of the past was a symptom of fear of the future. Hingham was entering an ordeal of growth and cultural strain. Total war's ardent solidarity had disintegrated.

While the town debated its costly option to buy the shipyard, some looked with "anxious concern on shipyard communities" nearby. The old debate over industry was heard again, heated by fears of a flood of low-cost housing and industrial strife. The town named a "Wait and See" Committee, but local business could not afford to wait and see. It pressed against the narrow confines of zoning. Younger men formed a Progressive Club and won seven offices in the 1946 election, led by Lewis Perkins for selectman and "Winker" McKee for the Planning Board. The divisive mood was sadly displayed that year in the confrontation over Greenfield's. The town's one surviving industry wanted to replace its building. McKee led the support. Morton Smith, wise uncle to many a young Hinghamite, was loudly booed when he sounded the old note about threatened property values. More fireworks went off the following year when Earle Robinson and William McNulty won a zoning change for a new mill and lumber yard off Summer Street, and nearby "estaters" sued. "Billy" was asked if he expected a building boom. "'Man, dear,' said Bill, 'why do you suppose Junior and I put up a fight for that lumber storage space down at Nantasket Junction?'"

He was right, of course. Hingham had opened ten new subdivisions since January, 1946, compared with two in Brookline, three in Waltham and Lincoln, and four in Concord. Housing was acutely scarce. Dentist Ross Vroom, eager to move into George Walker's "corker" of a development "down at World's End," bought a house and moved it by water from Gallops Island to Seal Cove Road. Old Crow Point was changing. "I can remember when, after Labor Day, the whole section was folded up." Now, in 1946, few houses were vacant all year. By the summer of 1947, the "little row of houses" had appeared across from the dance hall on Route 3A, and the skeptic was invited to

> drive up Butler Road and take in the Higgins development. Then swing south into Smith Road and look over the numerous offerings of the Hingham Realty Company. Keep on South into High Street and swing into the Jim Kimball extension.

Bradley Park applied to expand, and houses higher on Otis Hill leaked sewage into new ones below. Between 1946 and 1949, the number of homes increased from 2781 to 2901. A survey predicted an increase of 1550 families by 1970.

The same survey foresaw a jump of over seven hundred in school enrollments in the next five years. Hingham had had more than its share of total war and more than its share of the baby boom that followed. The state's birthrate had grown by half, but Hingham's had almost doubled. Aging school buildings had been neglected during the depression, and new construction had been postponed by the war. When South School was finally built in 1948, inflation had added $150,000 to the cost. In 1946, funds to expand the high school were noisily denied; so, in 1947, classes were being taught in the cafeteria, offices, and fourth floor men's restroom. Kindergarten classes were initiated the same year. The Navy provided temporary quarters at the shipyard. Fifth and sixth graders were bussed to North School, while town engineers tried to install adequate heating.

Hingham's cost per pupil was only the Greater Boston average. Even so, between 1938 and 1947, the school budget had more than doubled, owing chiefly to increased enrollments, the inflationary pressure on salaries caused by a shortage of teachers, and pay parity for women. The rate of increase was exceeded only by that of the Fire Department, whose popular and persuasive new chief, Albert "Kimmie" Kimball, was noted for convincing town meetings that the Advisory Committee's figure for his department was too low.

The superintendent of schools was less successful. In 1947, the school picture was depressing. The new high school principal resigned after one year; within a week of being appointed, his successor asked to be released. Coach Bill Cronin was feuding with the director of athletics, and both resigned. In 1948, the student editor of "High School Highlights" wrote: "In the past few years school spirit here in Hingham has become a serious problem. It . . . is at its lowest ebb in a long time." The cause cited: the forming and abuse of social cliques.

If in the schools, so, too, in the town at large, there were signs of exacerbated social and moral division. One small symptom was a "babysitter debate," provoked by one babysitter who charged that Hingham parents were "godless" and declared she would leave "this haughty town." A larger manifestation in the same year was the division of the Baptist Church between "modernist liberals" and conservative fundamentalists and the forming of a new South Shore Baptist Church.

A traditional communality was hard to find amid new streets and subdivisions. One witty young townsman, Mayo Shattuck, Jr., made a graphic if impressionistic analysis of Hingham society in 1948-49. He described a class structure topped by a "protestant outlander elite" of great wealth with "tea-party etiquette," debutante daughters, and prep school sons. This class clustered at lower Main Street estates and was ritualized at an annual Christmas Eve party given by the heiress to a food fortune for two dozen families, few of them active in town affairs. "Upper older middle outlanders" lived near the Centre and on Glad Tidings Plain. Finding them too sedate, some of their younger kin had moved to Bradley Hill, near their exclusive venue, the Yacht Club, alleged to be the locus of bibulous parties that scandalized the proper. "Lower middle outlanders" were settled in Cape Cods, on Otis Hill, for example, where they specialized in poker, bridge, radio, the movies, and public school children. Irish Catholic families had their parallel hierarchy. The "Lace Curtain" had their centers at St. Paul's and at the Country Club, from which the "upper protestants" had fled to a lesser golf course in Cohasset to play with "their own." A typical "lower"

Irish family might be found in a five-room house near the square, the husband a fireman, the wife a part-time maid. The wife "absolutely denies, when asked bluntly, that there is any social scale in Hingham. She said, 'Just the other day, Mrs.____ waved to me in the First National.'"

Most poignant is Shattuck's stereotype of "natives," people with Hingham ancestors. Their children were moving away. They had, with a few exceptions, turned inward, frugal, and defensive. They had "seen a radical change in Hingham during their lives" and did not "like it in the slightest." In the 1930s, they had kept power through their spokesman, Selectman Foster, who retired in 1945. They had done "more harm to Hingham than anyone now realizes," cutting services, neglecting buildings, preserving solvency at great cost to the future. Our young satirist sums up a dying politics in an exchange between Foster and engineer Lewis Perkins. Perkins had secured state and county pledges for a new road. "The state and the county could go to the devil," said Foster. "Hingham will take care of itself."

The study concludes as follows: "No longer are the citizens of the small New England town united in single purpose; no longer do citizens know each other intimately. Furthermore, the individual class in Hingham cannot understand the interests and desires of the other classes." Had the writer been a historian, he might not have idealized the community of the past to such a degree. "As Francis Lincoln would say, 'Huh, it's all in the history books! . . . But—who nowadays reads a history book?'" Instead, young Shattuck was a student of politics, and his sketch was intended to make the case for radical changes in town government.

At the time, some people believed that the open town meeting had outlived its effectiveness, and they proposed changing to a "limited" or representative town meeting. Many towns had made this change. Problems and finances had become too complex, populations too large, interests too narrow, and civic responsibility too weak. It was not hard to make the case in Hingham: maximum turnouts at town meeting amounted to only 20 percent of the voters; it was physically impossible to admit more; special interest votes were followed by a mass exodus; late evening decisions were fortuitous when a few weary minutes and a bare quorum might undo months of work and planning. In 1948, study committees were approved to consider changes.

Town meetings resumed their struggles with nagging issues postponed during the war. The "dump question" resurfaced. New housing was going up off Hersey Street, and "the old fester spot," the "rat-infested place," was summarily closed. A new dump at the northeast corner of French and Hobart Streets, costing $750 for land and $3015 for equipment, opened on Christmas Eve, 1945. The more expensive "sewer question" was studied, "continued," and tabled. Attention was deflected to a more visible and age-old drainage problem.

In December, 1946, while wintering in Florida, retired Selectman Foster checked his two-volume index of town meetings. He had typed it letter by letter with the blunt end of a pencil in place of his arthritic fingers. He estimated that "our odious and unsanitary brook" had come up at town meetings *sixty* times since 1800; the mill pond had been debated twenty-five times. They would come up once more; only this time action would be taken.

The proposal was to carry the Town Brook through pipes under the tidal mill pond to a harbor conduit at Water Street. Simultaneously, yachtsmen were campaigning for harbor dredging. Why not go further, link the projects, and use the dredging to fill the pond? "Gone—and let us hope forever—will be the mill pond as a receptacle for," etc. etc. A special town meeting of October, 1947, approved the step. Not even the need for an additional $40,000 would block the making of history. In June, 1948, a special town meeting took only twenty minutes to vote the extra funds.

But what a meeting it was! By 7:30, only 160 voters had arrived. Fire Chief "Kimmie" Kimball sounded the fire alarm, but "only the young fry on bicycles fell for the ruse" and thought "Ag Hall" was on fire. Contractor Frank Barbuto, his brook project in jeopardy, urged the moderator to send folks home to their telephones. Fred B. Cole phoned his radio station, and WHDH broadcast Hingham's political emergency. An announcement was also made at Loring Hall, and a few moviegoers answered the call to civic duty. "After more than two hundred years, something was about to be done about the odious question," and at last fewer than 10 percent of 5380 voters showed up to take action. The long history of the "question" had come to a conclusion.

As 1948 ended, Hingham's ancient political character appeared to be in peril. It was facing a population explosion that would threaten its institutions. Its majestic old elms were falling victim to the blight that had reached Hingham in 1947. Its sense of the past had reached a low ebb. Memories of D-Day and its casualties were fading. "T-Day" had arrived, and young and old were "swarming around Woody's [store] like bees around the hive" to see baseball games on the new marvel, television. Television came just in time for the Louis-Walcott fight and for the astounding election upset of Thomas E. Dewey by Harry S. Truman. Charlie Marble did not live quite long enough to see "T.V." at the Wompatuck Club. He died on November 27, 1948, at the age of ninety, the club's oldest member, the town's oldest man. The repository of the town's memory, he had been born before the Civil War, had graduated in Hingham High School's second class, and had lived to play the Patriarch in 1935. His nearest surviving relative was a grand-nephew in Indiana.

Sounds of change awakened coastal residents to the hammer of harbor dredges and to the sight of the mill pond being filled. The sounds of the auctioneer's gavel were heard at the Cushing House as old furnishings were sold off. An antiaircraft unit and a Seabee reserve company were drilling at the armory. Along the cow path to Triphammer Pond, army reservists were being trained in "nuclear instruments." Congress had enacted a new draft law, and Hingham men were once more registering. The decade of war had come full circle. Change and *déjà vu* mingled oddly, frighteningly.

CHAPTER TWENTY-FIVE

※

Decade of Numbers

I WILL always be grateful," said Margaret McSweeney, "that I lived in Hingham when it was still small." By the 1950s, that time was past. In 1953, from Observation Post "Echo Nectar Zero One Black" in "Ag Hall" tower, an Operation Skywatch volunteer

> thought of days gone by, when the hollow to the east, a nursery now to baby elms and maples, was the only playground in Hingham; when the elm-lined streets seemed wide and cool and quiet; when the town was still a village, and the people on the street or in the market all were friends and acquaintances; when there were no airplanes in the sky, no cars streaming on the highways; when Russia, China, Germany, Japan were, to most, names in a geography book, colored areas on a map; when there was never a thought, much less an expectation of an "emergency."

The airplane-watcher was reflecting on the twin impulses driving the 1950s in town and nation, one a dream, the other a nightmare. "Emergency" meant the terror that nuclear attack would come from without, that spies and subversion would undermine from within. The other impulse was a rush to suburbia, "middle landscape between town and country," to realize the American "dream deferred" by depression and world war. The dream was made realizable by the affordability of cars, the $150 billion in the nation's war savings, and, for countless veterans, the security of a family home with low down payments and long amortizations. The result was "one of the greatest land rushes in our country's history."

One kind of suburbanization had occurred in the late nineteenth century; another, before the Great Depression. The suburbanization of the

1950s differed profoundly in the sheer numbers of those pursuing the dream, in their socioeconomic circumstances, and in their ages. In this decade, Hingham's population grew by 44 percent from 10,665 to 15,378. The population was younger than ever before or since. The number of homes increased dramatically, and so did the number of streets. The developer was in his heyday. More and more land was paved. Natural resources and waste systems were strained. Public buildings, neglected for two decades, were bulging and aged, while the costs of their repairs and replacements spiraled upward. A town government that had functioned reasonably well for a small population with fewer expectations responded to numbers by growing more complex. In short, the *quantitative*—the sum of numbers—brought *qualitative* change, change in the nature of community more radical than in any prior time.

Many factors determined the way Hingham grew. Unlike the developers of *sui generis* suburbs such as the Levittowns, Hingham developers were excluded from large tracts held by the federal government, by families such as the Brewer-Walkers and Thayers, by dairy farmers, and by the town. Perhaps the most influential factor was geology: the descending slope from south to north, with gravel sites, streams, marshes, and waterways, most lying near the Town Brook and the mill pond or on a spongy aquifer running under much of the central corridor. This aquifer supplies most of the town's water. Geology continued to haunt the town after every heavy rain and particularly during the hurricanes of 1954-55.

Almost all of the major new home development lay west of Main, Central, and Lincoln Streets, and on Crow Point. The one exception was a small subdivision north of Prospect Street and west of the town forest. Across Main Street from this, and behind the South Elementary School, Investment Realty Trust and Holden Realty began the largest development, Liberty Pole. Across Cushing Street to its north, James Kimball continued building south of High Street. Further up the west side and south of Lincoln Street, Alfred Cole was expanding Bradley Park. And at the northwest corner of Crow Point, Bayview Realty and Best Realty were building large homes at what became known as Bel Air and Kimball Beach.

Regulating what land was available were zoning and the Board of Health's new powers relating to water supply, sewage disposal, and drainage. Despite these restrictions, the number of dwellings increased between 1949 and 1958 by more than a thousand, from 2961 to 3980.

The dream of the single family home on a large, grassy space with lots of fresh air, "for the sake of the children," belonged not just to the professional and middle-management families who came. There were others, part of the exodus from crowded triple-deckers in South Boston and Dorchester. These new populations with their numerous cars and children created and then collided with other forms of crowding: inadequate numbers of classrooms, roads clogged with commuters, too few parking spaces. Their largest expectation, as in other suburbs, was that there would be good schools.

The school problem was most immediate and overriding. In the twenty years leading up to 1950, enrollment had jumped 62 percent from 1294 to 2098. In one more year, it reached 2231. By 1952, there were 298 kindergartners, almost three times the number graduated from high school in 1951. By 1956, the school population had doubled in eleven years, reaching 3047. This does not include Hull students, who had attended Hingham High for seventy years. 1956 was to be their last year, and the change would mean the loss of annual receipts from Hull of $80,000.

Except for South Elementary, no schools had been built since the 1920s. Despite the urgency, the prelude in 1949 to a large building program was rancorous. South Elementary, later nominated for an architectural award, was thought by some to be a school with Lincoln and Rolls-Royce trimmings when a Ford or Chevrolet model would have been more appropriate. When the same architects received a $1,125,000 contract to enlarge and renovate the high school on Central Street, two School Committee members objected, even though six parent-teacher associations, later called "organizations," and a majority of the Advisory Committee agreed it was needed.

The town was "literally agog" over the issue. For the first time, the telephone company installed lines between the armory and the high school's Sanborn Auditorium to handle an overflow crowd of 1557. As the 1949 town meeting stretched past midnight, Keelah Bouvé, lawyer, Advisory Committee member, and long-time Scout leader, suggested sending the plans back to committee for something more affordable. He was met with foot-stamping. The meeting adjourned until Friday. Then, the School Committee minority prevailed with the passing of a motion to re-study.

The "hornet's nest" buzzed even more noisily when, in May, a majority of the committee ousted the high school principal of two years, Harold Rice. The high school "PTA," of which Mason Foley was president, sent Rice a letter of sympathy and vote of confidence. Almost

250 students went on strike. They left school, marched down Central Street to the square and up Main to Superintendent Anson Barber's home on Water Street, and asked for a public explanation. Such explanation, advised Moderator Arthur Whittemore, could be made public only with the principal's consent. Rice gave it to the senior class president. Many meetings followed. Press and radio coverage was substantial. Dudley Alleman objected to the laundering of so much dirty linen in public. Hingham's wrangling was receiving statewide attention.

The School Committee finally issued its explanation, faulting Rice for administrative failures. Over seven hundred voters petitioned for a special town meeting to decide whether to "demand the immediate resignation of the entire school committee." The petitioners now learned what legal power was vested by the state in school committees: they were not "agents of the town" and were "accountable to no higher authority." The voters' warrant article was "not in order."

Reaction to the student strikers suggests much about the decade. Even though class presidents and the president of the Student Council represented the strikers at meetings, the leaders were charged with being truants and products of the pernicious influence of progressive education. At masses, the curate of St. Paul's declared his abhorrence:

> to stage a revolt against lawful authority is bad. Since when do we have to give a reason for our action to children? . . . The seeds of Bolshevism and Communism are sown, when we can revolt against anything we don't like, and be approved for it.

The strikes had been orderly, the *Journal* conceded, but

> they smack of something that is un-American . . . . When the time comes that the children refuse to abide by the conventional standards set for them by those in authority whose professional lives have been devoted to those ends, then . . . there is danger.

The young were the cynosure of suburban life, but they were not to question authority. The seeds of the 1960s were being sown. Forgotten was early Hingham history, when the defiance of civil authority was sometimes viewed as a defense of liberty. Past were the unofficially sanctioned, innocent "Freak Days" of early June, when high schoolers paraded in outlandish garb. Hi-jinks were out; conformity was in.

Local alarmists were expressing the growing national fear of communism. Stalin had blockaded Berlin, Mao Tse Tung had conquered China, and President Truman vied with the political Right for leadership of anticommunist action. "Cold War" split the nation between those later to be called "hawks" and "doves." These were the years of hearings by the House Un-American Activities Committee and of the rise of Joseph McCarthy. Subversion seemed possible even in schools.

In the fall of 1949, a new high school principal, Marine veteran John Redmond, took office. Superintendent Barber left for a larger district. Committeeman Wallace Marden resigned to move to his "suburban farm" in Hanover. Lawyer Stuart Macmillan succeeded him. Macmillan would chair the committee until September, 1955, when his wife died, and two children at home took priority over the numerous nighttime meetings that are the obligation of School Committee members. Under his leadership, a tremendous program of school construction began.

New elementary schools and additions appeared in quick succession between 1951 and 1958: Foster, then an addition; two additions to South; and East. Construction was problematic. Foster, its addition, and the first addition to South were held up, first by the shortage, then the lack of steel, brought on by what is often called "the forgotten war" in Korea.

In 1954, the old high school on Central Street became Central Junior High, and at Pleasant and Union Streets, a new high school arose. An appropriation of $1,895,000 had been voted for it, without controversy, in June, 1952. Its land, however, presented problems. For the site, the town had taken by eminent domain a prime twenty-seven-acre parcel owned by cattleman Harry Michelson. The land had been appraised at $65,000, and Michelson was not happy about the $25,000 the town intended to pay. At the same time, it was rumored that he might donate the land if the high school was named after him. Moderator Arthur Whittemore, who had often represented the town in litigation, reminded the town that suits were expensive. Another $10,000 was voted for the land, and the playing field was named after Michelson. The new building quickly began to serve community groups such as the nine-year-old Theatre for Children, the Civic Chorus, and the Orchestra. Town meeting was first held here in 1957.

Other schools were increasingly crowded. Eight kindergarten classes were sometimes scheduled in four double sessions. A first class for special education students, mandated by the state in 1954, met at little Elm Street school. In what was called "no man's land" were fifth through eighth graders, shuffled around almost yearly due to the shortage of space. "Which school will my child go to next year?" was a frequent question. The only parents who knew for sure were those with approximately three hundred children in grades one through six at St. Paul's parochial school, which had opened in the fall of 1952.

By 1958, total enrollments had soared to over 3800, and next year, all seventh graders were at North School (leased from the federal government), and ninth graders were at the high school. The town struggled to keep teachers, now in great demand; but despite pay raises, many left for the more generous pay-scales of communities with higher property taxes and incomes, or tax-producing industries, or less land held by the federal government.

School growth meant more management and bureaucracy. By 1958, on the secondary level, both mathematics and English programs were directed by department heads. The English supervisor also served in a quasi public relations role, "marketing" the schools through press releases. Educational policy emphasized the togetherness of the team, "Working Together" for "Middle-of-the-road" education, which developed the child as a "product" who would take his or her place as a "right-thinking member of a democratic community." Samples of "the work done in our high school to preserve and encourage the American Way of Life" won a medal from the Freedom Foundation. But when that Way, "the power of America and her role for good in the world," seemed threatened in 1957 by the launching of "Sputnik I," educators tried to meet new expectations. The "middle-of-the-road" team approach was modified by "gifted child" classes in the fourth and fifth grades, "homogeneous grouping" in the junior high school, and a senior math seminar for college-bound high school students, who now constituted 65 percent of the graduates.

School programs expanded to include such subjects as driver education and remedial reading, and a summer school was opened. The high school added an audio-visual department with its own director. Television was introduced, and students watched the immensely popular new President Dwight D. Eisenhower deliver his inaugural and State of the Union addresses. These students were the first generation who could scarcely remember life without television. How rapidly its influence seeped into local consciousness and shaped local culture can be extrapolated from the amazing fact that in 1956 Americans were purchasing sets at the rate of 20,000 a day. By 1960, 90 percent of America's homes had television sets. Although busily occupied in their many supervised activities, Hingham children also had glimpses of Elvis Presley, the violence at Little Rock, Arkansas, and the Hungarian Revolution.

Like other burgeoning suburbs, Hingham was turning into a town "for the good of the children." By 1958, of a population of about 15,000, about 5500 were under seventeen years old. As children grew in numbers and importance, so did efforts to keep them happily involved in activities that developed the group loyalty of "team players" according to the "togetherness" ethic of the new American Dream. Mothers stayed home to carry on hectic new roles, and fathers became coaches. Team sports expanded to include the littlest boys. With television heroes such as Ted Williams and Jimmy Piersall, they were expected to imitate adults. Over three hundred boys played in the Minor, Farm, Little, and Babe Ruth Leagues. After player "auctions," those not making a team could attend a "clinic" at Foster School. Businesses, churches, and fraternal organizations sponsored teams. The Hingham Playground Commission formed a Cracker Barrel League; its team names, "Saltines," "Animal Crackers," "Graham Crackers," "Oysterettes," and "Dog Biscuits," gave a leaven of whimsy to a time when parents feverishly played their roles in this new democracy focused on children and sports.

In 1957, for the first time in twenty-nine years, Hingham High's football team was undefeated and won the "Class C" state championship. A thousand people attended Sports Award Night in the high school gym. The hockey team was South Shore champions. How this would have pleased William R. ("Bill") Cronin, who had coached baseball and football and initiated the enthusiasm for schoolboy hockey on the South Shore, and who had died the year before. On the playing field named in his memory, summer basketball games were played under lights installed by the Light Board free of charge.

At the harbor, expanded Red Cross programs included boating. Hundreds participated in swimming classes. At mid-decade, a band of Crow Point parents, excluded from the Yacht Club, formed a sailing club and hired an instructor, and their young sailors soon began winning prizes in the new Hingham Bay Turnabout Racing Association. How fast Crow Point had filled with young families was signaled when the selectmen set aside Howe Street and Whiton Avenue, in addition to Mann Street, for sledding.

Scouting, that stalwart of child life, grew and grew. There were continuities: Chauncey Burr, chairman of the Hingham Boy Scout Committee for twenty-five years, holder of the adult award of "Silver Beaver," presented the Eagle Scout award to his grandson Peter Burr, whose father, too, had been an Eagle Scout. But to avoid placing boys on a waiting list, Scout leader Malcolm Ripley asked them to indicate their interest early. Mrs. Winston Hall, elected president of the Girl Scout Council in 1951, oversaw troops growing from twelve to twenty in one year. In four years, the number of Scouts including Brownies almost doubled to six hundred, and there were now seventy-four leaders, including Bertha Stringer. When she retired in 1957, she had worked with Troop I, now the "Mariners," since its beginning forty years before.

Those other bulwarks of family life, the churches, were also growing. In 1957, Archbishop Richard Cushing established a second Roman Catholic parish in Hingham to serve those living south of High and Free Streets. The South Shore showed the largest growth in the archdiocese, with ten new parishes since 1948. Resurrection Church was built on what had been Fletcher Wason's poultry farm, the farm of Selectman Seth Sprague in the nineteenth century, and in 1637, the Great Lot of "Goodman" Edmund Pitts. In 1954 at 16 Hull Street, Glastonbury, a Benedictine monastery, opened on a site which, a few years before, had been refused by the town for a mini Boys Town. At New North Church, a membership once chiefly made up of Barneses, Bouvés, Blackmars, Hoyts, Lincolns, Stringers, and Thaxters, grew by 50 percent. St. John's Episcopal parish dedicated an enlarged church and a new church school building and added a curate to assist Rector John Gallop with its four hundred families. The Congregational Sunday School enrollment grew from 125 in 1937 to 820 twenty years later. The Methodists built ten new Sunday School classrooms. At the First Parish, a campaign to raise funds for a "new" parish hall was underway by 1958. In the past, the work of such campaigns was carried on by volunteers. Now, for a first time, the campaign was managed by a professional fundraising organization. The Archer mansion across Main Street was purchased. And the Second Parish added a hall on land given by a descendant of those Cushings who had caused such consternation when they built the meetinghouse in 1742. In Abel Cushing's house lived the new minister with his wife Carol Howard Robinson, who, he said, was virtually his associate minister.

Donald Robinson's preparation for his twenty-year ministry is an unusual story. He grew up on a farm in Wilmington and went to Harvard. He had early ancestral roots in the town, but he knew nothing of them until his parents moved to Hingham in 1923. Years later, he "picked up" his divinity training in Philadelphia. During the depression, he lived alone in Maine, "cutting my own fuel, growing my own vegetables . . . . I worked my taxes out on the road and functioned with very little money," doing a "lot of studying and writing." During World War II, he was a conscientious objector. Then, married to Carol Howard, he settled in Cooperstown, New York, where he ran a music business. In 1953, they moved back to Hingham and became active in the Second Parish. "When its minister left," Robinson recalled, "I think I received a

unanimous call. I believe there were two people who weren't very enthusiastic, but they didn't vote."

This wise, independent man was the right minister for his parish and
his times. He was installed in 1957 in a period of extraordinary growth:
"There were 480-odd families in the South Hingham area in 1936, and
forty years later, there were 2400." His idea of the church, as he explained it in 1979, would be a force for community through twenty
challenging and sometimes discordant years.

> I see the church as basically an instrument of reconciliation, and its
> purpose is to accept everybody . . . try to understand everybody, and
> as far as possible see *how* you can reduce or eliminate the tensions
> . . . . I have never gone along with the kind of aggressive social action
> that has been so prominent particularly among certain Unitarians and
> also in a number of other churches . . . the trouble with the aggressive
> social action thing is it somehow makes people into sheep and wolves
> . . . . My idea is to find the solution in which the sheep and wolves
> live together in harmony. It sounds perhaps absurd but I don't think
> it is . . . . The whole history of humanity has been possible because of
> the ability of one human being to cooperate with another . . . . Now
> this doesn't mean there isn't tension. There's a certain amount of
> tension that is constructive and that makes the thing possible, not a
> tension that tends to pull it apart.

There were numerous signs, during the 1950s, of the kind of con-
structive social outreach and ecumenism that Robinson was advocating.
All the Protestant churches continued their Thanksgiving Union services. Under the sponsorship of the Hingham Council of Churches,
Halloween trick-or-treaters appeared on doorsteps with UNICEF cartons on behalf of the world's needy children. St. Paul's, the First Parish,
and St. John's sponsored displaced families from eastern Europe, who
were warmly welcomed and settled into furnished homes.

A Hingham chapter of the American Field Service was founded. Its
program was designed to further international understanding by exchanges of high school students, who lived with host families in other
countries for a year. Mrs. Marge Farrell, a later president, recalled that
most of the founders were members of the Yacht Club and of St. John's
Church. When discouraged about funds, the group was reminded by
the Rev. John Gallop that "The Lord will provide." The Carl Harrises
were the first host family in Hingham. Among the earliest to cross the
Atlantic in the other direction was Alexander Macmillan. By 1979,
when the AFS marked its twenty-fifth anniversary, forty-six students

from twenty-six countries had come to Hingham, and thirty-six Hingham students had lived in twenty-two foreign countries.

Outreach and understanding were fortresses of hope during the 1950s, together with team spirit and youth, church and school, home and family. In its prizing of these values, Hingham was like many other American towns at the time. Whatever its limitations and blindspots, the decade has sometimes been unfairly stereotyped. Contemporary social critics found the emergent "culture of suburbia" a wasteland of materialistic conformity. Later analysts have rejected this caricature. It soon became easy to sentimentalize the 1950s, but for many a Hingham child, this *was* a golden time.

It is tempting to think of 1950s Hingham as a new version of the ancient ideas of the town seal: Church, School, Trainband, and Town Meeting. The difference was that now the magnitude of numbers strained such institutions from within, while threats from without—the possibility of atomic annihilation, of the destruction of democracy by communist expansion—were unthinkable but nevertheless perceived as real and immediate. The stability of this new way of life seemed further menaced when a Soviet atomic explosion in 1949 produced world-wide radiation and when, in 1950, the North Koreans strengthened fears of communist expansionism by invading the South and capturing Seoul.

Without waiting for Congress, President Truman ordered forces to Korea. Hingham's Marine Reserves, its National Guard Battery D, and the Quincy-Hingham Naval Reserve Battalion were called up. Private Arthur McLean wrote home. He had been slightly wounded, but fifty-eight men in his platoon had been lost in a trap.

> I am just one of the lucky ones. I guess God is with me. Three Chink divisions went through the 38th Regiment and surrounded the 23rd. I lost contact with my company so myself and two GI's from Love Company hid in a Korean house for a day and a half. Rice tastes pretty good when there is nothing else around.

Army Nurse Patricia Duffy wrote about the poverty, filth, and disease in Pusan. McLean and Duffy survived Korea. Richard Powers, a Marine pilot, did not. His helicopter crashed in Tokyo Bay in 1954, just a few weeks before he would have been twenty-one. His body was returned home a month later on his mother's birthday.

For some families, World War II and Korea were a continuum of horrific double jeopardies and losses and sad reminders. A refitted World War II ship was recommissioned in the name of Albert Tweedy, Jr., posthumously awarded the Navy Cross for action at the Battle of

Midway. Air Force pilot Eugene Merrill, like his brother in World War II, was decorated for flights in enemy territory. Jet pilot John Laskey, who had survived fifty-five combat missions over North Africa, Italy, and France, was killed when his plane crashed into a mist-enshrouded Korean mountain. The most excruciating loss was of two brothers, the first townsmen to die in enemy action in the two wars. When their sister unveiled the World War II plaque which bore, among many others, the name of William Rhodes, killed at Pearl Harbor, she could not know that their brother Victor would be killed in Korea a year later.

Nationwide, this was "Red Alert" time. Defense policy included a Strategic Air Command, missile rings around major cities, and civil defense. Turkey Hill became the site of a Nike missile installation. High school students were shown "Operation Crossroads," an official film of A-Bomb detonation at Bikini. The PTA sponsored a talk on "Living with the Atom." At Loring Hall, "Invasion U.S.A." depicted what things might be like after a bombing. A veteran of both wars told the South Shore Council of Rotary Clubs that "we must fight Communism by every means including all-out war." From "Teddy" Berg, father of the Latvian family sponsored by St. John's, the warning was, "The American People think too much about sports and television and the high price of groceries. They do not realize the Russian threat to their way of life." Even after Stalin's death in March, 1953, the execution of Julius and Ethel Rosenberg, the Korean cease-fire, and the censure and demise of chief witchhunter Senator Joseph McCarthy, anxiety remained understandably high. By 1954, both the United States and the U.S.S.R. had the hydrogen bomb.

Hingham reorganized itself into the presumed safety of a volunteer civil defense network, a modern unarmed "trainband." The town felt vulnerable to attack with those prime targets the Depot and the Annex and their stores of high explosives. Evelyn Cheney, president of the local Red Cross, presided over disaster planning. Buildings were selected for shelters and hospitals. Fire Chief Kimball succeeded Albert Tweedy as director of what was now a town department of civil defense. The degree of organization was remarkable. In the event of attack, eight "divisions" were ready and would mobilize. Fire horn signals, for use in case of "imminent air attack," were published, and a civil defense booklet was issued. Divisions and fire departments joined in metropolitan alerts and drills. All was "ready at a minute's notice to protect us against any disaster."

This organization of defense against the man-created terror of *possibility* proved of inestimable service during three *real natural* disasters:

[376]

hurricanes "Carol" and "Edna" in 1954 and "Diane" in 1955. Rainfall for the two years, 62 inches and 56 inches, was far above the annual average of 42 inches. During "Diane," over 13 inches fell in three days.

"Carol" (August 31, 1954) did even more damage than the hurricane of 1938. At his uncle Norman Hersey's house at 17 Hersey Street, young John P. Richardson wrote in his diary:

> 11 A.M. I hear the snap of branches; some large branches give a report like a rifle as they snap . . . . The house vibrates . . . . There are clapboards—yellow clapboards hitting the house . . . . I nearly shout to Hersey to be heard above the din . . . . I see two or three shutters blowing end over end down the street. We are now sitting in the middle of the dining room and there is a crash of glass—a limb broke through the kitchen window onto the kitchen table—the catalpa tree is leaning over—I watch it go slowly then it crashes down . . . .
>
> 1 P.M. The atmosphere has a strange sweet odor from all the crushed vegetation.

Leaf-covered branches and tree trunks had to be removed from the town's 125 miles of road before electric and telephone service could be restored. The Light Department still had only one truck and seven men. Further, only linemen from other *municipal* companies could help, some from as far away as Pennsylvania and Ohio. Compared to 1938, there were more trees, more roads, more telephones, more refrigerators full of food, more garbage disposals and appliances, and more impatient customers.

The declaration of a state of emergency allowed departments to spend beyond their appropriations. Highway Superintendent Herbert Cole hired eighty men beyond his regular twenty. Auxiliary police and firefighters, trained for civil defense, assisted the regular police and coordinated with permanent and "call" firefighters. None of the fire alarm circuits was working, so civil defense radio operators took up the fire watch. A canteen group served meals, coffee, and doughnuts. Ice, candles, and flashlights were newly appreciated. With the help of payloaders, cranes, and an "emergency illumination truck," almost 80 percent of the town's power was restored in a little over a week. On September 11, all of this work was undone by "Edna."

During "Diane" in 1955, three families at Main and Friend Streets had to be evacuated, and the Fire Department pumped out 450 basements. In South Hingham, well water was unpotable, and hydrants were spigoted to provide safe drinking water. The Highway Department had begun blasting to straighten, widen, and deepen the Weir, and reconstructing, resurfacing, and re-engineering the drainage of many streets. Nevertheless, the Weir River was rampaging, Crooked Meadow River overflowed, and many streets were washed out. Yet another dangerous effect of growing numbers became apparent. The spreading town was settling itself on its water bed, paving over the land mass, which, under normal conditions, could absorb most precipitation. In the ten years from 1949 to 1958, almost always unanimously, the town voted to accept as town ways fifty-four new developer-built streets. Beginning in 1954, the selectmen published a disclaimer for damages on these streets.

Numbers also meant more formal regulation, bureaucracy, and professionalization. Hingham's well-admired Chief "Kimmie" professionalized his department by trying to "cover more fires with the permanent personnel . . . on silent alarm boxes"—that is, without signaling for the volunteers. His energy and diplomacy paid off in more permanent staff, increased salaries, a shorter work week, a second aerial ladder to cover West Hingham and Crow Point, and an alarm cable to South Fire Station. But added regulations required manpower. One firefighter spent almost full time checking compliance with safety rules for oil burner installations, nursing homes, and all public buildings.

Tree Warden John Fee was busy, too. The nursery operation, the selling of thinned wood, the spraying of trees for private customers, all saved money or added to the town treasury. His department maintained the beach, about fifty acres around Triphammer Pond, and the park areas, which grew in number from fifty to sixty. By 1958, there were almost two hundred miles of tree-lined streets, but the warden had eight instead of nine men.

After the abnormal rainfalls of 1953-55, mosquitoes were breeding everywhere. Saltmarshes were drained, culverts cleared, catchbasins sprayed. Fogging machines were used near sensitive areas such as the water supply, henneries, the dairies of the eighteen licensed milk dealers, and pasteurizing plants. Two thousand six hundred fifty acres of the town were sprayed with DDT. A federal, state, and county program of aerial spraying had begun in 1950 to prevent the ravages of gypsy moths. To stop army worms, the tree warden sprayed the hay crops of some local dairymen with methoxyclor. He sprayed three times a year with DDT to control elm bark beetles, carriers of the fungus which was destroying Hingham's magnificent elms. The town was being bombarded with chemicals, in which the 1950s had unquestioning faith.

Despite the spraying, pruning, and feeding of healthy elms and the prompt removal of sick ones, marked on their trunks with a painted circle, a sign of death, the recorded count of elms lost in the decade was over nine hundred. Fee tried to balance the loss with hundreds of plantings of other species. Elms were lost in the hurricanes, too, and so were many trees in the town forest. One family, near the forest on Prospect Street, lost a hundred trees during "Carol," many of them old pines. The owner watched as the top of a huge one snapped off and aimed directly at the house. A miraculous gust of wind sailed it over the roof.

Growth in numbers finally forced the town to take action in the long delayed matter of sewers. Soil in the north section did not percolate well, and after big storms, septic tanks and cesspools caused problems. Continued warnings from state and town boards of health resulted in nine unanimous votes at the town meeting of 1955. The town committed itself to the complex and expensive project of sewering, connecting North Hingham to the South Metropolitan Sewer District. Abuttors were assessed $5 a linear foot, about a third of the cost. Mains were laid on North, South, Thaxter, and Lincoln Streets, and in the Otis Hill area. It remained for the Board of Health to order recalcitrant major polluters of the former channel of the Town Brook to connect with the system. It did so in 1958.

Increasing regulation was seen in other areas of public health. The health officer now inspected the milk supply, seven child-care centers, four nursing homes, and eating and drinking establishments. Other measures included the fluoridation of water and immunization, with Salk vaccine, against polio. During the largest polio epidemic in Massachusetts history (1955), there were twenty cases in Hingham, eight of the paralytic form. On the advice of the Massachusetts Polio Advisory Committee, the ongoing immunization was postponed, and school opening was delayed, but after that, there were no recorded cases. In 1958, for the first time, there was no whooping cough, and there had been no diphtheria for eight years. These achievements were credited to immunization and the "enforcement of pasteurization." If science had created terror by splitting the atom, it was also eliminating some of nature's old scourges.

The scourge of garbage remained. There were few bidders for the garbage collection contract, and none was local, for raising pigs was now taboo. In two years, some three hundred homes were added to the route for twice-weekly collection. The collector asked for an amendment to his contract. He had many new stops, but he found "there is not much garbage, and the quality of it is poorer." The Advisory Committee and the town voted "no action." But he was the only bidder for an ensuing contract, and there was no choice but to accept his more than 50 percent increase in charges. In what may have been the last bit of tongue-in-cheek humor in town reports, Richard Barrett, chairman of the Garbage Committee, reported:

> The customary inland tests were conducted regularly at the Committee's experimental laboratory and established that the quality of Hingham's garbage remains high, markedly superior to that of Cohasset and other neighboring communities.

> There was one innovation consisting of individual tests by various members of the Committee . . . . Each member of the Committee, after foregoing collection of garbage at his own residence for periods ranging from ten days to two weeks, reported in favor of continuing to collect.

The inexorable *qualitative* changes produced by numbers were stunningly evident in town government. The town still sought to act as if it were small. In 1949, the committee to study the advisability of representative town meeting and of a town manager had been discharged. When the issue surfaced again in 1956, a new committee thought open town meeting was still functioning well, mainly due to the work of the Advisory Committee, but also because groups such as the Taxpayers Association, Civic Council, and League of Women Voters were keeping citizens active and informed. A representative town meeting, it argued, would make government more remote. The concept of "true democracy," which holds that every person is part of the legislature, would be lost. Many towns had adopted representative town meeting chiefly because they had no large building, whereas Hingham now had the high school. The proposal in Hingham for a representative town meeting assumed that delegates would be elected from precincts. When, in 1958, a committee recommended precincts to increase voter participation, the motion was defeated. For one change there was consensus. To control the long-winded, town meeting voted unanimously to limit a speaker on any subject to ten minutes the first time and five the second. There was little time for oratory in a decade of numbers.

In hope of preserving open town meeting, Charles Barnes left the town a bequest of $50,000, required to be matched within ten years, for a new town hall. In a eulogy of Barnes, Arthur Whittemore, by then a justice of the Supreme Judicial Court, said that if open town meeting was to work, there would have to be, as in other large legislative bodies, reliance on the work of committees. He urged voters to attend sessions of the Advisory Committee and arrive at consensus *before* town meeting. It was a very old idea of commonalty, and it should have worked in a time when togetherness and amiability were national suburban ideals. But the consensus principle, quite effective in the town's early years, was grounded in each person's knowing and influencing his neighbor. In the 1950s, a person could not know many neighbors.

These years marked the growth of what have recently been described as two constituencies: those who go to town meetings and those who go only to the polls. A third constituency, we suggest, also emerged: the elected or appointed members of town government. They grew in numbers. Not counting committees working on school expansion, or others that merged, or those formed and discharged, committees increased by nine. Their proliferation distributed power but also coalesced it. Of the members of the new Capital Outlay Committee, one was selected from the Planning Board by its chair, and two from the Advisory Committee by its chair. Three were chosen by Moderator Earle Carr, who, in his first year, made eighty-seven appointments. The appointive responsibility of the moderator is a little-noted but crucial political fact of modern Hingham.

The Capital Outlay Committee's first report appeared in 1956. Working on a six-year cycle to avoid a wildly fluctuating tax rate, it recommended the priority and sequence of capital needs above $5000. This was light years away from the late nineteenth-century Committee of Fifteen, with Amos Humphrey as a leading member, that evaluated any anticipated expenditure over $300. The permanent new committee gave needed relief to the Advisory Committee, the Planning Board, and the selectmen. It is claimed that this committee has never been influential, but influential or not, the Capital Outlay Committee offered intelligent, comprehensible explanation of town financing, much needed when numbers were puzzling and costs were spiraling.

In 1956, by a strange confluence of dates, the committee's *ex officio* member, Town Accountant Irving Botting, resigned and died within two weeks. In his last year, he had watched the Excess and Deficiency Fund become so depleted that the town had to borrow, for the first time in many years, to meet operating expenses before the collection of taxes. Like its people and the nation, Hingham was working on credit. With a debt ratio of 12 percent (the "ratio of outstanding indebtedness to assessed valuation"), the town's credit rating dropped from AA to A. It would have to pay higher interest.

A suburb's *bête noire*—the "major determinant that shapes the physical, political, and social character of suburbia"—is the property tax. New homeowners felt their taxes were unfairly high relative to those of owners who had purchased homes before the war. In 1950, Hingham voted for an independent assessment, but when a booklet of assessments was published in 1952, it included only the valuations made by town assessors, not the results of the independent survey. People had trouble getting access to these results, and suspicions worsened. The outcome was another committee, on Assessors' Office Practices, which recommended assessing all property at 55 percent of fair market value and predicted this would add $7 million in revenue to the $30 million being collected. A full-time lawyer was hired to work with the committee and new assessors, and by 1958, the projected tax rate of $79 was down to an actual figure of $73.

Other efforts to make government more efficient included streamlining and shortening the annual town book. Everyone was urged to abbreviate. School reports became much smaller. Amendments to the job descriptions and payscales of town employees were no longer published but put on file at the town offices. Human particulars were abstracted into numbers. Birth, marriage, and death records became merely a numerical account and remained so for eighteen years. The selectmen hoped the reports would be "more interesting reading." Instead, they became dense, clinical, depersonalized numbers: statistics, accounts, charts, and projections. The town meeting warrant, as a result of new kinds of articles, became a more legalistic document, with mushrooming citations of laws and provisos. Unlike his predecessors, lawyer-moderator Carr would not give legal counsel as he conducted meetings. He was "moderator only." Legal counsel was a separate function.

The bureaucratizing and legalizing of government is seen vividly in the story of the Foster School Construction Committee. The contractor had gone bankrupt. The town faced the possibility of unfinished work and suits by unpaid subcontractors. The chairman recommended written, not oral, inspection agreements, a central authority for all accounting and paperwork, and a "floating" member to advise on paperwork required by the town and state. His chief recommendation, however, was that legal counsel be sought *before* any contracts were signed. Governmental bodies would increasingly defer to lawyers.

And accountants. However astronomical appropriations appeared, however much the town was spending beyond its income, accountants understood how much money also came from federal, state, and county governments: all or part of the monies for road work and sidewalks, civil defense, school construction (almost 40 percent), purchases of school buses (33 percent), school lunches, public assistance (69-74 percent), rebuilding seawalls, dredging mooring basins, and stocking waterways and woodlands for sportsmen. Only accountants and business people would understand the complex statements of the Light Board, which paid back interest and loans, began to pay small profits into the treasury, and paid a "hidden dividend" by absorbing all costs for street lighting except a charge for the electricity. Could growing numbers of voters understand enough to play active roles? Would they believe that the magic could go on forever, or, by inertia, choose to remain in the dark?

To the "government constituency," voters appeared apathetic. Two "special issues," however, drew crowds at town meetings, reflecting a suburb's priorities. One, discussed earlier, was schools. The other was zoning. Zoning, in part a modern variant of a Puritan town's mechanisms of walling in and warning out, was almost the only means by which a suburb could control developers. But zoning grew more complicated. Many zoning articles tinkered with small areas, others with "grandfathering," others with controversial "spot zoning"—for example, the defeated move for a skating rink at the Country Club. Larger changes involved creating new districts or switching, say, from "Residential A" to "Industrial" or "Industrial Park," as happened in Hingham's southwest corner. These changes were made in anticipation of the Southeast Expressway, whose completion to Derby Street in 1959 opened a new chapter.

Equally portentous was a change whose effects no one could anticipate: the release by the federal government of some three thousand acres of Hingham land. At the close of 1958, the Navy peremptorily announced it would declare the Ammunition Depot, the Annex, and the shipyard surplus. National defense now relied increasingly on guided missiles and aircraft. By 1957, the aircraft industry was the nation's biggest employer. The need declined for the conventional ammunition stored and reworked in Hingham. Townspeople lost jobs; businesses lost customers. The town, once a federally impacted area, would no longer receive hefty amounts of federal aid for educating children of those living or working on property of the federal government. The land declared surplus was still nontaxable and would remain so for years while the Navy kept changing its mind about future ownership. Land, for so long a measure of citizen wealth, had become a burden for the town.

Hingham had, however, been spared much rapid and/or exploitative development. Fenced and off-limits for recreation, especially for hunters, federal land had become a refuge for wildlife. Mason Foley could still take pleasure in seeing a grey fox go over his stone wall, an otter on the way to Turkey Hill Run, and deer prints in the place he loved best, Triphammer. The days of this wildlife were numbered. The new young people filling the town would scarcely know them.

They were too young as well to know much of Hingham's human past. "In 1950, when I was sixteen," John Richardson remembers,

> I did some yard work in the summer. One of my customers was Elizabeth R. Gates [born 1859] and Lillian C. Thayer [born 1872]. They lived in a tall, pale yellow house at 33 Lincoln Street . . . . The wheel barrow was old, the rakes were old, the hand cultivator was ancient and bore a date of 1857 on the iron handle . . . . One day while I was cultivating the roses, Miss Thayer appeared with a big, wide sun bonnet. She informed me that Miss Gates wanted to see me . . . . Miss Thayer took me through the cellar and up the stairs to the kitchen . . . .

> Everything was spic and span but ever so old. There was a wooden ice box, tinware and graniteware pots and pans, and a huge soapstone sink, half covered by a wood top and exposed brass pipes and faucets all gleaming bright like gold . . . . I followed Miss Thayer upstairs . . . . Miss Gates was in a small chamber sitting in a rocking chair by the window . . . . I can recall vividly how old she looked—long white hair, a long plain dress, nylon stockings rolled down, and old white shoes.

> "So you are Mr. Hersey's boy?" "Yes, ma'am," I said, "he's my uncle." "Miss Thayer," she said, "tells me you are doing good work in our yard—my father [dry goods dealer John D. Gates had died in 1885] planted the roses long years ago." I can remember thinking that "even the roses were old." . . .

> I never saw Miss Gates again. Little did I know then that I was face to face with history . . . face to face with those who knew George Lincoln, who walked by Hingham's rotting wharves, who perhaps had tea in the home of John D. Long. In 1950, Miss Gates and Miss Thayer were in themselves two of Hingham's most valuable unrenewable resources.

What could the young know of the shapers of the town where they realized their dream? A number had departed: Tim Murphy, who had made the town forest; Morton Smith, conservationist and planner; moderator Charles Barnes; J. Irving Botting, town accountant for thirty-nine years; William L. Foster, selectman for forty. Who remembered, when old blacksmith Matthew Huntley died, his wrought iron work for the Arts and Crafts Society?

Fourth of July parade, with Francis Wright as "Uncle Sam": oil, 1961, Esther Lovell.

Crow Point Sailing Club. Kathleen Curtis identifications, left to right, the children: Catherine Sheehan, Gayle Allen, ?, Meridith Munzig; the fathers: Gerry Bruin, Harry Roberts, Thomas Munzig, Thomas E. Curtis.

The site after the demolition of the Railroad Depot (1849–1949) in Hingham Square, today the location of Bowl and Board and British Relief. Two buildings directly ahead have since vanished: Donovan Drug Company and Ford's Block.

Moving (May, 1949) the house built (1803) by Jacob Beal, from South Street to 7 Bates Way. Contractor James Gordon set the house on two sixty-foot wood beams, rollers, and a crib of wood blocks to move it.

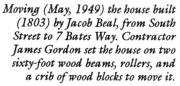

The Booket Brigade (November, 1966). School children and Boy Scouts helped move 60,000 books in two days.

The Board of Selectmen and five former chairmen of the board (photograph taken late 1962–early 1963). Left to right: Willis Butterworth (1962–1970), Albert Tweedy (1942–1950), James Gordon (1951–1969), Herman Stuetzer (1955–1961), George A. Cole (1931–1946), Lewis Perkins (1946–1955), Mason Foley (1961–1968), Harold Downing (1950-1962).

Albert W. Kimball (1908–1980), Hingham's first permanent fire chief (1942-1980). He served in the department for forty-five years.

Sam (Salvatore L.) Amonte on a frigid December morning in the Square in 1961. He served in the Police Department from 1953 until his retirement in 1988.

"Hornstra's Barn": watercolor, 1980, Barbara Menzies. The barn was demolished in 1981. The farm is now the site of the condominium park "The Meadows."

Aerial view of Cushing's Neck, World's End, the Brewer-Walker farm, and Nantasket, July, 1928.

How many knew of their great loss with the death of William A. Dwiggins? Internationally renowned, he had worked in his home at Hingham Centre for half a century as a book designer for Knopf, a designer of typefaces for Merganthaler Linotype Corporation, a calligrapher, painter, author, playwright, and whittler of marionettes. His life was wholly integrated and centered. His wife Mabel said of "William," he "loved his work so much [that] no day was long enough." Infinite patience, a whimsical, sunny disposition, and complete originality underlay his huge *oeuvre*. Although childless, the Dwiggenses never lost their own childlike sense of play. They created unforgettable memories for some fortunate local children, who came with their elders to marionette shows, first in the theatre in the Dwggins garage, and later in the tasteful, small theatre, seating about fifty, which Dwiggins built in 1937 across from his home on the corner of Leavitt and Irving Streets. At Christmas time, they carolled there, and a tiny marionette Santa distributed candies. Above the proscenium of the stage was Dwiggins's cut paper transparency of Ho-Tai, the God of Happiness and patron of little children. On those Christmases, Mabel Dwiggins recalled, the building's seams almost burst with joy. On Christmas Day, 1956, Dwiggins died. Carved on his gravestone are these words: "It was a grand adventure—I am content."

From the square disappeared the bulky silhouettes of the railroad depot and the Cushing House (in 1949) and of Ford's Block (1952), its place later used for the Talbots parking lot. Two small waiting stations replaced the depot, but they would be redundant when passenger trains ended in 1959. The Cushing House site, location of the present post office, temporarily became a merchants' parking lot. The tidal mill pond had just been filled and covered to become Station Street and another parking lot, this one for three hundred cars. The pipe which ran beneath to the Home Meadows was undersized and failed to allow a monthly floodtide to surge and rinse the meadows adequately with salt water. The salt meadow became a "brackish freshwater marsh." The depot, the hotel, the pond, even the meadow had surrendered to the automobile.

Fourth of July fireworks ended; the bonfire flickered and expired forever. Too many roof tops were too close. But the parade grew larger, and the auto's half-century gave birth to a special feature: antique cars.

Much farm land was sold for development, but there were still the dairies of Hornstra, Kress, Peirce, and Threlfall; Penniman Hill and Delmar Farms; Saponaro's stable on Turkey Hill; the Josselyn Nurseries. On High Street, Michelson still traded cattle. What soon would happen was explained later by elderly farmer Harold Newcombe: in the 1960s, the cost of grain, higher wages, and taxes that "kept going up and up . . . just put them [farmers] out of business. I don't think there's a cow left in Hingham now." Some land was saved. The gift to the town of John D. Long's eleven-acre estate from his daughter Margaret was finally accepted after a surprising six-year delay. His home off Cottage Street and his barn, with the revolving wooden platform for turning carriages, were promptly demolished. Charles Barnes's gift of Button Island was accepted with less delay. All four harbor islands now belonged to the town. In the next decade, a remarkable campaign would be mounted to save more land from the development mania.

The lost opportunity of the 1950s, as so often in the past, was the failure to purchase the Water Company. Water prices rose. In 1958, the town appropriated $40,000 for hydrant "water rental" and was short of hydrants and mains. But town and company again could not agree on a price; efforts to break the 1879 charter failed again; and no law allowed the taking of a water company by eminent domain. Officials and committee members had worked hundreds of hours. At an adjourned town meeting in 1958, with fewer than three hundred voting, a motion for a municipal water supply lost. The night before, fifteen hundred had turned up to vote negatively on an addition to the junior high school.

One of the decade's gains was a number of new businesses. In 1946, there were 134 businesses; by 1957, 248. On Green Street, to serve the many new businesses and households, the telephone company erected a building for its new dial system. The Chamber of Commerce revived, and the *Journal* was filled with advertising. Even so, rising costs necessitated raising the subscription to $3.50 annually, the first hike in almost a century. Single copies cost ten cents and were still available at Hennessy's. In 1953, Kitty had sold the business, with her blessings, to two Holbrook brothers, who kept the old name. When the shop opened in 1903, it carried a total of forty copies of daily newspapers for sale; fifty years later, it carried 700 in the morning and 750 in the evening.

Hingham remained, consistent with the theme of the tercentenary pageant, a town of families, now living in four thousand homes. Socially, however, it was less like its prewar self than it was like our present. Social life was less public, more home-centered; picnics and street fairs gave way to the cocktail party and the backyard barbecue. The informality of the barbecue included dogs (their population grew by over 40 percent), the games of children, and visits with neighbors, whose conversations played on all the themes of this chapter: school, church, sports, services, homes, cars, television, the young, and other components of the "dream".

Signs of flaws, however, appeared. The dream was "for the good of the children," but some children grew restless. They began defacing gravestones, pulling up flags and markers of the war dead, and breaking windows. Break-ins, thefts, and homemade bombs followed. The Girl Scout house was defaced with paint bombs. The boys' lavatory at the high school was partly destroyed. A bomb scare was phoned to the police. An elaborate murder hoax tied up local and state police and sent a diver to explore the bottom of the quarry. In 1954, Police Chief Oscar Beck said, "We have no juvenile delinquency in Hingham." Four years later, he had one hundred cases involving minors, together with confiscated zip guns and switch blades. He blamed the availability of cars, increased drinking among the underaged, and too-lenient parents. A new chapter of social upheaval was in sight.

Social organizations were also changing in number and nature. The Kiwanians (1951) and the Lions (1955) joined the Rotarians among chapters of international service organizations. Countless drives of charitable societies were merged in a metropolitan United Community Fund. The dwindled membership of the Wompatuck Club made a gift of what is now the Community Center. A Library Association formed to upgrade the collection, and in 1958, a young Simmons graduate, Walter Dziura, became librarian. At the Congregational Church, the elderly joined a Golden Age Club, started by Ruth Spencer.

The voices of other women were heard beyond the kitchen, family room, backyard, and playground. Members of the League of Women Voters still met at the home of Mrs. Morton Smith. For the first time, women served as jurors, were elected as library trustees, and appointed to the Advisory Committee. After ham radio operator Larry Stein picked up signals from Russia's spy satellite, "Sputnik I," in 1957, two women took out a half-page ad in the *Journal* calling for a South Shore branch of the National Committee for SANE Nuclear Policy.

That year, from Pleasant Street, a wise lady, the first woman elected to the Planning Board, made a salutary plea. In sorting out the confusion of issues and needs of the times, she said, citizens should think not in personal terms, but of the effects public decisions would have on the future. She would not live to see the new decade—she died in 1958—but her admonition would be much needed. It was the voice of Amy Howard.

CHAPTER TWENTY-SIX

The Shocking Sixties

It was the best of times, it was the worst of times.

Bliss was it in that dawn to be alive,
But to be young was very Heaven [or Hell?].

IN the 1950s, the Developer was king. In the 1960s, he was confronted by the Planner. Together through the decade, they did an uneasy dance. With the dramatic increase of Hingham's population between 1948 and 1958, planning took on urgency. Planners projected a population by 1975 of 30,000 with 6600 in the schools. A legion of volunteers, activists in an activist decade, struggled with the future. Some people realized that there were places, resources, and values to be conserved. An elusive essence, "Hingham's character," they strongly believed, must be saved. But in a decade so shocking, many shocks sent planners off the track.

On June 30, 1959, after 110 years, the last passenger train ran over the track through Hingham. The trains were decaying. John Richardson remembers his ride from Boston on January 6: "In the dirty old cars with lights flickering on and off . . . . Hardly any heat. My feet were nearly frozen and there was heavy frost coating the interior of the train's windows." Old George Melcher wrote from New Hampshire to reminisce about the 7:32 smoker of long ago, the card-players, conductor Fred Hersey, Wash James prudently meeting the Boston partygoers at the midnight train, and the thoughts of "a small boy going down to the station with a lantern to meet my father." And at noon, September 9, 1959, seven and a half miles of the Southeast Expressway opened from Braintree to a barrier at Derby Street. Already it seemed too small. Some felt like poor John O'Kane:

[388]

Three years ago I had a dream of a nice home in a quiet town near the water, where I could go boating and fishing and have good transportation to my office in Boston . . . . Since August my wife and I have had to drive. . . . After two months of trying to stay alive and drive at the same time, we are ready to quit. I reach home at night a nervous wreck, and my wife has worn out the floor mat helping to steer and put on the brakes. My dream . . . has evaporated in less than a year— apartment, anyone?

In the spring of 1959, entering its rapid transit phase, the government on Beacon Hill had proposed expansion of the Metropolitan Transit Authority line to terminate at Water Street, Hingham. Subway cars would be "thundering into our midst," under overpasses, on a depressed roadbed through the square, to turn around in Home Meadows. Here was the "gravest crisis in one hundred years." An "elongated Times Square shuttle" would transform the town into "another Dorchester or Everett" and encourage odious developments such as multistory housing projects. Petitions flew, opposers of the opposers raised their own chorus, and "acrimonious feeling" was as rampant as it had been "a score of years ago when the subject of zoning split the town." A minister admonished from his pulpit: "I do not want Hingham to become a slum. But Hingham will become a slum if her citizens . . . persist in resorting to the language of the slums." When selectmen did a turnabout and endorsed a "T" terminus at West Hingham, there was unprecedented talk of impeachment. Finally, in 1969, the Quincy "T" terminus was settled on, and one part of the ordeal of planning was temporarily over.

The expressway had turned Hingham's historical geography on its head. Expressway traffic menaced Main and Cushing Streets, and a struggle began for an alternate north-south highway. Liberty Plainers were now "most convenient," linked to a phenomenon of industrial relocation that made Route 128 into Electronics Highway. "Massachusetts means Progress," the state's Commerce Commissioner told Hingham, and "those who would attempt to maintain a 'status quo' or are content to pursue the 'even tenor of their ways' are caught in a continuing process of adjustment and adaptation." Developer Wallace Marden agreed, and a majority of voters did, too. They zoned about six hundred acres in the expressway's path as industrial park.

Commerce arrived before industry. The expressway soon split the park, and on the east side, in 1961, Marden began Hingham Plaza. Great ditches, ten to twenty feet deep, were dug through dense hemlock and white cedar swamp to drain off water. Industrial development was slower. The breakthrough came in 1964, when the Merriman Company planned its factory for yacht fittings and textile rings. Before it was finished (1966), it had a neighbor under construction, Spencer Press. Lounge Inc. followed next year, and North Terminal in 1968. Such operations were moving out from the city, where blighting was already underway. As 1968 closed, the Development and Industrial Commission, established in 1962, could point with pride to twelve new industrial plants in as many years.

The town wanted such arrivals to be "desirable" and remote. But hardly out of sight was the shipyard, its 223 acres and seventy-two buildings still owned by the federal government, leased and subleased to small businesses and industries. Abruptly, in 1963, it was again declared "surplus," and the General Services Administration negotiated a bargain sale to Grossman's for only $553,000 when an appraisal estimated the value of the yard at $9 million. The Planning Board asked indignantly: how could one federal agency spend millions on urban renewal while another sold "a now run-down, blighted area, in such a manner that the local community is unduly burdened" by its condition and low valuation?

The ordeal of planning was repeatedly aggravated by the Navy's changes of mind. At the start of the 1960s, it still owned almost one third of Hingham. The selectmen were "much concerned with the orderly growth of our town, and when in the future the West Hingham Ammunition Depot and the Annex are released by the GSA, we want no radical expansion that will change the character of Hingham." The Depot was set to haul down its flag in 1962, but when the town asked for the flagpole, the Navy cited "potential further use of the Depot," and the reply was similar when Depot land was sought for the garaging of school buses. In 1966 came another scare: the Navy announced $9 million plans for six to seven hundred housing units. Not until 1972 would the town acquire most of the Depot. Cat and mouse games over the Annex ended in 1966 when the state obtained title to most of it for what would become Wompatuck State Park. Years would pass before it was improved for park use. So went the ordeal of planning.

The magnitude of the ordeal could be seen in the number of bodies involved, a roster of civic volunteerism unexcelled in the town's history. In addition to standing boards and committees, more than twenty groups, official and unofficial, worked endless hours on problems and emergencies. In one way or another, most of them related to land, its use, its acquisition, or its protection. In addition, groups worked on emergencies in transportation, waste disposal, historic and environmental preservation, and new issues in education. Three different moderators and seven different selectmen served during these years. Last but not least, the Capital Outlay Committee tried to guide the town through a huge program of public investment.

As remarkable as this record of volunteerism was the willingness of the town of the 1960s to pay the costs. School construction was the biggest item. East School opened as the 1950s closed. South Junior High (1961-63) was the first project of the new decade, followed by additions to Central (1963-64) and the High School (1964-65). The town bought the Schirmer property on the south side of High Street in 1966, and in 1968, it voted almost $2 million for Plymouth River School, which opened in 1969. In the same years, the new library and town office building were greeted with balks and grumbles, mostly aesthetic, at architect Carl Koch's plans. What was touted as "classic hip roof" style reflecting Old Ship sparked such outbursts as "Good Lord! Is that the best they could do?" "Mongrel architecture, pure ranch with an Old Ship roof," and "color it orange and call it Howard Johnson's." "Dodge City's inhabitants would love . . . so many hitching posts!" Yet, in 1965 funds for the office building passed "without so much as a bleat," and funds for the library were approved unanimously. In half an hour, voters approved over $1 million in capital outlay.

On a March Saturday in 1965, citizens went for the last time to vote in the "creaky confines" of Agricultural Hall, now in its ninety-eighth year. The following week, "If you want to get a fair idea of what a place looks like after it has been hit by a bomb or by heavy gunfire, just take a peek . . . at Agricultural Hall." Late in 1966, town officers turned over their old building on lower Main Street to the School Department; and stretched along three-tenths of a mile from the once-controversial old library to the controversial new,

> with yeoman help from the Highway Department, the tireless work of Friends of the Library and a devoted staff, and above all with the fabulous "Booket Brigade" consisting of Boy Scouts and School Children, nearly 60,000 books were transported . . . in two days' time.

Soon the ornate old building was "no longer even an ailing ghost, but the liberal spirit of Albert Fearing lives on in this new building."

Voters were liberal in other expenditures, too. Appropriations had first topped $1 million in 1946. By 1958, they were over $3 million, and by 1970, when taxpayers revolted, over $8 million. In the two decades from 1949 to 1968, the budgets of town departments rose by 200 percent to 500 percent, maturing debt by 1045 percent, debt interest by 1319 percent. America, both public and private, was on its great credit-spending spree.

The major jump was in education. In each of these decades, the appropriations for the schools increased by the same percentage. However, the enrollment increase in the second decade was less than half the increase in the first. What, other than increased enrollment, could explain the rise in costs? The answer was America's optimistic obsession with education in the 1960s. With the launching of "Sputnik" in 1957, complacency about American schools had suffered a shock. Education became a priority of national defense. President Eisenhower signed the National Defense Education Act, and governments poured money into education. America felt sure of winning, sure of solving every problem, domestic and international, with new resources, new programs, in space, in the War on Poverty, in Vietnam. This faith did not survive the decade of shocks.

Hingham was caught up in the passion. Schools and their committees, proud of their "modern educational philosophy," "ever watchful and tuned to the constantly changing and advancing tide," believed that "progress in education is continuous." Technology demanded new facilities and equipment. Teachers and pedagogies were constantly "updated" and curricula expanded, especially in science and "New Math." Revisions in social studies simply squeezed more in; the Grade Twelve *history* course, titled "Contemporary Issues," was stretched to include a half-year of economics. History education had reached a nadir in America:

> we learned little about human endeavors, past or present . . . we had little connection with the past . . . . Instead, ignorant of history, students of social studies find it easy to accept exclusivity . . . . We find it easy to accept our isolation from one another . . . . History proclaims our common humanity.

Forgotten was George Santayana's warning that "Progress, far from consisting in change, depends on retentiveness . . . . Those who cannot remember the past are condemned to repeat it." "Memory," said Elie Wiesel, "is the basis of all culture."

Schools were expected to solve all problems. New specialists served students with all needs: "the retarded, the gifted, the average, the physically handicapped, and the emotionally disturbed." It soon became clear, however, that the schools could not solve all social problems. The optimism paled in the face of a disturbing trend: a phenomenal rise in juvenile delinquency. In the mid-1960s, a presidential commission found youth "apparently responsible for a substantial and disproportionate part of the national crime problem." By then, the problem had come to Hingham.

As meetings and speeches multiplied, the problem mushroomed: vandalism (with a special fondness for new school windows); theft—of cars, liquor, even Christmas light bulbs from the square; shoplifting by affluent kids; desecration of memorials; obscene phone invitations to sex parties; teenage pregnancies; rival gangs; beer blasts at World's End, Triphammer, and the town forest. A policeman was stationed nights at the library. Sergeant Raymond Campbell, juvenile officer, sighed, "We need a separate police department just to handle the kids alone." No wonder police budgets grew almost as fast as school budgets. In a decade when the population grew by only 20 percent, arrests by Hingham police—not all of Hinghamites, of course—climbed by 1900 percent. The case load per year at Hingham District Court grew between 1966 and 1969 from 5760 to 12,288. In 1965, twenty minors were arrested with liquor in their cars; in 1968, 185. In 1966, drugs arrived. "My God!" cried the *Journal* editor. "What kind of kids are we raising in Hingham?" What had gone wrong?

Non-plussed parents in countless comfortable towns were asking the same questions. At first, the tendency was to see the problem as one of impoverished areas such as inner cities, as "deviant," not "mainstream." But it was mainstream. Meetings and conversations offered many diagnoses: parental life-styles, breakdown of authority in the home, contempt for law, contempt for the church, the Supreme Court, a new-thrills consumer culture, "sordid Materialism," peer pressure, militarism and media violence, Communist conspiracy, progressive education, cars.

In retrospect, we can only try to understand. Certain facts, by no means peculiar to Hingham, may help. The number of young had grown prodigiously. Baby-boomers were reaching adolescence. In Hingham by the mid-1960s, almost half of the population was under twenty-one. Their numbers and affluence made them targets of a media marketing blitz. American culture had become obsessed with Youth, and adolescents were encouraged to think themselves "different," with their own styles, values, and rights. Parents had invested their dream in their children and paid for it extravagantly. When children reacted with ingratitude, parents were hurt and confused. The result: a growing alienation. The 1960s called it a Generation Gap.

The nation was confronting a moral revolution. 1960: *Lady Chatterley's Lover* was ruled not obscene, and the Food and Drug Administration approved "the pill." 1962: the Supreme Court ruled compulsory school prayer unconstitutional. 1963-64: Beatlemania brought long hair, and the Free Speech Movement began in California. 1965: the end of Vatican II left Catholics divided on contraception. In 1966 came the first Hippie festival and the Supreme Court's Miranda decision. 1967: *Bonnie and Clyde* made youthful violence poignant, and the San Francisco "Be-In" prepared for the "Summer of Love." 1968: the love-rock musical "HAIR" opened, and feminists picketed Miss America. 1969: the Manson murders were followed by the Woodstock Festival. 1970: Jimmi Hendrix and Janice Joplin died of drug overdoses, and another presidential commission called the gap between youth counterculture and established society a threat to national stability. Many mainstream Americans reflected, as the *Journal* expressed it in 1963, "Somehow or other it all seems . . . to be part and parcel of a general disintegration . . . of an insidious erosion."

Mainstream parents found it hard to recognize their complicity. They had encouraged adolescents to follow adult models but denied them adult status. In 1960, the Hingham Mothers Club and the Community Center offered a "Charm" course for junior highschoolers, and nearly a hundred girls signed up. Responding to the controversy that followed, the curate of St. John's spoke out about parental pressure toward "going steady" and early dating. Parents encouraged a party-life for their children out of fear that they might become "antisocial" or nonconformists, and thus nourished the very peer pressure that later seemed so dangerous. Many Americans, wrote David Riesman, had given up their traditional inner-directedness to become "other-directed." Robert Linder wrote, "Our teenage mutineers present us with a travesty of ourselves." Having been "liberated" early from childhood, the "children" found adulthood further delayed. They were "kept in school," denied adult work, meaningful social roles. Paul Goodman called it "growing up absurd."

At first, they were "rebels without a cause." In the 1960s, they found their causes in a culture no longer able to hide its flaws under labels of deviance and delinquency. Black students sat-in in Greensboro, North Carolina. The Freedom Riders were met by violence, and the Birmingham marchers faced Bull Connor. A great crowd in Washington heard Martin Luther King's dream. In the fatal year of 1963, notable deaths included those of Pope John XXIII, a Vietnamese monk by self-immolation, and South Vietnam's president and his brother. In Dallas, President Kennedy was shot, and Lee Harvey Oswald as the nation watched. In Mississippi, Medgar Evers, and four black girls in the bombing of a church. The wave of violence was rolling.

In 1962, Louis Bonitto, lifelong Hingham resident and black realtor, spoke to the South Shore Citizens Club, an outgrowth of the committee that entertained segregated black servicemen in World War II Hingham. After discussion of his efforts to obtain listings and place black families in homes, a Fair Housing Committee was formed. In January, 1963, the committee offered in the *Journal* a Good Neighbor Pledge for townspeople to sign. In its last printing almost three years later, the signers totaled about 7 percent of registered voters.

The Hingham Council of Churches sponsored a first "integration" meeting in 1963 and heard its president, Dudley Alleman, call the drive for racial integration "a challenge to both Christianity and American democracy." The League of Women Voters tactfully posed "provocative questions" to the town, such as, "If there are not significant racial minorities [here], is this because there are barriers to their coming? . . . what are they? . . . If these do exist, should there be a Council of Human Relations?" If responses came, they did not appear in the *Journal*. In 1964, the national struggle reached local consciousness. John Gallop and other clergymen took students to one of the day-long "Freedom Schools" held in Boston to protest school conditions there. Following the violence in Mississippi that summer, a Hingham Chapter of the Massachusetts Freedom Movement was formed. As the year ended, the public was invited to hear Hingham's Francis Wright, Jr., and his wife Judith describe their work for minority rights in Mississippi, their harassments and arrests, and her six months in jail.

March, 1965, saw the march from Selma to Montgomery; March the seventh was "Bloody Sunday." A clergyman, Orloff Miller, a Hingham resident, was beaten by the same group that killed Rev. James Reeb. Home again, Miller spoke at the First Parish House and stirred resentment when his statement that he had come home "to work for civil rights in my own Selma of the South Shore" was garbled by Boston newspapers into the proclamation that Hingham was THE Selma of the South Shore. One listener to Miller's talk recalled the meeting's "most important statement . . . lost in all this hullabaloo," the statement by an unnamed

> Negro lady in the audience who also had grown up and had gone to school in Hingham, and she had raised her family in Hingham. When her grown son, who was educated in the Hingham schools, married, he could not rent a home in Hingham because of his color and had consequently to move to Holbrook.

[395]

One more "hullabaloo" closed the year. The High School PTA invited antibusing leader Louise Day Hicks to speak. The plans were withdrawn, but tempers flared over both the invitation and its cancellation.

Efforts of the Freedom Movement's Hingham chapter were now focused on persuading Hingham to participate in the new "METCO" Program, established in 1966 to send small groups of black school children from Boston to suburban classrooms. Kenneth Janey, a leader of the local movement, appealed to the Hingham School Committee in 1967: "As a black man in Hingham for twelve years, I speak in behalf of the white children, who could benefit most from METCO. They will graduate into a multi-ethnic world and this program could help prepare them to live in it." Assurances were given that the program would not affect the classroom space situation and would cost the town nothing.

In the fall of 1967, fifteen school children began the long daily bus rides to and from Hingham. With Mrs. Camilla Roundtree chairing the local supervisory committee, the program grew annually by small increments, and by 1969, sixteen black city students were enrolled in Hingham High School. One dramatic event of April, 1970, was indicative of what the program was meant to initiate. The First Parish sponsored a "Lock-In" at the parish house. Fifty-five students, a mixture of METCO commuters and their white Hingham classmates, together with ten adults, were "locked in" for thirteen hours to discuss racism in America.

Other efforts in the local campaign for social justice were directed at such obstacles as housing costs, zoning laws, and the resistance to low-cost housing and apartment development. None of the active local groups—and they were numerous, including church groups of all faiths, from the First Baptist Church Social Relations Committee to the St. Paul's Human Rights Committee—could overcome these obstacles.

One significant factor in the social ferment of the 1960s was religious renewal. Woven into the "new consciousness" was a thread of religious quest. New religious institutions appeared or grew. Glastonbury Monastery flourished and in 1961 was elevated to independent conventual status. In 1964, it was joined by the Maryknoll Novitiate on Charles Street, and in 1965, by Notre Dame Academy. The Jewish congregation of Temple Beth Am, formed in 1958-59, held services at the shipyard, then at the First Parish house. In 1962, the Thayer estate on Turkey Hill became a center for retired Friends. In 1968, the Mormons dedicated a chapel on Gardner Street. The Lutherans began services in 1964, and in 1968 they dedicated their House of Prayer with representatives of all Hingham faiths present.

Inspired partly by Pope John XXIII and Vatican II, ecumenism flowered. "Altogether," remembers John Gallop,

> it was a time full of joy, new friendships (which overcame apprehension), a new vision of possible fulfillment of Christ's prayer "that they all may be one." Enthusiasm cannot of course be "on a high" forever .... How easy it is to revert to the "ghetto mentality."

The first joint worship of Catholics and Protestants took the form of a Bible Vigil in 1965 at Glastonbury, whose "Father Ed" Campbell carried on his own "ecumenical movement" in suppers for Kiwanians, Rotarians, and Lions. In 1967, Catholics joined for the first time in Union Thanksgiving Eve services at Old Ship. A week of Prayer for Christian Unity started at St. Paul's and ended at the Congregational Church. "Octave of Unity" weeks were followed by "Living-Room Dialogues," and a first Ecumenical Conference on Racial Understanding (1968) was sponsored by nine churches and a synagogue.

Some clergymen were social activists, John Gallop and the Methodist minister Ross Lilly prominent among them. Pastor Robert Lawson of New North was one of three Hinghamites in the 1963 Washington march. The First Parish called Texan civil rights activist Brandoch Lovely as pastor in 1965; then, in 1969, Paul Treat, veteran of the Selma march, activist in the National Association for the Advancement of Colored People, the American Civil Liberties Union, the Wisconsin campaign of Eugene McCarthy, and the peace movement. In 1969, the Congregationalists called Earl Alger, who had worked with minority groups, prisoners, and teenagers in Lawrence.

Clerical activism drew fire from those dismayed by current causes and demonstrations. Police Chief Raymond Campbell listed among his "Citizens' Rights" the "right to expect their clergymen to dedicate themselves to all their parishioners and not just to those who practice civil disobedience and anarchy." By then (1968), many clergymen had added to their commitments the most divisive cause of all: peace in Vietnam.

The Cold War had entered a new phase with the presidential election in 1960 of a cold warrior seen by some as more aggressive than the cautious Eisenhower. Hingham's vote was John F. Kennedy 3141; Richard M. Nixon 4500. Following the Bay of Pigs debacle, President Kennedy urged Americans to take seriously the prospect of nuclear war, and Hingham responded to advertisements for fallout shelters. Warren Noble and Thomas Dowd opened a shop, the first of its kind in the area:

Before any of you folks who are fallout shelter minded get too far along with the buying of the many things which go to stock it, better wait a few days until Warren opens his place on South Street next to Nese's cobbler shop. As a matter of fact, Warren's having a shelter built in his yard in Norwell.

By May, 1965, the Hingham Rotary Club's auction included a $500 bomb shelter unused and perfect for "an excellent outdoor playhouse." But that was long after the Cuban missile crisis when the world stood on the brink and Hingham learned how to prepare basement survival shelters. Attention had shifted to the other side of the world. Kennedy sent more advisers and technicians to South Vietnam, then hesitated, and suddenly it was November 22, 1963:

When the news of this tragedy reached Hingham shortly after two o'clock in the afternoon, it was almost received in disbelief . . . . People were stunned. Little groups . . . were seen to gather on the sidewalks and speak in subdued tones. "President Kennedy has been shot. Isn't it horrible?"

A new President promised to carry out Kennedy's policies. Lyndon B. Johnson declared War on Poverty, signed the Civil Rights and Economic Opportunity Acts, cut taxes by $13 billion, and pushed the Tonkin Gulf Resolution through Congress—such was the tragic mixture of Johnson's presidency. Still, he was seen in 1964 as a peace President, and when, as the *Journal* reported, "Senator Barry Goldwater and his legion of staunch supporters took over lock, stock and barrel" at the Republican convention of 1964, Hingham did what it never had done. It voted (4684 to 2959) for a Democratic President. After his landslide, Johnson increased the draft by 400 percent, awarded huge defense contracts, and began bombing North Vietnam. By the end of 1965, 185,000 U.S. troops were in Vietnam. Draft cards were burned. The antiwar movement gathered strength. By 1966, Americans were profoundly divided.

In well-to-do towns, largely insulated from the draft by the high percentage of men in college, consciousness grew slowly. The summer of 1965 brought an ominous signal: the flag by the War Memorial was stolen and found in the mud of Hingham harbor. As former health officer Win Wade wrote from south of Saigon, "The war is easy to understand once you're here, but difficult to explain." Army medical specialist Richard Perkinson wrote home of the "unpopular war":

My mother quite naturally started asking questions as to why we were in this mess over here . . . . All I can say in closing is, talk to an American soldier who has served here before you criticize our government's involvement. If this sounds like flag-waving, you're damn right.

The *Journal*, no doubt speaking for many, held to Perkinson's sentiments for an editorial policy while divisions deepened and homecoming servicemen were even "snubbed by citizens and businesses" in some parts of America. We do not know why the *Journal* printed no Honor Roll, but anecdotal evidence suggests that some families were actually afraid to let it be known that their men were fighting in Vietnam. In November, 1967, South Junior High students completed a list of Hingham men in Vietnam and sent Christmas gifts. The *Journal* did not print it.

Adding to the men's anguish was the weird, disorienting nature of jungle guerrilla fighting. Casualties, even deaths, seemed random. Curtis Chase, the first Hingham man to die, was burned when his helicopter was hit by small arms fire, causing a grenade to burst. Robert Galluzzo was wounded by a grenade thrown by mistake into a hut supposedly occupied by the enemy. Lt. Richard Perkins tripped on a vine and fell on a spear rigged to a booby trap. Edward Rizzotto was wounded in both legs when a land mine exploded near the Cambodian border. William Terry died in Formosa when his C130 crashed coming in to land. On the memorial boulder at Hawke Park appear the names of six Hingham men who died:

JAMES BYRNE	ROBERT RYAN
CURTIS CHASE	WILLIAM TERRY
CHARLES MC NUTT	BARRY WOLK.

Over Vietnam hamlets hung a life-death uncertainty: who were friends? who enemies? To the letters of Craig Steen, Hingham owed its most tragic word-picture of the moral nightmare, the war in miniature. May, 1967:

About 9:30 a.m. we came across a small village. We crept towards it slowly . . . . I got my first shot in when I saw Charlie [generic for Viet Cong] jump into a hole in the hamlet . . . . I found out later much to my sorrow that one of my bullets had hit a girl that had been hiding in the hole too. Of course I would have held my fire if I had known . . . . I was about to let go a grenade into the hole when I heard the crying . . . . This girl was found at the bottom . . . . A grenade was thrown in to finish the job . . . . The other fellows and I had to search through the connecting tunnels by crawling in on hands and knees with a flashlight . . . . I guess it was my first known killing, but why did it have to be a girl? The VC probably had grabbed her and thrown her into the entrance of the hole just as I let loose with the fire power . . . . I feel so sick about this, but as all the guys here say, "She would have grown up to be a VC too." Please do not think I am a merciless killer. I didn't want this to happen, but it did, and it's always happening. I hope I can forget it . . . . Why did *this* have to happen to me?

The next day, Steen was hiking through brush, falling on slippery ground, soaked and blackened with mud, aching all over:

My hands and arms were ripped apart from the thorns. My legs ached from falling on them so much, plus my feet were blistered and skin shriveled from being so wet so long and covered by my jungle boots . . . . A squad is going out to check on the wounded or killed. Now I really AM mad! It may sound crazy, but I really do want to cut down some of those Charlies . . . . Whoops, while writing this a lizard just ran over my legs! Well, it gave me a change of mood I guess . . . . The whole area resembled a dead planet and just looking at it gave me the willies . . . . Somehow sleep won't come. I keep remembering things.

At high school games that fall, it was "pretty much commonplace" when the band played "The Star Spangled Banner" for some to turn the other way. Richard Perkinson sent thanks to Hingham boys and girls for his Christmas package with its little card, "We support you." "Amidst all the uproar, protests, and draft-dodging, these young boys and girls thought enough to wish me well." If "memory is the basis of all culture," we must never forget the anguish of those who bore the scars of the tragedy.

As 1967 ended, many still believed their leaders' assurances that the war was being won. Then came 1968, *annus terribilis*, when the nation seemed to come apart, and Hingham was torn by stresses both local and global. In April, it was scandalized by an article in the far-off London *Sunday Times*. Reporter Pauline Peters, after a hasty visit, pictured this "ideal American small town" chiefly in terms of its drinking, divorce rate, cocktails at the dump, Mafia homes, racism, drugs, and wife-swapping—she called it "backyarding." She stirred up a hornet's nest and inspired the much-needed humor of Margaret McSweeney:

Aw! Gee whiz, I wonder if the person who wrote this piece would send me the names of the folks who give out the Bloody Marys before breakfast. I've lived in Hingham for fifty years and no one has ever given me a Bloody Mary, leave alone before breakfast . . . . About that other thing: "backyarding." I wish I'd heard of that before. I wonder if it's too late now! Did your writer notice that there's a store downtown that has a sign "Women's Exchange?"

The reviled journalist had not overlooked the idyllic aspect: the town was a "beautiful Aspiration." Had she stayed through 1968, she might have changed her mind. For, as one letter-writer ranted, "At last the lid has been blown off and Hingham has been exposed to the rot that is eating away at the rest of the world."

The year opened in Vietnam with the Tet offensive, mocking the administration's claims of success. *Time, Newsweek*, the *Wall Street Journal*, and Walter Cronkite became critics. In Hingham, the year began with a series of Vietnam lectures, in one of which Noam Chomsky charged that "a particularly destructive form of antipersonnel weapon" was being produced at the Annex. The report brought angry exchanges. Some spoke of "genocide against the Vietnamese people"; others charged these critics with giving "comfort to a ruthless enemy." As news came of casualties and the death near Hue of twenty-four-year-old Hingham man Barry Lee Wolk, plans were made for a conference on draft resistance. Political opposition attached itself to the candidacy of Eugene McCarthy. Dustin Hoffman spoke at the high school, while McCarthy's supporters canvassed the town. In New Hampshire, his youthful forces brought about an impressive primary showing. President Johnson announced he would not run again. Hingham voters re-registered and crossed over, and the primary results showed the strength of anti-war sentiment: of 946 Democratic and 801 Republican ballots cast, McCarthy received 579 on the Democratic ballot and 113 on the Republican.

In the midst of primary season, tragedy struck in Memphis. Martin Luther King was killed, and in America's cities, black anger brought looting and burning. In Hingham, there were mixed reactions to his death. However, twenty clergymen issued a statement urging every citizen "to recognize this tragedy and what it portends for us and the future of our free country." Three hundred people marched in silence from the Congregational Church down Main Street to the First Baptist Church. They were joined there, the crowd overflowing onto the lawn, by hundreds more, including the selectmen, for a memorial service and a eulogy by Kenneth Janey.

Demonstrations were held on hundreds of college campuses. Hingham's school crisis came in April, when four high school teachers suddenly "resigned." It was rumored that the actions were due to "personal appearance or a conflicting educational philosophy." Students assembled in the cafeteria to seek explanations but were ordered back to their homerooms. Twenty concerned parents confronted the School Committee with questions. Are schools examining white racism and preparing children for a world in which they are a minority? Are exams and grades inimical to real learning? What is the role of students in the choice of curriculum and dismissal of teachers? Brandoch Lovely, minister of the First Parish, sounded the keynote: "It is time to listen to all of our citizens, not just those who are over twenty-one."

The next night, June 18, 1968, five hundred attended another meeting; the subject, drug abuse. Like other troubles, this one had been wishfully seen as a problem "elsewhere." In 1966, there were two drug-related arrests in Hingham; in 1967, twenty; in 1968, sixty-four. The problem had arrived. Marijuana, children told their parents, was cheap and easy to get. Pharmacist Arnold Shapiro reported an increased demand for cough syrups and old-fashioned cigarette papers. The plague of the cities came to town in May when a motor cycle gang tried to invade World's End. It came again in July when a caravan of "Harassed Hippies Hankering for Hingham Haven" were halted at the gates of the Annex by Officer Sam Amonte. One townsman suggested sowing the area with poison ivy. It would take more than Sam Amonte and poison ivy to keep youth counterculture out of town. All over the western world, this was the Year of the Young Rebels.

In 1968's second assassination, Robert Kennedy was shot hours after his victory in the California primary. Though no friend of the counterculture, the *Journal* felt the magnitude of the shock:

> With the pillars of life and decency as we have known it crumbling all around us, it would appear that the time has come when we should all fall down upon our knees and implore almighty God to once more show us the way, His way. For let there be no mistake about it, we are floundering, and are as so much flotsam upon the troubled seas. Our way of life is failing, miserably so.

As Hingham was paying its last respects to "Bobby" Kennedy, Mason Foley died of a second heart attack. For many, this "slight, rather small-ish man" with the "wry smile" exemplified what the town loved and trusted most in its people. Born in Cohasset in 1902 just over the town line from "Tugmanug," he grew up in Hingham to become familiar with its "every nook and cranny" and to sense the oneness of its past and present, its natural beauty and well-being. Teacher, historian, conservationist, bookseller, and selectman, he labored indefatigably "to save from attic, cellar, and old barn, the vestiges of past records." He was "interested in Hingham, interested in everything." Yet, as Donald Robinson said during the packed services for Foley at the Second Parish, he was "always and delightfully himself" with a "gift . . . inherited perhaps from some Celtic minstrel of a thousand years ago . . . for expressing his thoughts in unusual and often whimsical ways." He was, said Margaret McSweeney, "an awful nice guy . . . . And he had a grand time." Some felt with gratitude that "in times of rapid change," he had been a "steadying influence and Hingham has been the better for it." To some others, he represented a conservatism "interested in preserving property values at their present level in the face of pressing human needs."

Fairness was *not* a virtue of the 1960s. With fine aptness, when Hingham civil rights groups planned a second conference on racial understanding, their theme was "Whites Understanding Whites." The goal was elusive in times of extreme polarization. Police Chief Campbell spoke for outraged, fearful people when, in January, 1968, he published his "Citizens' Rights": "Now that the courts have assured Communists, murderers, rapists, robbers, mobs, hoboes, vagrants, night prowlers, drug and filth peddlers of their rights—it's time decent citizens demand their rights." In July, a showing of "underground films" was scheduled at the library. The chief suggested to Librarian Dziura that the show be canceled, and it was. Letters poured in to the *Journal*, attacking Campbell as self-appointed censor and defending him as guardian of public morals. The selectmen heard from the Civil Liberties Union. City media carried reports, and Hingham was again the target of bad publicity. Before this furor faded, the selectmen received an "open letter" from 272 young people, charging police brutality. The selectmen backed the police but promised an investigation. Henry Stokes, candidate for selectman, said, "I seem to sense a breakdown in communication."

The breakdown had climaxed. The young accusers had just seen a frightful spectacle on TV. At the Democratic convention in Chicago, antiwar protesters were met in the streets by police brutality. Inside the hall, Mayor Richard Daley shouted obscenities at Senator Abraham Ribicoff, and Hubert Humphrey was nominated to lead a party in shambles. Not surprisingly, Richard Nixon was elected President as a "law and order" man with a mandate to "bring us together" and a "secret plan" to end the war. The Hingham vote was surprisingly close: with a 91 percent turnout, Nixon won by 4336 to 4062. The other surprise was the election of young Democrat William Spence as state representative. "The status quo has failed," he had said, "and unrest in America will be the worst in the nation's history . . . . The old politics must go." Incumbent Representative Alfred Shrigley went.

[403]

Shrigley had been hurt by his involvement in the most divisive local issue of this boisterous year, the relocation of Route 228. After years of persuasion, the state seemed ready to build a highway to draw traffic off Main Street. But which route would be chosen? A highway that would run north from Gardner Street, then over the crucial aquifer on the west side of town to the old Ammunition Depot at Route 3A? Or an easterly route skirting Prospect Hill and the state park? Norwell mobilized against the easterly route; Hingham charged "narrow and selfish localism." People near Gardner Street were up in arms. People on Prospect Street grieved to see "divided, conflicting positions . . . attack our community spirit." A special town meeting narrowly voted, 559 to 506, against any relocation. The state decided to do nothing. Main Street remains Route 228.

In 1969, Vietnam returned to center stage. Some troops were withdrawn, but little changed. Hingham groups planned for Peace Day, October 15. The prelude was controversy, but the day was peaceful and prayerful, with church bells ringing, twenty-four hour vigils at the Common and the Lincoln statue, the wearing of black armbands, and a quiet candlelight march. The High School Student Council issued a nonpartisan statement and held an assembly on American values. "I was proud of those kids," said the superintendent. In a speech nearby, State Senator William Weeks praised a "generation that is fighting its way back from the luxury of alienation to the burden of leadership and taking an entire people with them." Prophetic words.

Suddenly, in the spring of 1970, against opposition within his administration, the President ordered the Cambodian invasion. A divided peace movement was galvanized. Nervous, immature National Guardsmen killed four students at Kent State University. On more than a third of American campuses, strikes were called. But the change from earlier militancy was striking. The time had come to *communicate* with the folks back home. In the *Journal* of May 21 there appeared a copious collection of letters from Hingham students, as moving as any documents in the history of American youth.

Paul Kimball wrote from Hiram College, "Students remained on campus, to work long and hard in writing letters, giving talks, and staging sit-ins and teach-ins all without violence." Virginia Miller wrote from Smith, "The educational process has not been stopped; it has just been revised to include the main issues of today"; Thomas Belyea from American International, "We hope that the residents of Hingham will consider the sincerity of the students' actions and will join us in an honest evaluation of the United States' commitments in Southeast Asia."

"We don't want to overthrow our government," wrote Sheryda Collins from the University of Massachusetts. "We just realize that there are many things wrong in our country, many inequalities which must be corrected if we are to survive as a nation." "We are not revolutionaries," declared John Cavanagh and Jeffrey Runge at Bowdoin. "We do not wish to die fighting for ideals which many Americans wave about like flags, though few understand." Finally, "this is not a venture by radicals bent on destruction. It is a moderate movement." The signers were Philip Worrick, Charles Vickery, and Robert Petrie. Bob Petrie's credentials were beyond question. He was a Vietnam veteran with a Bronze Star.

Troops came home, negotiations dragged on, and Nixon's China policy unfolded. The draft ended. Youth activism faded, went underground, turned to pastoral communes, or worked for George McGovern. McGovern's strength in Hingham was seen in the presidential primary votes of 1972: he received 1055 to Muskie's 213, while on the Republican side, Nixon led with only 730. In November, Nixon beat McGovern in Hingham by a margin of only five to four.

And yet, town and nation were entering a new conservative era. Even activists breathed a sigh of relief. Chastened out of the fanaticism of Progress, disillusioned with the crusade for Change, many began to focus on conserving. The new conservatism had various faces. Its first face was turned to the natural environment, and the face was both old and young. The same young Hingham man who led a drive that sent twenty-five hundred letters to Hanoi on behalf of POWs in December, 1970, had, in the previous January, led a student petition drive for environmental legislation. He was president of the Central Junior High Science Club, Francis R.—"Sam" or "Santa"—Mahony, Jr.

In 1970, America celebrated its first Earth Day. As early as 1963, a year after Rachel Carson's *Silent Spring* had awakened the nation to environmental peril, Hingham was already one of four towns recognized nationally for leadership in conservation. The movement had opened with the decade in 1960. The urgent letters of John P. Richardson, a latterday Thoreau, began to appear in the *Journal*. In January, a Conservation Commission was established. Its first chair was Edgar T. P. Walker, the Hingham architect and artist. Its first project was to save Home Meadows. Another project was to conserve the shores of Foundry Pond and the Weir River. Selectman "Jimmy" Gordon offered acres of "beautifully marshy lowland virtually connecting Cushing Pond and South School property." A gift from Helen Burns added eight acres bordering Fulling Mill Brook. The Hingham Friends of Conservation, founded in 1965 with Laurence Stein as president, reached a membership of two hundred in 1966. In 1966, over ninety acres were acquired.

That year's best news was the saving of most of the Naval Ammunition Depot Annex for a state park and wildlife reserve. In 1961, the annex had been considered for the site of a "Project Apollo" Space Center, and the Hingham Business and Industry Committee promoted the idea. Mason Foley led an effort to organize conservationist forces in Hingham and adjacent towns. The battle was on. In January, 1963, a letter to the federal government signed by selectmen of Hingham, Cohasset, Norwell, and Scituate urged that "this land should be kept in its natural state." By 1966, the battle was won, and in May, 1967, the land, valued at $11,000,000, was purchased by Massachusetts for $311,000.

Another triumphant climax came in 1967. After the death of Fannie Brewer in 1936, the 249 acres of World's End became the object of speculation for many years. Houselot divisions had seemed likely before 1944, when Helen Walker became the owner, then again when the estate was put up for sale in 1949. Following World War II, there was talk of a home on World's End for the United Nations, even of using it as a site for a nuclear power plant. In the 1950s and 1960s, developers made offers. Then, in 1967, the Metropolitan Area Planning Council recommended its preservation, and the Trustees of Reservations issued their challenge. In a few weeks during November and December, an extraordinary drive led by Samuel Wakeman, once manager of the shipyard, raised over $200,000 toward the sale price of $650,000. The trustees matched with $200,000. The rest would be paid over ten years. World's End had been saved.

Less visible in years when history seemed buried by an avalanche of crises was conservatism's second face, which was turned toward the past. How short and moribund local memory had become. When Old Ship sexton Frank Reed died in 1960 at eighty-seven, one of few remaining links with the lore of the past was gone. When the new post office was dedicated in May, 1964, it took former townsman George Melcher in New Hampshire to remind people of the old post offices, and of the little Centre post office run by Peter Sprague, then by Seth Sprague, which got the mail by barge driven up by Eddy Sprague, and to offer this melancholy note: "Spragues were numerous in Hingham in those days."

Some were wise enough to know that natural and historic conservation went hand in hand, that "the principle of conservation in a community is indivisible." No one articulated it better than Francis Leonard in 1963:

> Who wants to live in a town where there is no wild land? No sense of breathing space? No feeling of communal belonging that discourages lawlessness? No awareness of an unbroken thread with the past that is now a kind of folk-wisdom inherited by the people who live here? Where would progress have led us but to a sterile complex of living units, like the cells in a wasp's nest, no longer communicating with each other, no longer part of the living tissue of a town?

In March, 1963, a Historic Survey Committee was formed, and in May, the National Park Service provided impetus when it designated Old Ship Church as a national historic landmark. The Historic District Study Committee was voted into being a year later, even though Norman Bouvé asked, "Why not declare the whole town an historic district and let every home owner be his own curator?" In 1966, the Lincoln Historic District was approved, and a year later the Historic Districts Commission was created.

The Historical Society campaigned to save Old Derby Hall from joining other "tired old landmarks" in oblivion. Derby Academy had come a long way since the late nineteenth century, when its time seemed past. It entered the twentieth century "in search of an identity." After a 1914 campaign to enlist the support of alumni, a "new awakening" took place. By 1920, with nine grades and one hundred students, Derby Hall was overcrowded. In 1923, the Upper School moved to its "temporary" new buildings on Burditt Avenue and was transformed by a progressive headmaster into a country day school. His successor had the task of insuring its survival through the depression. During the 1940s, it grew again. Edward McEachron began his long and energetic tenure, "established the identity of the school nearly as it exists today" (1984), and raised funds to replace the "temporary" upper school buildings. In September, 1966, a new lower school unit was ready. Old Derby Hall was obsolete.

The dire words had been heard: "once the old school is razed." Those of the obliterative mind-set wanted the land for town office expansion. John Richardson sounded the alarm: "Citizens of Hingham! Let us not be hasty with the arm of destruction." The Historical Society launched its drive, and on November 1, 1966, Old Derby became the Society's headquarters. Since there was no single major benefactor, as with the Old Ordinary or the town forest, this success was no small achievement.

A decade that had begun infatuated with youth ended with a new respect for age. Again, 1970 marks a transition: the Hingham Council on Aging was formed. Six years before, over 40 percent of elders surveyed had identified their most pressing need: lower-cost, apartment housing. Panicked by the thought of "housing projects," the town again and again rejected apartment proposals. Hingham's elderly suffered. A sad anecdote belongs to 1966. School Committeeman David Miller was forced to resign because he was no longer a resident. "What with the family gone, the present house near Accord Pond is just too big for my wife and me, and we just couldn't find a suitable apartment in Hingham." The Millers moved to Weymouth.

In 1967, after submission of his fifth plan, Wallace Marden's application to build the town's first apartment building—twenty-three units at the corner of North and Station Streets—was approved. Easement problems delayed completion until well into the 1970s. And in the summer of 1967, a Housing Authority was appointed to plan elderly housing. In 1969, West School closed forever, and the town approved plans for Thaxter Park—after, as a supporter said, a "rather shameful" history of "foot-dragging." Construction was held up until 1972 while state funds were awaited.

By then, Hingham's elderly were pinched in their pocketbooks as well as their housing. The elderly, wrote Marjorie Lincoln, were "being squeezed out by the ever-increasing burden." She referred to the third face of conservatism to show itself: taxpayer revolt. How late it appeared is surprising. Warnings had been heard with each new capital outlay, but town meetings continued with little dissent to approve ever larger outlays and budgets. Some people simply gave up, stayed away, even left town: "Our house is sold and we are getting out . . . . The town is run by a spendthrift group which only bankruptcy or a finance board can stop," or even a "taxpayers' strike." At a meeting of 1969, Water Company worker Albert Calvi said of the "big spenders," "The place nearest their hearts is to have taxes so high that the small people will have to move out of town." In 1970, in the wake of broad increases in assessments, a two-year jump of $11 in the tax rate, and a rise of more than $1.5 million in proposed appropriations, the revolt was organized. "TAXES" was a citizens' group intending to "hold the line." The tax shock was the final shock of the 1960s.

In the late fall of 1970, young minister Paul Treat gave a series of three sermons in the ancient venue of the old meetinghouse. The title of the series was "Time Shock." In the first, "Past Shock," he explored what many young people thought at the time: they had *no past* which they could affirm as meaningful. The story of his second, "Present Shock," has just been re-told. The third, taking Alvin Toffler's timely bestseller as its text, was "Future Shock." The sermons were a fitting close to a shocking decade.

Epilogue
(1971-1990)

I: 1971–1984

✠

The Costs of Saving the Future

HINGHAM's present and America's opened with the 1970s. The trends and the problems that emerged then are still with us in the 1990s. A small, residential New England town struggled with the problems of saving its future: saving the environment and its resources; saving the land while needing to provide affordable homes for its people; serving the growing numbers of its elderly; preserving its long tradition of volunteerism; finding alternative forms of transportation and energy; preserving, or perhaps modifying, its traditions of small town government; saving the monuments and memories of its long and rich past in the face of demographic changes that made a shared past elusive.

In 1971, the League of Women Voters met for lunch with local political representatives to discuss environmental quality and affordable housing. Both were taking prominent places on the political agenda. They were connected.

There was good news for environmentalists in the 1970s. The Conservation Commission still had funds to acquire land. Mrs. Winthrop Cushing gave the commission nineteen acres on the southeast side of Cushing Pond. Garden Club members successfully petitioned to exclude picnic tables from the area. They also made the earliest efforts toward recycling at the landfill and worked actively for the passage of a state Bottle Bill. In 1974, the one-hundred-member club celebrated its fiftieth birthday. It has continued to provide floral arrangements for the library and for the Old Ordinary during annual house tours and to tend the Old Ordinary's prize-winning garden.

[413]

The "greening of Hingham," so strikingly displayed by the Hingham Land Conservation Trust on its 1982 map, proceeded. The Trust, established in 1972 and supported liberally by Helen Burns and others, received gifts of land from donors wary of public ownership. The federal government returned 461 acres of the old Depot along the Back River to the town, and in October, 1974, "after months of clean-up and demolition," the north section of Bare Cove Park opened. A gravel path led through fields dotted with bayberry and cedar. A bicycle path bordered the river, with picnic sites and abundant land and shore birds. The remainder of the park would open in October, 1977. In June, 1973, developed at last with state funds, Wompatuck State Park formally opened. In 1979, the Bouvé land on Huet's Cove, the last open private shore space, was saved from developers by town purchase with state assistance. The climactic success in saving open space would come a decade later at the South Shore Country Club.

Saving the land and its resources was a constant battle. The bad news included the final loss of farms. In 1979, a campaign to save the Hanlon farm off Charles Street failed. Next year, the fate of the Hornstra farm was sealed. "That the face of this scenic landmark farm," a productive dairy until 1970 and

> a mecca for artists for many years, was due to change was practically a foregone conclusion. Several of the buildings are in a state of disrepair, and the extensive fields are used almost entirely for the planting of corn by a Hanover farmer who leases the holdings.

Even John Hornstra, whose family had bought the farm in 1917, supported a plan to build clustered condominiums instead of rows of houses. John Richardson warned in vain: "We have treated our agricultural resources as if they were totally expendable . . . . Our lives are now dependent upon fragile lifelines that pump in our energy and food . . . . The party appears to be over."

The environment was increasingly threatened by waste. In 1971, Hingham highschoolers warned the town that the United States, with less than 6 percent of the world's people, consumed 40 percent of its resources and produced nearly a million tons of trash daily. Hingham witnessed the birth of recycling: its first facility opened in the spring of 1972, with "balloons, a band, and much festivity." This modest start could not solve the landfill problem. Richardson warned that expansion of the dump would destroy the wetland feeding Cranberry Pond and its brook, victims of "man's total mania for developing the clouds themselves." After long controversy, a baler facility opened at the landfill in

1984. But each remedy was temporary. Each remedy caused new problems or aggravated old ones. The ban against trash-burning only filled the dump faster, just as the salting of roads for winter safety menaced trees and the water supply. Our present was made of dilemmas.

Environmental and economic priorities collided over the handling of other kinds of waste. In the 1970s, the north sewer project remained uncompleted. In 1982, amid a "raging" dispute, a $4 million project was approved at town meeting by about 5 percent of the registered voters. In the *Boston Globe*, Ian Menzies called "that wasteful institution," open town meeting, "ridiculous," and "because it is ridiculous, it is ill-attended, and because it is ill-attended, it can be manipulated." A group sued to block the project. The state threatened to withhold its share of the costs if Hingham did not improve its record in affordable housing, thus forcing a political linkage between housing and the environment. But more housing would require more sewer connections. Quincy sued the Metropolitan District Commission for polluting its bay. Hingham sewage went to the source of the problem at Nut Island, yet Hingham joined the suit. A Boston judge ruled that over four thousand Hingham homes could no longer have their septage carried to a facility en route to Stodder's Neck. Town meeting, despite the opposition and threats, persisted in the sewer project. Water, clean and otherwise, had become a pivotal issue of public policy.

So had affordable housing. Hingham remained fiercely opposed to the development of small homes and apartments. In 1971, contemplating the return of old Depot land on the Back River, town meeting considered numerous plans for such projects. Most startling in its scale was a high-rise apartment complex proposed for the shipyard land by its current owners. No promise of tax revenue or shipyard reclamation could overcome the horror felt at such a vision. Rejected, too, were plans for apartments off Lincoln Street and for homes on Baker Hill, whose projected grids of streets and intersections would only worsen the flood problem in West Hingham. The 1971 meeting approved only a "package deal" for land use at the Depot, including 84.8 acres for town house and garden apartments. The solution was temporary. Beal's Cove Village, a rental apartment complex, was built in 1978; within ten years, it had "gone condo."

A further proposal for land use at the West Hingham Depot aroused controversy of a different sort in 1973-74. The Boston Indian Council petitioned for some of the still-federal land for a national college of Indian culture. This Back River community would have included 250 Native Americans and their families. Local support was mobilized by the

League of Women Voters, the First Parish, and the Jewish Community Center. The selectmen were opposed, and, in behind-the-scenes negotiations with the federal government, they won the day. "The Indians," observed the *Journal* wryly, "will have to look elsewhere as they have throughout our nation's history." Old "NIMBY"—Not in My Back Yard—has been a prominent fellow in our present. Kenneth LaFleur, new minister of Old Ship, wrote: "Perhaps we feel one more degree of estrangement from politicians at all levels. This is sad." He wrote during the days of Watergate.

What gave the problem of affordable housing its local urgency were not the needs of those outside. What gave it urgency was the most significant of changes in the town's demography during the 1970s. How would Hingham "take care of its own?" Its own most rapidly growing population was its elderly, a change it shared with the nation.

Organized concern for the Greying of America was born with the 1970s. Elders were now called "Senior Citizens." America's attention was shifting from youth to age. Birthrates fell; life expectancy rose. By 1970, one of nine Americans was over sixty; by 1976, one of nine was over sixty-five. Most were women, and many were poor. But Senior Citizens were organizing politically into Grey Power. In 1971, they discussed their agenda in preparation for a White House conference on aging. Ten years before, there had been 300,000 organized elders in the nation; now there were six million.

A Hingham woman of foresight had anticipated the trend. In the mid-1950s, Ruth Spencer had founded the Golden Age Club at the Congregational Church. By 1972, it had grown so large that additional organizations were called for: a Senior Citizens Association and a chapter of the American Association for Retired Persons. Under Ruth Spencer's leadership in 1970, the Hingham Council on Aging was created to "stimulate community concern for the welfare of its older citizens and to identify and work toward solutions of their problems." The council surveyed the town's 2314 "seniors"; they now comprised 12½ percent of the town, above the national average, and 1550 were sixty-five or older. Some said they would like a hot lunch program, and one was set up for Thursdays at Central Junior High. Some would like a "Drop In Center," and it opened at the Community Center. "FISH" began delivery of meals to the shut-ins. The free Senior Shuttle, a yellow-and-white microbus, began its shopping runs and circular routes in December, 1971. The first year, volunteer drivers carried a weekly average of one hundred: a man to visit his wife at a nursing home; a talented painter to art classes and waterfront scenes; a couple to shop.

Paula Levinson enjoyed the "jaunty little bus" and its "spunky little driver," Dotty Mahoney, with her "shiny white jacket." "Thank you, Ruth," she wrote, "for making your dream a reality."

The most urgent need of Hingham's older citizens was for convenient and affordable housing. At Thaxter Park (site of the 1894 school), after a wait for state funds since 1968, construction began in the spring of 1972. By September, 135 elderly had applied, and a year later, there were 255 applicants for the sixty-eight units. In April, 1974, tenants began moving in. Though a start, this was obviously not enough. Abbot "Father Ed" Campbell of Glastonbury Abbey—it had become an abbey in January, 1973—suggested that abbey land might be used.

In 1979, Father Ed saw a dream realized. In February, Lincoln School, no longer needed for a dwindling school enrollment, became surplus. Town meeting approved the sale for $52,500, the deed was signed in December, and construction began. Landscaping preserved a playground for the young and sunny seats for the old. Over 540 applied for the sixty units, and in October, 1980, tenants began to arrive. Genevieve Wigmore, retired telephone operator formerly of Hingham, came home. Helping her to unpack, a niece found Miss Wigmore's Lincoln School graduation pin in an old jewelry box.

A further plan for elderly housing was swamped for years in the legal quagmire of the 1980s. Elder Care, a private company, proposed to build three hundred self-care apartments and a 120-bed nursing home on the site of the now-closed missionary school of the Maryknoll Fathers on Charles Street. Some environmentalists were alarmed: septage from a nursing home would be an unwelcome neighbor to Accord Brook. Elder Care proposed to build a sewage processing facility. There was also concern about the increased traffic on narrow roads. Nothing seemed to settle the issue of "Brandon Woods" once it became tangled in a web of litigation, appeals, revised plans, and delays. Whatever the objections to the plan, the frustration of Hingham's elderly was heard in a moving letter from Margaret McSweeney in 1983:

> the proposed facility would be the answer to the prayers of many in my age group. Comes a time—too soon—when household and yard chores, shopping and cooking, become too burdensome. The privacy of a small apartment, the availability of a dining room plus some transportation, seems like a bit of Paradise . . . . I'm hoping for one in Hingham for I would be sad to leave this town where I have been for sixty years.

In a way, this is a special appeal to people like Charlie Cushing at his Centre Gas Station, to Whit Price at the Centre Pharmacy, to Sam

Amonte one of our good police officers whose kindness and friendly greetings over the years have meant so much to me. Gentlemen, I would hate to leave the town where you are.

Others, more angry than sad, found a spokesman in retired Police Chief Raymond Campbell:

Where are the minorities? Why do so many town workers live outside town? Because they can't afford to live here. We're too good for low income housing, McDonald's, and elderly housing. Let's stop this nonsense and get this thing off the ground. Everyone wants it.

Maryknoll still sat vacant. There were no longer enough men to train for foreign missions. Perhaps the need for missionaries at home had become more pressing.

Meanwhile, Hingham's elderly population continued to grow. By 1976, there were about twenty-five hundred retired people in Hingham, one in eight. That year, Hersey House on North Street, like Lincoln School no longer needed by the School Department, became the Senior Center. Its director, Sandra Kent, expanded programs year by year. By 1979, Hingham's three thousand senior citizens had their Retired Senior Volunteer Program, with Edward Corea and Rose Berman as coordinators.

Youth, too, needed volunteers for its own outreach. The problems of youth were now on the national agenda; mere dismay and condemnation were giving way to supportive action by the young themselves. In June, 1971, a "Hingham Hotline" began its emergency phone service. "Call 749-2430 between 6 P.M. Friday and 2 A.M. Monday, and a teenage voice will answer, 'Someone cares. Can I help you?'" In its first month, Hotline answered no fewer than 150 serious calls for help, the largest number about teenage pregnancies, parent "hassles" second, drugs third. Another youth group raised funds for a drug rehabilitation program, "Project Turnabout," which was moving into the old almshouse off Beal Street.

The new calls for volunteers, however, came at a time when Hingham's traditional volunteerism was about to face a serious new challenge. The challenge was posed by the most momentous social revolution of these years: the change in the roles and priorities of women. By 1979, there was a note of urgency in the theme of the July Fourth parade—"Volunteers Make America"—and in the proclamation of its prize-winning float that "America Grows with the Volunteer Mother." Growing numbers of mothers were taking paid jobs.

Nationally, the proportion of women in their early twenties who held paying jobs rose from 50 percent in 1964 to 61 percent in 1973—and, of greater moment for a town like Hingham, to 86 percent among women who were college graduates. By 1979, Hingham's labor force had risen in six years by 41 percent and women constituted most of the increase. The impact was seen in the expansion of day care, career counseling, news columns with titles like "Security for Women Who Live Alone," and workshops in "Time Management for the Overcommitted Woman."

Some local women encountered problems. The career of Hingham's first woman police officer was brief. Officer Carolyn Lacombe resigned after four months in 1975, reportedly to "devote more time to her family." School Committee member Doris Ford announced she was moving to Maine, "where my husband is presently employed. In supporting the 'rights of today's women,' I am not just following him . . . but came to a joint agreement that although my [paying] job was more important, his job offered a better salary."

Nonetheless, Hingham women entered public life in growing numbers. Mary Fee was treasurer-collector; Joan Oates joined the Planning Board; Arlene Lewis was elected to the School Committee, chaired by Edna English. Barbara Sullivan became second vice president of John Hancock; Martha Reardon, economic development manager of the South Shore Chamber of Commerce; and Geraldine Lombardo, clerk-magistrate and later a judge of the District Court. In 1982, Janet Gifford-Vernon became the first woman minister of the First Baptist Church. When interviewed, she said that part of her role was to ask timely and difficult questions: "What does the Christian word have to say about the preservation of the earth, integrity in politics, the military budget, being a single parent, a working mother, a housewife, or a teacher in front of thirty screaming children?" Amid such revolutionary change, two events speak volumes. In 1979,

> As so many changes take place around us daily nowadays, it is noticeable that many clubs of all types are going out of existence. The Hingham Women's Club with its many enthusiastic workers has been fortunate in being able to plan programs for the coming year. The club is opening its membership to women in neighboring communities who do not have such a club in their town.

And in 1981, the Women's Exchange on South Street closed after twenty-four years.

Some young women followed their new models in professional sports. It is symbolic that the Old Colony Tennis Club hosted championship women's tournaments in 1972 and 1973; the rise of professional women stars—King, Casals, Wade, Goolagong—was an index of the changing status of women. By the end of the 1970s, young local athletes were rising to fame: running stars Liz Murphy and Melissa Lang, basketball star Paula Ayers, gymnast Kathy Taurasi, Denise deSautels and Wendy Anderson in field hockey, and Liz Hills in olympic rowing. It is also symbolic that the Old Colony Club closed in 1982 allegedly because so many women players "had gone to work."

They were joining the force of commuters at a time when commuting seemed ever more nightmarish and other forms of transportation were being sought. "Do you suppose," asked the *Journal* in 1975, "the day will come when the Southeast Expressway will be so glutted with traffic that commuters will be clamoring for some other mode of transportation? Does anyone know how effective or well-patronized were the boats from Hingham to Boston?"

In October, 1975, new commuter boats began a trial period, with fire boats sending up plumes of water, whistles blowing, a band playing, and about three hundred commuters aboard. Soon there were sixty-four "regulars." Edward Gelsthorpe found that

> it's a sheer delight for the fifty to seventy folks who have been regularly availing themselves of this experience . . . . There is a real spirit of camaraderie on the boat; a number of total strangers have become friends . . . . The boat is just that, a simple, uncomplicated pleasure which twice each day allows us to enjoy each other's company and the absolute beauty of Boston's island-filled harbor.

Not many listened. Service ceased, returned, ceased again, returned in May, 1977, with "120 hardy souls" braving winds gusting to forty knots and seas running at six feet. Loyalists took out a big advertisement in September. The signers, fifty-one from Hingham, included sixteen women, among them the boat's energetic promoter on Beacon Hill, Caroline Stouffer, and May Vuilleumier on her way to work at Massachusetts General Hospital. "Don't Let Us Sink!" they pleaded. Don't believe rumors that the boat will stop for the winter!

The winter of 1978 tested their mettle. A storm on January 20, the worst in half a century, was followed by a blizzard that arrived on Monday, February 6, beginning eight days of emergency. Over two feet of snow emptied the streets of all but emergency vehicles. Hurricane-force winds brought down power lines. High tides swept over Rockland Street and Route 3A and up North Street. Ernie and Dick had three feet of water in Barba's cellar at the square. Townspeople on foot, their groceries in backpack, sled, or toboggan, passed and chatted. When the commuter boat *Amberjack* turned back to Long Wharf in Boston, a few hardy souls set out for home by the "T", but their bus got stuck in Weymouth. Kaye Bennett made it to St. Jerome's Church, haven of 250 for two days and nights. An anxious father, trapped in Framingham, sent a message through Civil Defense to Fire Chief Fletcher Patch, and Deputy Robert Garvin was dispatched with food, milk, and diapers to the young mother and her two-week-old baby. Gordon Sears at Walsh and Packard sold out two hundred snow shovels by Wednesday morning. Highway Superintendent Herbie Cole, Tree Warden Frannie Ford, and their men worked round the clock, and kids had memorable no-school days playing on a snow mountain in front of Loring Hall, where the only words visible on the marquee were "Oh God!"

When the "infamous blizzard" marked its first anniversary in 1979, subzero temperatures had brought an epidemic of frozen pipes, and the town was in the midst of an energy crisis. Crises in transportation and energy marched together in the 1970s. Hingham had suffered through its first energy crisis in 1973-74, a winter of severe discontent. The Watergate investigation was on the verge of impeachment proceedings. As confidence in government sank, flag-stealing in Hingham became epidemic. Gas and oil prices skyrocketed. Thermostats were lowered, rooms closed off. Emergency Daylight Savings Time sent people to work and to school in the dark. Long lines waited at gas stations—those that were open. On February 4, 1974, the line waiting at the Old Colony station at the harbor was backed up to the bathing beach.

Nineteen seventy-nine was another year of crisis, with hostages in Iran, Soviets in Afghanistan, oil spills in the Atlantic and the Gulf of Mexico, double-digit inflation and mortgage rates, and, perhaps most frightening, the accident at Three Mile Island nuclear plant in Pennsylvania. One local effect was the politicizing of nuclear energy. The ownership of shares in the Seabrook, New Hampshire, nuclear power project by the Hingham Light Board was attacked by a new organization, "REACH," the Responsible Energy Alternatives Coalition of Hingham, headed by Alice ("Pat") Granahan. As a result of their efforts, an "anti-nuke" article received 44 percent of the vote at a special town meeting in September, 1979. In 1980, Mrs. Granahan ran for a place on the Light Board; in 1983, she won, the first woman elected to the board.

Her election is one signal of how Hingham's political landscape was changing in the 1970s and early 1980s. No longer its staunch old Republican self, the town had been affected by upheaval in the national parties. In 1972, conservatives and moderates were fighting for control of the Republican party, and traditional Democrats were alienated by the followers of George McGovern. Increasing numbers of voters were adopting a wait and see attitude. In the summer of 1972, Hingham registrants divided as follows: 3340 Republicans, 3011 Democrats, and 4376 independents. The election results in November suggested the strength of the new independency. With a turnout of 92 percent, Republican Senator Edward Brooke received 7000 votes; Republican William Weeks beat Democrat Gerry Studds for Congress by 5658 to 4129; President Nixon ran behind his ticket in Hingham, defeating McGovern by only five to four; while Democratic State Representative William Spence won reelection by better than two to one and Democratic State Senator Allan Mackinnon by five to four.

The results in 1976 were similarly mixed. Hingham preferred President Gerald Ford over Jimmy Carter by five to four, but voted for Democratic Senator Edward Kennedy by the same margin. Liberal Democrat Caroline Stouffer won a race for state representative by a plurality; her closest opponent was a former Democratic town committee chairman running as an independent. The day's top vote-getter was a Stouffer ally, Representative Gerry Studds. Among referendum questions, the women's Equal Rights Amendment and the bill to require bottle and can deposits both passed, while proposals for a graduated state income tax and for a ban on hand guns both lost. Liberal and conservative forces were almost equal.

By 1980, however, a new conservative coalition had taken shape. Ronald Reagan carried the town with 50 percent of the vote against Carter's 35 percent and John Anderson's 15 percent. The nation's new mood was aptly expressed that year in the theme of Hingham's Fourth of July parade: "America First." The winning float celebrated motherhood, apple pie, popcorn, and peanut butter.

In Hingham and the nation the conservative revolution had gradually gathered strength during the 1970s. One moral and constitutional issue in particular galvanized this revolution. In December, 1971, the U.S. Supreme Court first heard arguments in the case of *Roe v. Wade*. By the fall of 1972, the "abortion issue" had entered "the rough and tumble of national politics." In January, 1973, the Court handed down its decision holding choice to be a limited constitutional right of privacy. That month saw the fading of the most divisive of 1960s issues, Vietnam, and the emergence of the issue that would replace it.

[422]

Like abolitionism early in the nineteenth century and temperance later, the right to abortion became an overarching issue. Its local impact was felt in the split of the Hingham League of Women Voters, whose leaders had followed state leaders in supporting choice. Some members fought back, and some resigned. A new organization, "Birthright," was formed in 1971, and a year later, the Hingham Chapter of Citizens for Life was founded. The issue mobilized conservative reaction against the 1960s. Consider this letter from Dorothy James, written a few days after the *Roe v. Wade* decision:

> Our America where intellectuals introduced drugs as a way of medication, where family magazines are polluted with pornography, where free love has produced an epidemic of venereal disease, where the destructive protest has been thought to be rightful dissent, where the murder of unborn babies is thought a small price to pay for the pleasures of sex, where life cannot be protected in the Supreme Court, where the purpose of law is forgotten and the letter of the law is worshipped like a plastic god, where tradition's moral sense is spat upon, such is the atmosphere of present America.

It would be hard to find a fuller synthesis of reawakened conservatism.

The new conservatism was also heard in criticism of the schools. In 1973, when a deteriorating Foster School needed more classrooms and expensive repairs, the angry attacks were not just financial. Some were aimed at the spread of what was called "the Plymouth River School philosophy" of open classrooms, seen by the critics as fostering a lack of discipline and failing to "teach the basics." By 1976, the reaction against curricular innovations of the 1960s was in full swing. As School Committee Chair Edna English said, "The curriculum must not be cluttered with trivia," and she sounded the new battle-cry: "Back to Basics."

Many educators of those years agreed with Dean Wayne Booth of Chicago: "Perhaps most of us want to get back to basics, in one sense or another, but . . . we are not exactly united in a single conception of what the basics might be." Nonetheless, the Back to Basics movement was a powerful historic phenomenon—and not only in education. It said, "In our compulsion to amplify and liberalize, we have lost sight of priorities." America could no longer afford uncritical growth; its expansionist days were ending. It faced tough choices. It needed to identify or reaffirm priorities. This was a fueling motive of the conservative revolution.

Two other local issues energized the reaction: charter reform and tax limitation. The first ran its futile course during 1972 and 1973 in attempts to codify the town charter. Most towns in the state were still governing themselves by old and confusing accumulations of bylaws and statutes. The state Home Rule Amendment of 1966 called for codification and clarification into town charters. In 1972, Hingham elected charter commissioners with Jane Malme as chair. Only eight people ran for nine positions, indicating a lack of broad support. The group began eleven months of study, hearings, and roundtables. The process allowed for review of town government, and the commission recommended what it thought were a few moderate changes. To conservatives, they appeared to be radical alterations of traditional Hingham democracy.

The commissioners decided early not to challenge the open town meeting form, perhaps because they were sure that Hingham would never approve its demise, or perhaps because the alternatives appeared even more flawed. Their controversial suggestions were three. First, they would "strengthen" the selectmen by giving them the power to appoint a few officials who traditionally had been elected. Second, they would provide for a "recall" of officials deemed unsatisfactory. And third, in response to the selectmen's call for an executive secretary, they proposed that this position carry responsibility for coordinating the budget process and require professional and technical qualifications.

The selectmen, evidently dismayed, saw no difference between this office and that of a town manager. No "recall" was needed and certainly no "financial czar" administrator. Officials should be elected. Present operations were "quite satisfactory," needing no such "drastic changes." Counsel for the town suggested that the charter commissioners had not lived in Hingham long enough to understand its government. It has also been suggested that the group was inexperienced in the building of consensus. The handwriting was on the wall. By "complete surprise," the Advisory Committee opposed the charter, and in the town election of 1973, it lost: 3795 no, 1785 yes. Politically, the timing was unfortunate, the signs of reaction against "drastic changes" were many, and the commission's leadership was liberal.

The conservative movement for limited taxation, the second energizing issue, grew throughout the 1970s. Early in the decade, citizen efforts to monitor the budget process had limited and temporary success. From 1973 on, national inflation spiraled upward, fueled in part by the energy crisis, and town budgets escalated. Finally, in 1978, a dramatic sign of change appeared three thousand miles away. California passed the first state tax-cap law, Proposition 13, and the trend swept eastward.

"Prop 2½" was a revolution waiting to happen. Town meetings, sometimes with bare quorums, passed budgets rising to over $18 million by 1980. Hingham's Richard Manley, president of the Massachusetts Taxpayers Foundation, warned that the state's taxes had become the "laughing stock of the nation." "Some noble soul once said that being a taxpayer in Massachusetts is not unlike making love to a gorilla—you don't stop when you're tired, you stop when the gorilla is. And who ever heard of a gorilla getting tired?" South Shore realtor Jack Conway led an attack on the gorilla, and Citizens for Limited Taxation pushed Proposition 2½ for statewide referendum in 1980.

The measure would (1) eventually limit or cut back property taxes to 2½ percent of market value of all assessed property in the town, (2) limit their annual increases to 2½ percent "plus new growth" unless "overridden" at a town election, and (3) cut auto excise taxes by 60 percent. As November approached, dire warnings were heard of "drastic layoffs" and "cuts in services." A task force of town officials sounded the alarm. But many citizens no longer listened to their officials. "Prop 2½" passed in the state with 60 percent of the vote and in the town with 56 percent.

In November, 1980, the impending fiscal crisis coincided with an epochal event in Hingham's history. Selectman Oscar Beck, marking his fiftieth anniversary as a town employee, announced his retirement, and in December, Kate Mahony announced her candidacy to replace him. She won with 42 percent of the vote against four men. She had campaigned as a businesswoman who "knows how to watch the bottom line." She thought that, with careful management, "Prop 2½" might be a boon.

In 1981, Hingham had its first woman selectman in 346 years. Kate Mahony preferred to be called "selectman," but the post-victory interviewer found her busy with domestic chores: "there's nothing like washing to bring you down to earth." In the years to follow, laundry must sometimes have seemed a welcome holiday. She would retire in 1990 to campaign for an override of "Prop 2½."

In her first years, Kate Mahony faced a fearful array of problems: the impact of the new tax law, rampant inflation, climbing home costs, declining home starts, gypsy moth infestation and disputes over the safety of spraying, distress over plans to build a casino in Hull, and crises of water pollution and hazardous waste. In May, 1981, Police Chief Raymond Campbell returned from three months incommunicado on sick leave—perhaps, as Selectman Eugene Bickford suggested, "a victim of Prop 2½." The selectmen voted to force his retirement, then reversed their stand, but the damage was done, the chief charged a "conspiracy to destroy my name," and a highly contentious public tone was set for 1981-84.

The growing complexity of town government was now aggravated by internal dissension and by a rising tide of litigation. Disputes traditionally settled by political debates and institutions were referred to the courts for solution, and our "peaceable kingdom" joined in a national trend. "We live in a litigious society," said Kate Mahony at the close of 1982, and Selectman Joseph Daley echoed her: "People sue the town at the drop of a hat, whenever they are dissatisfied with the decision of a town department or board." One board sued another. That year, Daley's successful challenger, Edward Lewiecki, noted that

> Our town counsel has been placed in a position of making day-to-day decisions that should be made by our elected officials—we have involved ourselves in unnecessary litigation which compromise, commonsense, and executive leadership could have avoided.

The most newsworthy "official" of these years was George Ford, counsel to the town.

There was dispute over the purchase of nuclear energy, with the Light Board publicly divided. There was dispute over the alteration of a dangerous intersection after a multiple fatality in the summer of 1982, and the town was sued on behalf of a surviving child for police negligence. When retired Chief Campbell made remarks on the radio about the accident, the police union threatened to sue him. McDonald's sued and lost when denied a permit at Hingham Plaza. Boat owners refused to pay mooring fees, but when Harbor Committeeman Frank Mahony urged they be taken to court, counsel Ford warned of "impending litigation" by the owners. In a new tactic of intimidation, a condominium converter threatened to bring personal suits against those who spoke out against his project. Several housing projects remained in litigation for years. Members of the Police Department sued over alleged discrimination in promotions. The department seemed stabilized with the appointment of William Cushing as chief in June, 1983, but the new chief died at his desk three months later. Choice of his successor was delayed pending the next civil service exam. When the selectmen suggested removing his office from civil service, they were attacked. Their efforts to end inter- and intra-departmental disputes were met with charges of usurpation. Two members of the Conservation Commission were replaced, and Kate Mahony was "personally affronted" by charges that she was carrying out a "vendetta."

Two disputes, discussed earlier, became labyrinthine. One was over the sewer project issue, with its acrimonious history of suits, counter-suits, and court orders. The other was over the Elder Care/Brandon Woods project. The Zoning Board of Appeals denied a permit but neglected to put its denial in writing. Elder Care sued for its permit "by default" and then offered to negotiate. But the rule now, enunciated by counsel Ford, was that no issue in or close to litigation should be publicly discussed. In such a labyrinth of legalism, how could political discourse continue? Town meeting ignored Ford's warning and voted the needed zoning change. The board issued a permit for a smaller project, which the court found in "contravention" of its order. The town appealed again, lost, and capitulated, whereupon abutters brought their own suit. Brandon Woods would remain in the labyrinth for several years. As of 1990, the project remained "on hold" for financial reasons.

Into this maze in September, 1984, stepped the town's first administrative assistant, Daisy Janey. At sixty-three, she had been a teacher, a paralegal, and an administrator, and she held a degree in psychotherapy, a timely qualification. She would earn her $18,000 in a year marred by dispute and acrimony, by investigations of a building commissioner, a sewer commissioner, and the town clerk. One might conclude, said a writer to the *Journal*, that "our town government has followed Alice through the looking glass, but without amusing results . . . . I look forward with trepidation to your next accounts." In the fall of 1984, Selectman Bickford turned over the chair of the board to Kate Mahony and turned with visible relief to plans for the town's upcoming birthday. A party was sorely needed.

Each half-century since 1835, Hingham had directed its attention to its past. Each commemoration suited in mood and tone its changing circumstances. In 1835, the continuity of pioneer past and progressive future did not seem in doubt. By 1885, the days of ancestral independence and character seemed remote and quaint. In 1935, amidst depression, the town's past and present came together in a grand folk festival. As the twentieth century grew old, something of the mood of the 1880s returned.

Preparations for 1985 had actually begun a decade before, when the town participated in the national bicentennial of 1976. It is revealing to contrast the book published for this occasion with the book of 1935. Mason Foley's elegant essay brought the past vividly to life in fusion with the present and the future. Michael Shilhan's haunting *When I Think of Hingham* (1976) preserved old photographs and reminiscences

[427]

of a simpler, lost world. A renewed nostalgia pervaded celebrations of the 1970s. In 1974, Central Junior High celebrated "Life in the 1950s," and the theme of the 1975 cabaret was "Yesterday."

The bicentennial of 1976 climaxed with a parade of forty-eight floats and retiring Fire Chief Warren Lincoln as grand marshal. Symbolically, it had a new "Uncle Sam." Francis Wright had died two days after the last of his thirty-five parades in 1974. In 1975, there was only a small Uncle Sam hat on top of a black-draped vehicle, and "Frannie" Wright's reminiscences evoked nostalgic memories:

> All that night fire crackers and racing motorcycles kept the sleeper tossing feverishly, and he would awake with a shudder, fearing that he had overslept, his heart beating with the throb of the big brass drum . . . . The spirit gum had a very heady, hospital smell and stung his tender, fresh-shaven chin. The whiskers tickled his nose and lips maddeningly . . . . Just as he lit his stogie, his wife would dab his cheeks with rouge.

> It was nearly 9:30 now, and he had posed a dozen times or more with someone's tot—usually in tears—and he hailed a passing marshal. There was a delay, said the marshal, a band hadn't arrived from Dorchester . . . . In the interim, there were three dogfights, a riding academy horse "spooked" at a float of near-naked Indians and bolted through the shrieking crowd, and three kids fainted dead away, overcome by heat, nervous excitement, and several frankfurters hastily consumed . . . .

> The drums started a spirited beat . . . and the parade swung up past the garages and the paper store and headed straight up the Main Street to the tune of "Hey, Look Me Over" . . . . At the foot of that long, steep hill he halted the parade in front of a friendly pediatrician's house, and he disappeared quickly into the house. There, the good doctor had a strong bourbon highball ready . . . . The hill had become suddenly much less long and much less steep . . . .

> Up a long residential street to the High School, where the parade literally fell apart. The marcher tottered over to a station wagon parked inconspicuously in the shade behind third base . . . stripping off whiskers and necktie as he went. As he finished his first can of beer, someone asked him if he would do it again.

Along with nostalgia, however, there awakened a newly authentic sense of the past. Programs began to inventory a heritage rich in architecture and document. The Hingham Historical Commission was formed. Norman Hersey and John Richardson, his nephew, reminded the town of its real history behind popular myths. Old name signs were posted. Six men, including James Jamieson, organized a new Hingham Militia Company in 1973. Anthony Macmillan, its first commander, led the company in Boston's bicentennial parade. Occasionally he would rest, removing his artificial leg. Unlike many companies, which faded after the nation's bicentenary, Hingham's modern militia remained active and growing as of 1990.

The strength of the impulse to conserve could be seen in the liveliest controversy of 1977. The First Parish House of 1890 on lower Main Street had been purchased by the cooperative bank next door to be razed for space for a drive-in window. The parish had moved to its elegant "new" quarters in 1959, but the old building lived on for a while as office space and a doughnut shop. The plans to demolish it were vigorously opposed. Voices of some of the over eight hundred petitioners lamented the "transient, faceless" recent past and its destructiveness. The plans were halted, and alternatives were sought. The bank offered the building for a dollar to anyone who would move it. "Feasibility" prevailed at last. As scores watched in April, 1977, a giant wrecking crane did its work. But the sense of the past had changed since the days when demolition of "tired old landmarks" was hailed in the name of "progress." Many Americans had lost faith in that shibboleth.

The programs of preservation in 1975-77 were the start of planning for Hingham's 350th birthday. A committee was appointed in 1980, and four of its members, Winston Hall, Robert Garvin, and Robert and Brenda Beal, continued their work for five years. Winston Hall compiled a slide show about the 1935 celebration and took it "all over town to drum up interest in the 350th." Later they were joined by Judy Hardy, Jeanne Murphy, Judy Kimball, and others. Their labors would produce an occasion significantly different from the festivities of 1935. They faced challenges never before faced by such a group: how to reawaken and nourish the communal memory when sweeping demographic changes had seriously weakened a shared sense of local tradition? Their answer, while initially controversial, was appropriate.

II: 1985-1990

✠

Hingham on Its Birthday and After

IN his speech at Hingham's 350th birthday, Governor Michael Dukakis declared, "Hingham is an example of what community really means." The committee had set out to prove it with a year-long party. The party began suitably with a selectmen's ball on November 24, 1984. After the ball, Selectman Eugene Bickford was seen wearing a broad grin: "It was wonderful to see the cross section of people and all of them out there dancing." Bored at the next selectmen's meeting, he asked, "After the Ball, what is there?" Bickford, "Mr. Hingham," presided over the year's festivities as honorary chairman. Ironically, he lost his office as selectman in the 1985 election. Retiring, he recalled his first interest in town office, growing up next door to William L. Foster on Middle Street and riding with him about town in his electric car. "I think," he said, "a lot of him rubbed off on me."

New Selectman John Brady set out with verve and publicity in a confrontational style. He challenged his fellow selectmen on issues and procedures and battled the Yacht Club over parking arrangements. He clashed with counsel Ford, who responded with the puzzling pronouncement that "Hingham has not been a political town." Brady gave the birthday party some of its best fireworks. John Richardson, also at war with Selectmen Lewiecki and Mahony, provided it with a salutary birthday message. The occasion was local community opposition to a halfway house near his home on Fort Hill Street. He recalled the "entities" he had worked to preserve:

Yet all of these entities that bring quality to the experience of life are worth very little if we tend toward idolizing them and selfishly close the door upon the less fortunate. I have no desire to live in a com-

[430]

munity that is pretty veneer with no substance or compassion . . . . I urge my neighbors to stop and think for a while and dream dreams of what might be accomplished by reaching out rather than closing out.

The 350th Committee, at any rate, adopted the "reaching out" principle. Their budget request was challenged with the interesting complaint that their plans had little to do with "history" and were not "commemorative in nature." Judy Hardy explained that the committee was trying to serve everyone's interests, *including* those who "might not necessarily identify with the historical significance of the occasion, but would find the excitement of the Celebration memorable."

Judy Hardy perfectly described what took place. The point was celebration—not as in "mass," though Cardinal Bernard Law did celebrate mass, but as in "party." It was a party where every group could "do its thing": elderly picnic; eaters banquet; musicians play and sing; skateboarders, runners, cyclists, and sailors race; dancers dance; history buffs perambulate a colonial encampment; and all join as spectators of parades, fireworks, and five thousand balloons with ribboned messages, rising—thanks to Jeanne Murphy's arrangements—into skies briefly clear of Logan Airport's planes. The party declared that "all is well"; the theme was "pride."

At the high school field was a Revolutionary War encampment in its daily life, with visiting Colonial and British troops, cannons, and mock battles. At the old meetinghouse was a colonial wedding. The bride, descended from Aldens and Lincolns, and the groom, an EMT fireman, entered together. The bride received symbolic herbs; wheat, not rice, was thrown as they left. Feasting and maypole dancing followed. Central Junior High friends researched for a July Fourth float, "350 Years of Kids," with a message of sad insight: 1635—Colonization; 1735—Farming; 1835—Child Labor; 1985—Laziness (the loss of meaningful work). The prize-winning float was the Water Company's. Designed by Nancy Jermyn, its over two thousand handmade flowers had been stored by her mother, Anna Calvi, in the cellar: "I didn't dare wash my clothes for fear of the steam ruining the flowers." The birthday reached its climax on Labor Day weekend, 1985. Sunday's parade was a spectacle of exotic color. Down streets awash in white-on-red anniversary flags and three styles of T-shirts marched Benjamin Lincoln's Hingham Militia Company, four hundred Shriners in Arab garb and fez with a pipe band, and from England, wilting in the heat, wool-clad, armored seventeenth-century pikemen of the Sealed Knot Society.

Among the permanent birthday presents was a lovely garden, ninety feet long, in front of the public library—a gift from the Garden Club.

The Wilmon Brewers, marking the sixty-fourth anniversary of their betrothal, gave the 107-acre More-Brewer Park. Hingham, England, sent a replica of their handcarved market place sign, which stands in a triangle of land in front of the library. Nature's present arrived at the end of September in the shape of Hurricane "Gloria," leaving eighty-two hundred Light Plant customers in the dark and filling the town with firewood and the voice of the buzz-saw. In November, Halley's Comet carried the heavens into the party. A belated gift from the state lottery was $1.4 million, and at Christmas, a Massachusetts entering its brief Miracle repealed the income surtax.

What was Hingham on its 350th birthday? Its population, 20,648, was no longer growing. It was 99 percent white, as compared with 91 percent in southeastern Massachusetts. People who claimed a single ethnic ancestry were 38.3 percent Irish, 25.1 percent English, and 15.2 percent Italian. In recent years, its ethnic make-up had diversified a little. The Country Club had been described as a "virtual melting pot," its "Italian night" followed by the "Sons of Erin," and then by "signs of the Star of David." And what would old Myer Greenfield, one of the "boys" of Greenfield's knitting mills a half century before, have thought as he lay dying in Chestnut Hill in April, 1980, had he seen the completion that month of Temple Sha'Aray Shalom on south Main Street? Within a decade, the congregation included 250 families.

In 1985, with 30.4 percent of registered voters, Democrats outnumbered Republicans by four points, but over 43 percent called themselves Independents. School enrollments had dropped from 4044 to 3489 in three years. Among the elderly, the fastest growing group was eighty-five and older. Between 1981 and 1984, jobs had increased by 1443, and eighty-five new businesses had been established. Junior high students could study the "world of business," seniors at Notre Dame Academy checked their shares on Wall Street, and "Home Ec" high-schoolers studied the restaurant and fashion businesses and operated a nursery school. Daycare centers were in demand. Plans for a center at Plymouth River School were delayed when no company would write the large liability insurance for a private owner, and the center was operated by the public schools. Career women were feeling the stress of crowded lives:

> I reached every goal I had at twenty—my career is where I hoped in terms of status and financial reward—I have two children, a boy and a girl, just as I dreamed. I have a home I never even hoped for, but I'm enjoying it all less than I thought. There never seems to be enough time.

There was too little time for traditional town democracy. Attendance at town meetings had shrunk in recent years from 7.9 percent, 7.3 percent, under 6 percent, to 4 percent of registered voters. Many voters apparently were feeling the sentiments expressed in a hypothetical conversation printed in the *Mariner*: "Are you going to town meeting?" "No, I never go to those. They're boring. Everything is decided already, so what's the point? I don't understand what they're talking about. All that zoning."

There was still ample time for Hingham's long love affair with sports. Basketball vied with hockey for wintertime popularity, but youth hockey held its fascination, and the "Squirt B's" were state champions. The high school's football Harbormen were suffering a lapse from their late 1970s glory days as league champions, but soccer for boys and girls was phenomenally popular. Since 1978, when over five hundred signed up for soccer, one devoted soccer father tells us, "the Youth Soccer League had come to dwarf all other sports programs. Soccer has few injuries, and boys and girls can play together. Most important, the League rules prohibited coaching from the sideline!" And of course, Hingham on its birthday remained a home for passionate sailors, a place to which many had come for its sailing. In the year of the town's 350th, the Yacht Club was ninety years old, with almost four hundred members. Its younger partner, the Lincoln Sailing Club, had replaced it at the Cove. Founded in 1971 by Tom Curtis, Virginia Gray, and others, the club sailed its Turnabouts from Barnes Wharf, renovated by Rotary Club. By 1982, more than two thousand had learned to sail here. By 1988, when the Curtis pavilion was dedicated, the number would reach five thousand.

Also alive and growing was Hingham's traditional love of music. The South Shore Conservatory, founded in 1970, moved to handsome new quarters, the Depot Commandant's house, in 1974. And next year, newly arrived in town, Margot Euler formed the Broad Cove Chorale at the Barnabas Lincoln homestead on Lincoln Street. In the early 1980s, Conservatory enrollments reached 1900, and Mrs. Euler's Unicorn Singers graced festivities in the square.

On average, 1985 Hingham was a wealthy town. Median family income was over $30,000, compared with under $23,000 in southeastern Massachusetts. Over 18 percent of families earned $50,000 or more, 22 percent between $35,000 and $49,999. The average price of a home reached $200,000, 50 percent above the Greater Boston average, and prices were still rising. By 1986-87, the average was $225,000, and the least expensive home cost $130,000.

[433]

Hingham's 1985 was a year of stretch limousines, foreign cars, careening skateboarders, wheelchair ramps and ice cream shops, new flashing lights at the intersections of South, Main, and Central Streets, more protective house alarms and cocaine users, new high voltage transformers containing dangerous PCBs, IRAs, blow haircuts, and story hours for Toddlers and *Dads*. The citizens of 1985 saw the death of Paragon Park, read of plans to build homes on the just-sold South Shore Country Club, and heard the first disputes about the train's possible return. Streets were torn up for new water pipes and wired for cable TV, just in time for a debate between Bickford and Brady. They were asked, What is Hingham's greatest asset? its greatest liability? Both singled out the remarkable cadre of volunteers as the asset. For Bickford, the liability was not owning the Water Company; for Brady, it was Hingham's location between Boston and the mushrooming towns further south, which bred dilemmas of transportation.

A number of people were asked to prophesy the Hingham of fifty years hence. We will not be here to see the time capsule, donated by the Peter Murphys, unearthed, but posterity, we hope, will have fun doing so. Projections of the town's size ranged from Bickford's 35-40,000 down to John Studley's 27,000. Appraiser Nazzareno DeVito predicted that a $150,000 house would cost $1.5 million and expected more "condos." Overcrowding frightened Kate Mahony most: "All the 'good' land . . . is already built on." Already, said Alan Devine of the Planning Board, "the value of property is so high that . . . they're blasting pure ledge to put in a septic system." Conservation Commissioner Robert Beal warned, "The town is under siege." Brady believed, "We'll never be another Braintree." Bickford envisioned the shipyard with motel, marina, apartments, and shops.

Of most urgency for the prophets were water, waste disposal, and the railroad. Would the Metropolitan District Commission ultimately admit the whole town to its sewer system? John Brandt, chairman of the Sewer Commission, thought not. Would the water supply "become an overnight horror show caused by pollution . . . by toxic materials"? Edward Lewiecki prayed not. Would the railroad return? Warren Noble thought not. Lewiecki dreamed of a monorail down the center of Route 3, and Bickford of a line from Braintree to South Hingham. Carl Achille, former president of the Hingham Merchants Association, and Mary Stein, bookseller in the Sprague Building, thought the square would change little.

Pat Granahan envisioned a town free of pesticides and hazardous waste, with wind farms on Turkey and Baker Hills, wave energy from

Hull Gut, and every home with a rainwater collector and solar spaces. Jack Studley projected a pension fund still unfunded, a charter in need of revision, talk of private police and fire departments, and two or three people "experts on what happened in '85, and it would be possible for all of them to be correct." A healthy town needs both visionaries and cynics.

As the 1980s drew to a close, both visions and doubts were tested. Alarms old and new competed for attention. Some students claimed there was a serious drug problem at the high school; a study committee found them mistaken. Hingham's first two cases of AIDS were reported in April, 1987. There were alarms over incinerators in Weymouth and Braintree, and alarms over the Light Board's new high voltage substation close to the landfill. Town officials tried to expand the landfill, but town meeting said no. In the summer of 1990, mandatory trash separation for recycling began, and at the landfill, Hinghamites learned new maneuvers: plastic here; white and colored bottles here and here; papers, cans, over there; compost through the gates.

Four topics, however, were dominant: the development of affordable housing, trains, the Country Club, and Proposition 2½ overrides. Human inclusiveness, transportation, land use, and taxes—the quartet had persisted through Hingham's life history. Linking them still was the struggle for local control.

"One neighborhood after another" was "walking down to the Conservation Commission . . . trying to stop increased development." Suits and appeals held up plans, and a depression in the real estate market made some moot. In 1988, 250 people waited for space in the Lincoln apartments, thirty for Thaxter Park, and 120 other families were on the list of the Housing Authority. As one critic calculated, 70 percent of Hingham's homeowners could not afford to buy their own homes now. Another remarked, "Hingham is too homogeneous a town, which makes us poorer and less rich in ways other than economic." In late 1988, the attention of the media focused on Kitty Montgomery and her four children living in tents in Wompatuck State Park, denied admission to Hingham schools but admitted by Norwell. Developer Martin Murphy was at odds with the building commissioner over whether homeless families could live temporarily in the old Universalist meetinghouse on North Street. The commissioner, unfairly treated by the media, was concerned about the safety of the building. A brighter spot was the Interfaith Shelter in the Church of the Nazarene on Rockland Street. In five years, the Rev. J. Scott Newell and his wife Dorothy had sheltered many homeless families. People like the Newells, Ruth

Spencer, and Gretchen Condon of the Housing Authority did what they could. But Hingham had not solved its problem of inclusiveness.

In commercial development, a few new office complexes arose at the far corners of town. "There was a time when Hingham was a bedroom community . . . . In recent years, more and more companies have come to town," and "Hingham is becoming an employment center." One of its largest employers, Talbots opened the 1980s with a workforce of almost nine hundred. The small specialty shop opened by George Talbot in 1946 had moved to the Soule mansion in 1950. By 1985, it was expanding further into its surplus store on Lincoln Street near the shipyard. The shipyard had finally begun its face-lifting. Here, by the summer of 1985, the commuter boats drew about 11,000 riders a day; by the summer of 1989, that number would more than double. Across Route 3A on new William B. Terry Drive stood new professional offices. The Water Company closed its doors on South Street after 107 years and moved to Terry Drive; the Hingham Fire Insurance Company, to a site near the Back River. Their old buildings remained in the square.

Not so a younger one. By late evening, January 16, 1988, the sixty-year-old Sprague Building was engulfed in flames. Oil tanks in the basement exploded, sending thick black smoke into the air and polluting the rubble. Five firemen were hospitalized. The brick facade had to be demolished. "If this had happened four or five days ago," said Acting Fire Chief Garvin, recalling subzero temperatures, "we might have lost Hingham Square." Richard Bartlett, owner of the popular bakery and doughnut shop, said, "That business was my life." The owners of Hingham Galleries, Mary Ann and Gary Hayden, had put their life's savings into the business two years before, and now, irreplaceable art works and heirlooms were gone. The bookstore had been transformed by the new owner William Soderberg into an imitation salon complete with a piano and the cockatoo "Parnassus." He had taken Parnassus home that night because the building was so cold.

The new Pride Building arose with a "Newbury Street look" in time for late Christmas shopping in 1989, when cold days sent some passers-by shivering into the "glitzy new hallways," its rents 50 percent above the square's average. Fashionable new tenants moved in. No more doughnuts. Yogurt instead. The new building's name was chosen during the week of town meeting and election in 1989, when some detected irony in the old adage, "Hingham for its pride."

Another danger threatened to return to increase the anxiety of merchants in the square. Discussion of the possible return of the railroad had been heard early in the 1980s. In 1985, offered a vague referendum question, local voters favored the idea by 2558 to 1074. But in 1987, concrete plans evoked frightening images: two stations, one near the Country Club, the other near Hingham Lumber Company, with traffic and parking problems; trains every half hour at peak times, every hour and a half at other times, running fifty-five to sixty miles per hour except at grade crossings—fourteen of them with train-activated gates and flashing lights; traffic back-ups at crossings with emergency vehicles stuck in them; newly renovated homes close to the track in West Hingham, their dishes rattling, walls shaking, values falling.

Towns further south, facing no such dangers and seeking relief from worsening traffic, supported the idea, as did the South Shore Chamber of Commerce. In 1988, the project seemed moving toward realization, and radical models for the transformation of the square were weighed: barriers, gates, a closed-off Main Street, one-way traffic on North and South, and a parking deck behind the Hingham Institution for Savings. For two more years, the town awaited the Environmental Impact Report of the Massachusetts Bay Transit Authority. When, finally, it was released in the spring of 1990, Brian Noble "congratulated" the "T" on admitting that the "price of the Greenbush Line" would be the death of the square. Merchant Vito Nardo recalled the days when his predecessor "Ace" Loud "had a system rigged up to protect bottles from falling off the shelves when the trains came through." Merchants displayed their anti-train flags and supported the efforts of Alexander Macmillan, chairman of the Historical Commission, to protect the Lincoln Historic Districts, now extended along North and South Streets. Some residents near the track in West Hingham foresaw their neighborhood becoming once more "the slums of Hingham."

Elsewhere in town, many remained apathetic or supported the railroad's return. The selectmen were cautious in taking positions. The *Journal* surveyed its readers and found that three out of four were opposed, but only sixty-four readers had bothered to respond to the survey. As our narrative closed in the spring of 1990, the Environmental Impact Report was being distributed, and the town was planning its official response. We can only wonder about the outcome and about what posterity will say of its consequences. Whatever they are, Hingham's destiny will remain inseparable from its geography.

The third dominant issue of the late 1980s has been resolved—a remarkable fact since "some issues seem to last forever in Hingham." The South Shore Country Club challenge coalesced enduring sentiments: the love of open space, the fear of siege by developers, the passion for sports and recreation. News broke in the fall of 1985 that the club had been sold. The new owners planned to build homes there. The town negotiated with the owners in February, 1986. In April, a packed town meeting voted by secret ballot 1216 to 327 to approve $7 million for "taking by eminent domain." On town election day, the results, while narrower, were still decisive: 2993 to 2341. As 1987 closed, a court-appointed panel set the price at $7.5 million. At a special town meeting in February, 1988, 1538 voters—two and one half times the attendance at some regular meetings—voted an additional $1.25 million for purchase and development of the Country Club by a margin of almost six to one.

One major question remained: whether to apply for state assistance. If the state contributed, nonresidents would be eligible for memberships, and the land would have to remain open space. At another special meeting, conservationists agreed with Alexander Macmillan. Describing himself whimsically as an "old fuddy duddy Yankee," he supported state aid to protect the land against future development. Robert Falvey expressed concern over "agreeing with Alec Macmillan about anything" but agreed: "We cannot afford not to take it." Edward "Tuck" Wadleigh, often the spokesman for lower-income Hinghamites, said he was "not a golfer (it's like playing catch with yourself)" but told Hingham to "get down off its high horse." Here was a rare and unbeatable coalition. In July, 1988, over five hundred people applied for memberships—some of them waiting in line for hours, some mothers with lawnchairs, games, and kids—to begin playing golf on the first of August. In November, 1989, the town's Country Club Committee reported sixteen hundred family memberships and a first-year profit of $87,297.

This was one bright spot in the gathering fiscal gloom. In the spring of 1986, the fourth key issue emerged, and the ominous term "override" entered common parlance. For two years more, "something," in the phrase of Dickens' Micawber, always "turned up." Drops in state aid to cities and towns were "depressing," but property values still climbed. At town meeting in 1988, the Advisory Committee was reassuring: "The town's economy is healthy. No override this year." Two months later, the bad news broke, and in September, James Welch, chairman of the Advisory Committee, summarized it to the Rotary Club: "the bloom is off the rose"; the town faced uncontrollable costs, decreased revenue and property growth, and ever decreasing state aid. The Advisory Committee worked for level funding and warned of drastic cuts. The town had seven months' warning.

Around the world, 1989 was an *annus mirabilis.* Freedom was breaking out: elections were held in Poland, in the Soviet Union, in Nicaragua; millions demonstrated in Beijing; Communist regimes were overthrown in Budapest, Warsaw, and Prague; the Berlin wall toppled. President George Bush's first year was a year of populist revolt. It was in Hingham, too. Skeptical voters asked of the proposed override, "Why this year when we had the money for the country club last year?" It was small comfort to hear that as many as two-thirds of Massachusetts cities and towns were facing the same crisis. Department heads worked on alternative budgets in the event the override failed, and perhaps the news of such options encouraged the skeptics. Selectmen, divided, made the controversial decision to offer two override choices: the full $1.9 million actually needed, or "half is better than none."

"Tuck" Wadleigh, running for selectman, spoke for some: "No more blank checks . . . . We are tired of being held over a barrel by scare tactics." At town meeting, as the line items in the proposed budget were read, Robert Macdonald led the attack, calling out "holds" to require separate discussion later. Lengthy debate over garbage collection muddled the process with dark humor. After three hours, the budget passed. On the second evening, Robert Falvey led in a futile fight to reconsider, favoring "people dollars" over old buildings, garbage, and this history of the town. The town found itself on the eve of an election at which all of the debate at the meeting might be rendered irrelevant by thousands who had not been there.

On the following Saturday in April, 1989, it was. With a more than 50 percent turnout, both override options lost, 56 percent to 44 percent and 52 percent to 48 percent. The weeks that followed were among the more dismal in the turbulent history of Hingham democracy. Teachers, administrators, firemen, policemen, and highway workers received layoff notices. Central Junior High School closed, with fond memories of its sixty-one years and none of its controversial birth. Marion Carnes would not return for her twenty-eighth year as cook-manager of the cafeteria: "2½ put me out of a job." At North Fire Station, the flag was lowered, and Warren Lincoln struck Box 45 four blasts, then five, to signal closing. The theme of Memorial Day was "sacrifice." At the old meetinghouse, the new minister, Kenneth Read-Brown, descendant of Peter Hobart, preached on a "day of hope." At the Methodist Church, the sermon was "Calming the Storm."

The mood was not hope, and less storm than dismay. A seventh-grader wrote, "What kind of a cheap town is Hingham?" Soul-searching began. Driving around town, the usually philosophical Philip Swanson saw

> the handsome old houses with shining new paint, newly shingled roofs . . . additions . . . . The newly built houses typically ostentatiously oversized . . . . Foreign import cars . . . . Our harbor . . . clogged with expensive pleasure craft. Our many restaurants with their parking lots full . . . . We accumulate so many things that we have had to invent the yard sale to shunt them about. Golf . . . courses are crowded. Peripatetic parents dish out megabucks for the approved uniforms and glorified sneakers.

He recalled the closings, layoffs, and reduced hours, and asked, "Because we could not afford to do otherwise? How come?" His conservationist ally John Richardson struck a different note:

> Those who wring their hands and shed tears . . . should not despair. Hingham is not coming apart at the seams. It is a return to common sense. There are many of us living here who purchased homes long ago when they were relatively cheap. Many Hinghamites do not make big bucks. Many Hinghamites would like to continue to live here after retirement . . . . From where I walk, the voice on the street was "No override" many weeks ago.

Both were truth-tellers.

In 1990, the battle was fought again. Committees on opposing sides fought to persuade. A program of "civic reeducation" was mounted. On election day in April, the largest number of voters ever at a town election, 8119, went to the polls. The current override proposal was approved by a vote of 59.4 percent to 37.9 percent. Obviously, the struggle was not over—the struggle of a self-protective small town to pay the costs of its future, the struggle of sincere combatants over the town's character, the struggle for safety, solvency, beauty, social equity, and affordability. The soul-searching would continue.

Perhaps the soul-searching and dismay of 1989 were aggravated by an almost mythic sense of Hingham's past. A mythic past can be a burden. Perhaps the newly named Pride Building hinted at the burden, or perhaps Daniel LeClerc, chairman of the town's social studies department, unconsciously reflected it when he said, "We live in the perfect New England town." Does "perfect" mean "without flaw," or does it mean "quintessential, warts and all"? The truth of the past might foster a beneficial humility.

In the gloomy spring of 1989, Dan and Robin Brewer wondered if Hingham had forgotten the principles of covenant and interdependence on which the town had been based "since the beginning of our history." It had forgotten them before. On the occasion of his twenty-fifth anniversary as town moderator in 1992, Thomas L. P. O'Donnell identified his "biggest worry": "That a sense of community and trust is diminished in Hingham, as it is in the nation." Such diminution has run in cycles. Hingham's past was human. We remember the panics and depressions it weathered with the human blend of the noble and the ignoble. We remember the strife of the 1640s; the dispute over where to place the meetinghouse; the struggles with Cohasset and South Hingham in the early 1700s; the rancor of rival oligarchies in the early 1800s; the pre-Civil-War discord over abolitionism; sectional feuds about high school, railroad, water company, electrics; the clashes over zoning; earlier taxpayer revolts. If Hingham's long history of rational religion has led it to idealize human nature, it has done a disservice. The first settlers knew better.

Past Hingham was no less human and no more perfect than present Hingham. Past Hingham could not avoid occasional betrayals of covenant and community. Past Hingham, blessed in environment, in dedicated servants, and in much else came through them and rediscovered its community, its love in the face of flaws. Not all is changed.

Its greatest virtue has always been found in the dedication of those who have served it. Its roster of dedicated servants is astonishing. The qualities it admires most are epitomized in the *Journal*'s first four Citizens of the Year (1985-88): conservationist and teacher Philip Swanson; policeman Sam Amonte, "the mayor of Hingham"; Ruth Spencer, advocate for the elderly and for affordable housing; and Virginia Williams, Welcome Wagon lady and founder of the Newcomers Club. They were kindly, humane, cheerful, and uncontroversial in their advocacies. They were chosen from lists that included other deserving people perhaps too closely linked to political life, in a town which likes to think of itself as non-political. The lists also included some "boat rockers." When he lost his bid for reelection in 1988, a resident praised Town Clerk John Studley as a man "who rocked the boat" and expressed the hope that Hingham would "never let the jellyfish on board!" Boat rockers, so indispensable to the life of a community, are rarely appreciated.

In the election of 1990, Hingham appreciated a young townsman, Kevin Costello, and elected him selectman at the age of thirty-three. Costello was a year older than General Lincoln when he became a selectman. Lincoln's father and several other eighteenth-century selectmen were even younger. It is good for the present to think itself young. It is also good to remember that the past was once as young as we.

On that election Saturday in 1990, landscaping and renovation were going on at Old Derby on its fractured hillside. The Historical Society had completed its diamond jubilee drive and was restoring a jewel of the past. John Richardson climbed the hill and began his search for artifacts unearthed by the work. From that vantage point, he recalled how the main street had once run in separate rough cart roads above and below the hillside, which had sloped uninterrupted to land below where the Pride Building now stood. The divided roads had created a hillside island. On that island, long ago, rose Hingham's first meetinghouse, its first school, pound, and burial ground. Gradually, after 1681, when Hingham built its new meetinghouse, its first pride building, the first cemetery fell into disrepair and neglect. There was little time then for the past, as there is little time now for the past.

When the hillside was cut away in 1831, the traffic of that bustling year ran straight through the site of the burial ground. Watching this obliteration, a boy named George Lincoln felt stirrings of curiosity about the town's past. Older friends such as Solomon Lincoln and Fearing Burr fostered them. Because of such people and their modern followers, without whom this book could not exist, Hingham's story can be preserved. The life of a community depends on the sharing of its story. If its story lives, its character will, too. Not all will change.

Thomas L. P. O'Donnell, Town Moderator since 1967.

John H. Studley, Town Clerk (1973–1988), present Town Historian.

Eugene Bickford, Selectman (1968–1985). The little flag reads "Don't tread on me."

Kate Mahony, Selectman (1981–1990). First woman elected to the board in 346 years.

The last of the elms (1969), Main Street.

The blizzard of 1978. Children play on the snow mountain in front of Loring Hall on Main Street. The movie title could not have been more timely.

BELOW: *the Sprague Block (1928–1988) general alarm fire, Saturday, January 16, 1988. The photograph was taken around midnight, about an hour and a half after fire was discovered, from the roof of the Lincoln Building.*

*Katharine and Wilmon
Brewer, Grand Marshals
of the Fourth of July
parade in 1985, the
350th anniversary
of the town.*

*Foster School children just
before the balloon release,
350th anniversary.*

*Flag raising by members of the
South Shore Country Club
Development Committee, July,
1988. Left to right: Robert
Garrity, George Kay, John
Barry, and Robert Di Censo,
chairman.*

The new Hingham Militia and the Old Ship Church, at the February, 1988, celebration of the birthdays of General Benjamin Lincoln and President Abraham Lincoln.

The buttonwood tree and Charles H. Cushing's gas station: oil, 1945, Wes Downing.

NOT ALL IS CHANGED

Notes on Sources

IT is unlikely that many readers will want to take the trouble to retrace our steps to sources, but for those who do and for those who wish to do their own research, we provide detailed notes. Rather than bespatter our narrative with countless distracting little numbers[1] like[2] these,[3] we simply note sources according to pages of the narrative with identifying quotations or tag phrases. A printed source is identified merely by the author's last name and the year of publication—e.g.,"Hart (1993)". Armed with these details, you can find the source's full identification in the bibliography that follows these notes. The bibliography also includes a list of people who talked with us or were interviewed by others. Naturally, we cannot verify the accuracy of all the memories of those interviewed.

It will be obvious that our most frequently used sources have been Hingham's weekly newspapers, published with a one-year lapse (1849—the year of the railroad's opening and of the building of the Congregational Church) from 1827 on. Newspaper reports—Philip Graham of the Washington Post called them the "first rough drafts of history"—are not always reliable. But neither, in different ways, is any other kind of historical evidence, and often, in local history, they are all we have. Besides, a town weekly, with sharp-eyed readers always ready to write corrective letters to the editor, is unusually self-corrective.

NOTE ON THE CHANGING VALUE OF MONEY

How much would one dollar have "bought back then"? What would a worker have been paid? In the many "back thens" of this narrative, there were many ups and downs in the economy, so we cannot offer a simple, single formula. Here is an approximate rough guide, taking as a reference point the values of 1985, the town's 350th birthday. What $1 bought in 1985 cost about 9¢ in 1860, about 20¢ in 1865 (war inflation), about 7¢ in 1895 (long deflation), about 20¢ in 1920 (war inflation), about 16¢ in 1935 (Depression), about 21¢ in 1945 (war price controls), and about 35¢ in 1965, after which inflation "took off." During the same 125 years, wages rose 3,000% or more—say, from $10 to $300-plus per week. A worker in 1985 would appear much better off were it not for the major costs of living added in recent decades—for example, in taxes, insurance and health care.

A few abbreviations are used in these notes.

ATB	Annual Town Book of reports and accounts published by the town
B-L	Burr and Lincoln (1876)
GL	George Lincoln
GL Gen	GL's *Genealogies*, Vols. II-III of *History* (1893)
GL Hist. Note	One of the historical notes by GL in the *HJ*
HHS	Materials in the possession of the Hingham Historical Society
HJ	*Hingham Journal*
Hist Coll HPL	Historical Collection in the Hingham Public Library (materials on microfilm are identified by reel number)
History (1893)	*History of the Town of Hingham, Massachusetts*, published (1893) by the town in 3 vols., 4 parts bound separately. This abbreviation refers to the historical parts, Vol I, Parts i and ii
JLN	Notebooks of Julian Loring tracing land and house ownership, arranged according to streets
JPR	Materials in the archives of John P. Richardson or information based on his own knowledge and memory included in memoranda to us
SL (1827)	Solomon Lincoln's *History of Hingham* (1827)
TCR and TR	Town Clerk's Records and other Town Records on microfilm in Hist Coll HPL
Trans. Ag. and Hort.	*Transactions of the Agricultural and Horticultural Society* on microfilm in Hist Coll HPL.

PRELUDE: *"The Home of My Heart"*

The principal sources of information about Hingham in the Civil War are *HJ*, B-L, and W. Bouvé in *History* (1893). In conversation, Richard Shaner offered corrections about men in service from his ongoing research, but errors and omissions are our responsibility. The story of the war in its broader contexts is drawn from Brogan (1986), Burns (1986), Catton (1963), Catton (1965), Hicks and Schultz (1989), McFeeley (1981), Paludan (1988), and Wiley (1952).

Page 3: B-L say the Lincoln Light Infantry was organized Oct. 19, 1854. In July, 1855, the company was attached to the Mass. 4th Regiment. In command was Capt. Hawkes Fearing, Jr., until he was promoted to Lt. Col. in the 4th and was succeeded as captain by Joseph T. Sprague. In Dec., 1857, the old male schoolhouse at the Common was renovated as an armory for the company. Here, on April 16, 1861 (not the seventeenth, as Stephenson recalled), the company mustered, departing the next morning. Capt. Sprague was ill, and Lt. Stephenson replaced him. Stephenson's memoir is in a speech at the dedication of the Tower Monument, repr. *HJ*, 7/24/1914.

Page 4: Gill in B-L, 142, 356; Marsh in B-L, 148, 384, and quotation from *HJ*, 8/2/1861. Quotations from Andrew: "home of my heart," Hist Coll HPL, Reel 76:15; "we march an ARMY," *HJ*, 9/20/1861. "Now that shoe-making," *HJ*, 12/27/1861. "When the war broke out," *HJ*, 7/17/1863.

Page 5: "indefensible bounty . . . vicious," Catton (1963), 207-8. The L.L.I. disbanded, *HJ*, 9/19/1862. The account of Hingham recruiting, B-L, Chaps. Two and Three. The extensive and eloquent letters of A. J. Clark (originals went to the Essex Institute) are most accessible in reprint in *HJ*, Jan.-June, 1913. Clark, "I think," *HJ*, 8/8/1862. Trask, "afraid the fault," *HJ*, 8/15/1862. "a town so wealthy," *ibid*. "arrangements to fill," *HJ*, 9/12/1862. "the banner town," *HJ*, 10/29/1862. The "heavily inegalitarian" draft and "poor man's fight," Burns (1986), 14. Boston gangs, *HJ*, 7/24/1863. Hingham draftees, B-L, 81-82, 396, 415.

Page 6: Melzar Clark, *HJ*, 9/12/1862. French's sons, *HJ*, 2/10/1865. Joneses, *HJ*, 10/7/1864. Horace Burr, B-L, 333. Wallace Sprague, *HJ*, 7/31/1863. Peter N. Sprague, *HJ*, 9/9/1864. Benj. Thomas, *HJ*, 12/25/1863. Tom Conway, *HJ*, 7/31/1863. James Healey, *HJ*, 9/4/1863. "little village of Liberty Plain," *HJ*, 9/23/1864.

Page 7: "quaint old place," *etc.*, *HJ*, 6/8/1860, 3/18/1864. "a town decayed," Long (1956), 78. Fire at Broad Bridge, *HJ*, 5/9/1862. Clark, "I know it would," *HJ*, 5/30/1862. New buildings, *HJ*, 11/27/1862, 8/14/1863. New lighting, *HJ*, 4/20/1860, 11/6 and 11/13/1863, 8/4/1864. Page 8: Demography: *HJ*, 2/20/1863, 8/19/1864 (report of the 1860 Census). Relative wealth, *HJ*, 1/18/1861, 3/10/1865.

Page 8: Mackerel fishery, *HJ*, 11/16/1860, 11/18/1864. *Rose Standish*, *HJ*, 9/2/1864. Revived agriculture and festivals, *HJ*, 6/22/1862, 2/19 and 12/30/1864 (and see Chapter Ten). Street scenes and animals, *HJ*, 5/2/1862, 4/2 and 4/10 and 9/14/1863.

Page 9: Railroad, *HJ*, 9/23/1864. Trees—"one street nearly," *HJ*, 9/28/1864. Gardens, hothouses, *etc.*, *HJ*, 4/18/1862, 5/29/1863, 7/15/1864. Wounded veterans, *HJ*, 1/2/1863. "The past year," *HJ*, 1/1/1864. Summer resorts, *HJ*, 7/31/1863. "outrageous extortion," *HJ*, 4/22/1864. "Dashed hopes," *etc.*, Wiley (1952).

Page 10: Clark, "They may keep us," *HJ*, 12/27/1861. "one sight of a wounded man," *HJ*, 3/28/1862. Estimates of men in service, B-L, W. Bouvé in *History* (1893), Richard Shaner conversation. Occupations, B-L and *HJ*, 8/22/1862. Corthell, "The war will end," *HJ*, 3/14/1862.

Page 11: Hingham men "for the first time," *HJ*, 1/2/1863. Bates, "Oh shame," *HJ*, 4/24/1863. "most brilliant victory," Catton (1963), 131. Humphrey, "Hingham boys," *HJ*, 5/15/1863. "cauldron of noise," Burns (1986), 11. "a performance no human," *HJ*, 7/31/1863. The 32nd home, *HJ*, 1/22/1864. Stephenson on "the terrible campaign" and Laurel Hill, B-L, 186-90.

Page 12: Victory in Hingham, *HJ*, 4/13/1865. Lincoln's death, *HJ*, 4/21/1865. Andrew and the flags, Pearson (1904), II, 256. Clark, "As the people of Hingham," *HJ*, 9/12/1862.

Page 13: Homecoming men and their genealogies, GL Gen. and B-L. Helen Dyer, B-L, 343-45.

CHAPTER ONE: *First Memories and Modern Guesses*

Chief sources include Hosea Sprague's "fair copies" of TCR, in Town Records, Hist Coll HPL, Reel I. Reel III includes Hobart's Journal; the original was given to the Mass. Hist. Soc. (1912) by Mrs. Francis Lincoln. See also GL Gen., W. Bouvé on military history, and F. Lincoln on ecclesiastical history in *History* (1893); Smith (1973) for population and demographics; SL (1827) and JLN for early land grants and settlement patterns; and Waters (1967-68). Though we must question Waters' reasoning, and sometimes find it self-contradictory, his article remains informative and provocative. For colonial history and culture, we draw on Breen (1980), Richard Brown (1978), Lockridge (1970), Wertenbaker (1947), and especially Labaree (1979). The picture of early agricultural life is drawn from Russell (1976). Of special interest regarding Hingham's challenge to Winthrop and the colonial government, in addition to Winthrop himself (1946), is Wall (1972), whose primary source on these events is *Records of the Governor and Company of the Massachusetts Bay in New England*, 5 vols., ed. N.B. Shurtleff (Boston, 1853-54). We are also indebted to JPR, who drew on "an exact copy (1833) of Hingham's Great Book of Land grants" (MS. in his possession), a plan of Lincoln Street by General Benjamin Lincoln, and Cummings (1979).

Page 17: SL (1827), 22n. J. P. Richardson, *HJ*, 10/16/1975. Earlier settlements, Labaree (1979) and Russell (1976). For early arrivals, SL (1827) and GL Gen. The SL lists are readily accessible in *History* (1893), I.i.201-3.

Page 18: "Invasion" hypothesis, first argued by Waters (1967-68), though some ideas are anticipated in Coolidge (1961). Wilson (1984) accepts the Waters hypothesis as dogma and elaborates it. On ethnic conflict, Waters; on different dialects, note to the authors from George Smith.

Page 19: For the calculation of families, SL (1827), based on Daniel Cushing, third town clerk, who, as a loyal Old Hinghamite, is unlikely to have missed many East Anglians. The "modern scholar," Waters (1967-68), 332n. For the "conservative" stereotype, see Waters, Wilson (1984), Coolidge (1961). The "recent historians of Massachusetts Bay" include Allen (1981), Breen (1980), Heyrman (1984), and Labaree (1979). The "population ratio" argument, though it contradicts his main thesis, is Waters'

(361). The "apparently determined" fancy is found in Wilson (1984), 35. Wall (1972), Chap. Three, gives a much more cautious account. The quotation is from SL (1827), 47 & n.

Page 20: "Early sifting out," Smith (1973), 215. On Dedham, see Lockridge (1966). "The picture of the early time," *History* (1893), I.i.207. "Truly the burdens," Russell (1976), 44. The sketch of early crops and work is based on Russell, who is speaking of other towns as well as Hingham. Information on houses, JPR based on Cummings (1979).

Page 21: "A strong man might carry," Russell (1976), 81. On predators, livestock, regulations and the quarrel, see H. Sprague's "fair copies" of TCR in Hist Coll HPL, Town Records, Reel I. A "deal of human nature," Long in *History* (1893), I.i.207. Our few glimpses of John Tower (see this chapter and the opening of Chap. Two) suggest a man not to be trifled with. "An inviting shore," Russell (1976), 22. See Richard Brown (1978), 11-12, quoting Morton's *New English Canaan*, for a catalogue of edible wildlife, rainfall, *etc.*

Pages 22-24: "The mind of any period," Rutman (1965), 3. On economic conditions in England, see Wertenbaker (1947), Chap. One; Labaree (1979), 15-28; Richard Brown (1978), 21. "Spectacles of misery" quoted from Winthrop in Rutman (1965), 6. Wertenbaker (189) cites the court order of 1635. On Watertown, see Lockridge (1970), Chap. One. The attempt to sketch the settlement patterns is based chiefly on JLN, with corrections and additions from JPR based on the "Great Book" cited in the headnote above, diagrams by GL and Gen. B. Lincoln (also in his collection), and GL Gen. Any brief attempt is bound to oversimplify, but there is no point in attempting here simply to list original landholders. For a more detailed account of early Centre settlers, see Foster (1925).

Page 25: On land accumulations, GL Gen. and JLN. On land swaps and particularly land policy and distribution, H. Sprague's "fair copies" of TCR, Town Records, Hist Coll HPL, Reel I.

Page 26: Other towns: Plymouth, in Richard Brown (1978), 32-33; Dedham, in Lockridge (1970), Chap. One; Sudbury, in Labaree (1979), 64-65. Regarding the request for a piece of Nantasket, SL (1827), 53. On the dispute with Scituate, Hurd (1884). "Fodder for an Englishman's cattle," Labaree (1979), 45. "Famous for lumber," quoted from Johnson's *Wonderworking Providence* in SL (1827), 54.

Page 27: "The settlers departed" and their conservative "localism," Breen (1980), 5. On "visible saints", see below. On assigning plantations only to groups, Richard Brown (1978), 44. Peter Hobart may have been a "hothead" as Wall (1972), 99, concludes, but the only evidence is from the journal of his adversary Winthrop. On local covenanted institutions, Breen (1980), 34.

Page 28: On the men's change of mind, Winthrop (1946), II, 229-30. For a fascinating account of the colony-wide significance of the militia affair, see Wall (1972), Chap. Three. For the threat of excommunication, Eames's leaving the congregation, and Winthrop's acquittal, see Winthrop (1946), II, 230-31, 237 and 245. On the petitioners, see SL (1827), 69. The aftermath of the Eames dispute is puzzling. No death record indicates his remaining in Hingham. Presumably he was the "Anthony Eames Senr." who lived in Medford in the 1650s. Yet, his three daughters all married early settlers of the town, East Anglians John Jacob and Edward Wilder, and west countryman William Sprague, son of Eames's neighbor near today's Union Street. It may be noteworthy that Jacob and Wilder were among the first to move to South Hingham. Did their geography suggest deliberate distance from the Hobart domain? The Jacobs were among the first old Hinghamites to arrive (1633). Is it accident that west country offspring married their children—an Otis son marrying a Jacob daughter, a Loring son marrying another Jacob daughter, an Eames daughter marrying a Jacob Son? Waters (369-70) notes that ethnic intermarriage grew common by the end of the 1640s. In view of the short time between the militia fight and the marriages, perhaps the hypothesis of ethnicity as the root of the conflict should be set aside. Waters asserts (368), "The split in the militia unit reflected the regional origins of the Bear Cove planters." The evidence given is that, of the eighty-one petitioners, all fourteen of those known or identifiable were *not* west countrymen. What of the other sixty-seven?

Page 29: On the Native American situation, see Richard Brown (1978), 8; Labaree (1979) 101; Russell (1976), 4-5. Breen (1980), 34-39, interprets the significance of the militias. Hobart's argument, "but as a corporation," from Winthrop (1946), II, 265. On the "plot," Wall (1972), 102, 157-58.

Page 30: On the complaints and petition of Child and others, Wall, Chap. Five. On the denial of the vote to many, Wertenbaker (1947), 299. For Winthrop's suspicion of Hobart,

Winthrop (1946), II, 289-90. Appeals to England "not allowed," Wall, 184. Wall, 191, 194, on the actual vote. Vassall, whom Wall sees as masterminding, did not sign the petition, but he went to England with Fowle. Solomon Lincoln says Child went, too; but he did not. He was kept under house arrest for almost ten months. "The Pastor of Hingham," Winthrop (1946), II, 321. On Fast Days, Hall (1989), 166, 169-73. On Thomas Joy, GL Gen. and Wall (1972), 202, 255. First grist mill site, JPR based on MS. letters of Solomon Lincoln to GL in his collection. On forbidding Hobart to preach and "a bold man," Winthrop (1946), II, 330. On the Cambridge synod, Wertenbaker (1947), 298-99.

Page 31: On "ecclesiastical independence": the sad irony perceived by Wall (1972) should be noted. The efforts of Hobart and others to win greater liberty and flexibility simply hardened the reactionary rigidity of the Bay Colony's leaders. "The [Child] Remonstrance of 1646 and the reaction to it by orthodox Puritans would force upon Massachusetts the major tragedies of the next decade and the frustrating failures of the decades beyond" (233). "Until 1664," Greene (1942), 262. Hobart "did manage all affairs," Winthrop (1946), II, 244. On "visible saints" and the "halfway covenant," Rutman (1965), 115-16, 147-53, and Deetz (1977), 135. On the need for forty members to elect a deputy, Richard Brown (1978), 51. For the number of men over twenty-one, Wall (1972), 39. On Hobart and broader membership, Waters (1967-68), 362. On the 1662 Synod, Wertenbaker (1947), 312. On Hobart's inclusiveness in baptism, Wilson (1984), 35-36.

Page 32: "Hannah Burton baptized," Hobart's Diary, Leaf 7, in Hist Coll HPL, Town Records, Reel III. On the town's liberality to Hobart, SL (1827), 24 and 79, and TCR in Hist Coll HPL, Town Records, Reel I.

CHAPTER TWO: *Land of the Puritans' Children*

Page 33: The account of the war and the attack is drawn from W. Bouvé in *History* (1893), I.i.235-47. The Tower petition (231) is dated "March 10th, 1675." We must assume this is "Old Style" ("O.S."). The calendar changed in 1752 from "Old Style," which began the year on March 25, to "New Style" ("N.S."), which (after dropping eleven days) began the year on January 1. Up to 1752, January 1 through March 24 were considered part of the prior year. Thus, while Lehner and Fannin (1989) say the decision to build the new meetinghouse was made in January, 1679, we would say (N.S.) 1680. Figures on war casualties are from Russell (1976), 105.

Page 35: The reconstruction of the divisions is based on H. Sprague's "fair copies" of TCR in Hist Coll HPL, Reel I. Hobart's grant was given at the town meeting, May 17, 1669. The January, 1670, meeting is N.S.; the record by Sprague is dated 1679. We compute on the basis of 32.1 square miles for seventeenth-century Hingham (including Cohasset), a total of 20,544 acres. The vote was taken Jan. 10, 1669/70 (1670 N.S.). E. Bouvé states in *History* (1893), I.i.163, that the Fourth Division (along the Weymouth line) was not made until slightly before the middle of the eighteenth century. Town Records, however, indicate otherwise. To avoid confusion for the reader, let us explain that the Cohasset lands were divided into three tracts, each essentially behind the other——hence, "three divisions." In fact, the third division was a two-stage operation because of the extreme variability of the land.

Page 36: The requirement regarding "selling 'his whole seat,'" voted Jan. 24, 1669/70 (1670 N.S.). The quadrupling of property requirements, Breen (1980), 45. The deed with Wompatuck is printed in *History* (1893), I.i.203-6. The declaration of fidelity to the King is dated April 10, 1666, in TCR.

Page 37: Restrictions on oaks, Usher in Hart (1928), II, 398. "One historical geographer": Brown, Ralph (1948), 108. Cf. Russell (1976), 175: "an ordinary dwelling needed twenty cords a year." The value of mast trees, Labaree (1979), 92. On offices and powers of J. Hobart, see Bouvé in *History* (1893), I.i.219, TCR 4/7/1670 and 5/20/1650, and SL (1827), 163-64. Hobart's captaincy was secure. The local nomination of trainband officers had become so rancorous that in 1668 the General Court took the power to itself. This ended for a number of years what had been the most democratic franchise in the colony (Breen [1980], 42-44). On clergymen and marriages, Greene (1942), 192. Ralph Woodward, one of Hingham's first two deacons, was authorized in 1649 to marry couples (GL Gen., III, 332).

Page 38: On "well-rooted and extended families," Wilson (1984), 36. Ratios from Coolidge (1961), 442. Selectmen, Smith (1973), 154. More stable life, Heyrman (1984), 42. New regulations, Foley (1935), 14. "No inmigration," birth-death rates, fertility control, Smith, 35, 37, 239.

Page 40: Threat from overseas, Richard Brown (1978), 51, 56. "Little is known" of Norton, *History* (1893), I.ii.21. Norton's doctrine, Wilson (1984), 36-38. On Ipswich, Wall (1972), 71, 171-73.

Page 41: Cushings from GL Gen. Cushing homestead: JLN dates it 1678; Fearing Burr, 1679. Industries, GL Gen., GL in *History* (1893), I.ii.155-69, and Hartwell (1954). The aqueduct, JPR, who conducted on-site archaeological exploration, and Robinson (1980), 9. On late seventeenth century houses, Lehner and Fannin (1989), 816-17, and (1990), 4-5. They warn: "Extant seventeenth century Hingham houses no longer" exhibit original external features, "as they have all been encased in eighteenth century colonial envelopes." On the "boom" in new meetinghouses, Coolidge (1961), 444. The "bell," Stark (1951). The "unceilinged loft," Sinnett (1963), 32-33. Stockbridge is identified in Coolidge (1961), 446-47.

Page 42: On whether the culture was changing, Bailyn (1959), Deetz (1977), Heyrman (1984), and Zuckerman (1970). Coolidge (1961), 455 n. 19, estimates the capacity. On heading off separatist moves, Wilson (1984), 36. *History* (1893), I.ii.22, dates the vote to proceed Jan., 1679/80. The count of taxpayers, Stark (1951). The spread of wealth, Coolidge, 448. On the seating plan, Coolidge (1961), 452, and Wilson (1984), 37.

Page 43: On the site conflict, *History* (1893), I.ii.23. The schoolmaster "hired cheap," *History* (1893), I.ii.84. On the schools, *History* (1893), I.ii.85-88. On Cohasset's "rebellion," Wilson (1984), 39.

CHAPTER THREE: *Parson Gay and His Times*

Chief sources for town history in this chapter are Robinson (1980), Smith (1973), and Wilson (1984). For other towns and the colony, Richard Brown (1978), Labaree (1979), Lockridge (1970), and Zuckerman (1970). For the franchise and currency matters, Robert Brown (1955), R. D. Davis and M. W. Jernagan in Hart (1928), and Hoerder (1972). For change and expansion in agriculture, Russell (1976). For black history and slavery, context from Greene (1942) and Twombly and Moore (1967). Military history from W. Bouvé in *History* (1893).

Page 44: Population, *etc.*, from Smith (1973). Agricultural figures and trends from Hersey in *History* (1893), 182-83, and Russell (1976), 109ff.

Page 45: Journal of Joseph Andrews as transcribed in Russell (1976), 158, 193.

Page 46: Locations of farms from JLN, with a memorandum from JPR on Third Division lands, based on his *Wompatuck State Park Natural and Historic Resource Inventory* (Boston: Mass. Dept. of Environmental Management, 1982). "Towns that would not," Labaree (1979), 131.

Page 47: On South Hingham, Robinson (1980), 1-6, and Wilson (1984), 49-50 and 114-16. The "Hingham manner" is described in Wilson, 49. On the growing socio-economic inequality, Smith (1973), 103-4 and 127-41, and Wilson (1984), 194.

Pages 48-49: On the franchise, Labaree (1979), 309-12, and Robert Brown (1955), 21-24, 80-83. The enigmas and ambiguities of the franchises have occasioned much scholarly disagreement. We cannot accept Brown's conclusion that requirements were so low that provincial and local voting rights were consistently available up to the Revolution. However, his description and explanation of the qualifications are useful. On the charter and changes in the franchise, Labaree (126) gives 1691; others give 1690, '91, and '92. See Breen (1980), 95, on property qualifications. Jernagan in Hart (1928), II, 14, on the confusing terminology. Robert Brown (1955), 21-23 & n., on the textual discrepancy; and 80-83 on the 1735 law. On the currency, Dewey, II, 206-13, in Hart (1928); and Lockridge (1970), 154. Hingham votes are from SL (1827), 108, 110. The population count is in *History* (1893), I.ii.379. Here is why the vote was so exclusionary: by this time, "one had to have real estate valued at £3 per annum . . . or other property worth £60" (Labaree, 311-12). If the £3 seems small, it refers only to *rental* value, not full value of the property. How much land did a family need to subsist? Consider McManis (1975), 100: "An average of fourteen acres of plowed land plus an average of seventy-five acres of other types of land was the minimum in late colonial or early national times for a family to live above subsistence levels . . . unless it had other sources of income . . ." It is unlikely that a family with little or no land could meet the alternative requirement of £60.

Page 49: On economic differentiation, Smith (1973), 103. On black history, Deetz (1977), 138. The following reconstruction of slave history is documented in detail below in order that the nature of this evidence and research will be seen by anyone interested in pursuing this subject. As we say, eighteenth century record-keeping about the black/Indian population was erratic and haphazard and sometimes contradictory.

Town Record dates and Gay's do not always coincide. According to the TR, Cesar and Candace were married in 1757; Gay says 1767. According to the TR, Prince and Pat were married in 1774; Gay says 1783. The research must cope with vagaries of spelling and handwriting (Gay's is often hard to read), with town clerks who were "volunteers," and with errors of copyists and indexers. Within these limitations, however, it is possible to work with some reliability. For example, there were *three* black men named Prince in eighteenth century Hingham. One, a servant of Benjamin Lincoln, died in 1750. A second died in 1786 at the age of forty-three. But the Prince of our story appears again and again in almsworkhouse records through the 1820s. (It is somewhat unusual to find such repetition of names among this population.) But the same uncertainty applies to ages of blacks/Indians at their deaths. TRs state that "Patience an Indian" was "95 years" in 1803. George Lincoln states she was even older. These people may have been uncertain about their own ages. However, much could be learned from extant documents through persistent, careful research. On the legal status of blacks before 1690, Twombly and Moore (1967), 226-27, 229; Greene (1942), 167. On interchangeable terms, Greene, 290. For the seating plan, Coolidge (1961), 455 n. 80. Sneaking in at Nantasket, Twombly and Moore, 239. Slaves' children, A. B. Forbes in Hart (1928), II, 262. The 1733 order, Cushing MSS, Hist Coll HPL, Reel 76:1. Deaths 1723-27 and description of slaveholders from JLN, Reel 76:21 (which names the slaves) and GL Hist. Note #17 in *HJ*, 1/12/1883. Hersey will, GL Gen., II, 300.

Page 50: The legitimized marriage, TR, Births-Deaths-Marriages, I, 305. Gay's list and baptisms, Wilson (1984), 41-42 and 249 n.27. The Suffolk County listing is in Greene (1942), 339. *N.B. HJ*, 7/26/1850: in 1749, the number of slaves "between twelve and fifty years of age" taxed to their owners was thirty-nine. *HJ*, 7/5/1850, citing Am. Statistical Soc., Book I, for the colonial census. Primus Cobb, *History* (1893), I.i.292; Squire, Foster (1925), [5]. For the Barneses, GL in *HJ*, 4/12/1877 and JLN, Reel 76:21. Black Sam and Black Dick, from GL *ibid*. On Fearing's Prince, HHS Family Papers 15:1. The marriage of Prince and Pate, Gay Records, TR, Reel III, Leaf 312. Almshouse furloughs, JLN, Reel 76:21. Black Patty, *History* (1893), I.i.179. Birth of Cesar, JLN, Reel 76:21. Humphrey will, GL Gen., II, 361.

Page 51: Cesar's marriage, Gay records, TR, Reel III, Leaf 305. "Cesar was an athlete," GL Hist. Note #35, *HJ*, 2/14/1890. Nineteenth century property records from GL Hist Coll HPL, Reel 80:7. Chloe Ward from GL Gen., III. 372. Deeding of the eight-year-old from HHS Family Papers 15:1. Candice in the almshouse, JLN, Reel 76:21. Death of Candice, TR Births-Deaths-Marriages, III, 70. On Patience Pometuck (or Pometik or Pometick), *History* (1893), I.i.179, and Coatsworth (1948), 82; GL Hist. Note #9, *HJ*, 12/2/1881; *HJ*, 2/13/1880; JLN, Reel 76:21. On the "growing repugnance," Richard Brown (1978), 173; Greene (1942), 76-77; Labaree (1979), 305. On Freedom Fearing, Uncat. Reel from Town Clerk's office in HPL, and *HJ*, 12/31/1852.

Page 52: The Massachusetts Bill of Rights of 1780 declared that "all men are born free and equal." The practical application of this clause was first made in a Worcester trial in 1783. Judge Levi Lincoln, a native of Hingham and later Jefferson's attorney general, and William Cushing, Chief Justice of the Massachusetts Supreme Judicial Court and a descendant of the Scituate branch of the Hingham Cushings, are both credited with interpreting the clause to call for an abolition of slavery in the state. Cushing later became the first associate justice named to the United States Supreme Court. His Hingham connection is commemorated in the name of the highway (Route 3A) leading from Hingham to Scituate. Town officers, Smith (1973), 149-51; Wilson (1984), 49-50, 195. Majority rule, Labaree (1979), 129-30. Zuckerman model, Zuckerman (1970), 6, 123, 167-68.

Page 53: Schools and the special meeting, Wilson (1984), 91. Lawsuits and barristers, Zuckerman (1970), 89-92. On the constable's office and the "crisis," Smith (1973), Chap. Five. On "tythingmen" and the "alarming increase," Wilson (1984), 49, and Smith (1957), 25. Taverns located, JLN.

Page 54: Ann Whiton (Witon), from a note loaned to JL by Mrs. Shute of 1242 Main St. and GL Gen., III, 292. Symptoms in the south parish, Robinson (1980), 16-17, 24.

Page 55: Gay and "enthusiasm," Wilson (1984), 106-19; on the anti-Baptist riot, Wilson, 233. The brief summary of Gay's changing doctrines is based on Wilson, especially pp. 43, 52, 65, 68, and 77—the sources of the quoted phrases.

Pages 56-57: Rise of the waterfront, Wilson (1984), 192-95, and JLN. Images of Gay, Wilson, 196, and Roscoe (1984), 43-44. "Old Punk," GL Gen. (Leavitt) and Hist. Notes #25 and #54. Letter from Souther, JLN (notebook for Ship Street). On the wars, Labaree

(1979), 202ff.; W. Bouvé in *History* (1893), I.i.249-69 (the story of Major Thaxter is on 262).

CHAPTER FOUR: *More Than One Revolution*

Page 58: Summary of colonial events leading up to the Revolution based on Richard Brown (1978), 66-101, and Labaree (1979), 241-89. Sprague's reminiscence provided by JPR, from Francis S. Drake, *Tea Leaves* (Boston: Crane, 1884), clxiii.

Page 59: On Gay and Hingham, Wilson (1984), 211-29; quotations appear on 216, 218-19. War history, Bouvé in *History* (1893), I.i.280-81, 288-89, 294-96.

Page 60: The verses of Thaxter courtesy of Frederic Hills, who owns a copy.

Page 61: Bouvé's estimate is in *History* (1893), I.i.326. The impact on farming, Russell (1976), 214-15, 226. Reminiscence of Lydia Bates Lincoln provided by JPR from his archival notes, Solomon Lincoln to GL, 11/19/1871. On the Haswells, GL Hist. Note #17 (*HJ*, 1/12/1883); Parker (1986), 2-8; and Rowson's novel *Rebecca*, 2nd edn. (1814). The Introduction identifies the "realities," including "the imprisonment of the family, the friendship experienced by them in the most distressed circumstances, the removal farther into the country" (iv). In the novel, Susanna is "Rebecca"; her father, "Apthorpe." For Hingham events and names, see 152-53, 160-64, and 162n. We deduce first names with the help of GL and by a process of elimination. Haswell's home in Nantasket had been the Rev. Samuel Veazie's. In the nineteenth century, it was purchased and renovated by John Boyle O'Reilly and later became the Hull Public Library (Parker, 126 n.9). An intriguing question remains: who was the kindly stranger, the "respected and benevolent being" in Hingham ("delicacy" forbade Rowson's giving his name), who offered Rowson-"Apthorpe" a commission (declined) in the Continental Army, and warned that they would be moved inland the next day? We think it could only have been Gen. Benjamin Lincoln.

Page 62: The Leavitt incident, Bouvé in *History* (1893), I.i.288. We quote the version of the Gay rejoinder given in Coatsworth (1948), 128. Costs of war, *History* (1893), I.i.306-7, 311, 319, 322, 324. Shays' Rebellion, Richard Brown (1978), 116-21, and Russell (1976), 230-31. "The response of the . . . elites," Burns (1983), 21.

Page 63: On General Lincoln, *History* (1893), I.i.302-306 and GL Gen. On the surrender, Tuchman (1988), 289. His "little low carriage," GL Hist. Note #17 (*HJ*, 1/12/1883). Margaret Hazlitt's *Journal* (1967), 69-72. Eliot to Belknap in *Belknap Papers*, Mass. Hist. Soc., 6th Series, IV (1891), 274. "Paddy" from Wilson (1984), 237.

Page 64: The account of Ware, *Dictionary of American Biography*. "their stately procession" and "steer the Old Ship," Wilson (1984), 234, 238. The Ware ordination ball, "a number of the lads," J. Q. Adams (1903), 52-54.

Page 65: "That dancing hall," Roscoe (1984), 31. Sarah Derby, T. P. Smith (1957), *passim*. "Pure bosh," GL Hist. Note #31 (*HJ*, 7/9/1886). The "load of boards," Sidney H. Gay, letter dated 5/29/1847, reprinted from Gay's *N.Y. Anti-Slavery Standard* in *HJ*, 6/18/1847. Bouvé story in *History* (1893), I.i.198.

Page 66: Early history of Derby, Roscoe (1984), *passim*. Ware's poverty, GL Hist. Note #55 (*HJ*, 3/4/1898). Ware at Harvard, Parke (1957), 77-80; "particular religious principles," 78.

Pages 67-68: This condensed account of the battle over Richardson is an attempt at fairness based on a critical comparative reading of the opposing pamphlets, Thaxter's *Narrative* (1807) on the side of the opposition, and the *Vindication* (1807) of the Richardson supporters in response. On his exclusion from the Bay Association, see Richardson, *Complaint* (1818). On pulpit exchanges, see Richardson, *Letter* (1847). On Stearns and the baptism, *HJ*, 10/4/1850. Fearing's marriage, GL Diaries, 5/24/1875. Little boys behind walls, Coatsworth (1948), 146. Doctors of their own parish, Roscoe (1984), 31. George Lincoln states: "The New North meeting-house was raised and boarded when Mr. Richardson was ordained. Some students of the Derby Academy undertook to burn him (Mr. R.) in effigy but were prevented by the citizens. So says Rev. Henry Hersey Sept. 14, 1868." (GL Scrapbook, HPL Hist Coll, Reel 76:13.) "The Derby family" and "resurgence of orthodox," Roscoe, 31, 33.

Page 69: Lists of antagonists drawn from the signers of the opposing pamphlets; other facts from GL Gen. For Col. Cushing, see JLN (School Street).

Page 70: Federalists and Republicans (a very different party from the one formed in the 1850s), Burns (1983), 126-33, 151-55. The rival packets, Morison (1921), 231. The embargo and reaction, Burns, 199-203. On Lincoln and Cushing, see above, note to

Page 52. The "appearance of stillness," Dwight (1969), III, 79-80. Dwight described Hingham as of 1790 as a "pretty village," alas on ground "unpleasantly broken by several small elevations formed by collections of rocks . . . thrown together in a disagreeable confusion." For General Lincoln's last years, see the note to page 63. The quoted phrase, "the venerable age of a good man," is from *Vindication* (1807).

Page 71: The local tradition that the battle was "watched" off Scituate is recorded in Coatsworth (1948), 100.

CHAPTER FIVE: *Entrepreneurs and Evangelicals*

In this period, two valuable new sources for historians appeared, themselves symbolic of the times: the town newspaper and the regular census report. With a hiatus in 1849, the three newspapers were published as follows: *Hingham Gazette* (1827-38), *Hingham Patriot* (1838-48), and *Hingham Journal* from 1850 on. There were also town maps printed in 1830 and 1857, appropriate to an era of road building and naming. The account of the growth of villages, roads, *etc.*, is based chiefly on JLN. A main source for the story of national politics is Burns (1983).

Page 72: The image of the mackerel fleet, *HJ*, 10/14/1870. The mackerel industry, SL (1827), 2-3 n., and GL in *History* (1893), I.ii.171-73. See also "The Old Saltworks," HHS Pub. #1 (1916). Stoddard's poem is reprinted in *HJ*, 10/11/1889.

Page 73: R. H. Dana (1936), 381-82. On industries, GL in *History* (1893), 155-80, Hartwell (1954), and Robinson (1980), 112-15. The industries are mentioned only briefly here because there is a full account in Chapter Nine. On coaches, roads, *etc.*, see Wood (1919); Russell (1976), 264-66; Schreiber (1961), 172; and Bagwell (1974), 43, on the impact of Elliot's elliptical spring. R. M. Hartwell in Cipolla (1973), 375, writes: "'a transport revolution' preceded and accompanied all industrial revolutions." The impact on Hingham of road development can be inferred from the charge of a new town committee in April, 1827, to *give names* to streets, lanes, plains, and bridges. As of May, 1827, there were thirty-five streets, twelve lanes, seventeen bridges, and three plains.

Page 74: On the destruction of Great Rock, see E. Bouvé, *History* (1893), I.i.191-92. On Gen. Lincoln's trees, *HJ*, 1/21 and 1/28/1852 and 2/4, 2/11, and 2/18/1853. On new bridges and Abigail Adams, Wood (1919), 176-79. The boys' poem appeared in *The Cabinet*, Hist Coll HPL, Reel 76:9 (1853). For easy access to the full poem, see Robinson (1980), 113-15.

Page 75: On M. Wilder, *HJ*, 11/22/1901. On Hall, F. Burr in History (1893), I.ii.208; GL Gen.; and the ongoing research of Eugene Chamberlain. On Brooks, see the excerpt of the S. Lincoln memoir in *History* (1893), I.ii.50-53.

Page 76: On the banks and insurance company, "Historic Hingham" brochure, Hist Coll HPL, Reel 76:8, and Hersey (1926). Black Patty, E. Bouvé in *History* (1893), I.i.179. Helen Thomas's story, *Patriot*, 9/10 and 12/17/1847, and "H.W." in *HJ*, 1/5/1923. On the railroad, Hersey (1969). On rates, timetables, and mismanagement, *HJ*, 5/17 and 10/12/1850. The story of the fight, from *HJ*, 10/19/1855.

Pages 77-79: Population and demographics, Smith (1973) and table of census reports in *History*, I.ii. 379. Stories from the villages are from JLN, according to the streets involved. Locations of shops, JLN. See also Marble (1928). On Hunt the baker, *HJ*, 7/1/1853.

Page 80: Jefferson-Madison majority, reported in SL (1827), 112. Details of new office holders from GL Gen. On Richardson and J. Q. Adams, Falkner (1967), 22-26. Letter from Solomon Lincoln to John B. Davis (dated Oct. 1, 1830), in *Massachusetts Historical Society*, Feb., 1916, 234-35.

Page 81: On Webster and the statue, memorandum from JPR, based in part on his interview with Ardra Soule Wavle (1975), and quotation from Coatsworth (1948), 42. On national parties and "the dance of factions," Burns (1983), espec. 227-28, 320-24, 422-29. For Hingham votes, *Gazette*.

Page 82: The impact of the "diffusion of sects," Nelson (1981), *passim*. The quotation regarding Kingston is from 137-38. Memories of the old meetinghouse, *HJ*, 8/29 and 9/12/1851. Lane journal, copy provided by JPR from MS. in his archives.

Pages 83-85: On new Hingham churches, SL (1827), 39-40, and *History* (1893), I.ii.34-35, 57-64. Bassett and the Episcopalians, Gallop (1983), 2-3. Charles Cushing and the Universalists, Hist Coll HPL, Town Records, Reel I 326A, and E. Hersey, 2d, in Hurd (1884), 1076. "Mobbing" of Baptists, Wilson (1984), 232-33. Harassment of Baptists, Hurd (1884), 1077. "Pull for the shore, boys," Coatsworth (1948), 10. See also *HJ*, 7/20/1877 (Baptist history from the Rev. Jonathan Tilson) and *HJ*, 3/20/1868 (Methodism Remembered). See Souther in Hist Coll HPL, Reel 76:10, pamphlet "History of the Methodist Episcopal Church," for the building and financing of the Methodist Church by the Puffers, the number of members, and the account of reharnessing the horses. Also, Anna Gilman, pamphlet "History of the First Baptist Church" (1930), copy in the possession of the authors. "Trinitarian congregational presence," Edson (1988), 6.

CHAPTER SIX: *"The Great Principle of the Age"*

Pages 86-87: Epigraphs from Mann: "The Great Principle," from a speech in the U.S. House of Representatives, reported in *HJ*, 3/1/1850; on "a free man," quoted in Burns (1983), 510, from Mann's farewell to Mass. teachers in 1844. On "all Christian and pacific means," *Patriot*, 8/16/1844. Folsom quoted in *Gazette*, 3/31/1837. On the 1808 federal law, Brogan (1986), 290. The "drop of Prussic acid," J. Q. Adams, quoted in Burns (1983), 465. On early anti-slavery activists, *Patriot*, 7/26/1844, and Robinson (1980), 108. Other early Society members included Caleb S. Hunt, Quincy Hersey, printer E. B. Gill, Edward Cazneau, David H. Abbot, Joseph Sprague, Captain Reuben Eldridge, and Captain Ephraim Harden. Women involved in the cause early included Mrs. Rhoda Beal, Mrs. Evelina Smith, Mary W. Lincoln (wife of Jairus), Elizabeth W. Lincoln (Jairus's daughter, who died in 1845 at the age of twenty), Maria A. Sylvester, Mary L. Gardner, Susan F. Wilder, Martha E. Sprague, Mary H. Lincoln (daughter of Barnabas), and Elizabeth T. Davis.

Pages 87-88: The "Jim Crow pews" (Douglass), *Patriot*, 11/20/1841. "Unus" in *Patriot*, 9/18/1841. The meeting is reported in *Patriot*, 9/11/1841. The 1820 "colored" population from SL (1827), 9. The 1855 population from Lainhart (1988). For versions of the history of Lucretia Leonard, see ATB, 1904, Deaths, 54; "Brief Historical Sketch of New North Church," 1932 and 1935, in Hist Coll HPL, Reel 76:11; *Boston Evening Transcript*, 6/18/1932, on the same reel; S. B. Willard, "Early Hingham and the Thaxter Family," Part Four, *HJ*, 5/10/1907; and interview with Bertha Stringer (Wheaton, 1975). On the galleries, see also *Hingham Magazine* (1898) and the same article significantly revised in DAR, *Hingham* (1911). The unanimous resolution, reported in *Patriot*, 11/20/1841. The "Great Catouse" from *Transcript* story (above). The Thaxter sisters' house next to the present site of the Methodist Church was razed in 1906 by Ira Hersey to enlarge his grounds (present Hersey House)—see *HJ*, 5/1/1931. The account of N. Q. Thaxter's death is in GL Diaries, 3/11/1873. Leonard and the out-of-almshouse poor, ATB, Report of Overseers of the Poor, 1886, ff. The Gould party, *HJ*, 6/10/1887. The burial of Mrs. Smith, *HJ*, 10/19/1894, repr. from *The Woman's Journal*. Regarding the endurance of Lucretia's memory, see a letter from George Melcher, a Hingham native living in New Hampshire, in *HJ*, 4/25/1968. He wrote in response to the study of the black community written shortly after the death of Martin Luther King, Jr. He remembered seeing Lucretia in the Thaxter pew when he was a young child. She was, he wrote, "one of the best known members of the church." On the burial, *HJ*, 2/26/1904, and S. B. Willard in *HJ*, 5/10/1907. "The general sense of the community," *Patriot*, 11/13/1841.

Page 89: On the meeting at Derby and the "mobocratic spirit," *Patriot*, 4/9/1842. Stringer of Raleigh is identified in GL Gen., II, 345. Jairus Lincoln's memories of Derby Hall, *HJ*, 2/21/1873. Non-support of parties and candidates, hardening of positions, and charges of "sowing disunion," *Patriot*, 1/16/1841, 3/4/1843, 7/16/1842, and 10/3/1845. The prediction of filling the almshouse, *Patriot*, 1/29/1842. Gardner's death and funeral, *Patriot*, 4/8/1843, and (quotation from Wilder) 4/22/1843. For Clark's memories of the procession, see reprint in *HJ*, 10/25/1912.

Page 90: Arrangers, participants, *et al.*, are named in *Patriot*, 7/26/1844 and 8/16/1844, which also prints the first two banner sentiments. The third banner sentiment, from S. B. Willard, *HJ*, 5/10/1907. "ruined the choice retreat," *HJ*, 10/4/1850. On Evelina Smith, *Patriot*, 2/14/1845. On S. H. Gay and the constitution, *HJ*, 6/29/1888. Gay (1814-88) was a great grandson of Parson Ebenezer. He was a neighbor on Staten Island of the parents of Robert Gould Shaw, who commanded the (black) 54th Regiment. Gay was the actual author of W. C. Bryant's *Popular History of the United States*. J. Lincoln's pew #16, second from the left front as one faces the altar, became Governor Andrew's. Offending local Whigs, *Patriot*, 11/3/1843. J. Lincoln's home sale, *Patriot*, 1/5/1844 (and JLN). "If you wish to be popular," *HJ*, 2/21/1873.

Page 91: The move to Northborough, GL Gen., II, 484. The little bathhouse is remembered in
HJ, 12/17/1926. Adams's memorial, *Patriot*, 1/19/1839. The "confession of
wrong," *Patriot*, 6/29/1839. Slavery a "cancer," *Patriot*, 3/19/1842. On the
charges and threats against Adams, *Gazette*, 2/17/1837; *Patriot*, 2/9/1839 and
2/5/1842. Adams and the abolitionists and colonizers, from a speech in the House
(1/23/1839) reprinted in *Patriot*, 2/9/1839. On women as his constituents,
Patriot, 8/4/1838. Word of the petitions giving hope, *Patriot*, 11/13/1841. "It was
mainly owing," *Patriot*, 1/12/1839.

Page 92: On the "simple majorities" and the events of 1845 regarding Texas, Burns (1983),
460, and Fehrenbach (1980), 262-67. Hingham's delegates to the "great Texas
meeting" reported in *Patriot*, 1/24/1845. Stearns's sermon, "The Duty of Moral
Reflection with Particular Reference to the Texas Question," is in Hist Coll HPL,
Reel 76:11. On the forty-member committee and the 40 percent vote, *Patriot*, 11/21
and 12/5/1845. Browne's letter to Polk, *Patriot*, 7/30/1847. On the loss of
Southern patronage, *HJ*, 3/14 and 5/28/1851.

Pages 93-94: The five Presidents in ten years were W. H. Harrison (d. 1841), succeeded by
John Tyler (1841-45); James K. Polk (1845-49); Zachary Taylor (d. 1850), succeeded by Millard Fillmore (1850-53). On the last Whig parade, *Patriot*,
11/10/1848. The Great Compromise of 1850, Burns (1983), 472-75. "This bill
derides," *HJ*, 5/10/1850. The bill's passage in Congress, reported in *HJ*, 8/30 and
9/20/1850. J. Lincoln's letter, *HJ*, 5/10 and 5/24/1850. Stearns's sermon, "The
Gospel applied to the Fugitive Slave Law," March 2, 1851, is in Hist Coll HPL, Reel
76:11. On Parker and the inevitability of violence, Richard Brown (1978), 178-79,
and Parker lecture at South Hingham, *HJ*, 1/2/1857. Lincoln on aiding fugitives,
HJ, 3/14/1851. Hingham not on routes, Wilbur H. Siebert, "The Underground
Railroad in Massachusetts," *American Antiquarian Society*, April, 1935, 25-100. Ten
other townsmen joined Andrew in signing the request that the sermon be published:
Gorham Lincoln, John Lovett, Joseph Sprague, David Abbot, Perez Lincoln, David
Lincoln, Eben Gay, Isaac Winslow, David Andrews, and George Lincoln, Jr. (the
later historian). On Andrew's marriage, *Patriot*, 12/29/1848.

A summary note to this chapter is necessary. The chapter can only suggest, from a local perspective, the corrosive and chaotic politics, the class warfare and sectional fears, the complexities
of that anarchic and violent time, which remains imperfectly understood by most of us today.
Burns (1983) has described the issue of slavery as one that the political process could not make
acceptable by "morselizing"——that is, by breaking up and "devouring" it in small bites (p.
467). Slavery was built into the Constitution, a document rejected by radicals such as Garrison
and Wendell Phillips, who burned a facsimile at a Framingham rally in 1854 (Richard Brown
[1978], 177). Anti-slavery advocates favored the Bill of Rights, the first ten amendments, and
protested their violation in the denial of free speech, a free press, and trial by jury. The mobbing
of Garrison, editor of *The Liberator* (founded 1831), and the murder (1837) of the gradual
abolitionist editor Elijah Lovejoy while he was defending his presses, catapulted Phillips into
prominence as an abolitionist spokesman. Lovejoy's death moved a lukewarm Increase Smith
into the more distinct anti-slavery position of his wife. Sidney Howard Gay risked being killed
when he spoke against slavery in the border states. J. Q. Adams's difficulties in presenting
petitions, which were "tabled" so that they could not be read, debated, or printed, denied many
the right of free speech. The illegal slave trade and the violations of treaty obligations with
foreign nations added to the distress of his old age. The havoc at polling places in Kansas, the
caning of Sumner, the Dred Scott decision, viewed today as entirely political, were events
without precedent. Modern historians too often leave the impression that of the opposed
factions, pro-slavery forces were the more reasonable until provoked by abolitionist fanaticism.

CHAPTER SEVEN: *John Albion Andrew*

The account of Andrew's life and personality is based on Browne (1868), Chandler (1880),
Clarke (1918), and Pearson (1904). See also J. D. Long's sketch in B-L. Andrew's speeches are
included in Hist Coll HPL, Reel 76:15.

Page 96: Andrew's advertisement, *HJ*, 9/1/1854. On the officers of the Republican Party, *HJ*,
9/15/1854. On "Stebbings," *HJ*, 7/9/1852. The mock battle is reported in
Spunkville Chronicle, 7/4/1854. A second *Chronicle* (7/5/1858) was on sale at
"Sprague's periodical depot" for five cents. We are indebted to Helen and Eugene
Chamberlain for materials about a "Spunkville" offshoot, the "Clams, Oysters, and
Plum Pudding Corporation." It held an annual evening festival with much the same
cast of characters. It was abandoned until after the War, by which time the sharply

satiric political allusions had given way to wild punning, and participation was less exclusively Centerite. On the "murder" of Jeheil, *HJ*, 8/13/1858. On "pulpit politics," *HJ*, 10/10/1856.

Page 97: The Constitutional Union stalwarts are listed in a report of their meeting, *HJ*, 9/7/1860. On Richardson's "sentiment," *HJ*, 11/2/1860. It is an ironic fact of Hingham history that the First Parish leadership was opposed to the election of Abraham Lincoln in 1860. It is also intriguing to speculate about the timing of the establishment of the Congregational Church in the late 1840s with an abolitionist pastor at a time when the First Parish pastor was noticeably absent from abolitionist rallies. The founding of the Ag. and Hort. Society is reported in *HJ*, 11/19/1858. For its history, see Chapter Ten. Andrew's Charles Street house, originally numbered #71, is now #110, between Pinkney and Revere Streets. "All the victories of life," Pearson (1904), I, 230. On Bouvé's aid to Kansas and Brown, Hurd (1884), 1102; on Parker's, Richard Brown (1978), 179. Report of the Kansas free-state vote, *HJ*, 1/11/1856.

Page 98: Andrew on Dred Scott, from Pearson (1904), I, 78-79. Andrew's reply to Cushing, Pearson, I, 86. On the "infernal statute": Judge Edward Loring, Probate Judge for Suffolk County and a U.S. Commissioner, was finally removed by the controversial Personal Liberty Law. No man who held a state judicial office in Massachusetts could henceforth serve as a U.S. Commissioner; no state courts, jails, or militias could be used in a fugitive slave case. On Andrew's refusal to speak, letter to Garrison in Hist Coll HPL, Reel 76:15 (7/31/1860). Sumner on Andrew's integrity, Pearson (1904), I, 128. For Andrew's actions regarding John Brown, Pearson, I, 96-104.

Page 99: For Andrew's Senate testimony, Hist Coll HPL, Reel 76:15. For an analysis of the Southern perspective on events of 1859-60, including Brown's raid, the activities of abolitionists, the Senate investigation, and the genesis of the Constitutional Union Party, see Fehrenbach (1980), 335-43. "The home of my heart" from Andrew's speech in front of his Hingham home at the time of his nomination, late August, 1860, Hist Coll HPL, Reel 76:15. Election results, *HJ*, 11/9/1860.

Page 100: Sargent's speech is in a booklet describing the inauguration of the Andrew statue in Hist Coll HPL, Reel 76:15.

Page 101: On Howe's "Battle Hymn," Pearson (1904), I, 270; Howe (1899), 271-75; Clifford (1979), 142-47; and Tharp (1956), 241-45. Evidence for attribution of the tune and the words of "John Brown's Body" is conflicting. Brogan (1986), 319, claims that Thomas Bingham Bishop, "composer of a successful camp-meeting chorus 'Gone to be a Soldier in the Army of the Lord,'" quickly set new words to the tune either after Harper's Ferry or after John Brown's hanging. Boni (1952), 145, states that the original words began "Say, brothers, will you meet with us" and that the tune "is credited to a Southern composer, William Steffe . . . . This Southern camp-meeting song was a favorite with American soldiers before the Civil War." Frederic Hills of Hingham believes that the words of "John Brown's Body" originated with Col. Fletcher Webster's 12th Massachusetts Volunteer Infantry while it was stationed at Fort Warren in Boston Harbor. The 12th marched down State Street in July, 1861, singing "John Brown's Body" and continued to sing it along the Potomac. Webster, the son of Daniel, was killed at the first battle of Bull Run.

Page 102: "A poor, despised," *etc.*, from Andrew's letter to Lewis Haydn, a Boston black freedman (12/4/1863), in Pearson (1904), II, 70. On Shaw and his regiment, Burchard (1965) and Emilio (repr. 1969). Hingham men in black regiments from B-L.

Page 103: "The government, which found" from Andrew's letter to Lincoln in Pearson (1904), II, 109. The "comic incident" quoted in Pearson (1904), II, 248n. A "hater of seemings" from Andrew's letter to his sister (3/27/1847) in Pearson, I, 53.

Page 104: "He worked like," Clarke (1918), 31. "Principles" from Andrew's letter to John Binney in Pearson (1904), II, 321.

Page 105: "Duty of a citizen" from Andrew's address (1864) to the Harvard Medical School graduating class, Browne (1868), 11. "My only anxiety" from Andrew's letter to Binney in Pearson (1904), II, 322-23. "There were periods," journalist John Robinson quoted in Pearson, II, 329. "Never mean enough," Andrew's statement at a Methodist Camp Meeting on Martha's Vineyard (8/10/1862) quoted in Chandler (1880), 25.

Page 106: On the removal of Andrew's remains to Hingham, *HJ*, 10/29/1869. On the statue controversy, see note to Chapter Fourteen.

CHAPTER EIGHT: *A Changing Hingham*

The reconstruction of human geography, house locations, ages, and anecdotes, is based chiefly on JLN and Plymouth County Atlas (1879). Also used were maps of 1857, 1882 and 1885; GL Diaries; E. Bouvé in *History* (1893); early photographs in Shilhan (1976); and reports in *HJ*. It should be emphasized that George Lincoln's ride is a composite construction and not the account of a single event. The account of the monument's dedication is from B-L. Quotations from GL Diaries are as follows: 10/22/1876, 5/13/1877, 10/12/1873, 11/12/1871.

Page 110: On the buttonwood tree: JLN say it was planted by Sprague in 1793. T. T. Bouvé (*HJ*, 10/14/1859) says Fearing Burr told him the buttonwood tree "in front of Mr. Fearing Burr's store had been set out by Daniel Souther about seventy years since" — *i.e.*, 1789. Hall (1985), 11, discusses the conflicting attributions. Was there another tree across Main "in front of" Burr's store?

Page 111: "A house is a story," Italian proverb.

Page 112: "The neatest little cottage", *Patriot*, 9/5/1845. Old Colony House history, JPR, based on MS. letters, Solomon Lincoln to GL in his collection. Joe Lincoln, *Boston Sunday Globe*, 11/3/1918. See also Mosher (1992). JPR adds the following from William J. Mackey, Jr., *American Bird Decoys*, 85-87: "Joe Lincoln was a fastidious workman who strove for perfection in the fashioning, finishing, and painting of every decoy. His wooden ones are of perfect symmetry . . . . They are literally streamlined to a degree that no other maker, with the possible exception of Keyes Chadwick, attained . . . . Lincoln's ducks, geese and now his shore birds make secure his position as one of America's top decoy makers." "The people coming up from the Cape," interview with M. Annette Loring.

Page 113: "gathering meanwhile a basket," GL Diaries, 10/12/1873. "quiet village" survey, *HJ*, 4/4/1867. "grandfather in Hull," Loring interview.

Page 114: Fort Hill history, GL Gen. For a view of Broad Bridge, *HJ*, 3/19/1869.

Page 115: House history, JLN and JPR, based on MS. *Hingham Houses and Other Buildings*, etc., by GL, in JPR's collection. Information on the Soule mansion from JLN is ambiguous.

Page 116: The account of St. Paul's, *HJ*, 3/6 and 11/3/1865, 3/2 and 8/10/1866, 6/17/1870, and 7/28/1871, and GL Diaries, 7/23/1871. Irish families, GL Gen.; home locations, JLN.

Pages 117-18: Population figures from census table in *History* (1893), I.ii.379. Appropriations and tax rates, ATBs 1865-95. Demographics computed from reports of the Town Clerk and the School Committee.

CHAPTER NINE: *A Half-Century of Work*

This reconstruction and interpretation is based in part on analysis of Directories (1867, 1885, 1894, 1908), Census Reports, and Lainhart (1988). *HJ* has numerous accounts of leading industries and factories, permitting amplification of GL in *History* (1893) and Hartwell (1954). Occasional reports in *Trans. Ag. and Hort.* interpret trends. For broader contexts, we draw chiefly on Richard Brown (1978), Burns (1985), and Tager and Ifkovic (1986). The survey of changing occupations is based on hand counting and conflation of statistics. We avoided the usual broad categories, which are misleading. We traced numbers of individual workers (recording their ages) and all descriptive categories of work, then followed the revealing general trend of workers' descriptions of themselves as "employed" by a firm or an individual. Commuting patterns were evident from the Directories. The tracing of women in the workforce was more difficult because some sources, such as the *Plymouth County Directory* of 1867, excluded them. Here, we relied on post Civil War censuses (women worked at paid labor before, but the 1855 state census did not list them), GL's chapter, "Manufactures and Commerce," in *History* (1893), ATBs and *HJ* articles.

Page 119: Longfellow (1975). "The Ropewalk" is dated 1854. "Fate seems to have put," *History* (1893), I.ii.180.

Page 120: Gould as "capitalist dragon," Burns (1986), 177. "Dealers in country towns," GL Diaries, 12/10/1873.

Page 121: Under 2 percent growth, *HJ*, 2/6/1891. "Other towns in our vicinity", *Trans. Ag. and Hort.* for 1873, Comm. on Manufactures. On shoe manufacture, *History* (1893), I.ii.167; Hartwell (1954), 12-13; GL Diaries, 12/31/1877; *HJ*, 2/4/1870,

8/3/1872, 7/31/1874, 1/30/1880, 12/14/1883, 12/18/1885, 9/29/1887, 3/2/1888.

Page 122: Elijah Burr is remembered in *HJ*, 10/1/1858. For Stephenson's, *HJ*, 11/26/1884; *History* (1893), I.ii.160; Hartwell (1954), 5.

Pages 123-24: On Jacobs', *History* (1893), I.ii.159-60; Hartwell (1954), 5; *HJ*, 5/23/1883; D.A.R. Paper #3, History of the Jacobs Family, reprinted in *HJ*, 4/3/1908. On woodenware, *History* (1893), I.ii.163-64; Hartwell (1954), 5; *HJ*, 2/27/1891; Marble (1928, no pagination). On Hersey's box manufacture, *HJ*, 4/18/1868 and 3/8/1872. Local boxes seen in Chicago, *HJ*, 12/16/1859. "Elsewhere for their worklife," *HJ*, 9/12/1856.

Pages 125-26: On Tower toys, *HJ*, 8/20/1869, 5/13/1870, 3/31/1893, 5/12/1899, and Elwin Fearing interview. On cordage, *History* (1893), I.ii.175-76; Hartwell (1954); *Trans. Ag. and Hort.* for 1873; *HJ*, 9/16/1881 (history of ropemaking in Hingham); and 6/9/1865, 1/30/1880, 7/22/1887, and 6/15, 9/21, and 11/2/1894.

Pages 126-27: On Burr Brown, *History* (1893), I.ii.161-62; Hartwell (1954), 11; Horton (1949); *HJ*, 1/19/1872 (detailed description); 12/14 and 12/21/1894, 2/13/1899, 4/3/1903. Mrs. A. P. Soule, *HJ*, 12/21/1894.

Pages 127-28: On woolen mills, *History*, I.ii.161-62; Hartwell (1954), 11; *HJ*, 4/2/1880; GL Diaries, 9/18/1875; *HJ*, 11/12 and 12/31/1875, 12/31/1886, and 6/3/1887. Seymour and Hersey's ideas, *HJ*, 3/25/1887.

Page 129: Barnes and Ripley, Shilhan (1976), 8; Levi Hersey, *HJ*, 5/14/1897.

Page 130: Members of the town labor force, from ATBs, 1870-94.

Page 131: Nurse Patterson's celebration, *HJ*, 8/3/1883; retirement, *HJ*, 2/20/1891. The poor, from ATBs, annual reports of Overseers of the Poor, and GL Gen. Sketch of the poorhouse, Board of Health Report for 1881.

Pages 133-36: Tower's store, GL Diaries, 4/12/1879; Hobart's traveling shop, Elwin Fearing interview; "Quilp" quoted from *HJ*, 9/22/1871, 10/17 and 10/24/1873. Burr's new wagon, *HJ*, 5/21/1891. The sled ride of Todd and Loring, *HJ*, 2/3/1893. "Choices are the essence," Chafe (1986), 486.

CHAPTER TEN: *The New Agriculturalists and Their Society*

Page 137: The Wilder statement, *HJ*, 1/27/1860. SL (1827), 9. Smith (1973), 82.

Page 138: Foley (1935), 30, 36-37. Sketch of Fearing based on GL Diaries, 5/24/1875 and 1/12/1876; GL Gen.; obit. in *HJ*, 5/28/1875.

Page 139: For Cushing, GL Gen. For Brewer, Walker (1973). The "expert" was seedsman Aaron Low, later owner of the Whiton farm. "In a farming town," Russell (1976), 391.

Page 140: "Hereditary rust," *HJ*, 9/18/1857. J. C. Wilder, *HJ*, 3/18/1859. On gentlemen farmers, Russell, 409. Aims of the society, *Trans. Ag. and Hort.* for 1858-61, 1869, and 1872. The poem appeared in *Trans.* for 1861.

Page 142: The roosters, *HJ*, 2/14/1868.

Page 143: "The committee cannot but feel," *Trans. Ag. and Hort.* for 1877. On the impact of canning: the vacuum method of preserving perishables was patented by Amanda Jones in 1873 (see Macdonald, 1992, 67). "Thirty years ago," *HJ*, 7/26/1878. GL on roses, *Trans. Ag. and Hort.* for 1882. Mercy's cereus, *HJ*, 8/7/1885. Hingham Institute, *HJ*, 5/7 and 6/25/1869.

Page 144: Visit to Cushing, *HJ*, 12/21/1877. "The writer of this report," *Trans. Ag. and Hort.* for 1882.

Page 145: Farm memories from interviews with M. Annette Loring and Elwin Fearing. "Peddling strawberries," JPR conversations with E. Fearing.

Page 146: "What should be the aims?" *Trans. Ag. and Hort.* for 1872. "True results are to be," *Trans.* for 1883.

CHAPTER ELEVEN: *The Sociable Life of George Lincoln and his Neighbors*

Most quotations from the chief source, GL Diaries, are located by date in the text.

Page 147: On the idea of the "social," Arendt (1958), 38-39. The C.O. & P.P. announcement appears in *HJ*, 12/14/1866, twelfth anniversary of the founding. Centre humor deserves a chapter unto itself.

Page 148: Provincetown memories, GL Diaries, 2/26 and 6/12/1872, 7/22 and 8/7/1873.

Page 153: "Would by no means advocate," *HJ*, 11/2/1860.

Page 155: Musical orgies, GL Diaries, 7/14, 9/30, and 10/7/1877.

Page 156: "forefathers," *HJ*, 12/2/1870. Winter picnics, *HJ*, 1/23/1874. Dunbar "raid," *HJ*, 1/5/1872. "Velocipede madness," *HJ*, 2/19 and 4/30/1869.

Page 157: "Base Ball," *HJ*, 7/31/1868. The "tadpoles," *HJ*, 4/28/1871. The Agricultural Society, *HJ*, 3/13/1868. The new high school, *HJ*, 5/24/1878. The Catholic youth society, *HJ*, 2/27/1874. Hanaford, *HJ*, 9/20/1867. "Few things tend," *HJ*, 2/13/1871. "A parish that cannot," *HJ*, 3/4/1870.

Page 158: "Bringing South Hingham to life," *HJ*, 2/20/1880. On the bands, see Baumgartner (1980). "Nothing so tends," *HJ*, 9/25/1866. Stephenson, *HJ*, 5/8/1868. Loring Hall items from program collection, Hist Coll HPL, Reel 76:9. Universalist ladies tea, *HJ*, 1/23/1874. "Who Dar Minstrels," *HJ*, 3/12/1875.

Page 159: Little Plain humor: the "ball," *HJ*, 2/10/1883; Cushing's trial, *HJ*, 8/21/1891. Fourth of July, *HJ*, 7/9/1886. It is worth noting that on 12/2/1892, *HJ* claimed that Mrs. Cleveland, Frances Folsom, was a direct descendant of John Folsom (or Foulsham), who came to Hingham in 1638.

Page 160: "To slip up to Boston," *HJ*, 2/5/1885.

CHAPTER TWELVE: *Revolutions in Moving About*

Sources other than *HJ* and ATBs are "Public Conveyances" in *History* (1893), I.ii.141-56, and, for "Downersville" and Melville Garden, six articles by Adelaide Hunt (1961) and one by JPR in *Hingham Mirror* (8/4/1982). For broader contexts of transportation, Andrist (1972), Burns (1986), Harlow (1946), Hersey (1969), and Horton (1948).

Page 161: The *Rose's* arrival, *HJ*, 9/1/1866. For the rival Litchfield, *HJ*, 2/22 and 5/10/1867, 5/29/1868, and 9/3 through 9/17/1869.

Pages 162-63: "Steamboat excitement," *HJ*, 8/23 and 9/1/1868; GL Diaries, 8/13/1872. Aground in mud and fog, *HJ*, 9/6/1867, 4/23 and 8/13/1869, 9/22/1871, 6/28/1872. Litchfield's whale, *HJ*, 3/15/1872, 4/24/1874. "Beautiful hills," *HJ*, 4/13/1866. "Rip Van Winkle," *HJ*, 7/4/1867.

Pages 164-66: The brief account of Downer is drawn from his own lay sermons, *HJ*, 9/10/1875, 7/27 and 8/17/1877, 8/14/1881, the obit. in *HJ*, 6/27/1884, and Hunt (*Patriot Ledger*), 9/30/1961. Note an interesting Hingham connection: Samuel Gridley Howe, also a close friend of John A. Andrew, was backed by Downer in the founding of Perkins Institute for the Blind. Charles Sumner's Hingham ancestry, GL Gen., II, 306. "Across the outspread meadow-lands," reprinted in *Hingham Magazine* (1898). Growth of Melville Garden, *etc.*, *HJ*, 6/9/1871; GL Diaries, 6/23/1871; *HJ*, 5/30/1873, 7/30/1875, 6/9/1876, 4/27/1877, 6/21/1878, 7/4/1879.

Page 167: Kelly the "holy terror", Hunt (1961). James's wedding, *HJ*, 11/28/1875. "Humanitarian success," *HJ*, 6/27/1884.

Page 168: Later history of steamboats, *HJ*, 7/2, 8/20, and 9/24/1880, 1/12/1883, 7/6/1894, 6/7/1895. Railroad, Hersey (1969); *HJ*, 5/18/1877, 2/7/1879, 8/20 and 9/24/1880, 1/7/1881. Old Colony House fire, *HJ*, 10/11/1872. Pastor Cargill, *HJ*, 5/3/1867. Jotham Lincoln, Jr., *HJ*, 9/18/1868.

Page 169: Railroad ten years ago, *HJ*, 5/18/1877; growth: *HJ*, 8/8/1879, 4/4 and 6/15/1883. "We'll have a railroad," *HJ*, 10/15/1869. Proposed route, *HJ*, 1/14/1870. "strangled to death," *HJ*, 3/22/1872. "destroy the wholesome," *HJ*, 12/25/1874.

Page 170-72: Central Street, *HJ*, 5/14/1869, 10/14 and 11/18/1870, 4/6/1871; Thaxter estate, *HJ*, 9/22/1876. Downer's plea, *HJ*, 3/16/1877. "The town's nearness," ATB, 1880. Traffic and accidents, *HJ*, 8/26/1870, 1/12/1872, 8/1/1873, 1/2/1874, 7/8 and 8/5/1880, 9/9/1881. Town meetings, ATBs, 1870, 1876. The "system" of repairs, *HJ*, 8/7/1868, and ATBs 1869, 1871, 1872. "Reckless extravagance," *HJ*, 2/28/1873. Stephenson's warning, *HJ*, 5/16/1879. "The plea of public good," *HJ*, 7/15/1881.

CHAPTER THIRTEEN: *The Political World of John Davis Long*

All quotations identified as "Long" are from Long (1956). References to this edition are unavoidably confusing. Where diary entries and letters are dated in the edition, we give dates; where they are not, we simply cite page numbers. State and national contexts are drawn chiefly from Bailyn (1981), Brown (1978), Burns (1986), Hofstadter (1959), and Tager and Ifkovic (1985). On temperance, see especially Gusfield (1963); on women's rights, Flexner (1959).

Page 173: "We trust that," *HJ*, 3/1/1872; the warning was probably occasioned by the high school fracas the year before (see Chap. Fourteen below). Report of 1879 town meeting, *HJ*, 3/14/1879.

Page 174: The Long victory procession, *HJ*, 11/7/1879. The words "brilliant illumina-tions" and "illuminated houses" occur frequently in the nineteenth century in descriptions of nighttime political celebrations, patriotic ceremonies, and parades. "Illuminations" were made from thin sheets of colored paper, folded many times. The makers, often children, then scissor-cut geometric and other shapes into the folds. When the folded sheets were opened and placed in windows, the light of oil and kerosene lamps, candles, and gas light flickered through the cut-outs. "Chinese gong-beating," and "harassed," Long, diary entries dated 12/17/1882, 10/24/1877.

Page 175: On Buchanan, Long, p. 51. On Phillips, 10/4/1859. On Lincoln, 9/7/1860. Day-dream of a daughter, Long, p. 98. "ambition to be a poet," 2/14/1858. "Mrs. Johnson's attic," 5/21/1867. "home in the village," 12/2/1868.

Page 176: "push, energy, verve," "faithful," *etc.*, *HJ*, 2/11/1876, 6/1/1877. "carried down with our bundles," Long, 4/12/1875. "Get up at six," 4/18/1877; letter from father, 4/14/1872. "My campaign," 11/18/1879. On the *Maine*, Long, pp. 214-15; letter to his wife, 1/4/1899. "The Vice President business," 4/17/1900.

Page 177: "The slightest turn," 2/21/1906. Physical images of Long, *HJ*, 2/12 and 10/8/1886. "One could not but notice," *HJ*, 3/29/1889. The ex-Confederate chaplain, *HJ*, 5/29/1891.

Page 178: The "old white horse," McCall (1916), 14. "Long is a small man," reprinted *HJ*, 12/23/1887. "travesty" and "only a chip," *HJ*, 10/8/1886, 10/22/1886. "Love of home," Long, p. 40. "merry walk", 2/14/1892. "long ago evening," *HJ*, 7/27/1934. "clustering in the vestibule," Long, 1/6/1906; "social element," *ibid.*

Page 179: St. Patrick's Day, 3/17/1906. "dance of factions," Burns (1983), 327. "The irate Democrat" charged was Charles B. Leavitt. However, the private detectives who arrested him and reported his confession were later indicted for several false arrests and perjury in other cases.

Page 180: "Symbolic crusade," Gusfield (1963). "bullies a poor man," *HJ*, 8/27/1869.

Page 181: Weymouth beer peddlers, *HJ*, 5/10 and 8/23/1872. "groggery at the Cove," GL Diaries 12/18/1870. Arrests: Margetts, *HJ*, 3/22/1867; Overton the "ice cream autocrat," *HJ*, 4/26 and 8/30/1867, 5/28/1869, 6/30 and 7/28/1871; J. L. Hunt, *HJ*, 4/19/1867. Cushing House, JLN and JPR based on GL, *Hingham Houses and Other Buildings*, etc., MS. in his collection. "pressed too hard," *HJ*, 3/19/1872. Henry W. Lincoln, *HJ*, 10/23/1874. "Mr. Cushing believed," *HJ*, 12/4/1874. Space of the stage coaches, *HJ*, 10/13/1876. The "trap," *HJ*, 12/20/1876.

Page 182: Votes on licensing, ATBs. Law and order meeting and other temperance societies, *HJ*, 3/30, 5/4, and 11/2/1883, 1/4 and 9/12/1884, 4/1 and 11/14/1887. "Spotting" as "entrapment," *HJ*, 11/28/1883. The Collier speech, *HJ*, 3/16/1888.

Page 183: On the temperance crusade, Gusfield (1963). The W.C.T.U. "studied and agitated," Burns (1986), 279. Willard "saw the possibility," Flexner (1959), 182. The account of the women's movement is based on Flexner. The quotation, "veritable domestic revolution," opens her Chap. Thirteen.

Page 184: Hanaford, *HJ*, 2/14 and 2/21/1870, 6/11/1869, and 5/29/1868. Ordina-tion, "I was the first," *HJ*, 9/16/1904.

Page 185: "The year in the pulpit," Shaw (1915), 106. See the biography in Willard and Livermore (1897), and Flexner (1959), 237-39. Livermore, "one of the foremost," Gusfield (1963), 88n. See the biography in Willard and Livermore (1897), and Flexner (1959), 107.

Page 186: For the battered letter, *HJ*, 10/7/1887. Shaw's anecdote, Shaw (1915), 95. On Livermore's preaching, *HJ*, 12/21/1877, 12/19/1873, and 6/12/1874.

Pages 187-88: On the suffrage campaign, Flexner (1959) and *HJ*, 9/5 and 11/21/1884, 11/18/1887, and 1/20/1888. Peterson, "Women who believe," *HJ*, 4/26/1895. The "remonstrance," *HJ*, 5/10 and 5/24/1895. Record of the vote, ATB, 1896 and *HJ*, 11/8/1895. "Brave liberalism in thought," D.A.R., *Hingham* (1911), 8.

CHAPTER FOURTEEN: *Transforming the Schools*

Sources, unless otherwise indicated, are reports of the School Committee and Superintendent in ATBs (dated in the text). For context, see Benjamin (1969), particularly useful, and Cremin (1961), Good (1962), and Roscoe (1984).

Pages 189-90: Interviews with Thomas (1971), Loring (1969), and Wilder (1969).

Pages 190-91: For school buildings, ATB for the year ending February, 1874. Jairus Lincoln letter, *HJ*, 4/3/1873. "The idealist notions," Roscoe (1984), 34; see also Benjamin (1969), 40, and *passim*.

Page 192: The "sham" of laws, Cremin (1961), 127. Forty other towns, Good (1962), 242. For the traditional account of the high school, see *History* (1893), I.ii.136.

Page 193: School Committee complaints are in annual reports for 1867 and 1868. For the impact on Derby, see Roscoe (1984), 50. Signs of a storm, *HJ*, 3/3/1871. Snyder letter, *HJ*, 9/15/1871.

Page 194: Cushing reply, *HJ*, 9/26/1871; Snyder reply, *HJ*, 10/13/1871. "Sectional prejudices," *HJ*, 3/13/1874. Opposition to the Andrew monument, *HJ*, 10/20/1871. This story is both perplexing and unpleasant. Andrew's body, buried first at Mount Auburn Cemetery in Cambridge, was moved to Hingham Cemetery in November, 1869. A state-wide drive for funds was headed by General Stephenson and Colonel B. F. Meservey, local Democratic leaders. As of June, 1872, even the local G.A.R. had not voted to contribute (*HJ*, 6/14/1872). A writer (*HJ*, 3/21/1873) signing herself (?) "Women's Rights" asked somewhat derisively what had become of the drive, and a week later, State Rep. John Cushing proposed state aid. Both were angrily put down by Stephenson. In *HJ*, 7/4/1873, someone noted it had taken five years to raise the "contemptible sum of $6000." But by October, 1873, sculptor Thomas Gould had been commissioned and departed for his Florence studio to make the Carrara marble statue at a cost of $10,000. In September, 1875, it was in place. When, on October 8, it was dedicated, General Stephenson acknowledged the aid of *Boston* businessmen and cited the cold shoulder with which solicitations had been met locally. Controversy had broken out over the facing of the statue, with its *back* to the Civil War monument and the town. Perhaps Stephenson's confrontational style, outspoken conservative politics, and notoriety as an antagonist of women's rights had caused the trouble.

Pages 195-96: On Jennings, Robinson (1980), 137, 139, 155-56. His philosophy is set forth in Supt. Reports, ATBs for 1872-80. On the "progressive impulse" and Parker, Cremin (1961), 21-25, and Good (1962), 219-21.

Pages 197-98: Changes in the schools, from reports of the Committee and the Superintendent, ATBs. Locations of new sites for old buildings, JPR, based on *History* (1893), I.i.103-10; MS. letters of Solomon Lincoln to GL (JPR collection); and the MS. Fearing Burr's Memoranda Notes (JPR collection). "Do our schools meet?" School Comm. Report, 1881. "leading our youth away," Supt. Report 1883. "make out bills, notes," full program outline published 1889. "a thorough mastery," Comm. Report 1883. "learn to make a good biscuit," Comm. Report 1887. "the business of any system," Supt. Report 1890. "a boy or girl just out," Supt. Report 1893. Shift from "the concrete and practical," Comm. Report 1894.

CHAPTER FIFTEEN: *The Rise of Convenience and Safety*

For national context, we draw on Andrist (1972).

Page 199: Bicknell's report, *History* (1893), I.ii.26.

Pages 200-01: "Hingham, spare that pond," *HJ*, 10/6/1876. Hayward's report is reprinted in *HJ*, 3/19/1875. Votes on the water issue from ATBs. On the first customer, Robinson (1980), 152. For the opening of the water system and the Fourth of July trial, *HJ*, 6/25 and 7/9/1880. GL's observations in his diaries, 9/15/1877, 9/10 and 9/19/1879. For a contemporary history of the waterworks, see *HJ*, 7/30/1880. The Water Company bought Fulling Mill Pond in October, 1885. On the turtle, *HJ*, 11/5/1886.

Page 202: The counts of subscribers, *HJ*, 12/23/1887 and 7/29/1892. Melcher's reminiscence, *HJ*, 1/6/1949. Company directors, a mixture of old family, year-round, and summer residents, included E. Waters Burr, Ebed L. Ripley, Charles B. Barnes, George Hayward, Morris Whiton, and contractor Charles L. Goodhue. The taste of "newly shingled roof," *HJ*, 6/15/1888. Mrs. Nye's faucet, *HJ*, 1/17/1890. The struck main, *HJ*, 6/27/1884.

Page 203: Lowering the main, *HJ*, 5/23/1884, 2/25/1887. On Bradley's fertilizer works, *HJ*, 1/1 and 4/23/1869, 4/2/1870, 11/19/1875, and especially 6/23/1876. Accounts of public health from annual reports of the board in ATBs, which also describe the pond and the brook. See also *HJ*, 6/27 and 7/4/1873.

Page 204: The winter flood and muskrats, *HJ*, 2/19/1886 and 8/21/1888. The "surface wash," Board of Health in ATB 1883. "immediate cessation," *HJ*, 2/25/1887. The "open sewer," *HJ*, 12/4/1885. The "piggery behind," *HJ*, 10/2/1885. The 1887 report and Spalding's response, *HJ*, 2/25 and 3/4/1887.

Pages 205-06: Street conditions and dangers, *HJ*, 1/9, 3/19, and 10/22/1880, 4/1 and 8/26/1881. "Tinkering up," *HJ*, 3/15/1888. North St. abutter, *HJ*, 5/4/1888. Railroad tickets, *HJ*, 9/6/1889. Beal's blasting, *HJ*, 6/28/1889. Beal's unearthing, GL in *HJ*, 10/19/1894. Beal's operations and machinery, *HJ*, 5/15/1896.

Page 207: Central St. extension, *HJ*, 1/26/1894, 2/22 and 10/4/1895, 11/1/1895 (opened). Kimball appropriations and salary and sixty miles of road, *HJ*, 4/12/1889, 7/24/1891, 2/26/1892.

Page 208: On vandalism and rowdyism, *HJ*, 10/16/1885, where they are blamed on the vote against police. The history of night police is given in *HJ*, 11/19/1886. "Young roughs," *HJ*, 4/1/1887; the Baptist prayer meeting, *ibid.* Zion Hill, *HJ*, 1/11/1884. Town and Depot safes, *HJ*, 4/1/1887. Ufford's sermon, *HJ*, 11/9/1885. Fourth of July report, *HJ*, 7/8/1887. Robberies of Long, *HJ*, 7/12 and 7/26/1889. Lahee and Eady, *HJ*, 7/1/1887. Street lighting, *HJ*, 2/15, 5/10, 6/1, 7/26, 8/30, and 10/25/1889, 2/28/1890.

Page 209: Whiton's tour, *HJ*, 1/11/1889. Domestic lighting, *HJ*, 1/23/1891, 8/12/1892, 5/29/1883.

Page 210: Telephones: *HJ*, 6/7/1878, reports that Fearing's is probably the first in town. See also 7/4/1878 (Rose Standish), 6/20/1879 (Cushing House), 7/1/1881, 6/2/1882, 3/2, 6/22/1883. Litchfield's complaint, *HJ*, 9/23/1892. For all the "strikers," see *HJ*, 11/15/1889.

Pages 211-13: On fire-fighting, see *History* (1893), I.ii.257-60, updated in *HJ*, 10/13/1922, and Pitcher (1946), supplemented by ATBs and Robinson (1980). On fires, Fearing Burr's Notebooks, Hist Coll HPL, Reel 76:19; *HJ*, 4/10/1885, 1/1/1886, 4/12/1889; the new "steamer," *HJ*, 2/15/1895; Cushing House precautions, *HJ*, 9/23/1892; Whittemore fire, *HJ*, 1/1/1897; barn of Barnes, *et al.*, *HJ*, 8/22/1890.

CHAPTER SIXTEEN: *The Wider World Touches the Island Community*

Page 214: Miles, "finer issues," *HJ*, 2/5/1885.

Pages 215-16: Dying off of buttonwoods, JPR, based on *HJ*, 4/3/1847 and 5/11/1855. Bela Tower, the Gay elms, and Stoddard's maples, *HJ*, 1/12 and 11/28/1883, 9/12/1890. On forming the Tree Club, *HJ*, 8/6 and 8/27/1880; papers of the club in Hist Coll HPL, Reel 76:11; and Reardon (1987). On plantings and the nursery, *HJ*, 10/1, 10/15, and 12/3/1880, 4/15, 4/22, and 5/6/1881, 10/28/1882, 12/14/1883, 11/21/1884.

Page 216: On rubber hoses, Panati (1987), 164-66. The lawnmower (1830) was developed by a foreman at an English textile plant, Edwin Budding, who realized that the rotary cutting blades used to shear the nap from fabrics could be applied to cutting grass when it was dry. Previous to this time, grass was cut with a scythe. The grass had to be damp "to give it body against the 'blow' from a scythe." Panati (1987), 162.

Page 217: Factory paints, Panati (1987), 151. On the "spectator," Sennett (1977), 195 and 205ff. Four Hingham photographers, JPR based on his collections and on collections of HHS and HPL. Forming of the Camera Club, *HJ*, 11/2/1888.

Page 218: Greek evening, *HJ*, 3/15/1889. Choral Society and "Creation," *HJ*, 11/2, 11/25, and 12/4/1885, 4/4/1888. Philharmonic, *HJ*, 2/3/1882. Morris Whiton, *HJ*, 11/17/1882. The "Clarion," *HJ*, 10/21 and 12/19/1884. Musical Association, *HJ*, 11/23/1888, 1/18/1889. Cushing's barges, Cohasset, Clapp Hall, *HJ*, 1/16 and 4/10/1885. "Music preaches better," *HJ*, 4/20/1888.

Page 219: Henry Miles, *HJ*, 6/5 and 8/21/1885. On Wilder Hall, "Hingham's finest" and "an ornament," Lehner and Fannin (1989), 821, 825. Second Library, *History* (1893), I.ii.153-54; *HJ*, 1/2, 1/16, and 1/23/1880 (the architect defended), and 1/30/1880. G.A.R. Hall, *HJ*, 1/1, 7/1, 9/2, and 10/21/1887, 1/6 and 5/25/1888. On St. John's, Gallop (1983), 7-10, and *HJ*, 3/12/1881, 5/5 and 12/22/1882, 2/9 and 6/8/1883, 7/18, 8/29, and 12/12/1884. The interior is described in Hurd (1884). The mission was organized at a meeting convened by William O. Lincoln, Jr., a parish founder and long-time treasurer.

Page 220: Coolidge, "The people of Hingham," *HJ*, 11/9/1888. On the stained glass of Baptists and Congregationalists (1886), *History* (1893), I.ii.60, 68. Marriage of Long's daughter, *HJ*, 9/14/1883. Gifts from England, *HJ*, 5/4/1883. On the Cemetery Chapel, *HJ*, 2/3/1882, 4/20/1883, and 10/28/1887, which reports the dedication ceremony and the chapel's history. GL in *History* (1893), I.ii.369, dates the erection in 1886, the year of the wooden numerals on the building. Since the dedication did not occur till a year later, we infer that completion was delayed. See also HHS House Tour Program, 1988. Collier, *HJ*, 2/17/1887, 12/31/1886, 12/2/1887. Simpson funeral, *HJ*, 12/17/1886.

Page 221: For "ripe tomatoes," *etc.*, see the children's descriptions of the old fairs, Chap. Seventeen below. Tuttleville at Wilder, *HJ*, 10/8/1886. The black veterans' reunion, *HJ*, 8/5/1887. Gardner St. Chapel, *HJ*, 11/14/1890, 5/15 and 5/22/1891, 1/27/1893; *Patriot Ledger*, 5/4/1967.

Pages 222-23: E. Andrew, *HJ*, 2/19/1897; M. Long, *HJ*, 6/4/1898. Floral Sunday, *HJ*, 6/25/1885. Children's missions, *HJ*, 11/2/1888, 6/22/1883, 7/22 and 11/11/1887.

Page 223: On Nursey Souther, *HJ*, 8/26/1887, repr. from the *Springfield Union*. A century later, the eighty-three-year-old daughter of Winthrop Lincoln, Lucy Bates, remembered her maternal grandmother as we talked to her on the House Tour at the Methodist Church (1991). Sara Tower ("Nursey") Souther "was a lovely woman. She was BIG." Country Week, *HJ*, 4/22/1887. St. Paul's confirmation, *HJ*, 4/27/1888. Henry Miles, *HJ*, 4/27, 6/5, and 8/24/1885.

Pages 224-25: On croquet, Pick (1952), 46; *HJ*, 10/14/1881 and 6/21/1895. "Future Mike Kellys," *HJ*, 5/20/1887. Problems of local baseball, *HJ*, 8/24/1888. On the Music Hall, *HJ*, 6/21/1889. On Kelly, Macmillan, *HJ*, 3/2/1989. Kelly appears often in *HJ*, 1890-92. For the gifts of house, *etc.*, *HJ*, 8/15/1890, 5/15/1891. The house is chronicled in JLN. Kelly's "last slide," Okrent and Wulf (1989), 17. G. Edmands, *HJ*, 3/16/1888, 7/17 and 12/24/1891, 8/3/1894.

Page 226: "Island Communities," Dumenil (1984), 89; Wiebe (1967), 44. "Secure the shadow," *Directory* (1894), 12.

CHAPTER SEVENTEEN: *The Old, the Young, and the End of An Epoch*

Pages 227-28: For the Centennial Fourth of July, *HJ*, 7/14/1876; GL Diaries for 7/4/1876 identify him as author. Proceedings and speeches of the 1881 event are in *Commemorative Services* (1881). Lincoln (1835)—see Bibliography.

Page 229: Proceedings and speeches of the 250th Anniversary are in *Celebration* (1885). GL's stories, *HJ*, 2/13/1880, 5/30/1884, and 2/6 and 9/25/1885. On the elderly, *HJ*, 6/10/1887, 3/24/1888, and 12/24/1891. The safe at GL's store, *HJ*, 12/12/1884.

Page 230: "Ancient Landmarks," *History* (1893), I.i.157-200. It deserves reprinting as a separate pamphlet.

Page 231: Long, "that sturdy, educating," *History* (1893), I.ii.208. F. Lincoln in *History* (1893), I.ii.31. Eighty years and upward: in sequential entries, *HJ*, 6/12 through 11/6/1896, GL lists them all alphabetically. On the collection of artifacts, *HJ*, 10/29 through 12/24/1897, JPR. Recovery of GL MSS., JPR.

Pages 232-33: Changes in the schools, reports of the School Committee and the Supt., ATBs. Nash, Supt. Report, ATB 1889. Growth of the electrics nationwide, Burns (1986), 250-51, and Andrist (1972), 75. Miles, "Perhaps the only remedy," *HJ*, 2/5/1885. On the coming of the electrics to Hingham, *HJ*, 8/17/1889, 11/16, 11/25, and 12/28/1894, 1/7 and 5/24/1895. See *HJ*, 1/17/1896, for planned routes: (1) Broad Bridge to Queen Ann's Corner, *via* Main, to connect with Norwell-Hanover line; (2) *via* Fort Hill Street to East Weymouth; (3) *via* Lincoln Street to connect with the Quincy-Boston line; (4) spur track up Downer to the Landing; (5) branch *via* Summer and Rockland to "the Beach."

Page 234: On construction, *HJ*, 2/27/1896, and weekly reports through 5/22. Opening celebrations, *HJ*, 6/12 and 7/3/1896. Ground had been first broken for tracks on March 27, and the engineers' trial run took place May 28. For technical specifications of buildings, machinery, and cars, *HJ*, 6/5/1896.

Page 235: For the count of passengers, *HJ*, 12/4/1896. For the mock town meeting of 1900, *HJ*, 3/30/1900.

Pages 236-37: "How eagerly, when farming," Preface to *Trans. Ag. and Hort.*, 1893. "The rich man is there," *HJ*, 11/2/1894. Essays by Griffin, Gibbons, and Kimball, *Trans. Ag. and Hort.*, 1895. "how to improve," *Trans.*, 1896.

Pages 237-39: On Melville Garden's last years, see especially *HJ*, 8/7/1891, 6/3, 6/17, and 8/15/1892. For the naughty cadets, *etc.*, *HJ*, 7/20/1888 and *Patriot Ledger*, 9/2/1961. "Pleasure Seeker and Weary Worker," *HJ*, 8/1/1884. Singing black waiters, *Patriot Ledger*, 8/31/1961. Architect Francis F. Brewer from Maine should not be confused with Francis Brewer, son of John and tree enthusiast. Obit. of Scudder, *HJ*, 5/15/1896. On Edmands and his tenants, *HJ*, 6/21/1895 and 4/2/1898. Crow Point Improvement Association, *HJ*, 9/17/1897.

Page 239: On Boston annexation and the "metropolitan" movement, Merino (1968) and Warner (1978). "The grid plan," Warner (1978), 158-59.

Pages 240-41: State politics, Richard Brown (1978) and Tager and Ifkovic (1985). Election results from ATBs. Wilder interview. On Buttimer, *HJ*, 10/18/1895. Showdown 1896" in national politics, Burns (1986), 223-32.

CHAPTER EIGHTEEN: *Memories of Childhood and Youth*

The account of the child's walk home is an imagined composite, with events ranging over a generation (1898 to the early 1920s). The chronicle of a typical year is woven from sources too numerous for complete documentation. Unless otherwise indicated, they are interviews, written reminiscences, and *HJ*. Memoirists are identified in the text; for a complete list, see Bibliography.

Page 246: Brewer (1985), I, 80.

Page 248: The blacksmith shop and the mill, Coatsworth (1948), 62, 63.

Page 249: On the Italians, Horton (1945), 27. "wheel out of the firehouse," Horton (1945), 22.

Page 250: Fair of 1900, *HJ*, 9/28/1900. "Break her down, boys," Shilhan (1976), 133. Storm of 1898, *HJ*, 12/2/1898.

Page 251: Punging (in addition to Clark), Shilhan (1976), 99. Sledding, *HJ*, 3/9/1917. Skating at Cushing's Pond, Shilhan, 136.

Page 252: "The atmosphere," JPR interview with Bertha Stringer. "We would sit," Ruth Marsh interview. "Quite a spirited scene," *HJ*, 12/17/1910. Ice-harvesting, Sharp (1916), 30, 36; Shilhan (1976), 136. "As soon as grandfather," Shilhan (1976), 71.

Pages 253-54: Notes of E. Fearing talk with JPR. Foley's visit to Mullein Hill, *HJ*, 1/5/1950. Information on West's Corner, reminiscences of Kathleen Reichardt. Horton on Mullein Hill, *HJ*, 7/28/1955.

Page 255: Smelt catches, *HJ*, 9/21 and 9/28/1917. "bathhouses," Horton (1945), 26.

Pages 256-57: Forget-me-nots, Hall (1985), 7. Boys on running boards, *HJ*, 7/3/1914. Eddie Long's trade continued into World War II; Herbert Hirsch was a supplier at age eleven or twelve. Cadets (in addition to Clark): Hall (1985), 9; Shilhan (1976), 24; Horton (1945), 5. Yacht Club regatta and Open Race Day, *HJ*, 8/7/1914, 8/17/1910. "only ten more days," *HJ*, 8/25/1911.

CHAPTER NINETEEN: *Years of Improvement*

Page 258: On the Progressive era, Hofstadter (1963), 2-9; Brogan (1986), 479-80; Burns (1986), 245-46. Village Improvement Society formed, *HJ*, 5/27/1910.

Page 259: Fourth of July, *HJ*, 6/24/1910. Lane journal excerpt from MS. in archives of JPR. *HJ*, 2/2/1912: "The child is the special ward of the civic improvement effort." Incident of the boys at the Common, *HJ*, 6/17/1910. Forming of the Boy Scouts (meeting at Loring Hall, Oct. 21, 1910), HJ, 10/22/1910, 2/17/1911.

Page 260: "wave of improvement," *HJ*, 2/2/1912. The sick cow, *HJ*, 7/19/1912. The dead birds, *HJ*, 6/1/1909. Rachel Carson was launched on her study of pesticides in 1957 by a report from a friend in Duxbury of dead robins on her lawn. (Warner [1984] 248-58.) Statistics from ATBs and U.S. and Mass. Census reports.

Page 261: Report of the 1912 town meeting, *HJ*, 3/8/1912. The ATB issued just prior to this meeting, at *272 pages*, was "the largest ever issued" to date. Conditions and changes in schools, from School Comm. reports in ATBs, 1898-1912. Whiton offer, *HJ*, 12/15/1899. Lincoln School, reports of town meetings of 1911-12 in ATBs and *HJ*, 3/24/1911 and 3/15/1912.

Page 262: "When fields situated," School Comm. report in ATB, 1909. "why the expenses of the town," *HJ*, 3/3/1916. Memories of A. Humphrey from interview with Oscar Beck, Jr. Mail delivery, *HJ*, 3/9/1917, 2/8/1918. Daylight Savings, *HJ*, 4/5/1918. Summer listings from Directories of 1885, 1894, 1908, 1912, 1920.

Page 263: Newhall obit., *HJ*, 6/14/1912. "Modern Hingham estate," *HJ*, 6/20/1913. For the real estate boom of ensuing years, see Chapter Twenty-Two below. On new styles, Kaplan (1987), 337-38, 358. "This lovely scene," *Hingham* (1911), 51-54.

Page 264: Sharp, "I have no quarrel," *ibid.*, 69. On Boston, Merino (1968), 13, 70, 78, 111; Handlin (1979), Thernstrom (1973), and Warner (1978). Filene Commission and reactions, Merino (1968), 10, 84. The "fearsome plan," *HJ*, 1/7/1916. Boston politics, Merino, 36-37, 43; Huthmacher (1973), 14-15. Election results, ATBs.

Page 265: "The ballots were carefully counted," *HJ*, 11/14/1902. Town elections and officials, ATBs.

Page 266: Long's funeral, *HJ*, 9/3/1915.
Page 267: James's chase, *HJ*, 9/8/1915. Accidents: *HJ*, 4/21, 7/28, and 12/22/1899, 4/18/1901, 7/28/1905, 4/29, 5/20, 7/29, and 8/5/1910. Advertisement for the horse, *HJ*, 5/3/1904. Early autos, Brewer (1985), I, 48, 79-80; Rich, *HJ*, 6/27/1902; Lane, *HJ*, 8/14/1903 and 1/10/1905.
Page 268: Kemp's account book entries, copy from MS. in archives of JPR. Horns and regulations, *HJ*, 4/1, 4/22, 5/6, and 7/15/1910. Whelan's saga, *HJ*, 3/18 and 7/1/1910; 3/29, 10/18, and 11/22/1912; 11/27/1914. "The most dangerous spot," *HJ*, 11/7/1913.
Page 269: Traffic, *HJ*, 6/5/1913, 7/17/1914, 9/17/1915, and 6/9/1916. The "boulevard" (Route 3A), *HJ*, 5/14/1915, 7/5 and 7/27/1917. On the "mania" of organizations, Kropotkin (1955), 279, Bryce quoted in Schlesinger (1949), 40; the Beards quoted in Dumenil (1984), xi.
Pages 270-72: Susan B. Willard, GL Gen. and obit. in *HJ*, 10/30/1925; interview with R. Marsh. Arts and Crafts Society: Willard in *HJ*, 8/21/1901, and *Hingham* (D.A.R., 1911), 121-23; Lane in *Craftsman* (1903), 277-78; Riley in *House Beautiful* (1905), 31-33; Kaplan (1987), 176-77; Clark (1972). Clark's Chronology is the basis for the claim that Hingham's society was the third in the state. Nationally, it came sixth, following Minneapolis, Deerfield, Boston, Chicago, and New York. Exhibit and *Sun* review, *HJ*, 8/21 and 8/28/1903. The Society sign, *HJ*, 12/4/1904. Visit to Roseneath Cottage, Coatsworth (1948), 116-17.
Page 273: "The public school," *HJ*, 5/5/1899. Sloyd, Supt. Howard's reports, ATBs, 1904, 1906. St. John's gift, ATB, 1907. Memories of Whidden, conversations with Ann Tolman and Herbert Hirsch. After retiring in the late 1940s, she went to live near her sister, Mrs. Nellie Preston, in Woburn. Many efforts to find a photo of her have been unavailing.
Pages 274-75: Cookbook, *HJ*, 7/19/1901. Willard as regent, *HJ*, 4/14/1905. Bell Tower, *HJ*, 11/29 and 12/30/1912. Historical Society, *HJ*, 8/1/1912 and 6/12/1914.

CHAPTER TWENTY: *Years of War*

Brief accounts of national and international events are based on Burns (1986), Ellis (1975), Friedel (1964), Hayes (1972), and *History of the Yankee Division* (1955).

Page 276: The march through Hingham, *HJ*, 5/22/1914. War headlines and the flight of Americans, *HJ*, 8/7/1914.
Page 277: John D. Long's plea, *HJ*, 8/21/1914. Orders from Europe, *HJ*, 11/6/1914 and 1/8/1915. Mexican border battles, Burns (1986), 403-06. Camp Cotton and watermelon feasts, photo album of George Melcher in Hist Coll HPL.
Page 278: Hingham town meeting, *HJ*, 3/16/1917. Public Safety Committee, *HJ*, 4/1/1917. "Come to the Armory," *HJ*, 3/23/1917. "The country is at war," *HJ*, 4/6/1917. Rebellion in Ireland reported in *HJ*, 7/3 and 7/17/1914. Reluctance to volunteer, *HJ*, 3/23 and 3/30/1917 and weekly through April and early May. The rally and the Aerie of Eagles, *HJ*, 4/19/1917.
Page 279: The curate of St. Paul's, *HJ*, 6/1/1917. Draft stories, *HJ*, 8/10 and 12/14/1917. Departure of Company K, *HJ*, 8/17 and 8/24/1917. Letters home began to appear in *HJ*, 9/28/1917. Letters quoted appeared in *HJ*, 10/19 and 10/26/1917, and 1/11/1918.
Pages 280-81: The Dill letter, *HJ*, 2/15/1918; the Tower letter, 2/22/1918. Ammunition Depot site selection, *HJ*, 3/25/1904. Growth of the Depot, *HJ*, 2/2 through 3/2/1917 and 5/4/1917. The swimming children, from a letter to the authors from Mrs. Richard Riddle, 1/18/1988. Crowding of workers, *HJ*, 8/2/1917. "Hingham's Klondike," *HJ*, 10/12/1917. Camp Hingham, *HJ*, 8/10 and 9/14/1917. YWCA speaker, *HJ*, 11/9/1917. Home Front shortages, Robinson (1980), 181-83, and *HJ*, April-June, 1917 *passim* and 9/2/1917. For Mrs. Emmons, Horton (1949), 29.
Pages 282-83: For Hingham residents in the war, see ATB, 1919. Reports of casualties, *HJ*, 12/14/1917, and 2/22, 3/29, 5/17, 6/28, 10/4, 11/29, and 12/20/1918, and 1/10 and 2/27/1919. An addition after these reports: Lt. Bradford Jones, a Hingham native, was living in Hyde Park when he enlisted. He was killed at Chateau-Thierry on 6/18/1918, and was buried in Hingham Centre Cemetery on 5/13/1921. For the Knowles letter, *HJ*, 12/20/1918. Other letters appeared 3/22 and 4/19/1918.
Page 284: Borland's account appeared *HJ*, 7/5/1918; Emma Stringer's, *HJ*, 4/19 and 8/23/1918; her work at St. Didier, *HJ*, 2/15/1935.

Page 285: Excerpts from Sibley, *HJ*, 8/16/1918. Cresswell's letter is dated 8/15/1918. Cresswell's decoration, *HJ*, 1/2/1923.
Page 286: Collins' account of Borland, *HJ*, 11/29/1918. False armistice report, 11/14/1918. Homecomings, *HJ*, 4/10 and 4/17/1919.

CHAPTER TWENTY-ONE: *Years of Anxiety*

Page 287: Reports of the police strike, *HJ*, 9/19/1919 through late December. See *HJ*, 11/21/1919: "almost everybody one meets these days has a story to unload about unrest in this country." For Brockton pay-cuts, *etc.*, *HJ*, 3/24/1922. Rhodes Ripley, *HJ*, 3/4/1921.
Page 288: The telephone strike was in June, 1923. On local hard times, lay-offs, pay-cuts, prices, *HJ*, 7/11 and 11/21/1919, 1/21, 6/10, 7/28, and 8/26/1921, 1/2/1922, and 10/26/1923. Count of autos, ATB 1924. On early radio: Pratt had his set prior to 1917, but could not operate during the war. The West Hingham fan, *HJ*, 4/14/1922. "Don't place the tickler," *HJ*, 6/23/1922.
Page 289: Advertising "has made," *HJ*, 4/10/1925. "Entering this election," *HJ*, 2/17/1922. On Nativism, see Higham (1955), espec. Chap. Seven. On the Friends of Irish Freedom, *HJ*, 7/25, 8/23, and 11/28/1919; 5/5 and 12/17/1920, and 1/17/1921. Last entries appear in April, 1922.
Pages 290-91: Local election results from ATBs 1914-28. On Walsh, Smith, and Mass. politics, Huthmacher (1973), Chaps. Five and Six. "Hollanders who came," Coatsworth (1948), 171; Directories; JLN for farm locations; Robinson (1980), 189.
Pages 291-92: "I have only a very vague," Coatsworth (1948), 172. On the Finns, interviews with Margaret McSweeney, Harold Newcombe, John McKee, and Warren Lincoln. Names and occupations from Directories of 1920 and 1928. Sharp, "This town's attitude," *HJ*, 10/31/1919.
Pages 292-94: Early Italian work gangs, *HJ*, 1/8/1895, 6/10/1894. "son of sunny Italy," *HJ*, 3/9/1917. Italian arrivals inferred from Directories and Census Reports. A further indicator: in the spring of 1914, Mrs. Starkes Whiton sold sixteen acres of land between Kilby and Weir Streets off Rockland to an unnamed man from Hull, who would "open up the tract for house lots" (*HJ*, 5/1/1914). Italian work life from numerous *HJ*s, interviews (A. Calvi, M. Calvi, P. Rando), Directory of 1920. General context, Lopreato (1970), 110-20; Gans (1962), 113, 201; Novak (1973), 106-07. P. Rando interview. "The indignant Irish," Lopreato (1970), 120. A. Calvi interview.
Page 295: Interviews, R. Marsh, Mrs. O. Beck, M. Calvi, A. Calvi. Coatsworth (1948), 172. Raymond Barba, from Directory of 1928. "The Italian still bore," Higham (1955), 160.
Page 296: Published versions of the two tragedies appeared in *HJ*, 1/21/1921, 6/3/1927, 5/18/1928, 9/4/1925, and 5/12 and 5/19/1933.
Pages 297-98: "We are living," *HJ*, 7/24/1914. Sacco in Hingham, *HJ*, 8/26/1927. Americanization "does not mean," *HJ*, 8/8/1919. "Not a large number," *HJ*, 4/25/1919. See also *HJ*, 8/15 and 10/31/1919, 1/2/1920. On the KKK in Mass., Huthmacher (1973), Chap. Four. "Hingham was all agog," *HJ*, 9/19/1924.
Page 299: Fiery crosses reported in *HJ*, 7/11/1924, 2/13/1925, 6/5/1925, and 6/24/1927. A sign of rising crime (*HJ*, 10/9/1925): "lock your doors and look well to the fastenings. All around us they are experiencing a series of breaks." Votes to stay "dry" from town meeting reports, ATBs 1896-1918. The "Vet shindig," *HJ*, 1/14/1916. "Oh listen," *HJ*, 3/28/1919.
Page 300: Prohibition stories, *HJ*, 10/3/1919, 1/16 and 6/17/1920, 4/1/1921, and 8/8/1924. The "local police station," *HJ*, 8/8/1924. The big raid, *HJ*, 12/14/1923. Mrs. Emmons' advertisement, 10/24/1924.
Page 301: "Had to confess failure," Burns (1986), 443. The "plucky little woman," *HJ*, 9/11/1914. A "clumsy, unwilling electorate," *HJ*, 4/2/1915. "So I'll stay and change," *HJ*, 8/23/1920.
Pages 302-03: Women's votes and women elected, ATBs 1919-26, and *HJ*, 9/3 and 10/29/1920. The high spirits and pink pajamas, *HJ*, 11/5/1920. The term "angels in the house," from the title of a book of poetry (1854) by the English poet Coventry Patmore. Women in the workforce, from Directory (1908).
Page 303: Interview by J. Wheaton with Mrs. Hattie Shute Wilder, 1969. This interview, on tape in Hist Coll HPL, is, in our opinion, the gem of Hingham oral history to date. Since it must be *heard* to be fully appreciated, we have tried in this transcription to suggest phonetically how it sounds.
Page 304: Interviews with Louise Cobleigh and Anna Calvi. The description of Kitty Hennessy, interview with Mrs. Evelyn Cheney. On the Pratt sisters, Coatsworth (1948), 76-77.

Description of Suzie Gates, Shilhan (1976), 64. On women's occupations, see Directory of 1928; Mass. Census of 1925.

Page 305: "Like little black knots," Gunn (1934), 321. On seeing Miss Cazneau, the Centenary booklet of the Hingham Methodist Church (1928), Hist Coll HPL, Reel 76:10. Pythian benefit, *HJ*, 8/18/1922.

Page 306: The account of Isabel Hyams is from Amy Howard, "Isabel Hyams and the Orchard House," *MIT Record*, 1958. (For a copy of this, we are indebted to Eugene and Helen Chamberlain.) The *JLN* identify Orchard House as #36 Pleasant Street, built in 1809 by Thomas and John Fearing. On the District Nurse, see a history of the Public Health Nurse in *HJ*, 3/18/1921. Reports of the hospital movement, *HJ*, 1/26 and 5/4/1923, and 7/25 and 8/8/1924.

Page 307: See *HJ*, 3/27/1925, for a history of the Andrew House. Girl Scouts, *HJ*, 3/9-3/23/1917; 5/27/1927; 5/29, 7/6, 8/31, and 9/28/1928. Hyams' donation, reported by Helen Chamberlain in conversation (1991). Women's Club, *HJ*, 2/24/1922.

CHAPTER TWENTY-TWO: *Boom and Identity Crisis*

Pages 309-10: "It is very obvious," *HJ*, 4/12/1912. For new housing development, see a long summary, *HJ*, 2/17/1922. The Crehan letter, *HJ*, 1/19/1923.

Pages 310-11: Continuity and growth in commerce, from commercial listings, announcements, and advertisements, *HJ*, 1919-28. See advertisements of new chain stores in *HJ*, 6/25/1920, 10/21/1921, 1/13/1922 (A&P opening), 6/23/1922, and 9/7/1923.

Pages 311-12: "Hingham - what is it?" *HJ*, 7/27/1923. On the demise of the electrics, see reports of regular and special town meetings, 2/20 and 3/26/1920; 3/11/1921; meetings, 1921-23, and special town meeting, July, 1923, in ATBs 1920-23. A political advertisement prior to the meeting of 1924 asks, "Why prolong their agony? Their time is up, let them retire." On "jitneys" (motor busses), *HJ*, 8/8/1924. On taking up North Street tracks, *HJ*, 10/25/1924. "Little by little," *HJ*, 7/15/1927. Last car on the Queen Ann-East Weymouth line, Sat. night, 9/11/1926 (*HJ*, 9/9/1926). On the town forest, see Howard (1956). On the new high school, see annual reports of the School Committee and reports of town meetings in ATBs: 1922, 1923 (postponed), 1925, 1926 (report accepted), special town meeting, June, 1926 (approved 312 to 91), town meeting, 1927 (additional funds); and a history of the high school, *HJ*, 9/14/1928.

Page 313: On the waterfront park, *HJ*, 10/16/1925. "The one time of year," *HJ*, 3/4/1927. Intersection of South and Main, special town meeting, *HJ*, 6/15/1928. Bathing beach, special town meeting, *HJ*, 12/7/1928. Water Company, *HJ*, 12/14/1928. Talks on planning and the forming of the joint committee, *HJ*, 2/23 and 3/2/1923, and 1/25/1924. On planning and zoning, ATBs 1922-26.

Page 314: On the Country Club: *HJ*, 1/13/1922, reports the option to buy the "Litchfield property" of about 140 acres; in May, 1922, construction of the first nine holes was underway; the course opened on Memorial Day, 1923; a fourteen-room clubhouse was finished during the winter of 1924; the second nine holes opened in 1925. See *HJ*, 3/10/1922, 1/19 and 6/1/1923, 2/8/1924, and 5/29/1925. Early history of the Yacht Club from *Hingham Yacht Club 50th Anniversary Yearbook 1895-1945*. The six founders were George A. Cole, George E. Hills, Charles Jefferies, Reginald L. Robbins, Roger L. Scaife, and Frederic A. Turner. See also Scrapbook of H.Y.C. Memorabilia 1898-1908, Hist Coll HPL, Reel 79:4. Founding of the Garden Club, from "Garden Club of Hingham 1924-1974" (unpub. typescript) by Katharine H. Davis, continued by Betty Watkins, a copy of which was provided to us by Mrs. Virginia Pearce.

Pages 315-16: "In the little one-room building," *HJ*, 7/6/1928. Second Parish membership lists, Robinson (1980), 197-99. On the Leavitts, GL Gen. and JLN.

Pages 316-17: Changes in identity, annual street lists, *HJ*, 1/12 and 9/21/1923, 7/18/1924, 8/7/1925, and ATBs 1921-28. Interview with S. Eldredge. Interview with H. Wilder. We have selected and arranged these excerpts from the Wilder interview, added italics for emphasis, and interposed a few phonetic approximations.

CHAPTER TWENTY-THREE: *"A Tough, Tough Time"*

Chief sources for national history in this chapter are Brogan (1986), Burns (1986 and 1990), and Phillips (1969).

Page 321: Number of shares computed from Brogan (1986), 526.

Page 322: "Nine million savings accounts" from Burns (1986), 524. Hingham business revenues, *HJ*, 9/25/1931 and 12/18/1936, citing U.S. Dept. of Commerce figures. Workers at Greenfield's, *HJ*, 1/23/1931, and A. Calvi interview. Policeman's job, O. Beck interview. O. O. Smith's job, ATB 1931. Janitor's job, *HJ*, 8/21/1936. Letter carrier positions, *HJ*, 2/14/1936. School teachers and undernourished children, ATB 1933. Milk consumption, ATB 1934. The quarter for electricity, S. Eldredge interview. "Heart-breaking," "brass bed," M. McSweeney interview.

Page 323: Brokers' wives, J. McKee interview. Thayer vegetables, H. Newcombe interview. The "potato patch," *HJ*, 6/17/1932. Firewood from the *Nancy*, *HJ*, 11/11/1932. Making soap, *HJ*, 12/23/1932. Survival strategy, McSweeney interview. Infirmary and outside aid and impoverished elderly, ATBs 1929-36. "Temporaries," ATB 1934. Grange, *HJ*, 5/8/1931. Sons of Italy, *HJ*, 12/14/1934.

Page 324: Second-hand shoes, *HJ*, 11/18/1932. Bags of flour and First National groceries, *HJ*, 11/18/1932. Loaves of bread, *HJ*, 1/1/1932. "Sensational silence," A. Calvi and S. Eldredge interviews. Emmons resignation, *HJ*, 1/29/1932. Horton's visit, Horton (1949), [29]. "Invaluable help," *HJ*, 3/3/1933, 2/2/1934. Cloth-ing for needy, *HJ*, 1/29/1932. Red Cross workers, *HJ*, 2/23/1934.

Page 325: Mabel Dwiggins, *HJ*, 6/9/1933. Uncollected taxes, *HJ*, 1/29/1932. Estimates of farms and acreage from two land study maps done by the firm of Lewis Perkins (copies in HPL): Roads and Buildings, and Land Utilization, Aug., 1936, WPA Project No. 65-14-1161. On local farmers' sentiments, see for example, *HJ*, 5/8 and 9/4/1931, 5/27 and 6/24/1932, 8/4 and 9/29/1933, 7/6/1934, 6/7 and 9/20/1935. On local prices, *HJ*, 6/3 and 9/9/1932. Tom Howe, *HJ*, 1/22/1932. The anonymous townsman, *HJ*, 9/30/1932. On the laborers, ATB 1932. The state census of Hingham unemployed is reported in *HJ*, 5/11/1934.

Page 326: The national average is estimated in Brogan (1986), 556, and Burns (1990), 18-19, 30. The Hingham presidential vote, ATB 1932. Week's wait for pay, *HJ*, 3/17/1933. The banker's explanation, *HJ*, 9/30/1932. Count of radios, *HJ*, 1/12/1934.

Page 327: Killing hopes for federal money, *HJ*, 9/13/1935. CCC men, *HJ*, 6/2 and 9/8/1933. The $15,000 and $70,311, *HJ*, 11/24/1933 and ATB 1934. Home delivery, J. McKee interview. Land survey, *HJ*, 3/6/1936. Loans for house repairs, *HJ*, 9/7/1934. One-third of houses, *HJ*, 12/13/1935. Bonus Bonds, *HJ*, 6/19/1936.

Page 328: "Half a million boots," from the depression song, "Brother, Can you Spare A Dime?" Recommended Water Company purchase, ATB 1936. "Not to proceed further," ATB 1938. Taking Whitney property, ATB 1931. Whitney's opinion, *HJ*, 4/3 and 4/17/1931. Hersey's opinion, *HJ*, 4/10/1931. Rescinding the vote, ATB 1931. Whitney obit. and bequest, *HJ*, 12/17/1937 and 1/14/1938. The statue was dedicated in 1939. Mock town meeting, *HJ*, 1/22/1932. The Bradley offer, *HJ*, 2/28/1936 and ATB 1935. The new station, ATB 1937 and *HJ*, 4/23/1937. Hingham's school ranking and number of students, ATBs 1932, 1934.

Page 329: Proposal defeated, ATB 1935. Raising the entry age, ATB 1938. Vocational training, ATB 1936.

Page 330: Tolman as paid officer, efficient and devoted, and the value of his salary, ATB 1933. Scarlet fever and the single source, ATB 1933. Diphtheria cases from Reports of Communicable Diseases ATBs 1929-36. Pulmonary TB, ATB 1935. Local dairymen's assoc., *HJ*, 12/29/1933. Slaughter of cows, ATB 1933. Mandated water metering, *HJ*, 8/31/1934.

Page 331: "non-existent" sewer, ATB 1934. Crow Point sewers too complex, ATB 1934. "Ideal combination," ATB 1936. Committee on Town Brook and Mill Pond, and Buttimer's opinion, ATB 1933. Selectmen's opinion, ATB 1933. Tolman and every abutter, ATB 1934. "Indefinitely postpone," ATB 1934. Bouvé's view, *HJ*, 3/9/1934. Weir River project, ATB 1935.

Pages 332-33: "Our 'best families,'" ATB 1934. Tossing garbage, ATB 1935. New committee and garbage collection, ATBs 1937 and 1938. "Due to lack of co-operation," ATB 1936; see also *HJ*, 6/12, 6/19, and 6/26/1936. Good roads, *etc.*, not enough, ATB 1935. "A pole cat," ATB 1931. The "fetish" and "unwisely proud," ATB 1935.

Page 333: Fifty percent of Melcher's salary, *HJ*, 2/19/1932. "Water wings," *HJ*, 3/11/1932. His "own badge," through "plenty of gold braid," ATB 1929. After this year, the selectmen, citing a need to economize, declined to publish reports from the "Navy Department," and Melcher published them in *HJ*. Saving George Cole, *HJ*, 2/19/1932. Ideas for employment, *HJ*, 1/29/1932. (Cities Service was in East Braintree.)

Page 334: A "few skins" and Tolman reply, *HJ*, 3/3/1933. Seth Stowers in *History* (1893), I.i.261.

Page 335: Meetinghouse restoration, *HJ*, 10/4/1929-10/10/1930. "Faithful copies," Stark (1951), 20. The bass viol, *HJ*, 1/8/1932. Unsuccessful reunion, *HJ*, 11/8/1935 and 4/17/1936. New North organ, *HJ*, 11/24/1933. Congregational Church, *HJ*, 9/4/1931. Old Ordinary, *HJ*, 12/7/1934. Harding-Whidden house, *HJ*, 10/30/1931 and 6/24/1932. "Ancestors' Sunday," *HJ*, 6/30/1933. Leavitt reunion, *HJ*, 6/22/1934. Leavitts and Towers, *HJ*, 7/12/1935. Whitons, *HJ*, 8/16/1935.

Page 336: Baseball game, *HJ*, 9/11/1934. Street fair, *HJ*, 6/28/1929. Revolutionary War graves and Foss celebration, *HJ*, 2/17 and 2/24/1933, and 1/30/1931. Foss died in Sept., 1937. Pageant appropriation, ATB 1934. Committee, *HJ*, 5/13/1932. Huet's Cove, dates, and director, *HJ*, 4/27 and 5/18/1934. Researches, ATB 1934. Coordinator, *HJ*, 1/19/1934. Poster, Gas Company, and banners, *HJ*, 6/7/1935. The float, *HJ*, 6/21/1935. Chamber of Commerce booth, *HJ*, 5/31 and 6/7/1935. Costume stitching, ATB 1935.

Pages 337-38: Shattuck's chorus, ATB 1935, and *HJ*, 4/26, 5/24, and 12/6/1935. Wire, cues, and call for horses, *HJ*, 6/14, 6/21, and 7/5/1935. For an official report of the Tercentenary, see ATB 1935. For the program and excerpted newspaper items, *etc.*, see Hist Coll HPL, Reel 76:14. Harpo Marx, E. Cheney interview. George Silipo, Jr., *HJ*, 7/5/1935. The "valuable lesson," ATB 1935. Magruder, *HJ*, 7/5/1935.

Pages 338-39: Foley (1935), 39, 24, and *passim*. On Dwiggins, Abbe (1970, 1979, 1988), Bennett (1960), and Dwiggins (1937, 1974).

Pages 339-40: List of proposals fulfilled as itemized in a memorandum from JPR. Unanimous vote to acquire Triphammer Pond, ATB 1945. The town got a ninety-nine-year lease from the Water Company and appropriated $1,350 to buy forty-seven acres surrounding the pond. In 1948, the town bought ten more acres and accepted the Ripley and McSweeney properties. In 1960, fifteen acres off Pope's Lane were also added.

Page 340: Dwiggins' pet show entries, *HJ*, 7/14/1933. On the town forest, see Chap. Twenty-Two above and Howard (1956). Land from Smith, and the firewood, *HJ*, 5/27/1932. Fully planted, ATB 1937. First municipal nursery, *HJ*, 8/12/1932. Howard's rich "contralto," M. McSweeney interview. "A beautiful person," J. McKee interview. "I think of her," E. Cheney interview.

Page 341: The street fair, *HJ*, 7/8 and 9/9/1938. On the hospital, *HJ*, 12/4/1932 (opening); edict on closing, *HJ*, 7/12 and 12/20/1935; ATB 1935 for Tolman's mystification as to why some had moved "Heaven and Earth to get rid of so modern and worthwhile an institution as a hospital." The fee, A. Calvi interview. Defence and testimonial, *HJ*, 1/31 and 2/7/1936. Brief history and closing, *HJ*, 11/12 and 12/24/1937. Shattuck letters on zoning, *HJ*, 2/25, 3/4, and 3/11/1938. Zoning article, ATB 1938.

Page 342: The meeting, *HJ*, 3/18/1938. "The illumined circle," Foley (1935), 73. Obits. in *HJ*: Jones, 1/23/1931; Buttimer, 6/2/1933; Sharp, 12/6/1929; Melcher, 2/21/1936; Bradley, 8/25/1933; Hennessy, 12/2/1938; McKee, 11/13/1931; Greenfield, 7/29/1938. Gates, *HJ*, 10/30/1931. Pratt closing, *HJ*, 1/27/1933. End of V.I.S., ATB 1933. Humphrey Post, *HJ*, 1/3/1930. Burr Brown, *HJ*, 6/21/1935. Cushing stable, *HJ*, 4/13/1934. On the hurricane of 1938, *HJ*, 9/23 through 10/28/1938.

Page 343: The reference to Bayside calls attention to a feature of the 1930s which this chapter does not have room to develop——the obsession with aviation, associated in part with the fame of Charles Lindbergh. South Shore Air Mail service was initiated from Bayside. Boys were busy making balsa model planes. The roof of the town hall ("Ag" Hall) was painted in big yellow block letters, "HINGHAM," for identification from the air. Curtiss, *HJ*, 10/29/1937. Studley, R. Marsh interview. "Ag" Hall dance floor, W. Lincoln and J. McKee interviews. Broad Cove Park, ATB 1937.

Page 344: League of Women Voters, *HJ*, 2/12/1932.

CHAPTER TWENTY-FOUR: *Small Town and Total War*

The depictions of America in World War II draw on Blum (1976), Davis (1965), and Phillips (1975). The account of the town draws on *HJ* and ATBs so widely that full documentation is not practicable. We have not located the history of the town in World War II on which Mason Foley was reportedly engaged for several years.

Page 345: Statistics from ATBs. New housing, *HJ*, 6/28 and 9/8/1939 and 8/1 and 10/28/1940.

Page 346: The Hingham scene in 1939 is sketched from *HJ* throughout the year. The emergency homecomings, *HJ*, 8/25, 9/22, and 9/29/1939.

Page 347: Finnish War Relief, *HJ*, 2/16 and 3/1/1940. March election day, *HJ*, 3/15/1940. British refugee children, *HJ*, 7/19, 10/10, and 12/26/1940. On the Sharps and their "religion of service" in Hingham (they left in August, 1933), *HJ*, 11/21/1930, 8/21/1931, 10/21/1932, and 4/21/1933. ABC-TV News, 12/21/1990, reported a reunion of Martha Sharp Cogan, age eighty-five, with the "children" the Sharps had brought from France in 1940. The forming of the Hingham committee, *HJ*, 6/7/1940. The "sensitive situation," *HJ*, 5/3, 6/28, and 8/1/1940. Election results, ATB 1940.

Page 348: Fore River and Depot growth, *HJ*, 8/1 through 8/15/1940. Bradley Woods and zoning, *HJ*, 11/7/1940, and 1/2, 1/23, 1/30, and 3/13/1941. In February (*HJ*, 2/6/1941), Engineer Lewis Perkins reported (1) there were thirteen or fourteen "home developments"; (2) of the town's 15,000 acres, only four or five thousand were available for home building; (3) there were already 2414 houses; (4) 160 permits had been granted for new houses in 1940; and (5) the proposed by-law set a minimum lot size of 12,500 sq. ft., allowing slightly over three lots to an acre, whereas Bradley agent Alfred Cole planned on over four to an acre. On the death of Amos Humphrey, *HJ*, 3/12/1942. On the Naval Annex, *HJ*, 7/31, 8/7, 8/14, 8/21, and 10/30/1941, and M. McSweeney interview.

Page 349: First draftees, *HJ*, 11/21/1940. For a list (with additions) of Hingham's war dead, see *HJ*, 8/23 and 8/30/1945, which give locations and circumstances. Additions, *HJ*, 12/13/1945 and 1/24/1946. Details of casualties in following pages come from these sources and specific reports in *HJ*, 1941-46.

Page 350: Regarding the day after Pearl Harbor in Hingham, *HJ*, 8/20/1942: "We woke the morning after Pearl Harbor to see long lines of trucks, filled with soldiers and guns, rolling down our tree-shaded streets to take up strategic defense positions in and around our town." Regarding Edward Howard, *HJ*, 1/17/1963, reports the finding of the crash site and the remains high in the Owen Stanley Range; the site had been located by Australians in 1961.

Page 351: Information on Mrs. Macgregor from herself in interview. On "the day" of the visit, Macmillan (1985).

Pages 351-53: On the shipyard, *HJ*, 1/15 and 5/28/1942. The quotation is from *HJ*, 4/9/1942. For later history, see 8/12, 11/4, and 12/23/1943. The end, Sept. 4, 1945, is reported in *HJ*, 9/6/1945: the last ship, the high speed transport *U.S. Francovich*, had been launched June 5. The yard closed with a "few shrill blasts," leaving "the absolute nakedness of the yard," its "big cranes idle," and a total production of 227 ships.

Page 353: The picture of the town, *HJ*, 1942, *passim*. Images of the black-outs, *HJ*, 2/26, 5/28, and 6/25/1942. Chief Ed Anderson, *HJ*, 7/2/1942.

Page 354: "This saving business," *HJ*, 8/21/1941. "For many years," *HJ*, 5/21/1942. Ingram on Tarawa, *HJ*, 4/6/1944.

Page 355: On the speed of change in Hingham, *HJ*, 8/20 and 8/27/1942. Statements of war workers, *HJ*, 1/28 and 6/3/1943, and 1/6/1944.

Page 356: To sense the activity of the Red Cross Motor Corps, consider January, 1944. Passengers transported totaled 547; hours of service, 625; miles driven, 2482 (*HJ*, 2/3/1944). On "Mother Quinn," see the obit. in *HJ*, 2/19/1948. One local nurse was former Visiting Nurse Frances Larkin, who served two years in the South Pacific, spending months in the steaming jungle working twelve-hour shifts (*HJ*, 8/9/1945). "Nellie Calvi", *HJ*, 4/29/1943. On Mary, Samuel Rizzotto's daughter, see *American Magazine*, April, 1948, and *Look*, September, 1948.

Page 357: "I watched one of the lassies," *HJ*, 3/11/1943. The gypsies, *HJ*, 6/10, 8/5, 8/19, and 9/30/1943; Coatsworth (1948), 161-64, and Peter Murphy interview. Segregation of black servicemen, *HJ*, 3/11/1943. "We left where we were," *HJ*, 7/15/1943.

Page 358: "Report immediately," *HJ*, 5/24/1943. "It will be no surprise," PFC Everett Linscott, *HJ*, 11/25/1943. On Hatten and the death of Seth Sprague, Jr., *HJ*, 3/8/1945. VE Day, *HJ*, 8/16/1945.

Page 359: "Dad, it's a far different war," *HJ*, 3/30/1944. VJ Day, *HJ*, 8/16/1945.

Page 360: "I just don't know," *HJ*, 7/4/1946. The Welcome Home sign, *HJ*, 6/20/1946. Town meeting of 1946, *HJ*, 3/21/1946. In January, 1947, Mrs. Winston Hall expressed the sentiments of many: "This memorial should be a living thing—a memorial not only for those who made the supreme sacrifice, but for those boys who fought and returned, and in so doing made it possible for there to be a Hingham today" (*HJ*, 1/16/1947). Rejection of the Legion's efforts, *HJ*, 3/13/1947. "It is less than three years," *HJ*, 3/18/1948. Memorial Day, *HJ*, 6/3/1948. The "anxious concern," *HJ*, 6/7/1945.

Page 361: The Greenfield's episode was followed just over a year later by Smith's death, 9/9/1947. For a long eulogy and record of his many services and benefactions to the town, see *HJ*, 9/11 and 10/16/1947. "Man, dear," *HJ*, 5/8/1947. New subdivisions, *HJ*, 7/3/1947. "I can remember when," *HJ*, 5/16/1946. "Drive up Butler Road," *HJ*, 9/11/1947. The survey (by the New England Telephone Company), *HJ*, 12/23/1948. Hingham's baby boom, *HJ*, 10/23/1947 and 1/8/1948. The school situation, *HJ*, 6/26, 7/24, and 7/31/1947.

Pages 362-363: "In the past few years," *HJ*, 3/4/1948. The "babysitter debate," *HJ*, 2/19/1948. The Baptist division, *HJ*, 3/11/1948. The analysis of Hingham society, Shattuck (1949). He includes real names; we omit them, since families are significant in this context only as representative. "No longer the citizens," p. 82. "Outlander elite," pp. 40-41. "Older middle," pp. 56-61. "Lower middle," pp. 62-63. Irish hierarchy, pp. 44, 68-69. The wife "absolutely denies," p. 72. The "natives," pp. 75-80, 123. Perkins and Foster, p. 151. "As Francis Lincoln would say," *HJ*, 5/5/1939.

Pages 363-65: On proposed changes in town government, *HJ*, 2/5, 2/26, and 1/11/1948. On other towns, Sly (1930). The "dump question," ATBs 1945 and 1946 and *HJ*, 4/19/1945. The sewer question, *HJ*, 3/21/1946. William L. Foster's topical index was accepted in 1949 (ATB). His typing letter by letter was described by Amy Howard after his death (*HJ*, 8/30/1951). "Gone and let us hope forever," *HJ*, 4/17/1947. The special town meeting, *HJ*, 6/17/1948. "Swarming around Woody's," *HJ*, 6/17/1948. Obit. of Charles Marble, *HJ*, 12/2/1948. Sights and sounds, *HJ*, 10/7 through 10/21/1948.

CHAPTER TWENTY-FIVE: *Decade of Numbers*

On the history and sociology of modern suburbia, we have consulted several recent studies; of special use were Joel Schwartz's opening chapter in Dolce (1976), William M. Dobriner in Kramer (1972), and Kaplan (1976). For historical context in the 1950s, we depend chiefly on Miller and Nowak (1977), Brogan (1986), and Burns (1990). Kathleen Curtis has shared with us her fine paper on the life of young families on Crow Point—see Curtis (n.d.) in the bibliography—but we are not free to quote from her oral histories.

Page 366: "I will always be," McSweeney interview. The anonymous skywatcher, *HJ*, 10/8/1953. The "middle landscape" of suburbia, Kaplan (1976), 8. $150 billion in savings, Miller-Nowak (1977), 114. The "greatest land rushes," Kaplan, 14.

Page 367: Hingham population and demographics, ATBs 1949-58. For the differences between the new suburbs and suburbanized old towns like Hingham, see Dobriner in Kramer (1972), 160. Dobriner's "Natural History of a Reluctant Suburb," treating a town renamed for tact "Old Harbor," in some respects describes Hingham. For the Board of Health's new powers, granted by a state law of 1952, see ATB 1952.

Page 368: The twenty-year jump in school enrollment, School Comm. report, ATB 1950. Further jumps, ATBs 1951, 1952, and 1956. Also, *HJ*, 1/12/1955. Loss of Hull receipts, ATB 1956. Nomination for an architectural award, *HJ*, 5/19/1949. A "Ford or Chevrolet model," *HJ*, 2/24/1949. "Literally agog," *HJ*, 3/10/1949. Telephone lines between the armory and auditorium, ATB 1949. The foot-stamping, *HJ*, 3/17/1949. The motion to restudy, ATB 1949. Ousting the principal, *HJ*, 5/26/1949; *ibid.* for the PTA/Foley message.

Page 369: The student march, Rice's permission, Alleman's objection, and the "blot," *HJ*, 6/2/1949. School Committee explanation, *HJ*, 6/9/1949; letter on "truants," *ibid.* Petition for special meeting and the powers of school committees, *HJ*, 6/16/1949. Warrant article, *HJ*, 6/23/1949. The curate's abhorrence, *HJ*, 6/9/1949. *HJ*'s concession, 6/2/1949. Ending of "Freak Days," *HJ*, 5/26/1949. "Prowler" evidently saw no connection between this ending and reactions to the strike.

Page 370: Appointment of Redmond, *HJ*, 8/11/1949. Barber's resignation, *HJ*, 9/29/1949. Macmillan's resignation, *HJ*, 12/1/1955. Foster School opened in 1951; the addition was built in 1957. South School opened in 1949, with additions in 1951 and 1956. East School opened in 1958. On Michelson's land and the "taking," ATB 1951 and *HJ*, 11/22/1951 and 7/16/1952. On the addi-tional $10,000 and the naming of the field, ATB 1954. We have not included—as based too much on "hearsay"—evidence that anti-Semitism played a part in discussions of naming after Michelson.

Page 371: The 1958 enrollments and distribution of seventh through ninth graders, ATB 1958. The English head as public relations director, *HJ*, 11/8/1951 and 11/12/1953. Concepts of "working together," "middle-of-the-road," "product," and "rightthinking," ATBs 1951 and 1955. The Freedom Foundation medal, *HJ*, 2/28/1957. The threat to the "way," ATB 1955. The percentage college-bound, ATB 1956. Grouping, the gifted child, and math seminar, ATB 1958. Inclusions in the curriculum, ATB 1956. For sales of and statistics on television sets, see Miller and Nowak (1977), 338 and appendix. Fifty-five hundred under seventeen years of age, *HJ*, 4/3/1958.

Page 372: Forming of the Little League, *HJ*, 5/15 and 6/24/1952. Other leagues, *HJ*, 6/13/1957. The "clinic," *HJ*, 5/12/1955. More and more teams, *HJ*, 5/24/1956. The Cracker Barrel League, *HJ*, 6/28/1956. The undefeated football team and sports night, *HJ*, 11/28 and 12/26/1957. Hockey team, *HJ*, 2/14/1957. Cronin obit., *HJ*, 3/22/1956. Naming of Cronin Field, *HJ*, 7/4/1957. Red Cross classes at the harbor, *HJ*, 7/12/1956. On the Crow Point Sailing Club, see Curtis, "Turnabout," in bibliography and *HJ*, 1/31/1957. Crow Point sledding streets, *HJ*, 2/20/1958. Chauncy Burr, *HJ*, 1/15/1953. Growth of Girl Scouts, *HJ*, 5/10/1951, 3/6/1952, and 3/17/1955.

Page 373: Bertha Stringer, *HJ*, 1/17/1957. Ten new South Shore parishes, *HJ*, 4/25/1957. Glastonbury, *HJ*, 8/26/1954. Mini Boys Town, *HJ*, 9/7, 9/14, 9/28, and 11/23/1950. New North membership, *HJ*, 5/19/1949 and 2/7/1957. St. John's building and curate, *HJ*, 6/16/1955 and 1/30/1958. Congregational Sunday School, *HJ*, 4/9/1953 and 3/21/1957. Methodist classrooms, *HJ*, 3/1/1956. First Parish Hall, *HJ*, 9/13/1956 and 5/2/1957. Second Parish Hall, Robinson (1980), 218, and *HJ*, 4/5/1956. Robinson's story and idea, interview with Robinson (1979).

Page 374: South Hingham growth, Robinson (1980), 219. Thanksgiving Union services, *HJ*, 11/20/1958. UNICEF cartons, *HJ*, 10/20/1955. Displaced families, *HJ*, 12/28/1950, 10/25/1952, and 1/31 and 10/31/1957. AFS: conversation with M. Farrell, 3/29/1992; *HJ*, 8/4/1955, 4/11/1957; AFS 25th anniversary, May 10, 1979.

Page 375: For attacks on the culture of suburbia, see especially Kramer (1972). The best-known attack was William H. Whyte's *The Organization Man* (1956). Marine Reserves, Battery D, and Navy Reserve Battalion, *HJ*, 8/17/1950 and 2/15/1951. McLean's letter, *HJ*, 6/7/1951. Duffy, *HJ*, 3/19/1953. Powers: conversation with his sister, Mrs. Helen Mansfield (3/24/1992). The *Tweedy*, 4/3/1952.

Page 376: Merrill, *HJ*, 9/17/1953. Laskey, *HJ*, 4/10/1952. The plaque unveiled, *HJ*, 5/25/1950. Victor Rhodes, *HJ*, 6/14/1951. Nikes on Turkey Hill, *HJ*, 11/17/1955. "Operation Crossroads," *HJ*, 1/18/1951. "Living with the Atom," *HJ*, 3/6/1952. "Invasion U.S.A.," *HJ*, 4/16/1953. The veteran of both wars, *HJ*, 10/1/1953. "Teddy" Berg, *HJ*, 3/1/1951. Cheney, *HJ*, 11/17/1955. Kimball and Civil Defense, ATB 1951. Buildings chosen, *HJ*, 3/10/1955. Fire horn signals, *HJ*, 12/21/1950. "Ready . . . against any disaster," ATB 1951.

Page 377: Hurricanes: "Carol" arrived Tues., Aug. 31, 1954; "Edna," Sat., Sept. 11, 1954. "Diane" reported, *HJ*, 8/25/1955. Rainfall, ATB 1955. "Carol" damage and restoration, ATB 1954, and *HJ*, 9/2, 9/9, and 9/23/1954. Pumping basements, *HJ*, 8/25/1955. Weir River, ATB 1954.

Page 378: Selectmen's disclaimer, ATB 1954. "Silent alarm boxes," ATB 1955. Tree Warden Fee's activities, ATBs 1956 and 1958. Spraying, ATBs 1950, 1951, 1954, 1955. Dutch Elm disease arrived in Hingham in 1948. The tally of lost elms (ATBs) was 803. No figures were given for 1952 or 1957, but figures tallied from *HJ* suggest a total loss of close to one thousand. Census in ATB 1955 suggests 2,700 elms then left in Hingham. The white circle painted on trunks, JPR reminiscence.

Page 379: The pine sailing over the roof, *HJ*, 9/9/1954. Nine unanimous votes, ATB 1955. On sewering, ATBs 1955 and 1958. Fluoridation, ATB 1953. Cases of polio, ATB 1955. No recorded cases, ATB 1957. In 1957, almost 3,500 children had been immunized against polio—about 62 percent. "Enforcement of pasteuriza-tion," ATB 1958. "Not much garbage and . . . poorer," *HJ*, 6/12/1952. "No action," ATB 1952. "No choice," ATB 1953.

Page 380: "The customary inland tests," ATB 1955. The committee to study representative town meeting, *etc.*, ATB 1949. Open town meeting still functioning, ATB 1956. Vote against precincting, ATB 1958. Limiting a speaker's time, ATB 1957. Whittemore on Barnes, ATB 1957.

Page 381: For the function and personnel of the Capital Outlay Committee, see ATB 1956. Carr's eighty-seven appointments, *HJ*, 6/7/1956. Committee of Fifteen, *HJ*, 3/11/1898. Alexander Macmillan (1992) contends that this Committee has been "generally ignored," with little impact on planning. Botting obit., *HJ*, 12/20/1956. The E.&D. Fund's depletion, ATB 1956. The debt ratio, ATB 1957. The property tax as "major determinant," Kaplan (1976), 167. Note: the 1911 classic *Essays in Taxation* by R. A. Seligman observed: "There is nothing wrong with the property tax, except that it is wrong in theory and does not work in practice" (quoted in Kaplan [1976], 168).

Page 382: On the independent assessment: the town had voted to include the survey results in the booklet (ATB 1952). Worsened suspicions, *HJ*, 3/5/1953. Assessors' Office Practices Committee, ATB 1957. Additional $7 million, ATB 1958. Figure of $73, ATB 1958. "Interesting reading," ATB 1957. Carr as "Moderator only," ATB 1956. Chairman S. Gunnar Myrbeck's recommendations, ATB 1957. Forty percent of school construction, ATB 1958. Thirty-three percent of school buses, ATB 1956.

Page 383: Interest and loan payments of Light Board, profits, and "hidden dividend," ATBs, 1956, 1957. On the rejected skating rink, *HJ*, 5/30, 6/13, 6/20, and 6/27/1957. On zoning articles, ATBs 1949-58. Release of federally-owned land, *HJ*, 5/31/1956 and 12/21/1958, and ATB 1958. On the aircraft industry, Miller-Nowak (1977), 44. Foley and wildlife, *HJ*, 6/6/1957.

Page 384: Memories of Misses Thayer and Gates, JPR. Human departures: Murphy 1947; Smith 1947; Barnes 1956; Botting 1956; Foster 1951; Huntley 1955; Dwiggins 1956.

Page 385: On Dwiggins, see note to Chap. Twenty-Three; "a man who loved his work," Mabel Dwiggins in Bennett (1960), 70. House history, JLN. Depot demolition, *HJ*, 12/1/1949 and ATB 1950. Cushing House, *HJ*, 10/20/1949. Pond and Home Meadows problems as interpreted in a memorandum from JPR. On disappearance of farms, Newcombe interview.

Page 386: John D. Long's estate: ATB 1951 (the offer); ATB 1957 (acceptance). Demolition of the house and barn, ATB 1958. The revolving platform, described by Herbert Hirsch in interview. Button Island, ATB 1957. Hydrant water rental, ATB 1958. Water Company non-purchase, ATBs 1949, 1950, 1954, and 1958. New businesses, *HJ*, 1/17/1957. New telephone building, *HJ*, 6/21/1956. Chamber of Commerce, *HJ*, 4/28/1955. *HJ* subscription increase, 11/13/1958. Sale of Hennessy's, *HJ*, 12/24/1953.

Page 387: On juvenile delinquency, see Chap. Twenty-Six and *HJ*, 9/16/1954 and 5/15/1958. United Community Fund, *HJ*, 10/3/1957. Wompatuck Club gift, *HJ*, 7/4/1957. Walter Dziura, *HJ*, 9/4/1958. Women jurors, *HJ*, 9/6/1951. Women HPL Trustees, *HJ*, 10/31/1957. Women on the Advisory Committee, ATB 1957. Larry Stein and Sputnik I, *HJ*, 10/10/1957. Two women and SANE, *HJ*, 5/13/1958. Amy Howard's counsel, *HJ*, 6/30/1957. Amy Howard obit., *HJ*, 8/14/1958.

CHAPTER TWENTY-SIX: *The Shocking Sixties*

Epigraphs are from Charles Dickens, *A Tale of Two Cities*, opening line, and William Wordsworth, *The Prelude*, XI. 108-09.

National history is based chiefly on Chafe (1986), Howard (1982), O'Neill (1971), and Shachtman (1983). On local matters in these years of intensive public policy work and debate, the ATBs are of special value. The diminished value of the *HJ* reflects changed times in local life. Such a newspaper could no longer embrace the life of so large and divided a community, as if the possibility of coherence were gone. There were over eighty social and other organizations, but little is printed about most. The "social" in *HJ* is confined largely to weddings, engagements, and sports. Political affairs, very controversial, are treated cautiously or avoided; editorial comments are curmudgeonly. Scanning *HJ* in these years suggests that local memory had become tenuous. Obituaries are brief and abstract, as if the memory of old-timers' early lives had been quickly "razed" like "tired old landmarks," a revealing phrase from *HJ*, 4/20/1961. In some respects, the *Hingham Mirror* (established 1957) filled the gap.

The growth of the 1950s became obvious in 1960, when the U.S. Census Bureau estimated a growth of 5,000 in Hingham's population in the 1950s. The following table of home building *permits* was published (note the big drop after 1955):

1948: 119	1951: 139	1954: 185	1957: 59
1949: 150	1952: 165	1955: 152	1958: 34
1950: 177	1953: 117	1956: 91	1959: 61

In the second half of the 1960s, population growth slowed markedly:

1955: 13,418;	1960: 15,378;	1965: 17,576;	1970: 18,867.

Page 388: For a fascinating essay on the "Tragedy of Development" and the developer as American prototype, see Berman in Howard (1982). The planners' estimate, *HJ*, 1/21/1960. Memory of last trains, JPR. Melcher's reminiscence, *HJ*, 7/9/1959.

Page 389: O'Kane's lament, *HJ*, 11/5/1959. The "gravest crisis," *HJ*, 4/16 through 5/7/1959. "Acrimonious feeling," *HJ*, 5/7/1959. "I do not want Hingham," the Rev. Sisson at the Congregational Church, *HJ*, 5/28/1959. It was familiarly known as the "White Church" until the interracial sensitivity of the mid-1960s made this name objectionable. On traffic off the Expressway, see, for example, *HJ*, 1/5 and 9/28/1961, and 2/7/1963. "Massachusetts means Progress," *HJ*, 1/5/1961. On the start-up and growth of Hingham Plaza and the Industrial Park, see especially *HJ*, 11/19 and 11/26/1959, 1/21 and 10/13/1960, 11/16 and 11/23/1961, 1/25/1962, 4/4 and 8/1/1963, 1/23/1964, 9/3/1970. "great ditches," memorandum from JPR. The first Plaza store, GEM, opened in March, 1962.

Page 390: On Merriman, see *HJ*, 8/6/1964 and 7/21/1966. On Spencer Press, *HJ*, 12/23/1965; Lounge Inc., 12/1/1966; North Terminal, 2/1/1968. On the sale of the shipyard and reaction, see especially *HJ*, 1/4/1962. The selectmen "much concerned," from ATB 1963, Report of the Selectmen. On the "flagpole," *HJ*, 9/27/1962 and 2/10/1966. On land for school buses, *HJ*, 10/18/1962. On proposed Navy housing, *HJ*, 9/9 and 12/16/1965; 2/3, 3/10, and 3/31/1966. On the Annex as state park, *HJ*, 9/24/1959, 4/28/1960, 1/3/1963, and especially 10/27/1966; also, 5/15/1969 and 10/29/1970, and the Epilogue below. See Epilogue also for later history of the Depot. On planning: the activity began with the issuing of the Blackwell Report on long-range planning, January, 1961. For the text, see *HJ*, 1/12 and 1/19/1961.

Page 391: East School, *HJ*, 1/15 and 10/15/1959 and 1/5 and 4/13/1961. On junior high schools, *HJ*, 2/5/1959; 5/5, 6/23, and 10/27/1960; 2/8/1962. On the high school, *HJ*, 10/22/1959 and 3/21 and 10/3/1963. On Plymouth River, *HJ*, 3/24 and 3/31/1966 and 3/28/1968. Balks and grumbles about town hall and library, *HJ*, 3/12 and 3/19/1964 and 4/22/1965. Ag Hall's "creaky confines," *HJ*, 4/1 and 4/8/1965. *The Patriot Ledger* reported it was "crumbling in places," its heating system long since failed; except as polling place and commuter parking area, it had served almost no purpose for years. Airplane spotters had kept vigil from its tower, and the Fire Department had used it for ladder drills. Hinghamites born as late as the 1930s remember dances there. For the "book-et brigade," ATB 1966. Appropriations and school enrollments from ATBs.

Page 392: On America's post-war faith, see Howard (1982), 497: "We embraced the ebullient vision of the developers as our own . . . with boundless confidence that everyone would adapt and everything would be fine, finer than ever, very soon." On how President Johnson epitomized this confidence, see Chafe (1986), 243. On school philosophy and programs, see especially the School Committee reports in ATBs 1963 and 1966. "We learned little about," Simon (1990). "Progress, far from," Santayana (1954), 82. "Memory is the basis," Wiesel, PBS-TV, 3/21/1990. "The retarded, the gifted," *etc.*, from School Committee report, ATB 1963.

Page 393: On the rise of juvenile delinquency, see "Growing Up" in Miller-Nowak (1977). It is significant that the ATB 1961 included an explanation of what juvenile delinquency is. On juvenile delinquency in Hingham, see, for example, *HJ*, 3/2/1961, 5/17/1962, 11/18/1965, 4/20/1967, and Police Department reports in ATBs. "We need a separate police department," *HJ*, 9/8/1966. Case loads at Court, *HJ*, 1/22/1970. "My God!" *HJ*, 11/18/1965. On possible "causes," see Miller-Nowak (1977), 287.

Page 394: Chronology from various sources such as Howard (1982), App. "Somehow or other it all," *HJ*, 5/30 and 9/5/1963. The "Charm" course, *HJ*, 10/1/1960. St. John's curate, *HJ*, 10/20/1960. Riesman (1950). Linder, from Miller-Nowak (1977), 277. Goodman (1960).

Page 395: Bonitto, *HJ*, 5/17/1962. The Pledge, *HJ*, 1/3/1963 and 3/18 and 11/11/1965. Characteristically, there is neither report nor editorial comment by *HJ*. Alleman's speech, *HJ*, 9/5 and 9/12/1963. The "provocative questions," *HJ*, 10/3/1963. Gallop and Freedom School, *HJ*, 2/27/1964. The Hingham Chapter, *HJ*, 10/15/1964. The Wrights, *HJ*, 12/31/1964 and 1/7/1965. Miller's speech, *HJ*, 4/1/1965. The "Negro lady," *HJ*, 4/8/1965.

Page 396: Louise Day Hicks, *HJ*, 11/18 and 12/16/1965. On METCO, *HJ*, 4/29/1965, 11/24/1966, 9/7 and 9/14/1967; K. Janey quoted, 3/3/1969; 4/30/1970. Interview with Camilla Roundtree. Glastonbury, *HJ*, 10/5/1961; Temple Beth Am, *HJ*, 1/18/1962 and 1/20/1966. Friends' Home, *HJ*, 3/1/1962; Maryknoll, *HJ*,

10/25/1962; Notre Dame, *HJ*, 5/16/1963 and 9/2/1965; Mormons, *HJ*, 10/31/1968; Lutherans, *HJ*, 8/5 and 10/28/1965, 7/6/1967, and 2/8/1968.

Page 397: "It was a time full of joy," Gallop (1983), 47. Ecumenical services and meetings, *HJ*, 1/19, 1/26, and 2/9/1967, 1/18 and 3/21/1968. Lilly, *HJ*, 7/19/1962; Lawson, *HJ*, 9/12/1963; Lovely, *HJ*, 6/24/1965; Treat, *HJ*, 5/8/1969. Alger, *HJ*, 5/22/1969. Campbell's "Citizens' Rights," *HJ*, 1/18/1968.

Page 398: "Before any of you folks," *HJ*, 9/28/1961. Auctioned shelter, *HJ*, 5/27/1965. JFK's death, *HJ*, 11/28/1963. "Senator Barry Goldwater," *HJ*, 7/23/1964. Vote, ATB. The stolen flag, *HJ*, 7/22 and 7/29/1965. "The war is easy to," *HJ*, 6/22/1966. "My mother quite naturally," *HJ*, 4/6/1967.

Page 399: "Snubbed by citizens," *HJ*, 8/24/1967. South Junior High's list, *HJ*, 11/16/1967 (report only). Reports of casualties and deaths: *HJ*, 1/19, 4/13, 5/4, 5/11, and 7/27/1967; 2/22/1968; 3/13/1969; and 1/1/1970. Steen's letters, *HJ*, 8/3 and 8/10/1967 (reprinted with his permission).

Page 400: "Pretty much commonplace," *HJ*, 10/12/1967. Perkinson, *HJ*, 12/14/1967. The Peters story, repr. *HJ*, 4/18/1968. "Aw! Gee whiz," *HJ*, 4/25/1968.

Page 401: "At last the lid," *HJ*, 5/8/1968. Chomsky charge and responses, *HJ*, 2/29, 3/7, and 3/14/1968. The McCarthy campaign, *HJ*, 4/4/1968. Hoffman at the High School, *HJ*, 4/25/1968. Primary vote, *HJ*, 5/2/1968. Twenty clergymen and the memorial march, *HJ*, 4/11/1968. High School "resignations," *HJ*, 4/25 through 6/20/1968.

Page 402: Drugs and drug arrests, Police Department reports in ATBs. The cycle gang, *HJ*, 5/2/1968. "Harassed Hippies," *HJ*, 7/11/1968. "With the pillars of life," *HJ*, 6/18/1968. On Mason Foley, *HJ*, 6/13/1968 ("in times of rapid change") and 10/3/1968; McSweeney interview.

Page 403: "interested in preserving," *HJ*, 8/1/1968. Second conference, *HJ*, 11/21/1968. "Citizens' Rights," *HJ*, 1/18/1968. Underground films, *HJ*, 8/1 through 8/22/1968. The "open letter," *HJ*, 9/5 and 9/12/1968. "I seem to sense," *HJ*, 9/12/1968. Hingham vote, *HJ*, 11/7/1968. "The status quo," *HJ*, 6/27/1968.

Page 404: The Route 228 relocation matter persisted throughout the year. See *HJ*, 2/22, 3/7, 3/14, 3/21, 4/4, 8/1, 8/15, 9/5, 9/26, and 10/3/1968 (the town vote: 506 for relocation, 559 against), and 10/24/1968. Peace Day, *HJ*, 10/16/1969. Student letters, *HJ*, 5/21/1970.

Page 405: Presidential primary, *HJ*, 4/27/1972. On "Sam" Mahony, *HJ*, 1/15 and 12/31/1970. On the Conservation Commission, see annual reports of gifts and purchases in ATBs 1962-68. Friends of Conservation, *HJ*, 2/18 and 3/11/1965.

Page 406: On the Annex drive, reminiscences from JPR. World's End campaign, *HJ*, 11/23 through 12/21/1967. History of World's End, Walker and Walker (1973), 50-54. Acreage of World's End: Greening of Hingham map shows 249; Walker and Walker say "some 248 acres and over five miles of shoreline"; A. Macmillan says 251. A 1949 brochure (in the possession of JPR) advertising World's End for sale says 245 acres. Reed's death, *HJ*, 1/28/1960. Melcher on post offices, *HJ*, 5/14/1964. The "principle of conservation," report of Historic District Study Committee in ATB 1965.

Page 407: "Who wants to live," *HJ*, 2/21/1963. Historic Survey Committee, *HJ*, 3/28/1963. Old Ship Church as landmark, *HJ*, 10/13/1960 and 1/17/1963; the dedication was on 5/26/1963. Historic District Study Committee, *HJ*, 3/26/1964 and 3/31/1966. "Why not declare," *HJ*, 3/26/1964. Derby Academy in the twentieth century, summarized from Roscoe (1984). "Once the old school," *HJ*, 1/14/1965. "Citizens of Hingham!" *HJ*, 1/21/1965. The campaign to save Derby, *HJ*, 11/18/1965 and 2/24/1966.

Page 408: Hingham Council on Aging: see Epilogue below. The survey of elders, report of Senior Citizens Survey in ATB 1964, and *HJ*, 2/25/1965. "What with the family gone," *HJ*, 7/21/1966. Marden's apartments, *HJ*, 1/5/1967 and 9/25/1969. Housing Authority, *HJ*, 3/30 and 7/27/1967. West School, *HJ*, 6/12/1969. "Rather shameful . . . foot-dragging," *HJ*, 9/25/1969. The elderly "being squeezed out," *HJ*, 10/22/1970. "Our house is sold," *HJ*, 4/1/1965. "The place nearest their hearts," *HJ*, 10/2/1969. Taxes and appropriations in 1970, *HJ*, 3/19 and 3/26/1970. The organizing of "TAXES," *HJ*, 9/3, 9/10, 10/1, 10/8, and 10/22/1970. The "Time Shock" series, *HJ*, 10/22/1970.

EPILOGUE

Pages 413-14: Ecology becomes political: report of LWV, *HJ*, 1/28/1971. Environmental news, *HJ*, 1/28 and 2/18/1971, 1/20, 4/13, and 5/12/1972, 4/12/1973, and

10/10/1974. Bare Cove Park described, *HJ*, 10/13/1977. Bouvé land, ATB 1979 and JPR. Hanlon farm, *HJ*, 3/15/1979 and ATB 1979. Hornstra farm, *HJ*, 5/1/1980 and 6/4/1981. "We have treated," *HJ*, 4/17/1980. Waste and recycling, *HJ*, 2/18/1971 and 4/29/1972. "man's total mania," *HJ*, 5/23/1974.

Page 415: Sewer dispute, *HJ*, 4/14, 6/30, 7/28, and 10/20/1983; 3/8, 3/15, 6/14, 6/28, 7/5, 9/6, and 9/27/1984. "That wasteful institution," *HJ*, 4/29/1982. Apartment and other developments, *HJ*, 1/7, 3/4, 3/11, 3/18, and 7/22/1971, and report of town meeting ATB 1971. Indian College, *HJ*, 6/7, 9/20, 11/22 through 12/13/1973, and 1/10, 2/21, and 3/7/1974.

Page 416: National growth of Grey Power, Gross (1978). Local elderly, *HJ*, 2/25/1971 (survey and statistics), 1/25/1971 (lunch program), 1/4/1973 (shuttle bus), and 6/29/1972 and 5/17/1973 (history of the Council).

Page 417: Thaxter Park, *HJ*, 3/2 and 9/14/1972, 8/9/1973, and 3/21/1974. Abbey land, *HJ*, 12/6/1973. Glastonbury's status, *HJ*, 1/18/1973. Lincoln School, *HJ*, 5/11/1978, 2/22, 3/15, and 4/5/1979, and 1/1/1980. Miss Wigmore, *HJ*, 11/20/1980. Elder Care, *HJ*, 8/27/1981, 4/22/1982, 4/14/1983, and 2/9, 3/29, 6/28, 8/23, 9/13, and 10/18/1984. The McSweeney letter, *HJ*, 4/21/1983.

Page 418: "Where are the minorities?" *HJ*, 5/19/1983. Retired people, *HJ*, 12/23/1976. Hersey House, *HJ*, 10/1/1976. "RSVP," *HJ*, 3/16/1978. Youth Hotline, *HJ*, 6/10 and 8/19/1971, and 5/31/1973.

Pages 419-20: National status of women, Hymowitz and Weissman (1978) and Ryan (1983). Labor force, *HJ*, 7/24/1980. Columns and workshops, *HJ*, 2/8 and 10/3/1979, and 2/7/1980. Women in the workforce, Chafe (1986), 435. Officer LaCombe, *HJ*, 1/2 and 5/15/1979. Committeewoman Ford, *HJ*, 3/20/1975. "What does the Christian word?" *HJ*, 2/18/1982. "As so many changes," *HJ*, 7/12/1979. Women's Exchange, *HJ*, 7/8/1981. Tennis Club, *HJ*, 12/16/1971, 12/14/1972, and 6/6/1974. The closing was announced in May, 1982.

Page 420: "Do you suppose?" *HJ*, 9/4/1975. Commuter boats, *HJ*, 10/9, 12/4, and 12/25/1975 (Gelsthorpe), and 3/18, 6/24, and 7/22/1976, and 5/12/1977. The advertisement, *HJ*, 9/29/1977. Blizzard, *HJ*, 2/16/1978.

Page 421: First anniversary (1979), *HJ*, 1/11/1979. Energy crisis, Chafe (1986), 447-48, and *HJ*, 11/8 and 11/29/1973, and 1/24 through 2/7/1974. "REACH", *HJ*, 6/28, 9/13, and 10/25/1979, and 3/13, 4/10, and 11/26/1980.

Page 422: Local registration and elections, ATBs 1972 and 1976 and *HJ*, 8/24/1972. 1980 election, ATB. On the history of *Roe v. Wade*, Faux (1989). "Rough and tumble," Faux, 267.

Page 423: LWV split, *HJ*, 2/8, 10/11, and 11/1/1973. "Birthright," *etc.*, *HJ*, 2/8/1973 and 3/14/1974. "Our America where," *HJ*, 2/1/1973. Schools controversy, *HJ*, 11/30/1972 and 1/25, 6/7, and 6/14/1973. "Back to Basics," Booth (1988), 30.

Page 424: Charter reform, *HJ*, 4/13, 11/30, and 12/21/1972. Charter vote, *HJ*, 3/29 and 4/5/1973, and ATB 1973. Tax resistance, *HJ*, 3/11 and 3/18/1971, and town meeting, ATB 1971. Economic troubles, Chafe (1986), 445-50.

Page 425: Manley's warning, *HJ*, 3/8/1979. Vote on Prop 2 1/2, ATB 1980. Mahony vote, ATB 1981. Mahony interview, *HJ*, 5/7/1981. Chief Campbell, *HJ*, Feb., 1981, through April, 1981, and 5/14/1981.

Page 426: Disputes and litigations: the sceptical reader can test the truthfulness of this mild, abbreviated sketch only by scanning *HJ* from 1982 to 1984 *passim*. Selectmen's statements on litigiousness, *HJ*, 12/23/1982 and the election campaign of Spring, 1983. "personally affronted," *HJ*, 6/7/1984.

Page 427: Elder Care/Brandon, see above, note to p. 417. Daisy Janey, *HJ*, 8/16/1984. "Alice through the looking glass," *HJ*, 7/19/1984. Local celebrations and commemorations, *HJ*, 1/23, 1/30, 4/10, 7/10, and 9/11/1975, and 6/10, 7/1, and 7/8/1976.

Page 428: Wright's memoir of Uncle Sam, written ten years earlier, reprinted in *HJ*, 7/17/1975.

Page 429: Old Parish House controversy, *HJ*, 1/20 through 4/7/1977. Demolition began 4/13/1977. On preparations for 1985, note to the authors from Winston Hall.

Page 430: "It was wonderful," *HJ*, 11/29/1984. "I think a lot of him," *HJ*, 9/12/1985. "Hingham has not been," *HJ*, 9/12/1985. "Yet all of these entities," *Hingham Mariner*, 4/11/1985.

Page 431: Not "commemorative in nature," *Hingham Mariner*, 2/21/1985. For the events and personalities of 1985, see *Hingham Mariner* Supplement 12/12/1985. "I didn't dare wash," *Hingham Mariner*, 7/11/1985.

Page 432:— The profile of 1985 Hingham draws chiefly on "Historic Hingham," *HJ* Special Supplement, 7/3/1985, especially pages 29A-30A by Hilary McCarthy. Other details from *HJ*, 1985, *passim* and ATB. "virtual melting pot," *HJ*, 1/26/1978. The temple was completed April 1, 1980, and dedicated June 6 (see *HJ*, 3/21/1980). On growth of the congregation, *HJ*, 11/22/1989. "I reached every goal," from "Calling All Women," *HJ*, July, 1985.

Page 433: "Are you going?" *Hingham Mariner*, 4/18/1985. Popularity of soccer, note to the authors from George Smith. Yacht Club, *HJ*, 5/24/1984. Lincoln Sailing Club, *HJ*, 4/1 and 6/10/1971 and 8/11/1988. South Shore Conservatory, *HJ*, 6/21/1979 and 12/1/1983. M. Euler, *HJ*, 1/18/1981.

Page 434: The predictions are on pp. 34A-38A of *HJ* Special Supplement.

Page 435: A drug problem? *HJ*, 11/25 and 12/3/1987, and note to the authors from W. R. Carr. AIDS, *HJ*, 2/26/1987. Incinerators, *HJ*, 6/25 and 10/8/1987 and 11/16/1989. Landfill expansion defeated at town meeting 1988 (ATB). Manda-tory recycling, *HJ*, 4/12/1990. Light poles, *HJ*, 10/15/1987. "One neighbor-hood after another," *HJ*, 12/31/1986. Affordable housing, *HJ*, 1/8, 2/5 and 5/28/1987; 4/7, 5/5, 5/12, 8/4/1988; and 2/16/1989. Report on housing and lists, Ruth Spencer, *HJ*, 4/14/1988. Seventy percent of owners and "Hingham is too homogeneous," *HJ*, 2/5/1987. Kitty Montgomery, *HJ*, 9/26/1988. Murphy, *HJ*, 1/5 and 1/12/1989. Interfaith Shelter, *HJ*, 2/9/1989.

Page 436: "There was a time," *HJ*, 3/5/1987. Talbots, *HJ*, 6/26/1980. Commuter boats, *HJ*, 8/17/1989. Water Company move, *HJ*, 11/22/1989. Fire Insurance Company, *HJ*, 9/11/1986. Sprague Building fire, *Hingham Mariner*, 1/21/1988. Pride Building, *HJ*, 10/19 and 12/7/1989.

Pages 437-38: Railroad: *HJ*, 8/6 and 8/27/1987, Jan., 1988, March, 1990. Country Club, *HJ*, 11/19/1986, March, 1987, 10/1/1987, 2/8, 5/5, and 5/26/1988, 7/14 and 10/13/1988.

Pages 438-39: "Overrides," *HJ*, 4/17/1986, 3/12/1987, 3/3, 3/17, 6/9, 9/22, and 10/6/1988, 2/2, 2/23, 3/9, 3/28, and 4/27/1989. "No more blank checks," *HJ*, 3/28/1989. Election results, *HJ*, 5/4/1989. "2 1/2 put me out," *HJ*, 6/15/1989. North Fire Station, *HJ*, 6/29/1989. "Day of Hope" and "Calming the Storm," *HJ*, 6/1/1989.

Page 440: "What kind of a cheap town?" *HJ*, 5/11/1989. "The handsome old houses," *HJ*, 9/14/1989. "Those who wring," *HJ*, 5/11/1989. Campaign of 1990, *HJ*, January-April, 1990. Report of town meeting, *HJ*, 4/26/1990. Election results, *HJ*, 5/3/1990. "We live in the perfect," *HJ*, 6/8/1989. Brewers' letter, *HJ*, 5/4/1989.

Page 441: O'Donnell quoted in *Hingham Mariner*, 5/14/1992. Citizens of the Year: see the photo of all four, *HJ*, 3/23/1989. The "men who rocked the boat," *HJ*, 5/12/1988. Ages of young selectmen in the eighteenth century from GL Gen.: John Beal (age twenty-nine), Thomas Gill (age thirty-one), Peter Jacob (age thirty), Enoch Lincoln (age thirty-three), Benjamin Lincoln, the general's father (age twenty-seven), Samuel Thaxter (age twenty-nine), John Thaxter (age twenty-four), Enoch Whiton (age thirty-three), Elias Whiton (age thirty-three).

Page 442: Richardson at Old Derby, *HJ*, 5/10/1990. On GL's curiosity, *HJ*, 8/31/1877. In the last week of August, 1877, excavation for a new storm sewer at Broad Bridge and Main Street unearthed human remains at the site of the old Acadian house (present School Department headquarters) and GL reminisced about the removal of the hill in front of Old Derby: "As late as 1831, when the hill was removed, there was standing in front of the homestead of Samuel Norton Esq., now the residence of Henry C. Harding [site of today's Granite store], a brick tomb into which we boys used to gaze with curiosity and awe." GL as usual says it well: the recovery of the past should always be gazed upon with a mixture of curiosity and awe.

Bibliography of Sources Referred to or Consulted

PRINCIPAL SOURCES

Annual Town Books. Financial reports, reports of the Selectmen, etc., 1833, 1849, 1856, and following.

Burr, Fearing, and George Lincoln. *Hingham in the Late Civil War.* Pub. by the Town, 1876.

Directories:

Plymouth County Directory and Historical Register of the Old Colony. Middleboro: Pratt & Co., 1867.

Resident and Business Directory of Hingham, Mass. Needham: Chronicle Press, 1885.

Directory of Hingham and Hull, Mass. Quincy: Hogan & Co., 1894.

Resident and Business Directory of Hingham and Cohasset, Mass. Boston: Suburban Book Co., 1908.

Resident and Business Directory of Hingham and Cohasset, Mass. Boston: Union Pub. Co., 1912

Resident and Business Directory of Hingham and Cohasset, Mass. Auburndale: Gordon, 1920.

Polk's Hingham and Cohasset Directory. Boston: Polk & Co., 1928.

Foster, William L. *Topical Index of Town Meetings since the Founding of the Plantation.* Typescript. 2 vols. Town Clerk's Vault, Hingham.

Hingham Gazette. Jan., 1827, through March, 1838, weekly.

Hingham Journal. Jan., 1850, to the present, weekly.

Hingham Patriot. July, 1838, through Dec., 1848, weekly.

Historical Collection, Hingham Public Library.

History of the Town of Hingham. 3 vols., 4 parts. Pub. by the Town, 1893.

Lainhart, Ann S. *Mass. State Census for Hingham, 1855, 1865.* Boston, 1988.

Lincoln, George. Diaries. Hist Coll HPL.

Lincoln, George. *Genealogies.* Vols. II-III of *History* (1893).

Lincoln, Solomon. *History of Hingham.* Hingham: Gill, Farmer & Brown, 1827.

Loring, Julian. Notebooks. Hist Coll HPL, microfilm.

Massachusetts State Census Reports.

Robinson, Donald F. *Two Hundred Years in South Hingham 1746-1946.* Hingham: Historical Society, 1980.

Town Monographs. Mass. Dept. of Commerce and Development, 1955 and following.

Town Records. Fair copies by Hosea Sprague. Hist Coll HPL, microfilm:

Reel I: Town Clerk's Record of Town Meetings, 9/18/1635 through 3/25/1700.

Reel III: Vital Records, Hobart's Journal, Gay's Record.
Transactions of the Agricultural and Horticultural Society. 1861, 1868 and following. Hist Coll HPL, microfilm.
United States Census Reports.

OTHER SOURCES

Abbe, Dorothy. "Concerning Dwiggins." *Journal of Decorative and Propaganda Arts*, Winter, 1988, 110-29.
Abbe, Dorothy. *The Dwiggins Marionettes.* New York: Abrams, 1970.
Abbe, Dorothy. *Stencilled Ornament and Illustration.* Boston: Trustees of Boston Public Library, 1979.
Adams, John Q. *Life in a New England Town.* Boston: Little, Brown, 1903.
Ahlstrom, Sydney E., and J. S. Carey. *An American Reformation: A Documentary History of Unitarian Christianity.* Middletown: Wesleyan UP, 1985.
Allen, David G. *In English Ways.* Chapel Hill: UNC Press, 1981.
Andrew, John A. Speeches. Hist Coll HPL, Reel 76:15.
Andrist, Ralph K. *American Century: One Hundred Years of Changing Life Styles in America.* New York: American Heritage, 1972.
Andrist, Ralph K., and Francis Russell. *The American Heritage History of the Confident Years, 1865-1916.* New York: Bonanza, 1987.
Arendt, Hannah. *The Human Condition.* Chicago: UC Press, 1958.
Bagwell, Philip S. *The Transport Revolution from 1770.* London: Batsford, 1974.
Bailyn, Bernard, *et al. The Great Republic.* 2nd edn. Lexington: Heath, 1981.
Bailyn, Bernard. *The New England Merchants in the Seventeenth Century.* Cambridge: Harvard UP, 1959.
Baumgartner, John D. *Bands and Band Music in Hingham, Mass. 1866-1876.* Ph.D. dissertation, U. of Colorado, 1980.
Benjamin, James M. *The School Question in Massachusetts, 1870-1900.* Ph.D. dissertation, U. of Missouri, 1969.
Bennett, Paul A., ed. *Postscripts on Dwiggins.* 2 vols. New York: the Typophiles, 1960.
Blum, John M. *V Was for Victory: Politics and Culture in World War II.* New York: Harcourt Brace Jovanovich, 1976.
Boni, Margaret B. *Fireside Book of American Folksongs.* New York: Simon & Schuster, 1952.
Booth, Wayne C. *The Vocation of a Teacher.* Chicago: UC Press, 1988.
Breen, T. H. *Puritans and Adventurers.* New York: Oxford UP, 1980.
Brewer, Wilmon. *Looking Backwards.* 2 vols. N.H.: Marshall Jones, 1985.
Brogan, Hugh. *The Pelican History of the United States of America.* New York: Penguin, 1986.
Brown, Ralph. *Historical Geography of the United States.* New York, 1948.
Brown, Richard D. *Massachusetts: A Bicentennial History.* New York: Norton, 1978.
Brown, Robert E. *Middle-Class Democracy and the Revolution in Massachusetts, 1691-1780.* Ithaca: Cornell UP, 1955.
Browne, Albert C., Jr. *Sketch of the Official Life of John A. Andrew.* Cambridge: Riverside, 1868.
Burchard, Peter. *One Gallant Rush: Robert Gould Shaw and His Brave Black Regiment.* New York: St. Martin's, 1965.
Burns, James M. *The Crosswinds of Freedom.* New York: Vintage, 1990.
Burns, James M. *The Vineyard of Liberty.* New York: Vintage, 1983.
Burns, James M. *The Workshop of Democracy.* New York: Vintage, 1986.
Burr, Fearing. Notebooks. Hist Coll HPL, Reel 76:19.
Catton, Bruce. *The American Heritage Short History of the Civil War.* New York: Dell, 1963.
Catton, Bruce. *Never Call Retreat.* Garden City: Doubleday, 1965.

The Celebration of the Two Hundred and Fiftieth Anniversary of the Settlement of the Town. Pub. by the Committee of Arrangements, 1885.

Chafe, William H. *The Unfinished Journey: America Since World War II.* New York: Oxford UP, 1986.

Chandler, Peleg W. *Memoir of the Hon. John Albion Andrew, LLD.* (repr. from *Mass. Hist. Soc. Proceedings*, April, 1880). Cambridge: Cambridge UP, 1880.

Clark, Andrew J. Civil War Letters. *HJ*, May, 1861, to May, 1864. Sel. repr. *HJ*, Jan.-June, 1913. MSS. Essex Institute.

Clark, Myron R. Autobiographical Notes. MS. (courtesy of Alexander Macmillan) in HHS Collection.

Clark, Robert J., ed. *The Arts and Crafts Movement in America 1876-1916.* Exhibition Catalogue. Princeton: UP, 1972.

Clarke, James F. *John A. Andrew.* Boston: Ellis, 1918.

Clifford, Deborah P. *Mine Eyes Have Seen the Glory: A Biography of Julia Ward Howe.* Boston: Little Brown, 1979.

Coatsworth, Elizabeth. *South Shore Town.* New York: Macmillan, 1948.

The Commemorative Services of the First Parish in Hingham on the Two Hundredth Anniversary of the Building of its Meeting House. Pub. by the Parish, 1881.

Conzen, Michael P., and G. K. Lewis. *Boston: A Geographical Portrait.* Cambridge: Ballinger/Lippincott, 1976.

Coolidge, John. "Hingham Builds a Meetinghouse." *New England Quarterly*, XXXIV (1961), 435-61.

Cremin, Lawrence A. *The Transformation of the School: Progressivism in American Education, 1876-1957.* New York: Knopf, 1961.

Cummings, Abbott L. *The Framed Houses of Massachusetts Bay 1625-1725.* Cambridge: Harvard UP, 1979.

Curtis, Kathleen. "Turnabout: A Portrait of the Crow Point Sailing Club." Unpub. paper loaned by the author.

Dana, Richard H. *Two Years Before the Mast.* New York: Modern Library, 1936.

D.A.R. Old Colony Chapter. *Hingham.* D.A.R., 1911.

Davis, Kenneth S. *Experience of War: the United States in World War II.* Garden City: Doubleday, 1965.

Deetz, James. *In Small Things Forgotten.* Garden City: Anchor, 1977.

Dolce, Philip C., ed. *Suburbia, the American Dream and Dilemma.* Garden City: Doubleday, 1976.

Dumenil, Lynn. *Freemasonry and American Culture 1880-1930.* Princeton: UP, 1984.

"Dwiggins Legacy." *Boston Public Library News*, Spring, 1974.

Dwiggins, William A. *The Work of W. A. Dwiggins.* New York: American Institute of Graphic Arts, 1937.

Dwight, Timothy. *Travels in New England and New York*, ed. B. M. Solomon. 4 vols. Cambridge: Harvard UP, 1969.

Eddy, Charles W. *Hingham Illustrated with Pen and Camera.* Ware, Mass., 1885.

Edson, Robert B. "The Effect of the Church in the History of An American Town." Copy provided by the author. Paper read to the H. Hist. Soc., April 14, 1988.

Ellis, Edward R. *Echoes of Distant Thunder: Life in the U.S. 1914-1918.* New York: Coward McCann & Geoghegan, 1975.

Emilio, Luis F. *A Brave Black Regiment: History of the Fifty-Fourth.* New York: Arno (reprint of 1874 edition), 1969.

Falkner, Leonard. *The President Who Wouldn't Retire.* New York: Coward-McCann, 1967.

Faux, Marian. *Roe v. Wade.* New York: New American Library, 1989.

Fehrenbach, T. R. *Lone Star: A History of Texas and the Texans.* New York: Collier/Macmillan, 1980.

Ferguson, Charles W. *Fifty Million Brothers.* New York: Farrar & Rinehart, 1937.

Flexner, Eleanor. *Century of Struggle: the Women's Rights Movement in the United States.* Cambridge: Belknap/Harvard, 1959.

Foley, Mason A. *Hingham Old and New.* Hingham: Tercentenary Committee, 1935.

Foster, William L. "The Old Training Field." Paper read to the D.A.R. Old Colony Chapter, April 25, 1925. (Pamphlet *HJ.*)

Friedel, Frank. *Over There.* Boston: Little Brown, 1964.

Gallop, John W. *Parish of St. John the Evangelist, Hingham, Massachusetts, Centennial History.* Boston: Spaulding, 1983.

Gans, Herbert. *The Urban Villagers.* New York: Collier/Macmillan, 1962.

Gilman, Anna. *History of the First Baptist Church of Hingham, Mass.* 1930.

Gist, Noel P. *Secret Societies.* U. of Missouri Studies, XV (1940), No. 4.

Goldston, Robert. *Suburbia and Civic Denial.* New York: Macmillan, 1970.

Good, H. G. *A History of American Education.* 2nd edn. New York: Macmillan, 1962.

Greene, Lorenzo J. *The Negro in Colonial New England, 1620-1776.* New York: Columbia UP, 1942.

Greetings from Hingham. 153 postcards. HPL Pamphlet File.

Gross, Ronald, *et al.*, eds. *The New Old: Struggling for Decent Aging.* Garden City: Doubleday, 1978.

Gunn, Neil M. *Butcher's Broom.* Edinburgh: Porpoise, 1934.

Gusfield, Joseph R. *Symbolic Crusade: Status Politics and the American Temperance Movement.* Urbana: U. of Illinois Press, 1963.

Hall, David B. *Worlds of Wonder, Days of Judgment: Popular Religious Belief in Early New England.* New York: Knopf, 1989.

Hall, Winston. *By the Wayside.* Hingham: Historical Society, 1985.

Handlin, Oscar. *Boston's Immigrants, 1790-1880.* Rev. edn. Cambridge: Belknap/Harvard, 1979.

Harlow, Alvin F. *Steelways of New England.* New York: Creative Age, 1946.

Hart, Albert B., ed. *Commonwealth History of Massachusetts,* Vol. II: *Province of Massachusetts.* New York: State History Co., 1928.

Hartwell, George H. *Hingham's Colonial Industries.* South Shore Nature Club, 1954.

Hartwell, R. M. "The Service Revolution" in C. M. Cipolla, ed. *The Fontana Economic History of Europe. The Industrial Revolution.* London: Collins/Fontana, 1973.

Hayes, Grace P. *World War I: A Compact History.* New York: Hawthorn, 1972.

Hazlitt, Margaret. *Journal,* ed. E. J. Moyne. Manhattan: U. of Kansas Press, 1967.

Hersey, Alan F. *The First Hundred Years of the Hingham Mutual Fire Insurance Co.* (1926). Hist Coll HPL, Reel 76:9.

Hersey, Alan F. *Old Colony Story.* Rev. edn. Old Colony Railroad, 1969.

Heyrman, Christine L. *Culture and Commerce: the Maritime Communities of Colonial Massachusetts 1690-1750.* New York: Norton, 1984.

Hicks, Roger W., and Frances E. Schultz. *Battlefields of the Civil War.* Topsfield: Salem House, 1989.

Higham, John. *Strangers in the Land.* New Brunswick: Rutgers UP, 1955.

Hingham Magazine. Boston: Ellis, 1898.

Historic Hingham. Brochure. Hingham Institution for Savings. Hist Coll HPL, Reel 76:8.

History of the 26th Yankee Division. Salem: Yankee Division Veterans Association, 1955.

Hoerder, Dirk. *Society and Government 1760-1780: the Power Structure in Massachusetts Townships.* Berlin: J. F. Kennedy-Institut, 1972.

Hofstadter, Richard, *et al. The American Republic.* Englewood Cliffs: Prentice-Hall, 1959.

Hofstadter, Richard, ed. *The Progressive Movement 1900-1915.* Englewood Cliffs: Prentice-Hall, 1963.

Horton, H. Leavitt. *Aspects of a New England Town (Hingham, Mass.).* Philadelphia: Raum, 1945.

Horton, H. Leavitt. *Melville, Downer, Railroads.* Pamphlet, 1948.

Horton, H. Leavitt. *New England Chronicle.* Typescript, copyright 1956.

Horton, H. Leavitt. *New England Scrapbook.* Typescript, copyright 1949.

Howard, Amy C. *The Hingham Town Forest.* Leaflet No. 21, South Shore Nature Club, 1956.

Howard, Amy C. "Isabel Hyams and the Orchard House." *MIT Record,* 1958.

Howard, Brett. *Boston: A Social History.* New York: Hawthorn, 1976.

Howard, Gerald, ed. *The Sixties . . . Our Most Explosive Decade.* New York: Washington Square, 1982.

Howe, Julia W. *Reminiscences 1819-1899.* Boston: Houghton Mifflin, 1899.

Hunt, Adelaide. Six articles on Melville Garden. *Quincy Patriot Ledger,* Aug. 28 through Sept. 2, 1961.

Hurd, D. Hamilton. *History of Plymouth County.* Philadelphia: Lewis, 1884.

Huthmacher, J. Joseph. *Massachusetts People and Politics 1919-1933.* New York: Atheneum, 1973.

Hymowitz, Carol, and Michaela Weissman. *A History of Women in America.* New York: Bantam, 1978.

Kaplan, Samuel. *The Dream Deferred: People, Politics, and Planning in Suburbia.* New York: Vintage, 1976.

Kaplan, Wendy. *The Art That is Life: the Arts and Crafts Movement in America, 1875-1920.* Boston: Museum of Fine Arts, 1987.

Kramer, John, ed. *North American Suburbs: Politics, Diversity, and Change.* Berkeley: Glendessary, 1972.

Kropotkin, Petr A. *Mutual Aid.* Boston: Extending Horizons Books, 1955.

Labaree, Benjamin W. *Colonial Massachusetts: a History.* Millwood: KTO Press, 1979.

Lane, C. Chester. "Hingham Arts and Crafts: Their Aims and Objects." *Craftsman,* V (1903), 276-81.

Larkin, Jack. *The Reshaping of Everyday Life 1790-1840.* New York: Harper & Row, 1988.

Lehner, M. B., and M. J. Fannin. "History in Towns: Hingham, Massachusetts." *Antiques,* Oct., 1989, 813-25.

Lehner, M. B., and M. J. Fannin, *et al. Historic Districts Handbook, Hingham, Massachusetts.* H. Hist. Comm. & H. Hist. Dist. Comm., 1990.

Lincoln, Jairus. *Anti-Slavery Melodies for the Friends of Freedom.* Hingham: Gill, 1843.

Lincoln, Solomon, Jr. *Address . . . on the two hundredth anniversary . . . of the town.* Hingham: Farmer, 1835.

Lockridge, Kenneth A. *A New England Town: the First Hundred Years of Dedham, Massachusetts, 1636-1736.* New York: Norton, 1970.

Lockridge, Kenneth A. "The Population of Dedham, Massachusetts, 1636-1736." *Economic History Review,* 2nd Series, XIX (1966), 321-23.

Long, John D. *Journal,* ed. Margaret Long. Rindge: Smith, 1956.

Longfellow, Henry W. *Poetical Works.* Boston: Houghton Mifflin, 1975.

Lopreato, Joseph. *Italian Americans.* New York: Random House, 1970.

Macdonald, Anne L. *Feminine Ingenuity: Women and Invention in America.* New York: Ballantine, 1992.

Mackey, William J. *American Bird Decoys.* New York: Dutton, 1965.

Macmillan, Alexander. "The Day Eleanor Roosevelt Came to Town." *Historic Hingham* (*HJ* Special Supplement, July 1, 1985).

Macmillan, Alexander. "Mike (King) Kelly: Hingham's Hall of Famer." *HJ,* March 2, 1989.

Marble, Arthur D. *The Country Store of Long Ago.* Hingham: Historical Society, 1928.

Mazotti, Louis H., and J. K. Hadden, eds. *Suburbia in Transition.* New York: New Viewpoints, 1974.

McCaffrey, Lawrence J. *The Irish Diaspora in America.* Washington: Catholic UP, 1984.

McCall, Samuel W., *et al. Resolutions in Appreciation of the Distinguished Services of John Davis Long.* Mass. House of Representatives, May 22, 1916.

McFeeley, William S. *Grant: a Biography.* New York: Norton, 1981.

McManis, Douglas R. *Colonial New England: a Historical Geography.* New York: Oxford UP, 1975.

Merino, James A. *A Great City and its Suburbs.* Ph.D. dissertation, U. of Texas, 1968.

Miller, Douglas T., and Marian Nowak. *The Fifties: the Way We Really Were.* Garden City: Doubleday, 1977.

Morison, Samuel E. *The Maritime History of Massachusetts 1783-1860.* Boston: Houghton Mifflin, 1921.

Mosher, Robert. "Joseph Whiting Lincoln." *News and Notes Out of the Ordinary,* Jan., 1992 (Newsletter of the HHS).

Nelson, William E. *Dispute and Conflict Resolution in Plymouth County, Massachusetts, 1725-1825.* Chapel Hill: UNC Press, 1981.

Novak, Michael. *The Rise of the Unmeltable Ethnics.* New York: Macmillan, 1973.

Okrent, Daniel, and Steve Wulf. *Baseball Anecdotes.* New York: Oxford UP, 1989.

The Old Saltworks. H. Hist. Soc. Pub. #1 (1916).

O'Neill, William L. *Coming Apart: an Informal History of America in the 1960s.* Chicago: Quadrangle, 1971.

Paludan, Phillip S. *"A People's Contest": the Union and Civil War 1861-1865.* New York: Harper and Row, 1988.

Panati, Charles. *Extraordinary Origins of Everyday Things.* New York: Harper and Row, 1987.

Parke, David B., ed. *The Epic of Unitarianism.* Boston: Starr Press, 1957.

Parker, Patricia. *Susanna Rowson.* Boston: Twayne, 1986.

Pearson, Henry G. *The Life of John A. Andrew.* 2 vols. Boston: Houghton Mifflin, 1904.

Phillips, Cabell. *From the Crash to the Blitz, 1929-1939.* New York: Macmillan, 1969.

Phillips, Cabell. *The 1940s: Decade of Triumph and Trouble.* New York: Macmillan, 1975.

Pick, J. B. *The Phoenix Dictionary of Games.* London: Phoenix House, 1952.

Pitcher, Albert L. *Origin and Growth of the Hingham Fire Department, 1635-1942.* (1946) Hist Coll HPL, Reel 76:8.

President's Commission on Law Enforcement and Administration of Justice. *The Challenge of Crime in a Free Society.* New York: Avon, 1968.

Reardon, Katharine W. "Land Conservation in the Town of Hingham: An Historical Overview." Radcliffe Seminars paper, May 19, 1987. (Copy in HPL.)

Richards, Leonard L. *The Life and Times of Congressman John Quincy Adams.* New York: Oxford UP, 1986.

Richardson, Joseph. *Complaint against the Clergy of the Bay Association.* Boston: Parmenter & Norton, 1818.

Richardson, Joseph. *Letter . . . on the Subject of Exchanges of Pulpit.* Hingham: Farmer, 1847.

Richardson, Joseph. *Sermon . . . June 28, 1856, in close of the fiftieth year of his ministry.* Hingham: Farmer, 1856.

Riesman, David, *et al. The Lonely Crowd.* New Haven: Yale UP, 1950.

Riley, Mary L. "Arts and Crafts Societies in Massachusetts." *House Beautiful,* XVIII-XIX (1905), 31-33.

Roosevelt, Eleanor, and Frances Cooke Macgregor. *This Is America.* New York: Putnam's, 1942.

Roscoe, Theodore S. *History of Derby Academy, 1784-1984.* Hingham: Trustees of Derby Academy, 1984.

Rowson, Susanna. *Charlotte Temple.* Intro. by Clara M. and Rudolf Kirk. New Haven: College and University Press, 1964.

Rowson, Susanna. *Charlotte Temple.* Intro. by Cathy N. Davidson. New York: Oxford UP, 1986.

Rowson, Susanna. *Rebecca or the Fille de Chambre.* 2nd American edn. Boston: Williams, 1814.

Russell, Howard S. *A Long, Deep Furrow: Three Centuries of Farming in New England.* Hanover: UP of New England, 1976.

Rutman, Darrett B. *Winthrop's Boston.* Chapel Hill: UNC Press, 1965.

Ryan, Mary P. *Womanhood in America: from Colonial Times to the Present*. 3rd edn. New York: Franklin Watts, 1983.

Santayana, George. *The Life of Reason*. Rev. edn. New York: Scribner's, 1954.

Schlesinger, Arthur M. *Paths to the Present*. New York: Macmillan, 1949.

Schreiber, Hermann. *The History of Roads*, trans. S. Thomson. London: Barrie & Rockliff, 1961.

Schwartz, Harold. *Samuel Gridley Howe, Social Reformer 1801-1876*. Cambridge: Harvard UP, 1956.

Sennett, Richard. *The Fall of Public Man*. New York: Knopf, 1977.

Shachtman, Tom. *Decade of Shocks: Dallas to Watergate, 1963-1974*. New York: Poseidon, 1983.

Sharp, Dallas L. *The Hills of Hingham*. New York: Houghton Mifflin, 1916.

Shattuck, Mayo A., Jr. *Hingham, Massachusetts: A Study of Democratic Thought and Institutions in a Small American Community*. Honors (A.B.) Thesis in Government, Harvard College, 1949.

Shaw, Anna H. *The Story of A Pioneer*. New York: Harper, 1915.

Shilhan, Michael J. *When I Think of Hingham*. Hingham: Historical Society, 1976.

Simon, Linda. "What Shall We Tell the Children?" *Boston Review*, April, 1990, pp. 9-11.

Sinnett, Edmund W. *Meetinghouse and Church in Early New England*. New York: McGraw Hill, 1963.

Sly, John F. *Town Government in Massachusetts, 1620-1930*. Cambridge: Harvard UP, 1930.

Smith, Daniel S. *Population, Family, and Society in Hingham 1635-1880*. Ph.D. dissertation, U. of California/Berkeley, 1973.

Smith, T. Page. *Sarah Derby: the Story of a Colonial Innkeeper's Daughter*. Hingham, 1957.

Souther, Shirley M. *A History of the Methodist Episcopal Church Hingham, Mass. 1828-1928*. Hingham, 1928.

Springer, L. Elsinore. *That Vanishing Sound*. New York: Crown, 1976.

Stark, Gladys. *The Old Ship Meeting House*. Design by W. A. Dwiggins. Illus. Edgar T. P. Walker. Hingham, 1951.

Stephenson, Luther, Jr. Speech on the Dedication of the Tower Monument (read by J. D. Long, July, 1914). Repr. *HJ*, July 24, 1914.

Stoddard, Richard H. *Recollections Personal and Literary*. New York: Barnes, 1903.

Tager, Jack, and J. W. Ifkovic, eds. *Massachusetts in the Gilded Age*. Amherst: U. Mass. Press, 1985.

Tharp, Louise H. *Three Saints and a Sinner*. Boston: Little Brown, 1956.

Thaxter, Thomas, *et al. Narrative of the Proceedings in the North Parish of Hingham.* . . . Salem: Cushing, 1807.

Thernstrom, Stephan. *The Other Bostonians*. Cambridge: Harvard UP, 1973.

Tuchman, Barbara W. *The First Salute*. New York: Knopf, 1988.

Twombly, Robert C., and R. H. Moore. "Black Puritan: the Negro in Seventeenth Century Massachusetts." *William and Mary Quarterly*, Series 3, XXIV (1967), 224-42.

Vindication of the Proceedings of the First Parish. . . . Boston, 1807.

Walker, William H. C., and W. B. Walker. *A History of World's End*. Trustees of Reservations, 1973.

Wall, Robert E., Jr. *Massachusetts Bay: the Crucial Decade 1640-1650*. New Haven: Yale UP, 1972.

Warner, Sam B. *Province of Reason*. Cambridge: Belknap/Harvard, 1984.

Warner, Sam B. *Streetcar Suburbs: the Process of Growth in Boston (1870-1900)*. 2nd edn. Cambridge: Harvard UP, 1978.

Warner, Sam B. *The Way We Really Live: Social Change in Metropolitan Boston Since 1920*. Boston: Trustees of Boston Public Library, 1977.

Waters, John J. "Hingham, Massachusetts, 1631-1661: an East Anglian Oligarchy in the New World." *Journal of Social History*, I (1967-68), 351-70.

Wertenbaker, Thomas J. *The Puritan Oligarchy.* New York: Scribner's, 1947.

[Whiton, Helen] "H.W." Reminiscences. *HJ,* Jan. 5, 1923.

Wiebe, Robert M. *The Search for Order, 1877-1920.* New York: Hill & Wang, 1967.

Wiley, Belle I. *Common Soldier in the Civil War.* New York: Grosset, 1952.

Willard, Frances E., and M. A. Livermore, eds. *American Women, Fifteen Hundred Biographies.* Rev. edn. New York: Mast, Crowell, & Kirkpatrick, 1897.

Wilson, Robert J. *Benevolent Deity: Ebenezer Gay and the Rise of Rational Religion in New England, 1696-1787.* Philadelphia: U. of Pa. Press, 1984.

Winthrop, John. *Winthrop's Journal "History of New England" 1630-1649,* ed. J. K. Hosmer. New York: Barnes & Noble, 1946.

Wood, Frederic J. *The Turnpikes of New England.* Boston: Marshall Jones, 1919.

Wright, Conrad, ed. *Three Prophets of Religious Liberalism: Channing, Emerson, Parker.* Boston: Beacon Press, 1961.

Zaitgevsky, Cynthia. *Frederick Law Olmsted and the Boston Park System.* Cambridge: Belknap/Harvard, 1982.

Zimiles, Martha and Murray. *Early American Mills.* New York: Bramhall, 1973.

Zuckerman, Michael. *Peaceable Kingdoms: New England Towns in the Eighteenth Century.* New York: Knopf, 1970.

INTERVIEWS AND CONVERSATIONS WITH THE AUTHORS

MANY people have been kind enough to talk with us about their knowledge of Hingham past and present. Some talks were conducted in person, and of these, some were recorded; others took place by telephone. Some were extensive; others were short and casual and are documented only in brief notes made later. Some informants spoke under conditions of confidentiality. Dates of talks are given below, but in a few cases, talks occurred serially over a span of months or years.

Dorothy Abbe (12/16/92, 2/19/93)
Lucy Bates (6/19/91)
Oscar Beck, Mrs. Beck and Oscar Beck, Jr. (7/9/88)
Anna Calvi (6/29/88)
Mary Calvi (6/29/88)
Robert and Beverly Cashman (10/12/92)
Eugene and Helen Chamberlain (1988-92)
Evelyn Cheney (6/29/88)
Louise W. Cobleigh (1987-88)
Ernest Colarullo (May-July 1988)
Kathleen Curtis (10/9/88)
Rev. Robert Edson (3/13/88)
Elizabeth Suzanne Belding Eldredge (7/10/88)
Marge Farrell (3/29/92)
Herbert Hirsch (1989-92)
William W. Howard (1/4/90)
James Jamieson (8/6/92)
Mildred Kimball (11/14/92)

Barbara and Josephine Lincoln (3/7/92)
C. Warren Lincoln (7/9/88)
Frances Cooke Macgregor (3/18/89)
Ann MacNeil (10/30/87)
Helen Mansfield (3/24/92)
Ruth Marsh (7/2/88)
John McKee (6/25/88)
Margaret McSweeney (7/10/88)
Peter Murphy (11/8/87)
Harold Newcombe (6/26/88)
William Quinn (11/25/87)
Peter Rando (1988-89)
Kathleen Reichardt (4/13/92)
John P. Richardson (11/15/87)
Rev. Donald Robinson (3/12/88)
David and Shirley Rogers (11/15/92)
Richard Shaner (5/31/88)
Alma Tinsley (10/29/87)
Solace Tobey (2/16/88)
Ann Tolman (1991-92)

Many have responded to our telephone calls, letters of inquiry, and public appeals for information and for help tracing graphics included in this work. We thank and list them as follows:

Andrew Adams
Elizabeth Melcher Anderson
Fred Baker
Claire Barnes
Marge Barry
Ellen Blaser
Susan Berry
Henry Bosworth
Mildred Walker Bickford
Jean Thaxter Brett
Katharine & Wilmon Brewer
John Carnes
Isabelle Cassidy
Elizabeth and Morton Cole
Ruth Curry
Elaine Cusker
Barbara Ruyl Daugherty
Robert Delorey
Susanne Eldredge
Mary Forester
Thomas Foster
Rita Gage
Diane Getchell
Jane Gibson
Mary Gilbert
Sally Goodrich
Linda Gordon
Dan Haff
Winston I. Hall
Esther Harlow
Marilyn Harrington
Paul Healey
Frederic Hills
Caroline Hobbs
Larrie E. Hurst
Helen Ingram

Helen Ireton
Edward G. Jones
Jean Kimball
Albert W. Kimball
Claire Kirsch
the Krall family
Barbara Lincoln
Ronald Lincoln
Wilfred A. Loring
Louise and Earl Mabel
Alexander Macmillan
Barbara Menzies
Robert Mosher
Jeanne Murphy
Robert Olson
Virginia Pearce
Sylvia Pope
Roberta Pitcher
Rev. Kenneth Read-Brown
Lorraine Rose
Gene Alan Seaburg
Captain William Schmitt
Robert Shea
Thomas Smith
Robert Stearns
George K. Stoddard
Neil Swidey
Nancy Tiffin
Ann Tolman
William Vanderweil
Christopher Walker
Willard B. Walker
Thomas J. Wallace Jr.
Helen Ware
James Zanello

INTERVIEWS CONDUCTED BY OTHERS

Elwin Fearing   (J. P. Richardson, 1961--notes owned by JPR)
Elwin Fearing   (J. Wheaton, 1969--tape in Hist Coll HPL)
M. Annette Loring   (J. Wheaton, 1969--tape in Hist Coll HPL)
Donald and Carol Robinson (E. Kelleher, 1979--tape in Hist Coll HPL)
Camilla Roundtree (P. Hart, 1981--notes in possession of the authors)
Bertha Stringer (J. P. Richardson--notes owned by JPR)
Bertha Stringer (J. Wheaton, 1975--tape in Hist Coll HPL)
Helen Thomas (J. Wheaton, 1971--tape in Hist Coll HPL)
Hattie Wilder (J. Wheaton, 1969--tape in Hist Coll HPL)

Index

�֍

In a book which will serve for reference, a thorough index is of major importance. This index includes over 2400 entries and subentries; even so, it cannot be complete. Nearby cities and towns are included, but more remote places, organizations, and celebrities are included only if they have local significance. Local places and villages are included, but it is not practical to index streets and roads. Passages about villages---South Hingham, the Centre, Liberty Plain, etc.---are indexed only when they deal with a village's special characteristics or problems. Specific industries are listed under Industry and Manufacturing; town boards and committees under Town Government; churches under Churches; schools under Schools and Education. If you do not find a particular institution in its alphabetical place, check under a general entry, especially "Hingham." Locations of military events are too numerous to index separately, but they can easily be found in passages indexed regarding particular wars. For those interested in tracing a general theme throughout the narrative, we provide a number of general topical entries, for example, Childhood and Youth, Politics and Elections, and Women's Occupations, Roles, and Rights.

The Maps

North Hingham
on eve of Civil War
*(Just before Thaxter Street cut through—
Methodist Church in old position)*
1857

BRIDGES

1. Derby	5. Thaxters
2. Marshs	6. Broad
3. Goolds	7. Magoons
4. Hobarts	8. Mill

South Hingham
1879

VILLAGE OF
SOUTH HINGHAM

TOWN OF HINGHAM
MASS.

Scale, 528 ft 1 Inch.

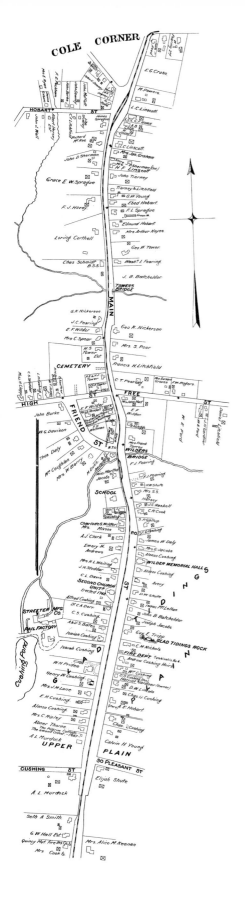

**South Hingham
1903**

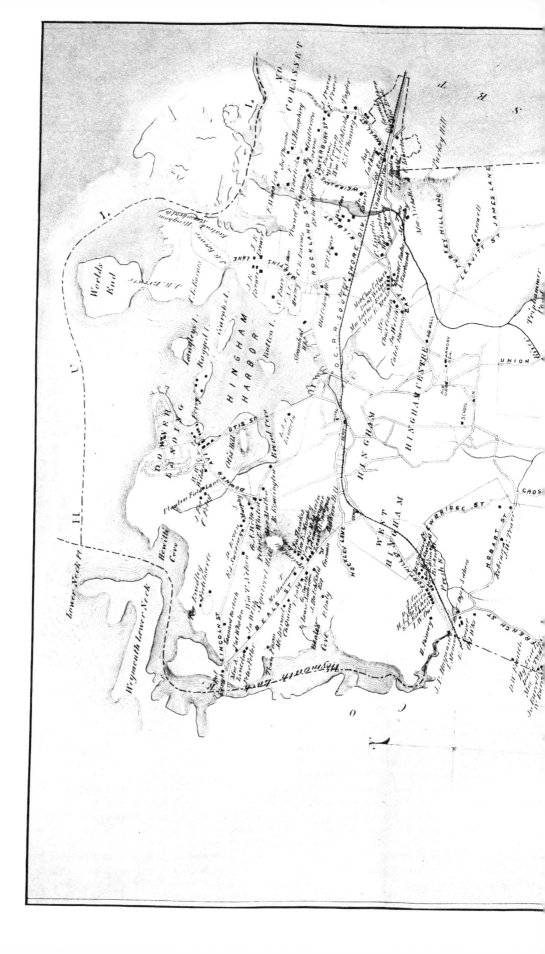

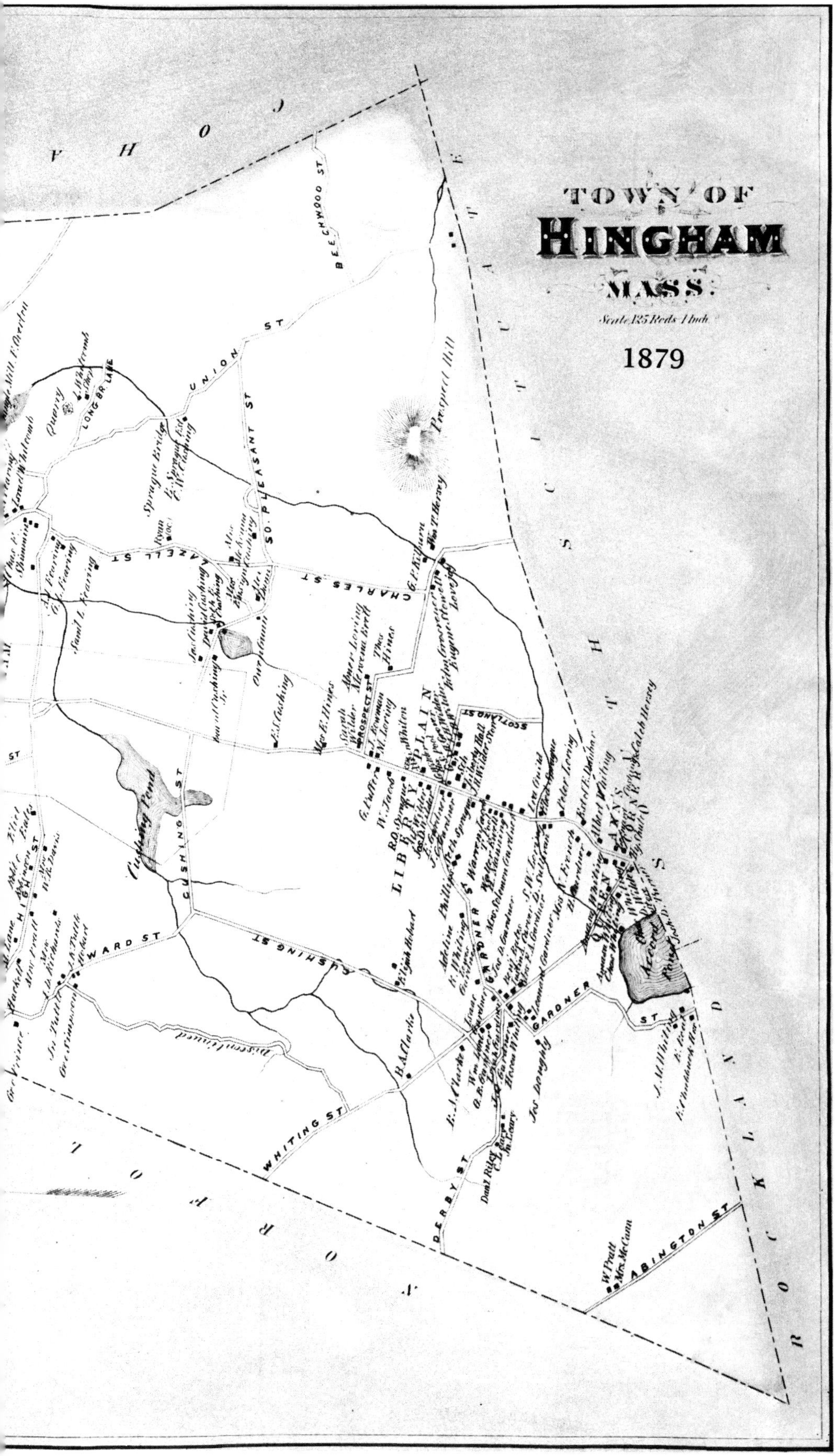

TOWN OF
HINGHAM
MASS.
Scale 125 Rods 1 Inch
1879
BEECHWOOD ST
UNION ST
LONG BR. LANE
Quarry
Sprague Bridge
SO. PLEASANT ST
Prospect Hill
LAZELL ST
CHARLES ST
PROSPECT ST
LIBERTY PLAIN
Cushing Pond
CUSHING ST
HIGH ST
WARD ST
GARDNER ST
Accord Pond
WHITING ST
DERBY ST
ABINGTON ST

VILLAGE OF
HINGHAM
MASS.
Scale 528 ft 1 Inch.

1879

WEST HINGHAM

SUB PLAN
CROW POINT
TOWN OF HINGHAM
Scale 500 feet to one inch.

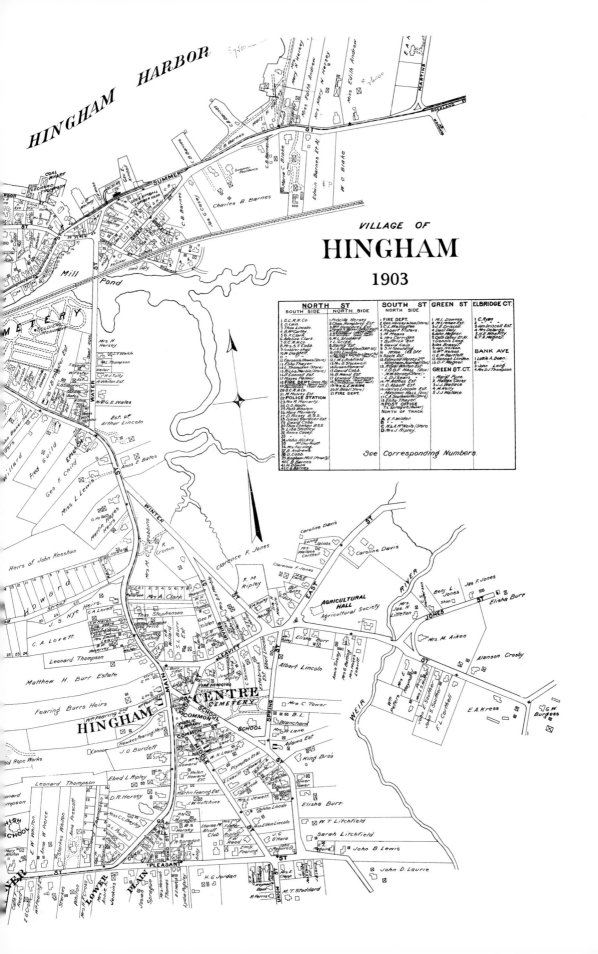

VILLAGE OF

HINGHAM

1903

See Corresponding Numbers.

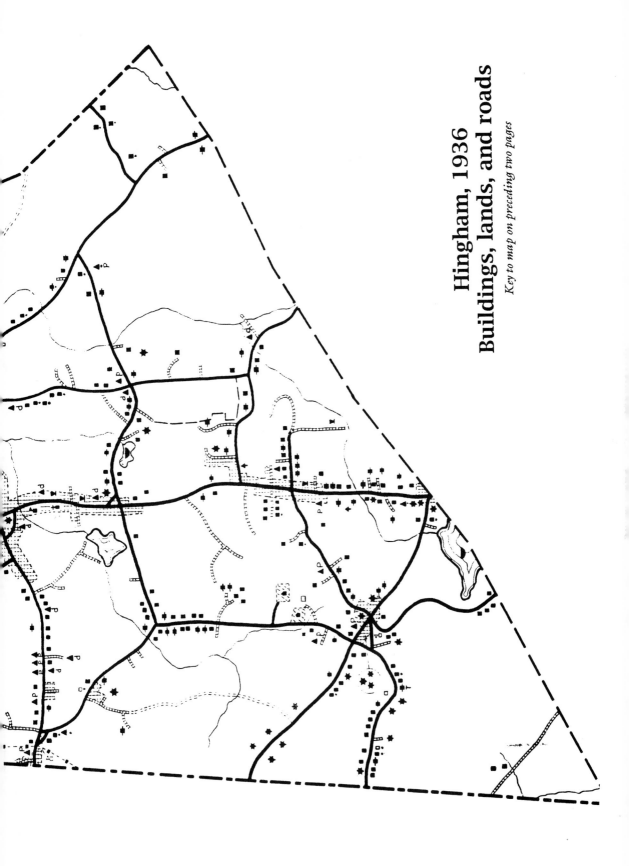

Hingham, 1936
Buildings, lands, and roads

Key to map on preceding two pages

Hingham, 1936
Buildings, Lands, Roads
Key to map on preceding two pages

Public buildings
    Churches
    Schools
    Other public, quasi-public

Commercial buildings, quarries,
    gravel pits

Agricultural buildings
    Dairy farms
    Poultry farms
    Farmsteads
    Semi-agricultural uses
    Greenhouses, nurseries

Residential buildings,
    including summer homes
    Occupied, good condition
    Occupied, poor condition
    Vacant, good condition
    Vacant, poor condition
    Tourist accommodations
    Private estates

Thickly settled areas
Playgrounds, ballfields
Bathing beach
Golf courses, country clubs
Cemeteries
Aviation field
Roads
    Hard surfaced
    Gravel or dirt
    Abandoned
Railroad
High tension line

Parks and Recreation Areas

Key to map on following two pages

1.	Grape Island	30, 31.	More-Brewer Park
2.	Slate Island	32.	Cassidy Field
3.	Webb Memorial State Park	33.	Burns Memorial Park
4.	Stodders Neck	34.	Central Junior High School Area
5.	Bouve Conservation Area at Hewitt's Cove	35.	Merrymount Road Conservation Land
		36.	Downing Street Water Company Land
5A.	Bradley Woods Playground	37.	High School Area
6.	Fee Pond	38.	Bradford Road Water Company Land
7.	Foster School Area	39, 40.	Triphammer Pond
8.	Ragged, Sarah & Langley Islands	41.	Leavitt Street Conservation Land
9.	Bathing Beach	42.	Wompatuck State Park
10.	Button Island	43-45.	Plymouth River Complex
11.	Monument Park	46.	Mildred Cushing Woods
12.	Barnes Wharf & Steamboat Lane Wharf	47.	Bucket Mill Lane Pond
		48.	Crooked Meadow River Area
13, 14.	Boulevard Border Park	49.	Jacobs Meadow Area
15.	World's End	50.	Wadleigh's Rill
16.	Lyford's Lyking	51.	Old Ward Street Conservation Land
17.	Hull Street Playground	52.	Swanson Hollow
18.	Foundry Pond Area	53.	Eel River Reservation
19.	Chief Justice Cushing Highway Border	54, 55.	Whortleberry Hollow
20.	Skating Club	56.	South Junior High School Area
21.	Great Esker Park	57, 58.	South School Area
22.	Bare Cove Park	59.	Fulling Mill Pond Area
23.	Hersey Field	60, 62.	Water Company Land
24.	Broad Cove	61.	George Washington Forest
25.	Governor Long Bird Sanctuary	63.	McKenna Marsh Area
26.	Home Meadows	64.	Kress Field
27.	East School Area	65.	Accord Pond
28.	Whitney & Thayer Woods	66.	Bradley Pond
29.	Cranberry Pond	67.	South Shore Country Club

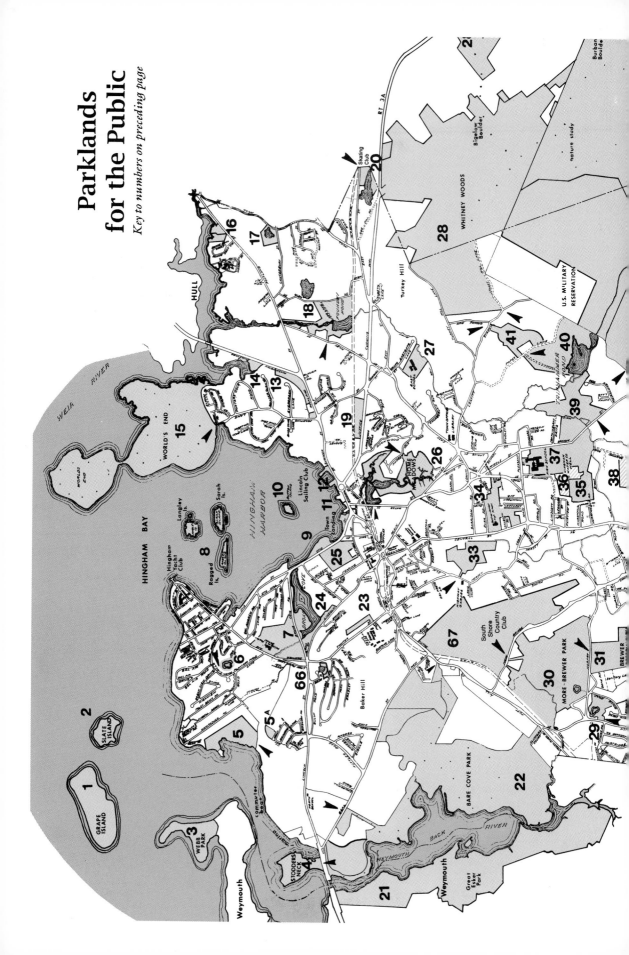

Parklands for the Public

Key to numbers on preceding page

PUBLIC : QUASI-PUBLIC OPEN SPACE

HINGHAM WATER COMPANY

ACCESS POINT

one square mile

100 acres

This book was set using Microsoft Word for Windows in ten and one-half point on thirteen Adobe ITC Galliard. Some of the line art was digitized and restored. Camera work, mechanicals and flats provided by Jay's Publishers Services. Printed on 70 lb Glatco Matte manufactured by P. H. Glatfelter Company and supplied by Pratt Paper Company. Printing and binding by The Maple-Vail Book Manufacturing Group. Design & production by Peter Carr.